PATHWAYS TO COMPETENCE

PATHWAYS TO COMPETENCE

Encouraging Healthy Social and Emotional Development in Young Children

by

Sarah Landy, Ph.D.
Hincks-Dellcrest Institute
and
Toronto East General Hospital
Ontario, Canada

·P·A·U·L·H·
BROOKES
PUBLISHING CO.®

Baltimore • London • Sydney

Paul H. Brookes Publishing Co.
Post Office Box 10624
Baltimore, Maryland 21285-0624

www.brookespublishing.com

Typeset by Integrated Publishing Solutions, Grand Rapids, Michigan.
Manufactured in the United States of America by Corley Printing Company, St. Louis, Missouri.

Individuals described herein are composites, pseudonyms, or fictional accounts based on actual experiences. Individuals' names have been changed and identifying details have been altered to protect their confidentiality.

Cartoons courtesy of Lynn Johnston, from *Do They Ever Grow Up?* (1978). Minnetonka, MN: Meadowbrook Press; reprint granted with written permission of Lynn Johnston Productions, Inc.

The following people were among the many who contributed the photographs that are used to illustrate points in the book: Ruth Blair, Anne Fraser, Jill Fraser, Alan Landy, Chris Landy, Jane Landy, Matthew Landy, Khan K. Liakat, Nilofar Liakat, Lesa Noonan, Sheikh Parvez Sleem, Jacqueline Mankiewicz Smith, and Lennox White of the audiovisual department at the Hincks-Dellcrest Institute and Treatment Centre. Photos are used with permission.

Library of Congress Cataloging-in-Publication Data

Landy, Sarah.
  Pathways to competence : encouraging healthy social and emotional development in young children / by Sarah Landy.
     p.   cm.
Includes bibliographical references and index.
  ISBN 1-55766-577-X
1. Child development.   2.   Child psychology.   3.   Child rearing.   I.   Title.
  HQ772. L242 2002
  305 .231—dc21

                                                                    2002018499

British Library Cataloguing in Publication data are available from the British Library.

CONTENTS

ABOUT THE AUTHOR

Sarah Landy, Ph.D., is a developmental and clinical psychologist at the Hincks-Dellcrest Institute and the Developmental Centre at Toronto East General Hospital in Toronto, Ontario, Canada. She is also Assistant Professor in the Department of Psychiatry at the University of Toronto and an Adjunct Professor at York University in Toronto.

Dr. Landy has worked for more than 20 years in the field of early intervention. Among her many published works, she has written several articles and contributed to books on various topics related to the assessment and treatment of infants, young children, and their families, including "Parenting Infants from Birth to Two Years," in *Parenting in America* (Landy & Menna, 2000, ARC Clio); "Assessment and Evaluation in Community Settings," in the *World Handbook of Infant Mental Health* (Landy, 2000, John Wiley & Sons); and "Difficult Behaviours: When Your Child Seems Out of Control," from *The New Baby and Child Care Encyclopedia* (Landy, 1995, Family Communications, Inc.).

Dr. Landy has been involved in a variety of aspects of early intervention, including program development, program management as director and clinical director, research, consultation, teaching and training, and clinical practice. The programs she has initiated and developed include a tracking system for infants and young children in which mothers and children were assessed for any risks during the children's first 5 years, developmental services, and community-based services for families at psychosocial risk. Her current interests and activities include assessment and treatment of young children with severe developmental, behavioral, and emotional disorders of various kinds, treatment of high-risk families with young children, program development, and training. Dr. Landy has always been interested in community-based early intervention programs and has been an advocate for programs that can reach and be relevant for the most at-risk families.

FOREWORD

With a focus on building strengths within a growth-promoting environment, *Pathways to Competence: Encouraging Healthy Social and Emotional Development in Young Children* addresses an important area for our understanding of children's development. Because so many children do not have the opportunity to live and develop in positive, nurturing environments, a focus on what is most important for the healthy social and emotional development of children is crucial.

Sarah Landy has been creative in including ideas for parents as well as professionals who deal with children. The ideas are consistent, and she forges a path in many new prevention and intervention directions focusing on crucial developmental issues, such as building secure attachments, self-esteem, morality, emotion regulation, and social competence. Helpful information for parents provides practical tools that they can use to guide them in developing and nurturing these capacities in their children.

The number of risk factors a child has, rather than any specific combination of factors, can significantly jeopardize the development of the infant's mental health. Most mental health interventions focus around children in poverty, adolescent parents and their infants, parents with mental illness and/or substance abuse, children exposed to violence and trauma, children with ongoing and/or severe medical conditions, and children in foster care. These interventions include prevention that may be specific, such as providing education and training; or global, utilizing a public health approach including early identification of risk, infant–parent intervention models, and interventions in a variety of environments. *Pathways to Competence* is especially useful in helping to guide child care providers, interventionists, mental health providers, parents, and others working with young children in understanding risk and resilience issues faced by all children growing up today, not just those in high-risk groups. Positive experiences in early development build competence. Mental health professionals emphasize the importance of both prevention and intervention approaches supporting the development of competence in children, as does Dr. Landy in this book.

Dr. Landy makes a strong case that relationships between children and parents and even parents and their own parents are crucial to understanding children's mental health. A focus on relationships includes recognizing and fostering reciprocity between child and caregiver, involving shared and complementary affects and experiences that are extremely important for the developing infant to build positive attachments. The importance of attachment relationships is emphasized throughout this book as a major factor contributing to competence. Emotional availability that accompanies a reciprocal relationship is a primary means of nonverbal communication for the infant and caregiver. Dr. Landy stresses that parenting effectiveness and adaptive parenting rely heavily on parents' ability to regulate their emotions. Reciprocity, or building mutually satisfying relationships between the young child and his or her parent, influences both behavioral and affective development. Bowlby (1973, 1980) emphasized the importance of early separation and loss as potentially disruptive to the development of the relationship. In addition to traumatic events, children may experience rejecting or overly frustrating events in their families, such as abuse and neglect, which may lead to disruptions in the development of reciprocity and, subsequently, significantly interfere with a child developing the trust that leads to competence and security.

The ability to share emotions is extremely important for affective development because it is through a caregivers' sharing of emotions with the infant that a feeling state is understood. If the parent is unable to share the infant's affective states, this may result in a lack of reciprocity in the relationship. These ideas are closely related to the sensitive work of Fraiberg, Adelson, and Shapiro (1975) centering on disturbed mothers' neurotic repetitive patterns that interfered with their ability to parent their infants. They termed these repetitive and maladaptive patterns "ghosts in the nursery" because of their tendency to be repeated generation after generation if no reparative work was done. All of these ideas form the "risk" background that interferes with the child's and parent's finding pathways to competence.

A very important risk factor in our society is violence exposure, which affects even the youngest of children and interferes with their normal development of trust and later exploratory behavior (Drell, Siegel, & Gaensbauer, 1993; Osofsky, 1997). In addition, parents and other caregiving adults may be numbed, frightened, anxious, or depressed by exposure to trauma. Parents or other caregivers experiencing these feelings make it even more difficult for children's healthy socioemotional development in that children's development of trust and security comes from caregivers who are emotionally available. Exposure to violence and trauma can lead children to withdraw, show disorganized behaviors, and also become aggressive. For some children, however, resilience or invulnerability appears to characterize their responses to even very difficult environments. These children are able to find the support and guidance they need and have less difficulty with finding pathways to competence.

Often, protective factors are more difficult to identify than risk factors. Frequently, conditions may increase resilience to later disturbance under conditions of adversity. Protective factors may exist within the infants or children, parents, or the environment. Again, one of the most important protective resources a child needs to build competence is a strong relationship with a competent, caring, positive adult—most often with a parent. When children have a supportive relationship with an adult as well as good attention and interpersonal skills of their own, many children can move toward competence despite their difficult environmental circumstances. Pathways to competence, the focus of this book, are paved with parenting skills that play a central role in children's risk-taking ability, resources, opportunities, and resilience.

The policy implications of work in the area of building children's competencies are clear when taking into consideration the body of work compiled by Landy and other researchers in this area. The future of infant mental health related to building competence has been considered carefully at the turn of the new century in the significant National Research Council publication, *Neurons to Neighborhoods: The Science of Early Childhood Development* (Shonkoff & Phillips, 2000). This report emphasized that all children are wired for feelings and are ready to learn, that early environment matters, that nurturing relationships are essential, and that society is changing and the needs of young children are not being addressed. Similarly, *Pathways to Competence* refocuses the attention of professionals who work with young children as well as parents who are their main nurturers on to ways that foster children's optimal development.

Joy D. Osofsky, Ph.D.
Professor of Public Health, Psychiatry, and Pediatrics
Louisiana State University Health Sciences Center

REFERENCES

Bowlby, J. (1973). *Attachment and loss, Vol. 2: Attachment.* New York: Basic Books.

Bowlby, J. (1980). *Attachment and loss, Vol 3: Loss.* New York: Basic Books.

Drell, M.J., Siegel, C.H., & Gaensbauer, T.J. (1993). Posttraumatic stress disorder. In C.H. Zeanah, Jr. (Ed.), *Handbook of infant mental health* (pp. 291–304). New York: Guilford Press.

Fraiberg, S., Adelson, E., & Shapiro, V. (1975). Ghosts in the nursery: A psychoanalytic approach to the problems of impaired infant–mother relationships. *Journal of the American Academy of Child and Adolescent Psychiatry, 14,* 387–421.

Osofsky, J.D. (1997). *Children in a violent society.* New York: Guilford Publishers.

Shonkoff, J.P., & Phillips, D.A. (2000). *From neurons to neighborhoods: The science of early childhood development.* Board on Children, Youth and Families, National Research Council and Academy of Medicine. Washington, DC: National Academy Press.

ACKNOWLEDGMENTS

The people who have contributed to the writing of this book are too numerous to mention them all. I would, however, like to acknowledge the National Health and Development Program, Health Canada Grant #6606–4806–102, which allowed me to develop and evaluate the parenting program on which the book is based.

I thank my friends and colleagues Dr. Rosanne Menna, Dr. Elizabeth Thompson, and Norma Sockett-Dimarcio, who helped *Pathways to Competence: Encouraging Healthy Social and Emotional Development in Young Children* come to fruition through their work with the Helping Encourage Affect Regulation (HEAR) parenting program. I am grateful for the support of the staff and management of the Hincks-Dellcrest Institute and especially Dr. Freda Martin, who always encouraged me to go in new directions and to develop new ways of providing services. I am also grateful for the support of the Hincks-Dellcrest Treatment Centre's Growing Together team (or "family" as we called ourselves), who always provided thoughtfulness, humor, and understanding for everyone who was a part of it, as well as for the hundreds of children and families whom they support and encourage to grow and to flourish. It was with these caring people, working with families in one of the most high-risk areas in Toronto, that many of these ideas were conceived, implemented, and further developed.

Many other people worked on this book and helped make it a reality, including Nikki Martyn, who helped find the many hundreds of references on which the book is based. I would also like to express my thanks to the fine professionals at Paul H. Brookes Publishing Co., including former Brookes editor Jennifer Kinard, who was the first person to believe in this book. Special thanks go to my editor, Jessica Allan, who made sure the book took shape and that the content was accurate and the format suitable. I am very grateful for her patience, understanding, and knowledge as she helped me form the book and made sure it did not grow to 2,000 pages in length! I am also grateful to Leslie Eckard, who transformed my writing into something that flowed and became coherent for the readers and who took the book through the process of final production.

My deep gratitude and respect go to those families who were in the many parenting groups on which the book is based. They helped by describing the parenting tips that had worked for them. Their input clarified my thoughts and ideas into useful and meaningful strategies to share with other parents.

I am fortunate in having the support of four special friends—Jacque Montgomery, Elizabeth Pederson, Carmel Hall, and Mavis Stonefield—whom I have known for more than 30 years as we have traveled down our own "pathways." They were always there for me, especially when the journey was most difficult.

My greatest thanks go to Mary Damianakis, who was my research assistant from the book's first draft to its final "birth." She was always cheerful, meticulous, and understanding while keeping me convinced that one day the book would be published. Without her work, support, and friendship, this book would never have been completed.

INTRODUCTION:
STARTING ON THE PATHWAY

Many professionals who provide services to young children and their families have taken courses in early childhood development. Translating that knowledge into practical ideas and strategies that can be used with parents and children in real-life situations can be difficult, however:

- A recently graduated child psychiatrist on a training fellowship decided he wanted to evaluate the effect of a parenting group for fathers. He quickly realized that his training had neither prepared him for the fathers' questions about preschool behavior that arose nor provided him with answers on advising about parenting strategies.

- A community home visitor and parent of three teenage daughters had begun to question her own strict style of discipline. She had smacked her girls when they were small but was looking for new ways to help the families she now worked with to deal with their children's negative behaviors. She knew she needed to consider and study alternative discipline methods before she could advise parents in new directions. She was particularly interested in learning about positive discipline techniques and ways to encourage self-regulation of aggression.

- A speech-language therapist found she was frequently encountering aggressive children in her practice who *could* talk but who failed to use language in their encounters with peers. She was interested in learning about the influence of attachment and negative self-esteem on children's aggression.

- A newly graduated psychologist found it necessary to spend a considerable amount of time finding answers to common parenting questions. Such information had not been provided in the child development graduate program she attended. She needed to translate knowledge about child development into ways to teach parents.

Despite the critical importance of the emotional and social development of children in overall development, in the past these areas received less attention than other areas of development in many early intervention, infant stimulation, and infant development programs. The importance of these areas was not widely acknowledged, and clear ways to optimize their development were less available. The importance of a secure attachment, healthy self-esteem, the ability to modulate intense emotions, and the capacity for empathy and prosocial behavior to healthy child development are becoming more widely researched and understood. Professionals are also more aware of both the process and the effects of compromised development, which can result in emotional problems and behavioral symptoms. As Daniel Goleman (1995) expressed it, how well people do in life is not only dependent on IQ scores but also on what he terms "emotional intelligence" or EQ, which includes abilities such as self-control, caring, expressing and understanding feelings, and self-esteem.

Pathways to Competence: Encouraging Healthy Social and Emotional Development in Young Children seeks to fill the gaps in knowledge in the literature of children's social and emotional capacities. The book closely examines what children need in order to thrive and move successfully from one stage to another.

FACTORS THAT INFLUENCE CHILD DEVELOPMENT

Before describing the contents of the book in depth, it is helpful to look at the many factors that influence child development and the challenges that parents face today. In many ways, parenting is more difficult today than it was in the past. More than 50% of marriages end in divorce, and families often split up when children are in their preschool years and are most vulnerable to being separated from a parent (Glick, 1988). This has resulted in an increasing diversity of living arrangements for children, including single-parent homes and blended families in which parents with children remarry (Shiono & Quinn, 1994). In addition, about 75% of young children spend most of their daytime hours with other caregivers in home or group child cares (Lero, Goelman, Pence, Brockman, & Nuttall, 1992). The effect of this experience on children varies according to the personal characteristics of the child and the quality of the child care, especially the caring and nurturing provided by the staff. Not only do many children find the child care experience difficult, but many parents also have a hard time coping as they worry about separation from their children and struggle to balance time for parenting, work, and relaxation (Hewlett, 1991; Lero et al., 1992; Steinhauer, 1996).

The Effects of Stress

An increasing number of children are also growing up in poverty (Carnegie Corporation of New York, 1994) and in neighborhoods characterized by crime, violence, and substance abuse (Dubrow & Garbarino, 1989; Garbarino, Kostelny, & Dubrow, 1991; Zuckerman & Brown, 1993). These factors place increased strain on families, especially those who have little support from the extended family or community. Finding the time and energy for parenting is increasingly difficult, and a growing number of parents report themselves as being psychologically and physically burdened by the experience (Statistics Canada, 1994).

These societal pressures can create stress. This stress can adversely affect neurological development in children and actually destroy synapses, the connections that enable neurons to work and to pass information from one area of the brain to the other (Sapolsky, 1994). This can result in deficits in memory and other cognitive processes. If stress is long term, it may also result in a hypersensitivity to certain experiences.

Parental Factors

Parental characteristics such as personality, level of self-esteem, and knowledge of parenting skills are also important influences. Another critical contributor is how parents' own childhoods influenced their parental styles. As a society, we are now far more aware that the way we were parented influences our interactions with our children. How many parents have heard their mother's or father's words coming out of their mouths as they talk to their children—words they were determined never to use with their own families? Parenting is said to come naturally, but it is natural to parent as one was parented. It is difficult to break negative patterns, even if one wants to (Benoit & Parker, 1994). As adults, we all have deep, underlying, sometimes unconscious, memory traces of how we were parented when we were very young (Grossman, Fremer-Bombik, Rudolph, & Grossman, 1988). Many of these memories were formed before we could speak and so consist of feelings and physical experiences. These can include wonderful warm feelings of being held and nurtured. Sadly, in other cases, we may also remember feeling ignored, rejected, or abused. These feelings and memories from infancy and childhood often remain buried for a long time and have little influence until one's own baby is born. At this time, the feelings or memories may come to the surface or remain unconscious but, nevertheless, may affect the way one raises his or her children.

Other Factors

Certain characteristics within the child, such as temperament, biological makeup, and level of responsiveness, also influence child outcomes. While all children differ in these areas and most still fall within what is considered typical, research has shown that as many as 4%–10% of school children and adolescents have a mental disorder (Offord, Boyle, & Racine, 1989). A substantial proportion of these children meet criteria for another disorder as well (i.e., the disorders are *comorbid*). For example, many children with anxiety disorders also show signs of depression, while those with conduct disorders often have symptoms of hyperactivity (Offord et al., 1989). These figures are consistent in surveys of child mental health carried out in several countries (Garralda & Bailey, 1986; Rutter, Tizard, & Yule, 1976; Velez, Johnson, & Cohen, 1989; Williams, Anderson, McGee, & Silva, 1990). Surveys of preschoolers conducted in the 1980s and 1990s identified a similar, or even higher, percentage of these children as having difficulties varying from excessive aggression and noncompliance to anxiety and withdrawal (Campbell, 1995; Landy, Peters, et al., 1998; Richman, Stevenson, & Graham, 1982; Tremblay, Pihl, Vitaro, & Dobkin, 1994).

Early help for young children and parents is, therefore, critical. Research suggests that 50% of preschoolers with severe problems will continue to have difficulties unless they receive intervention and their parents receive support, information about child development, parenting techniques, and sometimes, counseling (Campbell, Ewing, Breaux, & Szumowski, 1986; Rose, Rose, & Feldman, 1989).

REALIZING A CHILD'S FULL POTENTIAL

Although society increasingly confronts parents with challenges, the good news is that during the last two decades of the 20th century and beyond, researchers uncovered amazing information about early development and the characteristics of parenting that can optimize it. Most important, they learned that children needed to resolve certain developmental issues or stages before they can reach their full potential (Cicchetti, Ganiban, & Barnett, 1991; Landy & Peters, 1992). Fortunately, most parents are enthusiastic about learning about their child and helpful parenting strategies and are open to new ideas and information.

The fact that children progress through different stages of development in a particular sequence is well known. In the areas of physical and cognitive development, this sequence is relatively clear: Children cannot form words before they have learned to make sounds; walking only comes after sitting and standing have been mastered. With emotional and social development, the sequences are less obvious, although the principles are similar. For example, if a child does not develop a secure attachment or relationship with a caregiver, it is difficult for him to develop other social relationships. Children who develop a basic sense of being able to control their bodies and a positive body image have a foundation for establishing a positive sense of self-esteem. A child who does not have adequate communication skills will find it hard to negotiate, problem-solve, or be empathic—in other words, he or she will have difficulty learning to listen to and understand the perspective of someone else.

Children who develop a basic sense of being able to control their bodies and a positive body image have a foundation for establishing a positive sense of self-esteem.

As in other areas of development, children need to resolve a number of developmental issues and to obtain a variety of capacities that can lay the foundation for later mental health (Cicchetti et al., 1991; Greenspan, 1981; Greenspan & Greenspan, 1985). As a developmental capacity is acquired, it is not then discarded in favor of the next learning challenge but will continue to evolve and expand as the child deals with new issues. For example, after children learn to walk, they continue to elaborate the skill by running, walking up stairs, and so forth. After acquiring the ability to say a few words, a child continues to elaborate on language skills for many years to come. From observing caregivers with children, we know that they can assist children as they progress through the early stages of their lives. Although there is not a complete caregiving system that can be taught to every caregiver, *Pathways to Competence* does include clear guidelines and some "do's" and "don'ts" of caregiving that can be adapted to fit children and their caregivers.

DEVELOPMENTAL CAPACITIES

During the course of a child's early emotional and social development, some capacities achieved in the first 6 years of life have been shown to be critical in forming foundations for later development. These capacities, which continue to evolve throughout an individual's life, are outlined next and in subsequent chapters of this book.

A *sense of body self* is the first capacity to develop as the infant begins to be able to separate from the caregiver (see Chapter 2). As the infant acquires more control over gross motor capacities such as sitting, rolling, and grasping, a positive sense of body image and of body control is established (Gallagher & Meltzoff, 1996; Krueger, 1989; Rochat, 1997).

During the next few months, the infant begins to develop *an attachment* to one or more primary caregivers (see Chapter 3), and children look to these individuals' presence and comforting, which encourages the child to explore the world and to feel secure in times of stress (Main, Kaplan, & Cassidy, 1985).

As the child reaches the middle of the second year, an interest develops in *pretend play* and symbolization (see Chapter 4). The child attempts to try on new roles and to play out frightening or frustrating experiences. As play becomes more and more elaborate, it is increasingly used to symbolically ease and modulate tension and anxiety. Play becomes a medium through which the child forms new mental images of events and people and works on old ones (Singer & Singer, 1990).

In the second and third years of life, the child becomes increasingly interested in *using language and communication* (see Chapter 5). The use of language becomes more and more elaborate, both as a means of expressing wants and desires and as a way to interact with peers and caregivers (Kopp, 1982).

By 3 years of age, children are developing and establishing a sense of self as well as a subjective and qualitative evaluation of themselves (see Chapter 6). This is *self-esteem,* and whether it is positive or negative, it will have a great deal of influence on how the child develops later (Mack & Ablon, 1983).

In the third year of life, children become more compliant and begin to *internalize standards, limits, and rules* that are imposed by caregivers (see Chapter 7). Over time, this internalization allows children to control their own behavior and to be freed from a primary reliance on external control by caregivers (Vaughn, Koop, & Krakow, 1984).

At about the same time, the child becomes more able to express negativity and regulate *emotions* without resorting to physical expressions such as hitting, biting, and scratching (see Chapter 8). Gradually, children who are encouraged to do so can express their frustration, anger, sadness, and anxiety by talking about it. Children can also avoid throwing tantrums—at least most of the time (Bretherton, Fritz, Zahn-Waxler, & Ridgeway, 1986; Kopp, 1982).

In order to deal with conflict and fights with others, 4- or 5-year-old children can be taught *concentration, planning, and problem-solving* (see Chapter 9), all of which will enable children to contain frustrations and manage relationships (Lyon & Krasnegor, 1996; Quiggle, Garber, Panak, & Dodge, 1992; Shure & Spivack, 1978). Although such behavior begins to develop earlier, the child at 4 or 5 years of age is usually able to *socialize* well, show *empathy for* the feelings of others, and can gradually initiate helping or *prosocial behavior* (Eisenberg & Mussen, 1989; Yarrow & Waxler, 1976) (see Chapter 10). With this capacity to understand and empathize with the point of view of others, a child can now manage difficult emotions and is able to engage in cooperative social interactions. Both are critical components of a child's healthy emotional and social development.

The Growth-Promoting Environment

Although maturation and a child's personal characteristics establish the groundwork for an individual to acquire these skills, input from caregivers is crucial. For each capacity and at different stages of the child's life, various caregiving interactions, teachings, and methods of encouraging the capacity are critical. Some of these ideas and ways of reacting come naturally to parents; others provide challenges so that parents need assistance both to understand these strategies and to provide them in an optimal way. This process is particularly difficult when children are already developing emotional or behavioral difficulties or are developmentally or physically challenged (Greenspan & Greenspan, 1985, 1989). As pointed out in each chapter, how parents respond when encouraging a particular developmental capacity in their child—such as self-esteem, attachment, or communication—can vary significantly.

WHO IS THIS BOOK FOR?

Pathways to Competence: Encouraging Healthy Social and Emotional Development in Young Children is designed for professionals, paraprofessionals, and home visitors who work with infants, young children, and their families in various environments. All of the sections can be used in in-service training and in courses on early child development; however, some sections are also suitable for use with parents and other caregivers, either individually or in groups, to provide developmental guidance and strategies to optimize caregiver–infant/child interactions. Of particular relevance in working directly with parents are the sections dealing with the development of the capacity, principles of the growth-promoting environment, and group and individual activities included in the sections entitled "Working with Parents." Specifically, the activities in this section can be used with groups of parents and in parenting workshops. These workshops may target particular areas of caregiving, such as discipline or improving the self-esteem, empathy, and values of young children. The chapters can also form the basis for a more extensive course for caregivers or be used as a training package. These ideas and approaches are designed to work with all parents by taking into consideration parents' varying levels of comfort with

such activities. If these approaches are not successful, other, more intense early intervention approaches designed for working with very high-risk families may be needed (Erickson & Kurz-Riemer, 1999; Lieberman, Silverman, & Pawl, 2000).

The book can also be a tool for independent study and a resource for ideas for early child development enhancement. The ideas can be used clinically with individuals as they ask for advice about problems with children or about how to enhance particular aspects of development.

The materials were developed from a parenting program that has been field tested with a variety of parent groups and revised in response to comments and evaluations from parent participants and group leaders. One study found that parents who completed the tasks in a parenting program using these materials showed increased sensitivity and less intrusiveness in interactions with their children compared with pre-test measures. Children's negative behaviors were also significantly reduced at the end of the programs (Landy, Menna, & Sockett-Dimarcio, 1997). As well, parents found the program extremely useful and believed it helped them find meaningful, long-term approaches to parenting.

PURPOSE AND CONTENT OF THE BOOK

The overall purpose of *Pathways to Competence* is to give service providers an understanding of the basic dimensions of development in young children with an emphasis on emotional and social development. The book also provides a variety of practical, concrete suggestions for encouraging healthy development of children.

Pathways to Competence describes the development of a number of crucial skills and capacities in young children. Each chapter includes definitions and theories related to the capacity, and explains its importance in overall development. Each chapter follows the same basic structure and includes

- Definitions and theories related to the capacity

- The importance of the capacity in a child's overall development

- How the capacity develops through the stages of a child's life

- Important, up-to-date research findings related to each capacity

- Characteristics of the growth-promoting environment, including principles that foster the growth of the capacity

- Commonly raised issues

- Discussion questions to use in training early childhood professionals

- Ways to work with parents individually and in groups

Included, as well, are case vignettes and activities that can be used to support caregivers in positive interactions with their children. Each chapter ends with a list of sample measures that service providers might use in order to pinpoint potential problems or assess the effectiveness of various interventions (note that many of these should only be administered by trained professionals).

Children are eventually able to initiate helping or prosocial behaviors.

REFERENCES

Benoit, D., & Parker, K.C.H. (1994). Stability and transmission of attachment across three generations. *Child Development, 65,*1444–1456.

Bretherton, I., Fritz, J., Zahn-Waxler, C., & Ridgeway, D. (1986). Learning to talk about emotion: A functionalist perspective. *Child Development, 57,* 529–548.

Campbell, S.B. (1995). Behavior problems in preschool children: A review of recent research. *Journal of Child Psychology and Psychiatry and Allied Disciplines, 36,* 113–149.

Campbell, S.B., Ewing, L., Breaux, A., & Szumowski, E. (1986). Parent-referred problem three-year-olds: Follow-up at school entry. *Journal of Child Psychology and Psychiatry and Allied Disciplines, 27,* 473–488.

Carnegie Corporation of New York, Task Force on Meeting the Needs of Young Children. (1994). *Starting points: Meeting the needs of our youngest children.* New York: Author.

Cicchetti, D., Ganiban, J., & Barnett, D. (1991). Contributions from the study of high-risk populations to understanding the development of emotion regulation. In J. Garber & K.A. Dodge (Eds.), *The development of emotion regulation and dysregulation* (pp. 15–48). New York: Cambridge University Press.

Dubrow, N.F., & Garbarino, J. (1989). Living in the war zone: Mothers and young children in a public housing development. *Child Welfare, 68,* 3–20.

Eisenberg, N., & Mussen, P. (1989). *The roots of prosocial behavior in children.* New York: Cambridge University Press.

Erickson, M.F., & Kurz-Riemer, K. (1999). *Infants, toddlers, and families: A framework for support and intervention.* New York: Guilford Press.

Gallagher, S., & Meltzoff, A.N. (1996). The earliest sense of self and others: Merleau-Ponty and recent developmental studies. *Community Alternatives: International Journal of Family Care, 9,* 211–223.

Garbarino, J., Kostelny, K., & Dubrow, N. (1991). *No place to be a child: Growing up in the war zone.* Lexington, MA: Lexington Books.

Garralda, M.E., & Bailey, D. (1986). Children with psychiatric disorders in primary care. *Journal of Child Psychology and Psychiatry and Allied Disciplines, 27,* 611–624.

Glick, P.C. (1988). The role of divorce in the changing family structure: Trends and variations. In S.A. Wolchick & P. Karoly (Eds.), *Children of divorce: Empirical perspectives on adjustment.* New York: Gardner Press.

Goleman, D. (1995). *Emotional intelligence: Why it can matter more than IQ.* New York: Bantam Books.

Greenspan, S. (1981). *Psychopathology and adaptation in infancy and early childhood: Principles of clinical diagnosis and preventive intervention.* New York: International Universities Press.

Greenspan, S., & Greenspan, N. (1985). *First feelings: Milestones in the emotional development of your baby and child.* New York: Penguin.

Greenspan, S., & Greenspan, N. (1989). *The essential partnership.* New York: Viking.

Grossman, K., Fremer-Bombik, E., Rudolph, J., & Grossman, K.E. (1988). Maternal attachment representations as related to patterns of infant–mother attachment and maternal care during the first year. In R. Hinde & J. Stevenson-Hinde (Eds.), *Relationships within families: Mutual influences* (pp. 241–262). Oxford, UK: Clarendon Press.

Hewlett, S.A. (1991). Mainstream kids and the time deficit. In S.A. Hewlett (Ed.), *When the bough breaks: The cost of neglecting our children* (pp. 62–100). New York: Basic Books.

Kopp, C. (1982). Antecedents of self-regulation: A developmental perspective. *Developmental Psychology, 18,* 199–214.

Krueger, D.W. (1989). *Body self and psychological self: A developmental and clinical integration of disorders of the self.* New York: Brunner/Mazel.

Landy, S., Menna, R., & Sockett-Dimarcio, N. (1997). A pilot study to evaluate a treatment model for parents of preschoolers with behavioral problems. *Early Child Development and Care, 131,* 45–64.

Landy, S., & Peters, R. DeV. (1992). Towards an understanding of a developmental paradigm for aggressive conduct disorders during the preschool years. In R. DeV. Peters, R.J. McMahon, & V.L. Quinsey (Eds.), *Aggression and violence throughout the lifespan* (pp. 1–30). Beverly Hills: Sage Publications.

Landy, S., Peters, R. DeV., Arnold, R., Allen, A.B., Brookes, F., & Jewell, S. (1998). Evaluation of "Staying on Track": An identification, tracking, and referral system. *Infant Mental Health Journal, 19,* 34–58.

Lero, D.S., Goelman, H., Pence, A.R., Brockman, L.M., & Nuttall, S. (1992). *Parental work patterns and child care needs.* Ottawa, Ontario: Statistics Canada.

Lieberman, A.F., Silverman, R., & Pawl, J.H. (2000). Infant-parent psychotherapy: Core concepts and current approaches. In C.H. Zeanah (Ed.), *Handbook of infant mental health* (2nd ed., pp. 472–484). New York: Guilford Press.

Lyon, G.R., & Krasnegor, N.A. (Eds.). (1996). *Attention, memory, and executive function.* Baltimore: Paul H. Brookes Publishing Co.

Mack, J.E., & Ablon, S.L. (1983). *The development and sustenance of self-esteem in childhood.* New York: International Universities Press.

Main, M., Kaplan, N., & Cassidy, J. (1985). Security in infancy, childhood and adulthood: A move to the level of representation. *Monographs of the Society for Research in Child Development, 50* (1–2, Serial No. 209), 66–104.

Offord, D.R., Boyle, M.H., & Racine, Y.A. (1989). Ontario Child and Health Study: Correlates of disorder. *Journal of the American Academy of Child and Adolescent Psychiatry, 28,* 856–860.

Quiggle, N., Garber, J., Panak, W.F., & Dodge, K.A. (1992). Social information processing in aggressive and depressed children. *Child Development, 63,* 1305–1320.

Richman, N., Stevenson, J., & Graham, P.J. (1982). *Pre-school to school: A behavioural study.* London: Academic Press.

Rochat, P. (1997). Early development of the ecological self. In C. Dent-Read, & P. Zukow-Goldring (Eds.), *Evolving explanations of development: Ecological approaches to organism-environment systems* (pp. 91–121). Washington, DC: American Psychological Association.

Rose, S., Rose, F., & Feldman, J. (1989). Stability of behavior problems in very young children. *Development and Psychopathology, 1,* 5–19.

Rutter, M., Tizard, J., & Yule, (1976). Research report: Isle of Wight studies, 1964–1974. *Psychological Medicine, 6,* 313–332.

Sapolsky, R.M. (1994).*Why zebras don't get ulcers: A guide to stress, stress-related diseases, and coping.* New York: W.H. Freeman.

Shiono, P.H., & Quinn, L.S. (1994). Epidemiology of divorce. *Future of Children, 4,* 15–28.

Shure, M., & Spivack, G. (1978).*Problem solving techniques in child rearing.* San Francisco: Jossey-Bass.

Singer, D.G., & Singer, J.L. (1990). *The house of make-believe: Children's play and the developing imagination.* Cambridge, MA: Harvard University Press.

Statistics Canada (1994). *Parents' report of the experience of caring for their children.* Ottawa: Author.

Steinhauer, P.D. (1996). *Developing resiliency in children from disadvantaged populations.* Toronto: University of Toronto.

Tremblay, R.E., Pihl, R.O., Vitaro, F., & Dobkin, P. (1994). Predicting early onset of male antisocial behavior from preschool behavior. *Archives of General Psychiatry, 51,* 732–739.

Vaughn, B., Koop, C., & Krakow, J. (1984). The emergence and consolidation of self control from 18–30 months of age: Normative trends and individual differences. *Child Development, 55,* 990–1004.

Velez, C.N., Johnson, J., & Cohen, P. (1989). A longitudinal analysis of selected risk factors for childhood psychopathology. *Journal of the American Academy of Child and Adolescent Psychiatry, 28,* 861–864.

Williams, S., Anderson, J., McGee, R., & Silva, P.A. (1990). Risk factors for behavioral and emotional disorders in preadolescent children. *Journal of the American Academy of Child and Adolescent Psychiatry, 29,* 413–419.

Yarrow, M., & Waxler, C. (1976). Dimensions and correlates of prosocial behaviour in young children. *Child Development, 47,* 118–125.

Zuckerman, B., & Brown, E. (1993). Maternal substance abuse and infant development. In C.H. Zeanah (Ed.), *Handbook of infant mental health (pp. 143–158).* New York: Guilford Press.

● ● ● 1

UNDERSTANDING EARLY CHILD DEVELOPMENT AND TEMPERAMENT

Of all the things we do in life, raising children is one of the most exciting and fulfilling. This is especially true of children's early years, when developmental changes are particularly dramatic as new abilities constantly emerge, changing the way the little ones relate to the world and our interactions with them. The differences among a newborn baby who spends much of the time sleeping and eating, the toddler who can walk around and explore the world, and the preschooler who can use sentences to talk to friends are remarkable. Each stage has its particular challenges and can sometimes be confusing for caregivers. Consequently, all caregivers experience some frustration with children in their care from time to time. In fact, infants and young children are sometimes delightful, exasperating, and exhausting all at the same time: Few caregivers can claim that they have never become furious with a small child at one minute only to be overwhelmed with delight at some cute behavior soon after. Often, this roller coaster of emotion goes on until the little one is at last tucked into bed and sleeping peacefully.

A child's rapid changes in behavior or mood can be confusing for caregivers and leave them feeling inadequate and even rejected by the small child in their care. In fact, some parents become so upset that they may withdraw from or overdiscipline their young child because they do not understand how to deal with a new or challenging behavior that their child is exhibiting. Professional caregivers may experience similar frustrations.

In the first 6 years of life, children undergo extraordinary change. On one hand, although newborn infants have a number of exciting capacities that allow them to respond to caregivers, much of their behavior is reflexive and not under voluntary control. Moreover, they are so helpless that without constant caregiving, they would not survive. On the other hand, the competent 6-year-old is capable of maintaining warm, caring relationships with other children and adults; communicating with others; controlling negative emotions; and planning and problem solving.

Development, it is now widely recognized, involves a number of qualitative shifts or re-organizations that allow a child to increasingly adapt to the environment (Greenspan, 1985; Lieberman, 1993). When these shifts occur, capacities that developed earlier across various developmental areas are transformed and result in more sophisticated levels of organization. The shifts or changes include a child's abilities to establish attachments to consistent caregivers; develop representational capacity for language and pretend play; gain perspective-taking or an understanding of another's point of view, and exhibit empathy and caring behavior.

Although established in a rudimentary fashion during a child's first 6 years, these adaptations remain ongoing, lifetime, psychological issues. Throughout life we continue to gain understanding about relationships, and we struggle to find optimal ways to communicate and modulate negative feelings such as anger, sadness, or jealousy. Satisfactory resolution of developmental tasks at one stage tends to lead to better adaptation, however, and prepares the way for competence at the next stage. Conversely, failure to achieve a level of competency at an early stage can lead to the compromising of future development, and difficulty adjusting to the cognitive and social demands of child care and school.

While in most children qualitative shifts occur in sequence and become increasingly established and comfortable, at times regressions occur, and a child may temporarily seem to return to an earlier stage of development. Many children seem to become more irritable and to have problems sleeping while they are learning to walk, for example, which subsides once the new skill is achieved. These regressions can occur for a number of reasons and can vary significantly in their severity and continuity. Sometimes, early difficulties with developmental shifts can result in ongoing difficulties.

The following vignette illustrates how one child, Luke, had problems from a very early age that affected interactions with his mother. These issues and his delays in many areas of development continued to affect one another throughout his early years, and as a result Luke had difficulty adjusting to school.

● ●

Luke was a very irritable infant, who cried constantly and seemed inconsolable. He arched away from his mother when she tried to comfort him. Luke's "fussiness" and the sleepless nights his mother spent with him made her feel inadequate and exhausted. Unsure how to respond to Luke, his mother became increasingly distant, and Luke's attachment to her was insecure and avoidant. He tended to isolate himself and not to reach out for help when he was upset. As he matured with little opportunity for warm, meaningful interactions, Luke's social behavior was often alternatively aggressive or withdrawn. His ability to play and his language development were also delayed and showed little positive affectivity or richness. In fact, Luke seemed to have trouble playing with others and in controlling his anger and frustration. Consequently, when Luke started school his teachers found him to be an unhappy, isolated child who had difficulty concentrating and calming down, and who was inclined to act out toward the other children indiscriminately.

The kinds of outcomes described in this vignette are not unusual, unfortunately.

As Table 1.1 shows, similar regressive behavioral symptoms may reflect very different causes, some stemming from the child and others from the environment. Although some re-

Table 1.1.   Examples of regressions and possible reasons for them

Type of regression	Some possible reasons for the regression
Disruption of sleep in a 1-year-old who had been sleeping through the night	Parents were away for a few days, leaving the child with grandparents.
	Child is so focused on learning to walk that she finds it very difficult to settle down, and may refuse to lie down at night, wanting to walk around the crib instead.
	Family has moved and the child is feeling anxious in the new surroundings.
Child who was toilet-trained and drinking out of a cup now wants to have a bottle and has constant toileting accidents	A new sibling has come home from the hospital and the older child is upset by having to share the attention of his parents.
	Parents have separated and the child is feeling anxious.
	Child has started child care and is very upset by the separation.
A 2½-year-old, who at age 1 had a few words, shows a sudden loss of language and increasing inability to relate to other children and adults	Child may have pervasive developmental disorder-not otherwise specified (PDD-NOS).
	Family violence has become a significant aspect of environment and is very frightening to the child.
	A recent flood has meant the family has temporarily had to move out of the family home.

solve quickly, others may need further evaluation and treatment by a health or mental health professional. It is important to recognize that some of the regressions may be helpful. They may allow the child to return to an earlier, more secure level of functioning in order to integrate a change—such as the birth of a new sibling or starting child care, for instance—before the child is able to move on again.

DEFINITIONS OF DEVELOPMENT AND TEMPERAMENT

In this section, we define development and temperament generally as well as explain the aspects or components that make up each term. To develop, according to *The New Webster's Dictionary,* means "to unfold gradually," which describes quite graphically what happens in a child's first 6 years of life.

Definition of Development

When professionals observe or assess development, they consider how the child is achieving in different aspects of development. Seven major areas are usually considered:

1. *Gross motor:* What the child can do with large muscle groups, such as running, jumping, and climbing stairs.

2. *Fine motor:* What the child can do with small muscle groups, including building with blocks; picking up, handling, and fitting small objects into other containers; banging things together; and doing puzzles.

3. *Cognitive:* This describes, for example, the child's understanding of object permanence, concepts such as *large* and *small,* classification, and problem-solving.

4. *Language and communication:* This area includes skills in receptive language (i.e., what the child understands) and expressive language (i.e., what the child can say). Gestures and non-verbal communication are also considered here.

5. *Self-help:* Skills include independent feeding, dressing, and toileting.

6. *Emotional development:* This includes the child's affective display, regulation, and control of emotions.

7. *Social development:* Attachment, level of cooperative play, empathy, and relatedness are considered here.

Other important areas, discussed in the temperament section of this chapter, include auditory and visual processing, sensory integration, memory, and motor planning. Although all of these areas affect one another and are important, in this chapter the areas of a child's social and emotional development are emphasized.

Definition of Temperament

The word *temperament* has no universal definition at this time, and researchers have defined temperament in a number of ways. In general, the term has been used to describe individual differences in children or in their behavioral styles. Chess and Thomas (1996) explained temperament as the behavioral style ("how") of behavior and not the content ("what") or motivation ("why") for what the child does. Other researchers have defined temperament differently. For example, Derryberry and Rothbart (1997), and Rothbart (1999) described temperament as composed of differences in reactivity and regulation. Goldsmith (1993), Goldsmith and Campos (1986), and Goldsmith and Lemery (2000) described it as the expression of emotions; and Buss and Plomin (1984) and Goldsmith, Lemery, Aksan, and Buss (2000) as personality traits appearing early in life. Moreover, some researchers have emphasized the biological basis of temperament while others have been more interested in its impact on parent–child interactions.

Most temperament theorists agree on certain components, although their emphases may differ. These components on which theorists agree include the following:

• Temperament has various dimensions. Some of these are emotionality, reactivity and regulation, activity level, sociability, and adaptability.

• Major elements of temperament are present early in life but do not acquire stability until later.

• Temperament characteristics are displayed differently at different ages and stages.

• The dimensions of temperament are influenced by biological factors.

• The goodness-of-fit between the child's temperament and her environment—especially the parents' values and expectations—is considered by some researchers to be a crucial influence on a child's social-emotional well being.

THEORIES OF DEVELOPMENT AND TEMPERAMENT

The following theories of development and temperament have been established from years of research on young children.

Theories of Development

A numbers of theories have formed the initial basis for understanding how development unfolds (see Table 1.2). They differ significantly in their emphasis on the importance of biological processes as opposed to children's experiences, the role of stages, the involvement of the child in fostering development, and the factors and circumstances that are considered to affect development, however. None of the theories listed in Table 1.2 used alone can describe all of the changes and shifts that occur in a child's first 6 years of life. Consequently, an eclectic view that integrates the important aspects of and insights from many theories is most useful.

Other theories not included in Table 1.2 that have been developed in recent years and guide current thinking on development are discussed in the section on Important Research Findings in this chapter. They also are described in subsequent chapters of this book. These theories are based on information on brain development and neuroplasticity, the effects of trauma and resilience, and emotion regulation. Modern theories accept that genetics (nature) and environment (nurture) both have significant influence on developmental outcomes. Researchers and theorists have moved beyond efforts to document how much each contributes to development and consider instead the processes or causal pathways by which each operates on the final outcomes for children and adults. These include various areas of development as well as success in school and later in careers and relationships. Numbers of theories such as the transactional, contextual, and ecological have considered how the interplay among various contributors within the child and various aspects of the environment affect development. These theories are discussed further later in this chapter.

Theories of Temperament

Until the 1960s, the study of temperament or individual differences in children was practically ignored in the clinical literature. Differences in children's temperaments were considered as best explained by variations in children's past experiences, particularly those related to how their parents raised them. Parents (particularly mothers) were often seen as responsible for such problems as attention-deficit/hyperactivity disorder (ADHD), learning disabilities, and even autism spectrum disorders. In the 1960s and 1970s there was a resurgence in interest in viewing the infant or child as an important contributor to the parent–child interaction (Lewis & Rosenblum, 1974) and acceptance that caregivers could experience children differently from one another as a result of these individual differences or temperaments.

Another important trend was an upsurge in acceptance of the *ethological* position (most forcibly supported by Ainsworth, 1967, 1969; Bowlby, 1958, 1969a, 1969b; and Freedman, 1965, 1974, 1976). This position views the infant as inheriting certain species-specific behaviors or behavioral systems that are "strictly limited by the state of development of the brain" that predispose the infant to various types of reactions (Bowlby, 1969a, p. 156).

Table 1.2. Major theories of development

Theorist	Type of theory	Major constructs	Stages of early development
Freud (1964, 1975)	Psychoanalytic	Personality seen as consisting of id, ego and superego Levels of consciousness and importance of the unconscious are stressed Defense mechanisms (e.g., repression, denial) are emphasized Mother viewed as primary love object Resolution of Oedipal and Electra complexes during late preschool years seen as crucial	Birth to 1 year: Oral stage 2–3 years: Anal stage 3–6 years: Phallic-urethral stage
Erikson (1963)	Psychosocial/ego psychology	Both internal psychological and external social factors considered important in shaping development Ego growth and identity emphasized Continuing sense of mastery and achievement critical Primary importance is put on the mother–child relationship Psychosocial stages throughout lifetime are emphasized	Birth to 18 months: Basic trust versus mistrust 1–3 years: Autonomy versus doubt and shame 3–6 years: Initiative versus guilt
Ainsworth (1969) Bowlby (1969 a,b)	Attachment theory	Quality and consistency of parent–child relationships in early years is critical Security or quality of attachment of child to primary caregivers influences behavior and relationships with others Securely attached infants receive adequate care, warmth, and predictability from caregiver	Birth–3 months: Non-focused orienting and signaling 3–6 months: Focuses on one or more figures 6–24 months: Secure base behavior 24–30 months: Goal-directed partnership, Declining separation anxiety
Piaget (1970)	Cognitive	Adaptation is in response to ongoing environmental experiences and interaction with the environment Quest is for *equilibrium* using *assimilation* and *accommodation* Emphasizes the transforming of cognitive structures Learning also occurs through social contact and observation of others	Birth to 2 years: Sensorimotor period 2–7 years: Preoperational period

Theorist	Type of theory	Major constructs	Stages of early development
Lorenz (1971)	Ethological theory	Strong emphasis on biological foundation of children's development Behavior is tied to evolution and characterized by critical and sensitive periods Imprinting is rapid learning that occurs after birth Uses observations in natural settings for research	No stages proposed, although critical periods are defined for imprinting and so forth
Skinner (1974)	Behaviorist	Human beings shaped by the environment Development dependent on contingency of environmental consequences (reinforcement, absence of reinforcement, and punishment) following behavior Conditioning determines the probability that a response will occur again Child is passive reactor	No stages proposed. Development viewed as continuous
Mischel (1974) Bandura (1977)	Social learning theory	Behaviors are seen primarily as shaped by the environment, but the role of cognitive maturation also is acknowledged Focuses on observational learning, imitation, and modeling of behavior Cognition can be used to regulate and control behavior Child is an active participant in learning interactions	No exact stages proposed, but stages are mentioned
Bronfenbrenner (1979) Lerner (1991) Sameroff and Fiese (2000)	Ecological, developmental contextual, and transactional theories	Considers the child's developmental outcome as a product of the interaction between the individual's characteristic and the environment The social context is considered in terms of how it influences parent–child interactions Considers risk and protective factors in child and environment Goodness of fit between all levels of influence are seen as important Positive changes can occur if protective mechanisms are enhanced	No stages proposed, but child's development at any time is seen to be a result of transactions across time between child and family characteristics as well as the social context

The New York Longitudinal Study   The largest influence on the study of temperament, however, came from the New York Longitudinal Study (NYLS), which began in 1956 and extended for 3 decades (Thomas, Chess, & Birch, 1968). The study assessed 131 individuals from 3 months of age into adulthood on a number of temperament dimensions. Based on extensive interviews with the parents and later with the participants themselves, a theory was developed that proposed nine characteristics or dimensions of temperament (Chess & Thomas, 1996). These dimensions based on traits, described in greater detail in Table 1.3, are as follows:

1. Activity level

2. Regularity/rhythmicity

3. Approach/withdrawal/first reactions

4. Adaptability

5. Sensory threshold/sensitivity

Table 1.3.   Temperamental traits identified in the New York Longitudinal Study (NYLS)

Trait	Definition
Activity level	Refers to the level of motor activity and the proportion of active to inactive periods. While some children cannot sit still for a minute, others play for hours quietly with their toys.
Regularity/rhythmicity	Refers to how predictable or regular a child is in terms of biological functions such as hunger, sleep-wake cycle, and bowel elimination. For some children, bedtime and meal times run like clockwork, while others have little natural rhythm or regularity.
Approach/withdrawal/ first reactions	Applies to wariness, or how easily a child accepts new things such as foods, people, places, clothes, or going to school for the first time. Some are "plungers" and react enthusiastically to new things while others immediately back off from the unfamiliar.
Adaptability	Applies to more long-term responses to new or changed situations and the degree to which reactions to stimuli can be modified in a desirable way. Children who are low on adaptability have a great deal of difficulty with any changes and with transitions during the day.
Sensory threshold/sensitivity	Responses to differences in flavor, texture, and temperature. Some highly sensitive children are overstimulated by noise, touch, bright lights, texture, and the feel of clothes, while less reactive children may be very difficult to arouse and present as passive and uninterested.
Intensity of reaction	Refers to the energy level of response, whether positive or negative. Some children's emotions are intense and easy to read, while others express themselves far less clearly or loudly.
Mood	Applies to the amount of pleasant, joyful, and friendly behavior that a child displays as compared with unpleasant crying or unfriendly behavior. Some children generally seem happy while for others everything is a source of complaint.
Distractibility	Refers to how effective outside stimuli are in interfering with or changing the direction of a child's ongoing behavior. Some children can attend with noise all around while others have to be perfectly isolated to get anything done.
Persistence/attention span	Refers to the amount of time an activity is pursued without interruption and its continuation in the face of obstacles. A persistent child may spend hours getting something just right.

Source: Thomas, A., Chess, S., & Birch, H.G. (1968). *Temperament and behavior disorders in children.* New York: New York University Press.

6. Intensity of reaction

7. Mood

8. Distractibility

9. Persistence/attention span

These dimensions are usually apparent from a very early age, with biological rhythms most important in infancy and other characteristics, such as adaptability, distractibility, and persistence becoming more significant as the child gets older. On the basis of these dimensions or temperament characteristics and the results of the study, Thomas and Chess (1977) distinguished three major types of children (see Table 1.4 for a list of types of children based on the NYLS). It was found that when a child displays one of these groupings of traits, the characteristics tend to remain stable over time, although they are displayed differently at various developmental stages.

In recent writings, these dimensions of temperament and the resulting clusters have been seen as developmental risk or protective factors. A child with a number of dimensions in a negative direction (e.g., slow rather than quick to adapt to new experiences and highly sensitive) is usually experienced as more challenging or difficult, while a child with a number of dimensions in a positive direction (e.g., positive rather than negative in mood and not distractible) may be able to handle more stressful situations in a more adaptive way. It is also important to note that although some temperament characteristics may predispose a child to certain difficulties; some of the "difficult" children in the NYLS did not end up having emotional or behavioral difficulties.

Table 1.4. Types of children as found in the New York Longitudinal Study (NYLS)

The difficult child (10%)

    Is **irregular** and has unpredictable routines

    Is low in approach, **withdrawing** from novelty

    Is **slow to adapt**

    Is **intense in reactions**

    Displays a lot of **negative mood**

The easy child (40%)

    Is **regular** and has predictable routines

    Readily **approaches** new things

    Easily adapts to new situations

    Shows a **mild** degree of **reaction**

    Is **positive in mood**

The slow-to-warm-up or **shy child** (5%–15%)

    Withdraws in new situations

    Is **slow to adapt**

    Is **low in activity** level and intensity

    Displays a lot of **negative mood**

Source: Thomas, A., Chess, S., & Birch, H.G. (1968). *Temperament and behavior disorders in children.* New York: New York University Press.

Note: Percentages do not add up to 100. Approximately 40% of children combine these qualities and have been called intermediate or mixed.

Temperament and Goodness of Fit   In order to explain the reasons that some "difficult" children developed difficulties while others did not, Thomas and Chess (1977) emphasized the importance of *goodness of fit* between the environment—including the parents' personality and values—and the child's temperament as important determinants of the developmental outcome. "Consequently, any temperament characteristic or group of them can become a source of friction between caregiver and child, depending on the situation. Similarly, no temperament cluster is a universal source of distress or invariably acceptable" (Carey & McDevitt, 1995, p. 14).

Other theorists who have made important contributions to the study and understanding of temperament are Bates, Freeland, and Lounsbury (1979); Buss and Plomin (1984); Goldsmith and Campos (1986); Kagan (1994); Rothbart and Derryberry (1981); and Strelau (1996). Although these theorists differ in terms of the dimensions of temperament they emphasize, they all see them as inherited or genetic individual differences that are relatively stable. Most of the theories include as basic dimensions those of emotional reactivity or expression, activity level, sociability, and adaptability (Goldsmith et al., 1987).

THE IMPORTANCE OF OVERALL DEVELOPMENT AND TEMPERAMENT

When development is compromised in any area, it is clear that this can set off a chain of difficulties that will adversely affect the child's ability to function in other areas. For example, a child who has speech delays may well show social and behavioral difficulties as a result. For this reason, it is important to monitor development in all developmental areas on an ongoing basis and to provide strategies to ameliorate difficulties when necessary.

Areas of Development

A child's temperament (difficult or easy) can affect his development in practically all areas of development, but particularly in the following areas:

Social Relationships   Children who are more inhibited or less adaptable in new situations may find social situations more difficult and may withdraw, while children who are more active and intense may become aggressive with other children. Conversely, the easy and more adaptable child often finds it fun to interact with peers and makes friends more easily.

Emotion Regulation   A child's capacity to modulate reactions to negative emotions has increasingly been found to be critical for overall adjustment. A child who is very negative in mood and intense in reactions will find it much more difficult to modulate his emotional reactions than a child who is generally cheerful and less intense.

Academic Achievement   Children who are very active, distractible, and who have short attention spans often have a great deal of difficulty adjusting to school and learning, while those who can concentrate well and can sit still when necessary are much more likely to do well.

Self-Esteem   Children with easier temperaments often elicit more favorable reactions from peers and caregivers and, as a result, feel good about themselves. Children with difficult

temperaments may elicit the opposite kinds of reactions and, as a result, have lower self-esteem. As well, children who find they have difficulty controlling themselves in different situations also can feel bad about themselves.

Emotional Development and Behavior   Difficult temperament can result in a variety of emotional and behavioral problems. These can include anxiety disorders, excessive aggression, depression, oppositional disorders, and ADHD. Of course, the possibility that these difficulties will develop depends on how extreme a temperament trait is, the goodness of fit between the child and parent, and how much the environment (social and physical) can be adapted to the child's needs.

STAGES OF DEVELOPMENT

In this section, development is divided into six periods: birth–3 months, 4–7 months, 8–14 months, 15–24 months, 2–4 years, and 4–6 years. For each of these developmental phases, the salient emotional and social developmental issues are described and expected capacities in other developmental areas are outlined. These developmental tables (see Tables 1.5–1.17) are intended as a guide to expected development, and the developmental profiles given for each age should be considered as those that will typically be reached by the upper level of the age range.

Birth to Three Months

The first 3 months of a child's life are a very exciting time for parents as their infant's capacities unfold. At the same time, if an infant is colicky and only sleeps for very short periods or if a mother suffers from postpartum depression or other stresses it can be a challenging time for parents. Infants are extremely demanding and are so helpless that they would die without care, but from the moment of birth, they have a number of important capacities and reflexes that support their survival.

The primary emotional and social milestones attained by an infant in the first 3 months involve the acquiring and use of two important capacities. One involves the infant's ability to establish some level of physiological homeostasis or regularity and another is a beginning capacity to self-calm. During this period, many infants sleep for up to 18 hours, but it may take some time before a predictable eating and sleep–wake routine is established. During the sleep–wake cycle, infants need to be able to move smoothly between sleeping and crying with alert periods in between that allow the infant's other emotional and social milestones to be achieved. For this to happen, the infant needs to display periods, at first extremely brief and gradually lengthening, of interest in the world. During these times, typically developing infants are alert and responsive to both *animate* (i.e., human) and *inanimate* (i.e., objects) stimuli. Having achieved these milestones of establishing a routine and having periods of alertness and responsiveness, the infant is ready to move on to having increased interpersonal and emotional interactions.

Infants at this time show the facial expression of most of the basic emotions of happiness, sadness, anger, distress, and surprise. Although these emotions are observable, how the child actually experiences these feelings is less clear. Of course, although she can sometimes settle

Table 1.5. By 3 months: Emotional and social milestones typically attained

Self-regulation	Interest and responsiveness to the world
Able to calm down or self-quiet for brief periods	Reliably signals to caregivers about needs
Feels sense of oneness with mother	Brightens, alerts, focuses and tracks objects
Sleeps regularly	Brightens to sounds, especially the human voice
Has predictable eating schedule	Enjoys touch, molds if held
Quiets when picked up	Enjoys movement in space (up and down, side-to-side)
Uses thumb sucking, gazing at objects, or other sensory modalities to calm down	Enjoys responding to people and eye-to-eye contact
Cycles through various states (e.g., crying, responsive alertness) with less crying and more alert times	Responds to social overtures with smiling, vocalization, and arm and leg movements
	Is able to recognize caregivers

herself by sucking on her fist or a pacifier or can look at an object for a sustained length of time, an infant needs her parents to respond to her cries and to calm her and hold her when she is upset. See Table 1.5 and Table 1.6 for a list of capacities most typical infants develop by age 3 months. In addition, Table 1.7 outlines some capacities of newborn infants and implications for optimum caregiving.

Table 1.6. Other capacities typically attained by 3 months of age

Gross motor	Cognition
Gets fist to mouth	Watches hands
Holds head up in upright position	Usually explores environment by looking around
Makes thrusting leg movements	Can follow moving objects with eyes
Rolls from side to back	Can recognize familiar faces, voices, and smells
Turns head from side to side	
On stomach, can lift head by using arms	

Fine motor	Emotional
Will grasp objects placed in palm	Expresses all basic emotions (happiness, anger, sadness, distress, and surprise)
May pat at object	Quiets to soft reassuring voice and to being picked up
Has control of eye muscles	Uses sustained looking or sucking to calm down
Focuses eyes 8–10 inches away	Entertains self by playing with hands, feet, and toes

Language	Social
Coos with two or more different sounds	Available for responsive interaction with caregivers
Attends to human speech	Quiets when picked up
Moves in synchrony to language of caregiver	Recognizes caregiver and reaches out and responds with pleasure
Cries if hungry or upset	Smiles in response to friendly face or voice
Makes sucking noises	
Babbles; repeats simple vowel and consonant sounds	

Self-help
Explores environment visually
Opens mouth to touch of breast or nipple of bottle
Sucks efficiently
Enjoys bathing

Table 1.7. Newborn capacities and their implications for caregivers

Infant capacities	Implications for caregivers
Can retain memory for 5–10 seconds	Responses to infant's signals need to be immediate
Prefers human voice to other sounds	Talking to the infant can be soothing or can help alert infant into periods of responsiveness
Follows unusually bright moving objects	Child is attracted to toys that are bright and that move
Prefers human face, especially eyes, to other visual stimuli	Infant especially enjoys eye-to-eye contact and face-to-face interaction. Enjoys mobiles with black and white features of face
Can see best 9–10 inches away	The face and toys are best placed at this distance
Sensitive to touch and movement	Most infants enjoy gentle touch and being held and rocked
Responds to strong smells	Infants may be drawn to pleasant smells while unpleasant smells may lead infant to pull away
Turns to mother's breast pad as opposed to that of another woman	Is increasingly aware of and attracted to primary caregivers' signals

Four to Seven Months

The period from 4 to 7 months is a time of monumental change in all areas of a child's development (see Tables 1.8 and 1.9). With the achievement of a number of motor milestones, the infant begins more and more to get beyond the initial close, exclusive union with the primary caregiver. As he is no longer held primarily and can roll over and crawl and sit unsupported, the stage is set for more intentional action in the world. Such actions include reaching out to grasp objects and making things happen in a purposeful way. This capacity of acting intentionally can include shaking a rattle to make a noise, pulling a string to make something move, or crying to get a caregiver to come. Gradually, two-way communication develops as, for example, the baby cries, the caregiver responds, and the baby babbles back. At a more physical level, the baby increasingly begins to understand feelings through bodily sensations of being touched and held, and becomes more aware of what is going on inside his body or his body sensations. Of course, in the early months, the baby expresses his emotions primarily through physical means, such as flailing his arms when crying, and smiling and flapping his arms when happy or excited. During this time, many infants have the capacity to "woo" caregivers with smiles and gestures.

The Beginning of Attachment A number of new abilities heralds the beginning of attachment. Attachment, or the infant's growing relationship with significant caregivers, will develop gradually over the next few months. But by 7 months a number of capacities are achieved

Table 1.8. By 7 months: Emotional and social milestones typically attained

Increased attention to interpersonal interaction and communication	Emotions become more differentiated
Gazes at caregiver's face with great interest	Shows different emotions to caregivers
Distinguishes caregiver(s) from other people	Demonstrates increased differentiation of emotions to include laughing and anger
May cry if caregiver leaves or when a stranger is close by	Looks at caregiver with special joyful smile
Plays games such as Peek-a-Boo or Pat-a-Cake	Shows fear and sadness at separation from caregiver
Reaches to be picked up and held	
Cries for attention	
Will "woo" caregiver with sounds, smiles, and gestures	
Vocalizes when spoken to	

Table 1.9. Other capacities attained by a typical 7-month-old infant

Gross motor	Cognition
Rolls from back to stomach and stomach to back	Likes to make things happen
Sits up unsupported	Imitates gestures
Lifts head when lying on back	Follows and searches for objects
Creeps or crawls	Establishes object and person permanence
May pull to standing at furniture	Focuses on toy or person for 2 minutes
Bounces actively if held to stand	

Fine motor	Emotional
Imitates motor play	Laughs out loud
Brings hands to midline	Cries in response to another infant's cry
Exhibits purposive reaching and grasping	Beginning of felt-security and attachment to primary caregiver
Lets go of objects	Reacts to emotional displays of others
Puts objects in mouth	Gets upset at "still" face of caregiver or if caregiver does not respond
May bang objects together	
Can pick up small objects using raking motion	Shows fear of falling off high places
Demonstrates palmar grasp (all four fingers hold object against palm of hand)	Expresses emotions with different sounds and expressions
Transfers objects from one hand to the other	

Language	Social
Babbles with inflection	Shouts for attention
Vocalizes back to vocalizing	May cry if caregiver leaves
Tries to imitate sounds (e.g., coughing)	Plays interactive games like Peek-a-Boo.
Can reproduce a number of consonants (e.g., ba, da, ma) and repeats in sequence	Knows difference between familiar and unfamiliar people
Responds to a few familiar words like Daddy and bye-bye	
Responds to name	

Self-help	
Places hands on bottle or breast during feeding	
Enjoys making things happen such as squeezing a toy to make a noise	
Can pick up objects	

that make attachment possible. These are primarily cognitive and include *object permanence* (i.e., knowing that something continues to exist when it is out of sight) and a beginning capacity for *object constancy* (i.e., understanding that an object does not change and having a memory of it that can be retrieved at any time).

Object and person permanence allows the infant, by about 7 months of age, to know that something exists even when it is hidden. Babies by this age will search for something they are attracted to if it is hidden under a cloth and may cry when a caregiver moves out of sight. No longer is it a matter of "out of sight, out of mind." It takes a long while, however, before the infant can hold on to that memory long enough for it to be sustaining when the caregiver is away, that is, for object constancy to be truly in place. The capacity for object constancy develops very slowly and is subject to regression and is fragile under stress over the next 3 years of a child's life (Greenspan, 1992; Mahler, Pine, & Bergman, 1975).

Many behaviors signal the beginning of a child's attachment to a parent. For many infants today who are in child care for a number of hours a week, the signs may not be as dramatic as for a baby who has not been away from his primary caregiver as much. Nevertheless, usually

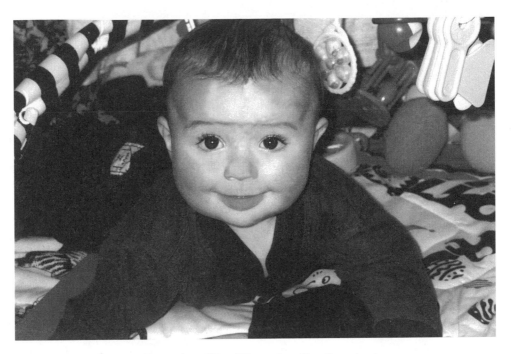

Between the ages of 4 to 7 months, an infant will "woo" his caregiver with smiles and gestures.

around 5 months of age we begin to see indications that the infant is trying to establish a retrievable memory of the caregiver. This is usually demonstrated as the infant becomes fascinated with the caregiver's face—gazing at it, pulling at hair, feeling the nose and eyes—all in an effort to "know" and remember the caregiver in great detail. Often, the infant will become upset if the caregiver's usual image is violated, if glasses are put on or taken off or a hairstyle is radically changed. The most dramatic behaviors are usually "making strange" or becoming upset if a person the baby does not know approaches. By 7 months of age, an infant usually cries when left in an unfamiliar place, which is caused by separation anxiety.

During this time, minute by minute, hour by hour, and day by day, the baby begins to identify herself in the context of the developing relationship with primary caregivers. The infant learns to define herself in the "mirror" of the caregiver. If the caregiver is depressed, she is depressed; if the caregiver is angry, she feels rejected; and if the caregiver is happy, she is happy. The baby becomes a reflection of the reactions shown in the caregiver's face. Babies of this age

Table 1.10. By 14 months: Emotional and social milestones typically attained

Secure attachment relationship is being established	Child is exploring the world
Continuously checks back to caregiver by touching, calling out, or looking	Knows no fear: Fearlessness is at its height
Communicates needs and feelings and establishes closeness	Explores the world with curiosity and excitement
Establishes a true sense of object and person permanence	Examines objects with great interest
Smiles specifically for attachment figures, not indiscriminately	Appears more alert and goal directed
Enjoys Peek-a-Boo game as a way to control separation	

become very upset or withdrawn if a caregiver presents with a "still face" or fails to respond to their initiations, which demonstrates how intense their need is for responsive interactions.

Eight to Fourteen Months

The stage between 8 and 14 months usually is a time of excitement and exhilaration for the infant, particularly as she becomes mobile and more capable of exploring the world (see Tables 1.10 and 1.11). Mahler, Pine, and Bergman have described the stage as one in which the infant has "a love affair with the world," and in which fearlessness and independence are at their height (1975, p. 70). As well, the infant becomes more alert, persistent, and goal directed—he is determined to make that tape recorder work or to rearrange those flowers (and sometimes to

Table 1.11.   Other capacities typically attained by 14 months of age

Gross motor	Cognition
Cruises around furniture	Understands causality and hands a mechanical
Walks	toy to caregiver to activate
Walks up and down stairs	Examines toys to see how they work
Throws a ball	Begins to use symbolic play
	Can point to objects in picture book
	Plays on own for 10 minutes or more
	Follows simple instructions

Fine motor	Emotional
Pincer grasp using thumb and forefinger to pick up tiny objects	Shows more control over display of emotions
Scribbles	Indicates social referencing or awareness of signals from caregivers
Builds tower with three blocks	Demonstrates fear of strange objects and events and separation
Targets objects and manipulates them	Develops fear of "visual cliff" or heights
Can handle two objects at a time	
Puts round piece in form board	
Places objects inside each other	
Drops and throws objects	

Language	Social
Is beginning to use words to communicate	Likes to hide
Uses two to three words (e.g., *Da-da, Ma-ma*)	Babbles or jabbers to get attention
Understands a few simple words and sentences	Can distinguish between *self* and *other*
Copies simple gestures such as waving	Parallel play with eye contact and occasional vocalization
Jabbers expressively	Joint attention with object
Shows communicative intent with gestures (e.g., waves *bye-bye*)	Recognizes peer as social partner, likes to be around other children
Likes rhymes and singing games	Capable of turn-taking
Understands "no" but does not always follow through	Imitates actions of another person

Self-help	
Sips from cup with assistance	
Begins to use a spoon	
Can ask for a drink by pointing or gesturing	
Removes food from spoon with tongue	
Can feed with finger foods	
Shows interest in pulling off clothes	

destroy the house!) In spite of this persistence, the stage is often a relatively easy one for caregivers because 1-year-olds are usually excited, happy, and even exhilarated.

For some parents, this need to explore can be seen as the infant not needing them or even rejecting them. On the contrary, the exploring toddler desperately needs caregivers to be available and will demonstrate this need by continually "checking back" to make sure someone is close by. In fact, a study in which toddlers and their caregivers were observed outside in a park found that 1-year-olds rarely wander far and are continually returning to home base for "refueling" before they move off again (Anderson, 1972).

By 12 months of age, children show what has been called social referencing when they look at their parents' faces and monitor the emotional expressions of their parents in order to decide how to act. For example, in experiments in which a child is close to what appears to be a drop (or visual cliff), if the parent shows encouragement, the child will go over, but will pull back if the parent shows fear (Sorce, Emde, Campos, & Klinnert, 1985). This provides evidence of how much children rely on their caregiver's emotional expression and containment.

This stage becomes a rehearsal for later stages in which the infant moves between attachment and separation, engagement and disengagement, as if they are opposite sides of the same coin. Interestingly, the more the caregiver is available to the child, the more the child becomes able to function independently and with confidence in the world.

During this time, children are fascinated by mirrors and the reflections of themselves or other people they see within the mirrors. They do not yet recognize themselves but do smile and show enjoyment at the images. In fact, they may be more interested in their parents' reflections than their own, as their parents' faces are more familiar.

Caregiving is not an easy task. (From Johnston, L. [1978]. *Do they ever grow up?* Minnetonka, MN: Meadowbrook Press; reprint granted with written permission of Lynn Johnston Productions, Inc.)

The more the caregiver is available to the child, the more the child becomes able to function independently and with confidence in the world.

Obviously, for parents who may be sensitive to rejection and who perceive the child's growing need to explore as a sign that they are not needed anymore, this is a difficult time. If the parent reacts by pushing the child away too early or by holding the child back and being overprotective, the trend can be set for the child to develop subsequent behavioral and emotional difficulties and ongoing relationship problems with his parents.

Fifteen to Twenty-Four Months

The stage between 15 and 24 months often is a time of great confusion for caregivers and may be the most difficult stage for many parents—with the exception of their child's adolescence.

Table 1.12.   By 24 months: Emotional and social milestones typically attained

Development of autonomous self	Beginning of understanding of intersubjectivity
Is more negative: "No-saying" is at its height	Demonstrates an increase in separation anxiety
Has more frequent tantrums	Begins to be aware of actions of self and others
Begins to initiate activities	Enjoys playing alongside other children
Wants to control others and order them around	Enjoys some interactive games
Uses "I" and "mine"	Understands that other people have ideas of their own, and that many feel and act differently than he or she does
Is beginning to actively resist discipline	
Uses transitional objects (e.g., stuffed animals, blankets) more frequently	"Shadows" caregiver
Wants to do things himself	Demonstrates increasing fears and strong anxieties
	May experience frequent sleeping problems; nightmares and night terrors may peak

Certain capacities develop at this time that create anxiety in a child about abandonment at the same time that he or she is pushing toward independence. In a child, these milestones include a growing sense of separateness from others and the capacity for *intersubjectivity*, or the understanding that other people think, feel, and act differently from the way the child thinks, feels, and acts (see Tables 1.12 and 1.13). The child still does not understand *what* those different perspectives are, however. All this makes the child much more aware that the person she is now attached to could decide to—and actually does—"go away" at times. The child is often

Table 1.13. Other capacities attained by a typical 24-month-old child

Gross motor	Cognition
Begins to run	Increasingly engages in pretend play
Climbs up and down stairs unassisted	Can play in a focused way for 20 minutes or more
Stands on tiptoes	Points to body parts
Throws and catches a ball	Can sort by color and classification (e.g., cars, animals)
Uses feet to pedal tricycle	
Climbs on chair and turns around	Can match by size and color
Jumps 8˝–14˝	Can sequence pretend play into scripts
Walks backwards	
Walks on a straight line	
Squats while playing	

Fine motor	Emotional
Climbs	Often demonstrates social referencing
Copies circles, lines, and crosses	Shows shame if does not succeed at a task
Stacks nine blocks	Recognizes self in mirror
Puts pieces in puzzles	Expresses anxiety if object is flawed
Nests objects	Complies approximately 45% of time
Puts tiny object in small container	Gets upset if cannot meet standards
Folds paper in half	Labels emotions of others
Strings beads	Temper tantrums peak
Opens doors by turning doorknob	Demonstrates self-conscious emotions of shame and embarrassment
Enjoys pouring and filling	

Language	Social
Expressive language increases to 50+ words	Demonstrates showing and pointing
Speaks in two- to three-word sentences	Attends visually to same stimuli as another person
Listens to a story	Engages in complementary play and physical proximity
Answers questions	
Joins in songs	Plays games such as hide and seek and rolling ball back and forth
May understand more than can say	Uses personal pronouns
	May comfort another child
	Is possessive with toys and sharing is difficult

Self-help
Uses cup with minimal spilling
Puts on shoes, socks and shorts
Can use spoon to feed self
May tell parent "wet," and may indicate need to use potty
Cooperates in dressing
Unbuttons large buttons; unzips large zippers

torn by a wish to be independent that conflicts with a concern that this separateness will result in the caregiver abandoning him. The following vignettes illustrate these dual feelings:

● ●

Jane is an 18-month-old who has been increasingly negative. Today has been a bad day, so her mother decides to take her outside. Jane screams for her mother to help her put her shoes on. As her mother bends down to help, Jane falls screaming to the ground. What is going on?

Jane is demonstrating the push and pull between wanting to be independent and becoming frustrated because she can't do things. Her mother's offer of help draws her attention to the fact that indeed she does need help.

● ●

At 20 months, Michael is determined to do things himself. He often will scream if his father cuts up his meat or tries to help. At bedtime he often cries, sometimes to the point of sobbing desperately, convincing his parents that he is very afraid of something. What is going on?

Michael is becoming increasingly aware of his own separateness, and is pushing for independence. He also is aware of the possibility that his parents could disappear. Going to bed can feel like abandonment and may arouse his fear that his parents will go away when he is alone in his room.

In both of these stories, we see examples of the push and pull between a child's wish for independence and wish for containment and security from the caregiver. Unfortunately, at this stage we often see battle grounds being set up as the child struggles for independence around such issues as eating, sleeping, and toileting, all areas over which children can maintain control and often push for control in order to keep some sense of independence from their parents' wishes.

Along with this internal struggle, the child shows an expanding sense of self, as he increasingly uses "I" and "mine" and insists that he do things "myself." Children may demonstrate this growing sense of self by an increased interest in their mirror images. Moreover, if their usual appearance has been violated, for example, if rouge has been smeared on their nose, they may demonstrate that they realize that they look different from the way they usually look. As a result, children may show indications of shame and embarrassment. As well, tantrums and negativism frequently begin to appear when their desires and wants are frustrated.

In fact, during this stage, as the child tries to be independent, there are a number of cognitive abilities that the child just does not have. Consequently, this makes it very difficult for him to understand the world and respond in a rational way; often, what appears to be irrationality is the order of the day! The following is a list of some cognitive characteristics of the toddler stage that make life difficult:

- *Egocentricity:* Child sees herself as the "center of the universe" (e.g., the moon is following *her* down the street). Does not see other people's point of view or perspective.

- *Animism:* Sees animals and objects as human (e.g., the table can rise up and hit him). Consequently, the child does not accept responsibility for his actions.

- *Splitting:* Has very "black and white" thinking, so people and situations are all bad or all good. This can change in quick succession.

- *Magical thinking:* Believes that things he wishes for really do come true.

- *Lack of impulse control:* Is not able to self-modulate or control intense feelings or desire to do things.

- *Lack of symbolization/concrete thinking:* Words and phrases are taken literally (e.g., "Fly to grandma's house" can mean flying like a bird to grandma's house).

- *Sense of omnipotence/grandiosity:* Believes he can do anything and is all-powerful.

- *No time sense or ability to plan:* Wants things immediately and has no sense of time, planning, or thinking ahead.

During this time, language and the capacity for pretend play increase and children begin to communicate what they want, often with increasing intensity. Although children like to be around their peers and some cooperative play is possible, in general play is more parallel than cooperative, and fights over possession of toys are common.

Consequently, caregivers are dealing with a little person who seems to be quite independent and is, for example, beginning to speak, but is still only capable of a very limited degree of self-containment and impulse control. The following vignette describes a toddler's reactions during a typical errand. His reactions are explained in parentheses.

● ●

Kim has decided to take her 24-month-old, Nicholas, to the store to buy him a pair of new shoes he desperately needs. She carefully tries to warn him ahead of time, but when it's time to go he becomes furious because he wants to play more (lack of time sense *and* slow adaptation to transitions). *He throws himself on the floor screaming, saying Kim is "bad"* (lack of impulse control *and* splitting). *As Kim gets him in the car seat he bangs his foot, screaming, blaming, and hitting the car* (animism). *He is then determined he will drive the car* (omnipotence), *and seems to feel that his wish for red tennis shoes will make them appear from nowhere* (magical thinking). *The visit to the shoe store is disastrous; Nicholas screams to get shoes right away because "I want them"* (egocentricity) *and suddenly starts to scream when the salesgirl says she could send away for some. It seems he understood this as that he would be sent away* (concrete thinking). *With Nicholas screaming, Kim decides that the best plan of action is to pick him up and go home to try again another day.*

Fortunately, some days are better than others, and with careful management in which the child neither wins nor loses all the battles, things will improve over time.

Two to Four Years

When a child is between 2 and 4 years of age, a number of developmental gains are achieved (see Tables 1.14 and 1.15). Three-year-olds are much more cooperative than they were at 2, and use "we" more than the oppositional "I" and "you." They even seem to enjoy the sense of sharing and will ask for help at times and to be shown something. Most of the time the 3-year-old wants to please, loves praise, and wants to be noticed for good behavior.

She now enjoys other people, especially her parents, and loves to do things with them. She may "help" with the yard or housework just to be close. She also enjoys being around other children, although it is not always smooth sailing, and she may engage in arguments at times. Socially, however, children now need and are capable of cooperative play in which they take reciprocal and complementary roles, so Johnny may be a sea captain and Mary, a pilot on the aircraft carrier, with roles being reversed at times. Watching children jointly playing out events that the family has experienced or fantasies about upcoming issues can be both fascinating and revealing.

Three-year-olds are confident performing a number of gross motor activities: They run hard and fast, love to jump, throw a ball, pedal a bike, and can balance on one foot. They also can use their hands well, like to draw, build with blocks, and make things out of playdough or clay. Toilet-teaching may be complete, and the 3-year-old can do a lot of things himself, such as dressing, brushing his teeth, and pouring from a pitcher.

Language has expanded enormously, and a 3-year-old's vocabulary may be as large as 300 to 1,000 words. She can now recite nursery rhymes and sing songs and keeps conversations going by asking an increasing number of questions. She loves big words and new ones and may call attention to herself by using them. She loves to listen to stories and can do so for increasing periods of time without losing concentration.

Life with 3-year-olds is not always easy, however. Some children question everything and argue with parents about various rules and routines. Other children may seem quite emotionally insecure and may develop fears; they may suck their thumbs, bite their nails, or even chew on their clothes. They may have an intense need to be included in everything, insisting on "me too."

By the time they are nearing age 4, children are full of energy and seem to be in constant motion: hopping, jumping, climbing, and running around. A child's bouts of being stubborn and argumentative may switch with periods when he wants to be helpful and cooperative with

Table 1.14. By 4 years: Emotional and social milestones typically attained

Sense of self and sociability strengthens	Symbolic representation increases
Fear of abandonment subsides and object constancy becomes more stable	Increasingly able to express thoughts and feelings in words
Gains in self-esteem and sense of own identity	Increasingly able to identify feelings
Is basically optimistic and cheerful	Increasingly able to engage in pretend play
Instigates activities based on own needs and desires	Engages in sociodramatic play and takes different roles
Is able to engage in cooperative play with peers	
Is able to take turns	
Has some ability to empathize	
Can begin to integrate "splitting" and remember "good" part of people	
Interacts in socially appropriate ways with adults	
Degree of compliance increases	

Table 1.15. Other capacities attained by a typical 4-year-old child

Gross motor	Cognition
Throws ball overhand	Engages in more elaborate pretend play
Skips	Can classify objects by their purpose
Walks on tiptoes	Can point to six geometric designs
Stands on one foot	Understands "nearest" and "longest "
Hops on one foot	Counts five objects and rote counts to 20 or more
Balances on walking board or plank of wood	Distinguishes between real and pretend
Walks on straight line	Distinguishes between genders
Enjoys throwing and catching games	Can name some letters and recognize a few words
Jumps over object 5 or 6 inches high	Understands the sequence of daily events
Demonstrates more control over speed of running	
Climbs stairs alternating feet	
Climbs on playground equipment	

Fine motor	Emotional
Can screw things such as lids on jars	Reliably evokes memory of caregiver
Builds tower of 10 or more blocks	Displays emotional reactions to distress of others (e.g., tries to help, demonstrates affection, comforts)
Inserts pieces in puzzle	
Threads wooden beads on a string	Understands rules about what to do and not to do
Cuts with scissors	
Paints with large brush	Demonstrates increased use of arguments and justification with parents
Manipulates clay	
Draws person with three parts	Integrates "good" and "bad" of self and other representations
Folds paper	
Copies some shapes and letters	

Language	Social
Language expands to include all parts of speech	Demonstrates some sharing behavior and cooperative play
Repeats three numbers	May exhibit fears
Knows more than 1,200 words	Imitates and follows the leader
Points to colors	Shows increased awareness of standards and rules
Uses five-word sentences	
Language and emotions are congruent	Shows reciprocal and complementary roles in pretend play
Use gender words (e.g., *he/she, boy/girl*)	
Understands *tallest*, *same*, and *more*	May have a friend
Uses prepositions (e.g., *in, on,* and *under*)	Emotions are less intense and switch less rapidly, so child is more likely to sustain social interactions
Uses possessives (e.g., *hers, theirs*)	
Knows first name and last name	Shows less aggression and more verbal anger (e.g., name-calling)
Recites simple songs and rhymes	

Self-help
Can dress and undress fully
Can do buttons
Can feed self with little spilling
Can pour from jug into cup
Is toilet taught; stays dry at night
Uses fork effectively

others in group activities. Many children now have a "best" friend, although they may tease and exclude other children from their play.

One of the most important expansions in this year is in symbolic representation, and the child is now much more able to express his thoughts and feelings through language. As language expands to include more and more words and all parts of speech, children become able to express quite complex and integrated ideas. Along with this children show an increasing capacity for pretend play, with play themes becoming much more complex.

These new representational capacities mean that gradually, the child becomes less egocentric in thinking and begins to develop a theory of mind (i.e., understanding that other people have thoughts and feelings that are different from their own, and what they are). This means that children begin to be better able to understand another person's point of view or perspective. By this age, children do not just experience others' emotions as their own—they react to others' distress by helping, comforting, and showing affection. They now have the capacity to clearly differentiate real and pretend, and they increasingly understand and follow the rules and standards of behavior in the home, school, or child care.

At this age, the child has an increasing sense of self and understanding of who she is. With this new sense of self, the child may begin to experience self-conscious emotions of shame and guilt, however. These emotions may occur if children do something that is against the rules, if they do not measure up against their own or parents' standards of achievement, and even when something is perceived as dirty or broken. Children now use many feeling words and can label feelings in illustrations or pictures. They have an increasing ability to understand the emotions of others, particularly happiness and joy. Feelings of sadness and anger are a little

Between the ages of 2 and 4, a child gains in self-esteem and sense of his own identity.

more difficult for a child to understand, and a child's ability to understand or recognize fear in others is acquired last.

Nevertheless, fears of monsters and animals, and of being alone—especially in the dark—are common. Separation anxiety occurs less frequently in children of this age than in younger children, partly because the child has now experienced some separations when Mommy came back. Also, the child can now maintain an internal image of his parents to sustain him when he's away from them. Thankfully, his representations of himself and of other people are becoming much more integrated, so his mother does not seem like the "wicked witch" whenever she says no and he can still remember, during times of frustration, some of the special good things his mother did for him. Also, when he does not do as well as he would like he no longer falls completely apart or sees himself as a total failure but can quickly remember the times he did well. Of course, for this integration to occur, a parent needs to interact with an upset child in a way that can help bring the child back to more positive thoughts and feelings.

Many children during this stage become very interested in their genital organs and particularly in the differences between boys and girls. Sex play may be common, as well as masturbation. Questions about babies and reproduction may proliferate, especially if a new sibling is on the way. Gradually, children become more likely to play with other children of the same gender and to prefer gender-specific toys.

Four to Six Years

During the years between the ages of 4 and 6, children gain increasing emotional control over anger and aggression, although they still need their caregivers' reassurances in frightening situations that typically include the dark, monsters, death, and imaginary creatures. Although many 6-year-olds understand increasingly complex emotions such as pride, shame, worry, jealousy, and gratitude, mixed or conflicting emotions are still difficult to understand and deal with. A child can still find it difficult to understand being simultaneously happy about a school holiday and sad because she won't see her friends for a while, for example.

Providing she has been encouraged to grow in self-esteem, however, the child's increasing fine motor control, language, and cognitive abilities, will now bring a growing sense of competence or a sense of "I can do that." Children can now count and understand number concepts and sort objects into various categories such as color, shape, size, and density. Their language and ideas are much more complex, and they are capable of a basic level of abstraction. During these years, children identify with a parent or other adult and begin to internalize and use their thoughts and behaviors. Many children become quite moralistic. When a child has a friend over to play, for example, she might be dogmatic about what the other child can or cannot do in her home.

Nevertheless, children are much more able to play together, engaging in games with rules and sharing. This is less likely to be the case with siblings, in which jealousy can still be a frequent cause of fights. Many children now have a best friend, and the friendship may last for some time. As well, they have the capacity to resolve conflicts with reasoned discussion and negotiation over arguments. Sometimes they try this a little too much with parents!

Not only is the child now more adept with social interchanges but also he is better able to contain his emotions during frustrating experiences or when an activity just will not work out as it should. Children now talk to themselves or use self-talk as they struggle through a diffi-

Children at this age are much more able to play together.

cult task: "You can do it"; "keep trying"; "do this piece first." Gradually, this will become more internalized, although all of us at times talk aloud.

The 6-year-old is typically delightful to be around and fun to watch. At this time, Mom and Dad and other caregivers are generally seen as great and are not blamed for everything that does not work. In fact, children at this age are much more able to problem solve, to judge what they can and cannot do, and even to plan ahead a bit how they will do it.

By 6 years of age (see Tables 1.16 and 1.17), the typical child is competent and has the capacity to follow rules and standards of behavior, contain negative emotions, and feel successful and good about herself. She is capable of understanding and communicating complex thoughts and emotions through language and play; of problem solving and planning; of having warm, reciprocal relationships; and of showing prosocial behavior. Strategies for helping children acquire these capacities are outlined in more detail in the rest of this book.

Table 1.16. By 6 years: Emotional and social milestones typically attained

Sense of competence	Beginning of conscience
Shows expanding pride in work and interest in learning new things	Demonstrates increasing sense of right and wrong and rules of society
Demonstrates predominant feeling of competence	Feels guilty if does not obey rules
	Enjoys games with rules
Shows ability to problem-solve when faced with difficulty	Identifies with adult
Curious and interested in learning about the world	Insists children who come to his home obey his rules
	Increased empathy for the rights of others
	Increased incidence of helping others

Table 1.17. Other capacities attained by a typical 6-year-old child

Gross motor	Cognition
Skips with rope	Knows colors, shapes, sizes
Skips with alternating feet	Writes numbers up to 5
Hops distance of 50 feet	Understands number concepts
Climbs, slides, swings	Begins to understand concept of conservation (e.g., that short and wide and tall and narrow containers can hold same amount)
Is learning to swim, swing a bat	
Is learning to kick, catch a ball	
Keeps time when dancing	Enjoys games with rules
	Understands concepts of left and right
	Compares concepts of bigger and smaller, part and whole
	Understands time concepts (e.g., *today, tomorrow, yesterday*)
	Recognizes seasons and major holidays

Fine motor	Emotional
Draws a person	Still has difficulty with mixed emotions
Uses scissors skillfully	Shows some understanding of pride, gratitude, shame, worry, jealousy
Folds and cuts out simple shapes	
Holds brush or pencil between thumb and forefinger	Shows pride in work
Likes to paint	Uses private speech to calm down
Handedness established	Anxious to please and follow the rules
Draws shapes	Can be upset by things that are "not right "
Cuts and pastes	Hates to be corrected
Prints name and writes some letters	May develop fears of the dark, dogs, and so forth

Language	Social
Uses a 10,000- to 14,000-word vocabulary	Usually plays with same-sex children and gender-specific toys
Constantly asks questions	
Speech is fluent and grammatically correct in verb tenses, word order, and sentence structure	Understands perspective of others and shows prosocial behavior
Knows birthday and name and address	Is able to and frequently shares
Memorizes songs, television jingles	Has best friend
Uses plurals, tenses, and questions	Engages in complex social pretend play
May recognize more words	
Likes "bathroom talk "	
Likes telling jokes and riddles	

Self-help	
Combs/brushes hair	
Blows nose independently	
Washes face and hands	
Hangs up clothes	
Cuts with knife	
Totally cares for toileting needs	
Ties own shoes	

How far the 6-year-old has come from the newborn, whose behavior was largely reflexive with little intentionality! Now, we have a young child capable of many important achievements in all areas of development. It is crucial, however, that caregivers have realistic expectations of young children during the early years and understand what they can and cannot do. In this way, both caregivers and children will be happier and less frustrated, and the child's social and emotional development is more likely to proceed smoothly over time.

IMPORTANT RESEARCH FINDINGS

Since the 1980s, a staggering amount of research has focused on the development of children in the first 6 years of life. As well, research has begun to delineate, using multivariate and non-linear models, the conditions that promote psychological health or contribute to psychopathology. In the 1990s and the beginning of the 21st century, there has been growth in research and understanding on a number of topics that have been crucial to this understanding. These areas of interest include

- How emotion regulation is developed, particularly the link between cognition and emotions and the significant role that emotions play in determining behavior

- The development of a secure attachment and its implications for other developmental milestones and particularly its effects on the capacities for sociability, empathy, and prosocial behavior

- The early development of social interest and capabilities

- The importance of theory of mind, perspective taking, and executive functioning in enabling the child to problem solve, plan, and delay immediate gratification

- The contribution of brain development, various physiological and temperamental characteristics of the child, and the relative contribution of these and other proximal and more distal factors such as parenting, community and family variables, and culture

- The capacities that a child needs to acquire so that research does not only emphasize outcomes of IQ and intellectual capacities but considers the abilities of the competent child or of "emotional IQ" as well

Much of this kind of research is described in subsequent chapters, so this section will emphasize research on risk and protective factors and how they contribute to development, brain development in the early years, and some of the more important parental characteristics that are known to enhance development. As well, it will examine various research areas related to the contribution of temperament.

Research on Development

For a long time, developmental outcomes were seen as the result of either genetic inheritance or exposure to environmental conditions. More recently, however, efforts are being focused on understanding the complex interactions of biology and context. Boyce (2001) has talked about needing to uncover the *symphonic causation,* or the interplay between biology and the environment, which can lead to positive development or human disease. In the next section, low risk and protective factors within the child and the close (i.e., proximal) or more distant (i.e., distal) aspects of the environment surrounding the child are discussed.

How Risk and Protective Factors Contribute to Development   Risk factors are variables that have been found to be associated with the development of intellectual delays, emotional or behavioral problems, and/or physical health problems of children. They are usu-

ally organized under four general headings: 1) child characteristics, 2) interactional or parenting variables, 3) parental history and current functioning, and 4) sociodemographic and societal factors. Throughout the world, a growing number of children contend with a variety of risk factors that can compromise their development (Steinhauer, 1996).

1. *Child characteristics:* One of the most significant risks for infants is extreme prematurity or very low birth weight (Allen, Donohue, & Dusman, 1993; Hack, Taylor, Klein, Eiben, Schatschneider, & Mercuri-Minich, 1994). A significant percentage (6%–24%) of infants with very low birth weight may have major disabilities including learning disabilities or attentional or academic difficulties (Weisglas-Kuperus, Baerts, Smrkovsky, & Sauer, 1993). Other biological and/or genetic conditions also are significant risks in terms of cognitive and other developmental areas. Chronic medical conditions and repeated illnesses have also been found to be related to later psychosocial difficulties (Offord, Boyle, Fleming, Blum, & Grant, 1989). Difficult temperamental characteristics can also challenge parents' caregiving (Garcia-Coll, Kagan, & Resnick, 1984; Thomas et al., 1968).

2. *Interactional or parenting variables:* Many researchers suggest that interactional style and caregiving variables such as discipline practices are the most important in predicting child outcomes (Hart & Risley, 1995; Rutter, 1989; Werner, 1989, 1993). These are discussed in detail in the next section so they will only be briefly mentioned here. Some of the variables that are considered important influences on the quality of attachment are the parents' degree of sensitivity and responsiveness to their infants' cues and attunement and necessary containment of their children's emotions. If attachment becomes secure it can serve to protect the child, but if it is insecure it can lead to the development of a child's later social and emotional difficulties. For some parents, lack of knowledge about development and parenting strategies can lead to difficulties with discipline and lack of encouragement of language and other areas of development.

3. *Parental history and current functioning:* A number of parental factors can place a child's development at risk, including drug and alcohol abuse (Reich, Earls, Frankel, & Shayka, 1993), having less than average intelligence (Luthar & Zigler, 1992), and criminality of either parent (Fischer, 1985; Gobel & Shindledecker, 1993). It is also clear that some less obvious or latent variables, such as the parent's own experience of being parented (especially if it was traumatic and included abuse, neglect, or significant loss), can dramatically affect the ability to parent. Parents' childhood experiences with their own parents may also influence the attachment security of their children (Benoit & Parker, 1994; Main & Goldwyn, 1984). When one or both parents have a psychiatric condition, the child's development may be compromised as well. The outcome, however, depends on several factors, including the nature and severity of the illness, whether the parent is frequently hospitalized, and whether there is another caregiver in the home to buffer the child from the effects of the parent's illness (Anthony, 1982; Bell & Pearl, 1982; Phares & Compas, 1993; Wieder, Jasnow, Greenspan, & Strauss, 1983). Another known risk factor is when a parent, particularly the mother, experiences a significant level of depression. This has been shown to increase the child's vulnerability to developing anxiety and behavior disorders (Beardslee, Bemporad, Keller, & Klerman, 1984; Carro, Grant, Gotlib, & Compas, 1993; Pape, Byrne, & Ivask, 1996). Other relevant aspects of parental functioning are discussed in the next section.

4. *Sociodemographic and societal factors:* According to researchers, 25% of children in the United States are living in poverty, as well as 21.3% of children in Canada (Carnegie Foundation, 1994; Doherty, 1997). Variables that are more sociodemographic or that relate to the family environment can significantly increase a child's risk of experiencing problems later in life. These may include problems with unemployment and repeating patterns of poor parenting. Low socioeconomic status, when the child is living below the poverty line, and particularly, in the lowest quartile with regard to income, has been shown frequently to be a significant risk factor (Offord & Lipman, 1996; Zyblock, 1996). The effects of chronic poverty have been reported to be twice that of poverty that is more transient. In a recent study, young children living in persistent poverty were twice as likely to have lower IQ levels and to exhibit behavior problems (Brooks-Gunn, Klebanov, & Duncan, 1996; Duncan, Brooks-Gunn, & Klebanov, 1994; Sameroff, Seifer, Baldwin, & Baldwin, 1993). Poverty was found in some studies to be an important predictor of later child psychopathology (Dubrow & Garbarino, 1989; Offord et al., 1989); possibly because children living in poverty often live in substandard housing or in violent neighborhoods. Similarly, a particularly high incidence of dysfunction has been found within the population of children from homeless families. (Dail, 1990; Schteingart, Molnar, Klein, & Lowe, 1995).

Not only do parents living in poverty find it difficult to meet their children's basic needs, they often find it difficult to talk to, spend time with, and read to their children. Nurturing interactions can be difficult to provide as parents' energy may be depleted and they may experience feelings of hopelessness and depression (McLoyd & Wilson, 1991).

Adolescent parenting increases children's risk of having physical and emotional problems (Hechtman, 1989; Weinman, Robinson, Simmons, Schreiber, & Stafford, 1989). Another significant risk is severe family dysfunction, especially if it results in spousal abuse (Fergusson, Horwood, & Lynskey, 1992; Pedersen, 1994). Isolation and lack of social supports can also result from impoverished environments and can contribute to the family's ongoing social difficulties (Allen, Brown, & Finlay, 1992; Moroney, 1987). As well, chronic family adversity has been found to correlate with infant attachment security, although researchers found variables related to parental personality problems to be the most powerful predictors of insecure attachment in the child (Shaw & Vondra, 1993; Shaw, Vondra, Hammerding, Kennan, & Dunn, 1994).

While several variables have been found to be associated with poor outcomes for children, multiple pathways and processes exist that determine children's ultimate patterns of adaptation or maladaptation (Cicchetti, & Rogosch, 1996; Zeanah, Boris, & Larrieu, 1997). One of the reasons for the divergence in outcomes is the influence of a variety of protective factors that have a complex interaction with the risk factors discussed above.

Protective Factors and Mechanisms   Protective factors are sometimes described as the opposite of risk factors. For example, isolation can be a risk factor, while having a warm, supportive network can be a protective factor. In this sense, protective factors can be organized under the same four headings as risk factors (i.e., child characteristics, interactional or parenting variables, parental history and current functioning, and sociodemographic and societal factors). In addition, researchers who have examined child resilience have identified conditions that can improve resistance to risk factors and contribute to successful outcomes and adaptation. Typically, these conditions are seen as falling into three main categories: 1) personal characteristics within the child, such as high intelligence, good social skills, and positive temperament qual-

ities; 2) relationship and caregiver variables that provide the children with a secure relationship with a warm, empathic adult either within the family or the community; and 3) a social environment or community that reinforces and supports positive efforts made by the child.

The relationship between risk and protective factors and the development of child resiliency is complex. As mentioned previously, some writers have described protective factors as the positive versions of risk factors, and researchers such as Rutter (1990) and Werner (1995) elaborated on possible protective mechanisms that may occur to create resilience in children. Rutter (1990) described a variety of ways to reduce a child's exposure to and involvement in risky conditions as well as to prevent the perpetuation of the risk effects. Situations that enhance the child's feelings of self-esteem and self-confidence and opportunities that are provided for the child also are seen as possible pathways to resilience. One example might be to provide a child whose own parents are disinterested and emotionally unavailable with opportunities to develop a relationship with an adult who supports and believes in him.

Because many factors may contribute to outcomes in any individual and myriad pathways to any particular outcome exist, both adaptive or maladaptive, predicting a child's developmental trajectory or assessing potential for difficulties is extremely challenging. Perhaps the most important and consistent finding from longitudinal studies of development has been the understanding that one or two risk factors, unless they are extreme, rarely have a negative impact on development. As the number of risk factors increases, however, the negative effect is not just additive but becomes multiplicative. The existence of four or more risk factors that relate to the child, parent, and sociodemographic situation can lead not just to four times the risk to development, but rather, to a sixteenfold increase in difficulties, for example. This result has been replicated in a number of studies (Rutter, 1979; Sameroff, Seifer, Barocas, Zax, & Greenspan, 1987; Sanson, Oberklaid, Pedlow, & Prior, 1991). In the mid 1990s, researchers considered the number of protective factors in the same way and identified what has been called a *cumulative protection index* consisting of three or more protective factors as contributing to early resiliency (Bradley, Whiteside, Mundfrom, & Casey, 1994).

It is also crucial to consider not only the predictive factors but the outcomes being considered as well. For example, on one hand, for children with severe developmental delays or certain mental disorders such as schizophrenia, biological and genetic factors are strongly implicated (Broman, Nichols, & Kennedy, 1975; Werner, 1993). On the other hand, for children with mild delays and behavioral and emotional difficulties, factors in the environment may be more critical (Offord et al., 1989; Sameroff et al., 1987).

Different factors within the environment and family are important at different ages, and certain developmental events experienced by the child can constitute turning points that can be negative or positive for a child's development. Parents can either view the toddler stage as a positive time or a period in which the child rejects them, for example, which may influence the child's subsequent outcomes.

In conclusion, variables that have the most effect on early development are likely to be those that are closest or most proximal to the child, such as parent–child interactions. The nature of the influence of other variables that are more distal or farther away—such as stressful life events, poverty, single-parent status, and marital distress—is poorly understood. When marital conflict is intense the effect may be direct in that it sensitizes the child to negative emotional expressions between people or may be more indirect because of the risk impact on parenting behavior and interactions. However, other, more distal variables may not directly influence the child but affect the parenting interactions he receives.

Brain Development in the Early Years   During the 1990s, a number of new brain imaging techniques, together with ongoing animal research and autopsy results, have significantly contributed to or produced more knowledge about the brain and how it develops (Nelson & Bloom, 1997). The brain is an extremely complex system, consisting of different levels of analysis from cellular to a more gross anatomical level. There are four major areas of the brain that become functional at different times during early prenatal and postnatal development. Starting from the base of the brain they are 1) the brainstem, 2) the diencephalon, 3) the limbic system, and 4) the cortical area. The lower areas are responsible for more basic and primitive functions such as breathing, sleeping, and hunger. The higher areas are responsible for emotional responses, thought, and modification of intense emotional responses (Greenfield, 1997). In addition, the neurochemicals of the moment-to-moment functioning of the brain are extremely complex and also mature over time, and are affected by experience. They include neurotransmitters, such as dopamine, serotonin, and endorphins, and hormones, such as glucocorticoids, which are increased during stress (Sapolsky, 1994).

At birth, the infant has about a billion brain cells or neurons. In order for "information" to be conveyed between the neurons or for them to be functional, however, it is necessary for connections to be made. This occurs when the axons (which "output") and the dendrites (which receive impulses from the neurons) form synapses or connections. The transmission of impulses at the synapses is facilitated by the neurotransmitters mentioned above (Singer, 1987).

During the first year of life, the growth of synapses between the cells increases twenty-fold, from 50 trillion to 1,000 trillion. Not only does the brain change in terms of the number of synapses but also there also is a process of sculpting, pruning, and eliminating excessive neurons and synapses. This process is not random and although much is canalized (i.e., determined by genetic factors) in the first years, it also is significantly influenced by early experiences (Kolb, 1989). As Shatz stated, "cells that fire together, wire together" (1992, p. 64). Although the density of connections reaches its peak at around age 2, dendrites and synapses continue to develop well into old age. What may be even more important is that different areas of the brain and the central nervous system become fully functional at different times during childhood (Singer, 1987).

Most of the popular articles about the brain have focused on the importance of these neural connections being formed in the first 3 years of life, and have suggested that certain experiences are necessary during this "critical period" for this to happen. The reality is much more complex. Different regions of the brain develop at different times, and the influence of genetic factors and experience varies at different ages. Much of the brain research that has implications for this topic has been carried out on the organization of the sensory system, and almost all of it has been carried out with animals. Although it is likely that other aspects of children's development, including their cognitive, emotional, and social development, have optimal critical or sensitive periods, the exact nature of these is not as clear (Greenough, Black, & Wallace, 1987; Kolb, 1989).

We do know, however, that between 8 and 10 years of age there is a notable decline in recovery and saving of functions following injury to the brain. Also, many children who experience deprivation of opportunities for attachment and are raised in institutions, even if they are adopted into loving and enriched homes, may continue to show chronic impairments in cognitive, emotional, and social development (Morison, Ames, & Chishold, 1995). Researchers have also shown that children who experience insensitive parenting or who are raised in extreme poverty and violent communities frequently show reduced cognitive levels and problems with

concentration and memory. As well, clinical experience and research from early intervention suggests that the environment an infant and young child is exposed to can have long-lasting effects on development. For example, well-funded and intensive early intervention programs that have carried out well-controlled outcome research have been able to demonstrate significant short-term and long-term differences among children who receive the programs and those who do not. These differences have been found for a variety of outcomes including IQ scores, social skills, impulse control, and academic functioning (Guralnick, 1997).

On one hand, research on stress and coping also has shown that some stressful events result in increases in the hormone glucocorticoid, which stimulates arousal and results in increased energy and ability to concentrate. On the other hand, extreme events, such as natural disasters, or prolonged exposure to stressful stimulation, such as abuse—especially if it is experienced as uncontrollable—can result in the opposite type of response. Namely, if a child is exposed to an extreme event it may cause the inhibition of various hormonal systems; overexposure to glucocorticoids; and physical symptoms including decrease in energy, loss of ability to concentrate, and feelings of depression (Glaser, 2000). Rats who have experienced extreme stress on a continual basis have been shown to produce a generalized, ongoing hyperemotional stress response. This reaction may explain posttraumatic stress disorder (PTSD) and the tendency for severely traumatized individuals to react very strongly to an increasing range of stimuli. For example, an abused child may become sensitized to any expression of anger—such as a loud voice—and react intensely, uncontrollably, and immediately, seemingly without rational control (McFarlane & van der Kolk, 1996).

The effect of stress may result in these dramatic reactions to various stimuli but may also produce excessive cortisol on an ongoing basis, which can cause dendrites to shrivel and thus affect a child's cognitive capacity, most particularly in remembering new information. It may also influence a child's ability to sustain attention and to focus, problems so often observed in children who have experienced ongoing stress or who have not received nurturing and soothing interactions with caregivers and help to manage their intense emotions and reactions (van der Kolk, 1994). Although most of the work on the effect of mother–infant interactions on functioning has been carried out on animals, it is very consistent with what we know about humans. Moreover, Gunnar and associates have shown that when infants who are being inoculated are held and comforted, their production of the stress hormone cortisol is reduced (Gunnar & Stone, 1994; Nachmias, Gunnar, Mangelsdorf, Parritz, & Buss, 1996).

In conclusion, what we do know about brain development and child outcome is the following:

- Synapse development is largely genetic, and although research indicates that ongoing experience in the early years appears to be important, neuroscience does not indicate that more stimulation is necessarily better.

- Certain experiences during the early years may be more beneficial than others; however, neuroscience has not been able yet to inform us about optimal parenting strategies for developing the brain (Bruer, 1999).

- It is likely that exposure to stress (particularly severe neglect, trauma, loss, or abuse) negatively affects brain development. No neuroscience data exist, however, that prove whether and under what circumstance, given optimal care, the cerebral pathology found in severely maltreated infants is reversible.

- Although the first 3 years of a child's life are important, many functions of the brain develop well into adolescence and adulthood. For example, although vision and other sensory systems develop in the first year and the frontal cortex connections are made with regions responsible for emotional reactions between 10 and 18 months, other functions and parts of the brain develop much later:

  — Mental development continues to be influenced by growth in the frontal lobes through age 16.

  — The emotional limbic system is not fully developed until puberty.

  — Acquisition of language develops up to age 10, although early stimulation up to age 2 has been found to be an important predictor of language acquisition in later years.

The Importance of Parent–Child Interactions   In a variety of longitudinal prospective studies with large groups of children (Egeland & Erickson, 1990; Garmezy, 1987; Radke-Yarrow, Richters, & Wilson, 1988; Sameroff & Fiese, 1990), and in a smaller study of high-risk families (Greenspan, Wieder, Nover, Lieberman, Lourie, & Robinson, 1987), the impact of early parent–child interactions on a child's later development was found to be highly significant. For example, when a caregiver is insensitive, unresponsive, and not attuned to the infant's cues, it can lead to the development of an insecure attachment. As has been mentioned previously, the quality of attachment influences various areas of development, and disorganized attachment is a known risk factor for later emotional and social difficulties (Ainsworth, Blehar, Waters, & Wall, 1978; Grossman, Grossman, Spangler, Suess, & Unzner, 1985; Main & Goldwyn, 1984). In a study that followed a sample of children from birth to 6 years, Sroufe, Egeland, and Kreutzer (1990) found that the early parenting environment predicted a child's adjustment to school and such capacities as social skills and problem-solving ability. The child's attachment security, seen as resulting from early parenting, seemed to mediate between the home environment and school adjustment.

The emotional aspects of parenting have received increasing attention (Dix, 1991; Estrada, Arsenio, Hess, & Holloway, 1987). For example, Kopp (1989), Landy and Peters (1992), and Roberts and Strayer (1987) found that when parents responded to children's distress in a comforting and acknowledging rather than a suppressing way, it fostered children's competence in social and nonsocial aspects of their lives. In an observational study of 2-year-old children, Denham (1993) discovered that maternal responsiveness to specific child emotions was related to children's social-emotional competence in interactions with others.

Children's development is also affected by parental behaviors concerning supervision, management, and discipline. Desirable child outcomes have been associated with discipline that provides consistent enforcement of rules and a democratic recognition of the child's point of view (Maccoby & Martin, 1983; Radke-Yarrow, Zahn-Waxler, & Chapman, 1983). Baumrind (1967, 1971) called this type of discipline authoritative and found that children benefit from this style in many ways, from having optimal self-esteem, to showing prosocial behavior, to developing internal controls over negative behavior. Roberts (1986) also found optimal development to be associated with parenting style, especially for those parents who demonstrated high levels of warmth and moderate levels of control.

A number of characteristics contribute to the emotional tone and style of parents' interactions with their children (Belsky, 1984). For some parents, lack of knowledge about expected developmental milestones and parenting techniques can lead to difficulties with discipline and failure to encourage language and other areas of development (Crockenberg & Litman, 1990). As well, parental perceptions or attributions—if they are negative or distorted—of their infants and preschoolers have frequently been associated with negative interactions and poor outcomes in children (Nover, Shore, Timberlake, & Greenspan, 1984). Research has shown that for some parents, these perceptions are formed in the prenatal phase, and continue into early infancy (Zeanah, Keener, Stewart, & Anders, 1985). It is likely that some of these distortions arise from the parents' state of mind with respect to attachment or their own experience of being parented and that they influence their behavior with their child and consequently their child's attachment quality. In fact, several researchers have found strong concordance between mother and child attachment classifications, suggesting this to be the case (Benoit & Parker, 1994; Fonagy, Steele, & Steele, 1991; Grossman, Fremmer-Bombik, Rudolph, & Grossman, 1988; Main & Goldwyn, 1984; van IJzendoorn, Kranenburg, Zwart-Woudstra, van Busschbach, & Lamberman, 1991).

Unfortunately, the number of children who are abused and neglected and placed into foster homes continues to increase. Depending on the timing, type, and severity of abuse, the effects can be varied but often include learning disabilities, difficulties with relationships, problems concentrating and controlling impulses, and a tendency toward acting-out or disorders of anxiety or depression (Cicchetti, 1989; Erickson, Egeland, & Pianta, 1989; Kinard, 1980; Mueller & Silverman, 1989).

In summary, parents' interactional style and affective tone have been found to contribute to both current, short-term, and longer term outcomes for children. Consequently, parenting interactions have often been the focus of early intervention strategies and these approaches have frequently resulted in improved interactions and outcomes for children.

Research on Temperament

Since the 1990s, there has been a dramatic increase in research on temperament and individual differences, particularly as they relate to social and emotional development. The emphasis of these studies has varied dramatically and has included examination of a variety of areas that are discussed in this review of research:

- Physiological bases of individual differences in behavior

- Genetic contributions

- Continuity and discontinuity of temperament dimensions

- The effects of particular temperament traits or factors

- Role of temperament in the development of behavior problems and psychopathology

Physiological Bases of Temperament   Temperament studies have stressed the exploration of various physiological systems in order to explain individual differences in behavior (Healy, 1989; Kagan, 1996; Porges, Doussard-Roosevelt, Portales, & Suess, 1994). Researchers have considered and measured a number of these systems in order to begin to understand the great variability in the way in which infants and young children react to similar events and situations. Some of the systems and methods of analysis that have been examined include frequency analyses of brain activity, amount of activity in one hemisphere of the brain relative to the other, measurement of the autonomic nervous system, and indexing of the activity of the adrenocortical system. In each of these systems, individual differences have been identified although they have not necessarily shown long-term continuity.

In those studies that have examined hemispheric activation using EEG measures, differences have been identified in the type and intensity of emotional expression. Researchers have found that there is greater left-frontal activation in response to "approach" emotions such as happiness and anger, while with "avoidance" emotions such as sadness and anxiety there is greater activation of the right hemisphere (Calkins & Fox, 1992; Fox, 1991; Fox & Davidson, 1987; Fox et al., 1996). Researchers have therefore predicted that the relative strength of left and right hemisphere activation may underlie temperament and differences in emotional behavior, with a stable pattern of right frontal asymmetry measured early in life possibly being associated with higher levels of negative affect and later more inhibited behavior (Kagan, 1989; Rothbart, 1988).

The patterning of the autonomic nervous system and the balance between its two branches, sympathetic and parasympathetic, have also been measured in the study of infant and child temperament (Stifter & Jain, 1996). In some studies, the pattern of heart rate variability has been found to be related to temperament, with inhibited children displaying higher resting levels and less variable heart rates as compared with more uninhibited children (Fox, 1989; Kagan, Reznick, & Snidman, 1986). There is also growing evidence that 15%–20% of children in the elementary school years show more rapid increases in heart rate and blood pressure in response to normal stressors than do their peers (Jemerin & Boyce, 1990). These children have been found to show a higher incidence of inhibited and/or aggressive behavior than children without these physiological patterns.

These types of measures have also been related to signs a child exhibits such as depression, lack of energy, and being anxious and high strung—in other words, to signs of reactivity (Fox, 1989; Kagan & Snidman, 1991; Kagan, Reznick, Clarke, Snidman, & Garcia-Coll, 1985). Porges and colleagues have studied vagal tone, which measures heart rate activity that occurs during changes in respiration (respiratory sinus arrhythmia) (Porges et al., 1994). These researchers and others have found vagal tone to be related to both reactivity and regulation of emotions, with infants with high vagal tone tending to have better self-regulation than have those with low vagal tone. Infants with high vagal tone have also been shown to exhibit better regulation of their attentional processes (Fracasso, Porges, Lamb, & Rosenberg, 1994). Conversely, measures of low vagal tone in 9-month-olds have predicted difficult behavior when the children are 3 years old (Porges et al., 1994) and less sociability and more wariness of novel situations (Jemerin & Boyce, 1990).

The last approach to be discussed examines temperamental differences by measuring the activity of the hypothalamic-pituitary-adrenal system (HPA), which plays a major role in emotional responding, stress resistance, and learning and memory. Measurement of this system usually involves the collection of saliva, urine, or plasma specimens, which are then measured for levels of cortisol. Cortisol is a primary hormone produced by the HPA system. Some suggest that differences in cortisol levels may be associated with temperament differences in children. Gunnar and colleagues have examined the association among levels of cortisol and effortful control in preschool children (Gunnar, 1998; Gunnar & Stone, 1994; Nachmias et al., 1996). Children with consistently high levels of cortisol are less controlled than are their peers, as rated by parents and teachers. They conclude that it is unclear whether "high levels of cortisol make it hard for the brain to perform effortful control, or whether their lack of control gets them into situations that are stressful. We suspect that both may be involved" (Gunnar, 1998,

p. 7). As well, if the brain is exposed to high levels of cortisol over time, changes in brain activity and brain structure may ensue (Sapolsky, 1994), producing memory and learning problems and lowering the level at which negative emotions are experienced.

In conclusion, many studies suggest that certain individuals show a "pattern of increased physiologic arousal and exaggerated reactivity to stressful and environmental events which may be observed in several systems simultaneously" (Jemerin & Boyce, 1990, p. 150). These patterns obviously contribute to certain behaviors and temperamental dimensions such as intensity of emotions, predominance of negative affect, low sociability, poor adaptation to new situations, and difficulty concentrating.

Genetic Contributions Claims for a genetic or biological basis for temperament have come from the use of various physiological measures and from twin studies. In order to determine the extent that individual differences are influenced by genetic factors, twin studies typically compare the similarity between monozygotic (or identical) (MZ) twins relative to the similarity between dizygotic (or fraternal, nonidentical) (DZ) twins. In other words, genetically identical twins (MZ) are compared with those who share only half their genes on average (DZ). Some of the important twin studies are described below.

- *Colorado Adoption Study (CAS):* The Colorado Adoption Study began in 1976 and compared biological mothers with their natural children who had been adopted, adoptive mothers and their adopted children, and a control group of nonadopted children and mothers matched to the adopted group (Plomin & DeFries, 1985). Genetic continuity into adulthood was measured by comparing characteristics of biological parents and their adopted-away children. Results showed that genetic influences were implicated most strongly for measures of physical development, mental development, and language development, with IQ scores showing the greatest similarity. Only limited genetic influence was found for a few temperament dimensions, specifically sociability and emotionality. As has been suggested by other continuity studies discussed later in this chapter, similarity in development was found to be less marked in infancy than in later stages, suggesting that the influence of genes on development is less obvious during infancy but becomes more influential beginning in the preschool years and continuing into adulthood.

  On the other hand, certain environmental variables measured by the Home Observation Measurement of the Environment (HOME) and Family Environment Scale (FES) at 12 months predicted mental development scores at 24 months. Temperament variables that were related to these scores included sociability, task orientation, and extraversion. Given the finding that both genetic and environmental factors influence some individual differences in children, analyses of the relationships between the two indicated that the genetic and environmental factors do not interact in their influence but rather combine in an additive manner to affect development. Even together, however, genetic and environmental effects on various aspects of development seldom accounted for more than 10%, and never for more than 20% of the variance in infancy (Plomin & DeFries, 1985).

- *Louisville Twin Study:* In the Louisville Twin Study, initiated in 1967, 500 twin pairs were assessed from age 3 months to age 15 years. The genetic influence increased over time for IQ scores, while the family environment influences decreased between ages 1.5 and 8 years. A temperament dimension, task orientation, which was extracted from a number of behavioral variables measured between 3 and 24 months, showed the most stable genetic determination across ages (Matheny, 1980, 1986, 1987).

- *MacArthur Longitudinal Twin Study (MLTS):* In the MLTS study (Emde et al., 1992) 200 14-month-old twin pairs were assessed in the home and laboratory with a number of observational measures of affect, empathy, shyness, and other temperament dimensions. Significant genetic influences were found for expression of negative affect, empathy, and behavior inhibition, as well as for some cognitive measures of memory. Although shared-rearing environment had little effect on temperament measures or on the emotional domain of development, the researchers noted that this does not imply that environmental factors are unimportant in other areas of development.

In conclusion, not all genetic characteristics are evident at birth; some emerge or turn off later and change at various points during the life span. When adopted infants are compared with their biological adult parents, however, genetic influences have been found for cognition, temperament, and physical characteristics. Although genetic influences affect individual differences, the environment—especially the family interactions—also influences outcomes. With both genetic and environmental influences affecting outcomes, the effects have generally been found to be additive, with each contributing independently to child outcomes.

Continuity and Discontinuity of Temperament Behaviors

The continuity of temperament behaviors has often been difficult to demonstrate because of the developmental transitions that occur over time and that influence the behavioral display of underlying temperamental traits. For example, in early childhood these include the shifts to motor control, intentionality, symbolic communication, and perspective taking. As a consequence, it often is difficult to identify the features of temperament that survive maturational changes and are "displayed with some consistency across situations" (Matheny, Wilson, & Nuss, 1984, p. 1201). It has also been difficult for researchers to develop adequate techniques for assessing temperamental qualities longitudinally.

Various studies have shown significant stability correlations from infancy to age 5 (Huttunen & Nyman, 1982), from preschool to primary grades (Hegvik, McDevitt, & Carey, 1982), and in the elementary years (Chess & Thomas, 1996; Maziade, Cote, Boutin, Boudreault, & Thivierge, 1986; Thomas & Chess, 1977; Thomas et al., 1968). In the NYLS, some stability was found for the categories of Activity, Rhythmicity, Adaptability, Threshold, Intensity, and Mood, with Activity Level having significant correlations for all inter-year correlations. The greatest continuity was found for the cluster of variables they called "Easy-Difficult," with Difficult showing correlation with early adult clinical diagnoses and "Easy" with better adjustment in early adulthood.

In the Dunedin Study, Caspi and colleagues followed children starting from age 3 and every 2 years thereafter into mid-adolescence. They found threads of behavioral continuity in children from 3 to 9 years of age for clusters of factors suggesting tendencies they called Lack of Control, Approach (rather than withdrawal), and Sluggishness. These, in turn, were found to be connected to personality differences in young adulthood (Caspi, Henry, McGee, Moffitt, & Silva, 1995). A number of factors showed continuity from 4 months to 8 years in the Australian Temperament Project. Rhythmicity (including eating, sleeping, and toileting behavior); Approach (shyness and reaction to new experiences); Persistence (quiet approach to tasks, stays with them until completion); Irritability (negative emotionality, cooperation), Manageability (how easily the child is managed); and Inflexibility (difficulty coping with frustration and anger) showed significant consistency over time. The researchers note a tendency for greater-than-expected stability at the extremes of the dimensions (Prior, Sanson, & Oberklaid,

1989; Sanson, Pedlow, Cann, Prior, & Oberklaid, 1996). The Fullerton Longitudinal Study, which followed children from age 1 to age 12, found activity, approach, intensity, and distractibility correlated at 2 years with assessments at all years up to 12 years, while rhythmicity, mood, threshold, and persistence showed cross-time correlations only through preschool into middle childhood (Guerin & Gottfried, 1994).

In conclusion, although the findings are mixed, the highest stabilities are generally found for scales that tap affective dimensions (e.g., intensity, mood, rhythmicity) and activity. Age of assessment generally determines the degree of stability or continuity found. Measures taken in the first 3 months generally show little predictability, with increasing stability being found for assessments taken from the second year onward. Stability increases dramatically past age 3 years. As well, clusters of variables or more global concepts of temperament (e.g., the difficult child construct) show more stability than individual dimensions.

The Effects of Particular Temperament Traits or Factors   The three temperament types of children that have been researched the most are the 1) inhibited, 2) high activity level, and 3) difficult.

• *The Inhibited Child:* Inhibition refers to the child's initial behavioral reactions of withdrawal from unfamiliar people, objects, and situations. This trait has been related to shyness, low sociability, timidity, and introversion (Daniels & Plomin, 1985). More specifically, the inhibited child shows behavioral signs of anxiety, distress, and disorganization in response to unfamiliar people and situations. This tendency to be hesitant to explore the unfamiliar is moderately consistent across different types of situations (Asendorpf, 1994). In fact, it was the only trait in the Fels Research Institute's longitudinal study that was preserved from 3 years to adulthood (Kagan & Moss, 1962).

In their studies, Kagan and his associates have generally selected and assessed children at the extremes of inhibition or lack of inhibition. Their research found stability in the traits over time, with 78% of children continuing in the predicted categories from 21 months to 5 years of age (Kagan, 1989; Kagan et al., 1986; Reznick, Kagan, Snidman, Gersten, Baak, & Rosenberg, 1987). Other researchers included Bronson (1970) who found continuity of individual differences in fearfulness and Emmerick (1964) who, in observations in preschools, found continuity in inhibited behavior from 3 to 5 years of age.

Researchers have found certain physiological correlates with these behaviors, including high and stable heart rate, larger pupillary dilations, and higher cortisol readings, implying a lower threshold or increased reactivity in the sympathetic nervous system. As well, increased cortical asymmetry in the right frontal cortex has been identified (Calkins & Fox, 1992; Dawson, Panagiotides, Klinger, & Hill, 1992; Fox, 1989).

• *The High Activity Level Child:* Early research identified individual differences in activity level during the neonatal period (Escalona, 1968; Fries, 1954; Fries & Woolf, 1954). Activity level was measured using motor reaction to a startle test. No stability was found immediately after birth, but higher activity on this test was found to be related to a child's expressions of negative affect and greater motor activity while waiting to be fed (Riese, 1987; Strauss & Rourke, 1978).

Stability increases with age in some studies. For example, some studies found stability in activity level, for example, from 4 to 8 months to 1 to 3 years (McDevitt & Carey, 1978; Peters-Martin & Wachs, 1985) and from 3 to 7 years (Thomas & Chess, 1977). In general, activity level does not show continuity in infancy but shows moderate stability from 12 months on. Carlson, Jacobvitz, and Sroufe (1995) found that once symptoms of hyperactivity were established by the time a child was 3 or 4 years of age they tended to show continuity across elementary school. They found relationship and contextual factors to be most predictive of hyperactivity, although there was also a strong correlation with distractibility. Some longitudinal studies have not been able to demonstrate stability of activity level from later infancy into adult years (Huttunen & Nyman, 1982; McDevitt & Carey, 1981), however.

• *The Difficult Child:* The idea of the "difficult child" was introduced by Thomas, Chess, and Birch (1968). This term originated with the NYLS, and since then has been generally accepted in the clinical and temperament literature as useful in order to predict future behaviors and particularly behavior problems. In the NYLS, 10% of children met the criteria for the syndrome.

Some researchers have found concurrent relationships among difficult temperament and other difficult behaviors such as colic and night waking (e.g., Atkinson, Vetere, & Grayson, 1995; Maldonado-Duran & Sauceda-Garcia, 1996); and frequency of injury, shyness, and negative reactions to the birth of a sibling and sibling rivalry (Brody, Stoneman, & McCoy, 1994). DeGangi, DiPietro, Greenspan, and Porges (1991) suggested that a group of infants who have regulatory disorders or who are often hyper- or hyposensitive to sensory stimulation may share many characteristics with the difficult temperament dimension, perhaps explaining some of the components of the syndrome. Kochanska and colleagues found that fearless children with difficulties in inhibiting behavior may have more problems in internalizing standards and require very "firm limits and a very warm relationship with caregivers as well as an emphasis on positive motivations and qualities in order to internalize rules" (Kochanska, Murray, & Coy, 1997, p. 275).

A number of studies have found that when mothers perceived to a high degree that their infants were difficult, this predicted problem behaviors later. For example, Thomas and Chess (1985) and Lee and Bates (1985) found a fair degree of stability of child difficulty in the preschool years and that children identified in this category were more likely to break rules or to cause mild damage to people or property later in childhood and adolescence. It is much less predictive into early adulthood.

Although some children may be constitutionally difficult, some studies suggest that certain parental behaviors or personality traits may contribute to what Patterson has described as coercive cycles in which the behavior continues to be perpetuated by parental reactions (Patterson, 1982). Some parental characteristics that have been suggested are a tendency to give in after initially resisting, intrusive control with the children, unresponsiveness (Van den Boom & Hoeksma, 1994), maternal depression and anxiety (Mednick, Hocevar, Baker, & Schulsinger, 1996), and parental external locus of control or low sense of self-efficacy (Bugental, 1985). Of course, in some cases it is very hard to determine the causality of these reported differences, as mothers of children with more difficult temperaments may feel less confident as parents, causing feelings of lower self-efficacy and depression (Gross, Conrad, Fogg, & Wothke, 1994). As well, some parents may be concerned that they will reinforce crying by being responsive, which can result in nonoptimal care and insecure attachment in the child (Mangelsdorf, Gunnar, Kestenbaum, Lang, & Andreas, 1991).

The Role of Temperament in the Development of Personality, Behavior Problems, and Psychopathology   One of the most important considerations about infant temperament has been its role in the development of personality, behavior problems, and childhood psychopathology. Thomas, Chess, and Birch (1968), in the NYLS, considered whether difficult temperament measured in infancy predicted behavior problems later. In fact, data showed that early measures were not predictive and that difficult temperament did not signif-

icantly predict behavior problems until it was manifested at 3 years of age, when interactional styles among parents and children were more established. Maziade and colleagues reported similar findings, with temperament ratings not becoming predictive until 4 years of age (Maziade, Cote, Boutin, Bernier, & Thivierge, 1988). Some researchers have found an association between difficult temperament and behavior problems, however (Barron & Earls, 1984; Earls & Jung, 1987). Cameron (1978) found that a combination of difficult traits and "poorness of fit" was most predictive of behavior problems, emphasizing again the joint contribution of genetic predisposition and the environment. As well, when lack of predictability is found it may relate more to a failure of the measures used in the early years to detect important temperament dimensions or behavior problems than an actual lack of association.

Other researchers have found that some temperament variables measured at 2 years of age do predict internalizing and externalizing behavior problems among 4- to 6-year-olds. The dimensions that did relate were intense expression of negative emotions, poor adaptability to new people and situations, and resistance to management of activity (e.g., Caspi et al., 1995; Persson-Blennow & McNeil, 1988). Caspi and colleagues found that lack of control and hyperactivity assessed in early childhood—in addition to the dimensions mentioned above—predicted personality difficulties in young adulthood.

The other temperament dimension that has most consistently been linked to internalizing behavior and adult psychopathology is the display of inhibited behavior in unfamiliar situations. Kagan (1997) suggested that children who exhibit early inhibited behavior are at higher risk for developing anxiety disorders, particularly social phobia, separation anxiety, or compulsive symptoms. Other researchers noted correlations of inhibition with subsequent depression and loneliness (Bowen, Vitaro, Kerr, & Pelletier, 1995).

Conclusions About Temperament Research

A number of difficulties with temperament research have emerged, and results are hard to interpret and compare because of disagreements about the definition of temperament and the various dimensions or variables that make it up (Goldsmith et al., 1987). Other concerns surround temperament measures, with parent-report questionnaires being seen, on one hand, as too influenced by the subjective bias of parental attributions of the child. On the other hand, laboratory observations may be subject to distortion, because a limited period of observation is used that may not represent the range of behaviors or reality of parent–infant, parent–child interactions that happen in the home. Both types of measures frequently have poor test–retest reliability, and often show only modest correlations among measures and across various situations such as the home and school. Perhaps of most significance is that most measures of children are taken well into the first or second year of life when children have already been significantly affected by the caretaking environment, which makes it difficult to assess the role of temperament alone.

In the 1990s, a few studies have studied the interaction of temperament and other important variables such as parent–child interaction, social support, family relations, and social context on child outcomes (Wachs, 2000). The results of these studies suggest that temperament is most likely to act as a mediator of the impact of the environment on the child. Wachs (1994) and Wachs and Gandour (1984) pointed out that the same environment or similar parent–child interaction may affect children with different temperament traits very differently. In their own research, they found that easy infants were more responsive to the environment, particularly in interactions with people, while difficult infants showed more sensitivity to "noise confusion" (Wachs, 1987). A number of other researchers have found that the child's temperament influences the way that parenting styles affect the child (e.g., Barron & Earls,

1984; Kochanska, 1997; Kochanska, Murray, Jacques, Koenig, & Vandegeest, 1996; Kyrios & Prior, 1991; Park, Belsky, Putnam, & Crnic, 1997).

Some attachment researchers have come to similar conclusions and see temperament as having an indirect effect on attachment classification through its effect on parent sensitivity and responsiveness to the child (Susman-Stillman, Kalkoske, Egeland, & Waldman, 1996; Van den Boom, 1989, 1994). As concluded by Mangelsdorf et al., "temperament does not cause an insecure or difficult mother–child relationship but it may narrow the range of caregiver environments in which the relationship can develop securely" (1991, p. 326). This narrowing of environments increases the likelihood of poorness of fit between parent and child and of the child receiving nonoptimal caregiving.

In conclusion, temperament may have a significant influence on child development. Some characteristics that make the child more difficult to manage may be risk factors that predict later poor outcomes, while characteristics that contribute to a child being "easy" help protect the child from the impact of more negative environments (Rutter, 1981).

THE GROWTH-PROMOTING ENVIRONMENT: PRINCIPLES OF DEALING WITH STAGE-RELATED AND TEMPERAMENT ISSUES

In this section, core principles are presented to help caregivers use developmental and temperament information in order to adapt optimally to the needs of infants and young children and, thus, to enhance their development (see Table 1.18).

PRINCIPLE 1:   *Spend time observing the child and relate his behavior to what you know about his developmental level.*

Young children's behavior can often be confusing for caregivers and even, at times, infuriating. When caregivers feel their blood pressure rising and their anger mounting or are confused about a new behavior, it is important to step back and try to figure out the meaning of the behavior based on the developmental stage of the child. The following vignettes illustrate reasons behind some observed negative behaviors:

Table 1.18.   Principles for dealing with stage-related and temperament issues

Principle 1	Spend time observing the child and relate his behavior to what you know about his developmental level.
Principle 2	Set up the environment and the child's schedule to accommodate the child's developmental characteristics.
Principle 3	Try to learn about the child's temperament characteristics and any physical characteristics that may be contributing to his behavioral style.
Principle 4	Spend time changing negative labels into positive ones that reflect the child's developmental stage and temperament type.
Principle 5	Identify behaviors that trigger anger and anxiety in yourself and see how you are affected by your own temperament characteristics.
Principle 6	Identify and adopt strategies that can help you adapt to the child's special temperament characteristics.

• •

Behavior: *5-year-old Reuven gets very bossy when he has friends over and is always telling them what to do.*

Developmental issue: *Reuven is becoming very interested and strict about the rules of his house and insists his friends obey them.*

Other factors: *Reuven could be feeling a lack of control in other areas of his life, such as having a new sibling.*

Behavior: *Two-year-old Dia has started to have difficulty napping at child care and she cries a lot.*

Developmental issue: *Dia could be going through increased anxiety about being separated.*

Other factors: *Dia could fear some loss or impending loss of loved ones at home.*

It is important that caregivers come up with some useful ways to react if a child's negative behavior reoccurs. Trying to discover the source of the behavior, sometimes by joining in her play, can provide excellent opportunities for understanding what issues she is confronting and struggling to resolve.

Principle 2: *Set up the environment and the child's schedule to accommodate the child's developmental characteristics.*

Some of the primary capacities that children need to negotiate in the first 6 years, along with characteristics of a conducive environment, are set out in Table 1.19 in the order in which the child usually acquires the developmental abilities.

The child's mastery of these issues and the qualitative shifts that occur in his development will have a continuing influence throughout his life. For the most part, the environment—which includes both people and objects—is adapted to provide these experiences. It is important to regularly monitor young children's environments, however, to make sure that their needs are being met. More information on these aspects of development is provided in the chapters that follow.

Self-Regulation and Ability to Calm Down   For self-regulation to happen, the environment has to be predictable, with a regular schedule, in which changes are the exception and not the rule. Infants will need to be calmed and responded to when they become upset. As she matures into toddlerhood and older, however, a child needs to gradually be given some opportunities to find ways to calm herself down. This can include having the caregiver talk to her to calm her rather than always running immediately to pick her up or embrace her. This would, of course, only be the case if the child is not extremely overwrought or seriously hurt.

Interest In and Responsiveness to the World   Although the periods of quiet alertness during the first 3 months are often brief, caregivers may need to make an effort to identify them and to provide appropriate interactions when the baby is available. A special type of speech called *parentese* can be helpful to keep an infant interested and responsive. When speaking parentese, the caregiver holds the baby upright, uses a more high-pitched voice and longer sounds, and looks into the baby's eyes at the optimal distance of 8–10 inches.

Table 1.19. Different capacities and the characteristics of the environment needed to attain them

Capacity	Characteristics of the environment needed
Self regulation, ability to calm down	Caregivers who are calm and provide consistent caregiving for the infant
Interest and responsiveness to world	Caregivers who respond to the infant when he is awake and provide sensitive interactions
Increasing attention to interpersonal interaction and communication	Increasing periods of interaction with consistent caregivers who talk and gesture to the child in response to the child's interactions
Differentiation of emotions	Caregivers who respond to various emotions and name them for the child
Establishment of secure attachment relationship and sociability	Caregivers who comfort child when she is upset and show interest and positivity toward child. Caregivers who provide experiences of being with other adults and children
Exploring the world/sense of competence	An environment that is safety proofed and that provides objects that the child can explore and act upon
Establishing a sense of self	Caregivers who allow the child increasing independence and choices and help the child have experiences of success
Beginning of conscience	Caregivers who provide firm limits and structures and who teach the child about morals and rules

Increasing Attention to Interpersonal Interaction and Communication As a child grows and is awake for longer periods of time, he becomes increasingly interested in human interactions. At this time, he will reach out to his caregiver in different ways and begin to seek out familiar caregivers. During this period, it is essential that the infant experiences animated and pleasurable interactions in which his actions and communications elicit a response. It is important not to be overwhelming or intrusive, but to—as far as possible—follow the child's lead.

Emotions Become More Differentiated By about 6 months of age, a child's emotions become much more easy to read and often more intense. The baby begins to show pleasure with laughter, and anger and sadness with clear facial expressions and gestures. These emotions need to be responded to appropriately so that the child feels acknowledged. One helpful strategy is to name emotions for the child, reflecting the emotion the child seems to be experiencing: "I can see you're feeling really angry"; "That makes you feel really sad, doesn't it?"; "When Mary has to be held all the time it makes you feel jealous and left out."

Establishing Secure Attachment Relationships and Sociability Although children need to explore and become independent, they can only do so when they feel safe. This sense of security or safety only comes when caregivers are emotionally and physically available to the child. In fact, small children find it hard to explore unless they can see and actually reach out to caregivers. Security is provided by consistent responsiveness when the child is upset as well as by warm, sensitive, positive interactions. In addition to parents and other adults, children need opportunities to be around other children.

Many children are in child care and have opportunities for interaction with other children on a daily basis. For children who spend most of the day at home, however, it is important to make sure they get opportunities to play with other children, at least from the age of 3 years on.

Exploring the World and Establishing a Sense of Competence   Burton White (1985) has talked about the need to safety proof the young child's environment so that he or she can explore without danger. He advised caregivers to get on their knees and to examine the child's play space from this perspective, then to correct any potential danger. As he pointed out, this process of making the play space safe for exploring will be essential in developing interest in the environment, and consequently, a competent child.

Children also develop a sense of competence by being noticed for their efforts and by being provided with opportunities to learn and to develop any special interests or capacities that they have. When time permits, following up on the child's questions can help her feel an increasing sense of control and knowledge. In fact, the most important part of developing a sense of competence may be a child's feeling that she can influence her environment. What a caregiver says to a child, how limits are set, what opportunities are provided for exploration and mastery, and even how the caregiver expresses emotions may all be contributing factors.

Establishing a Sense of Self   Children in the toddler and preschool years increasingly become aware of their separation from others and begin to understand that they can exert their independence and individuality. Children need to be provided with opportunities to become their own person. Sensitive caregivers begin to provide the child with some flexibility within boundaries and to acknowledge their child's abilities and specialness. Some examples are making sure that the child puts on a painting shirt but then allowing him to choose what he paints, insisting that sand not be thrown but encouraging children to use sand in ways that are their choice, and letting the children choose play and conversational themes.

Beginning of Conscience   To help children internalize a sense of right and wrong and rules, they need clear rules and structures, explanations of why the rules are important, and knowledge of the effects of hurtful behavior on others. These aspects of the caregiving environment will be explained in detail in Chapter 7.

PRINCIPLE 3:   *Try to learn about the child's temperament characteristics and any physical characteristics that may be contributing to his behavioral style.*

Underlying the temperament traits and behaviors that define children are a number of physical characteristics that may contribute to their expression. Some physical problems are obvious, and caregivers are able to identify them very easily. Others are much more subtle and harder to detect. These physical problems rarely show up in CAT scans, electroencephalographs, or even in more sensitive imaging techniques (e.g., MRI, PET scans). This does not always rule out some physiological basis for the behavior, however. It is very important for caregivers to be aware of any physical traits a child has that may influence behavior and then to find ways to adapt the environment, to empathize with the child, and to communicate with and to enjoy the child. Some physiological characteristics that may underlie some of the behaviors of the difficult child include

- Hyper- or hyposensitivity; excessive reactivity; or lack of reactivity to touch, sound, sight, smell and movement

- Motor difficulties

- Auditory and/or visual processing difficulties and sensory integration problems

Hypersensitivity, or Excessive Reactivity   Some infants and young children are very sensitive to various sensations such as touch, sounds, sights, smells, and movements. For these children who seem to be excessively tuned in to various types of stimulation, some stimuli may be overwhelming, disorganizing, and even painful. Some children may experience even normal sensations as if they are excessive and they tune into every stimulation around them. This kind of difficulty can result in a number of reactions:

- Demonstrating excessive startle reactions (infants and toddlers)

- Demonstrating sensitivity to air and object temperature

- Getting upset if they are tickled or held close and arching away from touch

- Not being able to tolerate wearing or being touched by the labels in certain clothes

- Not eating certain lumpy foods

- Disliking certain movements like swinging or going down a slide

- Overreacting to loud noises or even voices

- Overreacting to certain sights such as a flashbulb or a part of a scary picture

- Being very sensitive to the body language and feelings of others

- Being very sensitive to their internal feelings as well as outside sensations

- Presenting as over-cautious and anxious

- Having attentional problems as they react to the various sensations that they experience around them

Hyposensitivity, or Underreactive Child   Just as some children tend to overreact to everything around them, others underreact and need a lot of input to get them to become involved or to respond. Sometimes these infants and children seem to be in their own world and to be tuned inward. Parents and caregivers may describe or experience them as "easy" because they make few demands. These children may also cause concern, however, because they show little interest in other children and in being sociable. Some of the behaviors these children may exhibit include

- Having difficulty making eye contact and responding to people

- Demonstrating a lack of interest in toys and in other stimulation in the outside world

- Tending to withdraw into a corner and avoiding other children

- Being drawn to the rapid movements and colors of certain television shows and games

- Being content to be left alone to play in their crib or to manipulate certain toys

Children's different temperaments affect the way they react to others (From Johnston, Lynn [1978]. *Do they ever grow up?* Minnetonka, MN: Meadowbrook Press; reprint granted with written permission of Lynn Johnston Productions, Inc.)

- Seeming very caught up in their own thoughts and fantasies

- Failing to initiate interactions, although they may respond with effort

Motor Difficulties   Motor difficulties may be caused by a variety of aspects of the motor system, including motor tone, motor planning, and coordination. Motor tone may be very low, with the body appearing floppy and loose or high or tense, resulting in the child appearing to be rigid and even awkward. For either, it may require a lot of effort to master even routine motor activities, such as walking or jumping, which are easy for children without these difficulties. Children with motor planning problems may find carrying out a string of coordinated physical activities very challenging. Activities requiring coordination such as skipping, tying shoelaces, and crawling are examples of simple activities that the child may take a long time to learn.

Other children have difficulty with motor tasks that involve responding to visual images, such as copying letters. Difficulty with these activities may involve a number of problem areas or just one. That is, the difficulty may be with taking in the information, understanding it, or with the actual motor response required. Some resulting behaviors may include

- Having difficulty learning new motor skills

- Experiencing problems copying shapes, letters, or numbers

- Having difficulty attending to certain tasks

- Expressing frustration with sequencing actions

- Experiencing clumsiness and difficulty with balance

- Having difficulty engaging in two-way communication because the sequencing required may be challenging

- Bumping into people and things

- Difficulty going up and down stairs

- Having problems using scissors, eating utensils, and so forth

- Having problems riding tricycles, bikes, and so forth

- Having difficulty buttoning or zipping

Auditory and/or Visual Processing Difficulties and Sensory Integration Problems   Some children have difficulty with processing sounds and words. It is not that they do not hear them, but rather that they cannot hold the words in their minds. Such children may have difficulty making sense of the words and phrases they hear. Consequently, following simple instructions may be challenging, with certain children only remembering the first or the last phrase of a sentence. This can lead caregivers to believe the child is being disobedient when in fact he is not able to remember what was said.

• •

Adam's teachers at his French immersion school were very concerned about his behavior, specifically his tendency to be in his "own world" and to not follow through on instructions. Referral had been prompted because when a physical education teacher would ask him to "Go to the locker room, take off your pants, and put on your shorts," Adam consistently forgot the last part of the instruction and ended up running around the gym in his underwear. His behavior was perceived as very peculiar. Psychological testing showed extreme auditory processing difficulties, though he did well with other nonverbal capacities. With catch-up tutoring as well as a transfer to a school where the curriculum was in English and he did not have to deal with two languages, Adam began to function extremely well in school, especially in subjects that used his excellent visual motor skills, such as geography and art.

Visual processing difficulties are somewhat less common, but cause difficulties with understanding what is seen. Pictures may be too complicated and be ignored or sorting tasks or doing mazes may cause difficulty. Children may be weak in one area and strong in the other.

Some children have sensory integration problems and have difficulty integrating and making sense of the sensations they receive from various sensory systems. When the brain has problems integrating sensations, the child will require a great deal of effort to undertake even simple tasks. Children with these sensory processing difficulties and sensory integration dysfunction may

- Have difficulty following a sequence of directions

- Have speech delays and difficulty communicating

- Misread signals from others as negative, thus resulting in strong emotional reactions

- Be easily distracted when looking at words or pictures

- Have trouble learning simple motor tasks

- Be clumsy and frequently trip or fall

- Run, jump, and so forth awkwardly

- Have difficulty with fine motor tasks such as drawing, coloring, and cutting with scissors

- Be hyperactive or distractible

Some children may have difficulties in only one of these areas, while others may have challenges in several. It is important to have an adequate assessment of the child because understanding the child's underlying physical challenges may help caregivers provide more attuned interactions and environments for children that utilize their strengths, as well as help overcome their deficits. In general, these children need understanding; empathy; warm interactions; structure; and consistent, firm limits. Some intervention strategies are presented in this chapter. For children with severe difficulties, however, interventions provided by professionals such as sensory integrative therapy and physiotherapy may be necessary.

PRINCIPLE 4: *Spend time changing negative labels into positive ones that reflect the child's developmental stage and temperament type.*

Many adults who feel inadequate note that, when they were growing up, they frequently heard negative remarks and cruel nicknames and labels that were just as hard to deal with as other kinds of abuse. For children, negative labeling highlights their problems and hides and ignores their strengths and potentials. When caregivers and other adults change the vocabulary used to describe a child, this can help them to view him or her differently. This, of course, in turn, helps the child begin to feel more positive about himself and then to act differently. Some suggestions are set out in Table 1.20. Caregivers may want to identify the negative labels they use and to think of other, more positive words to express the same characteristic.

PRINCIPLE 5: *Identify behaviors that trigger anger and anxiety in yourself and see how you are affected by your own temperament characteristics.*

Many who talk about temperament have emphasized the need for looking at the "goodness of fit" between the environment and its expectations and demands, and the child's capacities and style of behavior. Because the young child is most influenced by the primary caregiver, it is important to consider the contribution of this interaction. This refers to the need to recognize that our own temperament characteristics may affect how we perceive and react to a certain child's behavior. Evidence also points out that our own backgrounds influence the way we react to children's behavior. A "poor fit" could occur whenever there is incompatibility between a child's temperament and the values and expectations of the caregiver. For example, a caregiver might expect a child to be quiet and attentive, but the child is very active and exploring. The

Table 1.20. Changing labels from negative to positive

Negative label	Positive label
Rude	Honest
Has a bad attitude	Knows what he wants
Distractible	Perceptive
Stubborn	Independent
Difficult	Spirited
Willful	Strong
Oversensitive	Very responsive
Overactive	Energetic
Wild	Very busy

same kind of mismatch might occur if a caregiver who was brought up with a depressed caregiver has a child who tends to be anxious, is slow to warm-up, and often whines. These behaviors may be infuriating as they bring to the surface memories of a caregiver who did the same thing long ago and the struggles they have been through to overcome these tendencies in themselves.

When there is a mismatch or poor fit between the child and parent, negative cycles may be set up that are difficult to break (see Figure 1.1). Here are some examples of how a caregiver can find a child's temperament difficult to manage:

• •

Margaret tends to be rather quiet and shy, but she looked forward to the birth of her baby with pleasure. From early on, however, she found Paul's behavior difficult. Paul was exuberant and intense from the beginning, constantly on the go and highly sociable. Whereas for Margaret a good time would be staying at home and reading, for Paul his greatest delight was a trip to the park, "chatting" with everyone and playing on the swings. Margaret had to make a significant effort to provide Paul with the social and physically active experiences he craved.

Jonathan played football in college and now enjoys all sorts of sports. He dreamed of a son he could take to sports events and who would enjoy going to baseball and hockey games. When Joshua was born, Jonathan was disappointed to find that his son was shy and had trouble adjusting to new situations and to noise and crowds. In fact, he gradually paid less and less attention to him, leaving the caregiving to his wife, who seemed to understand the boy better.

The fit can be improved when caregivers are given opportunities to understand both their own temperament and the child's. Also, they can be helped to tolerate their child's temperamental

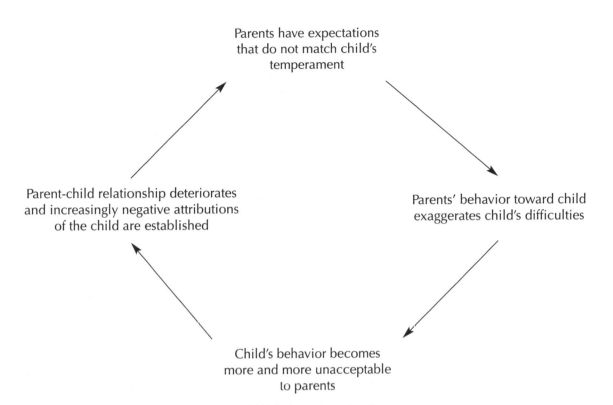

Figure 1.1. How negative cycles can be set up between child behaviors and parent reactions.

characteristics and to adjust the environment and their own interactions with the child to accommodate them. Providing caregivers with the suggestions under Principle 6 may also help them to do this. This will enable changes to be made at various parts of the cycle shown in Figure 1.1.

Problem-Solving Around Goodness of Fit If a caregiver is getting into very negative cycles with a child, it is necessary to step back, to problem solve, and to find new ways to react to the child in order to break the negative interactions. Negative cycles occur when an infant or child continually behaves in ways that frustrate and exhaust a caregiver, often making her feel helpless, inadequate, and out of control. As a result, the caregiver acts in punitive or helpless ways and the child's behavior escalates. Some examples are set out here.

• •

John had cried almost constantly since birth, and Mary was feeling exhausted, angry, and depressed. She sometimes left John to cry on his own because she was concerned that picking him up would spoil him, or she picked him up and rocked him vigorously in an attempt to soothe him. Neither response helped, and his crying continued unabated.

Emma had always been a quiet, shy little girl but her behavior became increasingly anxious and withdrawn when Kaye placed her in a preschool two mornings per week. Observing Emma's increasing unhappiness, Kaye became insistent that Emma socialize, and increased her days at the nursery. Emma became more and more withdrawn.

Michael was a very determined and demanding toddler whom both his mother, Irene, and his father, Roger, found very difficult to discipline. Limits usually resulted in Michael throwing intense temper tantrums and being defiant, refusing to do as he was told. His parents felt helpless and out of control sometimes—becoming so frustrated that they hit him or yelled at him.

It is important for these parents to consider the following:

1. *The child's characteristics*: What physical characteristics or temperament traits may be contributing to the child's behavior? Does John have a hypersensitivity to touch, which means he needs different ways to be soothed? Could Emma be drawn out with individualized, one-to-one, animated interactions adapted to her sensory processing strengths? Is Michael so intense because he finds it hard to concentrate and to enjoy his toys or pretend play? How may parents or caregivers adapt the environment and their behavior to deal optimally with the child's strengths and difficulties? Spending time observing the child and identifying strengths and problems can be very helpful.

2. *The caregiver's characteristics and history*: Sometimes caregivers get into negative cycles with challenging infants and children because the children's behavior clashes with their own personality or triggers painful memories from the past. Perhaps Mary is an upbeat, demonstrative person who is having a hard time accepting the fact that John is difficult to comfort. Perhaps Emma reminds Kaye of her own depressed and withdrawn mother. Maybe Michael reminds Roger of his stubborn, unyielding father with whom he continues to fight.

3. *The caregiver–child relationship*: If you are a caregiver, it is essential to find ways to repair the caregiver–child relationship. Unless the child feels secure in your responsive availability and caring, his behavior and your interaction will continue to deteriorate. Finding ways to have positive and happy times with the child can effectively break and stop the negative cycles. Possibly massaging John may help him calm down, for example, or talking calmly to him at an optimal distance may be an effective way to communicate. For both Emma and Michael, individual play sessions in which they are encouraged to take the lead in and choose the play themes may be helpful. It is important that these positive interactions are ones both parent and child genuinely enjoy, so they can continue to be effective.

4. *The environment beyond the family*: Adapting the environment to meet a child's needs includes considering aspects beyond the family to which the child may be exposed, including the child-care environment and those in the larger community. Perhaps the preschool Emma attends is too noisy and busy for her and a more optimal placement is necessary.

Perhaps Michael is being exposed to two different styles of caregiving, which can be very confusing for him.

5. *Structures, routines, limits, and family atmosphere*: As essential as it is to build relationships in the child's life, it will also be important to identify and consistently provide each of these children with a predictable routine, clear structures, and limits. These must be enforced calmly and consistently and be matched to the temperament of the child. These are discussed in detail in Chapter 7. It is also crucial to look at the way conflicts are resolved in the family between partners and among siblings. Calm negotiation, as opposed to yelling or hitting, can make a significant difference and improve the "goodness of fit" between a temperamentally sensitive child and the environment.

PRINCIPLE 6: *Identify and adopt strategies that can help you adapt to the child's special temperament characteristics.*

As has been noted, about 10% of children have temperaments that their parents rate or perceive as difficult and another 5%–15% of children are seen as slow to warm up. This requires caregivers to accommodate the adverse aspects of their child's temperament, to minimize conflict while still providing for the child's developmental needs.

Some strategies that can help young children with each of the extremes of the temperamental qualities are outlined here.

Activity Level

High activity level:

- Provide a child with opportunities for activities that "let off steam," such as running, jumping, and climbing.

- Demand quietness in certain places, but only expect it for brief amounts of time.

- Help the child experiment with going slowly by practicing moving "like a snail" or "like a lumbering elephant" so he can begin to experience some success in slowing down.

- Play games that have slow and fast movements in sequence, such as "Simon Says."

- Alternate running and jumping with fine motor activities such as drawing or cutting.

- Provide consistent limits and structure, as well as containment of any risk-taking behavior.

- Encourage use of words instead of constant action.

Low activity level:

- Allow sufficient time for the child to finish tasks.

- Do not criticize the child and do not allow a more active playmate who responds more quickly to take over.

- Notice what *has* rather than what has not been accomplished.

- Encourage physical activities that can improve motor tone and coordination.

Rhythmicity

Irregular rhythmicity:

- Accept that the child is not hungry or tired but impose social rules (e.g., you must sit at the table and eat one thing; you must stay in your bed).

- Impose a regular bedtime and waking time.

- Insist on regular mealtimes and on sitting at the table for an acceptable period of time.

- In general, give the child time to get up in the morning and assist him with a regular routine.

- Show the child how to talk to himself in order to calm himself and talk himself through routines.

Regular rhythmicity:

- Accommodate, as far as possible, the child's need for regularity; maintain as much of a routine as possible on holidays, outings, and so forth.

- Prepare well ahead for transitions.

- Talk about changes in routines that may be coming up.

- Use visual cues, such as calendars, to show the child how the day will be or how the summer holidays will be organized.

Withdrawal/Approach

Withdrawal:

- Insist on a timed-limited trial if you believe an activity fits with the child's interests or abilities.

- Provide opportunities for mastery and success by supporting the child during new experiences.

- Before beginning a task or a new activity, encourage the child to use her imagination and to pretend she is an astronaut or a caterpillar getting ready for an adventure.

- Help the child deal with disappointment when things do not work out. Sometimes replaying the episode in play sessions can be helpful.

- With a child who has become self-absorbed and withdrawn, use enthusiasm and animated interactions in order to draw him out to participate with others.

- Be encouraging when a child shows initiative, and follow his lead when appropriate.

- Remember the baby or child may take longer to warm up to new situations and stay around until he feels comfortable.

- Help her talk about her feelings.

- Invite a playmate (sometimes a younger playmate) over to play.

- Teach social entry skills and words to use such as "Can I play?" "Can I help?"

Approach:

- Watch that the child who tends to be a "plunger" is safe.

- If the child's first reactions to new experiences tend to be overenthusiastic and are often followed by negative views of the situation, try to prepare her by making sure she is more realistic about her expectations. Also support her if she becomes disappointed.

- Give the child appropriate ways to approach other children if he tends to be too pushy with others.

Adaptability

Slow to adapt:

- Provide multiple opportunities for brief, graduated exposure to new experiences (e.g., attending school for the first time).

- Provide predictable routines.

- Do not adopt a sink-or-swim approach because this can really frighten children and raise their anxiety levels.

- Talk about upcoming events, giving the child a chance to ask questions and be reassured.

- Use visual cues, such as calendars, to prepare the child for changes or new experiences.

- Provide plenty of warnings about transitions but do not give in if the child protests.

- Provide opportunities for social interactions and teach social entry skills (e.g., "Can I help you build with blocks?").

- Try playing out potentially difficult upcoming events, such as hospitalizations and entry to child care, in pretend-play situations.

Quick to adapt:

- For the most part, enjoy it and just make sure the new situation is safe.

- Make sure your child knows about possible dangers in the environment.

- Check that he is continuing to enjoy the new situation and is adjusting well.

- If the first positive response to a situation fades, remind the child that this sometimes happens but that it will be all right.

- Let the child know you appreciate how well he is managing.

Sensitivity or Threshold of Responsiveness

Low threshold:

- Avoid stimulation and situations that trigger intensive reactions (e.g., certain clothes or food).

- Give the child words to explain how she feels.

- Reduce stimulation whenever possible.

- Leave with the child, when situations get too difficult. This could be when there is too much stimulation, too many people, or the child finds it hard to play with other children.

- Notice the child's positive emotional reactions such as showing empathy and concern.

- Reduce television watching and use of computer games.

- Try and calm the child before he spins out of control. Signs that the child is becoming very anxious or overwhelmed, particularly if he is sick or tired, should be noticed and efforts made to reduce the immediate stresses if possible.

- Teach the child to use deep breathing techniques in difficult situations.

High threshold:

- Alert the child to cues he may be missing.

- Be careful to make sure the child understands what is being requested.

- In general, draw out the child by being enthusiastic and working hard to get his attention. You may need to speak in a very persistent way with a particular vocal tone to get the child's attention. Using a very animated facial expression may also be important with some children.

- Enter the child's world of play or television viewing in order to interact with her.

- Find out what does stimulate the child, for example, wrestling, listening to loud music, or going on the swings. Provide lots of opportunities for the activities.

- Provide opportunities for fun physical activities.

Intensity of Reactions

High intensity:

- Try and remain calm when soothing a crying baby. Avoid rocking too vigorously.

- Avoid responding intensely as well. Try and respond calmly.

- Listen to concerns and discuss them while looking for a solution.

- Persist in your limit-setting and do not give in to get "peace."

- Ask the child to talk about an upset in a calm manner.

- Step away from a situation sometimes.

- Provide calming activities such as playing with water, soft music, and so forth.

- Watch for cues that intensity is building, and intervene before things become too much.

- Provide activities that allow the child to touch, smell, hear, and see things.

- Use time-outs to allow everyone to calm down.

Low intensity:

- Listen to the child's opinions and requests even though they are expressed mildly.

- Take complaints or expressions of pain or upset very seriously.

- Encourage the child to express opinions and to talk about his feelings.

- Make sure the child is given an opportunity to receive soothing and containment even when reactions seem mild and low-key.

Quality of Mood

Negative mood:

- Help the child see the positive. Show her what she can do, not what she cannot do.

- Notice the child's distress and attend to it.

- Teach good manners and appropriate ways to express anger and frustration.

- Give practice in seeing both sides of a situation.

- Give the child a short time-out as a way to calm down when he becomes very upset.

- Provide a lot of opportunities for joyful, fun activities the child enjoys.

Positive mood:

- Enjoy it.

- Help the child to be a little more cautious about people and teach her some safeguards to protect against quick positive evaluations of people and situations.

- Let the child know that you really appreciate her good nature and positive mood.

Distractibility

High distractibility:

- Help the child concentrate by joining him in an activity. Play can be an excellent medium, especially in the company of an interested parent.

- For infants and young children, provide a small, enclosed space as a play area and only a very few toys at one time.

- Provide a table and chair and a place to enjoy an activity. Insist on some concentrated time (e.g., 10 minutes at a time at first) for doing some activities.

- Praise task completion and concentration.

- Make sure the child understands instructions and directions.

- Eliminate distracting stimuli as much as possible.

- Give the child periodic breaks, whether on long automobile trips or while doing homework.

- Insist that small tasks are completed by using firm structures and limits.

Low distractibility:

- Make sure the child hears instructions to stop an activity.

- Provide warnings when an activity must be stopped.

- Make sure that requests to do something or to follow through on a plan are given clearly and when the child is not concentrating on something else.

- Be aware if a child is isolating herself constantly in order to be alone to do something. Make sure social activities are planned and the child is included.

Persistence and Attention Span

Low persistence and attention span:

- Make sure the child returns to task after a break.

- Do not allow the child to leave everything unfinished and make sure the child returns to the task.

- Praise task completion and persistence.

- Plan brief periods of working on an activity in an uncluttered, consistent place.

- Offer guidance and assistance in completing tasks. Stay close while the child is working on a task and help out if it becomes too difficult.

- When getting a child to complete a task, use touch, pictures, and verbal instructions.

- Determine which sensations the child responds to best and use them to capture his attention.

- Encourage the child with good verbal skills to talk herself through fine motor tasks she finds difficult.

High persistence and attention span:

- Choose your battles carefully.

- Look for ways to say "Yes, you may."

- Use negotiation instead of absolutes.

- Make rules clear and have them stick.

- Notice persistence when it is positive, for example, sticking to a task.

- Give a warning when a task must be interrupted.

- Teach the child to estimate the time needed to complete a task.

- Let him know that sometimes he has to stop before a task is completed.

SOME COMMONLY RAISED DEVELOPMENT AND TEMPERAMENT ISSUES

Children develop at their own pace, and may be more advanced in one area of development than another. For example, one child may be particularly advanced in walking and other gross motor activities and slower in learning language. Another child however, sometimes in the same family, may be quite content to sit, but advances more quickly in terms of learning words and communicating.

When Delays Are a Concern

Although most differences are usually overcome, caregivers should monitor development and seek further assessment and consultation in certain situations, such as when the child

- Is delayed in all areas of development

- Has no or few words by 2 years of age

- Is not walking by 18 months of age

- Shows lack of responsiveness or very repetitive behavior

- Is extremely active, has difficulty attending to instructions, or has trouble concentrating on an activity

- Shows significant delays in any areas of development at 2 years of age

- Is excessively aggressive

- Is very withdrawn, anxious, or fearful, particularly with other children

When any of these delays or behaviors are noticed, it is important to consult a physician and/or a children's mental health specialist. A developmental assessment may also be recommended that will be carried out by a psychologist, developmental pediatrician, or a multidisciplinary team of specialists. Along with the pace of development, the child's temperament can significantly affect how readily he negotiates a particular stage of development. The "difficult" child, for example, may be more irritable and more intense about situations, and the "slow-to-warm-up" child may find new situations especially difficult. Regardless of the challenges or differences in temperament that characterize children, it is important that caregivers be aware of the developmental capacities that infants and young children need to achieve. It is also important that they make efforts to assure that during these first 6 years of life the children receive experiences that help them achieve these capacities. Sometimes, adaptations of the environment for different temperament characteristics may be necessary, but it is crucial to remember that achievements of these capacities can lay the foundation on which to construct other critical aspects of later development and competence.

What Children Need in Order to Develop and Acquire Competencies and Skills

Subsequent chapters outline the principles of caregiving or the interactions required in order for children to gain a variety of competencies and characteristics including optimal self-esteem, security of attachment, problem-solving skills, and social ability. From the previous discussion, it is clear that a number of aspects of the immediate caregiver–child interaction and family context and the community around the family can contribute to the attainment of these developmental shifts or gains. Nevertheless, for many skills a child acquires such as walking, talking, and even toileting, there are three primary aspects of an interaction necessary for learning to take place:

1. Adequate maturation or physiological readiness in the child

2. Competence, motivation, or a drive or desire to explore and achieve

3. Fueling and encouragement from the environment and particularly from interested and loving people

Analyzing the Acquisition of a Skill

Two examples of how children acquire a skill are described next.

Walking   In most situations, parents have to do little to encourage a child to walk. Maturation and a motivation to succeed seem to fuel the child to want to stand up, to take weight on his legs, and to cruise around furniture, and eventually to take off and walk alone. Nevertheless, the availability of a safe environment in which to explore and the presence of adults who show encouragement and containment enhance the child's experience and success (see Table 1.21).

Toilet Teaching   Toilet teaching can sometimes happen quite easily with some children; others may have far more difficulty with it. It is important to consider all of these areas if toilet teaching is being considered because all are important for the child to be successful. It is

Table 1.21. Analyzing the influences on acquiring a skill: Walking

Influences within the child	Child's motivation to succeed	Caregiver actions that influence the skill
Central nervous system has developed	Child keeps trying in spite of falling	Holds child's hands to practice walking
Spine and legs strong enough to support the child's weight	Child wants to explore environment from upright position	Provides physical environment that allows child to "cruise" around objects
Sufficient balance to remain upright	Child determined to take weight on legs	Shows excitement at efforts
		Encourages exploration

also important to consider the child's temperament as it can significantly influence the child's reactions to toilet teaching. If a child is being taught to use the toilet, it is important to be sure he is ready and motivated and to choose a relatively stress-free time for the child and caregiver. See Table 1.22 for the influences pertinent to a child's acquiring the skill of toilet teaching.

THE ROLE OF PARENTS IN DEVELOPMENT AND TEMPERAMENT

Although various principles of parenting are set out for each of the chapters and competencies explored in this book, some general principles apply about the kind of experiences that infants and young children need and the role that parents and caregivers play in helping them gain those experiences. Children need to experience a caregiver as

- A *teacher,* who assists him to learn about the world and about the values and rules of his family and society

- A *playmate,* who provides joyful interactions and joins in her fun activities, showing interest and acceptance

- A *nurturer,* who comforts the child when he is upset and helps modulate and contain his intense emotions

Table 1.22. Analyzing the influences on acquiring a skill: Toileting

Influences within the child	Child's motivation to succeed	Caregiver actions that influence the skill
Has enough physiological control of bladder and bowel movements	Shows an interest in learning to use the toilet	Caregiver encourages child by buying potty and "big kid" underwear
Can use a word to indicate need to use the potty	Wants to be "big" and not be in diapers	Sits child on potty when likely to have bowel movement
Understands what a potty is for	Dislikes being in a wet or soiled diaper	Praises or uses concrete rewards when child urinates or has a bowel movement in potty
		Never shames child if she has an accident
		Adapts to child's temperament style

Table 1.23. Adult characteristics and their effects on children

Adult characteristic	Effect on caregiving and children
Gets angry easily	Has a short fuse and may lose temper easily with the child
Tends to be introverted	May not expose child to necessary social experiences
Sensitive to criticism	May overreact to young child's negativism or temper tantrums
Distractible	May find it difficult to be firm and to follow through on limits and directives
Very anxious	May be very anxious and overprotective about child's behavior and find it difficult to relax and be positive and optimistic
Perfectionistic	May have very high expectations for their child's behavior and achievements

- *A limit setter,* who provides consistent structures and limits so that the child feels a sense of predictability and of being safe and can follow the rules and expectations of home and other settings

Of course, along with these types of caregiving, children also need to have adequate physical care and nutrition and a safe, stimulating physical environment. Caregivers will feel more competent in some of these areas than in others, and the child can experience them from different people in his world. Failure to receive any of these types of experiences could compromise the child's development in certain areas, however.

Just as with children, parents' areas of strengths and difficulties come from biological characteristics, their history of being parented, and temperamental traits. Consequently, each caregiver has certain areas in which they feel very confident in dealing with children and others in which they have more difficulty. It is critical that caregivers understand these personal signatures and how they may influence their interactions with children. In this way, they are far less likely to let their own difficulties get in the way of providing optimal interactions for children in their care. Some examples of how adult personality characteristics or temperament traits may influence caregiving and affect children are set out in Table 1.23 and discussed later.

DISCUSSION QUESTIONS TO USE IN TRAINING PROFESSIONALS

1. Discuss what might be particularly challenging about the stages between birth and 3 months and 14 months and 3 years of age.

2. What are the various areas of development and how might you identify delays and problem behaviors?

3. How would you define development and temperament?

4. What influences the development of an infant and young child? in the family? outside of the family?

5. How do these aspects or variables influence development?

6. What new information do we now have about brain development that can guide parents?

7. What types of caregiving do infants and young children need to experience?

8. Describe a resilient child you have met and point out how he or she is doing well.

9. What does "goodness of fit" mean? Describe some positive and negative examples of goodness of fit between children and caregivers you know.

10. Describe the "difficult child" concept and suggest what contributes to the behaviors that characterize such a child.

WORKING WITH PARENTS: GROUP EXERCISES AND SAMPLE HOMEWORK ACTIVITIES

Parents vary in the degree to which they can understand and accommodate the developmental and temperament needs of their children. Too often, parents do not have information about development and parenting strategies and, consequently, they feel uncertain and incompetent. It is important, therefore, that parents become informed about the development of young children and their child's inborn temperament characteristics. The information provided in this chapter and in the books listed in the bibliography can be useful in helping parents begin to understand and adapt to their child.

Carey and McDevitt (1995) have suggested three components that are needed when counseling parents who identify difficult behavior in their child:

1. *Recognition (or understanding) of the pattern of behavior by the clinician or educator:* This involves the counselor in an evaluation using observations, interviews, and questionnaires. A full developmental assessment of the child may be necessary sometimes in order to fully understand the contribution of the child to the presenting situation. The evaluation should assess the child, parent–child interaction, vulnerabilities of the parent, and the impact of the developmental stage and temperament on the parents.

2. *Revision of parental understanding and handling:* This entails the counselor's providing information to the parents about the child's needs and the coping skills they can adopt as caregivers. It may also require the counselor to assure the parent that the child's behavior is not "all his fault" and that there are ways to avoid a clinical disorder developing. Helping parents maintain hope that the child can do well over time can enable them to be more positive with their child. It is critical to teach parents and other caregivers coping strategies, which will enable them to adapt their interactions to meet their children's needs. It is also helpful to identify any areas of "poorness of fit" between expectations and the child's temperament and to provide information so a parent can adapt to a child. Then, it is important to give the caregiver suggestions for working with the child as teachers, playmates, nurturers, and limit-setters.

3. *Relief for parents by environmental intervention:* Caring for young children, and particularly for those who are temperamentally difficult, can be an exhausting process for parents. Professionals working with parents should therefore help them find ways to relieve stress and to build up support systems and find assistance from others.

GROUP EXERCISES TO HELP PARENTS RELATE TO THEIR CHILD'S STAGE OF DEVELOPMENT AND TEMPERAMENT

This section includes exercises that can be used with parents and other caregivers in groups and individually to encourage them to enhance their children's development and temperament.

What Would I Like My Child to Become?

Ask parents to list qualities that they would like their child to have as an adult. Then ask them to read them out, and have the group leader write them down on the blackboard or flipchart. The parents' hopes for their children can then be grouped into the primary categories shown in Figure 1.2.

Achievement/competence	Physical and emotional health
To find a satisfying job or career To work hard and to do well in school To be competent and to feel good about some ability	To be happy and content To be healthy and handle stress To establish good relationships with others
Courageous/determined	**Caring/moral**
To stand up for what he believes in To be brave in difficult situations To keep striving to achieve what he wants	To care about people in society who live in poverty, who are ill, and so forth To be honest and to follow the laws and moral beliefs of the family To help people in need

Figure 1.2. Sample completed worksheet: What would I like my child to become?

Each group typically provides different examples than the ones listed and places a somewhat different emphasis on each of the categories. But generally, parents are surprised to find out how similar their hopes and dreams for their child are to those held by other participants.

Parents are then asked to identify one or two characteristics that they want their child to develop, to think about any concerns they may have around their child achieving them, and to consider how they will help their child achieve them. Examples are given in Figure 1.3.

What Difficulties Do I Face With My Child, and How Can I Find Solutions?

Invite parents to identify temperamental traits of their child that they find difficult. Have parents complete the "Do you have a difficult child?" questionnaire shown in Figure 1.4. Have parents in the group suggest ways that have worked for them in dealing with some of the characteristics noted in the questionnaire (see Figure 1.5).

What Are the Stages of Childhood, and How Do I Feel About Them?

Most parents feel somewhat more comfortable with their infant and child at some stages than in others. Some may love the closeness of very young infants, while others prefer their children as they become toddlers and can walk and talk. Have parents choose the stage they find or expect to find most enjoyable, and the one about which they have the most concerns (see Figure 1.6).

Have parents discuss with which stages they feel the most and least comfortable and help them to identify some of the reasons for their preferences. Point out to parents any tendency they may have for discomfort with a stage. For example, some parents or caregivers are threat-

Desired characteristic	Concerns about acquiring characteristic	Strategies
Being happy and content	Child seems to be irritable a lot of the time.	Try to identify what may be causing the unhappiness and improving the environment where possible. Find fun times to be with child or activities he enjoys.
Helping other people	Child seems very self-centered and can be a bully.	Help child see others' point of view. Make sure child feels loved and recognized for his personality and behavior. Model caring behavior. Notice caring behavior whenever the child exhibits it. Have some family activities that involve helping others, such as taking some food to the food bank.

Figure 1.3. Sample completed worksheet: How can I help my child acquire this characteristic?

ened by the needs that infants have to be close. Some parents may feel rejected by the tantrums of a toddler. Still others find the demands of young children exhausting.

What Type of Parenting Do I Find the Most Challenging?

As mentioned previously, the four roles of parenting that infants and young children need to experience include teacher, playmate, nurturer, and limit-setter. Discuss with parents which of these four roles they find the most difficult to fulfill, and help them problem-solve as to how other people might meet their children's needs in that area. Figure 1.7 includes a form that can be used to record this information.

How Do I Rate My Own Temperament?

Building a relationship with a child is a two-way street, and parents need to understand their own ways of reacting as well as their child's. Understanding our own temperaments can help us

Do You Have a Difficult Child?

Family questions	Yes	No
1. Do you find your child hard to raise?	____	____
2. Do you find your child's behavior hard to understand?	____	____
3. Are you often battling the child?	____	____
4. Do you feel inadequate or guilty as a parent?	____	____
5. Is your marriage or family being affected by the child?	____	____

Child questions

The headings below identify areas of your child's temperament (his or her basic make-up).

Rate your child, in an overall way, on each item, using this scale:

0 = No problem
1 = Sometimes/moderate problem
2 = Often/definite problem
3 = Nearly always or always/extreme problem

High activity level

Very active; always into things; makes you tired; "ran before he walked"; gets wild or "revved up," loses control, hates to be confined   ____

Distractibility

Has trouble concentrating and paying attention, especially if not really interested; doesn't listen. Tunes you out, daydreams, forgets instructions   ____

Poor adaptability

Has trouble with transition and change of activity or routine; goes on and on nagging or whining for something he wants; stubborn; very persistent if he really likes an activity; seems to get "locked in"; tantrums are long and hard to stop; gets used to things and refuses to give them up; has trouble adapting to the unfamiliar   ____

Initial withdrawal

Doesn't like new situations—new places, food, or clothes; holds back or protests by crying or clinging; may tantrum if forced to go forward. Shy and reserved with new people   ____

High Intensity

A loud child—whether miserable, angry, or happy   ____

Irregular

Unpredictable. Can't tell when he'll be hungry or tired; conflict over meals and bedtime; moods change suddenly; wakes up at night; has good and bad days for no obvious reasons   ____

Low Sensory Threshold

Physically sensitive to sounds, lights, colors, textures, temperature, pain, tastes or smells (not necessarily all of these); clothes have to "feel right," making dressing a problem; over-reacts to minor cuts or scrapes; feels warm when everyone else is cold; easily overstimulated; doesn't like the way many foods look, smell or taste; picky eater   ____

Negative Mood

Basically serious or cranky; whines or complains a lot; not a "happy child"   ____

Negative Persistence

Stubborn, goes on and on nagging, whining or negotiating if wants something; relentless, won't give in, gets "locked in," may have long tantrums   ____

What Your Rating Means

If your Family "Yes" questions total is	And your Child questions total is	The conclusion is
0–1 +	2–5 points =	Basically easy child with some difficult features
2–3 +	6–12 points =	Difficult child
4–5 +	13 or more points =	Very difficult child

Figure 1.4. Blank questionnaire: Do you have a difficult child? (From Turecki, S., & Tonner, L. [2000]. *The difficult child* [2nd ed.]. New York: Bantam Books; reprinted by permission.)

Instructions: List your child's temperament traits on the left then some suggestions for dealing with the traits on the right. For example, if you listed "High activity level" on the left, you might answer "Provide lots of active toys and games" as coping strategies.

Temperament trait	What works

Figure 1.5. Blank worksheet: How do I deal with my child's temperamental traits?

Instructions: List the stages of childhood with which you are most and least comfortable below.

Stage with which I am **most** comfortable:

What I like about the stage:

Stage with which I am **least** comfortable:

What I find most difficult about the stage:

Figure 1.6. Blank worksheet: Stage with which I am most and least comfortable.

Instructions: For each of the roles below, list some of the ways that you carry out the roles.

Role	What I do
Teacher	
Playmate	
Limit-setter	
Nurturer	

Figure 1.7. The four areas of parenting and what I do with my child in each area.

in working with our children. Having this information can help in identifying differences and potential areas of conflict. Figure 1.8 provides a questionnaire to help parents and caregivers determine their own temperaments, and Figure 1.9 allows parents and caregivers to relate their characteristics to their child's. Have parents discuss how they think similarities or discrepancies influence their interactions with their child.

1. Activity level Are you always on the move, or do you prefer to be quiet? Do you need to exercise to feel good?	1 2 3 4 5 quiet .... active
2. Regularity or rhythmicity How regular do you like to be about eating, sleeping, and other bodily functions?	1 2 3 4 5 regular .... irregular
3. Approach/withdrawal/first reactions How do you react to new ideas, activities, places, or people?	1 2 3 4 5 reject at first .... jump right in
4. Adaptability How quickly do you adapt to new situations, changes in routines?	1 2 3 4 5 adapt quickly .... slow to adapt
5. Sensory thresholds/sensitivity How sensitive are you to noises, bright lights, emotions, differences in temperature?	1 2 3 4 5 very sensitive .... usually not sensitive
6. Intensity of reaction How intense are your emotional reactions? Do you laugh and cry intensely, or are you quieter with your reactions?	1 2 3 4 5 mild reaction .... intense reaction
7. Mood How much of the time do you feel happy and content compared to discontented and unhappy?	1 2 3 4 5 usually positive.... more serious ....negative
8. Distractibility How aware are you of things going on around you? Do you often get distracted from what you are doing?	1 2 3 4 5 hardly ever notice .... very distractible
9. Persistence/attention span Do you generally persist with an activity regardless of other people? Do you tend to hang on to ideas and feelings for a long time?	1 2 3 4 5 "locked in" .... easily stop don't let go

Figure 1.8. Blank worksheet: Understanding your own temperament.

Instructions: For each of the temperament characteristics on the left, list those you feel describe both you and your child.

Temperament characteristic	Myself (describe)	My child (describe)
Activity level		
Regularity and rhythmicity		
Approach/withdrawal		
Adaptability		
Sensory threshold/sensitivity		
Intensity of reaction		
Mood		
Distractibility		
Persistence		

Figure 1.9. Blank worksheet: Identifying your own and your child's temperament.

The Animal Game

One of the ways parents can help understand their own temperaments is to relate themselves to an animal. Ask group participants to choose an animal that is most like them in personality and to describe what they admire about the animal and how they are like it (see Figure 1.10). Discuss how some of the characteristics chosen may relate to their personality, temperament, or to experiences they have had. Repeat the exercise about one of their children, especially one that they may find more challenging.

Instructions: Choose an animal that is most like yourself, and fill in the columns below.

Animal: _____

Characteristics like me	How do these characteristics relate to my personality, temperament, or experiences I have had?

Figure 1.10. Blank worksheet: The animal game. Caregivers use this to help them identify and understand their own temperament traits.

How Is My Temperament Today Different from How It Was in the Past?

Ask group participants to describe how they may have overcome or improved certain temperamental traits they initially found difficult (e.g., shyness, hyperactivity), and ones with which they may still be struggling to improve (e.g., intensity of reaction). See Figure 1.11 for a form that can be used to record these characteristics.

What Are Some Labels People Assigned to Me During My Life?

Ask participants to share labels their parents used for them as they were growing up. These may be positive or negative. Ask them to think of how they influenced their own behavior.

My improved characteristics	How I can still improve

Figure 1.11. Blank worksheet: What am I like today and how can I improve?

Label	How it influenced me
"Lazy"	Sometimes made me not try very hard
"Stubborn"	Made me dig in my heels more
"Never amount to anything"	Made me give up trying or act out
	Made me feel helpless and depressed
"Mean and nasty"	Made me meaner to my sister
"Happy and positive"	Made me feel noticed and appreciated

Figure 1.12. Sample completed worksheet: Labels that have been applied to me and how they influenced me.

Also remember whom they were supposed to be like and identify how this has influenced their behavior. They could have been described as like a grandparent, aunt or uncle, or even a famous person. Be prepared to deal with some of the anger that may be identified with these labels. Figure 1.12 includes an example of what one person identified as the labels that influenced him.

SAMPLE HOMEWORK ACTIVITIES

It is helpful to give parents who are attending a weekly parenting group some activities to try during the week that can be discussed at the next group meeting. Assign only a small number to each group participant, or let them choose one or two they would like to do.

1. Observe your children's behavior and note characteristics typical of their developmental stage.

2. Read your child a story and discuss with the child the characters and what they are like.

3. Note examples of when your children managed their behavior well.

4. Find examples of positive behaviors or when your child really tried.

5. Sit back and watch your child and rate his temperament.

6. Rate yourself in terms of allowing the child to explore while keeping him safe.

7. Decide what kinds of behaviors and emotions your child exhibits that are most difficult for you as parents.

8. List your child's unique qualities that you enjoy.

9. Discuss appropriate routines and structures with your partner and agree on discipline strategies.

BIBLIOGRAPHY

REFERENCES

Ainsworth, M.D. (1967). *Infancy in Uganda: Infant care and the growth of love.* Baltimore: The Johns Hopkins University Press.

Ainsworth, M.D. (1969). Object relations, dependency, and attachment: A theoretical review of the infant-mother relationship. *Child Development, 40,* 969–1025.

Ainsworth, M.D.S., Blehar, M.C., Waters, E., & Wall, S. (1978). *Patterns of attachment: A psychological study of the strange situation.* Mahwah, NJ: Lawrence Erlbaum Associates.

Allen, M.C., Brown, P., & Finlay, B. (1992). *Helping children by strengthening families: A look at family support programs.* Washington, D.C.: Children's Defense Fund.

Allen, M.C., Donohue, P.K., & Dusman, A.E. (1993). The limit of viability: Neonatal outcome of infants born at 22 to 25 weeks' gestation. *New England Journal of Medicine, 329,* 1597–1601.

Anderson, J. (1972). Attachment behavior out of doors. In N.G. Blurton-Jones (Ed.), *Ethological Studies of Child Behavior.* London: Cambridge University Press.

Anthony, E.J. (1982). The preventive approach to children at high risk for psychopathology and psychosis. *Journal of Children of Contemporary Society, 15,* 67–72.

Asendorpf, J.B. (1994). The malleability of behavioral inhibition: A study of individual developmental functions. *Developmental Psychology, 30,* 912–919.

Atkinson, E., Vetere, A., & Grayson, K. (1995). Sleep disruption in young children. The influence of temperament on the sleep patterns of preschool children. *Child: Care, Health and Development, 21,* 233–246.

Bandura, A. (1977). *Social learning theory.* Englewood Cliffs, NJ: Prentice-Hall.

Barron, A.P., & Earls, F. (1984). The relation of temperament and social factors to behavior problems in three-year-old children. *Journal of Child Psychology and Psychiatry and Allied Disciplines, 25,* 23–33.

Bates, J.E., Freeland, C.A.B., & Lounsbury, M.L. (1979). Measurement of infant difficultness. *Child Development, 50,* 794–803.

Baumrind, D. (1967). Child care practices anteceding three patterns of preschool behavior. *Genetic Psychology Monographs, 75,* 43–88.

Baumrind, D. (1971). Current patterns of parental authority. *Developmental Psychology, 4,* 1–103.

Beardslee, W.R., Bemporad, J.V., Keller, M.B., & Klerman, G.L. (1984). Children of parents with major affective disorders: A review. *American Journal of Psychiatry, 140,* 825–832.

Bell, R.Q., & Pearl, D. (1982). Psychosocial changes in risk groups: Implications for early intervention. *Prevention in Human Services, 1,* 45–59.

Belsky, J. (1984). The determinants of parenting: A process model. *Child Development, 55,* 83–96.

Benoit, D., & Parker, K.C.H. (1994). Stability and transmission of attachment across three generations. *Child Development, 65,* 1444–1456.

Bowen, F., Vitaro, F., Kerr, M., & Pelletier, D. (1995). Childhood internalizing problems: Prediction from kindergarten, effect of maternal overprotectiveness, and sex differences. *Development and Psychopathology, 7,* 481–498.

Bowlby, J. (1958). The nature of the child's tie to his mother. *International Journal of Psychoanalysis, 39,* 350–373.

Bowlby, J. (1969a). *Attachment and loss. Vol. 1: Attachment.* New York: Basic Books.

Bowlby, J. (1969b). Disruption of affectional bonds and its effects on behavior. *Canada's Mental Health Supplement, 59,* 1–2.

Boyce, W.T. (2001). *Biology and context: Symphonic causation and the origins of childhood psychopathology.* Paper presented at the Millennium Dialogue on Early Child Development, University of Toronto.

Bradley, R.H., Whiteside, L., Mundfrom, D.J., & Casey, P.H. (1994). Early indications of resilience and their relation to experiences in the home environments of low birthweight premature children living in poverty. *Child Development, 65,* 346–360.

Brody, G.H., Stoneman, Z., & McCoy, J.K. (1994). Contributions of family relationships and child temperaments to longitudinal variations in sibling relationship quality and sibling relationship styles. *Journal of Family Psychology, 8,* 274–286.

Broman, S.H., Nichols, P., & Kennedy, W.A. (1975). *Preschool IQ: Prenatal and early developmental correlates.* Mahwah, NJ: Lawrence Erlbaum Associates.

Bronfenbrenner, U. (1979). *The ecology of human development: Experiments by nature and design.* Cambridge, MA: Harvard University Press.

Bronson, G.W. (1970). Fear of visual novelty: Developmental patterns in males and females. *Developmental Psychology, 2,* 33–40.

Brooks-Gunn, J., Klebanov, P.K., & Duncan, E.J. (1996). Ethnic differences in children's intelligence test scores: Role of economic deprivation, home environment, and maternal characteristics. *Child Development, 67,* 396–408.

Bruer, J.T. (1999). *The myth of the first three years.* New York: Free Press.

Bugental, D.B. (1985). Unresponsive children and powerless adults. In M. Lewis & C. Saarni (Eds.), *The socialization of emotions* (pp. 239–261). New York: Plenum.

Buss, A.H., & Plomin, R. (1984). *Temperament: Early developing personality traits.* Mahwah, NJ: Lawrence Erlbaum Associates.

Calkins, S.D., & Fox, N.A. (1992). The relations among infant temperament, security of attachment, and behavioral inhibition at twenty-four months. *Child Development, 63,* 1456–1472.

Cameron, J.R. (1978). Parental treatment, children's temperament, and the risk of childhood behavioral problems: II. Initial temperament, parental attitudes, and the incidence and form of behavioral problems. *American Journal of Orthopsychiatry, 48,* 140–147.

Carey, W.B., & McDevitt, S.C. (1995). *Coping with children's temperament: A guide for professionals.* New York: Basic Books.

Carnegie Foundation (1994). *Starting points: Meeting the needs of our youngest children.* New York: Carnegie Corporation of New York.

Carro, M.G., Grant, K.E., Gotlib, I.H., & Compas, B.E. (1993). Postpartum depression and child development: An investigation of mothers and fathers as sources of risk and resilience. *Development and Psychopathology, 5,* 567–579.

Caspi, A., Henry, B., McGee, R.O., Moffitt, T.E., & Silva, P.A. (1995). Temperamental origins of child and adolescent behavior problems: From age three to age fifteen. *Child Development, 66,* 55–68.

Chess, S., & Thomas, A. (1996). *Temperament: Theory and practice.* New York: Brunner/Mazel.

Cicchetti, D. (1989). How research on child development has informed the study of child development: Perspectives from developmental psychopathology. In D. Cicchetti & V. Carlson (Eds.), *Child maltreatment: Theory and research on the causes and consequences of child abuse and neglect* (pp. 377–431). Cambridge: Cambridge University Press.

Cicchetti, D., & Rogosch, F.A. (1996). Equifinality and multifinality in developmental psychopathology. *Development and Psychopathology, 8,* 597–600.

Crockenberg, S.B., & Litman, C. (1990). Autonomy as competence in 2-year-olds: Maternal correlates of child defiance, compliance and self-assertion. *Developmental Psychology, 26,* 961–971.

Dail, P.W. (1990). The psychosocial context of homeless mothers with young children: Program and policy implications. *Child Welfare, 69,* 291–308.

Daniels, D., & Plomin, R. (1985). Origins of individual differences in infant shyness. *Developmental Psychology, 21,* 118–121.

Dawson, G., Panagiotides, H., Klinger, L.G., & Hill, D. (1992). The role of frontal lobe functioning in the development of infant self-regulatory behavior. *Brain and Cognition, 20,* 152–175.

DeGangi, G.A., DiPietro, J.A., Greenspan, S.I., & Porges, S.W. (1991). Psychophysiological characteristics of the regulatory disordered infant. *Infant Behavior and Development, 14,* 37–50.

Denham, S.A. (1993). Maternal emotional responsiveness and toddlers' social-emotional competence. *Journal of Child Psychology and Psychiatry and Allied Disciplines, 34,* 715–728.

Derryberry, D., & Rothbart, M.K. (1997). Reactive and effortful processes in the organization of temperament. *Development and Psychopathology, 9,* 633–652.

Dix, T. (1991). The affective organization of parenting: Adaptive and maladaptive processes. *Psychological Bulletin, 110,* 3–25.

Doherty, G. (1997). *Zero to six: The basis for school readiness.* Hull, Quebec: Applied Research Branch, Human Resources Development Canada.

Dubrow, N.F., & Garbarino, J. (1989). Living in the war zone: Mothers and young children in a public housing development. *Child Welfare, 68,* 3–20.

Duncan, G.J., Brooks-Gunn, J., & Klebanov, P.K. (1994). Economic deprivation and early childhood development. *Child Development, 65,* 296–318.

Earls, F., & Jung, K.G. (1987). Temperament and home environment characteristics as causal factors in the early development of childhood psychopathology. *Journal of the American Academy of Child and Adolescent Psychiatry, 26,* 491–498.

Egeland, B., & Erickson, M.F. (1990). Rising above the past: Strategies for helping new mothers break the cycle of abuse and neglect. *Zero to Three, 11,* 29–35.

Emde, R.N., Plomin, R., Robinson, J., Corley, R., DeFries, J., Fulker, D.W., Reznick, J.S., Campos, J., Kagan, J., & Zahn-Waxler, C. (1992). Temperament, emotion and cognition at fourteen months: The MacArthur Longitudinal Twin Study. *Child Development, 63,* 1437–1455.

Emmerick, W. (1964). Continuity and stability in early social development. *Child Development, 35,* 311–332.

Erikson, E.H. (1963). *Childhood and society.* New York: W.W. Norton.

Erickson, M.F., Egeland, B., & Pianta, R. (1989). The effects of maltreatment on the development of young children. In D. Cicchetti & V. Carlson (Eds.), *Child maltreatment: Theory and research on the causes and consequences of child abuse and neglect* (pp. 647–684). New York: Cambridge University Press.

Escalona, S. (1968). *The roots of individuality: Normal patterns of development in infancy.* Chicago: Aldine.

Estrada, P., Arsenio, W.F., Hess, R.D., & Holloway, S.D. (1987). Affective quality of the mother–child relationship: Longitudinal consequences for children's school-relevant cognitive functioning. *Developmental Psychology, 23,* 210–215.

Fergusson, D.M., Horwood, L.J., & Lynskey, M.T. (1992). Family change, parental discord, and early offending. *Journal of Child Psychology and Psychiatry and Allied Disciplines, 33,* 1059–1075.

Fischer, D.G. (1985). *Family relationship variables, and programs influencing juvenile delinquency.* Ottawa, ON: Solicitor General of Canada.

Fonagy, P., Steele, H., & Steele, M. (1991). Maternal representations of attachment during pregnancy predict the organization of infant-mother attachment at one year of age. *Child Development, 62,* 891–905.

Fox, N.A. (1989). Psychophysiological correlates of emotional reactivity during the first year of life. *Developmental Psychology, 25,* 364–372.

Fox, N.A. (1991). If it's not left, it's right: Electroencephalograph asymmetry and the development of emotion. *American Psychologist, 46,* 863–872.

Fox, N.A., Calkins, S.D., Porges, S.W., Rubin, K.H., Coplan, R.J., Stewart, S., Marshall, T.R., & Long, J.M. (1996). Frontal activation asymmetry and social competence at four years of age. In M.E. Hertzig & E.A. Farber (Eds.), *Annual Progress in Child Psychiatry and Child Development,* 99–122.

Fox, N.A., & Davidson, R.J. (1987). Electroencephalogram asymmetry in response to the approach of a stranger and maternal separation in 10-month-old infants. *Developmental Psychology, 23,* 233–240.

Fracasso, M.P., Porges, S.W., Lamb, M.E., & Rosenberg, A.A. (1994). Cardiac activity in infancy: Reliability and stability of individual differences. *Infant Behavior and Development, 17,* 277–284.

Freedman, D.G. (1965). An ethological approach to the genetic study of human behavior. In S. Vandenberg (Ed.), *Methods and goals in human behavior genetics.* San Diego: Academic Press.

Freedman, D.G. (1974). *Human infancy: An evolutionary perspective.* Mahwah, NJ: Lawrence Erlbaum Associates.

Freedman, D.G. (1976). Infancy, biology, and culture. In L.P. Lipsitt (Ed.), *Developmental psychobiology: The significance of infancy.* Mahwah, NJ: Lawrence Erlbaum Associates.

Freud, S. (1964). *An outline of psychoanalysis.* Standard edition of the works of Sigmund Freud (Vol. 23, pp. 141–208). London: Hogarth Press.

Freud, S. (1905/1975). *Three essays on the theory of sexuality* (J. Strachey, Ed. and Trans.) New York: Basic Books. (Original work published 1905).

Fries, M.E. (1954). Some hypotheses on the role of the congenital activity type in personality development. *International Journal of Psycho-Analysis, 35,* 206–207.

Fries, M.E., & Woolf, P.J. (1954). Some hypotheses on the role of the congenital activity type in personality development. *Psychoanalytic Study of the Child, 8,* 48–64.

Garcia-Coll, C., Kagan, J., & Resnick, J.S. (1984). Behavioral inhibition in young children. *Child Development, 55,* 1005–1019.

Garmezy, N. (1987). Stress, competence, and development: Continuities in the study of schizophrenic adults, children vulnerable to psychopathology and the search for stress-resistant children. *American Journal of Orthopsychiatry, 57,* 159–174.

Glaser, D. (2000). Child abuse and neglect and the brain—A review. *Journal of Child Psychology and Psychiatry, 41,* 47–116.

Gobel, S., & Shindledecker, R. (1993). Characteristics of children whose parents have been incarcerated. *Hospital and Community Psychiatry, 44,* 656–660.

Goldsmith, H.H. (1993). Temperament: Variability in developing emotion systems. In M. Lewis & J.M. Haviland (Eds.). *Handbook of Emotions* (pp. 353–364). New York: Guilford Press.

Goldsmith, H.H., Buss, A.H., Plomin, R., Rothbart, M.K., Thomas, A., Chess, S., Hinde, R.A., & McCall, R.B. (1987). Roundtable: What is temperament? Four approaches. *Child Development, 58,* 505–529.

Goldsmith, H.H., & Campos, J.J. (1986). Fundamental issues in the study of early temperament: The Denver Twin Temperament Study. In M.E. Lamb, A.L. Brown, & B. Rogoff (Eds.), *Advances in Developmental Psychology* (Vol. 4, pp. 231–283). Mahwah, NJ: Lawrence Erlbaum Associates.

Goldsmith, H.H., & Lemery K.S. (2000). Linking temperament, fearfulness, and anxiety symptoms: A behavior-genetic perspective. *Biological Psychiatry, 48,* 1199–1209.

Goldsmith, H.H., Lemery, K.S., Aksan, N., & Buss, K.A. (2000). Temperamental substrates of personality. In V.J. Molfese, & D.L. Molfese (Eds.). *Temperament and personality development across the lifespan* (pp. 1–32). Mahwah, NJ: Lawrence Erlbaum Associates.

Greenfield, S.A. (1997). *The human brain: A guided tour.* New York: Basic Books.

Greenough, W.T., Black, J.E., & Wallace, C.S. (1987). Experience and brain development. *Child Development, 58,* 539–559.

Greenspan, S.I. (1985). *First feelings: Milestones in the emotional development of your baby and young child.* New York: Penguin Books.

Greenspan, S.I. (1992). *Infancy and early childhood: The practice of clinical assessment and intervention with emotional and developmental challenges.* Madison, CT: International Universities Press.

Greenspan, S.I., Wieder, S., Nover, R.A., Lieberman, A.F., Lourie, R.S., & Robinson, M.D. (Eds.). (1987). *Infants in multirisk families: Case studies in preventive intervention.* New York: International Universities Press.

Gross, D., Conrad, B., Fogg, L., & Wothke, W. (1994). A longitudinal model of maternal self-efficacy, depression, and difficult temperament during toddlerhood. *Research in Nursing and Health, 17,* 207–215.

Grossman, K., Fremmer-Bombik, E., Rudolph, J., & Grossman, K.E. (1988). Maternal attachment representations as related to patterns of infant–mother attachment and maternal care during the first year. In R.A. Hinde & J. Stevenson-Hinde (Eds.), *Relationships within families: Mutual influences* (pp. 241–260). Oxford: Clarendon Press.

Grossman, K., Grossman, K.E., Spangler, S., Suess, G., & Unzner, L. (1985). Maternal sensitivity and newborns' orientation responses as related to quality of attachment in northern Germany. *Monographs of the Society for Research in Child Development, 50* (Serial No. 209, pp. 233–256).

Guerin, D.W., & Gottfried, A.W. (1994). Temperamental consequences of infant difficultness. *Infant Behavior and Development, 17,* 413–421.

Gunnar, M. (1998). Quality of care and the buffering of stress physiology: Its potential role in protecting the developing human brain. *IMPrint, 21,* 4–7.

Gunnar, M., & Stone, C. (1994). The effects of positive maternal affect on infant response to pleasant, ambiguous, and fear-provoking toys. *Child Development, 55,* 1231–1236.

Guralnick, M. (1997). *The effectiveness of early intervention* (pp. 3, 11–12). Baltimore: Paul H. Brookes Publishing Co.

Hack, M., Taylor, H.G., Klein, N., Eiben, R., Schatschneider, C., & Mercuri-Minich, N. (1994). School-age outcomes in children with birth weights under 750 g. *New England Journal of Medicine, 331,* 753–759.

Hart, B., & Risley, T.R. (1995). *Meaningful differences in the everyday experience of young American children* (pp. 102–103). Baltimore: Paul H. Brookes Publishing Co.

Healy, B.T. (1989). Autonomic nervous system correlates of temperament. *Infant Behavior and Development, 12,* 289–304.

Hechtman, L. (1989). Teenage mothers and their children: Risks and problems: A review. *Canadian Journal of Psychiatry, 34,* 569–575.

Hegvik, R.L., McDevitt, S.C., & Carey, W.B. (1982). The Middle Childhood Temperament Questionnaire. *Journal of Developmental and Behavioral Pediatrics, 3,* 197–200.

Huttunen, M.O., & Nyman, G. (1982). On the continuity change and clinical value of infant temperament in a prospective epidemiological study. In R. Porter, & G.M. Collins (Eds.), *Temperamental differences in infants and young children.* Ciba Foundation Symposium 89 (pp. 240–251). London: Pitman.

Jemerin, J.M., & Boyce, W.T. (1990). Psychobiological differences in childhood stress response. II. Cardiovascular markers of vulnerability. *Journal of Developmental and Behavioral Pediatrics, 11,* 140–150.

Kagan, J. (1989). Temperamental contributions to social behavior. *American Psychologist, 44,* 668–674.

Kagan, J. (1994). Inhibited and uninhibited temperaments. In W.B. Carey & S.C. McDevitt (Eds.), *Prevention and early intervention: Individual differences as risk factors for the mental health of children: A festschrift for Stella Chess and Alexander Thomas* (pp. 35–41). New York: Brunner/Mazel.

Kagan, J. (1996). The return of the ancients: On temperament and development. In S. Matthysse, D.L. Levy, J. Kagan, & F.M. Benes (Eds.), *Psychopathology: The evolving science of mental disorder* (pp. 285–297). New York: Cambridge University Press.

Kagan, J. (1997). Temperament and the reactions to unfamiliarity. *Child Development, 68,* 139–143.

Kagan, J., & Moss, H.A. (1962). *Birth to maturity: A study in psychological development.* New York: John Wiley & Sons.

Kagan, J., Reznick, J.S., Clarke, C., Snidman, N., & Garcia-Coll, C. (1985). Behavioral inhibition to the unfamiliar. In S. Chess & A. Thomas (Eds.), *Annual Progress in Child Psychiatry and Child Development,* 280–303.

Kagan, J., Reznick, J.S., & Snidman, N. (1986). Temperamental inhibition in early childhood. In R. Plomin & J. Dunn (Eds.), *The study of temperament: Changes, continuities, and challenges* (pp. 53–67). Mahwah, NJ: Lawrence Erlbaum Associates.

Kagan, J., & Snidman, N. (1991). Temperamental factors in human development. *American Psychologist, 46,* 856–862.

Kinard, E.M. (1980). Emotional development in physically abused children. *American Journal of Orthopsychiatry, 50,* 686–696.

Kochanska, G. (1997). Mutually responsive orientation between mothers and their young children: Implications for early socialization. *Child Development, 68,* 94–112.

Kochanska, G., Murray, K., & Coy, K.C. (1997). Inhibitory control as a contributor to conscience in childhood: From toddler to early school age. *Child Development, 68,* 263–277.

Kochanska, G., Murray, K., Jacques, T.Y., Koenig, A.L., & Vandegeest, K.A. (1996). Inhibitory control in young children and its role in emerging internalization. *Child Development, 67,* 490–507.

Kolb, B. (1989). Brain development, plasticity, and behavior. *American Psychologist, 44,* 1203–1212.

Kopp, C.B. (1989). Regulation of distress and negative emotions: A developmental view. *Developmental Psychology, 25,* 343–354.

Kyrios, M., & Prior, M. (1991). Temperament, stress and family factors in behavioral adjustment of three- to five-year-old children. In S. Chess & M.E. Hertzig (Eds.), *Annual Progress in Child Psychiatry and Child Development,* 285–311.

Landy, S., & Peters, R. DeV. (1992). Towards an understanding of a developmental paradigm for aggressive conduct problems during the preschool years. In R. DeV. Peters, R.J. McMahon, & V.L. Quinsey (Eds.), *Aggression and violence throughout the lifespan* (pp. 1–30). Newbury Park: Sage Publications.

Lee, C.L., & Bates, J.E. (1985). Mother–child interaction at age two years and perceived difficult temperament. *Child Development, 56,* 1314–1325.

Lerner, R.M. (1991). Changing organism-contextual relations as the basic process of development: A developmental contextual perspective. *Developmental Psychology, 27,* 27–32.

Lewis, M., & Rosenblum, L.A. (Eds.). (1974). *The effect of the infant on its caregiver.* New York: John Wiley & Sons.

Lieberman, A.F. (1993). *The emotional life of the toddler.* New York: Free Press.

Lorenz, K. (1971). *Studies in animal and human behavior* (Vol. 2). Cambridge, MA: Harvard University Press.

Luthar, S.S., & Zigler, E. (1992). Intelligence and social competence among high-risk adolescents. *Development and Psychopathology, 4,* 287–299.

Maccoby, E.E., & Martin, J. (1983). Socialization in the context of the family: Parent–child interaction. In P.H. Mussen (Series Ed.) & E.M. Hetherington (Vol. Ed.), *Handbook of child psychology: Vol. 4. Socialization, personality, and social development* (4th ed., pp. 1–101). New York: John Wiley & Sons.

Mahler, M.S., Pine, F., & Bergman, A. (1975). *The psychological birth of the human infant: Symbiosis and individuation.* New York: Basic Books.

Main, M., & Goldwyn, R. (1984). Predicting rejection of her infant from mother's representation of her own experience: Implications for the abused-abusing intergenerational cycle. *Child Abuse and Neglect, 8,* 203–217.

Maldonado-Duran, M., & Sauceda-Garcia, J.-M. (1996). Excessive crying in infants with regulatory disorders. *Bulletin of the Menninger Clinic, 60,* 62–78.

Mangelsdorf, S.C., Gunnar, M., Kestenbaum, R., Lang, S., & Andreas, D. (1991). Infant proneness-to-distress temperament, maternal personality, and mother–infant attachment: Associations and goodness of fit. In S. Chess & M.E. Hertzig (Eds.), *Annual Progress in Child Psychiatry and Child Development,* 312–329.

Matheny, A.P., Jr. (1980). Bayley's Infant Behavior Record: Behavioral components and twin analyses. *Child Development, 51,* 1157–1167.

Matheny, A.P., Jr. (1986). Stability and change of infant temperament: Contributions from the infant, mother and family environment. In G.A. Kohnstamm (Ed.), *Temperament discussed: Temperament and development in infancy and childhood* (pp. 49–58). Lisse, Netherlands: Swets & Zeitlinger.

Matheny, A.P., Jr. (1987). Developmental research of twins' temperament. *Acta Geneticae Medicae et Gemellologiae, 36,* 135–143.

Matheny, A.P., Jr., Wilson, R.S., & Nuss, S.M. (1984). Toddler temperament: Stability across settings and over ages. *Child Development, 55,* 1200–1211.

Maziade, M., Cote, R., Boutin, P., Bernier, H., & Thivierge, J. (1988). Temperament and intellectual development: A longitudinal study from infancy to four years. In S. Chess, A. Thomas, & M. Hertzig (Eds.), *Annual Progress in Child Psychiatry and Child Development,* 335–349.

Maziade, M., Cote, R., Boutin, P., Boudreault, M., & Thivierge, J. (1986). The effect of temperament on longitudinal academic achievement in primary school. *Journal of the American Academy of Child Psychiatry, 25,* 692–696.

McDevitt, S.C., & Carey, W.B. (1978). The measurement of temperament in 3- to 7-year-old children. *Journal of Child Psychology and Psychiatry and Allied Disciplines, 19,* 245–253.

McDevitt, S.C., & Carey, W.B. (1981). Stability of ratings vs. perceptions of temperament from early infancy to 1–3 years. *American Journal of Orthopsychiatry, 51,* 342–345.

McFarlane, A.C., & van der Kolk, B.A. (1996). Trauma and its challenge to society. In B.A. van der Kolk, A.C. McFarlane, & L. Weisaeth (Eds.), *Traumatic stress: The effects of overwhelming experience on mind, body, and society* (pp. 24–46). New York: Guilford Press.

McLoyd, V.C., & Wilson, L. (1991). The strain of living poor: Parenting, social support, and child mental health. In A.C. Huston (Ed.), *Children in poverty* (pp. 105–135). New York: Cambridge University Press.

Mednick, B.R., Hocevar, D., Baker, R.L., & Schulsinger, C. (1996). Personality and demographic characteristics of mothers and their ratings of child difficultness. *International Journal of Behavioral Development, 19,* 121–140.

Mischel, W. (1974). Processes in delay of gratification. *Advances in Experimental Psychology (Vol. 7).* San Diego: Academic Press.

Morison, S.J., Ames, E.W., & Chishold, K. (1995). The development of children adopted from Romanian orphanages. *Merrill-Palmer Quarterly, 41,* 411–430.

Moroney, R.M. (1987). Social support systems: Families and social policies. In S.L. Kagan, D.R. Powell, B. Weissbourd, & E. Zigler (Eds.), *America's family support programs: Perspectives and prospects* (pp. 31–37). New Haven, CT: Yale University Press.

Mueller, E. & Silverman, N. (1989). Peer relations in maltreated children. In D. Cicchetti & V. Carlson (Eds.), *Child maltreatment: Theory and research on the causes and consequences of child abuse and neglect* (pp. 529–578). New York: Cambridge University Press.

Nachmias, M., Gunnar, M., Mangelsdorf, S., Parritz, R.H., & Buss, K. (1996). Behavioral inhibition and stress reactivity: The moderating effect of attachment security. *Child Development, 67,* 508–522.

Nelson, C.A., & Bloom, F.E. (1997). Child development and neuroscience. *Child Development, 68,* 970–987.

New Webster's Dictionary and Roget's Thesaurus and Medical Dictionary (n.d.). New York: Book Essentials Inc.

Nover, A., Shore, M.F., Timberlake, E.M., & Greenspan, S.I. (1984). The relationship of maternal perception and maternal behavior: A study of normal mothers and their infants. *American Journal of Orthopsychiatry, 54,* 210–223.

Offord, D.R., Boyle, M.H., Fleming, J.E., Blum, H.M., & Grant, N.I. (1989). The Ontario Child Health Study: Summary of selected results. *Canadian Journal of Psychiatry, 34,* 483–491.

Offord, D.R., & Lipman, E.L. (1996). Emotional and behavioral problems. In Human Resources Development Canada & Statistics Canada, *Growing up in Canada, National Longitudinal Study of Children and Youth* (pp. 119–126). Ottawa, ON: Human Resources Development Canada & Statistics Canada.

Pape, B., Byrne, C., & Ivask, A. (1996). *Analysis of the impact of affective disorders on families and children.* Submitted to the Strategic Fund for Children's Mental Health, Health Canada, Ottawa.

Park, S.Y., Belsky, J., Putnam, S., & Crnic, K. (1997). Infant emotionality, parenting, and 3-year inhibition: Exploring stability and lawful discontinuity in a male sample. *Developmental Psychology, 33,* 218–227.

Patterson, G.R. (1982). *A social learning approach to family intervention: Coercive family process.* Eugene, OR: Castalia.

Pedersen, W. (1994). Parental relations, mental health, and delinquency in adolescence. *Adolescence, 29,* 975–990.

Persson-Blennow, I., & McNeil, T.F. (1988). Frequencies and stability of temperament types in childhood. *Journal of the American Academy of Child and Adolescent Psychiatry, 27,* 619–622.

Peters-Martin, P., & Wachs, T.D. (1985). A longitudinal study of temperament and its correlates in the first 12 months. In S. Chess & A. Thomas (Eds.), *Annual Progress in Child Psychiatry and Child Development,* 315–331.

Phares, V., & Compas, B.E. (1993). The role of fathers in child and adolescent psychopathology: Make way for Daddy. In M.E. Hertzig & E.A. Faber (Eds.), *Annual Progress in Child Psychiatry and Child Development,* 344–401.

Piaget, J. (1970). Piaget's theory. In P.H. Mussen (Ed.), *Carmichael's manual of child psychology* (Vol. 2, pp. 703–732). New York: John Wiley & Sons.

Plomin, R., & DeFries, J.C. (1985). *Origins of individual differences in infancy: The Colorado Adoption Project.* San Diego: Academic Press.

Porges, S.W., Doussard-Roosevelt, J.A., Portales, A.L., & Suess, P.E. (1994). Cardiac vagal tone: Stability and relation to difficultness in infants and 3-year-olds. *Developmental Psychobiology, 27,* 289–300.

Prior, M.R., Sanson, A.V., & Oberklaid, F. (1989). The Australian Temperament Project. In G.A. Kohnstamm, J.E. Bates, & M.K. Rothbart (Eds.), *Temperament in childhood* (pp. 537–554). Chichester, England: John Wiley & Sons.

Radke-Yarrow, M., Richters, J., & Wilson, W.E. (1988). Child development in a network of relationships. In R.A. Hinde & J. Stevenson-Hinde (Eds.), *Relationships within families: Mutual influences* (pp. 48–67). Oxford: Clarendon Press.

Radke-Yarrow, M., Zahn-Waxler, C., & Chapman, M. (1983). Children's prosocial dispositions and behavior. In P.H. Mussen (Series Ed.) & E.M. Hetherington (Vol. Ed.), *Handbook of child psychology: Vol. 4. Socialization, personality, and social development* (4th ed., pp. 469–546). New York: John Wiley & Sons.

Reich, W., Earls, F., Frankel, O., & Shayka, J.J. (1993). Psychopathology in children of alcoholics. *Journal of the American Academy of Child and Adolescent Psychiatry, 32,* 995–1002.

Reznick, J.S., Kagan, J., Snidman, N., Gersten, M., Baak, K., & Rosenberg, A. (1987). Inhibited and uninhibited children: A follow-up study. In S. Chess, A. Thomas, & M. Hertzig (Eds.), *Annual Progress in Child Psychiatry and Child Development,* 256–290.

Riese, M.L. (1987). Temperament stability between the neonatal period and 24 months. *Developmental Psychology, 23,* 216–222.

Roberts, W., & Strayer, J. (1987). Parents' responses to the emotional distress of their children: Relations with children's competence. *Developmental Psychology, 23,* 415–422.

Roberts, W.L. (1986). Nonlinear models of development: An example from the socialization of competence. *Child Development, 57,* 1166–1178.

Rothbart, M.K. (1988). Temperament and the development of inhibited approach. *Child Development, 59,* 1241–1250.

Rothbart, M.K. (1999). Commentary: Temperament, fear, and shyness. In L.A. Schmidt and J. Schulkin (Eds.), *Extreme fear, shyness, and social phobia: Origins, biological mechanisms and clinical outcomes.* Series in affective science (pp. 88–93). New York: Oxford University Press.

Rothbart, M.K., & Derryberry, D. (1981). Development of individual differences in temperament. In M.E. Lamb & A.L. Brown (Eds.), *Advances in developmental psychology* (Vol. 1, pp. 37–86). Mahwah, NJ: Lawrence Erlbaum Associates.

Rothbart, M.K. & Derryberry, D., & Posner, M.J. (1994). A psychobiological approach to the development of temperament. In J.E. Bates & T.D. Wachs (Eds.), *Temperament: Individual differences at the interface of biology and behavior.* APA Science Volumes (pp. 83–116). Washington, D.C.: American Psychological Association.

Rutter, M. (1979). Protective factors in children's responses to stress and disadvantage. In M.W. Kent & J.E. Rolf (Eds.), *Social competence in children* (pp. 49–74). Hanover, NH: University Press of New England.

Rutter, M. (1981). Stress, coping and development: Some issues and some questions. *Journal of Child Psychology and Psychiatry and Allied Disciplines, 22,* 323–356.

Rutter, M. (1989). Intergenerational continuities and discontinuities in serious parenting difficulties. In D. Cicchetti & V. Carlson (Eds.), *Child maltreatment: Theory and research on the causes and consequences of child abuse and neglect* (pp. 317–348). New York: Cambridge University Press.

Rutter, M. (1990). Psychosocial resilience and protective mechanisms. In J. Rolf, A.S. Masten, D. Cicchetti, K.H. Niechterlein, & S. Weintraub (Eds.), *Risk and protective factors in the development of psychopathology* (pp. 181–214). New York: Cambridge University Press.

Sameroff, A.J., & Fiese, B.H. (1990). Transactional regulation and early intervention. In S.J. Meisels & J.P. Shonkoff (Eds.), *Handbook of early childhood intervention* (pp. 119–149). New York: Cambridge University Press.

Sameroff, A.J., & Fiese, B.H. (2000). Models of development and developmental risk. In C.H. Zeanah (Ed.), *Handbook of infant mental health* (2nd ed., pp. 3–19). New York: Guilford Press.

Sameroff, A.J., Seifer, R., Baldwin, A., & Baldwin, C. (1993). Stability of intelligence from preschool to adolescence: The influence of social and family risk factors. *Child Development, 64,* 80–97.

Sameroff, A.J., Seifer, R., Barocas, R., Zax, M., & Greenspan, S.I. (1987). Intelligence quotient scores of 4-year-old children: Social–environmental risk factors. *Pediatrics, 79,* 343–350.

Sanson, A., Oberklaid, F., Pedlow, R., & Prior, M. (1991). Risk indicators: Assessment of infancy predictors of pre-school behavioral maladjustment. *Journal of Child Psychology and Psychiatry and Allied Disciplines, 32,* 609–626.

Sanson, A., Pedlow, R., Cann, W., Prior, M., & Oberklaid, F. (1996). Shyness ratings: Stability and correlates in early childhood. *International Journal of Behavioral Development, 19,* 705–724.

Sapolsky, R.M. (1994). *Why zebras don't get ulcers: A guide to stress, stress-related diseases, and coping.* New York: W.H. Freeman.

Schteingart, J.S., Molnar, J., Klein, T.P., & Lowe, C.B. (1995). Homelessness and child functioning in the context of risk and protective factors moderating child outcomes. *Journal of Clinical Child Psychology, 24,* 320–331.

Shatz, C.J. (1992, September). The developing brain. *Scientific American, 267,* 60–67.

Shaw, D.S., & Vondra, J.I. (1993). Chronic family adversity and infant attachment security. *Journal of Child Psychology and Psychiatry and Allied Disciplines, 34,* 1205–1215.

Shaw, D.S., Vondra, J.I., Hammerding, K.D., Kennan, K., & Dunn, M. (1994). Chronic family adversity and early child behavior problems: A longitudinal study of low income families. *Journal of Child Psychology and Psychiatry and Allied Disciplines, 35,* 1109–1122.

Singer, W. (1987). Activity-dependent self-organization of synaptic connections as a substrate of learning. In J. Changeux & M. Konishi (Eds.), *The neural and molecular basis of learning* (pp. 301–336). New York: John Wiley & Sons.

Skinner, B.F. (1974). *About behaviorism.* New York: Vintage Books.

Sorce, J.F., Emde, R., Campos, J., & Klinnert, M. (1985). Maternal emotional signaling: Its effect on the visual cliff behavior of 1-year-olds. *Developmental Psychology, 21,* 195–200.

Sroufe, L.A., Egeland, B., & Kreutzer, T. (1990). The fate of early experience following developmental change: Longitudinal approaches to individual adaptation in children. *Child Development, 61,* 1363–1373.

Steinhauer, P.D. (1996). *Developing resiliency in children from disadvantaged populations.* Ottawa: National Forum on Youth.

Stifter, C.A., & Jain, A. (1996). Psychophysiological correlates of infant temperament: Stability of behavior and autonomic patterning from 5 to 18 months. *Developmental Psychobiology, 29,* 379–391.

Strauss, M.E., & Rourke, D.L. (1978). A multivariate analysis of the Neonatal Behavioral Assessment Scale in several samples. *Monographs of the Society for Research in Child Development, 43,* 81–91.

Strelau, J. (1996). The regulative theory of temperament (RTT): Current status. *Personality and Individual Differences, 20,* 131–142.

Susman-Stillman, A., Kalkoske, M., Egeland, B., & Waldman, I. (1996). Infant temperament and maternal sensitivity as predictors of attachment security. *Infant Behavior and Development, 19,* 33–47.

Thomas, A., & Chess, S. (1977). *Temperament and development.* New York: Brunner/Mazel.

Thomas, A., & Chess, S. (1985). Genesis and evolution of behavioral disorders: From infancy to early adult life. In S. Chess & A. Thomas (Eds.), *Annual Progress in Child Psychiatry and Child Development,* 140–158.

Thomas, A., Chess, S., & Birch, H.G. (1968). *Temperament and behavior disorders in children.* New York University Press.

Van den Boom, D.C. (1989). Neonatal irritability and the development of attachment. In G.A. Kohnstamm, J.E. Bates, & M.K. Rothbart (Eds.), *Temperament in childhood* (pp. 299–318). Chichester, England: John Wiley & Sons.

Van den Boom, D.C. (1994). The influence of temperament and mothering on attachment and exploration: An experimental manipulation of sensitive responsiveness among lower-class mothers with irritable infants. *Child Development, 65,* 1457–1477.

Van den Boom, D.C., & Hoeksma, J.B. (1994). The effect of infant irritability on mother-infant interaction: A growth-curve analysis. *Developmental Psychology, 30,* 581–590.

van der Kolk, B.A. (1994). The body keeps score: Memory and the evolving psychobiology of posttraumatic stress. *Harvard Review of Psychiatry, 1,* 253–265.

van IJzendoorn, M.H., Kranenburg, M.J., Zwart-Woudstra, H.A., van Busschbach, A.M., & Lamberman, W.E. (1991). Parental attachment and children's socioemotional development: Some findings on the validity of the Adult Attachment Interview in the Netherlands. *International Journal of Behavioral Development, 14,*375–394.

Wachs, T.D. (1987). Specificity of environmental action as manifest in environmental correlates of infant's mastery motivation. *Developmental Psychology, 23,* 782–790.

Wachs, T.D. (1994). Fit, context and the transition between temperament and personality. In C. Halverson G. Kohnstamm, & R. Martin (Eds.), *The Developing Structure of Personality from Infancy to Adulthood* (pp. 200–222). Mahwah, NJ: Lawrence Erlbaum Associates.

Wachs, T.D. (2000). *Necessary but not sufficient: The respective roles of simple and multiple influences on individual development.* Washington, D.C.: American Psychological Association.

Wachs, T.D., & Gandour, M.J. (1984). Temperament, environment, and six-month cognitive-intellectual development: A test of the organismic specificity hypothesis. In S. Chess & A. Thomas (Eds.), *Annual Progress in Child Psychiatry and Child Development,* 191–208.

Weinman, M., Robinson, M., Simmons, J., Schreiber, N., & Stafford, B. (1989). Pregnant teens: Differential pregnancy resolution and treatment implications. *Child Welfare, 68,* 45–55.

Weisglas-Kuperus, N., Baerts, W., Smrkovsky, M., & Sauer, P.J. (1993). Effect of biological and social factors on the cognitive development of very low birth weight infants. *Pediatrics, 92,* 658–665.

Werner, E.E. (1989). High-risk children in young adulthood: A longitudinal study from birth to 32 years. *American Journal of Orthopsychiatry, 59,* 72–81.

Werner, E.E. (1993). Risk, resilience, and recovery: Perspectives from the Kauai Longitudinal Study. *Development and Psychopathology, 5,* 503–515.

Werner, E.E. (1995). Resilience in development. *Current Directions in Psychological Science, 4,* 81–85.

White, B.L. (1985). *A parent's guide to the first three years.* Englewood Cliffs, NJ: Prentice-Hall.

Wieder, S., Jasnow, M., Greenspan, S.I., & Strauss, M. (1983). Identifying the multi-risk family prenatally: Antecedent psychosocial factors and infant development trends. *Infant Mental Health Journal, 4,* 165–201.

Zeanah, C.H., Boris, N.W., & Larrieu, J.A. (1997). Infant development and developmental risk: A review of the past 10 years. *Journal of the American Academy of Child and Adolescent Psychiatry, 36,* 165–178.

Zeanah, C.H., Keener, M.A., Stewart, L., & Anders, T.F. (1985). Prenatal perception of infant personality: A preliminary investigation. *Journal of the American Academy of Child Psychiatry, 24,* 204–210.

Zyblock, M. (1996). *Child poverty trends in Canada: Exploring depth and incidence from a total money perspective, 1975–1992.* Ottawa, Ontario: Human Resources Development Canada.

FURTHER READING ON THE TOPIC

Allen, K.E., & Marotz, L.R. (1994). *Developmental profiles: Pre-birth through eight.* New York: Delmar.

Ames, L.B., & Ilg, F.L. (1976). *Your two-year-old: Terrible or tender.* New York: Dell Publishing.

_____. (1976). *Your three-year-old: Friend or enemy.* New York: Dell Publishing.

_____. (1976). *Your four-year-old: Wild and wonderful.* New York: Dell Publishing.

_____. (1979). *Your five-year-old: Sunny and serene.* New York: Dell Publishing.

_____. (1979). *Your six-year-old: Defiant but loving.* New York: Dell Publishing.

Ames, L.B., Ilg., F.L., & Haber, C.C. (1982). *Your one year old: The fun-loving, fussy 12-to-24-month-old.* New York: Dell Publishing.

Barber, L.W., & Williams, H. (1981). *Your baby's first 30 months.* Tucson, AZ: H.P. Books.

Begley, S. (1996, February). Your child's brain. *Newsweek, 127,* (54), 7.

Brazelton, T.B. (1974). *Toddlers and parents: A declaration of independence.* New York: Dell Publishing.

Brazelton, T.B. (1983). *Infants and mothers: Differences in development.* New York: Delacorte Press.

Brazelton, T.B. (1994). *Touchpoints: Your child's emotional and behavioral development.* Reading, MA: Addison-Wesley.

Caplan, F. (Ed.). (1975). *The first twelve months of life: Your baby's growth month by month.* New York: Grosset and Dunlap.

Caplan, F., & Caplan, T. (Eds.). (1977). *The second twelve months of life: A kaleidoscope of growth.* New York: Grosset and Dunlap.

Caplan, T., & Caplan, F. (1984). *The early childhood years: The 2- to 6-year-old.* New York: Bantam.

Carey, W.B., & McDevitt, S.C. (1995). *Coping with children's temperament: A guide for professionals.* New York: Basic Books.

Chase, R.A., & Rubin, R.R. (1979). *The first wondrous year: You and your baby.* New York: Collier-MacMillan.

Chess, S., & Thomas, A. (1986). *Temperament in clinical practice.* New York: Guilford Press.

Chess, S., & Thomas, A. (1987). *Know your child: An authoritative guide for today's parents.* New York: Basic Books.

Chess, S., & Thomas, A. (1996). *Temperament: Theory and practice:* New York: Brunner/Mazel.

Chess, S., Thomas, A., & Birch, H.G. (1965). *Your child is a person: A psychological approach to parenthood without guilt.* New York: Viking Press.

Clarke, M. (1990). *The disruptive child: A handbook of care and control.* Plymouth, UK: Northcote House.

Cole, J., & Calmenson, S. (1989). *Safe from the start: Your child's safety from birth to age five.* New York: Facts on File.

Davis, L., & Kaiser, J. (1997). *Becoming the parent you want to be: A sourcebook of strategies for the first five years.* New York: Broadway Books.

Eisenberg, A., Murkoff, H.E., & Hathaway, S.E. (1994). *What to expect: The first year.* New York: Workman.

Eisenberg, A., Murkoff, H.E., & Hathaway, S.E. (1994). *What to expect: The toddler years.* New York: Workman.

Evans, J., & Ilfeld, E. (1982). *Good beginnings: Parenting in the early years.* Ypsilanti, MI: High/Scope Press.

Forehand, R.L., & Long, N.J. (1996). *Parenting the strong-willed child: The clinically proven five-week program for parents of two- to six-year-olds.* Chicago: Contemporary Books.

Fraiberg, S. (1959). *The magic years: Understanding and handling the problems of early childhood.* New York: Charles Scribner's Sons.

Gestwicki, C. (1995). *Developmentally appropriate practice: Curriculum and development in early education.* Albany, NY: Delmar.

Goldstein, S., & Goldstein, M. (1992). *Hyperactivity: Why won't my child pay attention?* New York: John Wiley & Sons.

Gonzalez-Mena, J., & Eyer, D.W. (1997). *Infants, toddlers, and caregivers.* Mountain View, CA: Mayfield.

Green, C. (1985). *Toddler taming: A survival guide for parents.* New York: Fawcett Columbine.

Greenspan, S.I. (1996). *The challenging child: Understanding, raising, and enjoying the five "difficult" types of children.* Reading, MA: Addison-Wesley.

Greenspan, S.I. (1999). *Building healthy minds: The six experiences that create intelligence and emotional growth in babies and young children.* Cambridge, MA: Perseus Books.

Holditch, L. (1997). *Understanding your 5-year-old.* Toronto: Warwick.

Kaye, K. (1982). *The mental and social life of babies: How parents create persons.* Chicago: University of Chicago Press.

Klaus, M., & Klaus, P. (2000). *Your amazing newborn.* Reading, MA: Perseus Books.

Kopp, C.B. (1994). *Baby steps: The "whys" of your child's behavior in the first two years.* New York: W.H. Freeman.

Kurcinka, M.S. (1998). *Raising your spirited child: A guide for parents whose child is more intense, sensitive, perceptive, persistent, and energetic.* New York: Harper Perennial.

Lake, A. (1985, July). Raising difficult kids: Rx for success. *Woman's Day, 44*(4).

Leach, P. (1989). *Your baby and child: From birth to age five.* New York: Alfred A. Knopf.

Lerner, C., & Dombro, A.L. (2000). *Learning and growing together: Understanding and supporting your child's development.* Washington, D.C.: Zero to Three.

Ludington-Hoe, S. (1985). *How to have a smarter baby.* New York: Rawson.

Martin, R.P. (1983). Temperament: A review of research with implications for the school psychologist. *School Psychology Review, 12,* 266–273.

Miller, L. (1997). *Understanding your 4 year-old.* Toronto: Warwick.

Miller, L. (1997). *Understanding your baby.* Toronto: Warwick.

Morse, M.B. (1990, July). Fitting into the family. *Parents Magazine, 65,* 58(5).

Munger, E., & Bowdon, S. (1993). *Beyond peek-a-boo and pat-a-cake: Activities for baby's first 24 months.* Clinton, NJ: New Win.

Nash, J.M. (1997, June). Fertile minds. *Time, 149,* (48), 9.

Reid, S. (1992). *Understanding your two-year-old.* Toronto: Warwick.

Rubin, N., & Vidal, B. (1987, September). Your child's temperament: Easy, difficult or slow-to-warm-up? *Parents Magazine, 62,* 94(8).

Rubin, R.R., & Fisher, J.J. (1982). *Your preschooler.* New York: Collier MacMillan.

Rubin, R.R., Fisher, J.J., & Doering, S.G. (1980). *Your toddler.* New York: Collier MacMillan.

Sammons, W.A.H. (1989). *The self-calmed baby: A liberating new approach to parenting your infant.* Boston: Little, Brown.

Sanger, S., & Kelly, J. (1987). *You and your baby's first year.* Toronto: Bantam Books.

Sears, W. (1991). *Keys to becoming a father.* New York: Barron's.

Sears, W., & Sears, M. (1987). *The fussy baby book: Parenting your high-need child from birth to age five.* New York: New American Library.

Segal, M.M. (1998). *Your child at play: Birth to one year.* New York: Newmarket Press.

_____. (1998). *Your child at play: One to two years.* New York: Newmarket Press.

_____. (1998). *Your child at play: Three to five years.* New York: Newmarket Press.

_____. (1998). *Your child at play: Two to three years.* New York: Newmarket Press.

Shore, R. (1997). *Rethinking the brain: New insights into early development.* New York: Families and Work Institute.

Silberg, J. (1993). *Games to play with toddlers.* Beltsville, MD: Gryphon House.

Silberg, J. (2001). *Games to play with babies* (3rd ed.). Beltsville, MD: Gryphon House.

Steiner, D. (1992). *Understanding your one year old.* Toronto: Warwick.

Stern, D.N. (1985). *The interpersonal world of the infant: A view from psychoanalysis and developmental psychology.* New York: Basic Books.

Thomas, A., & Chess, S. (1977). *Temperament and development.* New York: Brunner/Mazel.

Trowell, J. (1997). *Understanding your 3-year-old.* Toronto: Warwick.

Van der Zande (1990). *1, 2, 3—The toddler years: A practical guide for parents and caregivers.* Santa Cruz, CA: The Center.

White, B. (1993). *The first three years of life.* New York: Simon & Schuster.

Zimbardo, P.G., & Radl, S.L. (1986). *The shy child: A parent's guide to overcoming and preventing shyness from infancy to adulthood.* New York: Dolphin.

CHILDREN'S BOOKS ABOUT DEVELOPMENT AND TEMPERAMENT

Aliki. (1992). *I'm growing!* New York: Harper Collins Children's Books.

Bourgeois, P. (1987). *Big Sarah's little boots.* Toronto: Kids Can Press.

Carlson, N.L. (1996). *Sit still.* New York: Viking Children's Books.

Cohen, M. (1981). *Jim meets the thing.* New York: Greenwillow Books.

Cohen, M. (1983). *When will I read?* New York: Dell.

Cohen, M. (1995). *The real-skin rubber monster mask.* New York: Dell.

Goennel, H. (1987). *When I grow up ... .*Boston: Little, Brown.

Kraus, R. (1971). *Leo the late bloomer.* New York: Windmill Books.

Lasky, K. (1993). *The tantrum.* Toronto: Maxwell Macmillan Canada.

McPhail, David. (1980). *Pig Pig grows up!* New York: Dutton Children's Books.

Rockwell, A.F. (1995). *No! No! No!* New York: Macmillan Books for Young Readers.

Viorst, J. (1982). *Alexander and the terrible, horrible, no good, very bad day.* New York: Atheneum Books.

Waber, B. (1972). *Ira sleeps over.* Boston: Houghton Mifflin.

Wells, R. (1995). *Edward in deep water.* New York: Dial Books for Young Readers.

Wells, R. (1995). *Edward unready for school.* New York: Dial Books for Young Readers.

Wells, R. (1995). *Edward's overwhelming overnight.* New York: Dial Books for Young Readers.

Wells, R. (1997). *Noisy Nora.* New York: Dial Books for Young Readers.

Wells, R. (2001). *Shy Charles.* New York: Viking Children's Books.

Zagwyn, D.T. (1995). *Pumpkin blanket.* Toronto: Fitzhenry & Whiteside.

APPENDIX: SELECTED ASSESSMENT INSTRUMENTS

ASSESSING DEVELOPMENT

Tests of development vary from criterion-referenced instruments, which assess performance relative to a well-defined aspect of behavior, to more standardized, norm-referenced tests that examine development across various intellectual domains and show how a child compares to the standardization group or to the norm. Some rely on questionnaires that ask parents about the child's developmental capacities. Others require observation of the child and many involve direct administration of test items. Norm-referenced tests provide information about the developmental level of a child, while criterion-referenced tests emphasize what a child can or cannot do, not how his performance compares to others.

Many tests of infants and young children have failed to be predictive of a child's later development. Tests do give an accurate picture of the child at a particular point in time, however—and in extreme cases of delays or accelerated development—are often predictive of later developmental levels. Tests can be used to determine the need for early intervention and to evaluate the success of a program or intervention strategy. It should be pointed out, however, that successive assessments are more useful than a single test and will be able to show whether a child's development is catching up or dropping behind. As well, children who show an unusual or a complex array of symptoms should be observed at home and in a group environment as well as in the structured testing situation. Table A1.1 first describes the best-known standardized, norm-referenced tests in some detail, then other tests are briefly listed.

ASSESSING TEMPERAMENT

Three major categories of measures have been used to assess temperament: parent and teacher report questionnaires, observations in the home and laboratory, and physiological measures. In this chapter, the emphasis is on parent report measures as they are the most commonly used.

Parent Report Questionnaires

The following are questionnaires based on parental descriptions of children. Table A1.2 outlines studies using the New York Longitudinal Study (NYLS) categories and includes other temperament measures not based on NYLS categories.

Table A1.1. Selected developmental assessments

Tool/instrument	Age range	Items/administration time	General description
Ages and Stages Questionnaires (ASQ): A Parent-Completed, Child-Monitoring System, Second Edition Bricker, D., and Squires, J. (with assistance from Mounts, L., Potter, L., Nickel, R., Twombly, E., and Farrell, J.). (1999). *Ages and Stages Questionnaires (ASQ): A parent-completed child-monitoring system* (2nd ed.). Baltimore: Paul H. Brookes Publishing Co., Inc.	4 months–60 months	19 questionnaires	The *Ages and Stages Questionnaires (ASQ), 2nd Edition,* is a broad screening tool for overall child development that monitors five key areas—communication, gross motor, fine motor, problem-solving, and personal-social skills. The questionnaires are photocopiable and culturally sensitive, field-tested, and research-validated
Bayley Scales of Infant Development, Second Edition (BSID-II) Bayley, N. (1993). *Bayley Scales of Infant Development, Second Edition Manual.* San Antonio, TX: The Psychological Corporation.	1 month–42 months	25–60 minutes	The *Bayley Scales of Infant Development (BSID-II)* have two scales that assess mental and motor development. The Mental Scale assesses sensory-perceptual activities, object constancy and memory, learning and problem-solving ability, verbal communication, and early ability to form generalizations and classifications. The Motor Scale measures general body control, coordination of large muscles, and fine motor control of the hands.
Brazelton Neonatal Behavioral Assessment Scale (BNBAS) Brazelton, T.B., Nugent, K., & Lester, B. (1987). Neonatal Behavioral Assessment Scale. In J.D. Osofsky (Ed.), *Handbook of Infant Development* (2nd ed.) (pp. 780–817). New York: John Wiley & Sons.	Birth–4 weeks	27 items; 20–30 minutes	The *Brazelton Neonatal Behavioral Assessment Scale (BNBAS)* was designed to assess the infant's responses to his environment and to go beyond a neurological assessment. Skin color, motor maturity, hand–mouth coordination, tremors, startles, irritability, consolability, cuddliness, and the infant's ability to calm down on his own are measured. Also, the newborn's ability to orient to sensory stimuli is assessed. The scale is repeated at 3 and 10 days after birth and at other times during the neonatal period in order to assess the progress of the infant and his changing reaction to the postnatal environment.
Stanford-Binet Intelligence Scale, Fourth Edition Thorndike, R.L., Hagen, E.P., & Sattler, J.M. (1986). *Stanford-Binet Intelligence Scale* (4th ed.). Chicago, IL: Riverside.	2–adult	15 subtests; 45–60 minutes	The *Stanford-Binet Intelligence Scale, Fourth Edition* measures cognitive reasoning in four areas: 1) Verbal Reasoning, 2) Quantitative Reasoning, 3) Abstract/Visual Reasoning, and 4) Short-Term Memory.
Vineland Adaptive Behavior Scales (VABS) Sparrow, S.S., Balla, D.A., & Cicchetti, D.V. (1984). *Vineland Adaptive Behavior Scales (VABS).* Circle Pines, MN: American Guidance Service.	Birth–18 years 11 months	Interview Edition: Expanded form: 577 items; 60–90 minutes Survey form: 297 items; 20–60 minutes Classroom Edition: 244 items; 20 minutes	The *Vineland Adaptive Behavior Scales (VABS)* measure adaptive behavior in four domains: 1) Communication, 2) Daily Living Skills, 3) Socialization, and 4) Motor Skills. The test can be administered as a semi-structured interview or in survey form by a respondent who is familiar with the child. Standard scores, percentiles, and age equivalents are determined for each area, as well as a total Adaptive Behavior Composite Score (ABCS) obtained.
Wechsler Preschool and Primary Scale of Intelligence–Revised (WPPSI-R) Wechsler, D. (1989). *Manual for the Wechsler Preschool and Primary Scale of Intelligence–Revised.* San Antonio, TX: The Psychological Corporation.	4 years–6 years 7 months	11 subtests (six verbal and five performance); 75 minutes	The WPPSI-R provides a systematic appraisal of the mental ability of young children and is a downward extension of the Wechsler Intelligence Scale for Children (WISC-III). It provides an overall or global intellectual level.

Other commonly used measures	Age range
Battelle Developmental Inventory (BDI) Newborg, J., Stock, J., Wnek, L, Guidubaldi, J., & Svinicki, J. (1988). *Battelle Developmental Inventory*. Chicago: Riverside.	Birth–8 years
Brigance Diagnostic Inventory of Early Development-Revised Brigance, A.H. (1985). *Brigance Preschool Inventory*. North Billerica, MA: Curriculum Associates.	Birth–7 years
Child Development Inventory Ireton, H. (1992). *Manual of the Child Development Inventory*. Minneapolis, MN: Basic Books.	15 months–6 years
Developmental Profile II (DP-II) Alpern, G.D., Boll, T.J., & Shearer, M.A. (1980). *Developmental Profile II Manual*. Colorado: Psychological Development.	Birth–9.5 years
Diagnostic Inventory for Screening Children (DISC) Amdur, J.R., Mainland, M.K., & Parker, K.C.H. (2001). *Diagnostic Inventory for Screening Children (DISC)*. Kitchener, ON: Grand River Hospital.	Birth–5 years
Hawaii Early Learning Profile (HELP) Furono, S., O'Reilly, K., Hosaka, C.M., Inatsuka, T.T., Zeisloft-Falbey, B., & Allman (1988). *Hawaii Early Learning Profile*. Palo Alto, CA: Vort Corporation.	Birth–3 years
Kaufman Assessment Battery for Children (K-ABC) Kaufman, A.S., & Kaufman, N.L. (1983). *Kaufman Assessment Battery for Children Interpretive Manual*. Circle Pines, MN: American Guidance Service.	2.5–12.5 years
McCarthy Scales of Children's Abilities McCarthy, D. (1972). *Manual for the McCarthy Scales of Children's Abilities*. San Antonio, TX: Psychological Corporation.	2.5–8.5 years
Ordinal Scales of Psychological Development Uzgiris, I.C., & Hunt, J.McV. (1975). *Toward Ordinal Scales of Psychological Development in Infancy*. Champaign, IL: University of Illinois.	1–24 months
Transdisciplinary Play-Based Assessment Linder, T.W. (1993). *Transdisciplinary play-based assessment: A functional approach to working with young children*. Baltimore: Paul H. Brookes Publishing Co.	6 months–6 years

Table A1.2. Selected temperament measures

Tool/instrument	Age range	Items/administration time	General description
*Early Infancy Temperament Questionnaire (EITQ) Medoff-Cooper, B., Carey, W.B., & McDevitt, S.C. (1993). The Early Infancy Temperament Questionnaire. Journal of Developmental and Behavioral Pediatrics, 14, 230–235.	1–4 months	80 items; 20 minutes	The measure is used to assess infants' reaction to their environment. It uses parent responses to behavioral descriptions and assesses the nine temperament categories of the NYLS: Activity, Rhythmicity, Approach, Adaptability, Intensity, Mood, Persistence, Distractibility, and Threshold. Items are rated on a 6-point scale ranging from "almost never" to "almost always."
*Infant Temperament Questionnaire–Revised (ITQ-R) Carey, W.B., & McDevitt, S.C. (1978). Revision of the Infant Temperament Questionnaire. Pediatrics, 61, 735–739.	Birth–1 year	95 items; 30 minutes	The Infant Temperament Questionnaire–Revised (ITQ-R) assesses the behaviors of infants, such as how they react to new foods. These items are scored on 6-point scales ranging from "almost never" to "almost always." Dimensions include Activity, Rhythmicity, Approach, Adaptability, Intensity, Mood, Persistence, Distractibility, and Threshold to Stimulation. Dimensional scores are used to divide infants into various temperament clusters (i.e., easy, intermediate-low, slow-to-warm-up, intermediate-high, and difficult).
*Toddler Temperament Scale (TTS) Fullard, W., McDevitt, S.C., & Carey, W.B. (1984). Assessing temperament in one to three-year-old children. Journal of Pediatric Psychology, 9, 205–216.	1–3 years	97 items; 30 minutes	The Toddler Temperament Scale (TTS) is very similar to the Infant Temperament Questionnaire and includes the same nine temperament categories listed. It measures parents' perceptions of their child's typical behavior on a scale of 1 (almost never) to 6 (almost always). The five dimensions of regularity of biological functioning, approach/withdrawal, adaptability, mood, and intensity of affect are used to measure difficult temperament.
*Behavioral Style Questionnaire (BSQ) McDevitt, S.C., & Carey, W.B. (1978). The measurement of temperament in 3–7 year old children. Journal of Child Psychology and Psychiatry and Allied Disciplines, 19, 245–253.	3–7 years	100 items; 30 minutes	Response format uses a scale of 1–6 and the child is rated on each behavior from "almost never" to "almost always." The questionnaire yields scores representing the nine NYLS temperament dimensions. As with the other NYLS questionnaires, the dimensions can be combined into category cluster ratings that can place the child into one of the five categories (easy, low intermediate, slow-to-warm-up, high intermediate, or difficult). This questionnaire can be completed by the parent or someone else familiar with the child's behavior.
Infant Characteristics Questionnaire (ICQ) Bates, J.E., Freeland, C.A.B., & Lannsbury, M.L. (1979). Measurement of infant difficultness. Child Development, 50, 794–803.	4–30 months	32 items; 10 minutes	The items on the Infant Characteristics Questionnaire (ICQ) are rated by parents on a 1–7 scale, with 1 (optimal temperament) to 7 (difficult temperament). It consists of four factors or dimensions: 1) Fussy/Difficult/Demanding, 2) Unadaptable, 3) Persistent, and 4) Unsociable. Different scales may be used at 4, 6, 13, 24, and 30 months, allowing assessment of a wide age span.

*These questionnaires use the New York Longitudinal Study (NYLS) categories.

Tool/instrument	Age range	Items/administration time	General description
Parenting Stress Index (PSI) Abidin, R.R. (1995). *Parenting Stress Index-Manual.* Los Angeles, CA: Western Psychological Services.	Parents of children from birth–12 years	Child Domain: 47 items; 20 minutes	*The Parenting Stress Index (PSI)* was developed to identify stress levels in parent–child systems. Two domains include parent and child. The child domain consists of six subscales: 1) Adaptability, 2) "Demandingness," 3) Mood, 4) Distractibility/hyperactivity (which refer to the temperamental characteristics of children), 5) Acceptability, and 6) "Reinforces parent" (which are more the parental perceptions of the children). Questions are rated on a 5-point scale from 1 (strongly agree) to 5 (strongly disagree).

Other commonly used measures

Tool/instrument	Age range	Items/administration time	General description
Child Behavior Questionnaire (CBQ) Rothbart, M.K., & Ahadi, S.A. (1994). Temperament and the development of personality. *Journal of Abnormal Psychology, 103,* 55–66.	3–7 years		
Dimension of Temperament Scale-Revised (DOTS-R) Windle, M., & Lerner, R.M. (1986). Reassessing the dimensions of temperamental individuality across the life span: The revised dimensions of temperament survey (DOTS - R). *The Journal of Adolescent Research, 1,* 213–230.	4 years– adolescence		
Emotionality, Activity, Sociability Inventory (EASI-II) Buss, A.H., & Plomin, R. (1975). *A temperament theory of personality development.* New York: John Wiley & Sons.	3–6 years		
Infant Behavior Questionnaire (IBQ) Rothbart, M.K. (1981). Measurement of temperament in infancy. *Child Development, 52,* 569–578.	3–12 months		
Temperament Assessment Battery for Children (TAB) Martin, R.P. (1988). *The Temperament Assessment Battery for Children.* Brandon, VT: Clinical Psychology Publishing.	3–7 years		
Toddler Behavior Assessment Questionnaire (TABQ) Goldsmith, H.H. (1988). *Preliminary manual for the Toddler Behavior Assessment Questionnaire* (Technical Report No. 88–04) Eugene, OR: Oregon Center for the Study of Emotion.	16–36 months		

Observational Measures

Observational measures of temperament have included naturalistic observation of the child interacting with parents or other children in the home or school, or in structured laboratory or home situations.

In either case, various content areas of temperament are observed, usually based on a particular temperament theory. These include such aspects of behavior as anger proneness, task concentration, impulse control, joy, activity level, fearfulness, and delay of gratification. More structured observations use various predetermined episodes chosen to encourage responses involving the behaviors the researchers intend to measure. These episodes may include 1) briefly separating the child from the mother, 2) having the mother gently restrain the child while he is playing, 3) having the child play with toys, 4) having the child complete a task, 5) placing a desirable toy behind plexiglass, 6) not allowing a child to open a wrapped toy, 7) taking a toy away, and 8) having the child watch a puppet show.

These observations aim to give a view of temperament independent of parent perception. One measure that is available is the LAB-TAB, developed by Goldsmith and Rothbart: Goldsmith, H.H., & Rothbart, M.K. (1991). Contemporary instruments for assessing early temperament by questionnaire and in the laboratory. In J. Strelau & A. Angleitner (Eds.), *Explorations in temperament: International perspectives on theory and measurement* (pp. 249–272). New York: Plenum Press.

Psychophysiological Measures

A number of psychophysiological measures have been used as indexes of infants' and children's responses to particular stimuli. These are seen as underlying the various temperament dimensions. They include the following:

- Salivary measures of cortisol levels or adrenocortical activity

- Cardiac measure of heart rate

- Heart rate variability and vagal tone

- Differential EEG activity in the right and left lobes of the brain

- Other measures of the endocrine system such as levels of serotonin or norepinephrine

● ● ● 2

HELPING CHILDREN DEVELOP BODY CONTROL AND A POSITIVE BODY IMAGE

Until the 1990s, the psychology of the human body received very little attention. For some time, however, it has been clear that an individual's physical attributes and especially his or her own view of those attributes are critical aspects of personality development, psychopathology, and adjustment to disabilities. There is no question, for example, that one reason many people with the eating disorder anorexia nervosa continue starving themselves in advanced stages of the disease is because they perceive their emaciated bodies as obese. Similarly, children with visible disfigurements or physical disabilities often have considerable social and emotional difficulties as they enter middle childhood and adolescence and struggle with people's reactions and their own acceptance of their appearance. When children have less obvious difficulties with control of their bodies, such as problems with sensory integration or motor planning or illnesses such as diabetes, the effects on their development in other areas may be just as significant. This kind of body–mind connection became increasingly acknowledged in the 1990s and has led to a deeper understanding of the effects of certain experiences, stress, and emotions on brain development, production of certain neurochemicals, and the immune system. As explained in Chapter 1, traumatic events or chronic, stressful situations that are experienced as uncontrollable inhibit certain hormonal systems, increase others, and lead to decreased energy and even depression. Certain situations may trigger a state of hyperarousal, as well as certain intense reactions that can occur suddenly and unexpectedly.

The exploration of alternative treatments for a variety of physical symptoms and chronic illnesses also has burgeoned. Some examples of studies that have demonstrated these mind–body connections are outlined in Table 2.1. Certain treatments used with adults and children also illustrate the mind–body connection, including art and dance therapy; the use of

Table 2.1. Studies and evidence of the mind–body connection

The connection	Evidence of connection
Effects of religious commitment and prayer on physical and mental health (Matthews & Clark, 1998)	Health care outcomes positively affected by religious commitment for 75% of 212 studies (Matthews & Larson, 1995); frequent church attenders in a National Institute of Mental Health study of 2,679 people had lower rates of psychopathology (Koenig, George, Meador, Blazer, & Dyck, 1994).
Relationship between cognition and emotions and the function of the immune system (Sapolsky, 1996; Watkins, 1997)	68 individuals with melanoma were randomly assigned to control or supportive therapy groups. After 5 years, an increased rate of survival was found in the therapy group (Fawzy et al., 1990). In a prospective study of 2,000 men followed for 17 years, depression was the only predictor of cancer death that was significant (Shekelle, 1981).
Effects of psychological complementary treatments such as relaxation, visualization, and meditation (Caudell, 1996; Rossi, 1993)	Relaxation therapy was found to increase immune system functioning in geriatric adults (Kiecolt-Glaser & Glaser, 1988). Relaxation and visualization used with men who were HIV positive decreased anxiety and cortisol levels, although no effect on disease progression was found (Ironson et al., 1996).
Effects of being administered placebos, for example, sugar water (respondent believed he or she may have been receiving healing medication) or no treatment on recovery from disease (Gordon, 1996; White, Tursky, & Schwartz, 1985)	20% of patients with Crohn's disease improved when given a placebo (Greenberg et al., 1994). Reviews of 26 double-blind studies have shown that 35% of patients received significant pain relief with placebos (Beecher, 1959; Evans, 1985; White, Tursky, & Schwartz, 1985).
Effects of stress on the immune system (Dohrenwald & Dohrenwald, 1974; Holmes & Rahe, 1967)	Research on animals showed stressors result in immunosuppression and the development of illness (Riley, 1981). In humans, studies have shown the relationship between stress and illness (Locke, Krause, Leserman, Hurst, Heisel, & Williams, 1984).
Effects of mother–infant care and holding on stress reaction (Gunnar, 1998)	Research with infants during well-baby checkups that included immunizations showed that when infants are held and comforted by people they are attached to it reduces their physiological stress response or production of cortisol (Gunnar, 1998).

massage and touch with infants; and the use of biofeedback from physiological reactions, which gives patients some control over their responses to situations.

Given these important links between the body and mind, it is clear that adequate development of body control and body image is an important aspect of overall personality and behavior development. Importantly, some motor achievements significantly influence an individual's development in many other areas, including learning to sit up, to reach and grasp, to walk, and to control running. Other developments related to a child's body often cause significant anxiety in parents and are sometimes the source of parent–child conflicts. These behaviors may include—but are not limited to—sleeping, toileting, eating, and interest in gender differences.

DEFINITIONS RELATED TO BODY CONTROL AND A POSITIVE BODY IMAGE

A great deal of confusion and disagreement exist about many of the definitions and concepts related to a child's sense and control of his body. Theorists disagree about when an infant begins to be aware of himself as having a separate body self from his primary caregiver, for example.

Also subject to a great deal of discussion are how much cultural views of beauty, feedback from parents, and a child's sense of physical mastery contribute to a child's body image. The following are some concepts related to body self and their definitions as used in this chapter.

Body Self

Body self is used to describe a child's sense of a physical self. This sense of self is one aspect of self-concept that is gained early as the infant realizes her physical separateness by perceiving objects and other people in the outside world. A child also derives body self from internal sensations from the muscles and joints (i.e., *proprioceptive input*) that tell the brain how each part of the body is and how it is moving. This knowledge then acts as a bridge between purely physical and mental states. Later, a child's sense of body self is gained from her experiences of being able to control her body and from how attractive she believes her body to be.

Body Scheme and Body Control

Body scheme and *body control* refer to the subconscious understanding of motor capacities and abilities that enable movement, as well as the maintenance of body positions. Body schema are likely to be innate, but open to modification by sensorimotor experiences throughout life. Body control refers to an individual's subjective experience of his body, which evolves from perceptions, beliefs, and particularly his body control ability.

Body Image

Body image is a multidimensional entity, believed to be formed from multiple experiences. For example, body experiences and physical engagement with objects and people beginning in the early days of life are critical. The extent to which the infant or young child experiences a sense of mastery of bodily functions and control of motor skills also is significant. As well, the way caregivers interact with and talk to the child about his body will be important. Objective aspects of the child's appearance, as well as current cultural views of beauty, also are clearly significant determiners of how a child feels about his body. The following story of John illustrates how body image and a sense of body self is formed out of a sense of body control and body experiences and the way in which caregivers interact with the world.

• •

When John was born, he seemed to be a healthy and typical infant. But soon after birth he experienced multiple seizures that caused him to have difficulties later with achieving motor milestones, such as sitting up, walking, jumping, and catching a ball. Before he went to school, John seemed to be unaffected by his challenges and to have a good sense of self-esteem. When John entered kindergarten, however, his problems became much more obvious and he was teased about his clumsiness and difficulties in performing tasks. As a result, he felt inadequate and unpopular. With help from his teacher and an occupational therapist, John was able to master fine motor tasks. Also, his parents helped him by asking other children over to play. A year later, John was able to make a much smoother adjustment to first grade.

Other aspects of the body self that are important are *body cohesiveness* (i.e., sense that the body is a coherent whole and not fragmented or incomplete), *body integrity* (i.e., the ability to integrate parts of the body into a whole image), and *body boundaries* (i.e., a sense of being separate and apart from someone else, or "having one's own skin").

THEORIES OF BODY SELF

Few theories of development deal exclusively with the body or physical self, although many theories of development do address these concepts within a broader perspective. Many theories speak to the importance of the infant and young child acting on the environment (e.g., having toys and objects available that provide opportunities to feel a sense of mastery, such as mobiles the infant can activate and puzzles the young child can do) and receiving opportunities for responsive interactions in order to establish a sound sense of body self (e.g., Ayres, 1979; Greenspan & Lourie, 1981; Piaget, 1970; Rochat, 1997; Stern, 2000). They acknowledge the following:

- The child's body self develops in part from his actions on the environment that are innate and volitional.

- The development of self is embedded in relationships with significant caregivers.

- From birth, the infant has a number of action systems that are under voluntary control and she seeks out and reacts to certain stimuli in the environment.

- The infant, from birth, is aware of her separateness from the mother.

- Some infants have significant difficulties with body control and, consequently, with the development of a body scheme and positive body image.

These theories are summarized in Table 2.2.

THE IMPORTANCE OF BODY CONTROL AND A POSITIVE BODY IMAGE

From early on, infants use and move their bodies in ways that enable them to learn about them and to become effective in controlling them. As they get older, children develop a body image (see Table 2.3 for a timetable and descriptions of stages when developmental milestones occur). Caregivers play an important role in providing experiences that can enhance both body control and body image. Clinical literature describes infants and children who are deprived of adequate caregiving. Children who are brought up in isolation or in certain orphanages where they lack touch and holding as well as those whose bodies are violated through physical or sexual abuse

Table 2.2. Theories of physical/body self

Theorist	Type of theory	Major constructs
Piaget (1970)	Cognitive	The sensorimotor period from birth to 2 years; involves an emphasis on the importance of the young child's interaction with the world through perceptions and actions performed on objects
		Emphasizes that several senses of self exist in the preverbal infant, even before self-awareness
Ayres (1979)	Sensory integration	Emphasizes the effect of poor sensory integration—or the organizing of sensations from the environment—on gross and fine motor development, learning, and sense of self
		Has a well-developed assessment system and therapy that can be provided by occupational or physiotherapists
Greenspan (1992)	Developmental Structuralist	Has developed a detailed classification of the stage-specific tasks of infancy and early childhood. Stages that apply to the body self in this classification are explained next
		The first stage, from birth to 3 months, emphasizes the importance of attaining "homeostasis," or the "capacity for self-regulation and interest in the world" (1992, p. 743)
		Stresses the transformation of cognitive structures
Rochat (1997)	Ecological	Sees infant from birth as having basic "action systems" with which he actively seeks out certain features and objects of the environment
		Development occurs as a result of this linking between the infant's actions with his environment
Stern (1985)	Developmental	The body is the primary object of self-discovery for the infant
		The "emergent self," from birth to 2 months, is able to distinguish self from other
		Between 2–6 months, a "core self" develops that has a sense of agency (or making things happen), physical cohesion, and intentionality

often develop significant disorders. These disorders may include symptoms or feelings of bodily distortions or damage (Provence & Lipton, 1962; Weil, 1992).

Some infants and young children may experience caregivers as critical or nonaccepting of their appearance or bodies. Children need to see their caregivers as enjoying their bodies, hear them express in words and show in facial expressions their delight in their appearance, movements, and explorations. Without this, children do not develop a positive body image and a sense of themselves as attractive, accepted, and loveable.

Some of the disorders that are believed to be powerfully affected by abuse, lack of touch, and rejection of a child's body in infancy and early childhood include

- Anorexia nervosa and bulimia (eating disorders)
- Narcissistic and borderline personality disorder
- Character disorders manifested in criminal and violent behavior
- Promiscuity and sexual perversions
- Body dysphoric disorder
- Somatic delusions
- Self-mutilation

Table 2.3. Development of body self in typically developing children

| Age | Body control | | Body scheme and body image |
---	Fine motor	Gross motor	
Birth–1 month	Moves hand to mouth Looks at objects placed at a distance of 8–10 inches Moves arms when excited Makes a fist	Holds head up briefly when held on caregiver's shoulder or when lying on tummy Makes many movements that are involuntary and reflexive Turns head to follow moving object and tracks object briefly Turns head from side to side when face down	Begins to experience the body as defined and delineated Can be comforted and calmed through touching and rocking Already uses sensory modalities to learn about the world
2–3 months	Grasps objects with entire hand but cannot hold object yet Brings hands to midline Hands open 50% of time	Lifts chest off floor when lying on stomach Rolls from side to back and stomach to back Holds up head when propped in sitting position Kicks legs when lying on back Can be pulled to sitting position	Is increasingly aware of separateness through synchronized movement and eye-to-eye contact between caregiver and self Uses a variety of sensory modalities to get a sense of himself in the world Movements become increasingly more organized Muscle strength improves
4–8 months	Hands can now reach and grasp objects using entire hand or palmar grasp Transfers objects from one hand to another Bangs objects during play Has coordination in palm and fingers Puts objects in mouth Can now focus on small objects before reaching	Turns from back to stomach and stomach to back Crawls or creeps (i.e., locomotion) Sits alone Can bear weight on legs Lifts head when lying on back	Becomes aware of self as caregivers repeat "words" or babbling sounds that he makes Makes "bigger" movements such as banging Explores own body parts—and increasingly—caregiver's face and body Likes to look at self in mirror Perceives sense of self in space through locomotion Makes movements that are more planned and organized
9–12 months	Increasingly uses pincer movements and targets objects Bangs objects together Removes pegs from peg board Takes items out of container Claps hands Explores new objects by poking with fingers Stacks objects	Pulls up to stand Takes steps with hands held Stands alone Walks around the furniture Has good balance when sitting	Has cognitive sense of separate existence and of body self and physical whole
13–24 months	Grasps objects in a controlled way Releases objects Scribbles on paper Puts objects in container Turns pages of a book Stacks two to four blocks Puts pegs in peg board Imitates vertical and circular stroke Helps feed self with spoon	Walks alone Climbs Sits down from standing Walks backwards and sideways Throws a ball Pulls toy along Runs Stands on one foot Walks up and down stairs with hand held	Points to and names body parts Establishes accurate perception of body and recognizes self in mirror Is upset if mirror image is different (e.g., rouge on nose) Learns body is good, pleasing, and reliable

| Age | Body control | | Body scheme and body image |
	Fine motor	Gross motor	
2–4 years	Strings beads Holds pencil between thumb and fingers Cuts with scissors Imitates drawing a cross and a circle Puts small objects in container Folds paper in half Builds tower of 8–10 blocks Imitates a three-block bridge Puts simple puzzle together Copies block design Opens door by turning knob Unbuttons large buttons Builds tower of more than 10 blocks	Can run with ease Kicks ball Rides a tricycle Jumps up, forward, backward, and sideways Walks on tiptoes Throws and catches a ball Imitates movements momentarily Balances on beam momentarily Avoids obstacles Alternates feet on stairs Hops on one foot Climbs jungle gym Climbs on chair and turns around	Toilet teaching completed Loves body movement and rough-and-tumble play (which helps him gain a mapping or 'picture' of body in the brain) Shows intense interest in own body and in gender differences Engages in exploratory sex-play
4–6 years	Cuts on curved line with scissors Copies a square Reproduces several shapes and letters Draws stick person Spreads paste on one side of paper Cuts out square and circle Traces hand Puts complex puzzles together Ties own shoes Threads beads Hand dominance usually established	Runs and changes direction Can do forward roll Gallops and skips Walks on balance beam Does a somersault Does a sit-up Walks backwards heel to toe Touches toes without bending knees Pedals and steers a wheeled toy Climbs playground equipment, trees, and so forth with confidence Walks up stairs, alternating feet, unassisted	Shows continuing improvements in balance, planning of movement sequences, and sensory integration

Each individual case of these disorders is affected by a complex interplay of biological, interactional, and cultural determinants. Nevertheless, understimulation or overstimulation, excessive intrusiveness, and abuse in a child's early years often are implicated in a number of these disorders.

• •

Sally was a teenage mother whose symptoms included self-mutilation (e.g., slashing her arms), promiscuity, and drug addiction. In her childhood she had been severely neglected as well as physically and sexually abused. Her drawing of herself and her mother, depicted in Figure 2.1, dramatically indicates the lack of cohesiveness and experience of nothingness she had about her body. The despair and partial body self and the emptiness and lack of response from the mother figure graphically illustrate the effects of her early experience on her current body image and her sense of others.

MYSELF   MY MOTHER

Figure 2.1. Myself/my mother. This drawing by a woman who had been abused as a child illustrates the lack of cohesiveness and experience of nothingness the artist felt about her childhood self and body.

Areas of Development Affected by Body Control and Image

When children have difficulty developing body control and a positive body image, their development can be affected in these other areas.

Self-Esteem   Because a sense of physical attractiveness and competence has been identified as an important component of overall self-esteem, having difficulties with body image clearly can affect other areas of self-concept. A child who cannot make his body "work" as he wants to may experience a sense of frustration and inadequacy that will be more extreme if he receives criticism from parents or other caregivers and teasing by peers.

Academic Achievement   Difficulties with fine motor control may well influence early adjustment to child care or kindergarten and affect the ability to draw and print letters and numbers. If the difficulty is extreme, it could influence the ability to use a computer. Children with sensory integration difficulties who find it difficult to make sense of and integrate information from various sources can also have difficulty with early learning. Such early failures may create a negative experience of school and even lead to later failures and a tendency to drop out of school.

Social Competence   Because children increasingly rely on some ability for physical play to connect with their peers, children who experience difficulties with body control may withdraw from playing with peers—particularly on the playground during recess. Conversely, children who have physical prowess or sports ability may become popular and accepted by other children.

THE DEVELOPMENT OF BODY SELF

In this section, the development of gross and fine motor control—as well as of body scheme and body image—are outlined (see Table 2.3 on page 98). These are jointly considered as part of the process of developing a body self. The development of fine and gross motor abilities in the early years is well documented, but the process of establishing a body scheme and body self is less clear. A sense of a positive and coherent body self develops from the child's own sense of achievement as motor milestones are reached and body control becomes easier. It also results from caregivers' interactions with the infant and young child. Young children whose interactions include positive emotionality and sensitive responsiveness develop a more complex under-standing of their body parts. It also is clear that a positive body image develops at least partially from caregivers' reactions to children's movements and explorations and acceptance of their physical abilities and appearance. This approval or acceptance can come initially from holding, touching, and rocking; later it may come from looks of approval, verbal encouragement, and acknowledgment of the attractiveness of the child's body and his or her control over it. The se-quence of the development of a body self is outlined here.

Birth to One Month

Although much of the movement that goes on in the first month of life is reflexive and invol untary, a newborn infant already can interpret some of his body sensations. His sense of touch is well developed at birth and sets off many of the innate reflexes such as rooting and pushing a cloth off his face. The newborn also is responsive to the sensations of movement and gravity. Carrying and rocking can comfort and calm him, and when his head is held against someone's shoulder, the infant will try and lift it up. Similarly, the infant will practice using all senses during periods of responsiveness and will gradually improve his ability to use them in an or-ganized way. As the infant is held, fed, rocked and responded to sensitively in face-to-face in-teractions, he increasingly becomes aware of his body as separate from his mother's.

Two to Three Months

The infant's ability to control her muscle function develops from head to toe. The eyes and head are the first to be under voluntary control. First, the infant learns to hold her head up with her neck muscles and lifts her chest off the floor when lying on her stomach. During this pe-riod, the infant's hands are increasingly more open than clenched and she begins to reach out to objects, although her aim is lacking. She can grasp an object although she cannot let it go vol-untarily. Increasingly, the infant develops a sense of herself in the world as she rolls and begins the process of gaining control of her hands.

Four to Eight Months

The infant makes immense gains during this period, as locomotion becomes possible and the infant moves from one place to another. This experience gives him information about space and the distance between objects in the environment. Moving, in addition to seeing, allows the infant to understand what he sees. Big movements are now possible, and the infant reaches and grasps objects and bangs them, feeling a sense of control over his world. His play with objects is now more organized and shows the ability for motor planning. He becomes able to sit alone, making it possible for him to play with objects, particularly as he can now use his thumb and forefinger to pick up small objects. Also, he is now capable of planning hand movements to put objects together and to transfer them from one hand to another. He now enjoys looking at himself in the mirror and explores his own body parts and his caregiver's face. All of these experiences allow an increasing sense of independence and of understanding his body boundaries.

Nine to Twelve Months

This is a time of significant change as an infant crawls for longer distances and walks around the furniture, seeing a whole new view of the world and space. As she moves around and discovers more objects in the world, she can increasingly organize and integrate sensations and adaptive responses to them. During this period, she is increasingly interested in her own body and in examining that of her caregiver, particularly her face. As babbling increases and others respond to it, the infant becomes more and more aware of herself as a social and separate person.

Thirteen to Twenty-Four Months

At this stage, the infant increasingly reaches out to touch and feel objects. During this period, the child gains increasing awareness of how his body moves and how things in the world operate. He picks up objects and releases them, walks up and down stairs, throws a ball, and begins to run. He is into everything, including cupboards and shelves. Children at this age love roughhousing, wrestling, and piggyback rides. All of the information the toddler gains from these types of play helps increase his feeling of his body or body scheme. As the child is allowed to explore and learns how to do things, he feels good about his body. He now has an accurate perception of his body and recognizes himself in the mirror. He is upset or embarrassed if he feels his body scheme has been violated, for example, if blush is put on his nose when he is in front of the mirror. Climbing, although frustrating for parents, gives him an increasing understanding of visual space perception.

Two to Four Years

Children at this age are becoming increasingly aware of their body parts and gender differences. Exploratory play between children is common. A child continues to enjoy rough-and-tumble play and loves to kick a ball, ride a tricycle, jump, balance on a beam, catch a ball, and hop. She can also use a crayon and scissors, can string beads, and can copy a design made with blocks. Many skills that will be used in school are gained, including putting puzzles together and copying shapes and letters. During this time, toilet training is usually accomplished. At this age many children seem to be in constant motion as they run, hop, climb, swing, and jump.

Climbing gives a toddler an increasing understanding of visual space perception.

Four to Six Years

By the time the child is 6 years old he has acquired most of the gross motor skills, at least in rudimentary form. He now gallops and skips, can do a somersault, and runs and changes direction. There also are significant improvements in the child's ability to plan movements and to balance. For example, he can walk backwards, heel to toe; walk on a balance beam; and touch his toes without bending his knees. He is also much more able to control small objects and can target some of them, performing such tasks as tying his shoelaces and cutting on a line with scissors. The child now should have a full sense of body integration and constancy as well as of positive body image. He should perceive himself as competent and able to make things happen in physical space.

IMPORTANT RESEARCH FINDINGS

Although certain earlier theorists such as Freud and Piaget considered aspects of the body as important in development, much of the research that has addressed the development of the body self has been carried out in recent years. As well, the psychology of the human body had received very little attention until quite recently (Cash & Pruzinsky, 1990; Santostefano & Callicchia, 1992). As a consequence, the importance of body control or body image has often not been considered when treating social and emotional difficulties. This brief review of research will consider the following topics:

Many children seem to be in constant motion as they run, hop, climb, swing, and jump.

- Early development of the body self

- The effect of body image on development

- Various types of motor difficulties

- The effect of various interventions on body self and other areas of development

Early Development of the Body Self

New research techniques have spawned a resurgence of interest in understanding motor and physical development. Writers and researchers such as Meltzoff and Moore (1995a), Stern (2000), and Thelen and associates (Thelen, Corbetta, Kamm, & Spencer, 1993; Thelen & Ulrich, 1991) have analyzed movement at a molecular level and have challenged traditional models of the development of body schema. Through a variety of ingenious experiments, researchers have been able to consistently challenge the view that newborn infants are in a state of fusion or are undifferentiated from their primary caregivers and the rest of the environment. Instead, research has been able to prove that there are innate, basic action systems in place from the beginning that enable the infant to explore and to act upon the world and which provide the infant with an early sense of body self (Thelen et al., 1993; Thelen & Ulrich, 1991).

It is clear that among typically developing infants the five primary sensory modalities (smell, vision, hearing, taste, and touch) are functional from the moment of birth. Porges also has discussed an additional modality that he calls *interoception*. He describes this as "conscious feelings of and unconscious monitoring of bodily processes" (1993, p. 12). A great deal of research has documented the infant's ability to use these various sensory modalities.

Prior to the 1960s, many professionals believed that the infant could not see or hear at birth. A number of experiments that measured infant gaze were able to demonstrate not only that newborns could see objects placed at an optimal distance of 8–10 inches (Bronson, 1974; McCall, 1979; Salapatek, 1975) but also that they actually had preferences in what they looked at and sought out certain visual stimuli. Fantz (1963) was, for example, able to show that infants prefer looking at the human face to looking at other images, while Sherrod (1981) showed that they preferred images in the vertical (or top–bottom) plane, a characteristic of the human face. Hearing was explored similarly. In these studies, infants clearly demonstrated that from birth they could turn to and locate a sound (Sinnett, Pisoni, & Aslin, 1983). Infants were also found to prefer the human voice to other sounds and would suck more to activate the voice of their mother than the voice of other people (DeCasper & Fifer, 1980). Even more remarkable, it has been demonstrated by the use of habituation and sucking that 2-day-old infants can distinguish between the sounds of "ba" and "pa" (Morse & Cowan, 1982). The senses of smell and taste, which are intricately related in both children and adults, have been studied less than have the senses of vision and hearing. Infants detect and can distinguish among odors soon after birth, but it is not known which they find pleasant. Researchers have demonstrated that newborns turn more to the smell of their mother's breast pad than to that of another woman's (Macfarlane, 1975), however. In order to distinguish preferences for different tastes, researchers have studied the facial expressions of infants while they are being fed different substances. Newborns have been shown to distinguish three of the basic tastes—sweet, sour, and bitter—and to respond in a predictable way. Infants respond with relaxation and enjoyment to sweet tastes such as sucrose, and with facial grimaces to sour and bitter tastes. No distinguishable facial response has been shown to salty flavors (Ganchrow, Steiner, & Munif, 1983; Rosenstein & Oster, 1988; Steiner, 1977).

Sensitivity to touch has been demonstrated to elicit a number of reflexes in the newborn. For example, a touch on the cheek triggers rooting (or turning towards the location of the touch) and pressure on the sole of the foot elicits the Babinski reflex (i.e., spreading of the toes). Although the infant responds to touch over the whole body, the hands and mouth appear to be most responsive. Most infants respond positively to touch, snuggle in when held and, as will be outlined in the last section of the research findings in this chapter, actually show increased regulation and improved development when they receive properly administered massage. Evidence for the sixth sense or interoception noted by Porges (1993) has been more difficult to demonstrate because it describes the infant's subjective experience and involves very complex systems of various body organs and sensory and motor pathways in the brain. Research requires measurement and monitoring of these complex internal bodily processes, including the release of various hormones and vagal activity.

One area of research that has considered the infant's experience of his body has been the study of their behavioral and physiological responses to pain. Research since the 1980s has contradicted earlier observations that infants do not experience pain. Infants consistently cry and show painful facial expressions in response to inoculations, heel lances, and other medical interventions (Franck, 1986). Even more significant, infants show physiological responses to pain, such as increases in heart rate, blood pressure, and cortisol levels (Anand & Hickey, 1987; Owens & Todt, 1984). As well, memory research suggests that these experiences, although not available to immediate recall, can be more readily reactivated under subsequent stressful medical procedures so that the infant shows increased sensitivity to pain over time (Fitzgerald, Millard, & MacIntosh, 1988).

Even more important for the early development of body self is the infant's capacity for cross-modal perception (i.e., the ability to integrate the information gained from different senses). Evidence exists that infants have this capacity from birth; for example, they turn their eyes to locate a sound. In an interesting study conducted by Kuhl and Meltzoff (1982), infants were simultaneously shown two videos of the faces of people speaking with the sounds in one of the videos synchronized with the movements of the lips and not in the other. It was shown that they looked more frequently at the video where information from vision and sound were synchronized.

Vision and sound are not the only senses that have been tested for coordination. Vision and touch also have been studied. In one study using two sets of pacifiers (one smooth and another with knobby protrusions) (Meltzoff & Borton, 1979), infants sucked on one type of pacifier and were then shown the two types. They looked longer at the one with which they had had the tactile experience.

The capacities that have been outlined relate to sensory abilities. Others relate more to the infant's discovery and understanding of his body and movements and how this relates to other people. The study of imitation in the newborn has been a source of evidence for these innate action systems as well as infant's awareness of the bodies of others. In a fascinating series of experiments, Meltzoff and associates have been able to demonstrate imitation of tongue protrusions and facial expressions in infants as young as 42 minutes old (Meltzoff & Moore, 1983), a finding that has been replicated in approximately 20 studies. This capacity means that infants not only are able to recognize the independent movement of another person but also can match it with their own movements. Other studies have demonstrated that infants are capable of deferred imitation, and will imitate what they have seen up to 24 hours later (Meltzoff & Moore, 1995a, 1995b.) (See Figure 2.2.)

Other evidence for these innate action systems has come from the unusual examples of aplasic limbs and the body recognition of twins who were conjoined. Seventeen percent of infants who are born without limbs or who have limbs amputated very early have been shown to experience phantom limbs or to "receive messages" from limbs that do not exist, suggesting an innate body scheme that includes the missing limbs (Scatena, 1990). As described by Stern (2000), he and his colleagues carried out experiments with female conjoined twins who did not share organs but who were connected and always faced each other. The researchers noticed that sometimes they sucked on their own and the other twin's fingers. It was found that when the other twin's finger was removed from one of the twin's mouth she did not attempt any movements in order to reestablish the sucking. When sucking their own fingers, however, both twins resisted having their own fingers removed as well as the interruption of sucking, indicating that each twin knew when she was sucking her own fingers and was aware of a coherence of her fingers with her body self.

From very early on, infants learn about their own bodies and movement, at first by exploring with their mouths. By age 2 months, they systematically manually explore their own bodies, beginning with their heads and moving on to their mouths, fingers, trunks, knees, and feet. They also look at and explore a part of their bodies that is touched or tickled. In addition to this kind of self-exploratory behavior, infants learn about their bodies by self-produced movements and actions with people and objects in the environment. This can be sequential. Infants might spend hours *looking* at their hands, for example, before using them to reach for objects (Van der Meer, 1993).

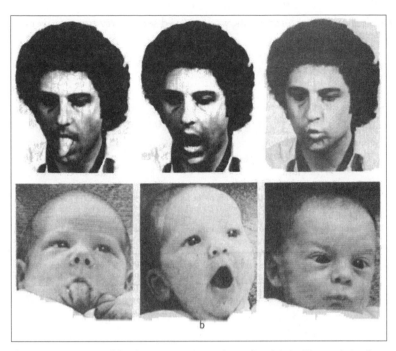

Figure 2.2. Imitation of facial expressions in newborns. (Reprinted with permission from Meltzoff, A.N., & Moore, M.K. Imitation of facial and manual gestures by human neonates. Copyright 1977 American Association for the Advancement of Science. *Science, 198,* 75–78.)

A number of studies have shown that infants have an inborn desire or volition to learn about the world and to make things happen. For example, very young infants move their heads or toes or suck more to activate interesting mobiles or sounds (Rovee-Collier & Fagen, 1981). Infants past 6 months recognize gestures that imitate their own and show more attention to those that are imitations of theirs and thus under their control than those that are not imitated (Meltzoff & Moore, 1995b). As well as touching and observing their bodies, infants learn about speaking by listening to their own voices while experiencing the kinesthetic and proprioceptive feedback of their actions. Researchers such as Stern (1985) have also noted that infants appear to move with the rhythm of the speech of caregivers, especially during face-to-face interactions.

By the time they are 3 months old, infants can recognize their own movements. Experiments have been carried out during which infants perceive themselves in the mirror and watch videotapes of their own leg movements as well as the leg movements of other infants. Although the infant does not recognize herself in the mirror until 18 months, she does, as early as 6 months, distinguish between herself, her mother, and a peer in the mirror (Field, 1979). At as early as 3 months of age, she is interested in watching her own movements reflected in that mirror image and will explore the visual movement seen in the mirror (Amsterdam, 1972). By 6 months of age, infants consistently look longer at images of the leg movements of other babies than at images of their own movements because of the novelty of the image, it is hypothesized (Bahrick & Watson, 1985). Other experiments by Rochat and his colleagues produced similar results; they found that infants looked longer at images of their legs that were distorted in some way than at those of their legs kicking in a normal position (Rochat & Morgan, 1993). These experiments have been noted by Rochat to be interpretable "as an early ex-

pression of a calibrated intermodal space of the body or, in other words, the early expression of a perceptually based body schema" (1997, p. 113).

The Effects of Body Image on Development

In the previous section, the development of the early body self and body schema is described. The development of body image takes much longer and requires an understanding of the body as 1) distinct from others, 2) stable and having continuity over time, and 3) cohesive and integrated.

Although, as noted previously, these understandings have their beginnings in the infant's perceptions and actions on the environment, in order to have a body image, the child requires the cognitive ability for reflection and evaluation of self (Butterworth, 1992). As described by Feiner (1987, 1988), children seem to pass through predictable stages, obtaining their body images by approximately 5 years of age. Inagaki and Hatano (1993) found that 6-year-old children who were asked to construct a puzzle of the human body and answer questions about parts of their bodies showed a capacity for understanding the cohesion and integrity of their bodies, but they expressed some anxiety about the possibility of losing body parts.

Recent research has shown that an individual's body image, or the way he views his body or physical appearance, has significant relationship with self-esteem, satisfaction with life, and other indices of personality and psychosocial functioning (Archer & Cash, 1985; Burns & Farina, 1990; Cash, Winstead, & Janda, 1986). Very little of this research has been carried out with young children, however.

In a *Psychology Today* survey of nearly 30,000 respondents, the authors selected a stratified, random sample that represented the population of the United States' sex by age distribution (Cash et al., 1986). In this survey, nearly one fourth of men and one third of women reported generally negative feelings about their appearance or body image. The respondents most commonly reported dissatisfaction with their weight. Adolescents, especially females, reported the most negative appearance evaluations. Another finding was that negative evaluations of fitness and health were associated with lower levels of social adjustment and even depression.

In studies carried out with children, body image has been linked with self-esteem. Krantz, Friedberg, and Andrews (1985) found that for fifth-grade children, self-perceived attractiveness was highly correlated with measures of self-esteem. Self-esteem also was related to popularity and ratings of physical attractiveness by peers, suggesting that children's subjective ratings of how they were perceived were quite accurate by this age. Studies have found links between body weight and body image, with overweight children and adolescents more likely to have negative body images (Flannery-Schroeder & Chrisler, 1996; Pierce & Wardle, 1993). In a study that examined this relationship, Mendelson and White (1985) noted that their findings varied with age and gender. At 11–14 years, being overweight was found to affect body image adversely for boys and not for girls. From 14 on, being overweight affected girls' body image, but not boys'. The researchers suggest that this difference may be related to the fact that society views the ideal size and shape of boys and girls differently, with the ideal girl being slender and the boy, bulky and strong. Studies with child populations have also found a link between having a low body image and depression. Nelson (1988) found that children with depression rated their body image lower than learning impaired or normal controls. Asarnow and Bates (1988) and McCabe and Marwit (1993) reported similar findings. In the latter study it was

found that dissatisfaction with one's body was the strongest predictor of depression for both boys and girls.

Although much of the research on body image has considered the effect of physical appearance (Patzer & Burke, 1988) and confirmed its importance, it also is clear that many children struggle with a variety of other difficulties with body control that significantly affect other aspects of their development. Some of these are identified later in this chapter, and research is described on therapeutic interventions that are effective or show promise in alleviating some of these difficulties.

The Effect of Motor Difficulties on Body Self

Children with hearing or visual impairments or physical or intellectual disabilities clearly face overwhelming challenges in developing a sense of body cohesion, integration, and control (Jennings & MacTurk, 1995). In addition, there are a number of other children who have less obvious disabilities but who face similar difficulties.

The growing body of knowledge surrounding sensory integration difficulties accelerated in the 1960s. Sensory integration problems have been called minimal brain dysfunction, although they seldom show up in brain scans and may not be diagnosed by many neurologists. Children with sensory integration difficulties may have problems processing information from any of the senses and with organizing the flow of sensory information to provide accurate information about the world and themselves (Rose & Orlian, 1991). These difficulties may result in problems with coordination of fine motor and gross motor activities and in motor planning. Learning disabilities also may occur and the child may have difficulties with fine motor control, speech, reading, spelling, writing, concentration, and behavior. Perhaps most significantly, children with these problems have a sense of a lack of body control, and have difficulties that interfere with many areas of daily life, such as understanding body language cues, understanding and processing language, and performing everyday activities such as writing neatly and clearly. They may eventually develop a poor body image as a result (Ayres, 1972, 1975; 1976; Chesson, McKay, & Stephenson, 1991; Hulme & Lord, 1986; Mailloux, 1980; Schaffer, Law, Polatajko, & Miller, 1989).

The Diagnostic Classification of Mental Health and Developmental Disorders of Infancy and Early Childhood (ZERO TO THREE/National Center for Clinical Infant Programs, 1994) has identified groups of children with regulatory disorders and with "multisystem developmental disorders" who may, in addition to other difficulties, have problems with sensory integration (DeGangi & Greenspan, 1988; Greenspan, 1992). DeGangi and Greenspan (1988) tested groups of infants between 4–18 months with difficult temperaments and learning delays, as well as typically developing infants for various aspects of sensory integration. They found that children with difficult temperaments showed problems with tactile defensiveness (64%–86%); adaptive motor responses, motor control (50%), and ocular motor control (43%–82%); compared with only 11%–19% of the typically developing infants. Along with these problems, DeGangi and associates described the infants with regulatory disorders as being fussy, irritable, lacking the ability for self-calming, hypersensitive to a variety of stimuli, and distractible (DeGangi, 2000; DeGangi, Craft, & Castellan, 1991; DeGangi, DiPietro, Greenspan, & Porges, 1991). Infants who have demonstrated difficulties in regulating their autonomic nervous systems, for example, have been found to have higher resting vagal tone (i.e., heart rate activity) and

inconsistent vagal reactivity (DeGangi, DiPietro, et al., 1991). Children with multisystem developmental disorder also have significant difficulties with processing sensations, motor planning, hyper or hyposensitivities, auditory processing, communication, and in establishing emotional and social relationships with primary caregivers (Greenspan, Wieder, & Simons, 1998).

The Effects of Various Interventions on Body Self and Other Areas of Development

A number of treatment strategies have been outlined to increase body control in children with sensory integrative difficulties. One type of intervention that has been used is multisensory teaching (Bradley, 1981; Hulme, 1981). The technique uses visual (seeing the shape), auditory (hearing the name), and kinesthetic (tracing and speech movements) sensations simultaneously for learning letters, shapes, and so forth. A study that used the technique with children ages 3.2–4.7 and 8 years found that the method, compared with visual stimulation alone, increased verbal recognition and word recall. The ability to correctly associate the letter with the visual stimulus was not improved, however (Hulme, Monk, & Ives, 1987).

A much more complicated and controversial intervention was originally developed by Ayres in which the child is provided with controlled "sensory input, especially the input from the vestibular system (i.e., a system of nerves in the brain that respond to changes in position and movement and is responsible for balance), muscles and joints, and skin in such a way that the child spontaneously forms the adaptive responses that integrate those sensations" (1979, p. 140).

During therapy, special equipment is used—such as a scooter board, ramp, and bolster swing—and children practice individually prescribed movements that respond to the vestibular, proprioceptive, and tactile sensations provided by the equipment and exercises. Ayres conducted various experiments to evaluate if the treatment was effective in remediating learning problems. Some of the research has been criticized because the originator of the theory conducted it and because the control groups did not receive the same amount of individualized time as the treatment groups. In general, however, children who received sensory integrative therapy made greater gains in reading and in overall academic achievement than those who received no treatment or a special education program that did not include this type of treatment. It was identified, however, that children with difficulties with the vestibular system were most likely to benefit from the intervention (Ayres, 1972, 1976, 1978).

DeGangi and associates have suggested that infants and young children with regulatory disorders can benefit from a number of approaches: sensory integrative therapy, parent guidance, and child-centered activities with parent–child interactions allowing the child to lead and choose the play. They also recommend that caregivers use specific techniques in order to work with children with special characteristics such as distractibility and hypersensitivity or hyperarousal (see Chapter 1). Providing parent guidance involves giving parents support and practical management techniques to help their child with sleeping, feeding, behavior problems, and so forth (DeGangi, 2000; DeGangi, Craft, et al., 1991; DeGangi, Wietlisbach, Goodin, & Scheiner, 1993). In a study that compared intervention to enhance the parent–child interaction with structured therapy with prescribed exercises for the child, it was found that fine motor skills were improved more when the focus was on the interaction, while, on the other hand, gross motor and functional skills improved more with the structured therapy. The researchers concluded that children need both types of treatment (DeGangi et al., 1993).

The types of interventions that have been used and evaluated the most are those using touch and ways to enhance closeness between parent and child (massage therapy), and kinesthetic (rocking) sensations. Many of these interventions have been carried out with special populations such as premature infants in neonatal intensive care nurseries, small-for-gestational-age infants, cocaine- and HIV-exposed infants, infants of depressed mothers, and children with autism (Field, 1995, 1998). Massage also has frequently been used as a part of child-care practices with typically developing infants and in many parts of the world (Field, 1998). Montagu (1971) was one of the first to write about the importance of touch and described it as being as necessary for a child's development as food and air. Infants as early as 7 weeks after conception have been shown to respond to tactile stimulation around the mouth cavity, and it has been shown that touch is more developed than eyesight or hearing at birth. Research on animals and on the outcomes of infants who have been living in institutions have clearly demonstrated how tactile deprivation adversely affects growth, learning, socialization, the capacity for empathy, and the capacity to raise children (Suomi, 1995). In a meta-analysis of studies of the use of massage carried out before 1987, it was found that medium-sized effects were found for children who received massage compared with children in control and comparison groups who did not receive the intervention (Ottenbacher, Muller, Brandt, Heintzelman, Hojem, & Sharpe, 1987). Studies of preterm infants who received massage therapy have shown that they gained weight, performed better on developmental tests, and, on average, were hospitalized far fewer days than those who did not receive massage therapy (Adamson-Macedo, Dattani, Wilson, & de Carvalho, 1993; Barnard & Bee, 1983; Field et al., 1986; Watt, 1990). With HIV-exposed infants, mothers were taught to perform the massage; again, infants gained more weight, achieved higher scores on the Brazelton Scales, and achieved better performance scores on a stress behavior test (Scafidi et al., 1990). Similar results were found for infants exposed to cocaine who received massage therapy; in addition, they had fewer postnatal complications and exhibited fewer stress behaviors (Wheedon, Scafidi, Field, Ironson, Valdeon, & Bandstra, 1993).

Although these results are interesting and encouraging, the underlying physiological changes that contribute to the identified improvements must be identified. At the time this book was written, Field was investigating whether massage stimulates growth because, as she suspected, it "leads to a release of gastrointestinal food absorption hormones, probably stimulated by vagal activity" (1995, p. 10). Some researchers have cautioned about the use of massage for all infants and the need to individualize touching and massage and to be aware of possible tactile defensiveness and the risk of overloading very fragile infants. It is also important to note that a light stroking that can be experienced as a tickle stimulation and aversive is not recommended; rather, massage should involve moderate to deep pressure and smooth stroking movements (Field, 1995; Gorski, 1991; Harrison, 1985).

Another approach to the use of touch has been to increase the amount of physical contact between mother and infant by encouraging the use of soft baby carriers. In a study in which mothers were provided with either a soft carrier or an infant seat in which babies can sit when not being held, researchers found that infants of mothers who used the carrier were significantly more likely to be securely attached (83%) compared to the control group who used the infant seat (38%). The researchers concluded that the close contact made mothers more responsive to their infants' cues, thus encouraging secure attachment (Anisfeld, Casper, Nozyce, & Cunningham, 1990). In a similar study, Field and colleagues compared the effect of holding an infant facing inward or facing outward. They concluded that both were important, with the inward position most useful for soothing and calming and the outward position encouraging active awake time (Field, Malphurs, Carraway, & Pelaez-Nogueras, 1996). Other researchers have found that individualized holding and handling of very low birth weight infants, if used to contain the infant, can improve the infant's state organization, especially in sleep states (Brecker, Brazy, & Grunwald, 1997). Also of importance are the findings in studies that show that when mothers provided touch during the still-face procedure (i.e., mother does not react to the infant's cues) infants smiled more and attended for longer periods than infants who were not touched during the procedure (Stack & Arnold, 1998; Stack & Muir, 1992). The researchers concluded that touch was able to compensate to some degree for lack of facial expressiveness and talking from the mothers in the still-face procedure.

These studies show that a variety of intervention models and techniques targeted at the level of the sensory system and other aspects of the body provide effective mechanisms to improve infants' and children's functioning when they have body control and other physical difficulties. What also is obvious is that when caregivers have children practice early motor skills, this can help them become more understanding of their bodies and assist them with the regulation of eating and sleeping. These skills can, in turn, serve as important ways to enhance growth and development in all aspects of functioning. In other words, a variety of approaches that emphasize the development of a child's body self and body control are important in order to encourage optimal development and a positive body image.

THE GROWTH-PROMOTING ENVIRONMENT: PRINCIPLES OF DEVELOPING BODY CONTROL AND A POSITIVE BODY IMAGE

Although much of an infant's or a young child's ability to control her body and to obtain a positive body image is gained by her own volition and excitement at exploring her body and the

Join the child in fun motor activities.

world, interactions and experiences provided by caregivers can help significantly. Principles of how to encourage the positive development of body self are described here in greater detail (see Table 2.4).

PRINCIPLE 1: *Provide the infant and young child with plenty of experiences of touch and physical contact.*

As pointed out previously, a significant body of research has demonstrated that touch and physical contact can enhance infants' and young children's development. Touch has been shown to be important for development in both nonhuman and human primates. Baby monkeys seek out touch or contact rather than milk when upset, and lack of touch has been implicated in failure to develop sociability in the same species (Champoux, Coe, Shanberg, Kuhn, & Suomi, 1989; Harlow, 1958; Suomi, 1991). In human populations, some researchers have claimed that touch and early contact immediately after birth encourage the mother's bonding with her newborn (Kennell, Trause, & Klaus, 1975; Klaus & Kennell, 1976). As has been discussed, touching in the form of massage improves weight gain in premature infants, and holding a young infant upright can encourage alertness. The effective use of therapeutic touch to reduce stress, speed healing, and improve the well-being of the acutely ill and elderly are increasingly acknowledged. With infants and young children, body experiences are one of the primary means for establishing relationships with others, and without touch, holding, and rocking, children may develop a body scheme that is distorted or that lacks integration.

Generally, during daily caregiving, the infant receives contact and touch as a part of bathing, feeding, and diapering. Holding and rocking need to be provided as a means of soothing or calming, particularly if the infant is fussy or crying. Toddlers and preschoolers continue to need to be touched and held and often seek out contact when tired or upset or during quiet, more intimate moments. It is important to be aware if a child is tactile defensive or very sensitive to touch or handling. Some of these children may respond to touch if it provides deep pressure, while other children may need to be held a little away from the body, using a soft voice, eye-to-eye contact, and hand holding instead of close holding.

Table 2.4. Principles for encouraging body control and a positive body image

Principle 1	Provide the infant and young child with plenty of experiences of touch and physical contact.
Principle 2	Encourage toddlers and preschoolers to get to know their body and body parts.
Principle 3	Provide interesting toys and fine motor activities that the infant and young child enjoys in order to encourage fine motor control.
Principle 4	Provide activities that allow for the integration of a number of senses.
Principle 5	Join the child in fun motor and movement activities.
Principle 6	Help the child to develop appropriate eating, sleeping, and toileting routines. Avoid creating battlegrounds around them.
Principle 7	Respond to children's early sexual curiosity by providing answers to questions, acceptance of their interest, and appropriate limits for sexual play.
Principle 8	Express delight in the child's body and her control of it. Adapt to her physical self.
Principle 9	Respond to body language and validate the reality of the experience being expressed.

Massage for infants and young children may relax them as well as making them more alert and attentive. A typical massage is given for about 16 minutes per day using baby oil, with the child first lying on her back. In this position, firm strokes are provided on the head, chest, stomach, legs and feet, and arms. The child then lies on her stomach, and her back is stroked along the length of back and on the sides (see Auckett, 1989; McClure, 1989; Schneider, 1989).

PRINCIPLE 2:   *Encourage toddlers and preschoolers to get to know their body and body parts.*

Teaching children the names of their body parts and engaging them in activities that encourage familiarity with their bodies facilitates the development of children's accurate body scheme.

In a study that assessed children between the ages of 11 and 25 months for their ability to point to body parts on themselves and a doll, Witt, Cermak, and Coster (1990) found the following results:

- At 12 months, the majority of children (about 70%) were unable to point to any body parts.

- At 24 months, the majority of children (90%) could point to 11 body parts.

- Children learned to identify *eyes, nose, mouth,* and *hair* first.

- Children quickly learned to identify *fingers, hands, toes,* and *feet* early, but *neck* and *chin* as well as joints such as *knee* and *elbow* were learned later.

- Girls tended to learn names of body parts earlier than did boys.

No significant differences existed between the children's *ability* to point to body parts on themselves or on a doll, but children do differ in their *preferences* regarding pointing out body parts on themselves or on a doll.

Most children are very interested in learning about their bodies, but some may have motor planning or language difficulties and find the learning more difficult. Most important is that the children enjoy the learning.

Activities for Encouraging Body Awareness   Here are some activities to help caregivers encourage a child's body awareness:

- *Mirror, mirror:* From very early on, an infant can learn about his body and distinguish it from someone else's. Using a full-length mirror, have your child look into it and show him his body parts. As he gets older, ask questions such as, "What do you see? What do you like best?" Also, use the mirror to help the child discover how he is different from other people. Stand with the child so you both can be seen in the mirror. Point to yourself and your child using his name and yours (e.g., "Alex," "Mom"). Point to all body parts.

- *Body tracing:* Have the child lie down on heavy brown wrapping paper and trace an outline of her body. Help her cut the outline out and color it. When it is cut out, hang it up where everyone can see it.

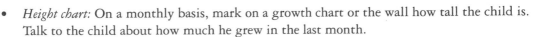

- *Height chart:* On a monthly basis, mark on a growth chart or the wall how tall the child is. Talk to the child about how much he grew in the last month.

- *Body knowledge:* This can be done at any time, but is particularly useful when the child is getting dressed or being bathed. The game consists of asking the child to name and describe the function of various parts of her body: "Show me your head. What is on your head? What is inside your head?" "Where is your heart? What does a heart do? What would happen if you didn't have a heart?"

The activity can be modified to suit the child's age, language skills, and knowledge of the human body:

- *My magic body:* Sit facing the child with music playing. Clap to the rhythm of the music. Start to pat individual body parts and call them by name. Begin with the most familiar ones: eyes, nose, mouth, and hair. Then move to knees, feet, toes, and so forth. Follow the child's lead if she selects a body part herself. Then, explore how the body part can move and compare this with objects like a swing or the hands on a clock.

- *Sing a song:* Action songs can be great ways to get children to know their bodies and learn about their body parts (see Figure 2.3).

It is also important that children learn the proper names for their genitals. The words can be introduced as the child learns the names for their other body parts. Parents who are uncomfortable with this can usually understand that it is important for the child to have the correct words in the event of inappropriate touching or even sexual abuse.

PRINCIPLE 3: *Provide interesting toys and fine motor activities that the infant and young child enjoys in order to encourage fine motor control.*

From a very early age, it is important that infants and young children are provided with toys, opportunities, and activities that give them a chance to learn and practice new fine and gross skills, so they have a sense of being able to control their bodies (see Table 2.5). Most children have the desire to reach out and to manipulate objects placed within their reach; others may need much more assistance and encouragement. It is important for caregivers to anticipate the next level of learning and to assist children to achieve it.

These activities may need to be adapted to the special characteristics of some children. When children have obvious physical challenges, the need for adapting the activities may be clearer than when children have less obvious difficulties, such as those of motor planning, eye–hand coordination, or sensory integration. Table 2.6 gives some activities for hands-on learning.

PRINCIPLE 4: *Provide activities that allow for the integration of a number of senses.*

The major sensory systems are *auditory* (hearing), *visual* (seeing), *olfactory* (smelling), *taste*, *vestibular* (gravity and movements), *tactile* (touch), and *proprioceptive* (muscles and joints). These systems are functional at birth, but develop significantly in the early years. As mentioned previously,

Action Songs

An Elephant Goes

The elephant goes
Like this, like that
(Move slowly like an elephant)

He's terribly big and he's terribly fat.
(Stand up, reach arms up high)

He has no fingers,
(Close hand over fist)

He has no toes,
But goodness, gracious
What a nose!
(Touch nose)

My Hands

On my head my hands I place
(Place hands on head)

On my shoulders,
(Place hands on shoulders)

On my face,
(Place hand on face)

On my hips,
(Place hands on hips)

And at my side,
(Drop hands to sides)

Then behind me they will hide,
(Hide hands behind back)

I will hold them up so high,
(Raise hands high above head)

Quickly make my fingers fly,
(Wiggle fingers)

Hold them out in front of me

Swiftly clap them. One, two, three!
(Clap, clap, clap)

Clap Your Hands

Clap your hands, clap your hands
Clap them just like me
Touch your shoulders, touch your shoulders
Touch them just like me
Tap your knees, tap your knees
Tap them just like me
Shake your head, shake your head
Shake it just like me
Clap your hands, clap your hands
Then let them quiet be.

My Body

My eyes can see
My mouth can talk
My ears can hear
My feet can walk
My nose can smell
My lids can flutter
My hand can write

Hands Clap

Hands clap
Fingers wriggle
Arms wave
Thumbs wiggle
Toes waggle
Heels thump
Legs run
Feet jump

These are _____ Fingers

These are Lisa's fingers
(Touch the baby's fingers)

These are Lisa's toes
(Touch her toes)

This is Lisa's bellybutton
Round and round it goes.
(Run your fingers around her bellybutton.)

Figure 2.3.   Some examples of action songs that can encourage children's sense of body self.

Provide interesting toys and fine motor activities.

many children who have emotional and social difficulties may have various types of sensory integration dysfunction. The problem is not with the sensory input itself but with the child's ability to process and make meaning of it, as well as to integrate information from the different sensory modalities. This makes learning difficult and may result in the child feeling uncomfortable about himself and his body.

Table 2.5. Activities and toys that encourage fine and gross motor skills

Gross motor		Fine motor	
Toy or activity	What it does	Toy or activity	What it does
Rocking	Calms child and provides kinesthetic stimulation	Rattle	Encourages grasping and auditory and visual processing
Running	Can provide release of energy and sense of joy and fun	Finger play songs	Fun way to use hands and fingers and to learn to control them. Also encourages imitation
Swinging	Improves balance and eye–hand coordination	Banging things together	Encourages the ability to cross the midline (or to play with objects) and transfer them from hand to hand across the chest
Waltzing	Integrates balance, listening, and motion when done to music	Copying lines and letters	Improves eye-hand coordination
Jumping	Aids control of legs and synchronizing with arms. Improves balance	Hammering pegs	Improves motor planning as child learns to control movement
Climbing	Integrates movement sensations with visual information and strengthens space perception	Large wooden beads	Learns to use pincer movement, improves fine motor control, and use of two hands
Tunnels	Encourages space perception, crawling activity, and sequencing of movements	Eating finger foods	Encourages eye-hand coordination and pincer movement. Integrates taste and sight and can be fun and rewarding

Table 2.6. Some activities for hands-on learning (activities are arranged from simple to more advanced)

Using one hand	Using two hands
Birth–1 year	**Birth–2 years**
Manipulates a toy placed in hand	Plays with toys placed in each hand alternatively
Reaches for and grasps interesting toy placed within reach	Transfers toys from one hand to another
Plays with feet and toes	Bangs toys together at midline
	Claps hands
1–2 years	**2–4 years**
Removes ring from stick	Screws and unscrews lids
Removes peg from peg board	Folds paper in half
Picks up small objects with pincer grasp	Holds bowl and stirs
Puts pegs in pegboard	Pulls apart large pop beads and then puts them together
Builds a tower	Buttons up buttons
2 years	Winds up toys
Plays with clay and playdough	Strings beads
Turns pages one at a time	Laces up shoes
Puts pellets in a bottle	Puts puzzles together
Uses a spoon	Makes simple forms with playdough
Turns a doorknob	
Imitates block designs	

Tool use	Pencil control
2–4 years	**2–4 years**
Transfers material with a spoon	Marks paper with pencil or crayon
Pounds with a wooden hammer	Scribbles spontaneously
Uses wooden tongs to transfer objects	Copies a single vertical line
Uses a rolling pin	Traces outline of a drawing
Uses spoon to eat	Copies a horizontal stroke
Imitates vacuuming, sweeping, mowing lawn, and so forth	Copies a circle, square, cross
	Begins to make other shapes and letters
	Writes name

Cutting	Representational drawing
2–5 years	**2–5 years**
Snips with scissors	Draws a person beginning with head
Cuts paper in pieces	Draws person with head and body
Cuts straight line	Draws a simple picture of an event
Cuts out a circle	Draws his or her family
Cuts out pictures	

Children with significant difficulties should be assessed and treated by an occupational therapist or physiotherapist. Some simple activities that provide multisensory input can be helpful for many children, however. Here are some activities integrating a number of these sensory systems:

- Imitate baby's sounds and faces while holding and touching baby.

- Gently stretch, bend, and stroke baby's arms and legs while smiling and singing or talking to baby.

- Walk around or dance with baby, looking into her eyes and singing or using music.

- Play simple rhyming games such as "This little piggy," while touching the baby's toes, singing the rhymes, and making sure baby is looking at you.

- Trace letters made of sandpaper while looking at them and repeating the name of the letter.

- Draw to music while having the child talk about the picture and his feelings.

- Use playdough to make objects and have the child name them.

- Make a "feely" box with objects in it that are identifiable by touch (e.g., sandpaper, toothbrush, block, cotton ball). Have the child reach in the box and try to identify an object from its texture by feeling without seeing it. Then have the child take it out, name it, and describe it.

- Have objects on a tray to taste (cheese, bread, crackers), to sniff (onion, coffee, spices), and to feel (a sponge, clay, emery board). First, let the children see the objects. Then, one by one, blindfold the children and encourage each one to taste, sniff, touch, and guess what the objects are.

PRINCIPLE 5: *Join the child in fun motor and movement activities.*

Infants and young children explore much of their world through movement and, in the early years, make sense of their world through sensorimotor experiences. The qualities and characteristics of the child's movement provide clues to her development of body self and express who she is. These include the child's tempo or pace, muscle tone, rhythm, sense of balance, and strength of movements. Observing a child moving and doing sensorimotor activities provides insight into how she organizes her experience and meaning of the world.

Movement activities are especially fun for children. When a caregiver joins in she can act as a catalyst and motivator for the child. For children who are very active, some movement activities may be crucial to help them "let off steam," while others can help them slow down and be calmer.

Activities Designed for Children of Different Activity Levels Depending on how active they are, children differ in terms of how they respond to various activities. Here are some suggestions for movement activities that help children of different activity levels both let off steam and calm down:

For all children:

- Dance with your child to some favorite music.

- Manipulate props such as a scarf or bean bag as you dance.

- Provide props to encourage large muscle activities such as climbing, running, and crawling. These can include large pillows, tunnels, parachutes, blankets, and large gymnastic balls. Provide objects to go over and to crawl under. Make use of small and large spaces.

- Do finger plays and interactive games such as Row, Row, Row Your Boat; Peek-a-Boo; and Hide-and-Seek.

- Encourage your child to be a character or an animal, such as a baby, a giant, a fairy, or a crocodile, as she moves around.

- Use musical instruments and encourage their use while marching or dancing.

- Encourage drawing or painting with very large sheets of paper so the child experiences the sensation of the movements.

- Lift, gently swing, and engage in rough-and-tumble play with the child (making sure you never shake the child).

For children who have difficulty slowing down:

- Ask the child to walk from one wall of a room to another (or one tree to another if you are outside) "in your regular way." Notice if he goes a regular route or gets lost along the way. Ask what it feels like, and ask him to describe his feelings. Ask him to move to a spot in the room very slowly. Have him describe the body sensations of this. Model taking steps and saying "slow . . . slow . . . slow . . ."

- Have a race with the winner being last.

- Teach the child to experience the difference between "your regular way like a deer" and the "slow way like an elephant."

- Join in a wiggle dance with rhythmic movements. Wiggle and shake your body all over. Slowly eliminate certain body parts from the dance such as legs and hips, then reverse it to wiggle all over. Do this reversal several times.

- Play imitation games such as Simon Says in which child is required to repeat one action.

- Play a statue game in which the child runs and then has to stay very still.

PRINCIPLE 6: *Help the child to develop appropriate eating, sleeping, and toileting routines. Avoid creating battlegrounds around them.*

One of the most important tasks of early infancy is to begin to develop some capacity for homeostasis—or regulation—of eating, sleeping, and toileting. Children differ significantly in their capacity to calm themselves or self-soothe and to set up regular and predictable routines. Of course, how their caregivers respond to them and the predictability of the environment around the child contribute significantly. Nevertheless, some infants and young children have more difficulty shutting out different stimuli and in reacting to various types of stimulation. As well, as children begin to individuate and become their own people, many may become oppositional in areas in which they can have some control. It is very difficult to make children eat, sleep, or go to the bathroom if they decide not to, so it is often around these important physical routines that conflicts between children and caregivers develop. Although in each of these areas different approaches are necessary, nevertheless, some important general rules apply. For all of these areas, it is critical that a consistent routine be established and that it be kept as calm and predictable as possible. Forcing and threatening around eating, sleeping, or toileting can have effects on emotional development. Sometimes it helps for caregivers to back off, observe the child's behavior, and problem-solve with other caregivers. It is also important to only work toward getting one area under control at any one time.

Feeding and Eating Problems   In a newborn, feeding takes place through reflexive sucking of the breast or bottle. Although initial problems with breast feeding are common, most are resolved, either naturally or with the assistance of friends or professionals. Difficulties may continue if infants have colic or are easily overstimulated. As many as 25% of typically developing infants and young children and 35% of those with developmental disabilities have feeding problems. Many infants may have certain types of medical problems that contribute to difficulties in establishing a feeding routine and in making progress in feeding. These include infants who have respiratory problems, structural anomalies of the mouth, or cerebral palsy. Infants who have experienced exposure to traumatic events (i.e., frightening experiences) involving the nose, mouth, throat, and esophagus such as surgery or internal tube feeding may also have feeding difficulties. Some infants seem to have difficulty with feeding because of more temperamental characteristics that include being more arrhythmic, hypersensitive, intense, and irritable. Some may be reacting to food allergies.

Whenever possible, it is important to stop eating problems from developing. Eating problems include refusing to sit at the table, refusing nutritional foods, throwing food, and having extreme food preferences. It is important for caregivers to remember that they can control mealtime routines (surrounding when, where, and what the child eats), however the child controls how much he eats. Here are some tips for encouraging good eating habits:

- Schedule meals and snacks at regular times.

- Do not use food in order to comfort the child.

- Keep meals to a time period the child can handle.

- Encourage your child to feed himself as much as possible. Praise him for his skill.

- Protect the floor from mess but do not fuss over it.

- If your child throws food, warn her once and if she persists, put her down from the table for a while.

- Do not watch television at mealtimes or allow the child to play with toys.

- Do not offer unplanned food between meals except water if the child is thirsty.

- Cut down on juice or milk if the child is drinking an excessive amount. Too much liquid can prevent him from eating.

- Encourage the child to eat nutritional foods. Serve them on something she likes, such as pizza. Use small, whole vegetables and fruits.

- Involve the child in food preparation.

- Let the child stop eating when she is full. Never insist that she empty the plate.

If you are concerned that your child is not eating enough, check with your family physician or pediatrician to see if his weight and height are acceptable compared with other children his age. Remember that all children have growth spurts and at times they may eat voraciously while at other times they may eat more sparingly. Keep a record or daily eating diary if you are really worried about your child's food intake, as it may reveal that she is eating far more than you thought. Such a record may also reveal underlying problems contributing to lack of appetite at mealtimes, such as the child's filling up on nonnutritional snacks or having too much juice or milk. If your child seems to be growing adequately and your concern is more that he is refusing to eat various foods, be patient and try to introduce more nutritional foods in appealing ways and only expect him to take very small amounts.

Sleep Problems　　Sleep problems can be the most difficult issue to deal with because parents and children need some uninterrupted sleep to give them the physical and emotional energy to deal with each day. Moreover, research has shown that sleep deprivation can cause depression, a low self-esteem, and—in extreme cases—disorientation. Almost all children go through periods of wakefulness due to teething, illness, fears of separation, and anxiety about changes within the family or in family routines. Sleeping difficulties include not being able to fall asleep, night waking, and nightmares and night terrors. Sleep problems are common in toddlers and preschoolers; 15%–20% of young children have them, and once established they tend to become chronic. About 70% of 2-year-olds with sleeping problems will continue to have problems at 5 years of age (Minde, Popiel, Leos, Falkner, Parker, & Handley-Derry, 1993). Parents vary in their beliefs and feelings about taking children into their bed. Sometimes, parents who are exhausted take a child into bed and find it very difficult to break the habit and reestablish the crib or child's bed as a place for the child to sleep. Although all children will sometimes try and come into their parents' bed, most parents want and need to have their child establish adequate sleep habits and to be able to sleep through the night. Researchers have found that children who have chronic sleep problems often had perinatal problems such as colic or severe allergies. These researchers found that both good and poor sleepers woke up during the night. Good sleepers were able to soothe themselves back to sleep, while poor sleepers needed to be soothed by a parent. They concluded that poor sleepers may have an overall difficulty with regulation and as infants were not encouraged to fall asleep on their own without rocking or feeding when they went to bed or woke up in the night. In other words, the problem was not that they did not sleep through the night but that they could not calm themselves and fall back to sleep if they woke up.

Avoiding sleeping problems should begin early by allowing infants to fall asleep on their own if possible and allowing them to self-calm whenever they can. Nevertheless, many children may develop difficulties during the second or third year of life because of teething or an illness or because they experience the separation of going to bed and falling asleep in their own bed as scary. Here are some ways to prevent sleeping problems:

- Have well-established bedtime routines and a set time. BE FIRM.

- Try and make sure children have a chance to calm down and have a pleasant *quiet* time before bed.

- Provide a night light.

- Encourage children to have a favorite toy or blanket that they always take to bed.

- Encourage infants and young children to calm themselves by allowing them to cry for a little while, before they fall asleep and when they first wake up.

- Let the child fall asleep on her own.

- Try and prevent the child from becoming overtired by continuing naps or at least a rest period during the day. Remember, a crying child may be tired.

Table 2.7. Strategies for overcoming sleep problems

Gradual method (Disadvantage is that this can span several days or longer.)	Put the child into bed awake, with no bottle but with a favorite toy(s). Stay in the room but do not talk or be responsive. Sit quietly, provide minimal contact, and read a newspaper. Move chair away from the crib toward the door. Gradually reduce time in the room. Put baby to bed and leave.
Extinction method (Disadvantage is that some parents cannot tolerate the crying, which may be long and intense.)	Put the child in the crib, kiss him goodnight, and leave the room. Let the child cry until she falls asleep. Once the child can fall asleep alone, do the same when he wakes up in the night.
Progressive method (Disadvantage is that it can take several days and the child will cry.)	Child is put to bed awake. Parent leaves the room. Parent returns after 5 minutes if child is crying but does not pick up child. Parent may pat or speak to her. Parent leaves room and waits 10 minutes before returning, then gradually extends this period (see Ferber, 1985, for chart). Use the same method for night wakings.

Note: None of the methods should be used with very young infants and may best be used when a child reaches 9 months and seems to be indicating that he is not interested in settling when put to bed.

- If a child appears fearful when going to bed and talks about monsters or other scary things in her room, take it seriously and reassure her by showing her that there is nothing in the closet, under the bed, and so forth.

Sometimes, even with these preventive measures, children develop sleep problems that become chronic and deprive the child and parents of adequate sleep. If this happens it is important to choose a time to correct unhealthy sleep habits when there is a clear period of at least two weeks coming up without any anticipated absences on your part. There are many books available that suggest ways to overcome sleep problems, and parents can choose from different approaches (see Cuthbertson & Schevill, 1985; Ferber, 1985; Haslam, 1992; Lansky, 1991; Weissbluth, 1999). All of these approaches aim to teach the child to fall asleep on her own. There are three main methods: 1) a gradual "fading" sequence, 2) "extinction," or a "cold turkey" approach, and 3) a progressive method that combines aspects of these two methods. In each case, it is critical that parents realize that if they occasionally give in (or intermittently reinforce) the bad sleeping habits, these habits will be immediately reestablished and more difficult to break later. Table 2.7 provides some strategies for eradicating sleeping problems.

The other most common sleeping problems are nightmares and night terrors. Explanations of the reasons for them and ways to deal with them are set out in Table 2.8.

Toilet Teaching With most children, toilet teaching occurs when a child is between the ages of approximately 3 and 4. Toilet teaching is most successful when children indicate readiness and parents stay calm about it. Children vary significantly in their readiness for toilet training, and girls are usually ready earlier than boys. The period from 2 to 3 years is often not a good time to begin unless the child indicates readiness. This often is a period of extreme negativism with many children trying to exert their independence from parents, and consequently toileting can easily become a battleground if begun at that age. It is also important to distinguish between daytime and nighttime control, because many children take much longer in staying dry throughout the night. A child is ready to begin toilet teaching when she

- Is able to stay dry for longer periods and bowel movements occur on a regular basis. In other words, she has enough physiological control.

- Can use a word to indicate the need to use the potty

- Indicates she is ready to urinate or have a bowel movement

- Shows curiosity, interest, and comprehension about bathroom habits

- Indicates disliking being in a wet or soiled diaper

- Shows understanding of what a potty is for

- Has enough coordination to pull pants up and down (if you expect her to be independent in using the potty)

Toilet teaching also is most successful during a period of stability within the household and not at the time of a major change (e.g., birth of a sibling, change of child care, move, loss of a family member). Ways to proceed with toilet teaching if the child shows readiness are outlined here:

1. Determine readiness to begin.

2. Choose a relatively stress-free time for you and your child.

Table 2.8.　Characteristics of nightmares and night terrors

	Description	Reasons	What to do
Nightmares	Begin usually between 2 and 6 years of age and occur in both childhood and adulthood. They are what most people call "bad dreams," and most often occur in early morning. Child can be awakened, and usually calms quickly with reassurance. May remember the dream.	Experts disagree about the reasons. Developmentalists see nightmares occurring as a result of the child's new ability to create mental images of the world, which can be scary. Some believe the dreamer is reworking events of the day or emotional issues such as normal separations, or is finding a way to handle anger and fears. Others see nightmares as more physiological than psychological.	Reassure the child; let him know the nightmare is not real. Hug and calm him. Let him know you are there to protect him. Gradually encourage the child to calm himself down. Sometimes talking about, playing out, or drawing a picture of the nightmare the next day can help, particularly if it is a recurring nightmare. If the child continues to have nightmares frequently, a consultation with your pediatrician would be helpful.
Night terrors	Usually begin in children between the ages of 2 and 6 years and occur in children up to 12 years old. Occur while the child is in deep sleep. Child may give a piercing scream; eyes may open; the child is frightened and may sweat with heart pounding. Child cannot be consoled and may push parent away. Child will have no memory of the incident the next day.	Tend to run in families, so phenomenon may have a genetic basis, but this is not proven. Are more likely to occur if the child is overtired and is perhaps changing naptimes and getting less sleep.	Do not try and wake the child. Stay calm, stand back, and make sure she is all right; do not intervene unless she wakes up. If she does wake, calm her and encourage her to fall back to sleep. If your child continues to have night terrors frequently, consult your pediatrician.

3. Encourage your child by buying a potty and "big kid" underwear and having the child pick them out if he would like to.

4. Sit your child on the potty at a time when he is likely to have a bowel movement.

5. Praise your child if he urinates or has a bowel movement in the potty. Some parents may wish to use more concrete rewards, such as stickers.

6. Never shame your child if he has an accident or if toilet teaching does not appear to be working. It is better to stop and try again later when he is more ready.

One potential source of problems is a fear about bowel movements being flushed down the toilet. Some children perceive this as a part of themselves disappearing. A child may be frightened by the prospect and think that he, also, will end up down the toilet. Emptying the potty when the child is not around may help. Also, if a child is suffering from constipation or recurring diarrhea, this may upset his confidence in controlling his bowels, and the process may take longer. If a child is still resisting well after his fourth birthday, a consultation with your pediatrician may be helpful.

PRINCIPLE 7: *Respond to children's early sexual curiosity by providing answers to questions, acceptance of their interest, and appropriate limits for sexual play.*

How parents react to their children's early sexual curiosity and interest will significantly affect children's attitudes towards their bodies, treatment of people of both genders, and attitude towards sexuality. Nevertheless, many parents do not have information about normal sexual behavior in young children and do not know how to respond to children's sexual questions and behaviors.

Development of Interest in Sexuality

Children have been shown to be sexual from birth—infant boys have erections and girls show vaginal lubrication. By the end of the first year, both boys and girls commonly touch their genitals. Children also are experiencing their bodies through the closeness and touching they share with caregivers and by sucking on the breast or bottle. Between 1 and 2 years of age, children can learn the names for their body parts, including their genitals. By 15–18 months, toddlers become especially interested in exploring and stimulating their genitals and may not understand that this is something that should be done in private. As 3-year-olds become more aware of themselves, they also become aware of body differences. This may lead children to engage in "doctor play" with children of the opposite sex as a way to explore these differences in what these children see as acceptable. Some children engage in "sex" play with dolls. At 3 and 4 years of age children become curious and concerned about sex differences. Little girls may wish they have a penis, while boys may want breasts and to be able to have babies. About this age, children may become very interested in toileting, as well, and may begin to use bathroom and sexual words to shock and to be funny. They may also want to peek at other children in the bathroom and may want to show their own nudity by leaving their pants down. As part of the understanding of gender differences, little boys may want to marry their mothers or another female they know well, and little girls, their fathers or another male they know well. Once they learn that this cannot happen, they generally identify with a same-sex parent, friend, or relative.

Three- and four-year-old children are more aware of and curious about body differences. (From Johnston, L. [1978]. *Do they ever grow up?* Minnetonka, MN: Meadowbrook Press; reprint granted with written permission of Lynn Johnston Productions, Inc.)

Often, by 5 or 6 years children become more modest about nudity and do not want to be seen naked. This will depend a great deal, however, on the attitudes of their parents around nudity.

Parenting Behavior and Sexuality   The principles outlined in this chapter should help parents provide their children with a positive attitude towards their bodies, including their sexuality. Research has shown that many parents have difficulty communicating with their children about sexuality (Hollander, 1988). One significant determinant appears to be that many parents feel uncomfortable talking about the issues and not knowing what children need to know at different ages. Moreover, many parents seem to conduct sexuality education in the same way that their parents did, even though they would like to do better (Furman, 1984). These are some ideas for answering questions about sexuality.

- Ask the child what she thinks is the answer to the question and build on the knowledge she already has of the subject.

- Keep answers simple and avoid overwhelming the child with too much information.

- Give the information gradually over time.

- If children ask questions about sexuality in public, tell them you will talk about them later at home, and follow through.

- Use appropriate books if you feel uncomfortable talking about the subject (see Andry & Schepp, 1984; Cole, 1994; Mayle, 2000, under Children's Books, in bibliography).

- Give children proper names for their genitals and use them naturally.

- Try not to be shocked by sexual behaviors or questions.

- Do not shame or punish children for using sexual words or behavior.

- Encourage children to act out female and male roles and to learn about the special satisfactions of both.

- Include information to safeguard children against sexual abuse. Discuss with the child what is appropriate regarding her private parts, touching, and keeping secrets, but avoid making the child unnecessarily fearful.

- Do not perpetuate the idea that the child will marry Mommy or Daddy and help them understand they will grow up and love someone else.

- Remember to restrict television viewing to avoid the child being presented with sexual information for which he is not developmentally ready.

Table 2.9 lists some suggested answers to some common questions that children ask regarding sex and sexuality.

It also is important that parents avoid being shocked about masturbation, nudity, and sexual play and deal with it as calmly as possible. By age 2 or 3 years, children can understand what is acceptable public behavior and can learn that they can only masturbate in their own room. With sex play, children do need to be stopped, making sure that there is no shaming of their behavior. Parents need to be especially vigilant around sex play between a much older child and preschooler or if it is very secretive or forceful, or both.

PRINCIPLE 8: *Express delight in the child's body and her control of it. Adapt to her physical self.*

A child's body image develops out of positive experiences with controlling his body and being able to make it do what he wants it to do. It also grows from the joy of movement—of being touched and held.

Many parents believe positive body image can be encouraged by telling children how good-looking or how pretty they are. This kind of message actually only reinforces the cultural message that physical attractiveness is the most important and necessary attribute to have, however. Instead, it is more important that parents comment on physical achievements and notice special attributes. It is critical that children are not made to feel ugly or ashamed of their bodies and are encouraged to feel positive about their appearance. Some encouraging remarks might be

- "What a bright smile you have."

- "How shiny your hair looks in the sun."

- "How lovely you look in green today."

- "How strong your legs are getting."

- "Wow, you can really jump high."

Just as important, caregivers need to understand and adapt to their infant's and young children's physical attributes at various ages and any special challenges they may be dealing with.

Table 2.9. Some suggested answers to common questions about sex and sexuality

1. Where do babies come from?
   —Babies grow inside the mother.
   —They come out of a special place inside the mother called the womb.

2. How do ladies get babies?
   —The baby starts from a little egg inside the mother. It grows in a *special* place inside, called a uterus.
   —Mothers have eggs inside that grow into a baby.

3. Can I make a baby from the egg inside?
   —It takes a man and a woman to make a baby from an egg.
   —Not until you (if the question is from a girl) are much older.
   —Only mothers can grow babies inside.

4. How do babies get out?
   —The mother has a special place where the baby can come out, called a vagina.
   —The vagina is very stretchy like elastic and can be stretched to let the baby out, and then gets small again. It's hard work, so the mom usually goes to the hospital to get some help.

5. What does the daddy do to make a baby?
   —The daddy has special cells called sperm cells and the mommy has egg cells and when they join, a new life begins.
   —Mommy and Daddy get close and have a special cuddle in bed.
   (Caregivers may wish to be more specific, but many parents will not want to explain sexual intercourse until the child is older.)

Although in certain situations special allowances may have to be made (e.g., helping a child use a pencil if he has fine motor control problems), it is crucial to emphasize strengths and to assure that children have experiences of success even in areas where achievement is more difficult.

When parents understand the physical characteristics of a child and are attuned to or recognize her mood at a particular time, this can contribute significantly to how comfortable a child is with her body. For example, in early infancy, attunement to feeding and the sucking rhythm may be critical, while toddlers need acceptance for their new rhythms of locomotion, climbing and making messes, which are usually done with great intensity. The preschooler's rhythms include running and chasing and catching games, which integrate high activity and more fluidity and variations in pace and intensity. Five-year-olds tend to enjoy activities with focused and controlled aggression such as jumping, pushing, and punching (Loman, 1994).

Difficulties children may face in controlling their body movements and perceptions were outlined earlier in this chapter in the section entitled Important Research Findings. Many caregivers become aware of these difficulties by observing the child, and in some cases formal assessment may be necessary. This would be the case especially if the child is showing emotional or behavioral symptoms that are intense and chronic. These may include excessive aggressiveness, sadness, difficulty in playing or socializing with other children, excessive fears, or anxieties. Around 5 and 6 years many children worry about their bodies and become concerned that parts will be lost or damaged. This can cause concerns about using the toilet, separations from parents, and gender differences. Children may react intensely to cuts, scrapes, and bruises, frequently demanding adhesive bandages whether they are actually needed. If a child expresses concern or shows it by various emotions or body language, let him know you and other caregivers are there to keep him safe. Assure him you expect to be around for him until he is really grown up. Some symptoms to look for and some possible problem areas that might be associated with these signs are set out in Table 2.10.

Some strategies for dealing with some of these difficulties are set out in Chapter 1 in the sections on temperament.

Table 2.10. Some possible difficulties associated with controlling body movements, functions, and perceptions

Difficulty	Symptoms
Auditory processing	May seem to switch off; cannot remember more than one request; at times seems unable to hear. May be slow learning to talk.
Visual processing	Has problems copying shapes or letters. May not be interested in pictures or puzzles or may have difficulty with them.
Motor planning	May seem clumsy or awkward. Falls over frequently. Has difficulty with many self-help skills such as tying shoelaces or drawing.
Hypersensitivities	May react strongly to loud noises, bright lights, certain foods, touch, and labels in clothes.
Regulation	Very intense in reactions, has difficulties with sleeping, extreme temper tantrums. Experiences difficulty calming and self-regulating.
Activity level	Constantly moving beyond what would be expected of a small child. May have concentration problems as well.

PRINCIPLE 9: *Respond to body language and validate the reality of the experience being expressed.*

Much of the activity of infants and young children is about play and movement. Nonverbal gestures and facial expressions can tell us a great deal about children, their needs, and their feelings. Body language can also inform us about how the child is experiencing and perceiving his environment. Sometimes, for example, muscle tension, apathy, disorganized movement, and negative facial expressions can tell us a child is afraid, angry, or discouraged far before he can express it verbally and sometimes before he is even aware of it himself! Often, to a child, physical responses such as holding, rocking, singing, and smiling can be as reassuring as any words of reassurance. In other words, letting the child know you understand how she feels and showing empathetic concern can help the child feel secure and confirm that her body is accepted and understood.

THE ROLE OF PARENTS IN DEVELOPING A CHILD'S BODY CONTROL AND IMAGE

Many caregivers are unaware of how critical it is for children to develop a sense of body control and a positive body image. Many are more concerned about issues of noncompliance and discipline and as a consequence do not see this early sense of self as critical. Some parents may be resistant to this topic because of feelings they have about their own bodies or even because of experiences of physical or sexual abuse.

For adults, physical appearance is extremely important as it is the most readily available information about a person, and immediately provides basic information about gender, race, age, weight, and height. Sometimes an individual's physical appearance allows us to guess his or her occupation and other circumstances of the person's life. Physical appearance variables have been shown by researchers to affect people's attitudes, attributions, and even actions. Unfortunately, some of these decisions are based on a belief that beautiful is good and on cultural stereotypes of what is beautiful. Many studies show that physical attractiveness makes a difference in people's responses to each other, beginning in infancy and continuing throughout life. Caregivers react more positively to good-looking children than they do to less attractive children. Attractive adults are more popular with the opposite sex and have an advantage in many

occupations. A person's body image does not always equate with how they are viewed by others, however. In other words, beauty does not always mean a favorable body image or homeliness, a negative body image.

DISCUSSION QUESTIONS TO USE IN TRAINING PROFESSIONALS

1. Discuss some links between the body and mind.

2. Define body scheme as opposed to body image.

3. Discuss some of the actions of caregivers that may assist the child in developing body scheme and body control.

4. Why may people with eating disorders have distorted body schema?

5. Describe how touch may help healing and body development.

6. Why may it be difficult for some parents to deal with sexuality issues with their children?

7. Why do some infants and young children develop sleeping problems?

8. What would you tell parents about toilet training?

9. What does sensory integration mean and why is it important for body control and body image?

WORKING WITH PARENTS:
GROUP EXERCISES, AND SAMPLE HOMEWORK ACTIVITIES

It is very important to explain to parents how important a child's sense of body self is before introducing some of the principles or ideas that they can use with their children. Exploring their own experience with their parents and other caregivers around being held and cuddled and how much they were encouraged to participate in physical activities can be helpful. As well, what might have been said to the parent about his body and how his body was treated may be most significant.

If parents feel negatively about their own appearance, it may affect the way they interact with children. Many parents may need encouragement to consider biases they may have toward the physical appearance of their children. These may be strongly influenced by the way they feel about their own appearance. If a parent feels overweight or has a history of struggling with weight issues, slimmer, more muscular children may appeal more to that parent, or the opposite. Asking parents how they want their children to experience their own bodies and what activities they plan to encourage for their children can open up important discussions.

Modeling your own comfort with holding their baby, remarking on how strong a child is, and demonstrating various types of fine and gross motor activities with the infant or child can be very helpful. Sometimes, answering parents' immediate questions about a young child's eating, sleeping, and toileting habits, or in older children, about their sexuality, may be an excellent way to allow parents to feel heard and to approach the topic of the importance of body control and having a positive body image.

GROUP EXERCISES TO HELP PARENTS ENHANCE THEIR OWN AND THEIR CHILDREN'S SENSE OF BODY SELF

This section includes exercises that can be used with parents and other caregivers to encourage them to enhance the body control and body image of children. As well, exercises to encourage caregivers to review their own sense of body self are provided.

The Meaning of Touch

In this activity, have parents talk about the amount of touch they experienced in their family as they were growing up. Did their parents touch and hold them? Was the touch ever experienced as too intrusive? (If parents report physical or sexual abuse, it will be important to show support and to ensure that appropriate counseling is available if they seem very distressed.)

Have caregivers identify some of the ways in which they provide experiences of touch for their infants and young children (e.g., holding during feeding). Child care providers may identify constraints on touching in their work and may need to discuss appropriate ways to touch without going beyond those limits.

Activities and Toys that Encourage Motor Control

Discuss some of the activities and toys that parents enjoy with their infants and young children that can enhance fine and gross motor development (see Table 2.5 for a list).

Establishing Good Eating, Sleeping, and Toileting Routines

Ask parents to identify the areas with which they have the most problems with their children such as eating, sleeping, toilet teaching, or another issue related to the body. Have caregivers identify relevant issues and have other parents suggest ways to help. Ask parents why they think the problem has arisen and how they plan to deal with it.

Educating Young Children About Sexuality

Ask parents to give an example of an early memory of how they learned about sexuality. Ask them to think about how this may influence how they plan to deal with sexuality with their children. Have them consider these questions:

- How will I deal with teaching my children about sexuality issues?

- What is very important to me about it?

- What will I avoid doing?

- What are my questions and concerns?

Share Table 2.9 with the group and go through the questions and answers and discuss them. Ask parents about other questions that their children may have asked and how they dealt with them.

Helping Children Learn Body Control

Have caregivers think about various difficulties children may have that affect their body control, and consequently, their body image. Table 2.11 explains some of the ways that problems with body control may affect a child's body image and should be shared with parents. Ask parents about other issues their children may have and discuss their influence.

Becoming a Role Model

In a society that idealizes perfect-looking people, most of us fall far short. In order to help caregivers feel more comfortable with encouraging appropriate role models for children, ask them to spend a few minutes thinking about friends, relatives, or public figures they admire. Then have them list the characteristics they like about them. The qualities that people admire typically relate to personal characteristics such as inner strength, kindness, a sense of humor, commitment, helpfulness, and so forth. Physical attributes and attractiveness are seldom mentioned. The group leader should point out that in personal relationships, personality characteristics are more important than physical attractiveness.

My Nickname

In this activity, ask parents to remember nicknames or words others called them when they were younger to describe the way they looked. Ask parents to think about how the words made them feel. Then, ask them to suggest ways that they would have liked their appearance to be described.

Table 2.11. Potential effects of body control difficulties on body image

Body control problem	Effect on an individual's body image
Hyperactivity	May experience life as chaotic and consequently, his body as out of control
Clumsiness	May feel out of control and that he cannot participate in gym and sports
Motor planning problems	May find simple tasks like buttoning clothes very difficult and slow-going, and may feel inadequate
Sensory integration difficulties	May find the world confusing and feel she cannot manage in learning situations
Hearing problem	May feel shut out of activities and conversations and thus, unaccepted
Enuresis or encropresis	May be teased for toilet accidents and feel out of control
Insomnia	Can become exhausted and dread bedtime because cannot control sleeping
Obesity	Will compare body to others and feel unattractive and unaccepted

Body-and-Mind Relaxation and Guided Imagery

Share with caregivers that there is growing evidence that thoughts and feelings can have a significant influence on the body, including the immune system (Caudell, 1996; Fawzy et al., 1990; Rossi, 1993). For this reason, it can be extremely helpful to use relaxation techniques and visual imagery in order to provide relief from stress and worry, to calm the autonomic nervous system, and to optimize physical and mental health.

Note that while using relaxation techniques, the person focuses on various muscle groups, tensing them and relaxing them several times and noticing the sensations. These techniques also may involve learning certain breathing techniques.

Guided imagery encourages people to relax and to imagine themselves in a pleasant place. Some types of imagery encourage people to re-experience the parts of the body that they are most uncomfortable with. Relaxation exercises also can be used to get in touch with the body and to reduce stress. One way that has been used to do this is to carry out a body scan. Instructions to do this are in the book by Kabat-Zinn (1990) and are summarized briefly here.

To carry out the guided imagery exercise, people are instructed to lie on their backs in a comfortable place and to close their eyes. They are then told to feel their body and to concentrate on their breathing. In order to bring attention to various parts of the body, they are then to imagine their breath going all the way from their nose and lungs to that part of the body. During this time, the instructions are to feel all the sensations in that part of the body. By maintaining the focus on the sensations of the body and on the breath, various parts of the body are scanned, beginning with the toes and progressing to the sole of the foot, heel, top of the foot, ankle, up each leg, and then through the rest of the body. It is suggested that the body scan is best done once a day and at a slow pace. Other books on the use of imagery are included in the Further Reading section of the Bibliography.

SAMPLE HOMEWORK ACTIVITIES

It is helpful to give parents who are attending a weekly parenting group some activities to try during the week that can be discussed at the next group meeting. Assign only a small number to each group participant, or let people choose one or two they would like to do.

1. Take your child on an outing that involves physical activity such as walking, climbing, swimming, or riding a bike.

2. With your child's other caregivers, discuss and decide on routines around eating and sleeping. Stick to the routine.

3. Make a list of some of the physical characteristics of your child. Consider less obvious aspects such as activity level, sensitivity to touch, coordination, and so forth.

6. Respond to your child's body language or facial expression and record what happened, including what you said and any response of your child.

7. Try talking with your child in front of the mirror and let him know how special he is.

8. Nurture your body with a special bath, sauna, exercise routine, body lotion, or a massage.

9. Use the relaxation exercise mentioned previously in this chapter when things become stressful and record how they made you feel.

10. Spend some time dancing with your child and participating in action songs.

BIBLIOGRAPHY

REFERENCES

Adamson-Macedo, E.N., Dattani, I., Wilson, A., & de Carvalho, F.A. (1993). A small sample follow-up study of children who received tactile stimulation after pre-term birth: Intelligence and achievements. *Journal of Reproductive and Infant Psychology, 11,* 165–168.

Amsterdam, B. (1972). Mirror self image reactions before age two. *Developmental Psychobiology, 5,* 297–305.

Anand, K.J.S., & Hickey, P.R. (1987). Pain and its effects on the human neonate and fetus. *New England Journal of Medicine, 317,* 1321–1329.

Anisfeld, E., Casper, V., Nozyce, M., & Cunningham, N. (1990). Does infant carrying promote attachment? An experimental study of the effects of increased physical contact on the development of attachment. *Child Development, 61,* 1617–1627.

Archer, R., & Cash, T.F. (1985). Physical attractiveness and maladjustment among psychiatric inpatients. *Journal of Social and Clinical Psychology, 3,* 170–180.

Asarnow, J.R., & Bates, S. (1988). Depression in child psychiatric inpatients: Cognitive and attributional patterns. *Journal of Abnormal Child Psychology, 16,* 601–615.

Auckett, A.D. (1989). *Baby massage: Parent–child bonding through touch.* New York: Newmarket Press.

Ayres, A.J. (1972). Improving academic scores through sensory integration. *Journal of Learning Disabilities, 5,* 338–343.

Ayres, A.J. (1975). Sensorimotor foundations of academic ability. In W. Cruickshank & D.P. Hallahane (Eds.), *Perceptual and learning disabilities in children* (Vol. 2). New York: Syracuse University Press.

Ayres, A.J. (1976). *The effect of sensory integrative therapy on learning disabled children: The final report of a research project.* Torrance, CA: Center for the Study of Sensory Integrative Dysfunction.

Ayres, A.J. (1978). Learning disabilities and the vestibular system. *Journal of Learning Disabilities, 11,* 30–41.

Ayres, A.J. (1979). *Sensory integration and the child.* Los Angeles: Western Psychological Services.

Bahrick, L.E., & Watson, J.S. (1985). Detection of intermodal proprioceptive—visual contingency as a potential basis of self-perception in infancy. *Developmental Psychology, 21,* 963–973.

Barnard, K.E., & Bee, H.I. (1983). The impact of temporally patterned stimulation on the development of preterm infants. *Child Development, 54,* 1156–1167.

Beecher, H. (1959). *Measurement of subjective responses: Quantitative effects of drugs.* New York: Oxford University Press.

Bradley, L. (1981). The organisation of motor patterns for spelling: An effective remedial strategy for backward readers. *Developmental Medicine and Child Neurology, 23,* 83–91.

Brecker, P.T., Brazy, J.E., & Grunwald, P.C. (1997). Behavioral state organization of very low birth weight infants: Effects of developmental handling during caregiving. *Infant Behavior and Development, 20,* 503–514.

Bronson, G.W. (1974). The postnatal growth of visual capacity. *Child Development, 45,* 873–890.

Burns, G.L., & Farina, A. (1990). *Physical attractiveness and adjustment.* Unpublished manuscript, Washington State University, Pullman, WA.

Butterworth, G. (1992). Origins of self-perception in infancy. *Psychological Inquiry, 3,* 103–111.

Cash, T.F., & Pruzinsky, T. (Eds.). (1990). *Body images: Development, deviance, and change.* New York: Guilford Press.

Cash, T.F., Winstead, B.A., & Janda, L.H. (1986). The great American shape-up. *Psychology Today, 20,* 30–37.

Caudell, K.A. (1996). Psychoneuroimmunology and innovative behavioral interventions in patients with leukemia. *Oncology Nursing Forum, 23,* 493–502.

Champoux, M., Coe, C.L., Shanberg, S., Kuhn, C., & Suomi, S.J., (1989). Hormonal effects of early learning conditions on infant rhesus monkeys. *American Journal of Primatology, 19,* 111–117.

Chesson, R., McKay, C., & Stephenson, E. (1991). The consequences of motor/learning difficulties for school-age children and their teachers: Some parental views. *Support for Learning, 6,* 173–177.

Cuthbertson, J., & Schevill, S. (1985). *Helping your child sleep through the night.* New York: Doubleday.

DeCasper, A., & Fifer, W. (1980). Of human bonding: Newborns prefer their mothers' voices. *Science, 208,* 1174–1176.

DeGangi, G. (2000). *Pediatric disorders of regulation in affect and behavior: A therapist's guide to assessment and treatment.* San Diego: Academic Press.

DeGangi, G.A., Craft, P., & Castellan, J. (1991). Treatment of sensory, emotional, and attentional problems in regulatory disordered infants. *Infants and Young Children, 3,* 9–19.

DeGangi, G.A., DiPietro, J.A., Greenspan, S.I., & Porges, S.W. (1991). Psychophysiological characteristics of the regulatory disordered infant. *Infant Behavior and Development, 14,* 37–50.

DeGangi, G.A., & Greenspan, S.I. (1988). The development of sensory functions in infants. *Physical and Occupational Therapy in Pediatrics, 8,* 21–33.

DeGangi, G.A., Wietlisbach, S., Goodin, M., & Scheiner, N. (1993). A comparison of structured sensorimotor therapy and child-centered activity in the treatment of preschool children with sensorimotor problems. *American Journal of Occupational Therapy, 47,* 777–786.

Dohrenwald, B.S., & Dohrenwald, B.P. (Eds.). (1974). *Stressful life events: Their nature and effects.* New York: John Wiley & Sons.

Evans, F. (1985). Expectancy, therapeutic instructions, and the placebo response. In L. White, B. Tursky, & G. Schwartz (Eds.), *Placebo: Theory, research and mechanism* (pp. 215–228). New York: Guilford Press.

Fantz, R. (1963). Pattern vision in newborn infants. *Science, 140,* 296–97.

Fawzy, F.I., Kemeny, M.E., Fawzy, N.W., Elashoff, R., Morton, D., Cousins, N., & Fahey, J.L. (1990). A structured psychiatric intervention for cancer patients. II. Changes over time in immunological measures. *Archives of General Psychiatry, 47,* 729–735.

Feiner, K. (1987). Development of the concept of anatomical constancy: Part 1. *Psychoanalytic Psychology, 4,* 343–354.

Feiner, K. (1988). A test of a theory of anxiety about body integrity: Part 2. *Psychoanalytic Psychology, 5,* 71–79.

Ferber, R. (1985). *Solve your child's sleep problems.* New York: Simon and Schuster.

Field, T.M. (1979). Differential behavioral and cardiac responses of 3-month-old infants to a mirror and peer. *Infant Behavior and Development, 2,* 179–184.

Field, T.M. (1995). *Touch in early development.* Mahwah, NJ: Lawrence Erlbaum Associates.

Field, T.M. (1998). Touch therapies. In R.R. Hoffman, M.F. Sherrick, & J.S. Warm (Eds.), *Viewing psychology as a whole: The integrative science of William N. Dember* (pp. 603–624). Washington, DC: American Psychological Association.

Field, T.M., Malphurs, J., Carraway, K., & Pelaez-Nogueras, M. (1996). Carrying position influences infant behavior. *Early Child Development and Care, 121,* 49–54.

Field, T.M., Schanberg, S.M., Scafidi, F., Bauer, C.R., Vega-Lahr, N., Garcia, R., Nystrom, J., & Kuhn, C.M. (1986). Tactile/kinesthetic stimulation effects on preterm neonates. *Pediatrics, 77,* 654–658.

Fitzgerald, M., Millard, C., & MacIntosh, N. (1988). Hyperalgesia in premature infants. *Lancet, 8580,* 292.

Flannery-Schroeder, E.C., & Chrisler, J.C. (1996). Body esteem, eating attitudes, and gender role orientation in three age groups of children. *Current Psychology: Developmental, Learning, Personality, Social, 15,* 235–248.

Franck, L.S. (1986). A new method to quantitatively describe pain behavior in infants. *Nursing Research, 35,* 28–31.

Furman, E. (1984). *Learning to feel good about sexual differences.* Cleveland, OH: Cleveland Center for Research in Child Development.

Ganchrow, J.R., Steiner, J.F., & Munif, D. (1983). Neonatal facial expressions in response to different quality and intensities of gustatory stimuli. *Infant Behavior and Development, 6,* 473–484.

Gordon, E.E. (1996). The placebo: An insight into mind-body interaction. *Headache Quarterly, 7,* 117–125.

Gorski, P.A. (1991). Promoting infant development during neonatal hospitalization: Critiquing the state of the science. *Children's Health Care, 20,* 250–257.

Greenberg, G.R., Feagan, B.G., Martin, F., Sutherland, L.R., Thomson, A.B., Williams, C.N., Nilsson, L.G., & Persson, T. (1994). Oral budesonide for active Crohn's disease: Canadian Inflammatory Bowel Disease Study Group. *The New England Journal of Medicine, 331,* 836–841.

Greenspan, S.I. (1992). *Infancy and early childhood: The practice of clinical assessment and intervention with emotional and developmental challenges.* Madison, CT: International Universities Press.

Greenspan, S.I., & Lourie, R.S. (1981). Developmental structuralist approach to the classification of adaptive and pathologic personality organizations: Infancy and early childhood. *American Journal of Psychiatry, 138,* 725–735.

Greenspan, S.I., Wieder, S., & Simons, R. (1998). *The child with special needs: Encouraging intellectual and emotional growth.* Reading, MA: Addison-Wesley.

Gunnar, M. (1998). Quality of care and the buffering of stress physiology: Its potential role in protecting the developing human brain. *IMPrint, 21,* 4–7.

Harlow, H.E. (1958). The nature of love. *American Psychologist, 25,* 161–165.

Harrison, L. (1985). Effects of early supplemental stimulation programs for premature infants: Review of the literature. *Maternal Child Nursing Journal, 14,* 69–90.

Haslam, D. (1992). *Sleepless children: A handbook for parents.* London: Piatkus.

Hollander, D. (1988). *News release, National Campaign to Prevent Teen Pregnancy, National Omnibus Survey.* Washington, D.C.

Holmes, T.H., & Rahe, R.H. (1967). The social readjustment rating scale. *Journal of Psychosomatic Research, 11,* 213–218.

Hulme, C. (1981). *Reading retardation and multisensory teaching.* London: Routledge & Kegan Paul.

Hulme, C., & Lord, R. (1986). Clumsy children: A review of recent research. *Child: Care, Health and Development, 12,* 257–269.

Hulme, C., Monk, A., & Ives, S. (1987). Some experimental studies of multi-sensory teaching: The effects of manual tracing on children's paired-associate learning. *British Journal of Developmental Psychology, 5,* 299–307.

Inagaki, K., & Hatano, G. (1993). Young children's understanding of the mind-body distinction. *Child Development, 64,* 1534–1549.

Ironson, G., Field, T., Scafidi, F., Hashimoto, M., Kumar, M., Kumar, A., Price, A., Goncalves, A., Burman, I., Tetenman, C., Patarca, R., & Fletcher, M.A. (1996). Massage therapy is associated with enhancement of the immune system's cytotoxic capacity. *International Journal of Neuroscience, 84,* 205–217.

Jennings, K.D., & MacTurk, R.H. (1995). The motivational characteristics of infants and children with physical and sensory impairments. In R.H. MacTurk & G.A. Morgan (Eds.), *Mastery motivation: Origins, conceptualizations, and applications* (Vol. 12, pp. 201–219). Norwood, NJ: Ablex.

Kabat-Zinn, J. (1990). *Full catastrophe living: Using the wisdom of your body and mind to face stress, pain, and illness.* New York: Delacorte Press.

Kennell, J.H., Trause, M.A., & Klaus, M.H. (1975). Evidence for a sensitive period in the human mother. In T.B. Brazelton, E. Tronick, & L. Admson, H. Als, & S. Wise (Eds.), *Parent—infant interaction* (pp. 87–101). New York: Excerpta Medica.

Kiecolt-Glaser, J.K., & Glaser, R. (1988). Psychological influences on immunity: Implications for AIDS. *American Psychologist, 43,* 892–898.

Koenig, H.G., George, L.K., Meador, K.G., Blazer, D.G., & Dyck, P.B. (1994). Religious affiliation and psychiatric disorder among Protestant baby boomers. *Hospital and Community Psychiatry, 45,* 586–596.

Klaus, M.H., & Kennell, J.H. (1976). *Maternal—infant bonding: The impact of early separation or loss on family development.* Saint Louis: Mosby.

Krantz, M., Friedberg, J., & Andrews, D. (1985). Physical attractiveness and popularity: The mediating role of self-perception. *The Journal of Psychology, 119,* 219–223.

Kuhl, P., & Meltzoff, A. (1982). The bimodal perception of speech in infancy. *Science, 218,* 1138–1141.

Lansky, V. (1991). *Getting your child to sleep—and back to sleep: Tips for parents of infants, toddlers and preschoolers.* Deephaven, MN: Book Peddlers.

Locke, S., Krause, L., Leserman, J., Hurst, M.W., Heisel, J.S., & Williams, M. (1984). Life changes, stress, psychiatric symptoms and natural killer cell activity. *Psychosomatic Medicine, 46,* 441–453.

Loman, S. (1994). Attuning to the fetus and the young child: Approaches from dance/movement therapy. *Zero to Three, 15,* 20–26.

Macfarlane, A. (1975). Olfaction in the development of social preferences in the human neonate. *Ciba Foundation Symposium, 33,* 103–117.

Mailloux, Z. (1980). *The relationship between self-esteem and praxis, visual motor integration and student role performance in learning disabled children.* Unpublished masters' thesis, University of Southern California.

Matthews, D.A., & Clark, C. (1998). *The faith factor: Proof of the healing power of prayer.* New York: Viking.

Matthews, D.A., & Larson, D.B. (1995). *The faith factor: An annotated bibliography of clinical research on spiritual subjects* (Vol. III). Rockville, MD: National Institute for Health Care Research.

McCabe, M., & Marwit, S.J. (1993). Depressive symptomatology, perceptions of attractiveness, and body image in children. *Journal of Child Psychology and Psychiatry and Allied Disciplines, 34,* 1117–1124.

McCall, R.B. (1979). *Infants.* Cambridge, MA: Harvard University Press.

McClure, V.S. (1989). *Infant massage: A handbook for loving parents.* New York: Bantam Books.

Meltzoff, A.N., & Borton, R.W. (1979). Intermodal matching by human neonates. *Nature, 282,* 403–404.

Meltzoff, A.N., & Moore, M.K. (1995a). Infants' understanding of people and things: From body imitation to folk psychology. In J.L. Bermudez, A. Marcel, & N. Eilan (Eds.), *The body and the self* (pp. 43–69). Cambridge, MA: The MIT Press.

Meltzoff, A., & Moore, M.K. (1983). The origins of imitation in infancy: Paradigm, phenomena and theories. *Advances in infancy research* (Vol. 2, pp. 265–301). Norwood, NJ: Ablex.

Meltzoff, A.N., & Moore, M.K. (1995b). A theory of the role of imitation in the emergence of self. In P. Rochat (Ed.), *The self in infancy: Theory and research. Advances in psychology* (Vol. 112, pp. 73–93). Amsterdam: Elsevier Science.

Mendelson, B.K., & White, D.R. (1985). Development of self-body-esteem in overweight youngsters. *Developmental Psychology, 21,* 90–96.

Minde, K., Popiel, K., Leos, N., Falkner, S., Parker, K., & Handley-Derry, M. (1993). The evaluation and treatment of sleep disturbances in young children. *Journal of Child Psychology and Psychiatry and Allied Disciplines, 34,* 521–533.

Montagu, A. (1971). *Touching. The human significance of the skin.* New York: Columbia University Press.

Morse, P.A., & Cowan, N. (1982). Infant auditory and speech perception. In T.M. Field, A. Houston, H.C. Quay, L. Troll, & G.E. Finley (Eds.), *Review of Human Development.* New York: John Wiley & Sons.

Naparstek, B. (1993). *General wellness.* Los Angeles, CA: Time Warner Audio Books.

Nelson, B.L. (1988). *Changes in children's body concept as a function of age, gender, and physical and emotional well-being.* Unpublished doctoral dissertation, Washington University, St. Louis, MO.

Ottenbacher, K.J., Muller, L., Brandt, D., Heintzelman, Hojem, & Sharpe, P. (1987). The effectiveness of tactile stimulation as a form of early intervention: A quantitative evaluation. *Journal of Developmental and Behavioral Pediatrics, 8,* 68–76.

Owens, M.E., & Todt, E.H. (1984). Pain in infancy: Neonatal reaction to a heel lance. *Pain, 20,* 77–86.

Patzer, G.L., & Burke, D.M. (1988). Physical attractiveness and child development. In B.B. Lahey & A.E. Kazdin (Eds.), *Advances in Clinical Child Psychology* (Vol. 11, pp. 325–368). New York: Plenum Press.

Piaget, J. (1970). Piaget's theory. In P.H. Mussen (Ed.), *Carmichael's manual of child psychology* (Vol. 2, pp. 703–732). New York: John Wiley & Sons.

Pierce, J.W., & Wardle, J. (1993). Self-esteem, parental appraisal and body size in children. *Journal of Child Psychology and Psychiatry and Allied Disciplines, 34,* 1125–1136.

Porges, S.W. (1993). The infant's sixth sense: Awareness and regulation of bodily processes. *Zero to Three, 14,* 12–16.

Provence, S., & Lipton, R. (1962). *Infants in institutions.* New York: International Universities Press.

Riley, V. (1981). Psychoneuroimmunologic influences on immunocompetence and neoplasia. *Science, 212,* 1100.

Rochat, P. (1997). Early development of the ecological self. In C. Dent-Read & P. Zukow-Goldring (Eds.), *Evolving expansions of development: Ecological approaches to organism-environment systems* (pp. 91–121). Washington, DC: American Psychological Association.

Rochat, P., & Morgan, R. (1993). Self-perception in 3 month-old infants. In S. Valenti & J.B. Pittenger (Eds.), *Studies in perception and action* (Vol. 2, pp. 14–18). Mahwah, NJ: Lawrence Erlbaum Associates.

Rose, S.A., & Orlian, E.K. (1991). Asymmetries in infant cross-modal transfer. *Child Development, 62,* 706–718.

Rosenstein, D., & Oster, H. (1988). Differential facial responses to four basic tastes in newborns. *Child Development, 59,* 1555–1568.

Rossi, E.L. (1993). *The psychobiology of mind-body healing: New concepts of therapeutic hypnosis.* New York: Norton.

Rovee-Collier, C.K., & Fagen, J.W. (1981). The retrieval of memory in early infancy. *Advances in infancy research* (Vol. 1, pp. 225–254). Norwood, NJ: Ablex.

Salapatek, P. (1975). Pattern perception in early infancy. In L.B. Cohen & P. Salapatek (Eds.), *Infant perception: From sensation to cognition* (Vol. 1). New York: Academic Press.

Santostefano, S., & Callicchia, J.A. (1992). Body image, relational psychoanalysis, and the construction of meaning: Implications for treating aggressive children. *Development and Psychopathology, 4,* 655–678.

Sapolsky, R.M. (1996). Why stress is bad for your brain. *Science, 273,* 749–750.

Scafidi, F.A., Field, T.M., Schanberg, S.M., Bauer, C.R., Tucci, K., Roberts, J., Morrow, C., & Kuhn, C.M. (1990). Massage stimulates growth in preterm infants: A replication. *Infant Behavior and Development, 13,* 167–188.

Scatena, P. (1990). Phantom representations of congenitally absent limbs. *Perceptual and Motor Skills, 70,* 1227–1232.

Schaffer, R., Law, M., Polatajko, H., & Miller, J. (1989). A study of children with learning disabilities and sensorimotor problems or let's not throw the baby out with the bathwater. *Physical and Occupational Therapy in Pediatrics, 9,* 101–117.

Schneider, V.S. (1989). *Infant massage: A handbook for loving parents.* Toronto, ON: Bantam Books.

Shekelle, R.B. (1981). Psychological depression and 17-year-risk of death from cancer. *Psychosomatic Medicine, 43,* 117–125.

Sherrod, L.R. (1981). Issues in cognitive-perceptual development: The special case of social stimuli. In M.E. Lamb & L.R. Sherrod (Eds.), *Infant social cognition: Empirical and theoretical considerations.* Mahwah, NJ: Lawrence Erlbaum Associates.

Sinnett, J.M., Pisoni, D.B., & Aslin, R.N.A. (1983). A comparison of pure tone auditory thresholds in human infants and adults. *Infant Behavior and Development, 6,* 3–17.

Stack, D.M., & Arnold, S.L. (1998). Changes in mothers' touch and hand gestures influence infant behavior during face-to-face interchanges. *Infant Behavior and Development, 21,* 451–468.

Stack, D.M., & Muir, D.W. (1992). Adult tactile stimulation during face-to-face interactions modulates five-month-olds' affect and attention. *Child Development, 63,* 1509–1525.

Steiner, J.E. (1977). Facial expressions of the neonate infant indication of the hedonics of food-related chemical stimuli. In J.M. Weiffenbach (Ed.), *Taste and development: The genesis of sweet preference.* Washington, DC: U.S. Government Printing Office.

Stern, D.N. (1985). *The interpersonal world of the infant: A view from psychoanalysis and developmental psychology.* New York: Basic Books.

Suomi, S.J. (1991). Early stress and adult emotional reactivity in rhesus monkeys. In D. Barker (Ed.), *The childhood environment and adult disease* (pp. 171–188). Chichester, England: Wiley.

Suomi, S.J. (1995). Influence of Bowlby's attachment theory on research on nonhuman primate biobehavioral development. In S. Goldberg, R. Muir, & J. Kerr (Eds.), *Attachment theory: Social developmental and clinical perspectives* (pp. 185–201). Hillsdale, NJ: Analytic Press.

Thelen, E., Corbetta, D., Kamm, K., & Spencer, J.P. (1993). The transition to reaching: Mapping intention and intrinsic dynamics. *Child Development, 64,* 1058–1098.

Thelen, E., & Ulrich, B.D. (1991). Hidden skills: A dynamic systems analysis of treadmill stepping during the first year. *Monographs of the Society for Research in Child Development, 56,* 1–98.

Van der Meer, A.L.H. (1993). *Arm movements in the neonate: Establishing a frame of reference for reaching.* Paper presented at the 7th International Conference on Event Perception and Action. Vancouver, British Columbia, Canada.

Watkins, A. (1997). *Mind-body medicine: A clinician's guide to psychoneuroimmunology.* New York: Churchill-Livingstone.

Watt, J. (1990). Interaction, intervention, and development in small-for-gestational-age infants. *Infant Behavior and Development, 13,* 273–286.

Weil, J.L. (1992). *Early deprivation of empathetic care.* Madison, CT: International Universities Press.

Weissbluth, M. (1999). *Healthy sleep habits: Happy child.* New York: Fawcett Colombine.

Wheedon, A., Scafidi, F.A., Field, T., Ironson, G., Valdeon, C., & Bandstra, E. (1993). Massage effects on cocaine-exposed preterm neonates. *Journal of Developmental and Behavioral Pediatrics, 14,* 318–322.

White, L., Tursky, B., & Schwartz, G. (1985). *Placebo: Clinical implications and new insights.* New York: Guilford.

Witt, A., Cermak, S., & Coster, W. (1990). Body part identification in 1- to 2-year-old children. *The American Journal of Occupational Therapy, 44,* 147–153.

Zero to Three/National Center for Clinical Infant Programs (1994). *Diagnostic classification: 0–3: diagnostic classification of mental health and developmental disorders of infancy and early childhood.* Arlington, VA: Author.

FURTHER READING ON THE TOPIC

Achterberg, J., Dossey, B.M., & Kolkmeier, L. (1994). *Rituals of healing: Using imagery for health and wellness.* New York: Bantam Books.

Barnard, K.E., & Brazelton, T.B. (Eds.). (1990). *Touch: The foundation of experience.* Madison, WI: International Universities Press.

Cash, T. (1990). *Body-image therapy: A program for self-directed change* (Cassette Recording) New York: Guilford Press.

Dalley, M. (1983). *Moving and growing: Exercises and activities for the first two years.* Ottawa, Ontario: Canadian Institute of Child Health.

DeGangi, G. (2000). *Pediatric disorders of regulation in affect and behavior: A therapist's guide to assessment and treatment.* San Diego, CA: Academic Press.

Fishel, E. (1992, September). Raising sexually healthy kids. *Parents Magazine, 67(6),* 110.

Fisher, S. (1968). Body image and personality. New York: Dover Publications.

Ford, C.W. (1993). *Compassionate touch: The role of human touch in healing and recovery.* New York: Simon & Schuster.

Geasler, M.J., Dannison, L.L., & Edlund, C.J. (1995). Sexuality education of young children: Parental concerns. *Family Relations: Journal of Applied Family and Child Studies, 44,* 184–188.

Gerard, P.G. (1988). *Teaching your child basic body confidence.* Boston: Houghton Mifflin.

Gibson, J. (1984, April). Hugs and kisses. *Parents Magazine, 59(1),* 140.

Gibson, J. (1988, February). Learning through touch. *Parents Magazine, 63(1),* 176.

Haynes, H., White, B.L., & Held, R. (1965). Visual accommodation in human infants. *Science, 148,* 528–530.

Kabat-Zinn, J. (1995). *Mindfulness meditation: Cultivating the wisdom of your body and mind* (Cassette Recording). New York: Simon & Schuster.

Kabat-Zinn, M., & Kabat-Zinn, J. (1997). *Everyday blessings: The inner work of mindful parenting.* New York: Hyperion.

Krueger, D.W. (1989). *Body self and psychological self: A developmental and clinical integration of disorders of the self.* New York: Brunner/Mazel.

Lansky, V. (1984). *Toilet training: A practical guide to daytime and nighttime training.* New York: Bantam Books.

Levy, R.B. (1990). *I can only touch you now.* Englewood Cliffs, NJ: Prentice-Hall.

Lynch-Fraser, D. (2000). *Danceplay: Creative movement for very young children.* New York: New American Library

Naparstek, B. (1993). *General wellness* (Cassette Recording). Los Angeles: Time Warner Audio Books.

Naparstek, B. (1994). *Staying well with guided imagery.* New York: Warner Books.

Shuman, W. (1984, November). Hugs and kisses: Your loving touch does more than comfort your children—it is essential to their healthy development. *Parents Magazine, 59,* 74(4).

Striker, S. (1986). *Please touch: How to stimulate your child's creative development.* New York: Simon & Shuster.

Summar, P. (1986, March). Shall we dance? *Parents Magazine, 61,* 90(4).

Suomi, S.J. (1995). Touch and the immune system in rhesus monkeys. In T.M. Field. (Ed.), *Touch in early development* (pp. 89–103). Mahwah, NJ: Lawrence Erlbaum Associates.

Thoman, E.B., & Browder, S. (1988). *Born dancing: How intuitive parents understand their baby's unspoken language and natural rhythms.* New York: Perennial Library.

Weissbourd, B. (1988, June). My body, myself. *Parents Magazine, 63,* 188(1).

ZERO TO THREE/National Center for Clinical Infant Programs (1994). *Diagnostic classification of mental health and developmental disorders of infancy and early childhood.* Arlington, VA: National Center for Clinical Infant Programs.

CHILDREN'S BOOKS ABOUT BODY CONTROL, SEXUALITY, AND BODY IMAGE

Aliki. (1990). *My feet.* New York: Harper Collins Children's Book Group.

Aliki. (1990). *My five senses.* New York: Harper Collins Children's Book Group.

Aliki. (1990). *My hands.* New York: Harper Collins Children's Book Group.

Andry, A., & Schepp, S. (1984). *How babies are made.* Boston: Little, Brown.

Bliss, C.D. (1995). *The shortest kid in the world.* New York: Random House Children's Books.

Brooks, R.B. (1993). *So that's how I was born.* New York: Simon & Schuster Books for Young Readers.

Cole, B. (1995). *Mummy laid an egg!* London: Arrow Books.

Cole, B. (1997). *Dr. Dog.* New York: Knopf.

Cole, J. (1994). *How you were born.* New York: William Morrow.

Fowke, E. (1969). *Sally go round the sun:* Three hundred children's songs, rhymes and games. Toronto, ON: McClelland and Stewart.

Frankel, A. (1999). *Once upon a potty.* New York: HarperCollins Children's Book Group.

Garth, M. (1991). *Starbright: Meditations for children.* San Francisco: Harper Collins.

Harris, R.H. (1996). *Happy birth day!* Cambridge, MA: Candlewick Press.

Hazen, B.S. (1978). *The me I see.* New York: Abingdon Press.

Herron, C. (1997). *Nappy hair.* New York: Knopf.

Isadora, R. (1985). *I see.* New York: Greenwillow Books.

Klipper, I. (1980). *My magic garden: A meditation guide for children.* Palo Alto, CA: Pathways Press.

Leaf, M. (1977). *The story of Ferdinand.* New York: Viking Press.

Leaf, M. (1985). *Wee Gillis.* New York: Puffin Books.

Mayle, P. (2000). *Where did I come from: The facts of life without any nonsense and with illustrations.* Secaucus, NJ: Stuart.

Miller, M. (1996). *Now I'm big.* New York: Greenwillow Books.

Moon, N. (1997). *Something special.* Atlanta, GA.: Peachtree Publishers.

Munsch, R. (1987). *I have to go!* Toronto, ON: Annick Press.

Munsch, R., & Daniel, A. (1990). *Good families don't.* Toronto, ON: Doubleday Canada.

Pearse, P., & Riddell, E. (1988). *See how you grow.* Hauppauge, NY: Barron's.

Rius, M., Parramon, J.M., & Puig, J.J. (1985). *Hearing.* Woodbury, NY: Barron's.

Rothman, J. (1979). *This can lick a lollipop: Body riddles for kids.* Garden City, NY: Double Day.

Sheffield, M. (1983). *Before you were born.* London: Cape.

Showers, P. (1991). *The listening walk.* New York: Harper Collins.

Stinson, K. (1988). *The bare naked book.* Toronto, Ontario: Firefly Books.

Tudor, T. (1988). *First delights: A book about the five senses.* New York: Platt & Munk.

Ward, L. (1991). *I am eyes: Ni Macho.* New York: Blue Ribbon Books.

Waxman, S. (1989). *What is a girl? What is a boy?* New York: Crowell.

APPENDIX: SELECTED ASSESSMENT INSTRUMENTS

ASSESSING BODY SELF IN CHILDREN AND ADULTS

Assessing Motor Development and Sensory Integration of Children

Subtests of some of the measures in Chapter 1 can be used to assess the gross and fine motor abilities of infants and young children. These are the

- Bayley Scales of Infant Development, Second Edition (BSID-II) (Motor scale)

- Vineland Adaptive Behavior Scales (Motor skills)

- Diagnostic Inventory of Screening Children (DISC) (Gross and fine motor scales)

More specialized tests that can be used include those described in Table A2.1. In this table, the best-known tests are described in some detail, then other tests are briefly listed.

Assessing Body Image and Body Scheme in Children

One of the four dimensions (Physical Competence) of the Pictorial Scale of Perceived Competence and Social Acceptance for Young Children (PSPCSA) can be used to measure body image. It is described in detail in Chapter 6.

Table A2.2 describes assessments used to better understand body image and body scheme in children.

OBSERVATIONAL MEASURES

The assessments set out here are not standardized tests but procedures that allow understanding of how the young child perceives him- or herself. Table A2.3 outlines one test in more detail, the Santostefano Schema Test.

Table A2.1. Selected motor development and sensory integration assessments

Tool/instrument	Age range	Items/ administration time	General description
Bruininks-Oseretsky Test of Motor Proficiency (BOT) Bruininks, R.H. (1978). *Bruininks-Oseretsky Test of Motor Proficiency.* Circle Pines, MN: American Guidance Service.	4–11 years	Long Form, 46 items; 60 minutes. Short Form, 15 items; 15–20 minutes	The *Bruininks-Oseretsky Test of Motor Proficiency (BOT)* is used to determine a child's level of motor proficiency for educational placement and to evaluate a training program. Four subtests measure gross motor skills, three measure fine motor skills, and one measures both. For example, subtests assess running speed and agility, balance, and upper limb coordination and control. No special training is required and people from various disciplines can administer the test. Standard scores, age equivalencies, and percentile ranks are provided for 1) gross motor composite, 2) fine motor composite, and 3) total battery composite.
DeGangi-Berk Test of Sensory Integration (TSI) Berk, R.A., & DeGangi, A. (1983). *DeGangi-Berk Test of Sensory Integration: Manual.* Los Angeles: Western Psychological Services.	3–5 years	36 items; 30 minutes	The *DeGangi-Berk Test of Sensory Integration (TSI)* measures areas of postural control, bilateral motor integration, and reflex integration. It is a criterion-referenced test to be used in order to identify children with delays in sensory, motor, and perceptual skills. It should be administered by a person who is familiar with pediatric and motor assessments.
Developmental Test of Visual-Motor Integration (Third Revision) (VMI) Beery, K.E. (1982). *The Developmental Test of Visual Motor Integration-Revised.* Cleveland, OH: Modern Curriculum Press.	3–18 years	24 items; 10 minutes	The *Developmental Test of Visual-Motor Integration (Third Revision) (VMI)* tests visual-motor integration. It consists of 24 geometric designs that are arranged in developmental sequence, from which the child copies as many of the designs as possible in the test booklet. The total raw score is converted into developmental equivalents and into scale scores. The test can be administered individually or to a group.

Tool/instrument	Age range	Items/ administration time	General description
Milani-Comparetti Motor Development Screening Test-Revised (MC) Milani-Comparetti, A., & Gidoni, E.A. (1967). Pattern analysis of motor development and its disorders. *Developmental Medicine & Child Neurology, 9,* 625–630.	Birth–2 years	27 items; 10 minutes	The *Milani-Comparetti Motor Development Screening Test–Revised (MC)* is a simple rapid neurodevelopmental exam to screen for motor delay and abnormal movement patterns in young children. It assesses the infant's positions, control, and movement or patterns of muscle activation. Locomotion and reflexes are also assessed. The profile obtained can be used to identify developmental delay, central nervous system dysfunction, or typical development. It incorporates both quantitative and qualitative judgments about motor development. Children who are judged to be at risk can be tested several times to monitor trends in motor development.
Peabody Developmental Motor Scales (PDMS) Folio, M.R., & Fewell, R.R. (1983). *Peabody Developmental Motor Scales.* Allen, TX: DLM Teaching Resources.	Birth–7 years	282 items; 60 minutes	The *Peabody Developmental Motor Scales (PDMS)* is an individually administered, standardized test that measures gross and fine motor skills. The tasks assess reflexes, balance, non-locomotor, locomotor, and receipt and propulsion of objects and are divided into four skill areas: 1) grasping, 2) hand use, 3) eye–hand coordination, and 4) manual dexterity.
Test of Sensory Functions in Infants (TSFI) DeGangi, G.A., & Greenspan, S.I. (1989). *Test of Sensory Functions in Infants (TSFI): Manual.* Los Angeles, CA: Western Psychological Services.	4–18 months	24 items; 20 minutes	The *Test of Sensory Functions in Infants* provides a measure of sensory processing and reactivity in infants. Five subtests are used to assess: 1) Reactivity to Tactile Deep Pressure, 2) Adaptive Motor Functions, 3) Visual-Tactile Inte-gration, 4) Ocular-Motor Control and 5) Reactivity to Vestibular Stimulation. The test is used to identify children with regulatory disorders and sensory integrative dysfunction who are at risk for learning and sensory processing difficulties. It can be used with the Bayley Scales of Infant Development. It is recommended that it be used by professionals with training in interpreting results in the domain of sensory functioning.

Other commonly used measures

Tool/instrument	Age range
The Primary Visual Motor Test (PVM) Haworth, M.R. (1970). *The Primary Visual Motor Test.* New York: Grune & Stratton.	4–7 years
Sensory Integration and Praxis Tests (SIPT) Ayres, A.J. (1989). *Manual of the Sensory Integration and Praxis Test.* Los Angeles, CA: Western Psychological Services.	4–8.11 years

Table A2.2. Selected assessments of body image and body scheme in children

Tool/instrument	Age range	Items/ administration time	General description
Mirror Self-Recognition Test Amsterdam, B. (1972). Mirror self-image reactions before age two. *Developmental Psychobiology, 5,* 297–305.	12–36 months	1 item; 5 minutes	During the *Mirror Self-Recognition Test,* the child's nose is surreptitiously dabbed with rouge, and the child is then placed in front of the mirror and asked "See?", and "Who's that?" Responses are recorded (e.g., smiling, vocalizing, gazing and touching). Full self-recognition is defined as self-directed behavior indicating awareness of the red spot on the nose. Children also may show "self-admiring" behavior (e.g., strutting and preening) and embarrassed behavior (e.g., blushing, coyness) as signs of self-recognition.
Self and Mother Feature Knowledge Pipp, S., Fischer, K.W., & Jennings, S. (1987). The acquisition of self and mother knowledge in infancy. *Developmental Psychology, 23,* 83–96.	6 months– 4 years	12 items; 10 minutes	These items or tasks were revised from recognition tasks previously developed. They include a sticker task (child pulls sticker off his and his mother's nose); and rouge task (detecting rouge on nose). The test has been used to assess the developmental sequence of the ability to perform the task.
The TacVi [tactile-visual technique] of Measuring Self-Concept in Preschool Children Rodriguez-Andrew, S., & Zurcher, L.A. (1986). The TacVi Technique: A tactile-visual method for exploring the self-concept of preschool children. *Child Welfare, XV*(3). 305–311.	2–6 years	5 items; 10 minutes	During the *The TacVi [tactile-visual technique] of Measuring Self-Concept in Preschool Children* the examiner uses his or her hand for illustrative purposes. The thumb of his or her left hand is identified as the most positive; index finger, next-most positive; middle finger as in between; ring finger as a "little bit" negative; and little finger as most negative. The child is asked to identify "Which one is you" on the following dimensions: 1) happiness (happiest as opposed to saddest), 2) physical size (biggest as opposed to smallest), 3) intelligence (smartest as opposed to dumbest), 4) physical attractiveness (best looking as opposed to ugliest), and 5) physical strength (strongest as opposed to weakest).

Table A2.3. Observational test to assess the capacity to imitate body movements

Tool/instrument	General description
The Santostefano Schema Test Santostefano, S. (1978). *A bio developmental approach to clinical child psychology: Cognitive controls and cognitive control therapy.* New York: John Wiley & Sons. Santostefano, S., & Callicchia, J.A. (1992). Body image, relational psychoanalysis, and the construction of meaning: Implications for treating aggressive children. *Development and Psychopathology, 4,* 655–678.	In *The Santostefano Schema Test,* the child is asked to assume certain body positions; to try out various movements; and to describe what he notices, feels, and what and who it reminds him of. In this way, the examiner can judge how well the child's body image is developing and how well she can tune into body sensations and experiences, which is a crucial step to really knowing her body and controlling it as well. Later, the child is asked to move his body through open space at various tempos and to construct images and fantasies. The therapist offers images to teach the child that tempos can be played out in fantasy rather than in constant movement. The child is asked to move slowly, like a turtle; then a little faster, like a deer. Then the child is asked to move like himself so his usual tempo can be determined. Children who are hyperactive will have a great deal of difficulty adjusting to the different paces of movements asked for here.

Table A2.4. Assessment of body image in adults

Tool/instrument	Age range	Items/administration time	General description
Body Esteem Scale (BES) Franzoi, S.L., & Shields, S.A. (1984). The Body Esteem Scale: Multi-dimensional structure and sex differences in a college population. *Journal of Personality Assessment, 48,* 173–178.	Adult	39 items; 30 minutes	The *Body Esteem Scale (BES)* uses self-evaluation of the body and has male/female subscales called Physical Attractiveness; Sexual Attractiveness; Upper Body Strength/Weight Concern; Physical Condition/Physical Condition.

Assessing the Capacity to Imitate Body Movements

Watch how well the 9- to 12-month-old can join in games such as: This Little Piggy Went to Market; I'm Going to Get You; and Row, Row, Row Your Boat. Most babies will try and imitate the movements and giggle while anticipating the next part of the game. As the child gets older, the game Simon Says will let the examiner see how well the child can imitate, for example, by raising his hands, jumping, and synchronizing movements.

Assessing Body Image in Adults

Table A2.4 describes one tool for assessing body image in adults.

● ● ● 3

DEVELOPING A SECURE ATTACHMENT

Baby Parames, almost 9 months old, sometimes gets upset when anyone other than her parents tries to pick her up. Her parents are also aware that she gets very excited when she sees them and that she seems to settle better when they are around. Parames is showing signs of having developed a secure attachment to both parents. This is a developmental achievement that research has shown to be a crucial foundation for much of the rest of development. Attachment research and theory have made a unique contribution to the understanding of child development. They have been particularly critical in demonstrating how important a child's relationships in the early years are on his or her later development, as well as suggesting a mechanism for transmitting styles of parenting across generations.

After more than 35 years of productive research using direct observations and extensive analysis of data, those who study concepts of attachment have been able to demonstrate not just that continuity exists in personality and social development, but more important, *how* this development takes place. Attachment theorists have been able to address issues that are critical for parents, child care workers, and a range of practitioners who provide early intervention services and other therapeutic approaches to children and adults of all ages.

Attachment theory has been able to at least suggest answers to a number of critical questions. Why do infants become attached to certain people? Does this attachment affect their ongoing behavior outside the home? What is the effect of child care on attachment quality and later adjustment? Does attachment help explain the tendency for parents who have been abused to repeat these patterns with their own children? And perhaps most fascinating, do these early attachments continue to affect other relationships in later life, even deciding the kind of partners individuals choose? Although attachment researchers do not yet have definitive answers for these questions, they are constantly testing hypotheses and, if necessary, adjusting theory and knowledge in light of their findings.

As explained by Goldberg (1991), attachment theory addresses four major areas of the development of close relationships: 1) social aspects, 2) the emotional bonds between people in

relationships, 3) the cognitive scheme and memories that are formed, and 4) the resulting behaviors that tend to maintain the attachment style and relationship.

Because research has been so prolific, making sense of the thousands of journal articles and books on the topic and the changes in understanding that have evolved and continue to change over time is, at times, confusing and challenging. In this chapter, some of the most important research findings and theories about attachment are described and translated into practical concepts that can inform parents and other caregivers about emotional and social development in infancy and early childhood. As well, readers are provided with strategies for how to optimize development through early relationships and styles of caregiving.

DEFINITIONS OF BONDING AND ATTACHMENT

The terms *bonding* and *attachment* have frequently been used in the popular press to describe some "magical" process that just happens and from which there are wonderful outcomes for children. In fact, as described by Bowlby, it is the "nature of the child's ties" or the security of the attachments that are critical (1958, p. 350). As is described later in this chapter, secure

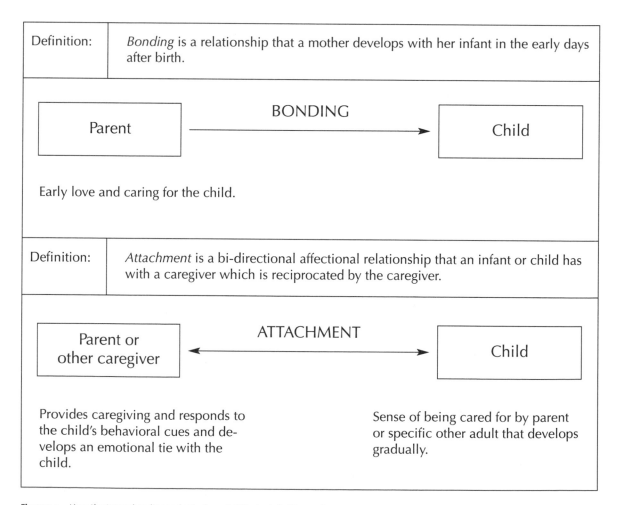

Figure 3.1. How the terms *bonding* and *attachment* differ in definition and process.

attachments are beneficial to infants and children as well as to adults, while insecure attachments can result in a variety of behavioral tendencies that can cause difficulties for an individual, especially in relationships. Although *bonding* and *attachment* have often been used synonymously, they actually describe two processes that are different in terms of direction and timing (see Figure 3.1).

Bonding

Bonding refers to the mother's tie to her infant, believed to occur during the early days or months after a baby's birth. Marshall Klaus and John Kennell originally described the process of bonding in 1976 as a process that happened immediately after birth. They believed that a period of heightened sensitivity occurred in the mother immediately after delivery, making this the optimal time for the mother to develop a relationship with her infant. In a study carried out in 1975, Kennell and associates reported that a period of extended contact at birth and in the days immediately following the delivery resulted in mothers demonstrating more nurturing relationships with their infants 13 months later. The study was conducted with a control group who only received the standard practice at the time of removing the babies to a nursery and only allowing the mothers to be with their infants at set times. Compared with mothers in the control group, the mothers who were allowed extended contact showed more closeness in feeding their infants, more responsive soothing during a medical examination, and an increased incidence of breast feeding. No differences were found for the infants on developmental tests (Kennell, Trause, & Klaus, 1975). Attempts to replicate the findings of the study have not been successful, however, and it is now generally accepted that the extended close contact described by Klaus and Kennell, although desirable, is not crucial for later attachment to occur. Still, some mothers, like Francina, described in the following vignette, expect a sudden rush of love on seeing their babies and may feel unnecessary anxiety and guilt if it does not occur.

• •

Francina telephoned a postpartum depression hotline in tears describing her experience after the birth of her first child 18 years ago. She also talked about the guilt that she still held all these years later! For Francina, her baby's birth had been traumatic and difficult and ended in an emergency caesarian section. When she was finally able to hold her baby she felt exhausted, worried, and a failure. These feelings worsened as she returned home to a colicky baby and little support. Instead of a flood of love and positive feelings, her early experiences were of depletion, depression, and, at times, resentment toward her baby. These feelings lifted after the first few months and she established a warm and loving bond with her infant. The guilt of those early weeks and her feelings remained, however.

Attachment

Attachment in the early years refers to an emotional tie between an infant or child and a caregiver. In infancy, the attachment system results in numerous behaviors on the part of the infant and the caregiver that help in establishing the relationship. Attachment is bi-directional and

goes from child to caregiver and caregiver to child. As illustrated in the vignette about Francina, attachment is not instantaneous for infant or parent, and for the baby, it is not established until about 8 months of age, when he has acquired certain cognitive abilities. Figure 3.1 depicts the differences between bonding and attachment and focuses on the bi-directional nature of attachment.

Attachment is a system of behaviors that the infant and young child displays in order to establish proximity and contact with a caregiver. It is a child's tendency to seek this contact with a *specific person* and to do this when he is frightened, upset, tired, or ill. As the child gets older and is capable of having a representation or image of self, attachment also includes working models of attachment or representations of others formed out of the child's interactions with caregivers. These working models, in turn, influence the child's self-concept as well as his expectations of future interactions with other relationships. Table 3.1 outlines behaviors used by infants and toddlers in attachment formation and the cognitions that are forming the child's working models of attachment.

THEORIES OF ATTACHMENT

Attachment theory originated in the 1950s with John Bowlby, a psychiatrist and psychoanalyst who trained with Melanie Klein, an eminent child analyst whose theory of child development was based on psychoanalytic principles. Bowlby himself abandoned the total focus of traditional psychoanalytic theory on internal mental processes and instead sought to prove that the child's actual experiences of early relationships were more critical in determining the child's development, and that these experiences and relationships could be the basic cause of emotional difficulties. Having rejected psychoanalytic principles, Bowlby was attracted to the concepts of ethology, which focuses on imprinting or a social bond. He proposed that an in-

Table 3.1. Behaviors used by infants, toddlers, and preschoolers in attachment formation and cognitions developed

Age	A behavioral system that attains or maintains proximity to attachment figure	Cognitions about attachment: A representational system or working model of attachment
Infants	Crying Sucking Clinging/grasping Responding to comforting Smiling Reaching out Affective sharing	Late infancy: General expectations of the caregiver's behavior developed
Toddlers and preschoolers	Crying/tantrums Following/locomotion Responding to comforting Using language to obtain contact (e.g., calling out) Affective sharing Smiling Initiating interaction Exploring from "secure" base of caregiver	Perceptions of self and caregiver(s) and other people Memory of events Processing of information Attributions of emotions and intent to others Expectations and attitudes towards social relationships in general

fant's attachment or tie to his mother (or substitute caregiver) is formed out of a number of behavioral systems or responses that develop during the first year of life and ensure survival by attracting the attention of caregivers. These behaviors become increasingly focused on particular caregivers or attachment figures by the time the child is 6 months or a little older. As part of his work on separation and loss, Bowlby formulated his ideas of the role of internal working models of attachment in the intergenerational repetition of attachment patterns or styles. He went on to use theories of information processing in order to elaborate on these ideas and to explain how—as a result of defensive processes—information is excluded from awareness that does not fit with the existing models.

Mary Ainsworth, who carried out a series of research studies, also made a significant contribution by developing a system with which to classify the relationship between children and their caregivers. This system was originally based on observations of school-age children following their prolonged stays in an institutional environment. The styles that she observed helped her formulate three classifications (secure, insecure–avoidant, and insecure–resistant), which she later elaborated on after she developed a way to measure attachment (Ainsworth, Blehar, Waters, & Wall, 1978). Also critical was her demonstration of how the quality of a child's attachment to a caregiver was related to how the caregiver had responded to the infant's signals in the 12 months following birth (Ainsworth & Wittig, 1969). Ainsworth's work is described in more detail later in this chapter.

Main and Goldwyn also influenced the field of attachment through their development of an interview and scoring system used to measure adults' "current state of mind in respect to attachment" (Main and Goldwyn, 1994, p. 1). Called the Adult Attachment Interview (AAI), responses are elicited that are used to evaluate the quality of the early experience with parents, state of mind regarding attachment, and evidence of unresolved loss or trauma. Scores assigned on the basis of the responses are used to make decisions about the person's attachment classification. These and other writers and researchers who have made significant contributions are outlined in Table 3.2.

ATTACHMENT CLASSIFICATIONS ACROSS THE LIFE SPAN

This section outlines how attachment classifications change over an individual's life span.

Attachment Classifications in Early Childhood

Infants and young children usually form an attachment to a caregiver unless they have no consistent caregiving or they experience extraordinary and ongoing deprivation or abuse. The quality of the attachment varies significantly, from secure to various types of insecurity (e.g., avoidant, ambivalent, disorganized). The attachment classification of children from 12 to 30 months of age can be assessed using the Strange Situation, a research procedure developed by Mary Ainsworth and associates in 1978. This laboratory situation consists of eight 3-minute episodes in which the child is either with the parent alone, the stranger alone, the stranger and parent, or totally alone. The stranger is someone the child has never seen before. The episodes present the child with increasingly stressful situations that are intended to evoke attachment-related behaviors such as seeking proximity with the parent, crying, and wanting to be held and comforted.

Table 3.2. Theories of attachment

Theorists	Major constructs
Bowlby (1958, 1965, 1980, 1988)	Focused on biological bases of attachment behaviors or an ethological theory, seeing the function of these behaviors as bringing the caregiver close in order to assure protection and survival
	Proposed that the attachment behavioral system also includes cognitive components or internal working models that—once formed—affect learning, information processing, attention, and interpretation of situations
	Proposed a developmental sequence for the development of attachment
	Contributed to the study of the effects of loss and separation, saw grieving as a normal reaction to loss, and proposed various stages that people go through following loss, including numbing anxiety, anger and denial, despair, sadness, and reorganization
Ainsworth, Blehar, Waters, & Wall (1978) Ainsworth (1982, 1989)	In two studies, one carried out in Africa and the other in the United States, observed mother–infant interactions during the first 12 months of life and assessed the infant's security of attachment using a laboratory procedure known as the Strange Situation, which she had developed
	Identified three classifications of attachment, one secure and two insecure
	Proposed that characteristics of maternal behaviors towards their infants in the home resulted in the three classifications of attachment
Main, Kaplan, & Cassidy (1985) Main (1990) Main & Goldwyn (1998)	Developed further the concept of internal working models
	With Goldwyn, developed the Adult Attachment Interview and a scoring and classification system, which allowed the study of attachment and collection of data to be extended into the adult stage
Main & Solomon (1986, 1990) Solomon & George (1999)	Identified the patterns of behavior for the disorganized attachment classification
	Examined the parental behaviors that can lead to the disorganized attachment classification
Hazan & Shaver (1987)	Expanded the attachment paradigm into adulthood
	Developed a brief questionnaire that can be used to identify the patterns of attachment or relationships of adults
	Used these patterns to examine their influence on the romantic relationships of adults
Crittenden (1988, 1992)	Examined the parental interactions and behavioral outcomes of abused, neglected, and abused and neglected children and identified particular patterns of behavior
	Developed a different attachment classification system for children in the preschool years that included six major classifications: secure, defended, coercive, defended-coercive, anxious depressed, and insecure/other
Fonagy, Steele, & Steele (1991) Fonagy, Steele, Steele, Moran, & Higgitt (1991)	Examined the intergenerational repetition of attachment patterns
	Identified the caregiver's reflective self as critical in determining her own attachment classification and her behavior with her infant

After participating in this procedure, children are classified in various attachment types on the basis of a variety of behaviors. These include

- The degree of exploration the child exhibits with the parent present

- Whether the child misses the parent when separated

- Relatedness with the parent compared with the stranger

- Type of behavior following reunion with the parent (e.g., proximity seeking, contact seeking and maintaining, resistance, or avoidance)

Table 3.3 outlines the kinds of behaviors shown in the Strange Situation by children of different attachment classifications. In most populations, approximately 60% of children have a secure

Table 3.3. Types of behaviors exhibited by children of different attachment classifications in the "Strange Situation"

B. Secure (60%)[a] (four subgroups, B1, B2, B3, B4, with B1 "most" secure)	A. Insecure/Avoidant (18%) (two subgroups, A1 and A2, with A1 more extreme in ignoring of mother)	C. Insecure/Ambivalent/ Resistant (12%) (two subgroups, C1 and C2, with C1 conspicuously angry and resistant, C2 unhappy, helpless and passive)	D.[b] Insecure/Disorganized/Disoriented (10–14%)
Uses mother as secure base to explore	Pays little attention to mother	Preoccupied with mother yet ambivalent toward her	Will try to stay close but may hit at same time/ contradictory behavior
Shows affective sharing with parent	Does not show affective sharing	Affective sharing intense	May be very concerned about mother's emotions
May or may not be upset at separation	May approach stranger as much as mother	Extreme distress at separation	Extreme distress at separation
Shows little or no resistance to interaction	Little distress at separation	Seeks and rejects contact	Attachment behavior directed to stranger
Explores toys and room from secure base	Explores toys and room but with no reference to mother	Has difficulty exploring room because of preoccupation with mother	At reunion seems dazed, confused, and frightened; shows freezing
Seeks proximity after separation	Snubs or ignores mother at reunion	May fuss or cry a lot even when mother is present	May control mother or comfort mother instead of being comforted him- or herself
Calms down quickly after mother returns and explores again within 3 minutes	Does not seek proximity	Refuses and resists or cannot be comforted at reunion	May gaze away while in contact with mother
	Does not need to be calmed at reunion		Repetitive, stereotyped gestures or motions
			Depressed or affectless facial expressions

[a]Percentages are only approximate and vary in different populations.

[b]The D category is usually only used as an adjunct of the three major classifications A, B, and C.

Adapted from Ainsworth, M.D.S., Blehar, M.C., Waters, E., & Wall, S. (1978). *Patterns of attachment: A psychological study of the Strange Situation.* Hillsdale, NJ: Erlbaum; and Main, M., & Solomon, J. (1990). Procedures for identifying infants as disorganized/ disoriented during the Ainsworth Strange Situation. In M.T. Greenberg, D. Cicchetti, & E.M. Cummings (Eds.), *Attachment in the preschool years* (pp. 121–160). Chicago: University of Chicago Press.

attachment; 18% are insecure/avoidant, 12% insecure/ambivalent-resistant, and 10%–14% are insecure/disorganized/disoriented. The percentages may differ in some cultures, and in high-risk populations the percentage of securely attached children may be much lower.

Behavior Patterns Associated with Attachment in Early Childhood

When children are observed in child care or in stressful situations, they tend to exhibit behaviors that are likely outcomes of their attachment patterns or classifications. It is important to note that actual attachment classifications can only be properly assessed using the reliable and valid assessment procedures listed in the appendix of this chapter. The behaviors described here are based on Ainsworth's rating scale for scoring the Strange Situation and follow-up research using observations of children in other situations such as in child care. These descriptions can be helpful to give service providers some ideas about the caregiving that children are likely to have received in infancy and in early childhood.

Securely Attached (B) Securely attached children usually manage well in child care and enjoy being around other children. Their social skills are more advanced and positive than those of insecurely attached children and elicit more positive responses from peers. Popular and empathetic with peers, they develop more friendships. They realize their attachment figure will return and are easily comforted if they get upset. For the most part they try and solve problems but seek out teachers to help in situations that they cannot manage alone. They are good problem solvers and manage conflict very well; in other words, they tend to be resilient under stress.

Insecure/Avoidant (A)   Insecure/avoidant children often manage well during separations and may learn well in child care and in school. They do not deal well with other people's feelings and tend not to show their own. They may be competent or aggressive and rejecting. They do not value friends and, as a consequence, are usually not well liked.

Insecure/Ambivalent/Resistant (C)   Insecure/ambivalent/resistant children often are very upset when they are left and very hard to settle. They tend to be whiny and unhappy and show high levels of attention-seeking behaviors mixed with impulsivity, neediness, tenseness, and helplessness. They find it hard to problem solve in frustrating or difficult situations. Quite intense and conflictual with other children and adults, these children may be angry one minute and seductive the next.

Insecure/Disorganized/Disoriented (D)   Children with disorganized attachments may show unusual, somewhat bizarre behavior at times. They may appear to freeze, dissociate, seem frightened, and want to be close but strike out at the same time. They are likely to have behavior problems or show ongoing sadness or anxiety disorders.

Table 3.4 outlines in more detail how children's attachment classifications relate to later behaviors.

Caregiving Patterns that Contribute to Behavior Patterns in Early Childhood

Caregiving patterns that contribute to these classifications were first identified by Ainsworth in her studies in Africa and the United States in which she observed infants and mothers several times in the first year of life (Ainsworth, 1967). She found four dimensions of the mother's behavior that predicted their infants' attachment classifications. These were 1) sensitivity versus insensitivity (i.e., the degree to which the mother understands her child's signals and interprets them correctly); 2) acceptance versus rejection (i.e., the degree to which the mother has positive feelings toward her child and displays happiness and delight in him); 3) accessibility versus being ignoring and neglectful (i.e., how much the mother focuses her attention on the child); and 4) cooperation versus interference (i.e., how much the mother takes her child's needs into account and respects his need to be separate and autonomous, as opposed to being intrusive in interactions with the child). These were scored from 1 to 9, with 1 being the least positive and 9 being the most positive.

Although these scales were developed several decades ago, they are still used by researchers today. Since Ainsworth's original work, however, researchers have identified other critical behaviors associated with caregiving that relate to a secure attachment, including

- Comforting the child, particularly when he is hurt, ill, upset, frustrated, or lonely

- Accepting the child's feelings such as anger, jealousy, sadness, and fear

Table 3.4. Attachment classifications and later behaviors associated with them

Secure	Insecure/Avoidant
Cooperative with parents and other adults	Tends to be noncompliant and to disobey rules
Affectively positive	Often very angry and hostile
Socially competent and seeks out friends	Isolated from group, does not seek interaction
Has good self-control	Can be excessively angry but has control in non-social situations
Can problem-solve with confidence	May be quite competent
Easily comforted if upset/ seeks help if overwhelmed	When in pain or upset, withdraws and does not seek help
Manages well away from parents	Manages well away from parents

Insecure/Ambivalent/ Resistant	Insecure/Disorganized/ Disoriented
May have behavioral diffi- culties and fluctuate between being tense and helpless	Usually has behavioral difficulties and is unpredictable
Tends to be fearful and tense	Is often both a bully and a victim
Has poor social skills, tends to be dependent on others	Has poor social skills
Impulsive, low frustration tolerance	Low frustration tolerance and self-control
Lacks confidence and assert- iveness and has little abil- ity to problem solve	Very disorganized and dis- oriented in approach to problems
Needs sensitive caregiving, often difficult to calm down	Needs specialized caregiving
Often misses parents and seems helpless and tense as a result	May miss parents and appear frightened when with them as well as away from them

- Being sensitive and responding to the child's cues

- Being careful not to overwhelm the child by being too intrusive or directive

- Showing positive feelings toward the child and expressing genuine love and joy

- Allowing the child to be as separate and autonomous in exploring the environment as pos- sible while keeping him safe

In summary, caregivers should be accessible but not overwhelming and in touch with the child but not overbearing or too directive. Such interactions provide a delightful dance in which par- ent and child are attuned to each other's emotional and behavioral agendas.

Caregiver Interactions with Insecure/Avoidant Infants and Children The beha- vior of caregivers toward insecure children is very different from that described previously. A child is likely to become insecurely or *avoidantly* attached when her caregiver ignores negative emotions and consistently fails to respond when the child is upset and crying. The caregiver may do quite well with teaching tasks and even with setting limits but may be hostile, ignoring, and even rejecting of any emotions that arise as part of these interactions. Thus, caregivers of avoidantly attached children tend to be accessible in some aspects of interaction but are insensitive and do not read the cues in others that particularly relate to neediness. In extreme cases, they may neglect all of the child's caregiving needs.

Caregiver Interactions with Insecure/Ambivalent/Resistant Infants and Children

The ambivalent resistant child is likely to have had a caregiver who is very anxious about the child and who can be overprotective and interfering at times. The caregiver tends to be inconsistent; sometimes she responds to the child, while at other times she does not notice or give the child the support she needs. The child may still expect nurturing during times of upset but cannot depend on getting her needs met.

Caregiver Interactions with Insecure/Disorganized/Disoriented Infants and Children

The disorganized/disoriented attached child has generally experienced caregiving in which the child is unable to predict what will happen. At times, the caregiver seems frightened and unable to manage the situation, including the child; at other times, she seems frightening, exhibiting extreme hostility and anger. This places the child in an unresolvable conflict when the attachment system is activated because the child wants to go to the parent but is simultaneously afraid to do so. Such caregivers may be depressed, alcoholic, drug dependent, abusive, or traumatized with a significant level of psychopathology. This may include character disorder, anxiety disorder, sociopathic tendency, or even psychosis. Although these patterns are frequently seen in chaotic, multiproblem homes in which children are exposed to violence and abuse, they are also found in lower risk homes. Sometimes the caregiving patterns are relatively subtle and low key but are always confusing and related to parents' unresolved loss or trauma.

Working Models of Attachment or Internal Representations of Self and Others

Working models of attachment—or the ideas that people internalize about themselves and other people—influence how individuals see the world, particularly other people, as well as how they perceive themselves. Children who are securely attached are more likely to perceive and remember events positively and to view their role and that of others in ambiguous situations as benign and unintentional. Children who are insecurely attached see the same event and the children involved in it as being rejecting and hurtful.

• •

Pierre, an insecurely attached child, was watching some other children playing tag but had not been asked to join in. He believed he was being rejected because the children did not like him. He first tried to get their attention by hitting one of them, and when this did not work, he ran away to the edge of the playground and hung his head, looking sad and dejected.

John, a securely attached child in the same situation, was watching some other children playing tag but had not been asked to join in. He decided that the group had not noticed him so he ran over, asked to join in, and began running around with the others.

As these vignettes illustrate, the insecurely attached child sees the world very differently from the securely attached child and acts negatively as a result. The kind of behavior elicited can either lead, on an ongoing basis, to cycles of rejection or to affirming interactions that result in enhanced experiences.

Adult Attachments

Most of us have heard our parents' words coming out of our mouths even when we had been determined to avoid this. Even as adults, early relationships with our parents continue to affect our personality and relationships with others, particularly our children. We tend to parent as we were parented.

An adult's classification of attachment, or the person's "state of mind with respect to attachment" can be assessed using the Adult Attachment Interview (AAI) that was developed by Main and Goldwyn. The AAI is comprised of a series of questions designed to "surprise the unconscious" (1994, p. 36). By doing so, the AAI is intended to reflect an accurate understanding of the person's internal representation of his experiences and relationships with his parents when he was growing up.

The interview takes 1–2 hours to complete and includes these kinds of questions:

1. What five adjectives describe your relationships with your parents when you were a child? (Give examples of why you chose the descriptors.)

2. What did your parents do for you when you were hurt or upset?

3. Did you experience the loss or death of someone close?

4. Did you experience abuse or other trauma?

5. Did your parents ever threaten separation?

6. Why do you think that your parents behaved as they did?

7. What changes have taken place in your relationships with your parents since childhood?

8. How have these experiences influenced your adult personality and functioning and your parenting?

The scoring of the interviews is time-consuming and complex. After it is completed, individuals are placed in attachment categories that parallel those of the children's classifications. Table 3.5 lists the major adult attachment classifications as categorized using the AAI and what they mean in terms of associated behaviors. In addition, Main and Goldwyn (1998) also noted several subcategories under each major category noted in Table 3.5 that reflect somewhat different patterns and degrees of attachment influencing parenting and current relationships.

Autonomous (secure) individuals seem to be at peace with and to understand their past experiences with parents and to have come to terms with them even if they were difficult. They also understand how these experiences have influenced their personality and can affect the way they parent. Most important, they value relationships and seek them out.

Dismissing adults do not value relationships. As well, they dismiss any idea that their early experiences affected them and may idealize their early caregivers or not have any memory of them.

Table 3.5. Types of adult attachment as categorized using the Adult Attachment Interview (AAI) and associated behaviors

F. Secure – Autonomous/Free (five subgroups, F1, F2, F3, F4, F5, with F3 most secure, F1, F2 some detachment, and F4, F5 some preoccupation)	Ds. Insecure– Dismissing (four subgroups, Ds1, Ds2, Ds3, Ds4)	E. Insecure– Preoccupied (three subgroups, E1, E2, E3)	U.[a] Insecure– Unresolved (three subgroups, U/Ds, E, F)
Values attachment relationships	Integrates positive and negative aspects of feelings	Sees relationships as unpredictable, wants great closeness	Little consistency; may change rapidly and be subject to extreme anger
Interview is coherent and objective	Devaluing of relationships and not seeing them as important	Striking incoherence	Interview is strikingly incoherent
Descriptions of parents supported by examples	Contradictions found in interview	Preoccupied with relationships with parents; often describes role-reversing experiences	Disorganized and distortions of thought patterns may be evident
At ease with description/ balanced view	May come up with few descriptions or examples of parents that do not fit together	Expresses anger and helplessness	Interview is disoriented
Reflective, not idealizing or angry and preoccupied	Restricted in feelings	Oscillates between good and bad evaluations	Angry and frightened emotions predominate
At peace with and understanding of past experiences	May idealize or not remember anything about early experiences	Influence of parents can neither be discussed nor coherently explained	Shows evidence of not having resolved death of loved one or trauma and abuse
Is cooperative and honest with interviewer	Dismisses idea that early experience has affected them		
Believes attachment experiences influence personality			

[a]Also assigned one of the three main categories. Patterns described here primarily occur in the interview in the context of discussing loss or abuse and do not necessarily occur throughout the interview.

Source: Main, M. & Goldwyn, R. (1998). *Adult attachment scoring and classification system.* Unpublished manuscript, University of California at Berkeley.

Preoccupied individuals want relationships but see them as unpredictable and strive for greater closeness. They are preoccupied with their past and/or current relationships with their parents and frequently continue trying to get the kind of consistent nurturing they crave.

When people are classified as unresolved, they often exhibit distorted, disorganized thought patterns as well as the emotions of anger and fear. There is evidence in the interview that they have not resolved the loss of a loved one by death or absence, or trauma or abuse that they experienced when they were growing up.

As Table 3.6 shows, the child and adult attachment classifications used in research are not called by the same names but refer to similar working models of attachment for the adult and child. The influence of these adult working models of attachment is described in the next sections.

Table 3.6. Similarity of terms assigned to child's and mother's attachment classification

Child's attachment classification	Mother's attachment classification
Secure (B)	Secure/Autonomous (F)
Insecure/Avoidant (A)	Insecure/Dismissing (Ds)
Insecure/Ambivalent/Resistant (C)	Insecure/Preoccupied (E)
Insecure/Disorganized/ disoriented (D)	Insecure/Unresolved (U)

Table 3.7. How a mother's attachment relates to the working model of the child

Mother's attachment	Working model of the child
Secure/autonomous	Balanced
Insecure/dismissing	Disengaged/impoverished
Insecure/preoccupied	Distorted
Insecure/unresolved	No category

The Significance of Parent's Perceived Attributions of Their Child on Attachment

Another area of research on attachment has been to consider how a parent's attachment to his or her parents and aspects of the child's personality contribute to the parent's attribution of the child. Whether a parent's perception is positive and realistic or negative and distorted significantly influences how she interacts with and parents her child. A commonly used measure of these caregiver perceptions and attachment to a child is the Working Model of the Child Interview (Zeanah, Benoit, & Barton, 1995). In this interview, parents answer questions about their perceptions of their child. They are asked several questions, and their answers describe the child by saying, for example, who he looks like and what kind of personality he has. On the basis of these responses, parents are categorized as balanced, disengaged, or distorted in their attributions of a child.

Balanced caregivers value their relationship with their child and give rich, generally positive descriptions. They also see their relationship with their child as affecting their child's behavior and development. Interviewees who are assessed as disengaged/impoverished display a lack of connection or involvement with the child. The parent shows emotional aloofness, distancing, and sometimes aversion to the child. The caregiver may also be hostile and rejecting. The caregiver who has a distorted view of the child presents as distracted and confused about him or her. There may be role reversal with the parent acting childlike and self-involved. There seems to be no real understanding of the child, and a number of inconsistent and conflicting statements are evident.

These classifications as they relate to the parent's attachment and working models of the child are illustrated in Table 3.7.

Intergenerational Transmission of Attachment

One of the most interesting aspects of attachment research has been the finding that parents' (particularly a mother's) attachment classification parallels her child's in 80%–85% of cases. This means, of course, that in some way the attachment classification and its characteristic representations and behaviors are passed across the generations through the caregiving a parent provides for her child.

As Figure 3.2 indicates, various aspects of the parents' situation influence how the parent perceives the child. Also, their experience with their own parents contributes significantly. Other influences are the child's characteristics—including temperament—and the parents' psychological status. These influence the parents' attributions, perceptions, or working models of their children that affect the kind of caregiving and interaction they provide, which determine

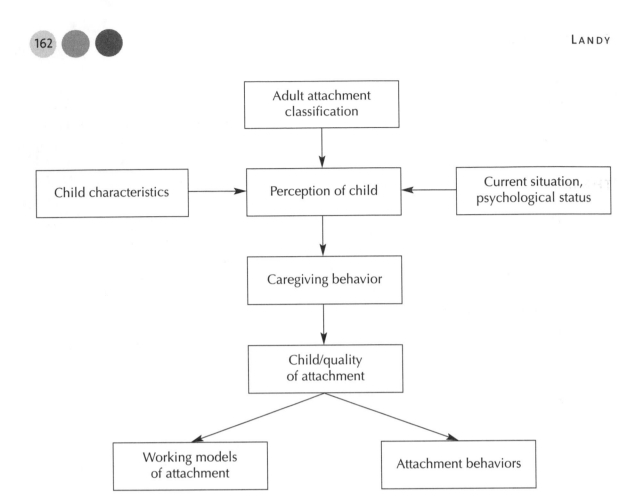

Figure 3.2. How attachment classification may pass from one generation to the next.

the children's quality of attachment. This, in turn, determines the children's behaviors and working models of attachment. Table 3.8, on pages 164–165, shows how similar attachment classifications can be transmitted from parent to child.

Continuity of Attachment Classifications

Many people, as they pass from infancy through early childhood and adolescence and into adulthood, maintain the same attachment style over time. Changes can occur, however, with secure attachments becoming insecure and insecure becoming secure when certain life experiences change. The percentages of people who change classifications vary in different populations, with those populations in high-risk situations being more likely to change. In relatively stable situations, in which patterns of caregiving remain consistent, as many as 80% continue with the same attachment classifications. In populations that experience many changes in life circumstances, however, as few as 40% may stay in the same attachment classification over time.

Attachments can change from secure to insecure when negative life experiences affect the parents' sense of security and, consequently, their interactions with their children. For example, attachments can change from secure to insecure as a result of experiences such as loss due to death or divorce or long periods of unemployment. Attachments can also go from insecure to secure when situations stabilize or people get into supportive, meaningful, new relation-

ships. Other people change from insecure to secure by being in successful therapy and by resolving and reintegrating previous negative memories into more positive memories and by forming integrated mental representations of the events. This is discussed further in a later section of this chapter.

THE IMPORTANCE OF ATTACHMENT

The theory of attachment has already influenced and changed the way many service agencies work with parents, children, and families. For example, various service providers

- Encourage family-friendly practices during childbirth, such as providing birthing centers, allowing fathers to be with their partners throughout labor and delivery, and rooming-in newborn infants with mothers

- Provide extended visiting hours for parents visiting children in the hospital

- Prefer the use of foster care families instead of institutions for children who are without parents or in protective care

- Make efforts to keep children with natural parents or extended family whenever possible and if not, try to ensure continuity of care and to avoid repeated moves and foster care placements for the child

- Promote increased understanding of the effect of loss and the stages of grieving in young children

- Pay attention to interpersonal issues rather than only internal conflicts in therapy

Attachment Theory and Interventions

Understanding of the role of attachment disorders in child development is growing, and greater use is being made of attachment theory in designing early intervention services. Specifically, research has confirmed the importance of secure attachment as a protective factor as well as a positive influence on later development in the following areas.

Social Relationships   As is evident from research, the quality of a young child's attachment can affect his relationships with others throughout life. Young children with secure attachments are more likely to form friendships and to be well liked by other children. As noted previously, insecurely attached children often either avoid friendships or are very demanding and conflictual in their relationships with others. Securely attached children also are more likely to respond to other children's distress in helpful ways. Similarly, adults with secure attachments are more likely to form long-term, fulfilling relationships with others in which comfortable negotiation and joint activities can occur.

Emotion Regulation   A child's attachment classification affects her capacity for self-regulation of negative feelings including fear, anger, sadness, and jealousy. In fact, attachment theory has sometimes been described as a theory of emotion regulation. Securely attached children have been described as being more emotionally expressive and as having better self-control.

Table 3.8. Intergenerational transmission of attachment quality

Parent's adult attachment or view of her own parents	Parent's working model of child (perception of child)	Caregiving behavior with child	Child attachment and attachment behaviors
Secure/ Autonomous (F)	Balanced		Secure (B)
Values relationships and regards them as influential on development Coherent and cooperative in interview Maintains objectivity and independence from any experiences Consistent descriptions whether experiences are favorable or unfavorable	Caregiver values relationship with child. Sees it as having effect on behavior and development of child Descriptions of child are generally positive	Shows sensitive and contingent responsiveness to child's cues Consistently comforting with child when upset, hurt, or ill Affectively positive with child Sees child in positive terms Allows exploration while keeping child safe Accessible to child	Explores around parent Toddler shows signs of missing parent if separated and in unfamiliar setting Actively seeks parent at reunion If upset, can be calmed and returns to playing and exploring Affectively positive Socially competent Manages well away from parents at day care Good self control
Dismissing (Ds)	Attributions: Disengaged/ Impoverished		Avoidant (A)
Mother dismisses, devalues or cuts off from attachment experiences and relationships Interview is not coherent and tends to be excessively brief Normalizes experience with parents without collaborating evidence	Show disengagement from relationship with child Emotional aloofness, distancing from child or aversion to child May be hostile and rejecting	Avoids emotional and physical contact with child Shows little delight in child Does not soothe child when he is upset Predictably unavailable, neglecting May be intrusive	Explores easily May be angry and hostile Little visible distress during separation Looks away from and avoids parent at reunion Seeks distance, may be isolated from group When in pain or upset withdraws and does not seek help

Note: Read information from left to right

They display more positive affect and are less dependent on adults for regulating their intense emotions. They are able to communicate negative affect in socially appropriate ways and, as a result, are more likely to receive a sensitive response. Insecure children may act inappropriately when they are upset, frequently expressing more anger and hostility, fear, or sadness than appears necessary. Because they are often impulsive and tense, they can be more difficult to care for and are more likely to be rejected by caregivers.

Information Processing and Problem Solving   Although security of attachment does not influence a child's level of intelligence, it does appear to influence how children pursue challenging cognitive tasks. Securely attached children do not need to expend as much energy on monitoring and dealing with attachment issues, which frees them up for coping with learning activities. As a consequence, they tend to be more self-confident, enthusiastic, persist-

Parent's adult attachment or view of her own parents	Parent's working model of child (perception of child)	Caregiving behavior with child	Child attachment and attachment behaviors
Preoccupied (E)	Distorted		Ambivalent/ Resistant (C)
Preoccupied with early relationships Goes between anger, and being passive or confused, to fear Not coherent Transcripts often excessively long Often meaningless phrases used	Distracted, confused Role reversal with child, self involved Inconsistency in representation, with conflicting statements No real understanding of child	Unpredictable, sometimes angry, passive, or confused Overinvolved, often conflictual Misreads cues and shows lack of synchrony with child May be role reversal and rapid changes of reactions	Child is visibly distressed and fretful and does not explore Unsettled and distressed at separation Less confident, assertive, and able to problem solve Does not settle during separations Tends to be fearful and tense
Unresolved/ Disorganized (U)	No category		Disorganized/ Disoriented
When discussing death of attachment figure or trauma, appears disorganized and irrational May indicate person is still alive Otherwise fits one of previous categories		May show chaotic interactions with child or more subtle atypical and inconsistent parent behaviors such as extreme misattunement to infant's cues May present as frightened and frightening at different times Preoccupied with unresolved loss and/or trauma Not available to child Distorts child's behavior	Contradictory behavior (freezing/stilling, fear, confusion) Lack of coherent attachment strategy May show some patterns of A, B, or C behavior Usually has emotional and behavioral difficulties and unpredictable behavior Poor social skills Poor self-control and low frustration tolerance

Note: Read information from left to right

ent, and effective in problem-solving situations. When a child is free to problem solve efficiently, she is better able to learn material and strategies necessary for adequate school and academic achievement. Research also suggests that attachment may influence information processing, and that secure individuals may be more flexible in attending to stimuli. Insecurely attached individuals may only selectively attend to and remember certain information and ignore other stimuli or information.

Other Influences   Although it is not proven, research does suggest that if a child is chronically stressed and does not have the support of a nurturing caregiver, this may have significant and detrimental effects on aspects of the child's biochemistry and neurological development. In some children this results in extreme hypersensitivities to some stimuli (McFarlane & van der Kolk, 1996). It is also likely that if the stress is intense enough, the child's immune system may become depleted.

THE DEVELOPMENT OF ATTACHMENT

This section outlines the sequence of the development of attachment and is based on Ainsworth's (1972) description of four phases of the growth of attachment in the preschool years. These were called the 1) preattachment phase, 2) attachment-in-the-making, 3) clear-cut attachment and 4) goal-corrected partnership. Table 3.9 expands on this sequence, and extends it beyond childhood into adulthood because of the influence of attachment styles throughout the life span. Of course, the sequence described would only unfold in what has been described by Bowlby as the "environment of adaptedness" (1969, p. 47), when at least one consistent caregiver is available to respond to the infant and sensitively provide for his care.

Birth to Three Months

Almost from birth, infants show a preference for the human face compared with other objects and tend to calm down and attend more to the human voice. In this early stage, the baby experiences his caregivers through various sensorimotor experiences such as being held and

Table 3.9. The development of attachment through various stages of an individual's life

Age	Stage	Behavior
Birth–3 months	Nondiscriminant eliciting of caregiving	Experiences caregiver at a sensorimotor level
		Infant's signaling behavior mainly reflexive
		Can be soothed by anyone
3–6 months	Differential responding to familiar caretakers	Smile is still indiscriminant
		By 6 months, can be soothed more readily by familiar caregiver
7–24 months	Establishment of attachment	Memorization or internal representation of sight, touch, smell and voice of attachment figure
		May be frightened in presence of stranger and be upset at separation
		Shows pleasure when caregiver returns and can be comforted
		Explores from "secure base" of caregiver
2–3 years	Partnership is established with attachment figure	Internal representation more established
		Can sustain separations more readily
		Can negotiate plans together with attachment figure
3–6 years	Goal-directed partnership	Physical contact not so central to relationship but still important
		Plans and perspectives shared
		Accepts values of the family
		Friendships with peers become important
6–16 years	New relationships formed but parental figures still primary attachment figures	Increased perspective-taking
		While moving out into the world more, very affected by internal representations formed in previous stages
16 years–adulthood	Old and new relationships coexist	Attachment relationships with parents continue to be maintained
		New relationships are formed
		Representational models continue to have an impact on later relationships, especially the parenting relationship

touched, feeding, being talked to, and seeing (particularly her face) and smelling the caregiver. It is likely that infants form memories of the sights, touch, and smell of the attachment figure and of the rhythm, style, and uniqueness of the interaction they have with each caregiver. It is also likely that through repetition, the preverbal or sensorimotor memories begin to be formed. At this stage, it is largely the caregiver who maintains closeness and protects the infant. If these interactions are well attuned to the infant, they are likely to lessen the infant's periods of crying and upset. During this phase, infants are nondiscriminating in their signaling and orienting to people. In other words, their attachment behaviors that elicit attention and caregiving from adults are not all directed toward a familiar figure. Although much of the very young infants' behaviors are reflexive or involuntary, such as crying, grasping, sucking—and a little later—smiling, they do draw the caregiver in, in order to ensure that the infants are provided the necessary care through feeding and so on that ensures their survival. At this time, the infant can usually be calmed equally by a variety of adults, as long as the soothing is sensitively provided.

Three to Six Months

From 3 months on, infants increasingly initiate and seek out caregiving and sociable interactions with their principal caregivers. Also, rather than passively responding in interactions, the infant may now make efforts to keep the interaction going. During this period, the infant's indiscriminate responding gradually shifts to more differential responding to familiar caregivers. This may occur at first through some sensory modalities more than in others. For example, infants can distinguish the smell of their mother's milk very early and will turn to her familiar voice more than to other sounds or, in fact, to other voices. Differential visual responding takes longer to develop and the baby continues to smile at strangers until the fourth or fifth month, when she gradually becomes less likely to respond to a stranger and instead becomes much more likely to readily smile at familiar faces. As well, usually by the end of this period, infants can be soothed more easily by familiar caregivers than by other people. Out-of-sight is still out of mind, however, and infants do not remember caregivers who are not around, so true attachment has not yet developed.

Seven to Twenty-Four Months

Around 7 months of age, an infant's indiscriminant responding changes rapidly. Just before and around this age the infant goes through a time of intense exploration of his primary caregiver(s). This can involve gazing at her face and touching and pulling at her nose, mouth, and hair. With the attainment of the cognitive milestone of object permanence and the active "memorization" of his caregiver(s), the infant can now remember them when separated from them, although the memory remains fragile for some time. Once this has occurred, many infants begin to "make strange" and resist being picked up or comforted by other people. They may also get very upset when separated from their familiar caregivers. For many infants who have spent time in child care from quite early on, the extent of this stranger and separation anxiety varies considerably. Whether the child gets visibly upset, until he gets to know the people he is left with, he usually has identifiable low-keyed or more cautious responses in the absence of the now-established attachment figure. As well, a special greeting and excitement is shown when a familiar caregiver approaches.

Another cognitive attainment that is achieved at this time is the differentiation of means from ends. This implies that the infant can now use behaviors intentionally to achieve a certain goal and can switch from, for example, crying to shouting out, to following after mother, if the first attempts for attention do not work. From 12 months on, infants usually become very excited about exploring the world from the secure base of their caregiver. The degree of contact the baby seeks during these times may vary according to how they feel (e.g., tired, stressed) and how familiar are the surroundings. Researchers that have observed mothers and toddlers in the park have found that the toddlers do not usually stray very far from their mothers and may call out or run back to literally touch their mothers as if to gain courage or to refuel. This may also enable the toddlers to set out exploring again. Of course, both temperament and the little one's quality of attachment will influence how far afield and relaxed the toddler is and how much he needs to refuel. By this time, toddlers will usually have attachments to a primary caregiver as well as to one other person in their social world.

Around approximately 14 months, as well as becoming quite assertive, the toddler can also become very upset by separation. Even going to bed can become quite anxiety producing. Along with a desire to separate, the toddler is now much more aware of the reality that caregivers can go away—and moreover—might not come back. So the push for separation and independence becomes both exciting and frightening, sometimes in quick succession. When attachment is secure, exploration happens smoothly and if the attachment system becomes activated because the child is tired, sick, or scared, the securely attached child will seek out the caregiver and will be comforted by the contact. For insecurely attached children, at this stage,

Toddlers are more aware that caregivers might not come back. (From Johnston, Lynn [1978]. *Do they ever grow up?* Minnetonka, MN: Meadowbrook Press; reprint granted with written permission of Lynn Johnston Productions, Inc.)

conflictual patterns of interaction between caregivers and children or avoidant reactions can be established, however, and will become increasingly entrenched over time.

Two to Three Years

In the third year of life, object constancy is fully established. Object constancy is the ability to hold on to the memory of a person for long periods of time, which can better sustain the child during separations. Separations are generally smoother, and the child is more relaxed and able to trust his world outside the home as well as the people in it. Because he now knows that his relationship with the caregiver continues even when she is not present, the previous goal of maintaining physical contact and proximity now changes into more of a representational mode. As a consequence, the relationship increasingly becomes one of fitting the caregiver's plans into his own, sharing ideas, and negotiating plans together, or as Marvin (1977) described it, an attachment partnership begins to develop and becomes increasingly characteristic of the attachment relationship over the next few years.

Three to Six Years

During this stage, usually by about 4 years of age, children begin to acquire a theory of mind and to advance beyond a totally egocentric way of seeing the world and other people. They now understand that their caregiver has thoughts, feelings, and plans that differ from their own. This can help the new partnership with their caregiver flow more smoothly. With this new insight and ability, a young child can understand that his mother has to finish the vacuuming before they go to the park or that they must do the grocery shopping before they can have an ice-cream together. At first, the caregiver needs to orchestrate this, carefully managing the succession of events and incorporating as much of the child's ideas into the plans as possible. Physical proximity is no longer the goal of the relationship but rather a mutual planning and a containment provided by the caregiver through a structure within which plans and perspectives are shared and decided. This does not mean that the child ceases to need or to look for physical proximity; in fact, he will still seek out closeness and enjoy physical contact on a regular basis and especially when ill, hurt, or frightened.

With this new ability for sharing in a partnership, the child gradually becomes more accepting of rules and more likely to cooperate with instructions and with requests for certain behaviors. The child gradually internalizes rules and values of the family and communicates them to others who come over to play. By 4 or 5 years of age, a child's interests are continuing to develop. He may now initiate separations and can manage to be away for extended periods of several hours so he can play with peers. Although peer relationships and friendships cannot substitute for relationships with parents, they do become increasingly important during this period and can be a great source of comfort for children living in stressful situations.

Six to Sixteen Years

By 6 years of age, the child has continued to gain in the ability to understand the perspectives of others and the capacity to process information. By this age, internal representations of *self* and *other* become more established as well as, to some degree, more conscious. By age 6 children are capable of self-reflection. These representations increasingly become organizers of a child's perceptions, memories, and behaviors—particularly in social situations. Research has shown that in secure children, these more-established models make them not only more positive about themselves and other people but also more flexible, available, and open for new information than those children whose attachment is based on less-established models. During this period, children develop close relationships with a number of other children and adults. Older siblings, teachers, extended family members, coaches, ministers, and others can become very important people in their lives.

Sixteen Years to Adulthood

Individuals who develop secure attachment relationships keep these relationships alive during adulthood, either through direct contact or through telephone calls and letters. Actual physical contact becomes less critical and cognitive processes become more central. Nevertheless, teenagers may still continue to want to refuel by returning home. This may be daily in early adolescence and gradually become less frequent as they move away to go to college or take a job and move away from their parents' home. In times of crisis, adults often seek care and protection from childhood attachment figures, especially parents. During this time, new attachments with partners and new families, while they do not totally replace early attachments, can become extremely significant and act as sources of stability, security, and nurturing during the adult years.

IMPORTANT RESEARCH FINDINGS

As mentioned previously, attachment theory has generated a remarkable amount of research resulting in an enormous number of articles and books. Although some of the research is methodologically sound, a great deal has been characterized by inadequate samples, multiple outcome variables, poorly conceived constructs, small effect sizes, and findings that cannot determine causality because they are based on correlational data. Nevertheless, because of the large numbers of studies that have addressed certain theoretical issues and sometimes through the use of meta-analysis, combined findings have been able to confirm and clarify theoretical constructs or dismiss them as without basis in fact.

In this brief review of the research, areas of particular interest to the understanding of development and parenting will be considered. The areas to be discussed are the following:

- The contributors to quality of attachment: sensitivity, temperament, and caregiver characteristics and the social environment

- Attachment disorganization and parental behavior

- Continuity and intergenerational transmission of quality of attachment

- Behavioral consequences of various patterns of attachment

- Attachment style and adult relationships and functioning

- Psychophysiology of attachment

Contributors to the Quality of Attachment

This section details factors that contribute to secure attachments between caregivers and children. Variables that have been researched as contributing to the quality of attachment fit into three main areas: parent–infant interaction, temperament, and contextual factors.

Parent–Infant Interactions

In the 1970s, Mary Ainsworth and associates conducted research using the Strange Situation and correlated the child's attachment classifications with mother–infant interactions in the home (Ainsworth, 1967; Ainsworth & Wittig, 1969; Ainsworth et al., 1978). Few studies have replicated these findings with naturalistic studies and extensive observations in the home as was done by the previous researchers. In laboratory studies and in-home observations of mother–infant interactions in feeding or play situations, however, researchers have found relationships between the degree of caregiver sensitivity and the child's quality of attachment in the Strange Situation (Grossman, Grossman, Spangler, Suess, & Unzer, 1985; Isabella, 1993; Pederson & Moran, 1996). As well, in a meta-analysis (van IJzendoorn, 1992) and a multisite study of 1,153 infants (National Institute of Child Health and Human Development [NICHD], 1997) maternal sensitivity was a predictor of quality of attachment, although the relationship in some studies was quite small compared with the original Ainsworth studies. There have also been studies that have not replicated the expected relationship (e.g., Seifer, Schiller, Sameroff, Resnick, & Riordan, 1996).

Other researchers have examined aspects of the quality of early interactions other than sensitivity and their relationship to later quality of attachment, including the degree of cooperation versus interference (Egeland & Farber, 1984), facilitation of exploration (Grossman, Scheuerer-Englisch, & Loher, 1991), and prompt responsivity to distress (Crockenberg, 1981). Generally, quite small but significant relationships to the child's attachment classification have been found, suggesting that other variables also make significant contributions to attachment security.

Temperament

An area of controversy within attachment theory has been the nature of the contribution made by infant temperament to quality of attachment. Early studies tended to ignore the relationship between temperament and attachment and the effects of temperament on attachment. When temperament has been considered, however, some studies have shown relationships between the two (e.g., Calkins & Fox, 1992; Goldsmith & Alansky, 1987), although other studies have not found direct effects (e.g., Bates, Maslin, & Frankel, 1985; Gunnar, Mangelsdorf, Larson, & Hertsgaard, 1989). Some researchers have explored the issue by looking at the effects of temperament on behavior in the Strange Situation. Again, results are complex, as a child's temperament has been found to influence the amount of crying during separation but not the reunion behavior and, consequently, the attachment classification (A, B, or C) (see Table 3.3). Some researchers, such as Thompson and colleagues (1988), have gone beyond considering the three classifications and have considered the subclassifications. Namely, Thompson and colleagues divided securely attached infants into two subgroups (B1 + B2 versus B3 + B4), linking infants with B1 and B2 classifications with avoidant infants and B3 and B4 subgroups with resistant infants. Findings have shown that the first grouping shows low distress during separation while the other group shows intense separation distress and crying (Thompson, Connell, & Bridges, 1988) (see Table 3.10). Some writers have therefore concluded that temperament predicts subcategories of classification but not security of attachment per se (Sroufe, 1985). This was confirmed in two studies (Belsky & Rovine, 1987; Susman-Stillman, Kalkoske, Egeland, & Waldman, 1996) but not in another (Mangelsdorf, Gunnar, Kestenbaum, Lang, & Andreas, 1991).

Table 3.10. How a child's attachment grouping affects his or her degree of distress during separation

Equation of attachment groups combined	Degree of distress during separation
B1 + B2 + A	Low distress during separation
B3 + B4 + C	Intense separation and crying

Key: B = Secure attachment (B1 and B2 = most secure; B3 and B4 = less secure; A = Insecure/Avoidant attachment; C = Insecure/Ambivalent

Other researchers have found that the effects of temperament on attachment are not direct but are mediated through their influence on caregiver behavior. In one study, infant irritability predicted mother interaction patterns with their infants, with mothers of irritable infants being less responsive and inconsistent in soothing their upset infants than mothers of less irritable infants (van den Boom, 1989). The same study found that when intervention was successful in increasing the sensitivity of the mothers to their infants, the irritable infants were more likely to become securely attached. Other research has shown a similar relationship between infant irritability and insecure attachment, but only when mothers perceived their social support as insufficient, again indicating that the relationship between the two variables may be mediated by the caregiving of the mother (Crockenberg, 1981; Crockenberg & McCluskey, 1986).

Infants with more difficult temperaments (i.e., those having high reactivity, proneness to distress, and high irritability) are seemingly more likely to elicit less responsive and sensitive interactions from their caregivers, which in turn may lead to the likelihood of more insecure attachments. This relationship from temperament to interactional style may be more significant in high-risk situations in which caregivers contend with higher levels of adversity and less supportive networks. An alternative possibility, suggested by Vaughn and Bost, is that "both attachment security and temperament depend (in part) on qualities of infant–parent interaction," although they note that "the nature and implications of relations between the two domains remain to be worked out" (1999, p. 221).

Caregiver Characteristics and the Social Environment   Along with considering the contribution of the child's temperament and caregiver interactions on attachment, researchers have also considered the effects of more distal variables such as the personality characteristics of the caregivers and the social environment. In general, parents with psychological difficulties, particularly with more extreme forms such as clinical depression, psychosis, severe anxiety disorders, and character disorders, are more likely to have children with insecure attachments (Belsky, 1999; Gelfand & Teti, 1990; Ricks, 1985). These effects are again mediated through parent–child interactions, particularly in terms of the degree of availability, responsiveness, and empathy the parent can provide for the child.

In general, findings from both longitudinal and cross-sectional studies indicate that children in families with parents with well-functioning marital relationships are more likely to have secure attachments, with the link likely to be both direct and indirect (Belsky, 1990; Erel & Burman, 1995). In families with extreme hostility or overt spousal abuse, the emotional impact of seeing or sensing the abuse or hostility may affect the child's sense of security with the parents more directly (Davies & Cummings, 1994). Indirect effects occur through the contribution of marital satisfaction on parent–child interaction. In considering the influence of social support outside the family, few studies have found a positive link with quality of attachment, however, when mothers live in very adverse situations or with infants with biological

difficulties, the effects of low social support may be more significant (Crittenden, 1985; Crnic, Greenberg, & Slough, 1986; Crockenberg, 1981). As Belsky and Isabella (1988) pointed out, one risk factor rarely contributes to insecure attachment, but a composite of risk factors shows a clear and significant relationship with insecure attachment.

Attachment Disorganization and Parental Behavior

Since 1986 when Main and Solomon first identified a disorganized, disoriented behavior pattern or type of attachment, there has been an explosion of studies and theoretical publications on attachment disorganization (Solomon & George, 1999). This section emphasizes the parenting behaviors that contribute to disorganized infant attachment. For many years before the category was actually identified, researchers noted that some infants did not fit into the three established patterns of attachment established by Ainsworth. These examples were either set aside as unclassifiable or forced into what was seen as the best-fitting category. Main and Solomon (1986) concluded that these children, unlike children in the other three categories, lacked any coherent or consistent strategy for dealing with the stress of separation. Rather, they showed contradictory movements that indicated uncertainty and confusion about what to do (e.g., approaching parent with head averted, dazed and trance-like responses, disoriented wandering).

The incidence of disorganized attachment has been found to range from 13% to as high as 82% in populations in which child maltreatment or serious parental psychopathology has been identified (Carlson, Cicchetti, Barnett, & Braunwald, 1989; DeMulder & Radke-Yarrow, 1991; Lyons-Ruth, Connell, Grunebaum, & Botein, 1990; Teti, Gelfand, Messinger, & Isabella, 1995). Other studies, including a meta-analysis, have shown only a marginally significant relationship between disorganized attachment and maternal depression (NICHD, 1997).

Exploring the mental representations of parents with the AAI, those who are found to be unresolved with respect to loss or trauma are more likely to have infants with disorganized attachment. It has been proposed that unresolved loss or trauma results in the parent engaging in frightened and frightening behaviors with their infants (Jacobvitz, Hazen, & Riggs, 1997; Thalhuber, Jacobvitz, & Hazen, 1998). Researchers have described these behaviors as, for example, the caregiver being in a trance-like state, acting like the baby could hurt her; baring teeth, looming at the baby, and pursuing the baby in menacing ways. In a few studies, although it would be expected that parents with secure/unresolved classifications would show less of this kind of behavior than insecure/unresolved mothers, the reverse has been found (Schuengel, van IJzendoorn, Bakermans-Kranenburg, & Blom, 1997). The reasons are unclear but the researchers suggest that the differences may relate to how old the mother was when the loss or trauma occurred and what her relationship was to the person involved.

Other, more subtle maternal behaviors have also been identified as related to disorganized attachment. These include expressing extreme misattunement to infants' cues and communications, and using competing caregiving strategies such as encouraging and then rejecting attachment-seeking behaviors. These mothers show "impaired ability to engage in well-attuned affective communication with their young children" (Lyons-Ruth & Jacobvitz, 1999, p. 53). These categories of frightened-frightening and disrupted affective communication have both been found to predict disorganized attachment in infants (Lyons-Ruth, Bronfman, & Atwood, 1999; Main & Hesse, 1992; Schuengel, Bakermans-Kranenburg, & van IJzendoorn, 1999; Schuengel et al., 1997).

Continuity and Intergenerational Transmission of Quality of Attachment

Research has shown that attachment classification tends to continue over time and is often predicted by intergenerational transmission.

Continuity Attachment theory predicts that an individual's attachment classification will remain constant over time. This may occur through the formation of working models of attachment (or internal representations or views of self and others); in other words, memories that the child forms that influence the child over time and tend to result in maintaining of the same attachment classification.

Most studies of the continuity of attachment over time have focused on short periods during early childhood. The findings from these studies have been mixed, with some studies suggesting a high degree of stability (Main & Cassidy, 1988; Main & Weston, 1981; Wartner, Grossman, Fremmer-Bombik, & Suess, 1994; Waters, 1978), although others have found much lower rates of continuity (Lyons-Ruth, Repacholi, McLeod, & Silva, 1991; Mangelsdorf et al., 1996; Schneider-Rosen, Braunwald, Carlson, & Cicchetti, 1985; Thompson, Lamb, & Estes, 1981). A few studies that have followed children into adolescence have also found somewhat mixed results, with one study finding no concordance between earlier patterns of attachment and those in adolescence (Zimmerman, 1994), while others have found a remarkably high level of stability (Hamilton, 1995; Waters, Merrick, Albersheim, & Treboux, 1995). In general, children in samples in very high-risk situations in which changes in circumstances may be frequent are less likely to show stability of attachment. Changes may occur in either direction, positive and negative. Factors that may contribute to these changes in attachment include significant changes in home environment, major family changes, beginning of out-of-home care, birth of a sibling, or new challenges of later developmental changes.

Intergeneration Transmission The development of the AAI has allowed study of the intergenerational transmission of attachment classifications from adult to child. In general, high levels of concordance, far above those expected by chance, have been found. In studies that administered the AAI to mothers during pregnancy and the Strange Situation to infants at one year, researchers have found that AAI classifications (secure versus insecure) of mothers predicted subsequent infant attachment patterns between 75% and 80% of the time (Benoit, 1991; Benoit & Parker, 1994; Fonagy et al., 1991; Steele, Steele, & Fonagy, 1996).

Similar concordances have been found when the two measures are collected concurrently in time (Ainsworth & Eichberg, 1991; van IJzendoorn, Kranenburg, Zwart-Woudstra, van Busschbach, & Lamberman, 1991; Zeanah, Benoit, Barton, Regan, Hirshberg, & Lipsitt, 1993) or when the infancy data is collected years earlier than the AAI (Grossman, Fremmer-Bombik, Rudolph, & Grossman, 1988; Main et al., 1985). The intergenerational associations are somewhat smaller for fathers and infants, with a prediction rate of approximately 65% (Main et al., 1985; Steele et al., 1996). The transmission has been conceptualized as when the parents' working models of attachment as portrayed in the AAI guide their views of their infants and their behavior in interactions with their children, which in turn influence their children's expectations of self and other and their children's behavior in the Strange Situation (Steele & Steele, 1994). This demonstration and understanding of how patterns of parenting can be repeated across generations may be one of the most important contributions made by attachment theory toward understanding child behavior patterns, especially in families who abuse and neglect their infants and other at-risk populations.

Behavioral Consequences of Various Patterns of Attachment

As outlined in a previous section, the quality of attachment has often been related to measures of children's self-confidence, problem solving, social relatedness, emotion regulation, and self-reliance. In a study that examined the effect of attachment classification on the development of children from 1 to 15 years, Sroufe and associates in the Minnesota Parent–Child Project found that security of attachment predicted behavior and interactions in preschool, middle childhood, and adolescence (Frankel & Bates, 1990; Matas, Arend, & Sroufe, 1978). Sroufe (1983) described securely attached children as more "ego resilient" and better able to deal with frustration by asking for help than anxiously attached children. Dependence was another characteristic that showed significant differences, with insecure resistant children far more likely to be dependent and to seek attention in negative ways. These differences were still evident when the children were 15 years of age (Sroufe, Carlson, & Shulman, 1993).

Other studies have found a relationship between earlier attachment and social competence with peers (Booth, Rose-Krasnor, & Rubin, 1991; Fagot, 1997; Jacobson & Wille, 1986; Kerns, 1994; Park & Waters, 1989; Pastor, 1981; Suess, 1987; Waters, Wippman, & Sroufe, 1979) and with empathy and concern for others (Denham, 1994; Kestenbaum, Farber, & Sroufe, 1989; Pierrehumbert, Iannotti, & Cummings, 1985). Elicker, Englund, and Sroufe (1992), in their research of social competence and attachment, concluded that securely attached children are more sociable and more enjoyable playmates, showing more cooperation and responding more positively to other children. Studies have not found that secure attachment is related to greater intellectual ability (e.g., Egeland & Farber, 1984; Pastor, 1981; Waters et al., 1979). It has been theorized that secure attachment requires less intensive monitoring of others and can free up the child's cognitive capacity to engage in various tasks. In fact, some studies have found securely attached children to be more able to problem-solve (Fagot, Gauvain, & Kavanagh, 1996), to do better on emotional understanding tasks (Laible & Thompson, 1998) and to be better able to process "affective-cognitive" information (Belsky, Spritz, & Crnic, 1996). As well, Slade (1987) found that secure toddlers had higher levels of symbolic play than did their insecure peers, suggesting an earlier shift to representational thought. Although these variables are not directly related to intellectual or language development, the greater ability to perform on these tasks suggests that securely attached children may be freer to explore situations and to understand accurately the task requirements without being overwhelmed by negative emotions and frustration.

Just as secure attachment has been related to better functioning in a number of areas of development, insecure attachment, especially disorganized attachment, has been found to predict a variety of behavior and emotion problems (DeKlyen, 1996; Lewis, Feiring, McGuffog, & Jaskir, 1984; Moss, Parent, Gosselin, Rousseau, & St-Laurent, 1996; Speltz, Greenberg, & DeKlyen, 1990). This is particularly true in very high-risk samples, although in low-risk samples the results are more equivocal. In two longitudinal studies of high-risk families, insecurely attached preschoolers (particularly those who had been rated disorganized earlier) were more likely to be hostile with peers and to have parental ratings of behavior problems (Lyons-Ruth, Alpern, & Repacholi, 1993; Shaw, Owens, Vondra, Keenan, & Winslow, 1996).

Compared with studies that have linked insecurity of attachment to aggression and behavior problems, little attention has been paid to the relationship of attachment to depression or anxiety later in childhood. In a recent study, LaFrenière, Provost, and Dubeau (1992) found that insecure attachment to mother was more likely than was secure attachment to be linked

to a child's withdrawal from peer interaction and anxiety in preschool, especially for boys. From these findings, it would appear that although studies have found a relationship between attachment classification and later behavior and emotion problems, it is clear that insecure attachment is not itself a measure of pathology. It may well constitute a significant risk factor for various forms of psychopathology, however, especially for children with disorganized classifications (Greenberg, 1999).

Attachment Style and Adult Relationships and Functioning

Just as adults' internal working models of attachment to their parents have been shown to affect their parenting styles, a number of other researchers have studied how these same attachment styles influence the way people conceive of and experience love and their adjustment in other social situations.

Much of the research that has explored individual differences in adult relationship styles has been conceptualized within the attachment perspective. In order to assess links among attachment styles and relationship styles, Hazan and Shaver (1987) and Mickelson, Kessler and Shaver (1997), using a brief self-report measure of adult attachment in a national survey, found that those who responded (of whom 79% were women) showed similar percentages in each attachment category to those generally found in infants (56% secure, 19% anxious/ambivalent, and 25% avoidant) (Mickelson et al., 1997). A refinement of the measure was introduced by Bartholomew (1990), who defined four attachment styles: 1) secure, 2) avoidant (dismissing), 3) avoidant (fearful), and 4) preoccupied. Considerable concordance has been found among these classifications and similar classifications on the AAI (Bartholomew & Shaver, 1998).

These measures have been used to link attachment style to dating behavior and relationships (Collins & Read, 1990; Mikulincer & Erev, 1991). Although the findings are complex, in general, secure individuals have been found to be more trusting, to have greater satisfaction in their relationships, and to be more committed compared with ambivalent and avoidantly attached individuals (Cohn, Silver, Cowan, & Cowan, 1992; Collins & Read, 1990; Fuller & Fincham, 1995; Kirkpatrick & Davis, 1994). Simpson (1990) and Kirkpatrick and Hazan (1994) noted that on the one hand, preoccupied people were very focused on their partner's degree of predictability, trustworthiness, and dependability, tended to have difficulty achieving the degree of interpersonal closeness they craved, and were more likely to be in troubled relationships. On the other hand, avoidant people were more interested in avoiding excessive commitment and intimacy in relationships and were generally less committed to and less trusting of their partners.

In research of adults that has examined the relationship of these attachment styles on functioning, association has been found for a number of aspects of adult functioning. These have related secure attachment to better emotion regulation (Kobak & Sceery, 1988) or to being able to acknowledge and to cope effectively with negative emotions (see Shaver & Clark, 1994; Shaver & Hazan, 1993, for reviews). Several cross-sectional studies have found links between attachment styles and personality (Collins & Read, 1990). Insecure attachment has been found to be related to job dissatisfaction (Hazan & Shaver, 1990); depression (Carnelly, Pietromonaco, & Jaffe, 1996); substance use (Brennan & Shaver, 1995; Senchak & Leonard, 1992); and domestic violence (Dutton, Saunders, Starzomski, & Bartholomew, 1994). Attachment status has also been related to psychiatric diagnoses and predicts success in treatment in adolescents and adults (Fonagy et al., 1996; Rosenstein & Horowitz, 1996; Tyrrell & Dozier,

1997). Because the studies are cross-sectional, however, it is not possible to determine the direction of the relationships.

Psychophysiology of Attachment

Although researchers have concluded that attachment classifications are not directly linked to temperament, the interest of attachment researchers in using psychophysiological concepts and measures that have been implicated in temperament studies has continued. Some of the measures that have been used include heart rate, cortisol level, and brain electrical activity (EEG) as it relates to brain asymmetry. Some research has tried to link changes on these measures to the infant's experiences in the Strange Situation. Sroufe and Waters (1977) reported that all the infants they studied had elevated heart rates during separation, although avoidant infants did not show behavioral reactions. Bono and Stifter (1995) found resistant infants displayed greater heart rate acceleration and less heart rate variability in the Strange Situation than secure infants.

In the largest study that has been conducted measuring cortisol levels in the Strange Situation, Spangler and Schieche (1998) found that resistant infants showed the largest increases in cortisol levels, while avoidant infants showed them only if they were temperamentally fearful. Gunnar and colleagues have also conducted studies in which the infants' attachment classification was related to cortisol levels and behavior responses to stressful situations. For example, when confronted by a boisterous clown, only the insecurely attached, inhibited toddlers showed elevations of cortisol (Nachmias, Gunnar, Mangelsdorf, Parritz, Hornick, & Buss, 1996; Spangler & Schieche, 1998). Similar findings were recorded when infants received inoculations (Gunnar, Brodersen, Nachmias, Buss, & Rigatuso, 1996), although Hertsgaard, Gunnar, Erickson, & Nachmias (1995) found that disorganized infants were most likely to have elevated levels of cortisol. Some studies have not found a link between security of attachment and cortisol levels following stressful situations, however. It may have been that the cortisol samples were taken too early to capture the peak responses (Gunnar et al., 1989; Gunnar, Colton, & Stansbury, 1992).

A number of studies have shown that the right frontal regions are activated during expression of negative affects (crying and sad expression) and the left frontal regions are activated during expression of positive affects (smiling and laughter). The two hemispheres have also been implicated in the regulation of different behaviors, the left with approach behaviors and the right with withdrawal (Fox & Davidson, 1984). There are no data directly linking attachment classifications to measures of frontal lobe activity asymmetry, although it has been linked to inhibition in infants, who in turn are more likely to have a classification of "resistant" (Calkins & Fox, 1992; Fox, Calkins, & Bell, 1994). Although data are mixed, it is probable that attachment security can act as a buffer for infants with a temperamental disposition toward inhibition or to distress and negative affect, particularly when the infant is faced with stressful situations (Fox & Card, 1999).

THE GROWTH-PROMOTING ENVIRONMENT: PRINCIPLES OF DEVELOPING A SECURE ATTACHMENT

Many early intervention approaches have focused on improving aspects of the parent–child relationship in order to optimize children's developmental outcomes. Some principles for enhancing caregiver–child interactions in order to lead to a secure attachment are set out in Table 3.11 and in greater detail here.

Table 3.11. Principles for developing a secure attachment

Principle 1	Comfort children when they are physically hurt, ill, upset, frightened, or lonely.
Principle 2	Respond to and notice children so they learn that their caregivers care.
Principle 3	Give children a sense of trust in the world and the people in it.
Principle 4	Help children review experiences and reenact frightening situations so that the memories can be integrated into their self-narratives.
Principle 5	Create and keep alive good, warm, and joyful memories because they can help develop secure attachment relationships. Establish predictable family traditions.
Principle 6	Let children know where you are going and when you will be back. Provide objects to give security and keep memories of you or the absent caregiver alive.
Principle 7	Try to be as predictable and as positive as possible in reacting to a child's behavior.

PRINCIPLE 1: *Comfort children when they are physically hurt, ill, upset, frightened, or lonely.*

An important aspect of parenting is learning to read infants' and young children's cues and distinguishing when they need comforting or some other response. Infants and young children become upset when they are physically hurt, ill, upset, frightened, or lonely. At these times they need comforting, usually in the form of holding, rocking, and calming reassurance. When this kind of response occurs regularly and predictably, infants learn to feel safe with their parents and secure that parents will be there when they are needed. Of course, no caregiver can be perfect, but being responsive and available as often as possible is extremely important.

Responding sensitively and reading the child's cues will determine if comforting is required in a particular situation. For example, an older child may be having a temper tantrum and may need a chance to calm down in a quiet, safe place before being ready to be comforted. After about 8 weeks of age, babies can begin to learn to self-calm or to regulate their upset for brief periods; for example, caregivers can delay the baby's need for feeding by waiting for a few moments when the baby begins to fuss. They may also try rubbing his back or talking calmly or watching to see if he self-calms by sucking on his hand or finger or by gazing at an object. These strategies work especially well if a baby was only just fed. This is very different from allowing a baby to cry inconsolably. It does, however, allow caregivers to read his cues and provides an alternative to immediate feeding. It can also encourage the child's capacity to calm himself, even if only temporarily.

PRINCIPLE 2: *Respond to and notice children so they learn that their caregivers care.*

Children need to develop a sense that they are important and that their caregivers will respond to them. This applies to babies and young children. In addition to being comforted when upset, it is important that babies and young children receive attention when they need it, or perhaps some help with a problem, or just someone to share a moment with. A special attach-

ment relationship can also build with this kind of sharing of interactions. Although it is often difficult to make time because caregivers are extremely busy or interactions with the child often end up in conflict, it is still critically important that children receive these times of special sharing. Ironically, this is particularly true for insecurely attached children with whom interactions may be the most conflictual. It is important to find activities that parent and child both can enjoy, to tune into the child, and to let him take the lead. These activities can often be quite brief, but they need to be warm and intimate to be meaningful.

The following examples, which are adapted from a number of examples of responses from AAIs of securely attached individuals, give us an idea of how these times may happen.

- "My mom made me feel important; we spent time talking, sharing time together, or even doing nothing."

- "My father took me places whenever he could—it really felt like he wanted me around."

- "My mom took time to listen to me, to help me with my homework, and to help me with my problems. I still go home to visit whenever I can."

- "My dad really cared about me—he showed interest in my activities and spent one-on-one time with me."

- "From an early age, my mother treated me as an individual and asked me how I felt about things."

As your child matures, it is critical to find special activities that you and the child enjoy doing together daily. These can include reading a story, having breakfast together, going for a walk, or playing a game. The activity itself is not the most important thing; what is critical is that both you and the child enjoy it and share good feelings about it and that the child feels important.

PRINCIPLE 3: *Give children a sense of trust in the world and the people in it.*

Although in today's dangerous times it may sound naive to talk about instilling trust in the world and the people in it, it is very important to find a coherent balance between encouraging children to explore the world in a trusting fashion and ensuring that they are safe. In the earliest years, children learn to feel safe when caregivers comfort them. Later on, caregivers instill a feeling of trust and safety when they are communicating a belief in children's ability to do things. Certainly, children need to be given some warnings about avoiding immediate dangers with strangers, and the home and the outside environment need to be as safe as possible to allow exploration. Children should not be exposed to terrifying accounts of tragic events on television or hear about acts of violence. If a child does actually experience an event he finds frightening, it is important to support the child and discuss what happened (see Principle 4). Only caregivers can keep children safe—and as far as possible—protected from knowing about overwhelming and dangerous situations. This becomes a balance of finding a way to be protective and encouraging independence without abandoning the child, such as when a toddler is allowed to run off a small distance away and to return to a watching caregiver.

Children need to develop a sense that they are important and that their caregiver will respond to them.

These vignettes show how parents can foster feelings of security or insecurity in their children:

· ·

Jane remembers her childhood in a very positive way, particularly the way she was able to do things for herself. When her daughter Grace was born, she treated her in much the same way as she had been treated. This meant encouraging Grace to try out new activities, to visit friends, to choose her clothes, and to go to preschool when Grace was ready and eager to meet new friends. Although Jane told Grace about certain dangers, she also taught her about the wonders of nature and the fun that being with friends, learning, and going to school would be. When Grace began school she did so with excitement and an expectation that learning would be fun and that she would meet lots of new friends. For Grace, adjustment to school was smooth and easy and she continued to enjoy it and to do well over the years.

Barbara barely remembers her background, though she knows she was abused when she was a child and placed in foster care. Eventually, she was returned home to a mother who tried hard to be a good caregiver, but who remained constantly vigilant and afraid that her daughter would be taken from her again. When Barbara's daughter Jill was born, she kept her at home, terrified that her daughter would be taken

away from her. Few people visited, and Jill was constantly told about strangers who would hurt her and people who would be likely to abuse her. When Jill reached an age that she must attend school, Barbara waited in the bushes outside the classroom to pick up her daughter in order to make sure she was safe. Jill, in turn, was anxious and concerned about school and the people she met. It was hard for Jill to do her work or to make friends—a situation that continued over the years of school, eventually negatively affecting her grades.

PRINCIPLE 4: *Help children review experiences and reenact frightening situations so that the memories can be integrated into their self-narratives.*

Caregivers can help guide recall of meaningful experiences by talking with children about things that have happened to them so they can develop autobiographical memories or a coherent script of past events. Research on adults' attachment to their parents has taught us that negative or traumatic experiences that are unresolved or scarcely remembered can continue to affect the personality, leading the individual to have distorted views of the world and difficulties in relationships, especially with their children. Moreover, it is well documented that recent traumas that directly affect children need to be reviewed, played out, and discussed when the child wants to do so in order to avoid nightmares, flashbacks, and other severe posttraumatic stress symptoms.

To integrate positive memories, parents can tell children stories about them when they were small, show photos of them when they were younger, and answer questions. Children often love to ask about when they were little. These memories can then become integrated into positive schemata or event scripts that give children a feeling of security through having a sense of a coherent past.

With difficult events, it is important that children be encouraged to talk about them before they happen if it's a predictable event, or after something that was not anticipated. These can be small events such as a friend leaving town, a trip to the hospital, or the birth of a sibling, to larger tragedies such as the death of someone close, a divorce, or a man-made or natural disaster. The techniques described in Chapters 4 and 5, which include strategies for encouraging play and imagination and language and communication, respectively, include some useful ways to review such events. It is often difficult for caregivers to discuss or reenact these scenes with their children, especially if they experienced the trauma or loss as well. Our tendency is often to ignore the event or to choose not to talk about it so the child will forget it. If doing the reviewing with the child is too difficult for an adult, it is important to seek treatment for the child, so someone less close to the event can help her.

PRINCIPLE 5: *Create and keep alive good, warm, and joyful memories because they can help develop secure attachment relationships. Establish predictable family traditions.*

Family traditions often vary from culture to culture and are frequently related to holiday times, to religious celebrations, or to festivities around birthdays, christenings, or weddings. They are important for instilling in children a sense of predictability and security.

Other ways to keep good memories alive *and* to make children feel valued and cherished include

- Keeping photo albums and looking through them with the child occasionally to remember special events and fun times

- Keeping special pictures and crafts that a child made at different stages

- Making a yearly calendar with photos of events that happened to each child or the whole family during the year, such as birthdays

- Maintaining a baby book or a diary of a child's special achievements

- Making videos of special events

- Keeping a record of special family holidays

PRINCIPLE 6: *Let children know where you are going and when you will be back. Provide objects to give security and keep memories of you or the absent caregiver alive.*

Strangely enough, if handled well, separations can strengthen a secure attachment. It is crucial to deal with the separations in certain ways, however. It is important that caregivers and substitute caregivers

- Establish goodbye rituals, but leave with confidence once the time comes. (Parents may also suggest things that the child might do while they are away.)

- Integrate the child gradually, with the caregiver present, during part of the initial days, if a child is very upset by separating for child care or school

- Allow the child to have a photo of parents or other mementos of home that can help ease the time away. Security blankets and other familiar toys can help a child keep calm.

- Talk about parents during the day, letting children know their parents miss them and are thinking about them

- Let the child know when the parent will return, then carefully adhere to the time

PRINCIPLE 7: *Try to be as predictable and as positive as possible in reacting to a child's behavior.*

Although being predictable or consistent in reacting to children's behavior is difficult, it is crucial for giving children a sense of security—an expectation that their needs will be met. Here are some suggestions for caregivers to foster this predictability:

- Set up a routine for getting up, mealtimes, bedtimes, and so forth.

- Give children a clear sense of the rules and consequences for misbehavior, and then follow through.

- Always comfort children if they are ill, hurt, or scared, and have things to soothe them, such as hot milk, soft touching or holding, or calming music.

- Develop strategies to calm yourself down if you find you are losing your temper frequently or become unable to respond predictably.

- Seek support or counseling if you find you are regularly ignoring, rejecting, or punishing a child and are unable to provide caring, predictable, and nurturing responses.

SOME COMMONLY RAISED ISSUES AROUND ATTACHMENT

As research about the importance of attachment has informed workers in service agencies, it can also be helpful in explaining and suggesting ways to maintain and enhance secure attachments between parents, other caregivers, and children.

Attachment and Child Care

When children first began to attend child care in large numbers and at earlier ages, many child development experts believed that children would be adversely affected and their attachments to their parents damaged. Much of the early research had flawed methodology because of small samples and the fact that little account was taken of variations in a child's care before he or she began child care. Also, the Strange Situation may elicit different reactions for children attending and not attending child care. More recent studies (NICHD, 1997; Rauh, Ziegenhain, Müller, Wijnroks, 2000) have tried to rectify these difficulties and have identified the following:

- The majority of infants in child care are securely attached, a percentage similar to those cared for by mothers at home.

- Children who were integrated into child care with extensive support and presence of parents rather than abruptly introduced were more likely to change from insecure to secure as a result.

- Some studies have shown slightly more anxious (specifically avoidant) classifications in children who attend child care than those in maternal care. The majority is secure, however.

- Infants who were least secure had experienced low maternal sensitivity and responsiveness at home, combined with poor-quality child care.

- The combination of temperament, maternal interactional quality, and quality of child care may be the most predictive combination.

Clearly, most infants can attend child care without becoming insecurely attached to their parents. In spite of these positive facts it remains crucial that child care providers take steps to meet the attachment needs of those in care. Some of these steps are the following:

- Make integration into child care as gradual as possible, allowing parents to stay for significant time periods at the beginning.

- Assign each child to a particular caregiver.

- Keep group size as small as possible.

- Encourage child care workers to respond sensitively to children who are upset. Also encourage them to respond by modulating other negative emotions such as anger or jealousy.

- When children are moved from one room to another within the child care, the transition should be prepared for and handled sensitively.

- Encourage contact between parent and child-care worker so that children perceive child care as part of an extended family.

- Let children know their parents are thinking about them if they want to talk about what they are doing.

- Provide child care providers with objects from the child's home, to make integration of the two environments more harmonious.

- Hold meetings and encourage contacts among parents and child care workers about any emotional issues that arise around separations.

The Quality of Attachment with Fathers and Other Caregivers

Infants develop attachments to more than one caregiver. Most commonly, these will be to a mother, father, child care provider, or grandparent. It is also true that the attachments are not necessarily of the same quality because they are formed out of the interactions, predictability and, to some degree, the amount of time each caregiver spends with the child. In other words, the child may know a number of other people, but only a very few will be attachment figures or provide security, care, or protection.

A father can do all the things a mother can do for her baby except breastfeed, of course. It may be that because of changes in hormones, a mother is more ready to care for her infant initially and may be more alert to her infant's cries and other cues than the father, however. Estimates of how much time fathers spend with their infants vary according to socioeconomic status, culture, time availability, and family beliefs but have been shown to vary from between 1 and 26 hours per week during their child's infancy. The time usually expands as the child gets older. In two-career families, mothers and fathers may spend similar amounts of time with their children. Also, roles are sometimes reversed when the mother works and the father stays home to care for the children. In more traditional families, many fathers assume the role of the playmate, and consequently may not become as much of a nurturing figure. In other words, the child might consider her father a fun person but not someone to seek out for care or comforting. Nevertheless, assessment of fathers in the Strange Situation does indicate that many infants do develop secure attachments with their fathers, and that their attachment style can be different from the one shared between mother and infant. Results of studies show that father–infant attachment distribution is about the same as that of mothers and infants (65% secure, 25% avoidant, and 10% resistant) (Steele, Steele, & Fonagy, 1996). As might be expected, such distributions are somewhat dependent on the amount of time the father spends with the baby. Although mother–infant and father–infant attachment classifications can be different, there is some degree of similarity, probably because partners often have similar beliefs and philosophies

A child's attachment to her father is enriched by doing all sorts of activities together.

about relationships and parenting and may spend approximately the same amount of time with their children.

Although infants and children often spend a great deal of time with other caregivers in home or group care, there is little research that examines the nature of the relationship. Moreover, the assessment tool available for assessing attachment, the Strange Situation, may not have the same meaning for measuring attachment quality among infants and mothers and infants and other caregivers. It seems likely that attachments do develop and that the relationships take some months to do so, however. It is important, therefore, to realize that once this kind of relationship has been formed, if the caregiver leaves, the child may show the same signs of loss and grieving as they would with the loss of a parent.

How these attachments coalesce or are integrated into one internal representation of others has been an area of disagreement among attachment researchers and theorists and one in which no agreement has yet been found. Most researchers have found that in episodes similar to the Strange Situation, when various caregivers are present the infant usually shows preference for the caregiver who has spent the most time and provided the most sensitive responses. Attachment theorists presume, therefore, that there may be an attachment hierarchy, with the infant preferring the primary caregiver, usually the mother, when distressed in any way. It also has been found that in terms of ability to function, infants with two secure attachments function best, while those with one insecure and one secure attachment function less well and children with two insecure attachments have the most difficulties (Colin, 1996; Howes, 2000; Main, 2000; Main & Weston, 1981). Even more interesting, when a child has one secure and one insecure attachment, they do better if the secure relationship is with the mother than with the father or another caregiver (Belsky, Rovine, & Taylor, 1984; Easterbrook & Goldberg, 1987; Howes, Rodning, Galluzzo, & Myers, 1988).

Security Blankets, Teddy Bears, and Other Soft Objects

It may seem that when a child wants to sleep with and hold onto a soft object, it is a sign of in-security. In actuality, this desire is quite healthy and common. Although statistics have varied from survey to survey, about 60% of young children are reported by their parents to have at least some attachment to a blanket or other soft object. Usually this desire for a soft object be-gins after 12 months and subsides after 48 months, although many children hang on to it for many years after that. Similar tendencies have been found in a number of other countries and cultures including Sweden, the Netherlands, Israel, Japan, and England, although American and British studies show a higher incidence than most countries.

The appeal of the soft "transitional object," as it was called by Winnicott, the British child psychiatrist (1971), is that as it is inanimate, a child is able to exert far more control over it than over the mother. Also, the object's warmth and softness may represent the mother—es-pecially during times of separation (including bedtime) and stress. In general, the objects ap-pear to serve an anxiety reducing, calming, and soothing purpose.

In one of the few studies that identified a link between security objects and attachment, Lehman, Denham, Moser, and Reeves (1992) found that at 12 and 30 months of age, children with soft object attachments were more likely to be securely attached to their mothers than children who did not have such a security object. They also noted, however, that children with insecure attachment do develop attachments to objects but suggest that this may be due to the fact that many children switch attachment classifications, and attachment to objects may have occurred during a time of secure attachment to the mother.

Whatever the case, it is clear that having an attachment to a blanket or a soft object may be an important advantage, especially in the sense of assisting with the developmental step of moving from intense closeness with the mother into more independence and a differentiation of self. It can serve to provide security by its presence during that time when the child's mem-ory of her mother is still fragile during times of separation. Therefore, parents need to be in-formed that these objects are helpful for their children and that the need for the objects gener-ally falls away naturally, only to return perhaps during times of stress or change. Of course, it is important to make sure that the soft object is safe (e.g., that there are no buttons or other po-tentially chokable pieces that can be pulled off), and infants should not have stuffed animals in their cribs.

The Effects of Loss and Separation

As was identified by John Bowlby in the 1950s, during a child's first 5 years the effects of loss or separation from attachment figures by death, divorce, or permanent separation can cause children significant upset on a short-term basis and potentially, on a longer term basis. This can place the child at risk for psychopathology if the loss is not resolved. Following a signifi-cant loss, children have been identified as going through a number of stages, although there will certainly be individual differences in terms of the intensity, order, and length of the stages (Bowlby, 1980). These have been identified as

- *Shock and denial:* During this stage, the child may deny that the loss has happened; further-more, any feelings about it are subdued. There may be little emotional expression of grief.

- *Anger and protest:* At this stage, the emotional response is typically one of anger. This may be diffused or directed at the lost person or someone seen as responsible for the loss. Other emotions of guilt, blaming, or frustration may be played out, and the child may act irrationally with those around him.

- *Bargaining and yearning:* Children will openly express or change their behavior in ways that they think will make the loved one come back to them, often through magical thinking. This may particularly be the case for young children, who see themselves as causing the breakup or even a death. Children may also search for the lost person, unable to accept that she will not return.

- *Depression and despair:* This stage is characterized by feelings of hopelessness, despair, and sometimes fear and withdrawal from other people. Eating and sleeping patterns may be disrupted, and the child may be difficult to comfort.

- *Understanding, acceptance, and resolution:* Eventually, the intense emotional pain will subside and the child will begin to redirect her energies to establishing relationships with others and in the future.

How successful the resolution of loss will be will depend on a number of things, including the quality of early relationships with attachment figures; other experiences; and certain child capacities such as social skills and athletic or intellectual abilities. The most critical determinant, however is likely to be how nurturing and containing the surviving or new caregiver(s) can be as well as the number of opportunities made to talk about or play out the loss and begin to gain some acceptance of it.

In summary, it is crucial to realize that a child will be significantly affected by a loss and to provide the following:

- As much stability in all other circumstances as possible

- A soothing and calming presence, physically as well as emotionally; providing warm milk, comforting food, a security object, and so forth can all be helpful

- Encouragement for the child to talk about or play out the loss

- A substitute caregiver, preferably another attachment figure. If that person is grieving as well, however, other caregivers may need to be provided.

- Assurance that the child will always be looked after by the family

- Help through counseling for the child if grieving fails to progress normally and becomes chronic or linked with intense anger or guilt

Attachment Disorders and Distortions

Lieberman and Pawl (1988) described three kinds of attachment disorders: 1) nonattachment, 2) disrupted attachment, and 3) anxious attachment.

Nonattachment   Nonattachment occurs when a baby has no opportunity to form emotional connections with other human beings. Fortunately, few children are unattached in North America because even minimal caregiving by a consistent person usually is sufficient for the child to form at least an insecure attachment. Nonattachment usually is due to severe abuse, multiple foster home placements, or institutionalization. It is also possible that children of mothers who have severe drug addiction, alcoholism, mental illness, or depression may be nonattached. Children who are nonattached often have extreme difficulties with impulse control and interpersonal relationships and may become psychopathic.

Disrupted Attachments   Disrupted attachments can occur when a child is separated from an attachment figure for a long period of time. Loss or repeated separations, as happens with placements in foster care rotating with returns home, may impair the child's capacity for forming ongoing, intimate relationships with others. This may be displayed in a child's behaviors as indiscriminant friendliness, extreme vigilance, or lack of social engagement or apathy in social interactions. Failure to thrive or other growth disturbances may also accompany these symptoms.

Anxious Attachments   Most anxious attachments should not be described as attachment disorders. Lieberman and Pawl (1988) described patterns of attachment that are extremely distorted, however. These patterns appear to result from parents' lack of availability or unpredictability as protective figures. They identified three major disturbances in children who have extremely distorted patterns of attachment. These are

1. *Recklessness and accident proneness:* This is manifested in children who run away or hurt themselves by falling, cutting themselves, and so forth and then do not appear to use caregivers as a secure base.

2. *Inhibition of exploration:* This disturbance is not the apprehension sometimes seen in children who are just naturally somewhat shy or inhibited, but rather a reaction in which the child withdraws from people and may be immobilized, showing very little affect in interactions with others.

3. *Precocious competence:* This occurs when there is a role reversal and the child is looking after the mother instead of the other way around.

Numerous intervention approaches have been used to treat these infants, young children, and their parents, and some activities for encouraging secure attachments are outlined in a later section of this chapter.

THE ROLE OF PARENTS IN ATTACHMENT

Caregivers may have difficulty providing the sensitive, responsive, affective responsiveness and comforting interactions that infants need in order to become securely attached. As this chapter demonstrates, this can occur for a number of reasons: lack of parenting experience, knowledge or confidence; a child's very difficult temperament; significant life stresses or lack of support; parental psychological or psychiatric difficulties; or unresolved issues from their own experience of being parented.

Some less obvious situations may lead to insecure attachments. For example, some parents may overinterpret or misinterpret recent information on the importance of brain development

and become quite intrusive with their infants, determined to make the "connections" happen in the brain. Other difficulties can occur when a parent has lost a child and may fear becoming emotionally involved with the new baby. Also, if a mother has lost a significant attachment herself close to the birth of her baby the grieving that she experiences can make it difficult for her to attend to her infant.

Sometimes parents may go to the opposite extreme in order to overcome parenting styles that they found destructive. One example is the parent who was abused and who then fails to set reasonable limits for fear of "hurting" the child or losing control. Another is the parent who was constantly told to excel in school who then backs off and fails to encourage his own child to do as well as possible in school or to help with school assignments. Another example might be an individual whose parents were more involved in their careers than in spending time with her; she then decides to stay at home with her own children, sacrificing her personal activities or career and some self-esteem and self-worth as a result. Sometimes, distortions of the mother's view of the child may be evident, making it difficult for the mother to be available and to interact positively with her child. Here are some question-and-answer examples that provide illustrative descriptions by mothers of their children, showing how different parents' attributions or views of their children can be.

Q: What was your first reaction when you saw him?

A: Well, he held his head up when he was lying on my stomach after he was born, and I knew right then that he was going to be trouble.

Q: How would you describe his personality or temperament?

A: I don't really know what to say . . . I haven't really noticed anything outstanding . . . He's just like any other kid . . . except he really is trouble like his father was.

Q: What was your first reaction when you saw her?

A: Well, she was all bloody so I didn't want to touch her, like she was all dirty.

Q: How would you describe her personality or temperament?

A: She is stubborn and has tantrums. Sometimes she tries to bother you, and she's whiney.

These examples of distorted attributions show how easily perceptions of a child can affect the tendency for providing sensitive interactions and result in negative interactions.

There is some suggestion that attachment security or insecurity remains a key feature of relationships throughout an individual's life. This idea has been supported by the extensive body of evidence showing that, on one hand, bereavement or loss of a loved one can be a powerful stressor throughout life. On the other hand, the presence of a close, confiding relationship protects adults of all ages as well as children against stress. Hazan and Shaver (1994) carried out a review of the features of adult relationships that are thought to reflect insecure attachment. They found that insecurely attached adults in relationships showed some of these patterns:

• Lack of self-disclosure or indiscriminant or overly intimate self-disclosure

- Undue jealousy in close relationships

- Feelings of loneliness even when involved in relationships

- Reluctance to commit in relationships

- Difficulties in making relationships in a new environment

- Tendency to view partners as insufficiently attentive

These characteristics make sense conceptually, but it has yet to be researched whether they have the same meaning as the qualities of insecurity observed in infancy. They do significantly affect adults' relationships with others, however, particularly romantic relationships, and consequently this has an indirect effect on the parents' children. Examples of an insecure and secure relationship are described next.

• •

John fell in love with Nancy the moment he saw her and asked her to marry him within a few weeks. He immediately told her all about himself and expected her to do the same. After they were married, he became more and more demanding of her attention and seemed to feel lonely even when they spent all of their evenings and weekends together. If Nancy wanted to spend time alone, John was suspicious that she had found someone else and refused to let her go out without him. Over time, the relationship became increasingly overbearing until Nancy insisted they seek counseling.

For Michael, there was no sudden "falling in love" with Caitlyn, but a gradual realization that he wanted to spend his life with her. They spent a great deal of time talking about values, ways they liked to spend time, and having children. They married, after both had completed their education and spent time working on the difficult parts of their relationship such as finding an optimal degree of intimacy for them both and resolving conflicts. Later, Michael and Caitlyn agreed they both wanted to have a child, and together they were both delighted when Caitlyn became pregnant.

DISCUSSION QUESTIONS TO USE IN TRAINING PROFESSIONALS

1. Describe the difference between attachment and bonding.

2. What is the biological function of attachment?

3. How are "working models of attachment" formed, and what influence do they have on the child's perceptions and behavior?

4. Describe the difference in behavior in the Strange Situation between a child with a secure, avoidant, resistant, or disorganized attachment.

5. What makes attachment classifications change from secure to insecure or insecure to secure?

6. Describe some ways in which the stages of development of attachment in infancy and the preschool years differ.

7. Describe some aspects of the environment that lead to secure or insecure attachments.

8. How may attachment affect an individual's behavior as an adult?

9. How many attachments is a child likely to have by 12 months of age, and how may they affect development?

10. How may cultural variations affect attachment classifications? What aspects of attachment are likely to be universal, and why?

WORKING WITH PARENTS:
GROUP EXERCISES AND SAMPLE HOMEWORK ACTIVITIES

When parents have difficulty responding sensitively to their infants and young children, various types of treatment may occur. Many interventions happen with the child and parent both present so that the interaction and the relationship are the focus of the work. Many of these interventions may work directly on the interaction by coaching the parent, providing developmental guidance, asking parents to play with their child, and allowing their child to lead in the play. Sometimes the intervention may be provided through psychotherapy, in which infants are present and parents' early experiences of abuse, neglect, or abandonment are explored and relived. Gradually, the mothers become able to recognize these feelings and to see links to problems they are having in feeding, nurturing, and interacting with their babies.

Sometimes other types of treatment may be necessary and could include individual psychotherapy for parents, group work, family therapy, and play therapy or placing the child in some form of out-of-home care. Of course, when difficulties are less serious and the parent's view of the child less distorted, providing parenting information individually or in groups can be very effective.

GROUP EXERCISES FOR PARENTS TO ENCOURAGE
POSITIVE ATTACHMENT BEHAVIORS WITH CHILDREN

This section includes exercises that can be used with parents and other caregivers to help them form secure attachments with children and better understand their own attachment background.

Describe Your Own Parents

Have parents list adjectives that describe their own parents and incidents from childhood that illustrate these adjectives (see Figure 3.3), and have them share the content with another group member. The group leader can then ask some of the group participants to share some of the information with the group.

My Family and Nurturing

Ask participants to discuss what happened when they were young if they were hurt, upset, ill, or frightened. To whom did they go, and why? Have them fill out a chart like the one in Figure 3.4 and share it with the group.

In the feedback and discussion following this exercise, emphasize that children need support when they are both physically and emotionally upset and that when children receive the nurturing they need at that time they become able to self-regulate more readily later. Make it clear that this kind of responding does not make children more whiny or spoiled but, rather, builds their sense of trust in other people. If parents bring up stories of rejection, listen and help them to also remember any positive aspect of their relationships with their parents.

Instructions: Choose five adjectives that describe your relationship with one of your parents and then relate incidents of how your parent displayed these characteristics.

Adjectives	Incidents for each word
1.	
2.	
3.	
4.	
5.	

Figure 3.3. Blank chart for listing adjectives that describe one's own parents and incidents from childhood that illustrate those adjectives.

My Favorite Place

In order to bring back some past memories, have parents draw a favorite place they have lived. Then ask them to show the drawing to others and describe it. Ask parents to expand on the importance of their chosen place and talk about any significant events that happened there. Also ask them to describe what it felt like when they moved away. Was there anything they missed? Did they feel sad?

The Love Experience

The questions given in Figure 3.5 were developed by two researchers, Hazan and Shaver (1987), and were included in a popular magazine with a large circulation. Parents are asked to complete the questionnaire as themselves, their partner, or a friend. Ask parents to discuss the category they chose for themselves or their partner or friend and how this category may affect the person's relationships with others, including their children. Also have parents think about the kind of experiences people may have had growing up that made them describe their feelings in these ways. Point out that the questionnaire is about distance in relationships and how it can be difficult if parents and children or parents and partners have very different needs in terms of closeness.

Who did I go to when I was hurt or ill?
What did that person do?
What happened if I was just upset, frustrated, or sad and not hurt or ill?
Was that person's reaction different?
Describe an incident you remember.
How has this affected your parenting with your own children?

Figure 3.4. Blank chart for recording what happened to parents in childhood when they were hurt, upset, or frightened.

Instructions: The following statements are about feelings in relationships. Which of the three descriptions best describe your feelings? Please check only one response.

_____ 1) "I find that others are reluctant to get as close as I would like. I often worry that my partner doesn't really love me or won't want to stay with me. I want to merge completely with another person, and this desire sometimes scares people away."

_____ 2) "I am somewhat uncomfortable being close to others; I find it difficult to trust them completely, difficult to allow myself to depend on them. I am nervous when anyone gets too close, and, often, others want me to be more intimate than I feel comfortable being."

_____ 3) "I find it relatively easy to get close to others and am comfortable depending on them and having them depend on me. I don't worry about being abandoned or about someone getting too close to me."

Figure 3.5. Sample questionnaire: My feelings about my relationships. (Key: 1=Insecure/ambivalent, 2=Insecure/avoidant, 3=Secure.) (From Hazan, C., & Shaver, P. [1987]. Romantic love conceptualized as an attachment process. *Journal of Personality and Social Psychology, 52,* 511–524; reprinted by permission.)

All Alone

Provide crayons and paper, and have parents imagine what it is like to be an infant or young child all alone in a great big room with a caregiver who responds when they cry, smiles at them, and soothes them to sleep when they are tired. Then ask parents to imagine what it is like to be all alone in a great big room, hungry, wet, and crying, with a caregiver who does not come for some time and then props a bottle in their mouth and walks away, leaving them alone again. Have the group participants draw how these situations felt and then describe the pictures, situations, and their feelings to other group members.

SAMPLE HOMEWORK ACTIVITIES

To strengthen the concepts and skills broached in the group meetings, it is helpful if parents can be given some homework tasks to do between sessions. The results can then be discussed the next week with the support of the group. Assign one or two of the suggested activities:

1. Spend time with your child in a way that is fun for you both.

2. Keep track of when your child is upset in some way. For a day, write down under what circumstances your child is upset and how often this happens.

3. Write down some positive and negative things that you may like to say to your parents about past events.

4. Watch how consistent you are and how much you follow through on what you promise or ask your child to do. Keep a diary of this during the week.

5. Look through a photograph album with your child and remember fun things together. Notice and comment on something special your child was doing in a photograph.

6. Write a description of your child that outlines his or her positive characteristics.

BIBLIOGRAPHY

REFERENCES

Ainsworth, M.D.S. (1967). *Infancy in Uganda: Infant care and the growth of love.* Baltimore: Johns Hopkins Press.

Ainsworth, M.D.S. (1972). Atachment and dependency: A comparison. In J.L. Gewirtz (Ed.). *Attachment and dependency.* Washington, DC: V.H. Winston and Sons.

Ainsworth, M.D.S. (1982). Attachment: Retrospect and prospect. In C.M. Parkes & J. Stevenson-Hinde (Eds.), *The place of attachment in human behavior* (pp. 3–30). New York: Basic Books.

Ainsworth, M.D.S. (1989). Attachments beyond infancy. *American Psychologist, 44,* 709–716.

Ainsworth, M.D.S., Blehar, M.C., Waters, E., & Wall, S. (1978). *Patterns of attachment: A psychological study of the Strange Situation.* Mahwah, NJ: Lawrence Erlbaum Associates.

Ainsworth, M.D.S., & Eichberg, C. (1991). Effects on infant–mother attachment of mother's unresolved loss of an attachment figure or other traumatic experience. In C.M. Parkes, J. Stevenson-Hinde, & P. Marris (Eds.), *Attachment across the life cycle* (pp. 160–183). London and New York: Tavistock/ Routledge.

Ainsworth, M.D.S., & Wittig, B.A. (1969). Attachment and exploratory behavior in one-year-olds in a Strange Situation. In B.M. Foss (Ed.), *Determinants of infant behaviour: Vol. 4. Based on the proceedings of the Fourth Tavistock Study Group on Mother–Infant Interaction* (pp. 129–173). London: Methuen.

Bartholomew, K. (1990). Avoidance of intimacy: An attachment perspective. *Journal of Social and Personal Relationships, 7,* 147–178.

Bartholomew, K., & Shaver, P.R. (1998). Methods of assessing adult attachment: Do they converge? In J.A. Simpson & W.S. Rhodes (Eds.), *Attachment theory and close relationships* (pp. 25–45). New York: Guilford Press.

Bates, J.E., Maslin, C.A., & Frankel, K.A. (1985). Attachment security, mother–child interaction, and temperament as predictors of behavior problems at age three years. In I. Bretherton & E. Waters (Eds.), Growing points of attachment theory and research. *Monographs of the Society for Research in Child Development, 50* (1–2, Serial No. 209), 167–193.

Belsky, J. (1990). Developmental risks associated with infant day care: Attachment insecurity, noncompliance, and aggression? In S.S. Chehrazi (Ed.), *Psychosocial issues in day care* (pp. 37–67). Washington, DC: American Psychiatric Press.

Belsky, J. (1999). Interactional and contextual determinants of attachment security. In J. Cassidy & P.R. Shaver (Eds.), *Handbook of attachment: Theory, research and clinical applications* (pp. 249–264). New York: Guilford Press.

Belsky, J., & Isabella, R. (1988). Maternal, infant, and social-contextual determinants of attachment security. In J. Belsky & T. Nezworski (Eds.), *Clinical implications of attachment* (pp. 41–94). Mahwah, NJ: Lawrence Erlbaum Associates.

Belsky, J., & Rovine, M. (1987). Temperament and attachment security in the Strange Situation: An empirical rapprochement. *Child Development, 58,* 787–795.

Belsky, J., Rovine, M., & Taylor, D.G. (1984). The Pennsylvania Infant and Family Development Project, III. The origins of individual differences in infant–mother attachment: Maternal and infant contributions. *Child Development, 55,* 718–728.

Belsky, J., Spritz, B., & Crnic, K. (1996). Infant attachment security and affective-cognitive information processing at age 3. *Psychological Science, 7,* 111–114.

Benoit, D. (1991, April). *Intergenerational transmission of attachment.* Symposium presented at the biennial meeting of the Society for Research in Child Development, Seattle, WA.

Benoit, D., & Parker, K.C.H. (1994). Stability and transmission of attachment across three generations. *Child Development, 65,* 1444–1456.

Bono, M., & Stifter, C.A. (1995, April). Changes in infant cardiac activity elicited by the Strange Situation and its relation to attachment status. In C. A. Brownell (Chair), *Early development of self-regulation in the context of the mother–child relationship.* Symposium conducted at the biennial meeting of the Society for Research in Child Development, Indianapolis, IN.

Booth, C.L., Rose-Krasnor, L., & Rubin, K.H. (1991). Relating preschoolers' social competence and their mothers' parenting behaviors to early attachment security and high-risk status. *Journal of Social and Personal Relationships, 8,* 363–382.

Bowlby, J. (1958). The nature of the child's tie to his mother. *International Journal of Psycho Analysis, 39,* 350–373.

Bowlby, J. (1965). *Child care and the growth of love* (2nd ed.). New York: Penguin Books.

Bowlby, J. (1969). *Attachment and loss: Vol. 1. Attachment.* New York: Penguin Books.

Bowlby, J. (1980). *Attachment and loss: Vol. 3. Loss, sadness and depression.* New York: Basic Books.

Bowlby, J. (1988). *A secure base: Parent–child attachment and healthy human development.* New York: Basic Books.

Brennan, K.A., & Shaver, P.R. (1995). Dimensions of adult attachment, affect regulation and romantic functioning. *Personality and Social Psychology Bulletin, 21,* 267–283.

Calkins, S.D., & Fox, N.A. (1992). The relation among infant temperament, security of attachment and behavioral inhibition at twenty-four months. *Child Development, 63,* 1456–1472.

Carlson, V., Cicchetti, D., Barnett, D., & Braunwald, K. (1989). Disorganized/disoriented attachment relationships in maltreated infants. *Developmental Psychology, 25,* 525–531.

Carnelly, K.B., Pietromonaco, P.R., & Jaffe, K. (1996). Attachment, caregiving and relationship functioning in couples: Effects of self and partner. *Personal Relationships, 3,* 257–277.

Cohn, D.A., Silver, D.H., Cowan, C.P., & Cowan, P.A. (1992). Working models of childhood attachment and couple relationships. *Journal of Family Issues, 13,* 432–449.

Colin, N.L. (1996). *Human attachment.* New York: McGraw Hill.

Collins, N.L., & Read, S.J. (1990). Adult attachment, working models, and relationship quality in dating couples. *Journal of Personality and Social Psychology, 58,* 644–663.

Crittenden, P.M. (1985). Social networks, quality and child rearing, and child development. *Child Development, 56,* 1299–1313.

Crittenden, P.M. (1988). Distorted patterns of relationship in maltreating families. The role of internal representational models. *Journal of Reproductive and Infant Psychology, 6,* 183–199.

Crittenden, P.M. (1992). Quality of attachment in the preschool years. *Development and Psychopathology, 4,* 209–241.

Crnic, K.A., Greenberg, M.T., & Slough, N.M. (1986). Early stress and social support influences on mothers' and high-risk infants' functioning in late infancy. *Infant Mental Health Journal, 7,* 19–33.

Crockenberg, S.B. (1981). Infant irritability, mother responsiveness and social support influences on the security of infant-mother attachment. *Child Development, 52,* 857–865.

Crockenberg, S.B., & McCluskey, K. (1986). Change in maternal behavior during the baby's first year of life. *Child Development, 57,* 746–753.

Davies, P., & Cummings, E. (1994). Marital conflict and child adjustment: An emotional security hypothesis. *Psychological Bulletin, 116,* 387–411.

DeKlyen, M. (1996). Disruptive behavior disorders and intergenerational attachment patterns: A comparison of clinic-referred and normally functioning preschoolers and their mothers. *Journal of Consulting and Clinical Psychology, 64,* 357–365.

DeMulder, E.K., & Radke-Yarrow, M. (1991). Attachment with affectively ill and well mothers: Concurrent behavioral correlates. *Development and Psychopathology, 3,* 227–242.

Denham, S.A. (1994). Mother child emotional communication and preschoolers' security of attachment and dependency. *Journal of Genetic Psychology, 155,* 119–121.

Dutton, D.O., Saunders, K., Starzomski, A., & Bartholomew, K. (1994). Intimacy-anger and insecure attachment as precursors of abuse in intimate relationships. *Journal of Applied Social Psychology, 24,* 1367–1386.

Easterbrook, M.A., & Goldberg, W.A. (1987). *Consequences of early attachment patterns for later social-personality development.* Paper presented at the Society for Research in Child Development, Baltimore.

Egeland, B., & Farber, E.A. (1984). Infant–mother attachment: Factors related to its development and changes over time. *Child Development, 55,* 753–771.

Elicker, J., Englund, M., & Sroufe, L.A. (1992). Predicting peer competence and peer relationships in childhood from early parent–child relationships. In R. Parke & G. Ladd (Eds.), *Family-peer relationships: Modes of linkage* (pp. 77–106). Mahwah, NJ: Lawrence Erlbaum Associates.

Erel, O., & Burman, B. (1995). Interrelatedness of marital relations and parent-child relations: A meta-analytic review. *Psychological Bulletin, 118,* 108–132.

Fagot, B.I. (1997). Attachment, parenting, and peer interactions of toddler children. *Developmental Psychology, 33,* 489–499.

Fagot, B.I., Gauvain, M., & Kavanagh, K. (1996). Infant attachment and mother-child problem solving: A replication. *Journal of Social and Personal Relationships, 13,* 295–302.

Fonagy, P., Leigh, T., Steele, M., Steele, H., Kennedy, R., Mattoon, G., Target, M., & Gerber, A. (1996). The relation of attachment status, psychiatric classification, and response to psychotherapy. *Journal of Consulting and Clinical Psychology, 64,* 22–31.

Fonagy, P., Steele, H., & Steele, M. (1991). Maternal representations of attachment during pregnancy predict the organization of infant–mother attachment at one year of age. *Child Development, 62,* 891–905.

Fonagy, P., Steele, M., Steele, H., Moran, G.S., & Higgitt, A.C. (1991). The capacity for understanding mental states: The reflective self in parent and child and its significance for security of attachment. *Infant Mental Health Journal, 12,* 201–218.

Fox, N.A., Calkins, S.D., & Bell, M.A. (1994). Neural plasticity and development in the first two years of life: Evidence from cognitive and socioemotional domains of research. *Development and Psychopathology, 6,* 677–696.

Fox, N.A., & Card, J.A. (1999). Psychophysiological measures in the study of attachment. In J. Cassidy & P.R. Shaver, (Eds.), *Handbook of attachment: Theory, research and clinical applications* (pp. 226–245). New York: Guilford Press.

Fox, N.A., & Davidson, R.J. (1984). *The psychobiology of affective development* (pp. 353–382). Mahwah, NJ: Lawrence Erlbaum Associates.

Frankel, K.A., & Bates, J.E. (1990). Mother–toddler problem-solving: Antecedents in attachment, home behavior, and temperament. *Child Development, 61,* 810–819.

Fuller, T.L., & Fincham, F.D. (1995). Attachment style in married couples: Relation to current marital functioning, stability over time and method of assessment. *Personal Relationships, 2,* 17–34.

Gelfand, D., & Teti, D. (1990). The effects of maternal depression on children. *Clinical Psychology Review, 10,* 329–353.

Goldberg, S. (1991). Recent developments in attachment theory and research. *Canadian Journal of Psychiatry, 36,* 393–400.

Goldsmith, H.H., & Alansky, J.A. (1987). Maternal and infant temperamental predictors of attachment: A meta-analytic review. *Journal of Consulting and Clinical Psychology, 55,* 805–816.

Greenberg, M.T. (1999). Attachment and psychopathology in childhood. In J. Cassidy, & P.R. Shaver (Eds.), *Handbook of attachment: Theory, research and clinical applications* (pp. 469–496). New York: Guilford Press.

Grossman, K., Fremmer-Bombik, E., Rudolf, J., & Grossman, K. (1988). Maternal attachment representations as related to patterns of infant–mother attachment and maternal care during the first year. In R.A. Hinde & J. Stevenson-Hinde (Eds.), *Relationships within families: Mutual influences* (pp. 241–260). Oxford: Clarendon Press.

Grossman, K., Grossman, K.E., Spangler, G., Suess, G., & Unzer, L. (1985). Maternal sensitivity and newborn orienting responses as related to quality of attachment in northern Germany. In I. Bretherton & E. Waters (Eds.), Growing points of attachment theory and research. *Monographs of the Society for Research in Child Development, 50* (1–2, Serial No. 209), 233–256.

Grossman, K.E., Scheuerer-Englisch, H., & Loher, I. (1991). The development of emotional organization and its relationship in intelligent behavior. In F.J. Mönks & G. Lehwald (Eds.), *Curiosity, exploration, and talent in young children* (pp. 66–76). München: Ernst Reinhardt Verlag.

Gunnar, M.R., Brodersen, L., Nachmias, M., Buss, K., & Rigatuso, J. (1996). Stress reactivity and attachment security. *Developmental Psychobiology, 29,* 191–204.

Gunnar, M.R., Colton, M., & Stansbury, K. (1992, May). *Studies of emotional behavior, temperament and adrenocortical activity in human infants.* Paper presented at the 8th International Conference on Infant Studies, Miami, FL.

Gunnar, M.R., Mangelsdorf, S., Larson, M., & Hertsgaard, L. (1989). Attachment, temperament, and adrenocortical activity in infancy: A study of psychoendocrine regulation. *Developmental Psychology, 25,* 355–363.

Hamilton, C.E. (1995). *Continuity and discontinuity of attachment from infancy through adolescence.* Paper presented at the biennial meeting of the Society for Research in Child Development, Indianapolis, IN.

Hazan, H.G. (1972). *Adolescent separation anxiety: A method for the study of adolescence separation problems.* Springfield, IL: Charles C. Thomas.

Hazan, C., & Shaver, P. (1987). Romantic love conceptualized as an attachment process. *Journal of Personality and Social Psychology, 52,* 511–524.

Hazan, C., & Shaver, P. (1990). Love and work: An attachment-theoretical perspective. *Journal of Personality and Social Psychology, 59,* 270–280.

Hazan, C., & Shaver, P. (1994). Attachment as an organizational framework for research on close relationships. *Psychological Inquiry, 5,* 1–22.

Hertsgaard, L., Gunnar, M., Erickson, M.F., & Nachmias, M. (1995). Adrenocortical responses to the Strange Situation in infants with disorganized/disoriented attachment relationships. *Child Development, 66,* 1100–1106.

Howes, C. (1999). Attachment relationships in the context of mulitple caregivers. In J. Cassidy & P.R. Shaver (Eds.), *Handbook of attachment: Theory, research, and clinical applications.* New York: Guilford Press.

Howes, C., Rodning, C., Galluzzo, D.C., & Myers, L. (1988). Attachment and child care: Relationships with mother and caregiver. *Early Childhood Research Quarterly, 3,* 403–416.

Isabella, R. (1993). Origins of attachment: Maternal interactive behavior across the first year. *Child Development, 64,* 605–621.

Jacobson, J.L., & Wille, D.E. (1986). The influence of attachment pattern on developmental changes in peer interaction from the toddler to the preschool period. *Child Development, 57,* 338–347.

Jacobvitz, D., Hazen, N., & Riggs, S. (1997, April). Disorganized mental processes in mothers' frightening/frightened caregiving and disoriented/disorganized behavior in infancy. In D. Jacobvitz (Chair), *Caregiving correlates and longitudinal outcomes of disorganized attachment in infants.* Symposium conducted at the biennial meeting of the Society for Research in Child Development, Washington, DC.

Kennell, J.H., Trause, M.A., & Klaus, M.H. (1975). Evidence for a sensitive period in the human mother. In T.B. Brazelton, E. Tronick, L. Adamson, H. Als, & S. Wise (Eds.), *Parent-infant interaction* (pp. 87–101). New York: Excerpta Medica.

Kerns, K.A. (1994). A longitudinal examination of links between mother child attachment and children's friendships in early childhood. *Journal of Social and Personal Relationships, 11,* 379–381.

Kestenbaum, R., Farber, E.A., & Sroufe, L.A. (1989). Individual differences in empathy among preschoolers: Relation to attachment history. *New Directions for Child Development, 44,* 51–64.

Kirkpatrick, L.A., & Davis, K.E. (1994). Attachment style, gender, and relationship stability: A longitudinal analysis. *Journal of Personality and Social Psychology, 66,* 502–512.

Kirkpatrick, L.A., & Hazan, C. (1994). Attachment styles and close relationships: A four-year prospective study. *Personal Relationships, 1,* 123–142.

Klaus, M.H., & Kennell, J.H. (1976). *Maternal-infant bonding: The impact of early separation or loss on family development.* St. Louis: Mosby.

Kobak, R.R., & Sceery, A. (1988). Attachment in late adolescence: Working models, affect regulation and representations of self and others. *Child Development, 59,* 135–146.

LaFrenière, P.J., Provost, M.A., & Dubeau, D. (1992). From an insecure base: Parent–child relations and internalizing behaviour in the preschool. *Early Development and Parenting, 1,* 137–148.

Laible, D.J., & Thompson, R.A. (1998). Attachment and emotional understanding in preschool children. *Developmental Psychology, 34,* 1038–1045.

Lehman, E.B., Denham, S.A., Moser, M.H., & Reeves, S.L. (1992). Soft object and pacifier attachments in young children: The role of security of attachment to the mother. *Journal of Child Psychology and Psychiatry and Allied Disciplines, 33,* 1205–1215.

Lewis, M., Feiring, C., McGuffog, C., & Jaskir, J. (1984). Predicting psychopathology in six-year-olds from early social relations. *Child Development, 55,* 123–136.

Lieberman, A., & Pawl, J.H. (1988). Clinical applications of attachment theory. In J. Belsky & T. Nezworski (Eds.), *Clinical implications of attachment* (pp. 327–351). Mahwah, NJ: Lawrence Erlbaum Associates.

Lyons-Ruth, K., Alpern, L., & Repacholi, B. (1993). Disorganized infant attachment classifications and maternal psychosocial problems as predictors of hostile–aggressive behavior in the preschool classroom. *Child Development, 64,* 572–585.

Lyons-Ruth, K., Bronfman, E., & Atwood, G. (1999). A relational diathesis model of hostile-helpless states of mind: Expressions in mother–infant interaction. In J. Solomon & C. George (Eds.), *Attachment disorganization* (pp. 33–70). New York: Guilford Press.

Lyons-Ruth, K., Connell, D.B., Grunebaum, H., & Botein, S. (1990). Infants at social risk: Maternal depression and family support services as mediators of infant development and security of attachment. *Child Development, 61,* 85–98.

Lyons-Ruth, K., & Jacobitz, D. (1999). Attachment disorganization: Unresolved loss, relational violence, and lapses in behavioral and attentional strategies. In J. Cassidy & P.R. Shaver (Eds.), *Handbook of attachment: Theory, research, and clinical applications.* New York: Guilford Press.

Lyons-Ruth, K., Repacholi, B., McLeod, S., & Silva, E. (1991). Disorganized attachment behavior in infancy: Short-term stability, maternal and infant correlates, and risk-related subtypes. *Development and Psychopathology, 3,* 377–396.

Main, M. (1990). Cross-cultural studies of attachment organizations: Recent studies, changing methodologies, and the concept of conditional strategies. *Human Development, 33,* 48–61.

Main, M. (1999). Epilogue attachment theory: Eighteen points with suggestions for further study. In J. Cassidy & R. Shaver (Eds.), *Handbook of attachment: Theory, research, and clinical applications.* New York: Guilford Press.

Main, M., & Cassidy, J. (1988). Categories of response to reunion with the parent at age 6: Predictable from infant attachment classifications and stable over a 1-month period. *Developmental Psychology, 24,* 415–426.

Main, M., & Goldwyn, R. (1998). *Adult attachment scoring and classification system.* Unpublished manuscript, University of California at Berkeley.

Main, M., & Hesse, E. (1992). Disorganized/disoriented infant behavior in the Strange Situation, lapses in the monitoring of reasoning and discourse during the parents' Adult Attachment Interview and

dissociative state. In M. Ammanati & D. Stern (Eds.), *Attachment and Psychoanalysis* (pp. 86–140). Rome: Gius, Laterza & Figli.

Main, M., Kaplan, N., & Cassidy, J. (1985). Security in infancy, childhood, and adulthood: A move to the level of representation. In I. Bretherton & E. Waters (Eds.), Growing points of attachment theory and research. *Monographs of the Society for Research in Child Development, 50* (1–2, Serial No. 209), 66–104.

Main, M., & Solomon, J. (1986). Discovery of an insecure-disorganized/disoriented attachment pattern. In T.B. Brazelton & M.W. Yogman (Eds.), *Affective development in infancy* (pp. 95–124). Norwood, NJ: Ablex.

Main, M., & Solomon, J. (1990). Procedures for identifying infants as disorganized/disoriented during the Ainsworth Strange Situation. In M.T. Greenberg, D. Cicchetti, & E.M. Cummings (Eds.), *Attachment in the preschool years: Theory, research, and intervention* (pp. 121–160). Chicago: University of Chicago Press.

Main, M., & Weston, D. (1981). The quality of the toddler's relationship to mother and to father: Related to conflict behaviour and the readiness to establish new relationships. *Child Development, 52,* 932–940.

Mangelsdorf, S.C., Gunnar, M., Kestenbaum, R., Lang, S., & Andreas, D. (1991). Infant proneness-to-distress temperament, maternal personality, and mother infant attachment: Associations and goodness of fit. *Annual Progress in Child Psychiatry and Child Development,* 312–329.

Mangelsdorf, S.C., Plunkett, J.W., Dedrick, C.F., Berlin, M., Meisels, S.J., McHale, J.L., & Dichtellmiller, M. (1996). Attachment security in very low birth weight infants. *Developmental Psychology, 32,* 914–920.

Marvin, R.S. (1977). An ethological-cognitive model for the attenuation of the mother–child attachment behavior. In T.M. Alloway, L. Krames, & P. Pliner (Eds.), *Advances in the study of communication and affect: Vol. 3. The development of social attachments* (pp. 25–60). New York: Plenum Press.

Matas, L., Arend, R.A., & Sroufe, L.A. (1978). Continuity of adaptation in the second year: The relationship between quality of attachment and later competence. *Child Development, 49,* 547–556.

McFarlane, A.C., & van der Kolk, B.A. (1996). Trauma and its challenge to society. In B.A. van der Kolk, A.C. McFarlane, & L. Weisgeth (Eds.), *Traumatic stress: The effects of overwhelming experience on mind, body, and society* (pp. 22–46). New York: Guilford Press.

Mickelson, K.D., Kessler, R.C., & Shaver, P.R. (1997). Adult attachment in a nationally representative sample. *Journal of Personality and Social Psychology, 73,* 1092–1106.

Mikulincer, M., & Erev, I. (1991). Attachment style and the structure of romantic love. *British Journal of Social Psychology, 30,* 273–291.

Moss, E., Parent, S., Gosselin, C., Rousseau, D., & St-Laurent, D. (1996). Attachment and teacher-reported behavior problems during the preschool and early school-age period. *Development and Psychopathology, 8,* 511–525.

Nachmias, M., Gunnar, M., Mangelsdorf, S., Parritz, R., Hornick, & Buss, K. (1996). Behavioral inhibition and stress reactivity: The moderating role of attachment security. *Child Development, 67,* 508–522.

National Institute of Child Health and Human Development (NICHD) Early Child Care Research Network (1997). The effects of infant child care on infant-mother attachment security: Results of the NICHD study of early childcare. *Child Development, 68,* 860–879.

Park, K.A., & Waters, E. (1989). Security of attachment and preschool friendships. *Child Development, 60,* 1076–1081.

Pastor, D.L. (1981). The quality of mother–infant attachment and its relationship to toddlers' initial sociability with peers. *Developmental Psychology, 17,* 326–335.

Pederson, D.R., & Moran, G. (1996). Expressions of the attachment relationship outside of the Strange Situation. *Child Development, 67,* 915–927.

Pierrehumbert, B., Iannotti, R.J., & Cummings, E.M. (1985). Mother–infant attachment, development of social competencies and beliefs of self responsibility. *Archives de Psychologie, 53,* 365–374.

Rauh, H., Ziegenhain, U., Müeller, B., & Wijnroks, L. (2000). Stability and change in infant–mother attachment in the second year of life: Relations to parenting quality and varying degrees of day-care experience. In P.M. Crittenden & A.H. Claussen (Eds.), *The organization of attachment relationships: Maturation, culture, and context* (pp. 251–276). Cambridge: Cambridge University Press.

Ricks, M.H. (1985). The social transmission of parental behavior: Attachment across generations. In I. Bretherton & E. Waters (Eds.), Growing points of attachment theory and research. *Monographs of the Society for Research in Child Development, 50* (1–2, Serial No. 209), 211–227.

Rosenstein, D.S., & Horowitz, H.A. (1996). Adolescent attachment and psychopathology. *Journal of Consulting and Clinical Psychology, 64,* 244–253.

Schneider-Rosen, K., Braunwald, K.G., Carlson, V., & Cicchetti, D. (1985). Current perspectives in attachment theory: Illustrations from the study of maltreated infants. In I. Bretherton & E. Waters (Eds.), Growing points of attachment theory and research. *Monographs of the Society for Research in Child Development, 50* (1–2, Serial No. 209), 194–210.

Schuengel, C., Bakermans-Kranenburg, M.J., & van IJzendoorn, M.H. (1999). Frightening maternal behavior linking unresolved loss and disorganized infant attachment. *Journal of Consulting and Clinical Psychology, 67,*54–63.

Schuengel, C., van IJzendoorn, M., Bakermans-Kranenburg, M., & Blom, M. (1997, April). Frightening, frightened and/or dissociated behavior, unresolved loss, and infant-disorganization. In D. Jacobvitz (Chair), *Caregiving correlates and longitudinal outcomes of disorganized attachments in infants.* Symposium conducted at the biennial meeting of the Society for Research in Child Development, Washington, DC.

Seifer, R., Schiller, M., Sameroff, A.J., Resnick, S., & Riordan, K. (1996). Attachment, maternal sensitivity and infant temperament during the first year of life. *Developmental Psychology, 32,* 12–25.

Senchak, M., & Leonard, K.E. (1992). Attachment styles and marital adjustment among newlywed couples. *Journal of Social and Personal Relationships, 9,* 51–64.

Shaver, P.R., & Clark, C.L. (1994). The psychodynamics of adult romantic attachment. In J.M. Masling & R.F. Bornstein (Eds.), *Empirical perspectives on object relations theory. Empirical studies of psychoanalytic theories, Vol. 5.* (pp. 105–156). Washington, DC: American Psychological Association.

Shaver, P.R., & Hazan, C. (1993). Adult romantic attachment: Theory and evidence. In D. Perlman & W.H. Jones (Eds.), *Advances in personal relationships* (Vol. 4, pp. 29–70). London: Jessica Kingsley.

Shaw, D.S., Owens, E.B., Vondra, J.I., Keenan, K., & Winslow, E.B. (1996). Early risk factors and pathways in the development of early disruptive behavior problems. *Development and Psychopathology, 8,* 679–699.

Simpson, J.A. (1990). Influence of attachment styles on romantic relationships. *Journal of Personality and Social Psychology, 59,* 971–980.

Slade, A. (1987). Quality of attachment and early symbolic play. *Developmental Psychology, 23,* 78–85.

Solomon, J., & George, C. (Eds.). (1999). *Attachment disorganization.* New York: Guilford Press.

Spangler, G., & Schieche, M. (1998). Emotional and adrenocortical responses of infants to the Strange Situation: The differential function of emotional expression. *International Journal of Behavioral Development, 22,* 681–706.

Speltz, M.L., Greenberg, M.T., & DeKlyen, M. (1990). Attachment in preschoolers with disruptive behavior: A comparison of clinic-referred and nonproblem children. *Development and Psychopathology, 2,* 31–46.

Sroufe, L.A. (1983). Infant-caregiver attachment and patterns of adaptation in preschool: The roots of maladaptation and competence. In M. Perlmutter (Ed.), *Minnesota Symposium on Child Psychology: Vol. 16. Development and policy concerning children with special needs* (pp. 41–83). Mahwah, NJ: Lawrence Erlbaum Associates.

Sroufe, L.A. (1985). Attachment classification from the perspective of infant-caregiver relationships and infant temperament. *Child Development, 56,* 1–14.

Sroufe, L.A., Carlson, E., & Shulman, S. (1993). Individuals in relationships: Development from infancy through adolescence. In D.C. Funder, R. Parke, C. Tomlinson-Keesey, & K. Widaman (Eds.), *Studying*

lives through time: Personality and development (pp. 315–342). Washington, DC: American Psychological Association.

Sroufe, L.A., & Waters, E. (1977). Heart rate as a convergent measure in clinical and developmental research. *Merrill-Palmer Quarterly, 23,* 3–27.

Steele, H., & Steele, M. (1994). Intergenerational patterns of attachment. In K. Bartholomew & D. Perlman (Eds.), *Attachment processes in adulthood: Advances in personal relationships* (Vol. 5, pp. 93–120). London: Jessica Kingsley.

Steele, H., Steele, M., & Fonagy, P. (1996). Associations among attachment classifications of mothers, fathers and their infants. *Child Development, 67,* 541–555.

Suess, G.K. (1987). *Consequences of early attachment experiences on children's competence in kindergarten.* Unpublished doctoral dissertation, University of Regensburg, Germany.

Susman-Stillman, A., Kalkoske, M., Egeland, B., & Waldman, I. (1996). Infant temperament and maternal sensitivity as predictors of attachment security. *Infant Behavior and Development, 19,* 33–47.

Teti, D., Gelfand, D., Messinger, D., & Isabella, R. (1995). Maternal depression and the quality of early attachment: An examination of infants, preschoolers, and their mothers. *Developmental Psychology, 31,* 364–376.

Thalhuber, K., Jacobvitz, D., & Hazen, N.L. (1998, March). *Effects of mothers' past traumatic experiences on mother–infant interactions.* Paper presented at the biennial meeting of the Southwestern Society for Research in Human Development, Galveston, TX.

Thompson, R.A., Connell, J.P., & Bridges, J.L. (1988). Temperament, emotion, and social interactive behavior in the Strange Situation: A component process analysis of attachment system functioning. *Child Development, 59,* 1102–1110.

Thompson, R.A., Lamb, M.E., & Estes, D. (1981). Stability of infant-mother attachment and its relationship to changing life circumstances in an unselected middle-class sample. *Child Development, 53,* 144–148.

Tyrrell, C., & Dozier, M. (1997). *The role of attachment in the therapeutic process and outcome for adults with serious psychiatric disorders.* Paper presented at the biennial meeting of the Society for Research in Child Development, Washington, DC.

van den Boom, D.C. (1989). Neonatal irritability and the development of attachment. In G. Kohnstamm, J.E. Bates, & M.K. Rothbart (Eds.), *Temperament in childhood.* Chichester, England: John Wiley & Sons.

van IJzendoorn, M.H. (1992). Intergenerational transmission of parenting: A review of studies in non-clinical populations. *Developmental Review, 12,* 76–99.

van IJzendoorn, M.H., Kranenburg, M.J., Zwart-Woudstra, H.A., van Busschbach, A.M., & Lamberman, W.E. (1991). Parental attachment and children's socio-emotional development: Some findings on the validity of the Adult Attachment Interview in the Netherlands. *International Journal of Behavioural Development, 14,* 375–394.

Vaughn, B.E., & Bost, K.K. (1999). Attachment and temperament: Redundant, independent, or interacting influences on interpersonal adaptation and personality development? In J. Cassidy & P.R. Shaver (Eds.), *Handbook of attachment: Theory, research and clinical applications* (pp. 198–225). New York: Guilford Press.

Wartner, U.G., Grossman, K., Fremmer-Bombik, E., & Suess, G. (1994). Attachment patterns at age six in south Germany: Predictability from infancy and implications for preschool behavior. *Child Development, 65,* 1014–1027.

Waters, E. (1978). The reliability and stability of individual differences in infant–mother attachment. *Child Development, 49,* 483–494.

Waters, E., Merrick, S.K., Albersheim, L., & Treboux, D. (1995, April). From the Strange Situation to the Adult Attachment Interview: A 20-year longitudinal study of attachment security in infancy and early childhood. In J. A. Crowell & E. Waters (Chairs), *Is the parent–child relationship a prototype of later love relationships?: Studies of attachment and working models of attachment.* Symposium conducted at the biennial meeting of the Society for Research in Child Development, Indianapolis, IN.

Waters, E., Wippman, J., & Sroufe, L.A. (1979). Attachment, positive affect, and competence in the peer group: Two studies in construct validation. *Child Development, 50,* 821–829.

Winnicott, D.W & Winnicott, C. (1971). *Playing and reality.* London: Routledge.

Zeanah, C.H., Benoit, D., & Barton, M. (1995). *Working Model of the Child Interview: Scoring and coding manual.* Unpublished Manuscript, Brown University, Providence, RI.

Zeanah, C.H., Benoit, D., Barton, M., Regan, C., Hirshberg, L.M., & Lipsitt, L.P. (1993). Representations of attachment in mothers and their one-year-old infants. *Journal of the American Academy of Child and Adolescent Psychiatry, 32,* 278–286.

Zimmerman, P. (1994). *Attachment in adolescence: Development while coping with actual challenges.* Unpublished doctoral dissertation, University of Regensberg, Germany.

FURTHER READING ON THE TOPIC

Atkinson, L., & Zucker, K.J. (1997). *Attachment and psychopathology.* New York: Guilford Press.

Biringen, Z. (1994). Attachment theory and research: Application to clinical practice. *American Journal of Orthopsychiatry, 64,* 404–420.

Bowlby, J. (1973). *Attachment and loss: Vol. 2. Separation, anxiety and anger.* London: Hogarth Press.

Cassidy, J., & Shaver, P.R. (1999). *Handbook of attachment: Theory, research and clinical applications.* New York: Guilford Press.

Crittenden, P. (1985). Maltreated infants: Vulnerability and resilience. *Journal of Child Psychology and Psychiatry and Allied Disciplines, 26,* 85–96.

Dunn, J. (1977). *Distress and comfort.* Cambridge, MA: Harvard University Press.

Durkin, L.L. (1987). *Special times for parents and kids together.* New York: Warner Books.

Egeland, B., Kalkoske, M., Gottsman, N., & Erikson, M.E. (1990). Preschool Behavior Problems: Stability and Factors Accounting for Change. *Journal of Child Psychology and Psychiatry, 31,* 891–909.

Gewirtz, J.L., & Kurtines, W.M. (Eds.). (1991). *Intersections with attachment.* Mahwah, NJ: Lawrence Erlbaum Associates.

Goldberg, S. (2000). *Attachment and development.* London: Arnold.

Greenberg, M.T., Cicchetti, D., & Cummings, E.M. (1990). *Attachment in the preschool years: Theory, research and intervention.* Chicago, IL: University of Chicago Press.

Jewett, C.L. (1982). *Helping children cope with separation and loss.* Harvard, MA: Harvard Common Press.

Karen, R. (1990, February). Becoming attached. *The Atlantic,* 35–70.

Karen, R. (1998). *Becoming attached: Unfolding the mystery of the infant–mother bond and its impact on later life.* New York: Warner Books.

Kraemer, G.W. (1992). A psychobiological theory of attachment. *Behavioral and Brain Sciences, 15,* 493–541.

Levine, S. (1982\3). Comparative and psychobiological perspectives on development. In W.A. Collins (Ed.), *The Minnesota Symposia on Child Psychology: The concept of development* (pp. 29–63). Mahwah, NJ: Lawrence Erlbaum Associates.

Main, M., & Goldwyn, R. (1990). Adult attachment rating and classification system. In M. Main (Ed.), *A typology of human attachment organization.* New York: Cambridge University Press.

Orlick, T. (1995). *Nice on my feelings: Nurturing the best in children and parents.* Carp, Ontario: Creative Bound.

Parkes, C.M., Stevenson-Hinde, J., & Marris, P. (Eds.). (1993). *Attachment across the life cycle.* New York: Routledge, Chapman and Hall.

Reite, M., & Boccia, M.L. (1994). Physiological aspects of adult attachment. In M.B. Sperling & W.H. Berman (Eds.), *Attachment in adults: Clinical and developmental perspectives.* New York: Guilford Press.

Rutter, M. (1995). Clinical implications of attachment concepts: Retrospect and prospect. *Journal of Child Psychology and Psychiatry and Allied Disciplines, 36,* 549–571.

Sameroff, A.J., & Emde, R.N. (1989). *Relationship disturbances in early childhood: A development approach.* New York: Basic Books.

Sammons, W.A.H. (1991). *The self-calmed baby.* New York: Yankee Publishing.

Sperling, M.B., & Berman, W.H. (1994). *Attachment in adults: Clinical and developmental perspectives.* New York: Guilford Press.

Sroufe, L.A. (1980). The coherence of individual development: Early care, attachment and subsequent developmental issues. *American Psychologist, 34,* 834–841.

Sroufe, L.A. (1988). The role of infant-caregiver attachment in development. In J. Belsky & N. Nezworski (Eds.), *Clinical implications of attachment* (pp. 18–38). Mahwah, NJ: Lawrence Erlbaum Associates.

West, M.L., & Sheldon-Keller, A.E. (1994). *Patterns of relating: An adult attachment perspective.* New York: Guilford Press.

Zigler, E.F., & Gordon, E.W. (Eds.). (1990). *Daycare: Scientific and social policy issues.* Boston: Kilburn House.

CHILDREN'S BOOKS ABOUT ATTACHMENT ISSUES

Best, C. (1996). *Getting used to Harry.* New York: Orchard Books.

Brown, M.W. (1991). *Goodnight moon.* New York: Harper Festival.

Brown, M.W. (1991). *The runaway bunny.* New York: Harper Festival.

Burningham, J. (1994). *The blanket.* Cambridge, MA: Candlewick Press.

Calmenson, S. (1997). *Tiger's bedtime.* New York: High/Scope Press.

Carrick, C. (1981). *Accident.* New York: Houghton Mifflin.

Caseley, J. (1986). *When grandpa came to stay.* New York: William Morrow.

Caseley, J. (1995). *Priscilla Twice.* New York: William Morrow.

Clifton, L. (1988). *Everett Anderson's goodbye.* New York: Henry Holt.

Cohen, M. (1995). *Lost in the museum.* New York: Bantam.

Cohen, M. (1996). *Jim's dog muffins.* New York: Turtleback Books.

De Paola, T. (1978). *Nana upstairs and nana downstairs.* New York: Putnam.

Denton, K. M. (1995). *Would they love a lion?* New York: Kingfisher Books.

Flack, M. (1997). *Angus lost.* New York: Turtleback Books.

Fowler, S.G. (1994). *I'll see you when the moon is full.* New York: Greenwillow Books.

Halevi, M. (1997). *Saying good-bye to grandma.* New York: Pitspopany Press.

Hazen, B.S. (1985). *Why did grandpa die?* Racine, WI: Western Publishing.

Hines, A.G. (1986). *Don't worry, I'll find you.* New York: Dutton Children's Books.

Hines, A.G. (1996). *When we married Gary.* New York: Greenwillow Books.

Joosse, B.M. (1993). *Mama, do you love me?* San Francisco: Chronicle Books.

Jordan, M.K. (1989). *Losing uncle Tim.* Niles, IL: A. Whitman.

Kandoian, E. (1990). *Maybe she forgot.* New York: Dutton Children's Books.

Keller, H. (1987). *Goodbye, Max!* New York: Greenwillow Books.

Keller, H. (1988). *Geraldine's blanket.* New York: William Morrow.

Keller, H. (1990). *What Alvin wanted.* New York: Greenwillow Books.

Kraus, R. (1970). *Whose mouse are you?* New York: Macmillan.

Kraus, R. (1986). *Where are you going, little mouse?* New York: Greenwillow Books.

Oxenbury, H. (1998). *Pippo gets lost.* New York: Little Simon.

Quinlan, P. (1994). *Tiger flowers.* Toronto: Lester.

Rogers, F. (1987). *Moving.* New York: Putnam.

Rogers, F. (1998). *When a pet dies.* New York: Putnam.

Selway, M. (1992). *Don't forget to write.* London: Hambleton-Hill.

Stinson, K. (1984). *Mom and dad don't live together any more.* Toronto: Firefly Books.

Stinson, K. (1988). *Teddy rabbit.* Toronto: Annick Press.

Turner, A.W. (1991). *Stars for Sarah.* New York: Harper Collins Children's Books Group.

Varley, S. (1984). *Badger's parting gifts.* London: Lothrop, Lee and Shepard Books.

Viorst, J. (1971). *The tenth good thing about Barney.* New York: Atheneum Books.

Viorst, J. (1988). *The good-bye book.* New York: Atheneum Books.

Wabbes, M. (1987). *Good night, little rabbit.* Toronto: Kids Can Press.

Waber, B. (1973). *Ira sleeps over.* Boston: Houghton Mifflin.

Waber, B. (1988). *Ira says goodbye.* Boston: Houghton Mifflin.

Watanabe, S. (1982). *Where's my daddy?* New York: Philomel Books.

Wells, R. (1991). *Max's dragon shirt.* New York: Dial Books for Young Readers.

Weninger, B. (1995). *Good-bye, daddy!* New York: North-South Books.

Yolen, J. (1994). *Grandad Bill's song.* New York: Philomel Books.

Zagwyn, D.T. (1995). *The pumpkin blanket.* Markham, Ontario: Fitzhenry and Whiteside.

APPENDIX: SELECTED ASSESSMENT INSTRUMENTS

● ● ●

ASSESSING ATTACHMENTS IN INFANTS, CHILDREN, AND ADULTS

The majority of the measures described in this section require extensive training to administer and, particularly, to score.

Assessing Attachment in Infants and Children

As mentioned in the text of this chapter, attachment in infancy (from 12 to 20 months) has traditionally been assessed using the Strange Situation, an observational measure that was developed in the late 1970s (Ainsworth et al., 1978). The laboratory procedure assesses attachment classification based on behavior of the infant in the various episodes of the procedure. Extensions of the measure have been made for use into the toddler and preschool years after 20 months. Other approaches that are used in childhood tap the representational system by having the child respond to pictures or to play out situations that relate to attachment themes. Still other methods have used Q-Sort methodology and a parent or researcher observer to describe the infant's or child's attachment behaviors in the home.

Table A3.1 details some instruments for assessing attachment in infants and children, including some measures that use symbolic forms of mental representations.

Assessing Attachment in Adults

Attachment in adolescents and adults is usually assessed using the Adult Attachment Interview (AAI), although a Q-Sort technique also is available. These types of measures are listed in Table A3.2.

Measures for Assessing Current Relationship in Adults

Table A3.3 lists some measures for assessing adults' current relationships.

Measures for Assessing Attachment History

Table A3.4 briefly describes measures that can be used to collect data on attachment history.

Table A3.1. Selected attachment assessments for infants and children

Tool/instrument	Age range	Items/ administratoin time	General description
Attachment Q-Sort (AQS) Waters, E. (1995). The Attachment Q-Set. In E. Waters, B.E. Vaughn, G. Posada, & K. Kondo-Ikemura (Eds.), Caregiving cultural and cognitive perspectives on secure-base behavior and working models. *Monographs for the Society for Research in Child Development, 60* (2–3, Serial No. 244), 247–254.	12–60 months	90 items are sorted following 2–6 hours of observation in the home	The *Attachment Q-Sort (AQS)* assesses attachment based on in-home observation. The Q-Set for the test consists of 90 items on cards that describe various attachment behaviors. The cards are sorted into 9 piles of "least characteristic" and "most characteristic" of the child. The sorts are done by a parent or an observer after 2–6 hours of observation in the home. Results are compared with a criterion sort for attachment security developed by the author.
*Attachment Story Completion Task Bretherton, I., Ridgeway, D., & Cassidy, J. (1990). Assessing internal working models of the attachment relationships: An Attachment Story Completion Task. In M. Greenberg, D. Cicchetti, & E.M. Cummings (Eds.), *Attachment in the preschool years* (pp. 273–310). Chicago: The University Press.	3 years	5 stories; 30 minutes	In the *Attachment Story Completion Task*, testers enact stories to mothers and children that introduce the following issues and situations: 1) *"spilling juice"*: How an attachment figure (the mother) responds in relation to a child who spills juice; 2) *"Hurt knee"*: What protective behavior is elicited when a child is in pain or when he hurts himself; 3) *"Monster in the bedroom"*: A child's fears and if or how it elicits protective behaviors from the caregivers; 4) *"Departure"*: The parents leave for an overnight trip, with grandmother remaining behind to look after the two children; and 5) *"Reunion"*: How the child responds on the return of the parents and the behavior that is elicited (Bretherton, Ridgeway, D. & Cassidy, 1990, p. 286). Detailed transcripts are made of the child's descriptions and acting out of each story and classifications are made on the basis of responses to the stories. Secure children show coping behavior, avoidant do not respond, ambivalent children show inconsistent patterns, and disorganized children show odd or disorganized responses.
Cassidy-Marvin System for Assessing Attachment in Children Older than 18 Months Cassidy, J., & Marvin, R.S. (1992). *Attachment organization in preschool children: Coding guidelines* (4th ed.) Unpublished manuscript, MacArthur Working Group on Attachment, Seattle, WA.	2–4 years	8 episodes of Strange Situation; 30 minutes	The *Cassidy-Marvin System for Assessing Attachment in Children Older than 18 Months* approach uses the episodes of the Strange Situation, although some researchers have lengthened the separations and introduced other laboratory tasks into the procedure. The behavior is scored for the quality of interaction including talking and negotiations engaged in by the parent and child around the separations. Scoring assigns children to one of five groups:1) Secure, 2) Avoidant, 3) Ambivalent, 4) Controlling/ Disorganized, and 5) Insecure/Other.
Main-Cassidy Attachment Classification for Kindergarten-Age Children Main, M., & Cassidy, J. (1988). Categories of response to reunion with the parent at age 6: Predictable from infant attachment classifications and stable over a 1-month period. *Developmental Psychology, 24*, 415–426.	4–7 years	One-hour separation and 3- to 5-minute reunion; 65 minutes	Scoring of the *Main-Cassidy Attachment Classification for Kindergarten-Age Children* is based on a 3- to 5- minute reunion following a 1-hour separation. Children are classified as 1) Secure, 2) Avoidant, 3) Ambivalent, 4) Controlling, or 5) Unclassifiable.

Tool/instrument	Age range	Items/ administration time	General description
*Picture Response Set Kaplan, N. (1987). Individual differences in six-year-olds' thoughts about separation: Predicted from attachment to mother at one year of age. Unpublished doctoral dissertation, University of California, Berkeley.	6–7 years	6 photographs, 10 minutes	In the Picture Response Set, children are presented with six photographs of attachment-related scenes ranging from saying goodnight to child in bed to child seeing a parent leave. Responses are scored for the child's ability to cope with separation in constructive ways, acceptance of feelings, and coherence of thought processes. Responses are scored as resourceful (B), inactive (A), and ambivalent (C) when they demonstrate a mixture of responses.
The Preschool Assessment of Attachment (PAA) Crittenden, P.M. (1994). Preschool Assessment of Attachment. Unpublished manuscript, Family Relations Institute, Miami, FL.	2–4 years	8 episodes of Strange Situation; 30 minutes each	The Preschool Assessment of Attachment (PAA) uses episodes of the Strange Situation and classifies children into five major groups: 1) Secure/ Defended (reduces emotional involvement); 2) Coercive (may threaten parent or be coy); 3) Defended/Coercive (both behaviors alternate); 4) Anxious/Depressed (stares, appears depressed and extremely distressed); and 5) Insecure/Other.
The Strange Situation Ainsworth, M.D.S., Blehar, M.C., Waters, E., & Wall, S. (1978). Patterns of attachment: A psychological study of the Strange Situation. Hillsdale, NJ: Erlbaum.	12–20 months	8 episodes; 30 minutes	The episodes of The Strange Situation are 1) Parent, Baby, and Observer (30 seconds); 2) Parent and Baby (3 minutes); 3) Stranger, Parent, and Baby (3 minutes); 4) Stranger and Baby (3 minutes); 5) Parent and Baby (3 minutes or longer if baby is still upset); 6) Baby alone (3 minutes or less if baby is very upset); 7) Stranger and Baby (3 minutes or less if baby is very upset); 8) Parent and Baby (3 minutes). Scoring and classification of the infant is based on 1) proximity seeking (how much infant seeks closeness with the parent), 2) contact seeking (how much the infant wants to be picked up), 3) avoidance (if infant pushes parent away, turns or walks away, refuses to be picked up), and 4) resistance to contact and interaction. As explained in previous sections, the infants are classified into secure (B), avoidant (A), ambivalent or resistant (C), and disorganized/ disoriented (D). Extensive training is necessary to use the measure.

*These instruments use symbolic forms of mental representations.

Table A3.2. Selected attachment assessments for adults

Tool/instrument	Age range	Items/ administration time	General description
Adult Attachment Interview (AAI) Main, M., & Goldwyn, R. (1985). *Adult attachment scoring and classification system.* Unpublished manuscript, University of California, Berkeley.	Adults, but has been used with adolescents and with children as young as 10 years of age.	21 questions (if a parent), 18 if not; 1–2 hours depending on responses	The *Adult Attachment Interview (AAI)* is intended to assess the individual's "state of mind" with respect to attachment and to elicit the unconscious material (Main & Goldwyn, 1994). Questions ask for descriptions of the individual's relationship with both parents. The individual is asked about what he did when he was upset; and about discipline, abuse, loss, and other trauma. Two sets of scales are used: parental behavior and state of mind. Interviews are classified as Secure/Autonomous (F), Dismissing (Ds), Preoccupied (E), and Unresolved/Disorganized (U) or (CC), Cannot Classify. In order to score the AAI, extensive training is necessary.
Adult Attachment Q-Sort Kobak, R.R. (1993). *The attachment Q-Sort.* Unpublished manuscript, University of Delaware.	Adolescents and adults	100 items, used to analyze the AAI transcripts; 1–2 hours	The *Adult Attachment Q-Sort* is a 100-item Q-Sort that has been used to analyze the AAI interview. It classifies individuals according to Secure versus Anxious and Dismissing versus Preoccupied. Items were selected from a discriminant analysis of the Main and Goldwyn system but do not include Unresolved and Cannot Classify categories.
Working Model of the Child Interview (WMCI) Zeanah, C.H., Benoit, D., & Barton, M. (1995). *Working Model of the Child Interview: Scoring and Coding Manual.* Unpublished Manuscript, Brown University: Providence, RI.	Adults expecting or who have an infant or young child	16 questions; 1–2 hours depending on responses	The *Working Model of the Child Interview (WMCI)* is a structured interview used to assess parents' "internal representations or working model of their relationship to a particular child" (Zeanah, Benoit, & Barton, 1995, p. 1). The interview is scored for six scales of parents' representation of their child: (1) richness of detail, (2) openness to change, (3) intensity of involvement, (4) coherence, (5) caregiver sensitivity, and (6) acceptance.

Table A3.3. Measures for assessing adults' current relationships

Tool/instrument	General description
Attachment Style Questionnaire (see the Love Experience in the Group Exercises in this chapter.) Hazan, C., & Shaver, P.R. (1987). Romantic love conceptualized as an attachment process. *Journal of Personality and Social Psychology, 52,* 511–524. Brennan, K.A., Clark, C.L., & Shaver, P.R. (1998). Self-report measures of adult attachment: An integrative overview. In J.A. Simpson, & W.S. Rhodes (Eds.), *Attachment theory and close relationships* (pp. 46–76). New York: Guilford Press.	Many adaptations to this brief *Attachment Style Questionnaire* measure have been made by using continuous rating scales for the three descriptions or by adding other items.
Relationship Questionnaire (RQ) Bartholomew, K., & Horowitz, L. (1991). Attachment styles among young adults: A test of a four category model. *Journal of Personality and Social Psychology, 61,* 226–244.	The *Relationship Questionnaire (RQ)* is a short instrument with descriptions of four types of relationships that incorporate the individual's view of self and other, as positive or negative.
Current Relationship Questionnaire (CRQ) Crowell, J.A., & Owens, G. (1996). *Current Relationship Interview and Scoring System.* Unpublished manuscript, State University of New York, Stony Brook.	The *Current Relationship Questionnaire (CRQ)* assesses adult attachment within close relationships.

Table A3.4. Measures for assessing attachment history in adults

Tool/instrument	General description
Attachment History Questionnaire (AHQ) Potthurst, K. (1990). The search for methods and measures. In K. Potthurst (Ed.), *Explorations in adult attachment* (pp. 9–37). New York: Peter Lang.	The *Attachment History Questionnaire (AHQ)* collects data on family history, inter-actions, and discipline techniques in family of origin as well as peers, friends, and support systems.
Inventory of Parent and Peer Attachment (IPPA) Armsden, G.C., & Greenberg, M.T. (1987). The Inventory of Parent and Peer Attachment: Relationships to well-being in adolescence. *Journal of Youth and Adolescence, 16,* 427–454.	The *Inventory of Parent and Peer Attachment (IPPA)* is a questionnaire to assess adoles-cents' perceptions of relationships with parents and friends.
Mother-Father-Peer Scale (MFPS) Ricks, M.H. (1985). The social transmission of parental behavior: Attachment across generations. In I. Bretherton & E. Waters (Eds.), Growing points of attachment theory and research. *Monographs of the Society for Research in Child Development, 50* (1–2, Serial No. 209), pp. 211–221.	The *Mother-Father-Peer Scale (MFPS)* includes dimensions of acceptance and rejection (of mother, father, and peers) and idealization (of mother and father) and independence/overprotection (by mother and father).

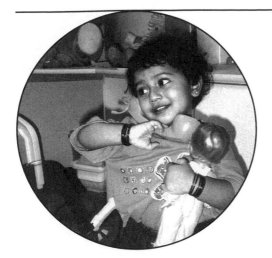

●●● 4

ENCOURAGING PLAY AND IMAGINATION

Whether they are at home, in child care, or in school, infants and children younger than 6 years of age spend a great deal of their time playing. Play comes in a number of different forms, from exploring objects, running and jumping, rough-and-tumble play, to elaborate make-believe in which children act out scenes from everyday life or from the world of their imagination, either alone or with others.

A WORLD OF PLAY OPPORTUNITIES

Here are some examples of the wide range and different types of play.

Social Games   Six-month-old Jack giggles with delight as his mother, Chandra, hides behind a blanket. "Where's Mommy?" Chandra says, and quickly removes the blanket. "Boo!" she says, not too loudly, and tickles Jack as she says, "Here I am." He watches in anticipation as she prepares again to hide and again he screams with delight as she reappears. Peek-a-boo is one game Jack can play repeatedly. He enjoys the fun, predictability, attention, and calming containment of his mother.

Exploratory Play   After several attempts, 4-month-old Megha is able to grab the rattle. She looks at it with great interest, mouthing and shaking it as she giggles with delight. Mother Rama is not far away and smiles and claps to encourage her exploration.

Play with Objects   18-month Matthew struggles to put a square block into the shape sorter. He becomes frustrated because he cannot get it to fit. His father wants to see if Matthew can manage it himself, but when it becomes obvious his son cannot make it fit, he helps Matthew adjust it just a little until it finally drops in, much to Matthew's delight. Next, Matthew strives to fit interlocking blocks together but decides that dropping them on the floor is more fun.

Play to Learn About the World   Maloona, who is almost 4, has become very interested in the gardening center at her child care. She loves to put potting soil in the basin and to plant some seeds so she can watch them grow. She is learning about how the roots appear and how the leaves and flowers grow later. She is also learning how important it is to look after the seeds, and she makes sure to water them every day.

Rough-and-Tumble Play   Denicia and Paul are outside at their child care center while their teacher watches carefully that their play does not get out of hand. They run around pretending to fight, chasing and pouncing on each other, obviously enjoying the game immensely. These 3-year-olds almost seem to have a prearranged script as they alternate between attacker and the one being attacked. They laugh with glee, chasing each other and finally rolling around on the grass together before it is time to go back in for snack.

Sociodramatic Play   In the pretend corner at preschool, an elaborate play theme develops as five 4-year-olds imagine an adventure in a big boat. Using an empty box, the captain organizes the trip during which they plan to be explorers sailing up a river where crocodiles live. They look over the edge and excitedly point out the sights—a snake crawling along the shore, a "tree as big as a house," a huge bear, and finally a campsite. They then get out of the boat and pretend they are cooking their dinner. Once this is over, they lie down to sleep for the night, tired but pleased about all the interesting things they have seen.

Other examples of types of play include games with rules (e.g., Mother May I?, Chutes and Ladders) and constructive play (e.g., building with blocks, making objects with paper). The benefits of play are numerous. Through play, children can

- Learn about the world

- Exercise small and large muscles

- Enhance sensorimotor understanding

- Meet emotional needs

- Enhance cognitive development

- Encourage planning and problem solving

- Enhance imagination

- Learn to concentrate

- Figure out how things work

- Learn about themselves, others, and the world

- Build strength and control of their bodies

- Enjoy opportunities for social experiences

Children engage in play at various ages. Play follows a fairly predictable timetable across a number of cultures, although the acceptance of play in cultures and families, and consequently the ability to play, may vary significantly. Although child care staff usually understand the importance of play and provide environments to encourage its various forms, some parents think

Children like to act out their imaginative fantasies.

of play as a waste of time and, as a consequence, do not encourage it or view it as an activity that is vital for their children's development. Instead, some families strive to create a "Super-baby," pushing infants and children to shake rattles, stack blocks, listen to classical music, repeat numbers, and name colors and letters rather than enjoying or joining in joyous spontaneous interactions with their children. This chapter emphasizes imaginative and pretend play—the type of play that is most influential for the emotional and social development of young children.

DEFINITIONS OF PLAY AND IMAGINATION

Play has been difficult to define. Because there are so many types of play, it is challenging to come up with a definition that is applicable to them all. For this reason, child development specialists have not been able to agree on a definition of play. Instead, they have talked about the essential characteristics that distinguish play from other behaviors in which children engage.

Play

One of the aspects on which theorists disagree is whether exploration of objects is considered play. As well, the differences between solitary and social play and physical and imaginative or pretend play have been hard to reconcile into one theoretical framework. For the purposes of this chapter, a simple definition of play will be used: an activity that is engaged in voluntarily and in which the child directs what happens. In addition, play has a number of components that most agree are important:

- Play is voluntary and spontaneous and not something imposed by caregivers. In other words, children give the play their own meaning and direct what happens.

- Play is pleasurable and fun and will come to an end when it is no longer interesting or engages the child's attention.

- Play has no particular goal, objective, or end in sight. It is the process or the "means" that is important.

- Play is characterized by active involvement on the part of the players and is not daydreaming or fantasizing only.

- Play is exploratory when the child uses toys and other objects to build, create, and learn about the world and the effects of her own actions on it.

- Players generate and adapt rules and establish roles and themes.

- Play is about something and expresses what the child is thinking and feeling.

There have been a number of attempts to categorize the many types of play. Piaget (1962), for example, talked about practice play, symbolic play, and play with rules; Smilansky (1968) added constructive play during which the child manipulates objects in order to create or build something. Pellegrini and Smith (1998) drew attention to the importance of rough-and-tumble and other physical play.

Imagination

Imagination is defined as the child's capacity to rise above reality by telling a story, fantasizing an event or situation, or engaging in pretend play episodes. In imaginative play, the child uses an object to represent or symbolize another or invents a play theme.

THEORIES OF PLAY

As outlined by Rubin, Fein, and Vandenberg (1983), early theories of play did not acknowledge its importance for many aspects of development. Before the 1960s, the most common view of play was that it was a way to "let off steam" and to deal with excess energy. Others saw it as a way to relax from the discipline and structure of work or school and to practice leisure and recreational activities. Today's theories of play, however, have their roots in some of the classical theories of development that emphasize particular aspects of its action.

Freud (1961) described play as "regression in the service of the ego" or as a regression that remained in the control of the more highly structured aspects of personality: the ego and superego. Play filled the "transitional space" between reality and conscious thoughts and the unconscious. As such, Freud saw play as a medium through which children could work out psychosocial conflicts and gain control over difficult events in their lives by repeating them over and over again so they could gain some resolution and so the events could be reintegrated into memories.

Theorists such as Piaget (1962) and Vygotsky (1966, 1978) were more interested in the way in which play can promote cognitive development. Piaget believed that children use ex-

ploratory play to master a problem. Children then assimilate what they have learned about events, objects, or situations into existing cognitive structures. These mental structures then accommodate in order to incorporate the new learning or information. Once children have mastered or solved a problem, they are seen as experiencing an increase in their sense of competence. Piaget also emphasized that children repeat successful action in order to experience the joy of mastery, which he called "a happy display of known actions," and it may have been from this perspective that the component of positive affect in many traditional definitions of play arose.

Vygotsky (1978), however, was more concerned with the building of higher mental processes or the learning that he saw occurring as a result of play. He talked about the zone of proximal development, which is the highest level of learning of which a child is capable—just above what has already been mastered and below a level that is not reachable. He saw this zone as including types of activity for which caregivers or more capable peers needed to provide guidance for the child. Play was an ideal way for learning to take place as it liberates the child from the constraints of the world, allowing higher order mental structures to operate and imagination to flourish. Vygotsky also emphasized the importance of the social characteristics of play. Montessori (1973) emphasized the importance of play for cognitive development, calling play "child's work."

In a classic study in which children's play and social behavior were observed, Parten (1932) described various types of play participation as appearing at successive stages. These were defined as onlooker behavior, solitary play, parallel play, associative group play, and—finally—cooperative play. These distinctions continue to be used today, although they have been expanded on and renamed by writers such as Howes and Matheson (1992).

Other theorists who have addressed play in a broader sense include Berlyne and Bruner. Berlyne's (1969) model of arousal was applied to play, with play seen as a mechanism to decrease arousal by decreasing stimulation to an acceptable level. Bruner (1972) described the importance of pretend play as its ability to generate novel, creative, and flexible ideas. According to Bruner, new combinations discovered in play can then be used in real-life situations. In Table 4.1, some of the more current writers and researchers in the area of play are listed and their major emphases or constructs noted. These more modern theorists emphasize different types of play and different effects that it can produce.

THE IMPORTANCE OF PLAY AND IMAGINATION

In spite of mixed results in research about the effects of play on various aspects of development, the importance of play has been established. In addition to the list of benefits mentioned previously, play enhances development in the following areas:

Encouraging Learning

Although the act of banging and shaking objects is a long way from solving an arithmetic problem or creating an elaborate design, various types of play form an important link from one to the other. As the infant explores objects, she discovers their parts and how they fit together, and as she constructs towers of blocks and creates houses or cities, she learns how to categorize

Table 4.1.   Theories of play and imagination

Theorist(s)	Type of theory	Major constructs
Erikson (1963) Elkind (1981) Fein (1981, 1989) Bettelheim (1987)	Emotional development	Suggests an "emotive theory," with pretense as a way that child regulates emotions
		Pretend themes are about the emotional aspects of living. They allow the child to gain self-regulation of the affect associated with difficult situations or normally occurring developmental shifts
		Arousal is converted into internal symbolic forms
		Play follows a developmental sequence
		Play allows children to express and cope with feelings and can give release from stress
Sutton-Smith (1985)	Cognitive–developmental	Suggests play helps produce novel associations with play objects and divergent thinking
		From play, the child develops a series of associations that can be drawn on in other situations
Garvey (1990)	Social and developmental	Emphasis on the social nature of play; solitary play is secondary to play with others
		Play is learned in the earliest interactions with caregivers
		Focuses on the development of a number of types of play, such as play with language and with rules
Singer & Singer (1990)	Cognitive-affective	Emphasis on make-believe play and its importance for emotional development
		Play cultivates creativity
		Imagery and fantasy are two of several major encoding systems
Pellegrini & Smith (1998)	Physical activity	Stresses the importance of rough-and-tumble and other kinds of physical play for motor, cognitive, and social development
		Emphasizes need for children to have the opportunity to practice different types of physical play to gain a sense of mastery

and combine, and about spatial relationships. Imagination and imaginative play actions allow for an increase in the capacity for flexibility of thought, reversibility, and divergent thinking. Play changes direction as objects are used in different ways and minds are stretched to solve the problems encountered during the play. Pretend and sociodramatic play provide practice in abstract and logical thinking and a chance to reflect and experiment with problems from a number of different angles. The fact that play is voluntary means that it often motivates children to learn and therefore enhances learning; the child *wants* to experiment and find out new facts.

Enhancing Self-Esteem

Physical play provides the child with an opportunity to experience mastery of his body, while explorative and constructive play often give a child a sense of immediate success and achievement. Play can give the child a sense of competence because during play he is freed from control of the immediate environment and can direct what happens himself. In a world where children look up to everyone and have little power or control, climbing a jungle gym, building a tower, making a toy work, or acting out grown-up themes allows them to feel successful and competent. As children imagine being different characters, they can believe that they can

achieve all sorts of things and overcome adversity. This belief can give them a sense of control and significantly enhance their self-esteem.

Reducing Physical Aggression

Not all play reduces aggression, especially if it is repetitive and violent, but children can use play to reduce aggression and to move from physical aggression and acting out to expressing their anger in more symbolic ways. So play can be physical or rough-and-tumble and a "letting off steam," or it can be more imaginative—involving assuming roles in exciting dramas. As well, play can give children a release from stress and reduce anger and anxiety that otherwise might lead to aggression and other acting-out behaviors. Often, when a child imagines being powerful this can reduce the child's need to act out aggressively and provide other avenues for the child to express anger.

Encouraging Language Development

Although in an infant's first year she is considered to be nonverbal, she can learn turn taking; rhythm of speech; and the meaning of actions, gestures, and sounds that form a basis for the beginning of speech in her second year. Early games such as Peek-a-boo, action songs, and re-petitive rhymes encourage the acquisition of these areas of knowledge. When caregivers name objects and verbalize actions while the children engage in exploratory play, children begin to learn language. Sociodramatic play, whether played with peers or parents, also provides a perfect opportunity for language to be used and for vocabulary to grow and expand. Children hear other children and adults use language during play and can then experiment with the new words.

Improving Social Ability

Play provides a common meeting ground for children to interact with one another without de-mands and structures. It lets children try out different roles and learn about their social world. Through play, children can acquire the social skills that can be learned only through experience with other children. Skills such as taking turns, sharing, cooperating, and compromising with others are practiced and friendships are made during play. Children who have difficulty play-ing will often find themselves on the sidelines and unable to enjoy all the fun and activity of the others' games. As the child plays out different social roles, she gains some understanding of the perspectives of others, laying the groundwork for the development of empathy.

Enhancing Attention and Concentration

Because play is fun and children are self-motivated to engage in it, they can often play for hours and may find it difficult to tear themselves away. For a child who has difficulty concen-trating and who tends to pass from one activity to another without settling into anything, play can help expand sequences, especially if an adult can join in and encourage and support the child to extend the play. Increasing a child's imagination and inner world also can enhance his ca-pacity to attend and increase his memory.

Offering Opportunities for Mastery of Physical Self

Preschoolers love play that lets them use their physical energy, and children who can play physically often are more popular with their peers. They learn body control through active physical play, running, hopping, climbing, balancing, and throwing. The feelings of fun, exhilaration, and agility, which are supportive of the learning process, are enhanced during play. As well, when a child's body is in motion it enables the discovery of spatial relations and patterns in space to take place. Children's eye–hand coordination is also developed as they paint, cut, and construct.

Enhancing Perspective-Taking and Negotiation

Imagination and imaginative play give children the opportunity to see other people's perspectives and to gradually begin to appreciate that other people have different thoughts, beliefs, and feelings from their own. Ideas for play themes and sequences have to be negotiated and agreed on, and the inevitable conflicts that arise must be explored and resolved if the play is to continue. Apart from these abilities, pretend play allows for planning ahead and sequencing events while integrating changes and the ideas of others. Children also can think about how the various characters in their story think and feel as they imagine sequences of events.

Enhancing Emotional Development

Make-believe can be a way for a child to unlock bottled-up feelings that are getting in the way and causing problems. Fantasy and imagination can provide an opportunity to handle feelings of helplessness, frustration, and anger. Play can also be used as a way to deal with the normal developmental issues of control and autonomy, attachment and separation, and so forth. If a child experiences a traumatic experience such as a move, loss of a nanny, birth of a sibling, or a more dramatic event, play can be used to help children begin to understand the situation by acting out and trying out different solutions. This process can help the child to feel in control again, to tolerate the frustration, and to feel less afraid. Experience shows that children who engage in make-believe are more joyful and smile and laugh more often than those who do not engage in make-believe. As they play, they come to understand their feelings better and deal with them in their play.

Developing a Healthy and Satisfying Inner World and Fantasy Life

As children get older, they engage in pretend play significantly less often, and instead, they play games with rules. The earlier experience of pretend play can enhance a child's private, inner world, and imagination that will form the basis for a child's later capacity for daydreaming, creativity, and hobbies. This inner world will be made up of images and metaphors formed out of the stories, games, and play of earlier life. It can also be a place to escape to for a while when the realities of the world temporarily become overwhelming. In fact, when people face great stress in their lives, visualizing and imagining being in a restful place can provide a respite from anxiety and stress. Adults spend about half their lives in this inner world of thoughts and imagination, and this fantasy world can be enriching and rewarding.

THE DEVELOPMENT OF PLAY AND IMAGINATION

For most children, the capacity for play develops in a predictable way and seems to be fueled from the inside. Because of the complexity and the many different forms of play that are available to a child, different types of play may develop at a different pace and reach different levels according to the child's interests and personality. A few children can get stuck along the way, however, and may have problems with moving into pretend play or into cooperative and sharing behaviors, for example. Table 4.2, which illustrates the development of play through the stages of a child's life, shows that play moves from simple to more complex, from concrete to more symbolic, and from parallel to more interactive. Although the sequence is usually invariant, as children develop and work on new structures or new achievements, regression may occur as previous structures are broken down. The same may happen during times of stress, trauma, or while the child resolves other new developmental issues or challenges. The following sections look at how play and imagination develop at each stage of a young child's life.

Birth to Three Months

From the moment a newborn is first held by his parents and they kiss and talk to him, they are encouraging their baby to engage in the first stages of play. As the baby begins to be alert for longer periods, he begins to notice sights, sounds, smells, and movements. At first, infants explore the world by mouthing, although occasionally they may try to pat at an object. Even at this young age, babies enjoy exercising their limbs and kicking and waving their arms. They also enjoy making sounds, especially when they are part of an interaction with their caregiver. These first interactions promote infants' capacities to smile from about 6 weeks on and to express some of the enjoyment they feel in these first playful interactions.

Four to Twelve Months

From the ages of 4–12 months, an infant becomes much more able to voluntarily explore objects and to play with them purposefully. She grabs, bangs together, and sometimes uses objects—such as a spoon—to feed herself or to bang on another object. Sometimes objects are put together that are usually not put together, such as a toy bed on top of the telephone and a ball in the dishwasher. Now she enjoys motor play, usually crawling and beginning to cruise around the furniture. She may be able to throw a ball as well and enjoys having it thrown back. Use of objects may include early scribbling, simple puzzles, building a tower, and pulling a string to get an object. She now loves playing hiding games with parents and a number of action songs and rhymes. She imitates her caregiver and also enjoys manually exploring her caregiver's face and body.

Thirteen to Twenty-Four Months

At this time, the child begins to be able to engage in simple pretend play. At first it is self-related (he may raise a cup up for a pretend drink or comb his own hair). Play is still only primarily parallel play with peers, although by 2 years of age he will show increasing interest in

Table 4.2. The development of play through the stages of a child's life

Age	Physical, sensorimotor, and cognitive play	Imaginative play	Social aspects of play
Birth–3 months	Predominately mouths objects (e.g., rattles and pegs) Enjoys making sounds Exercises limbs with kicking May pat an object Begins to explore environment with senses		Enjoys responsive interactions with caregivers Much of "play" is solitary Smiles at caregivers
4–7 months	Imitates motor play Bangs objects together Explores objects Uses objects functionally		Plays games like Peekaboo and Pat-a-Cake with caregiver Continues to enjoy responsive interactions
8–12 months	Begins to cruise around furniture Throws a ball Scribbles Builds a tower Can do simple puzzles Pulls string to get object Bangs on drum Plays hiding games		Enjoys manually exploring caregiver's face and body Plays primarily alone, with some parallel play Begins to imitate actions of caregiver Plays hiding games
13–24 months	Runs, climbs, jumps Does more complex puzzles Draws circles and crosses Stacks blocks and other objects Puts objects in container Mirror play is popular Picks up small objects Lines up and bangs objects Enjoys knocking things down Enjoys rolling on floor with adult Enjoys imitating movements Jumps off pillow or step with hands held Plays chasing games Pushes and pulls toys	Can now carry out simple pretend play Mostly self-related (e.g., raises pretend cup to mouth) Some play is directed away from child to others (e.g., pretends to give a cup of tea, pushes car along floor to go to work) Same play theme is applied to several objects	Begins to enjoy parallel play around other children but still cannot cooperate Can make some eye contact with other children May offer toys and smile Increased interest in and contact with caregiver Waves goodbye Likes to roll ball back and forth
25–30 months	Enjoys constructive play with blocks and Legos Enjoys playing with sand and playdough, makes objects with them Enjoys painting on paper Hops, marches Listens to tapes and music	Substitutes objects for one another (e.g., drinks from sea shell, feeds doll with pencil) Play becomes increasingly elaborate (e.g., cars go to garage to get gas, babies go to bed and cry) Doll play predominates	Pretend play often reflects the same theme as another child's, but still no real integration By this age, some cooperation becomes possible and gradually increases May take leader and follower roles
31–36 months	Enjoys making music Enjoys filling and spilling games Likes knobs and buttons Can string big beads Sorts shapes Likes sewing cards Likes to dance	Objects are used in sequence (e.g., may feed with spoon and then with stick) Double substitutions so two materials substitute for another in a single act Ascribes thoughts, feelings, and beliefs to play figures	Often enacts complementary roles such as mother-baby; doctor-patient Still plays alone at times

Age	Physical, sensorimotor and cognitive play	Imaginative play	Social aspects of play
3–4 years	Skips Likes throwing and catching games Likes to paint Cuts with scissors Manipulates playdough Likes pasting	Pretends to be someone else (e.g., superhero) Frequently engages in play themes of family Often plays out aggression through "good" and "bad" characters Masculine and feminine traits may be overexaggerated	Can usually distinguish between real and pretend By this age, 90% of pretend play occurs in cooperation with others Enjoys pretending to be someone else Can reverse roles
4–6 years	Climbs, slides, swings Is learning to kick ball Keeps time when dancing Draws letters and numbers Tests body competence by practicing running Can draw a person	Management of aggression continues to be major issue in play themes Increasingly plays out experiences that are difficult Complex pretend play themes are possible Play is less object dependent	Sexual curiosity can be expressed in doctor play Children often play joint games such as puppet shows or plays Play shows increasing intersubjectivity and players' assumptions about others' thoughts, roles Begins to be able to understand that others have their own thoughts and feelings Some children have imaginary companions

being around other children and may offer a toy and smile. The same play theme may be applied to several objects, so a banana is used as a telephone, followed by a block or spoon. By the time a child is 2 years old, his play begins to be directed *away* from himself and *to* others (e.g., pretending to give a doll a drink, combing a doll's hair, playing doctor). Motor or physical play is increasingly popular, as the child can now walk, run, and imitate movements. A child may find jumping off a cushion or step with hands held to be a lot of fun. Children enjoy rolling around the floor, chasing games, and pretend wrestling with adults, especially their fathers. They can now pick up small objects, and enjoy lining them up and knocking them down.

Two to Three Years

When children are between the ages of 2 and 3 years, their pretend play changes significantly. Children may follow one theme for a time, such as playing "house," for example. Objects are repeatedly substituted for others (e.g., drinking from a seashell, feeding a doll with a pencil). Play becomes increasingly elaborate (e.g., cars go out for a drive and "fill up" at a garage). Doll play is a favorite. Children now enjoy constructive play with blocks, Legos, and so forth. They also enjoy playing with sand and playdough, initially for the feel of it then gradually for its ability to be shaped into objects. Painting may be enjoyed, as well as drawing with markers. If given the opportunity, children enjoy all sorts of activities, including filling and spilling games, turning knobs and buttons, stringing big beads, and sorting shapes. Outside play activities, including running, jumping, climbing, and swinging are exciting, and children may cooperate in rough-and-tumble play and chasing games. They may also enjoy marching to music and making music with instruments.

At 3 years of age, children begin to understand the difference between real and pretend and to ascribe thoughts and feelings to play figures. Children now cooperate with others much more in their play, although some children may play more of a leader or follower role.

Three to Four Years

By 3 years of age, approximately 90% of a child's pretend play occurs in cooperation with others. Roles are often reversed and children become superman, a queen, a movie star, or a parent, with behavior sequences taken from real life, television, or books. Many parents have blushed with embarrassment as they hear their own words repeated with great gusto: "you'd better smarten up or else," or whatever their "favorite" threat may be. Play with "good" and "bad" characters is common and is often played out with much feeling and pretend aggression. Masculine and feminine roles are often exaggerated. At this age, children begin to play out significant occurrences, sometimes repeatedly. Motor skills become more sophisticated and skipping, throwing, and catching are common. Cutting out and pasting and painting continue to be popular, as do building with blocks and playing with sand and playdough.

Four to Six Years

Between the ages of 4–6 years, children's play becomes increasingly imaginative as they act out difficult real-life experiences and developmental issues they are experiencing. Complex play themes develop that are not so dependent on objects. Play is increasingly intersubjective, and children take on roles and share and understand others' thoughts, beliefs, and feelings that are different from their own. Some children may have imaginary friends. Joint games such as puppet shows and playacting are popular, and sexual curiosity may be expressed through doctor play. Children continue to love physical play and games with rules, and are able to work in teams beginning by approximately age 6. Children may also like to draw recognizable objects and people now, and to copy numbers and letters.

Gradually, after 6 years, little sociodramatic play will occur and games with rules will be more common. Although some dramatic play will continue, much of the representational activity is internalized to become part of an increasingly personal imaginative or fantasy life. Daydreams replace actions and are often about distant heroes and heroines and ideas about how to resolve issues and dreams about the future. This inner work is necessary for caring and empathy to develop and can help relieve a wide range of difficult emotions. Ultimately, these daydreams and fantasies become an essential component of every human being's emotional life.

IMPORTANT RESEARCH FINDINGS

Adequate research on play has only been carried out since the 1970s, and much of the voluminous amount that has been done has been of questionable quality. Lack of control groups, small sample sizes, and poorly defined constructs have characterized much of the research. This review will identify various important areas of recent research (as well as note any methodological difficulties within these areas), including the following:

- Effects of play on various areas of development

- Effects of context on children's play

- Effects of parenting interaction on children's play

- Difficulties in playing

- Focus for new research

The Effects of Play on Various Areas of Development

A number of correlational studies have sought to determine the effect of play on various areas of development. In these studies, statistical relationships were measured between different kinds of play and various developmental outcomes. Unfortunately, correlational studies like these do not allow researchers to say anything about the directionality of any relationships found (or what causes what)—only that a relationship has been found. Results of these studies that have looked at the relationship between play and developmental capacities such as problem-solving, socialization, and perspective taking have been mixed.

Several studies have examined the relationship between play levels and various cognitive measures. The methodology for these studies has primarily been to assess through observation either children's level of play or the amount of play in which they engage and to compare this with measures of cognitive development. Some studies have found a relationship between play and the amount and level of divergent thinking and problem solving in which children engage (Barnett, 1985; Dansky, 1980; Dunn & Herwig, 1992; Golomb & Cornelius, 1977; Rosen, 1974; Smith & Dutton, 1979). Studies have also shown correlations with the amount of play and IQ scores and school achievement (Dunn & Wooding, 1977; Sears, 1977; Shmukler, 1979), although effect sizes were small. In some studies, the type of play was examined to see if it differed in how it related to cognitive outcomes. On the one hand, Goodwin, Sawyers, and Bailey (1988) found that object play by 3- to 5-year-olds did not improve problem-solving skills. On the other hand, Li (1985) found that children who engaged in more pretend play did better in creative and divergent thinking, suggesting that pretend play may be particularly effective to improve some measures of cognitive functioning.

Although these studies—which have looked at concurrent measures of play and cognitive development—have not always found relationships, a few studies have found associations over time. For example, Caruso (1981) found that qualitative aspects of exploratory play were related later to persistence and success in solving problems. Similar effects were found in a study of exploratory behavior at 6 months, and cognitive skills at 19 and 42 months. That is, manipulation of novel objects at 6 months was related to Binet IQ scores at 42 months (Yarrow, Rubenstein, & Pedersen, 1975). A few studies have looked for associations between play and measures of socialization and social cognition. In one study, it was found that children who frequently engaged in pretend play tended to be more popular and to have higher scores on tests of social cognition (Connolly & Doyle, 1984). However, Li (1985), in his study of children and pretend play, did not find that children who pretended more scored higher on tests of empathy.

Consistent relationships have been found between play and language development. For example, one study found that test scores of a child's exploratory play at 12 and 18 months were related to vocabulary at 12 and 18 months and grammatical fluency at 24 months. The

researchers noted that early exploratory play and language have both been found to be related to childhood intelligence measures (McCall, Hogarty, & Hurlburt, 1972).

Because pretend play involves using mental representations in order to imagine a situation other than reality, it has been presumed to be related to the development of intersubjectivity (i.e., shared understanding) and a theory of mind and perspective taking (Dockett & Smith, 1995; Riblatt, 1995). Various researchers have noted that social play becomes more intersubjective after 3 years of age (Göncü, 1993). Nevertheless, some researchers have found no relationship between the capacity for pretend play and the capacity for intersubjectivity or having a theory of mind (Rosen, Schwebel, & Singer, 1997). In a related study, however, Taylor and Carlson (1997) controlled for verbal intelligence and found that 3- and 4-year-olds' level of fantasy was related to their theory of mind, with children rated in the "High Fantasy" group having higher scores on their theory of mind performance score. Although the findings from research have been mixed, failing to establish a precise relationship between the two abilities, commonsense would suggest that frequent and sophisticated pretending would enhance the development of these metarepresentations (Leslie, 1988; Lillard, 1993). Because these studies cannot prove a definite causal relationship between play and various child-development outcomes, a number of researchers have examined the effect of training children to be imaginative or to pretend on various developmental measures, instead. The studies again yielded mixed results, because in some experiments either inadequate procedures were used to encourage play or the wrong constructs were used to measure outcomes. The types of play training used have differed considerably and have included modeling, in which the teacher joins in the play; verbal guidance, using comments to encourage the play; thematic-fantasy training or helping children act out stories; and imaginative play training using puppets or role playing (Christie, 1985).

Early studies found significant improvements as a result of play training on variables such as perspective taking, problem solving, and language development (Freyberg, 1973; Li, 1985; Saltz, Dixon, & Johnson, 1977; Shmukler & Naveh, 1984–1985; Smilansky, 1968; Udwin, 1983). Later studies that tried to identify the most successful types of play training and to compare the effects of play training to just giving the child attention produced mixed results, however. Some studies suggested that children who received play training of various kinds showed more improved concentration and cooperation than those in an attention-only or in a social-interaction group (Doctoroff, 1997; Shmukler & Naveh, 1984–1985). Christie (1983) and Smith and Whitney (1987) found no significant differences between children who received play training and children who did not but spent additional time in social interaction with other children. This suggests that it may be the play itself that is most helpful and that it can be enhanced equally by play with peers or by coaching by an adult.

Effects of Context on Children's Play

Though interactions with others are most likely to influence children's play, the environment or context in which the child and her family live are also very important influences.

Socioeconomic Status and Culture A child's environment can significantly influence his ability to play. One variable that has consistently been found to influence the level of children's play is socioeconomic status. Children who live in disadvantaged circumstances and in families with lower socioeconomic status consistently score lower on measures of pretend

play (Doyle, Ceschin, Tessier, & Doehring, 1991; Freyberg, 1973; Griffing, 1974; Rosen, 1974; Rubin, Maioni, & Hornung, 1976; Shmukler & Naveh, 1984–1985; Smilansky, 1968; Udwin & Shmukler, 1981). Some studies have discovered that children in low socioeconomic circumstances do catch up in their capacity to pretend play by the second grade. This suggests that they may eventually reach the peaks of dramatic play seen in children from middle-class socioeconomic families but that they may do so at a later age (Melragon, 1973; Sears, 1977).

In addition, cross-cultural studies have found that in some cultures pretend play is rare, while in others it is very rich and varied (Udwin & Shmukler, 1981). One of the more critical influences in determining these differences is the beliefs of adults in the culture about the benefits of play, and particularly parental beliefs about play (Farver, 1993; Farver & Howes, 1993; Farver & Shin, 1997; Farver & Wimbarti, 1995; Gaskins, 1996; New, 1994). In a study comparing 44- to 63-month-old children of recent Korean immigrants with Anglo-American children of the same age, Farver and Shin (1997) found that the Korean American children engaged in less pretend play in preschool than did the Anglo-American children. The researchers noted that this may have been a result of the Korean preschool teachers' emphasis on culturally valued school readiness tasks rather than on pretend play; whereas, in the preschool attended by the Anglo-American children, social interaction and play activities were encouraged. Nevertheless, in an experimental play environment in which toys were made available, no significant cultural differences were found in the children's pretend play. These results suggest that there is a universality or "species-general" developmental maturation of play behavior but that the sociocultural environment has a significant influence on its occurrence. This finding was confirmed in a study of Argentinean children in Buenos Aires and American children in Washington, D.C. (Bornstein, Haynes, Pascual, Painter, & Galperin, 1999). Results pointed to more of a relationship between play and mother–child interactions than between play and cultural differences.

Environment   Various aspects of the environmental context in which play occurs have been found to relate to the frequency and quality of various kinds of play (Eaton & Enns, 1986; Fein & Apfel, 1979). Some researchers have studied the effect of the physical design of preschool play centers on play behavior (Droege & Howes, 1991; Petrakos & Howe, 1996). In the study by Petrakos and Howe (1996), they manipulated the design of the pretend-play centers by altering them by theme and in the design of equipment to encourage more solitary or group play. As expected, the "solitary-designed" centers encouraged more solitary play and the "group-designed," more group play. Adding a train with double seating, a car, and a ticket machine encouraged more dramatic play themes than there had been before. The study supports the idea that the physical design and availability of particular toys influence children's play.

As well as examining the effect of indoor environments on children, some researchers have explored the effects of outdoor playground design on pretend play. Susa and Benedict (1994) found that play areas that they called contemporary, in which pieces are joined and connected and some parts are left as undefined, encouraged more pretend play than did traditional playgrounds (with swings, slides, seesaws). Contemporary play spaces were also shown to encourage more play than "junk" playgrounds, where children are expected to create their own environments out of such things as old tires and cartons. Weinstein and Pinciotti (1988) found that various parts of the play space influenced imaginary play and noted certain aspects as important, such as having private space for joint play and varying levels of complexity in the play environment.

Effects of Parenting Interactions

Parenting interactions have been found to be the most powerful influence on the development of play. Parents who encourage, model, and show approval of play can enhance their child's play development (Belsky, Goode, & Most, 1980; Murphy, 1972; O'Connell & Bretherton, 1984; Smilansky, 1968). Disadvantaged children generally lack such parental modeling. Consequently, it is suggested that this lack of modeling rather than socioeconomic status is the mediator that results in the lower levels of play exhibited by the children studied (Feuerstein, 1979; Freyberg, 1973; Shmukler, 1981; Singer, 1973; Smilansky, 1968; Tower, 1980; Udwin & Shmukler, 1981).

Research on parental play interactions and their effects on the child's cognitive, emotional, and social development implies that certain characteristics might be central to the optimal development of children's play behavior. Sequential analysis has also been used to study the contingency and age-appropriateness of maternal interactions (Damast, Tamis-LeMonda, & Bornstein, 1996). The researchers found that parenting knowledge enhanced mothers' ability to respond at an appropriate level to their child's play. In another study that used sequential analysis, Fiese (1990) found that reciprocal forms of interaction and turn taking, rather than redirection, resulted in more complex symbolic play. Other researchers have found a relationship between play levels and the degree to which mothers participated in and guided their children's play (e.g., Bornstein, Haynes, O'Reilly, & Painter, 1996; Tamis-LeMonda & Bornstein, 1991).

Sigel (1986) found in a study of 367 children that those children with highly directive and didactic parents who insisted on teaching and who forced their own choices of activities on their children tended to have limited ability to play. Yet, when parents encouraged autonomy and when children used play to problem-solve, they tended to have more advanced development. The degree of sensitivity, reciprocity, and responsiveness of caregivers with infants and young children has consistently been linked to children's attachment classifications, with optimal levels associated with secure attachment. Kerns and Barth (1995) found that more play encouragement by parents was related to secure attachment in children, which in turn was related to children's friendly and cooperative behavior at school.

Much of the research on interactional influences on play has studied mothers and has ignored other family members, particularly fathers and siblings, as well as peers. Studies that have considered fathers have noted that although mothers and fathers are involved in equal amounts of play with their children, they usually engage in different types of play. Fathers, on one hand, tend to be more physical, tactile, and to have more peaks of excitement or boisterousness. Mothers, on the other hand, engage in games with less physical closeness and more toy play (Lamb, 1977). Youngblade and Dunn found that by the time children were 3 years old, they engaged in more pretend play with a sibling than with their mother, particularly if the sibling was older. They also found that pretend play was more related at this age to child–sibling relationship measures and discourse than to the same measures of the mother–child relationship and discourse. Measures of interaction with siblings were also more correlated with the task of understanding emotions than were measures of interaction with mothers. The researchers concluded, "The results support the argument that children's interactions with their siblings are particularly closely linked to development in understanding 'other minds'" (1995, p. 1486). This is particularly true when siblings are affectionate with each other. Other studies have examined the link between parent–child interactions or play and peer play. MacDonald

and Parke (1984) found that peer popularity was related to physical play with parents, and particularly with the positive affect that usually accompanied the play.

In summary, a number of contextual variables correlate with and contribute to the development of the child's play; however, early relationships with parents is likely to be the most critical.

Difficulties in Playing

As discussed previously, children from disadvantaged and deprived backgrounds in which play is not encouraged or modeled often show lower levels and less rich play themes. Similarly, children with developmental delays exhibit lower levels of play than do children of similar age; however, their level of play is usually correlated with their mental age or intellectual level. Other children show difficulties playing because of their physical characteristics; brain dysfunction; or emotional, social, or behavioral difficulties. In order to teach these children to play, it is important to determine their cognitive readiness and to begin at their developmental level.

One group of children who have significant difficulty with both solitary and social pretend play is children with autism spectrum disorders. Overall, their play lacks spontaneity and flexibility and instead usually consists of rigid, repetitive, and stereotypic actions that may be repeated for hours and even days (i.e., perseveration) (Tigerman & Primavera, 1981; Wing, Gould, Yeates, & Brierly, 1977; Wolfberg, 1995). Some children with autism engage in play with objects but rarely engage in symbolic or imaginative play (Sigman & Mundy, 1987; Wing & Attwood, 1987). Some writers suggested that the difficulties with pretend play are linked to a deficit in metarepresentation, or theory of mind, which has been found to relate to symbolic play level (Leslie, 1987). Other theorists have suggested that the deficit is related to difficulties with affective functioning (Hobson, 1986; Smalley & Asarnow, 1990). Both theories may be equally plausible.

Children with attention deficit-disorder, with or without hyperactivity, may also find it hard to concentrate on certain kinds of play and have difficulty continuing with pretend play for long enough to elaborate a play theme. They may show fragmentation and disorganization in their play because of difficulty with sustaining focused and quiet behavior (Wodrich, 2000). Many children with attention-deficit disorder or attention-deficit/hyperactivity disorder enjoy physical and rough-and-tumble play because it does not require the focused attention that other play does.

For different reasons, children who have been neglected or abused often find it difficult to participate in play of different kinds and may either play at a lower level than their peers or be unable to participate in social play (Alessandri, 1991; Cicchetti & Beeghly, 1987; Howard, 1986). In a study comparing the play behavior of children who had been physically abused, sexually abused, or physically and sexually abused with children who had not been abused, significant differences in play themes were observed (Harper, 1991). For sexually abused children, sexual themes and the need for protection dominated, while physically abused children displayed a great deal of aggressive and chaotic themes. The mixed group had the most diverse themes, with aggression and conflictual themes dominating. The children who had not been abused showed more family themes and expression of wish fulfillment. Alessandri (1991, 1992) examined mother–child play interaction of maltreated children and found the mothers to be less involved, to describe or demonstrate toys less often, and to engage in less turn taking with their children than mothers of children who have not been abused.

Other researchers have considered levels of motor proficiency and their effect on the ability to play. Bundy (1988) found that children with sensory motor integration difficulties were less playful than were children without these problems. In a study of children with rheumatoid arthritis, a cluster of factors was related to play level: locus of control, motor proficiency, and creative thinking. The researchers concluded that motor proficiency should be considered when evaluating the ability to play (Morrison, Bundy, & Fisher, 1991).

Focus for New Research

In this brief review of literature, a number of emerging research trends are mentioned. These include the relationship between play and normal or pathological development; increasing emphasis of the emotional components of play and its relationship to affective development; and the relationship of play to emerging cognitive functioning, especially perspective taking and theory of mind. Further research in these areas will eventually enable the enunciation of a theory of play that can incorporate individual and social, and cognitive and affective aspects of play.

THE GROWTH-PROMOTING ENVIRONMENT: PRINCIPLES OF DEVELOPING PLAY AND IMAGINATION

The principles presented here can be used to guide caregivers in ways to enhance infants and young children's capacity for play and imagination (see Table 4.3). Under each principle are ideas for putting it into practice.

PRINCIPLE 1: *Spend time observing the infant or child and learning about her style of play, how she interacts, what she enjoys doing, and her inner world and feelings.*

When an infant or child is playing or interacting, it is critical that caregivers stand back to observe her play, listening to her sounds or words and evaluating her mood in order to get to know and understand her. If the play is exploratory or constructive it can provide clues about her ability to concentrate as well as about her fine motor control and sensorimotor integration.

Table 4.3. Principles for encouraging play and imagination

Principle 1	Spend time observing the infant or child and learning about her style of play, how she interacts, what she enjoys doing, and her inner world and feelings.
Principle 2	Provide a special place(s) where children are free to play with objects, toys, and props that can encourage play and imagination.
Principle 3	Regularly assign time to join a child in play by giving the activity or game your undivided attention.
Principle 4	Follow the child's lead in pretend play, accept the feelings, join in the play, and—when necessary—extend play themes.
Principle 5	Encourage playfulness and joyous exchanges and experiences.
Principle 6	Provide children with the opportunity for a variety of different play experiences to encourage their imaginations.

Physical play can inform about balance and motor skills and about her ability to contain aggression, to interact with others, and to switch from leading to following. We learn the most about a child's feelings and desires from her imaginative play and fantasies, however. By watching play unfold, situations that the child may be finding difficult are reflected. These new insights can often help a caregiver to be more sensitive and understanding in reacting to a child. Some aspects of play to observe are the following:

- How long does the child remain absorbed in the play?

- What emotions are being shown (e.g., joy, anxiety, apathy)?

- Is the play creative and varied or repetitive, rigid, or obsessive?

- Is the play organized or does it appear fragmented or disorganized?

- How does the child interact with others? Can she share, cooperate, and accept roles in the group?

- How quickly does the child give up and become frustrated?

- How complex is the play, and what objects and toys are chosen?

- Does the child show the capacity for symbolic play and imagination?

- Does the child converse during play, and negotiate with other children over toys or play themes?

- What kind of play themes are predominant (e.g., doll play, family, "goodies" and "baddies," action figures and control, school, a hospital or doctor's office, death and destruction)?

- Are there any real-life stresses or developmental issues that the child appears to be struggling with?

- Does the child relate to other players?

- Can the child deal with difficult themes or emotions without the play becoming chaotic?

This process of standing back and observing will allow you to get to know and understand a child better and will provide the opportunity to problem-solve around areas in which a child may be having difficulties. It will also help you decide how to help a child who seems to be having problems playing.

PRINCIPLE 2: *Provide a special place(s) where children are free to play with objects, toys, and props that can encourage play and imagination.*

Research has shown that the child's play setting and toys can influence his ability to play. Homes need to be safety proofed to allow children to crawl, walk around, and explore without harming themselves or other people's possessions. This freedom to explore is crucial for the child to develop a sense of curiosity and excitement about the world.

If possible, provide a space in which the child can play, preferably with low shelves to display toys. Setting up a play space will let children know that play is something you approve of

Providing a special place where children are free to play encourages imagination to grow.

and encourage. Toys need to be matched to the child's developmental levels and some should clearly respond with an immediate sound, movement, or light when banged, pushed, or shaken. It is important that in the home the child is not overwhelmed with too many toys. For many children, too many toys can be distracting, making the children flit from one toy to another without settling down with anything. If it is possible, it is better to store some toys and periodically change them, putting away toys with which the child seems bored. This can increase the child's interest in and concentration with the toys. When a child is at the stage for engaging in pretend play, a variety of toys and dress-up clothes can help to encourage it. Some toys that encourage pretend play are the following:

- Miniature doll family

- Tea set

- Playdough or Plasticine

- Fierce toy animals (e.g., crocodile, dinosaurs, tigers)

- Doll furniture

- Baby bottle and large doll

- Vehicles (e.g., ambulance, tow truck, fire engine)

- Blocks

- Crayons, paints, and large paper

- Dress-up clothes

- Toy telephone

For children who enjoy other types of play media, it can be helpful to include musical instruments, a sand tray, and finger paint. A small table can be useful for children who enjoy drawing, painting, cutting and pasting.

PRINCIPLE 3: *Regularly assign time to join a child in play by giving the activity or game your undivided attention.*

To encourage their play, children need to experience interest and encouragement from caregivers. Getting down on the floor or at the child's eye level in order to join him in play is important. In order to facilitate play, caregivers need to respect the mood and respond to the signals of infants and children and to provide age-appropriate toys and activities. During infancy, babies can be introduced to play at first with kinesthetic (rocking) movement, by holding (touch), and by providing toys that enhance children's sensory reactions. Quite early, infants enjoy action songs and repetitive rhymes (see Chapter 2 for examples). By 4 and 5 months, infants may bounce up and down on their mother's lap in order to get a game such as Ride a Cockhorse started. Once the child begins to play with objects, joining in and adjusting to the pace and tempo of the child's play can be important. Activities that help a child try out and eventually master activities at the next level of ability can encourage a child to interact in different ways with objects and to experience a sense of competence. Show her how to put a few more blocks on the tower. Fit a more complicated shape into a shape box. Copy a stroke instead of scribbling. If the child's interest flags, try reengaging him by being playful and energetic. Remain

Encouraging and being interested in children's play helps foster their play capacities.

child-centered, and when the child initiates an action, respond by continuing the child's topic. While engaging in play with toys or pretend play, take the role of facilitator rather than director of the child's activity. Allow the child to take the lead and provide support and redirection if necessary. Scaffold, but do not take over. Model a solution from time to time and then have the child complete it so he can feel his own sense of competence or mastery. Age-appropriate toys and props to encourage play are set out in Table 4.4.

PRINCIPLE 4:   *Follow the child's lead in pretend play, accept the feelings, join in the play, and—when necessary—extend play themes.*

In order to encourage a child's ability to pretend play, it can be very helpful to set aside some time to play with the child and to follow the child's lead. During these times, some limits can be imposed so the play does not get out of hand; for example, the child can be forbidden to hit or hurt anyone or themselves or to intentionally break a toy or damage anything else in the room. Apart from these limits and restrictions, however, it is very important to accept the play and not to criticize, give advice, teach, or moralize. In other words, the child should be allowed to choose the play theme or activity and how the story unfolds.

It is important to not turn the session into a teaching experience but to make comments about the child's play in a helpful way without being intrusive. Talking for the toys and characters in the drama or assuming a role yourself will keep the play going and stimulate imaginative and symbolic thinking. Narrating the play for the child can highlight its value, show approval, and help organize the play of children who tend to be fragmented or disjointed in their play. Describing the feelings of the characters in the drama can be helpful for the child to begin to understand his own and other people's feelings. Here are some examples of caregiver responses based on children's play behavior:

Child is banging cars continuously into one another.

Parent: "My, these cars have a lot of energy and are moving very fast. I wonder where they want to go?"

Child is playing the doctor and preparing to give you a shot.

Parent: "Oh dear, will it hurt? I really don't like getting a shot. Could we forget it for today?"

Child is having the dinosaurs fight one another.

Parent: "That dinosaur looks really angry. I think he'd like the others to go away for a while."

Child is constantly building a tower and having a doll knock it down.

Parent: "I wonder why that doll keeps knocking the tower down?"

Table 4.4.   Suitable toys and props by age group

Age	Suitable toys and props	Age	Suitable toys and props
Birth–3 months	Rings made of plastic Rattles Mobiles Bells Squeaky toys Pictures of faces High-contrast, boldly patterned objects Wrist bands Foot finders or decorated socks Bumper pads with patterns Books Musical toys	25–30 months	Toy telephone Play equipment Sand and container Rhythm instruments Small wagon Push and pull toys Hammer boards Balls Pretend vehicles (e.g., cars, fire engine) Large wooden puzzles Pegboards
4–7 months	Toys with handles Furry animals Stuffed toys Rubber toys Bath toys Shiny saucepans Suction and roly poly toys Toys where an object pops up when a lever is pushed or pulled	31–36 months	Dress-up clothes Finger and hand puppets Toy brooms and mops Puzzles Art supplies Play table Play house Sand box Pretend stove Tunnels
8–12 months	Busy box/activity center Building blocks Newspaper to tear Nesting jars Shape sorters Suction cup toys Balls Plastic key chains Mirror Board and cloth books Pop-up toys Jack-in-the-box		Rocking horse Small human and animal figures Hammer and nails
		3–4 years	Doll stroller Glue Construction toys Picture story flannel board with people, houses, and so forth Bowling pins Wind-up toys Threading beads Plasticine
13–24 months	Toy cups, tea set Wooden spoons Ring stack Pull toys Toy telephone Musical instruments Finger paints Tricycles Feely box with objects of various textures (e.g., sand paper, grater) Slides and swings Pegboards Small trucks and cars Doll Bubbles Picture books Interlocking links	4–6 years	Stickers Lotto or matching games Dominoes Musical instruments Props for more elaborate pretend play (e.g., nurse/doctor kits, hats, cash registers, toy money) Puppet theater Doll houses Wagons All kinds of trucks Jump rope Tool box Magnetic letters and numbers

Sometimes, children seem to have difficulty moving beyond one or two sequences in play. You might see this evidenced in a child repeatedly running cars along the ground or serving imaginary tea in seemingly bottomless teacups. Joining the child's play theme is crucial, and when caregivers expand it by introducing a sequence or story it can work wonders in encouraging imagination. Having a car take someone to work and back again or introducing "guests" for a tea party can add richness while, at the same time, encourage the child to build on their own activities.

PRINCIPLE 5: *Encourage playfulness and joyous exchanges and experiences.*

Although research is still exploratory, there is growing evidence that the transfer of affect between caregiver and child influences the growing brain. Positive affective exchanges and interactions that can occur in play promote the development of cerebral circuits. The caregiver's positive facial expression enhances these neuronal connections and may trigger critical neurochemicals in the child's growing brain. Consequently, positive affective exchanges may be essential for the child's emotional development. In order to encourage playfulness, it is important to join the child in activities you both enjoy. A walk in the park, playing in water, swimming, going down a water slide, or a card game can all be fun activities and ones that can bring joy and great pleasure to a child. When children engage in physical, rough-and-tumble play, they may experience a wonderful sense of control, spontaneity, and special enjoyment.

PRINCIPLE 6: *Provide children with the opportunity for a variety of different play experiences to encourage their imaginations.*

If children are reluctant to play, it is helpful to introduce some different ways to encourage their imagination. Sometimes these different media may be ones that caregivers are familiar with, feel very excited about, or have experience using. Suggestions for these different play media are outlined in the next sections.

Puppets   Some children delight in puppet play, perhaps because it can give them some distance from scary and upsetting issues. A puppet can allow them to express their feelings, ideas, and concerns and to talk about issues they would find difficult to communicate directly about to an adult. Sometimes, puppets can be used by a child to express tabooed actions by making the puppet responsible for them. The adult can then discuss the child's feelings indirectly and may offer another point of view through the puppets. Children can be encouraged to pick up a puppet and to be its voice while another child or adult adopts the character of another puppet. Some children enjoy putting on a puppet show and telling their story through the puppets.

Reading Stories   Reading, unlike television, encourages children to imagine things and to conjure up pictures in their minds that can be internalized and remembered to be brought back later in quiet moments when they daydream and imagine events in the future. As well, reading stories about issues that may be troubling a child offers an opportunity to share a positive interpersonal experience while confronting issues that are universal and have a particular significance for the child. Dealing with these concerns in a symbolic or metaphorical format al-

lows the child to confront the issues in a more distant—and consequently safe—situation. The stories that will be most attractive to a particular child will depend on her age and will address concerns that she has, suggest solutions to things that are upsetting, and provide some confidence and hope in the future. Some of the common and universal issues that children may confront are listed here:

- Intimacy and trust
- Sibling rivalry
- Separation anxiety and attachment
- Individualization and growing up
- Fear of injury and death
- Struggles between good and bad
- Conflicts with parents
- Concern about sexual differences
- Control and compromise
- Fear of rejection or abandonment

Themes that certain children may confront include the following:

- Loss of a caregiver
- Divorce and separation
- Illness or injury
- Moving and change of school
- Death
- Fighting or violence in the family
- Natural disasters
- Adoption
- Witnessing a traumatic scene

Examples of children's books about a number of these topics are included in each chapter in this book. Reading a book or a fairy tale that deals with these tough issues and having the child talk about them and ask questions can often open up discussions that need to be brought into the open.

Traditional children's stories and fairy tales can provide meaning to many of the common and universal dilemmas of childhood. Although some of the characters can be cruel and the plots illogical, classic children's stories can simplify issues because the characters are clearly drawn and the child can identify with the hero and will feel comfort in his or her "goodness." As the stories are told, they make acceptable some of the child's unspeakable thoughts and emotions. Some of the common themes dealt with in fairy tales are outlined in Table 4.5.

Table 4.5. Some common childhood themes and issues in fairy tales

Fairy tales	Issues
Goldilocks and the Three Bears	Sharing with others and jealousy Respecting personal property
The Three Little Pigs	The shortcut or quick fix isn't always the best solution The seemingly small and weak can defeat the stronger enemy The security of family
Hansel and Gretel	Separation anxiety and individuation Love between siblings Don't talk to strangers!
Jack and the Beanstalk	Overcoming powerful, evil figures Respect for others (such as the poor)
Cinderella	Loss of loved ones Sibling rivalry Keeping hope alive
Little Red Riding Hood	Triumph of good over evil Don't talk to strangers!
The Frog Prince	Love can achieve all No one is too small or insignificant Character is more important than appearance
Sleeping Beauty	Fear of death Listen to the warnings of grownups
Snow White and the Seven Dwarfs	Struggle between mother and daughter Goodness and kindness Group unity

Storytelling   Storytelling is different from reading books because it follows no set script, but it can be a powerful way for children to organize thoughts, feelings, and experience. It can take many forms: A storyteller can use a flannel board to help tell the story or a tape recorder or microphone to give a little distance and to provide a record of what was said. By the time children are 3 or 4 years old, they will delight in telling stories about themselves and things that have happened, things they saw in photographs, or heard others talk about or have imagined. Telling stories can help children make sense out of masses of information and can organize it into meaningful, understandable self-narratives. The process of telling the story can help put events in sequence, set them in a time and place, and help the child understand about the past and the future. Sometimes it may be the parent that tells a story about the past, with photos and pictures of real events, or about imagined adventures.

Richard Gardner (1972) described a technique called mutual storytelling, which can be used for children from about 4 years old and older. In this method, the child is asked to tell a story, which will generally reflect some of the child's life situation because it was introduced by the child. After the child tells his story, the adult tells one too, using characters from the child's story but having it end differently and with the characters finding helpful solutions to the child's problems as revealed in the story.

Another method of storytelling that has been used successfully in classrooms as an intervention to increase children's play has been called "thematic-fantasy" training. In this approach, a story is read and children are coached to take different parts and to play out the story. It is helpful to have an adult facilitate the play.

Using Playdough, Plasticine, and Modeling Clay   Using media such as playdough, Plasticine, and modeling clay can provide children with a bridge between their senses and their feelings. Those who are insecure can enjoy the satisfaction of mastery and a sense of control as they make something, however simple. The object and feelings and thoughts that it generates can then form a bridge to verbal expression for children who either do not have language or who have difficulty expressing their thoughts. While creating an object, children often interact at a new level, sharing thoughts, ideas, feelings, and experiences. Some ideas for suggestions of things to make could be an imaginary animal, "something you'd like to be," the child's family doing something, a necklace, a snake, the child as a baby, and a scary monster.

Painting and Drawing   Young children who find it particularly difficult to put their ideas and feelings into words may find that painting and drawing offers them ways to express themselves in a different way. It can be a wonderful medium for self-expression and can be used therapeutically, to help some children deal with difficult issues and conflicts. Painting and drawing can be a joyful experience of self-expression if the child is given permission to make choices about the topic and the way it is expressed. Used in this way, finger painting can provide a way for discharging difficult feelings, uncovering defenses, and providing a channel to communicate about difficulties and anxieties. Materials that can be used include finger paints, water colors, tempera paints, chalk, crayons, markers, "paint sticks," and, of course, paintbrushes of all shapes and sizes.

Dress-Up Play   Providing a number of costumes can set the stage for dramatic play. In such play, children can play out different roles. Sometimes putting on mommy's or daddy's clothes can help them identify with parents and feel their closeness in a special way. Dressing

Painting can be a joyful experience of self-expression.

Children love to dress up, and it can set the stage for pretend play.

up can help children become transformed in their imagination into firemen, superheros, ballerinas, "bad guys," animals, or fanciful creatures. As they assume these roles, children can feel brave, graceful, or powerful and escape, for a while, feelings of being small and insignificant. When children choose costumes together it can also encourage cooperation, as children plan to act out parts and stage plays.

Sand Play   Sand can be a marvelous medium for children of all ages. The sand lends itself to the demonstration of a number of fears and fantasies. Activities that children can do in sand include tunnel-making, burying objects, or drawing in the sand. When small objects and toys are added, children can use them to play out situations in real life or fantasies that trouble them. They can be invited to make a picture in the sand and to describe it. Moreover, the sand feels wonderful to the fingers and hands, creating an ideal tactile and kinesthetic experience. Sand play is often used therapeutically with the child, using the same small animals and human figures over several weeks and creating stories and events that gradually develop over time. Play themes often change from very fragmented and disorganized stories to those that are meaningful, sequential, and rich.

Music   Children love dancing and moving to music. Songs and music can often encourage language, and for children with developmental delays and those with significant emotional difficulties, music may bring improvements when other approaches have failed. Music can be used in a variety of ways—as a background for other types of play or to encourage children to sing along with various children's songs. At early ages, very few children are constricted in dancing, marching, or moving to rock or other contemporary music and rhythms. Children also find rhythm instruments exciting and can quickly learn to create an acceptable beat. Tambourines, drums, and bells are all easy to use.

SOME COMMONLY RAISED QUESTIONS AND ISSUES SURROUNDING PLAY AND IMAGINATION

Following are some common questions and issues caregivers have regarding play and imagination.

Imaginary Friends

Imaginary friends are invisible characters who are named, talked about, and played with for a period of time. Most children who have an imaginary friend are between 3 and 7 years of age, and both boys and girls have them. Estimates of the percentage of children who have them vary from 13 to 16 depending on the measure used.

The child presents imaginary friends as real, although he knows they are not. There are some varying opinions in the literature about imaginary friends, both in terms of how frequently they occur as well as what they mean in terms of a child's overall adjustment. Imaginary friends may persist for up to 3 years, although some change over time so that the child has a series of imaginary friends.

Writers vary in describing children with imaginary friends. Some describe them as more intelligent, popular, mature, verbal, able to concentrate, and less aggressive. In one study conducted by Harter and Chao (1992), however, the researchers found children with imaginary companions to be rated as moderately competent by teachers, although the children rated themselves as highly competent. Some writers have noted that children with imaginary friends tend to be oldest or only children, and thus they may be lonelier and have fewer children to play with at home.

Imaginary friends are generally well tolerated by parents unless their "existence" causes problems with routines or errands. Imaginary friends take on various roles:

- The imaginary friend is very competent and independent. He is the child's ego ideal or represents the child's sense of omnipotence and grandiosity, which fades as he gets older.

- The imaginary friend is "bad" and does all sorts of things the child is not allowed to do and knows are wrong. The friend represents aspects of her personality that are less acceptable to others. By having her friend do these unacceptable things for her, the child can then identify with the parent by looking at herself from the outside in order to overcome these behaviors.

- The imaginary friend may be quite incompetent and may need to be looked after and nurtured by the child. Again, the friend represents unacceptable parts of the child or feelings of inadequacy and loneliness, and the child feels more adequate by comparison.

- The imaginary friend is safe, caring, and constantly available, unlike parents from whom he now needs to separate.

Usually, such imaginary friends go away by age 5 or 6, and the child replaces them with real peer friendships. Caregivers should not show too much enthusiasm or ask too many specific questions but, rather, accept the child's companion and enjoy listening and watching this window into the child's inner world. Make sure the child understands the difference between real

and pretend and occasionally remind the child of it. If the child refuses to play with other children because of the invisible playmate, if she displays disturbing behaviors, or if the imaginary friend does not fade at the expected time and is doing harm to others, there is cause for concern, however, and help should be sought.

Dealing with Aggressive Play

Many parents and child care workers are extremely concerned about children playing out hostile and aggressive themes. Playing with guns or other weapons is a particular concern because they believe it may encourage children to be aggressive and conjures up memories of the terrifying acts of violence that have become commonplace in too many parts of the world, including the United States.

● ●

Lee, Monica, and Gabeshan are playing an army game. Gabeshan has just "shot" Monica with a toy laser gun and stands over her. "Look I killed her—see, she's bleeding," he says, smiling. "Don't move," says Lee, "You're dead, I got you." "There are more soldiers coming." Then Lee and Gabeshan sing, "You're killed! You're killed! And you'd better look out." This scares them and they look at one another and say, "Aw, it's okay—she was smiling even though we killed her."

Many children become obsessed with movies, television, and comic book characters, and their play seems to become increasingly violent. They show a fascination with guns, shooting, and death. Sometimes, the games are repeated over and over again, seemingly without any resolution.

Aggressive play themes can vary considerably from those that are violent, repetitive, and escalate out of control to play that moves from aggression into more prosocial endings and resolutions and a greater understanding of the issues of war and violence. Developmentalists tend to see aggressive play as an important way for children to gain control of impulses; to integrate ideas of good and bad, compassion and evil; and to provide the child with a sense of competence (e.g., as he pretends to be a superhero). It is clear that this may be the case for some children who are highly fanciful, but for others, very aggressive play can be unhelpful and may in fact encourage violence. Another point of view is that children will learn the wrong values through war play and that through it they are developing acceptance of violence and a lack of compassion for victims.

In a study carried out by this writer, parents of preschoolers rated as aggressive or nonaggressive by parents and/or teachers were observed playing with their children. In the situations observed, children were provided with toy dinosaurs, a crocodile, cars, fierce animals, drawing materials, blocks, a small house, and miniature people. Significant differences were found in the ways parents reacted to their children's aggressive play. Parents of children who behaved aggressively did one of two things: Some cut off the aggressive play completely and refused to participate, making negative remarks such as "That's not nice," or "You hurt him," or they removed the toys from sight. Others let the aggressive play escalate out of control, allowing the

child to include images of blood and gore, death and destruction in his play, which frequently resulted in a great deal of observable anxiety in the child. Parents of children not rated as aggressive joined in their children's aggressive play, showing acceptance of the feelings, talking for the fierce animal, or expressing the feelings of the hurt animals or people in a natural way. If the play became repetitive or began to escalate out of control, they moved it to a more prosocial theme while still staying within the play metaphor or theme (Landy & Menna, 1997). The following is an example of the play between a nonaggressive child and his mother.

Child: "This is a bad guy." *Takes the dinosaur.* "Mummy, the crocodile is smaller, the dinosaur is stronger."

Mother: *Takes crocodile, smiling.* "But he's got a bigger mouth." *Both mother and child bang the animals together, laughing.*

Child: "My dinosaur is stronger than the crocodile." *Bangs the crocodile with the dinosaur.*

Mother: "I'm running away." *Takes the crocodile and makes him run away.* "I can outsmart you—you can't catch me. I can think!"

Child: *Tries to bang the crocodile with the dinosaur.*

Mother: *Moves the crocodile away, smiling.* "See? I'm coming to get you. My crocodile can be frightening, too." *Mother and child bang the toy animals together.* "I'm running away; I'll use the phone." *Gets the toy telephone.* "Help, help! Can you please come? Can you come? Let's see if the police are coming. What will you do if the police come?"

Child: "We could play."

Mother: *Talking for the crocodile.* "Are you going to be friends with me now?"

Child: "Yes, let's play." *Makes the dinosaur fall down.* "Oh, oh!"

Mother: "What's the matter? Can I help you?"

Child: "My name is Dinosaur."

Mother: "My name is Crocodile."

Child: *Makes the dinosaur fall down.* "Help me, help me!"

Mother: "Oh dear me, are you alright? Let me help you."

Child: *Smiles and takes the crocodile's hands, and then takes the dinosaur up in the air.* "See, I fly. I can go up in the air."

Mother: "Can you teach me to fly? Where will we go?" *Both fly the animals around together.*

Child: "Now we're friends. Let's not fight anymore."

As can be seen in this example, the mother accepts the aggressive play theme but does not let it escalate out of control, and she gradually brings it back to an interaction where the animals play together.

Parents and care child workers typically choose four alternatives as reactions to war play. According to Carlsson-Paige and Levin (1987), these are

1. Banning the play totally.

2. Ignoring it and letting it happen.

3. Allowing war play, but with certain limits such as only in one place and without guns.

4. Actively facilitating more elaborate play and a positive, prosocial resolution to the play.

Research on and theories of play and development suggest that option four is the most helpful. To ban the play totally would only frustrate the children and could increase aggression, while ignoring such play can let it escalate. Setting up certain limits can be difficult to enforce. Joining in the play and encouraging a more prosocial focus if play is becoming too aggressive can be very effective, however, because it demonstrates and models strategies that children can use to deal with aggression other than acting out physically.

Some positive strategies for dealing with aggressive play include

• Accepting that children need an avenue to express anger and frustration

• Joining the child at times in the play and talking for the aggressor or victim, which gives the child perspective on how others feel

• Taking on a role in the play if the play escalates out of control and introducing a more cooperative theme such as telephoning for help or going for a picnic in the park together. If this is unsuccessful and the play escalates out of control, it may have to be terminated by the caregiver.

The Effect of Television, Video, and Computer Games on Play

Many young children today watch a considerable amount of television, with preschoolers in the United States watching 3–4 hours daily. Many parents worry about its effect on development, although 85% report that they provide no guidance regarding the programs. There is ample evidence that viewing a significant amount of violence on television does increase aggressive play, at least immediately after watching, and some studies have shown a long-term effect over several years (Singer, 1997; Singer & Singer, 1990; Singer, Slovak, Frierson, & York, 1998). Children are prone to imitate and model behaviors they observe on television. Thus, children who see a number of violent shows or news programs that include several violent acts may become numb, or come to believe that the world is a hostile, scary place and that violence is acceptable and condoned by society.

What may be of even greater concern is that television presents children with numerous rapid-fire, disorganized stimuli that may lead to difficulty concentrating and in developing imaginative skills. It is hard to conjure up fantasies and to create dreams if the images are presented externally with few opportunities for fantasy play or storytime. Television can also lead children to believe in easy solutions and make them less likely to problem solve. Children younger than 3 or 4 years of age whose distinction between reality and fantasy is tenuous and

Table 4.6. Television's effects on children

Negative effects	Positive effects
Violence on television can stimulate aggressive behavior.	Certain shows can encourage compassionate behavior and provide positive role models.
Child does not have time to engage in other activities.	Sometimes teaches racial tolerance.
May lead to belief that the world is a very frightening place.	Source of information about an enormous range of topics.
Rapid-fire images can lead to more difficulty in concentrating, planning, and sequencing events.	Can be an opportunity for discussions about important topics.
May lead to apathy and lack of motivation.	Can be an excellent teaching tool.
Can become an addiction.	Some programs can stimulate imagination and pretend play.
May negatively affect reading ability.	Some television shows can actually encourage social interchange (e.g., *Sesame Street*).
May make it more difficult to imagine things and create inner worlds because images are all provided instead of encouraging child to think about them.	

who see the world from an egocentric position can become quite overwhelmed and confused by these television images. Certainly, most parents let their children watch television at certain times of day. In fact, some television programs (e.g., *Barney, Blues Clues, Sesame Street*) can actually exert a positive influence on the amount and complexity of imaginative play and decrease aggression. It is important for caregivers to watch shows with children when they can and to explain and discuss any material that may cause confusion and clear up any misunderstandings. Some control over content may also be gained by using videos instead of television.

To some extent, the effect of television on children will vary according to their temperament (including ability to attend), level of anxiety, aggressive tendencies, capacity for fantasy use, and what is going on elsewhere in their lives. Some negative and positive effects of television on children are outlined in Table 4.6.

Other concerns are now being expressed about the effects of video games and microcomputers on children. Neither has been proven to reduce imaginative play, perhaps because there is an interactive component that offers some involvement in the process. If video games or computer software include violent content, however, the same concerns noted above about violent television would apply. For some children, the immediate feedback that video games provide can help them learn and remember things and these games can be satisfying activities. Again, it is important for parents to monitor the content and amount of time that children spend with these activities.

Differences in the Amount and Style of Children's Play

As in just about everything that children do, they vary in their interest in and ability to play. Some of the differences, as noted previously in this chapter, relate to characteristics of the child, such as difficulty with concentration. Some children have problems staying with a play theme and pass rapidly from one to another. For others, internal conflicts or present circumstances may intrude on their ability to engage in any type of play. Gordon (1993) has suggested four types of pretend play inhibitions from her observation of children at play:

1. Children who can play symbolically but who seem unable to resolve disturbing themes or the negative affective arousal through the play

2. Children whose play is fragmented and disorganized and who fail to be able to coordinate separate play actions into meaningful play themes

3. Children whose play involves repetitive actions and perseveration of the same activity, and who may also have difficulty playing symbolically and expanding play schemes

4. Children who cannot engage in any pretend play or explore toys; children who are unmotivated to play and instead exhibit a great deal of anger and aggression

Gordon (1993) related these types of inhibition to emotional and behavioral problems in children and believed that mounting anxiety and anger interfere with symbolic functioning because of the difficult circumstances in which the children live.

Some children may pretend too much or lose the ability to distinguish reality and fantasy. These children do not realize that the game is just pretend, and make-believe becomes an escape from a world that they find too demanding, unpredictable, or frightening. They need the fantasies to survive and would rather escape into them than experience contacts with the real world. Unfortunately, children who continually live in a world of make-believe usually become outcasts and have few friends or social contacts. One little boy whose early life was characterized by severe abuse and his mother's drug addiction and sexual acting out could only maintain himself by becoming the leader of the "Power Ranger army," an army that could control the world and all the people in it. It took months of consistent and loving caregiving and play therapy before he was able to gradually and cautiously give up these defenses.

Ideally, as pointed out by Santostefano (1978), children should be able to pass freely between the world of pretend and reality, clearly distinguishing the two, but integrating information regularly from one into the other. As this happens, the child is aware of the differences and may remind us if we join in a game that "it's just pretend, you know."

Even within the group of children who can play for sufficient periods of time and cooperate with other children, there are different styles of players. Two styles have been proposed, the first by Wolf and associates, who talked about *patterners* and *dramatists*. Patterners enjoy playing with material and objects and often excel in visual-spatial tasks and building with blocks. Dramatists, on the other hand, love to pretend and play out roles or narrate various plays (Wolf & Gardner, 1979; Wolf & Grollman, 1982). The second styles of play were identified by another group of researchers who named sub-groups of leaders and followers. One type of follower, the "serfs," were not allowed to join in the play unless they did exactly what others wanted (Segal, Peck, Vega-Lahr, & Field, 1987).

Though researchers found that some children were both patterners and dramatists, other children seem to exhibit a dominant style of play. For children who are only patterners, their style of play may limit their ability to deal with conflicts and negative emotions through playing out dramas. Once they are adults, they may also be limited in their ability to develop imagination and a fantasy life.

Obviously, children who are always followers may have problems, especially "serfs," who were often observed by the researchers to become frustrated and aggressive when they could not join in play with the other children. Sometimes the researchers were able to modify the pattern by pairing the "serfs" with a compatible partner in order to encourage their joining in play with others.

A "dramatist" in action. (From Johnston, Lynn [1978]. *Do they ever grow up?* Minnetonka, MN: Meadowbrook Press; reprint granted with written permission of Lynn Johnston Productions, Inc.)

In conclusion, children vary significantly in the amount and style of play in which they engage. Some of the variation may be due to individual differences within the child, while some may relate to the environment and to the caregiver interactions to which they are exposed. When differences are extreme, as they are in children who either refuse to engage in pretend play or who seem constantly to be in a fantasy world, it is important to try to encourage children to moderate their play. Children can be encouraged either to engage in pretend play if they do not play at all, or if they pretend too much, to engage in activities that involve them in contact with other children. If the difficulties appear to persist, it could be useful to talk to a professional about more suggestions to help the child.

For children with different styles of play, it may be helpful to encourage "patterners" to pretend by introducing some pretend themes into their play, such as building a garage or house and playing with cars and miniature people. A building can become a castle with a king or queen or the place where Mommy or Daddy go to work. For children who are only followers, encouraging them to be more assertive by giving them some choices and making sure they have a role in the play can be very helpful.

The Use of Play as Therapy

Children who have emotional or behavioral problems or who have experienced a particularly traumatic event may be referred for play therapy. Parents may be confused about why play may

be used as a kind of therapy and what happens during sessions. Play therapy is often used with young children because they have difficulty talking about and verbalizing their worries and concerns; consequently, play becomes a better medium. In this kind of therapy, a trained therapist spends time playing with a child in a certain room, with certain toys, at a preassigned time. Different play therapists may use a variety of styles ranging from very nondirective to more focused approaches. In the focused or structured approaches pioneered by Levy (1938), specific stimulus situations are set up, which the child is then encouraged to play out. For example, these situations could be around sibling rivalry, peer conflicts, separation, gender differences, and so forth. In more nondirective approaches, the therapist does not organize the play to address a particular theme or topic, and instead follows the child's lead and responds to any feelings or play themes that are brought up. Sometimes a period of focused play therapy is used within a longer period of play therapy and after a relationship has been established. In spite of these differences, the primary goals of therapy are typically similar. These goals of play therapy are outlined in Table 4.7.

If the child has difficulty playing, the first part of the therapy may primarily deal with helping the child to begin to use play imaginatively. This can usually be done by joining in the play and helping to extend and elaborate play themes. For example, if a child is banging cars together, the therapist might take a car and start racing with the child's car to make the play more elaborate. Sometimes this first stage can take several weeks or even months. In the next phase, the therapist begins to understand the child's issues and a growing relationship develops. Later, as the child begins to introduce certain events, themes, or emotions into the play, the therapist can help the child understand them, integrate them into his "event scripts," and begin to consider how and why they happened. The child can be helped to become aware of feelings he has and to communicate them to the therapist and learn how to cope with them better. At this stage, there are often changes such as improvements in behavior, or unfortunately sometimes a temporary increase in anxiety about what is going on and even a deteriora-

Table 4.7. The goals of play therapy

To improve the child's capacity for using symbolization and pretend play to express feelings and solve problems	To improve view of self and others	To rework traumas and present conflicts
To encourage the child to play with extended themes and to move the play beyond repetitive stereotypic play	To provide the child with a positive relationship	To play out past traumatic events or situations in order to get some sense of control over them. To play out conflicts in order to begin to understand them
To allow ventilation of emotions and to move to more verbal or symbolic ways of expressing them	To help the child integrate "good" and "bad" parts of himself and others	To link past events to present actions and feelings the child may have
To open up dialogue and to break down resistance to discussion	To demonstrate that trust of and closeness to another person can be helpful	To help child to begin to understand recurring self-defeating patterns of relating that may affect the child's adjustment
To help the child distinguish between reality and fantasy and to move comfortably between the two	To allow child to re-experience certain developmental stages that may have been compromised	
To bring another perspective and to encourage the child to move beyond egocentricity	To allow child to get a sense of being understood and have negative feelings accepted	

tion in behavior. The last phase will be providing the child with different schemata with new and adaptive themes that can be used to help solve problems. Material will be interpreted so that the child understands the meaning of his play. As helpful as techniques are, however, there are no magic tricks for either therapist or child. Watching, joining in the play, showing empathy, and talking about what is happening are the best strategies for professionals and caregivers, and form a basis for emotional understanding of the child. As children become able to use pretend play and to express their inner concerns, they learn about themselves and can begin to make changes in their behavior.

THE ROLE OF PARENTS IN PLAY AND IMAGINATION

Many caregivers (including parents) find it difficult to play with children for a variety of reasons. Parents may not play with their children because of their beliefs about play, which may be cultural. Some other reasons behind a difficulty in playing might be that the caregiver

- Considers play a waste of time and to be competing with work

- Uses "play" as a way to teach the child, continually naming objects, colors, and shapes rather than following the child's lead and letting play themes develop

- May never have experienced the opportunity to play when growing up and does not know where to start

- May consider play as regressive and leading to an out-of-control situation and chaos that will be difficult to end

- May find it difficult to find time to play or may have too many children in their care to allow time for one-to-one interaction with a child

- May believe that children learn best by being taught their numbers and letters and that play will not help them academically

- May find play very tedious and boring because children often want to do the same thing over and over again

- May raise feelings of anger or anxiety

Usually, caregivers have these kind of difficulties because as children they were never played with or imaginative play was actually discouraged. As mentioned previously, pretend play, which can involve aggressive themes, may bring back memories of past traumas or acts of violence, making it too upsetting to engage in. It can also create anxiety because during pretend play some rules are temporarily set aside and parents may become concerned that their children's impulses will become out of control and overpower them. It is important to let parents know that not giving opportunities for pretend play can have the opposite effect, however, because children who do not experience interactive play often have a great deal of difficulty playing alone or in social situations. In fact, if parents can be encouraged to begin to play with their children, their children's behavior may actually *improve* and they may become more able to amuse themselves and less aggressive and angry.

DISCUSSION QUESTIONS TO USE IN TRAINING PROFESSIONALS

- What are the most important functions or uses of play?

- How can you define play and what are its essential qualities?

- Explain why some children may have difficulty with pretend play.

- List some of the main kinds of play.

- What do research findings have to say about the most important variables that can encourage play?

- Why do some caregivers have difficulty playing with children?

- How could you help a parent play with a child?

- How may culture affect a child's play?

- How does play at 1 year of age look different from play at 5 months of age?

- What can you do about aggressive play?

WORKING WITH PARENTS:
GROUP EXERCISES AND SAMPLE HOMEWORK ACTIVITIES

It is critical to convey to parents the importance of play and the idea that playing with children can help to enhance the parent-child relationship. Parents who see play as a waste of time should be reassured that it is fine to play for short periods, such as 20 minutes, three times per week, and that it is alright to set a timer to set boundaries for the child. It is important to make it clear that during that time they must give their child their full attention and not intrude or change the direction of what is happening. Parents also should be discouraged from giving assistance unless the child is "stuck" or needs help finishing an activity or solving a problem. If a parent is willing to engage in pretend play, explain that it should not be allowed to get out of control, and suggest ways to join in this kind of play as outlined in Principle 2 of this chapter. Once a parent has begun to enjoy the play, he or she should be encouraged to play at other times and to spend time spontaneously playing when the child initiates it.

Clarifying that there are a variety of ways to play with a child and that they can choose one they and their child enjoy is also helpful. If the parent has a partner, each may enjoy doing different activities with their child(ren) and, consequently, provide a variety of experiences for them. At times, parents may choose activities in which the whole family can be involved. Sometimes demonstrating different kinds of play to parents by using toys and activities with their infant or child can help model how to play with children. Bringing books and audiotapes of songs and games suitable to the child's age and using them to demonstrate the fun of playing can be helpful. Encouraging parents to join in can often spark their enthusiasm for a new way to be with their children. Using videotapes of play interactions can also be helpful.

GROUP EXERCISES FOR PARENTS TO ENCOURAGE PLAY

This section includes exercises that can be used with parents and other caregivers to help them learn to encourage play and imagination in children and in themselves.

Guided Imagery

To have parents experience how relaxing and enriching imagination can be, have them do the following:

> Close your eyes and imagine that you are in an ocean of blue light. Feel and believe that you are in a wave in the ocean. You float up and down with the wave and feel yourself relaxing into the water. You become like one with the waves and the blue light of the ocean. As you listen you can hear the seagulls and the waves pounding on the rocks and the sand. The waves keep forming into more waves and carry you into the shore where you land and open your eyes.

Ask parents to discuss how it felt and to describe their experience of visualizing and "listening" to the sounds. Point out that the freeing from stress, if only for a moment, can provide them with a "place" to relax and to escape from the pressures of the real world. Music, other imagined scenes, or relaxation techniques can be provided if parents find them useful.

251

Table 4.8.   Points to emphasize in drawing activity

Drawing can allow the individual to express feelings without necessarily talking about them.

Doing the drawing as a group is important for cooperation.

Drawing can express conflicts the person is experiencing and allow them to be "worked through."

The quality of the art is not important, but the process and the spontaneity that can be released are important.

Drawing a Picture

Give each parent a piece of paper and ask them to start a drawing. At a signal, tell them to stop drawing and to pass their paper to the next person who will add something to it. When giving instructions, emphasize the points shown in Table 4.8.

The cycle is completed when everyone has had a chance to add something to each picture. Next, have the participants put their pictures together and discuss the experience. Ask participants to describe the picture and what it reminds them of. Talk about some of the thoughts and feelings that were aroused by the pictures. This will give parents an opportunity to understand how others imagine things and can give them ideas about their own inner worlds. It is important to encourage parents to be as relaxed and as open as possible about discussing their thoughts and feelings as they create their pictures.

What Was My Own Childhood and Play History Like?

Here are some ways parents can use memories of their own childhoods and play history to help them become better playing partners with their children:

- Have parents think about any private games, magical rhymes, or play experiences they remember from their own childhood.

- Have parents talk about their favorite storybook when they were a child and what it meant to them. Ask them to think about why this book means so much to them, particularly the circumstances in which it was read and what the theme means to them now.

- Discuss some of their children's favorite books and why they think they enjoy them.

- Have them remember times their own parents played with them.

Videotape Parent–Child Interactions During Play   If possible, use videotapes of caregivers or parents in the group playing with their children. If they are not available, use videotapes of other parents and children playing. Play the videotape and ask caregivers to comment on what the child is doing and why they think he is playing in a particular way. Have the group comment on how the caregiver is playing with the child, and have her comment on how the interaction felt and what was going on. Make sure that comments do not become negative and that positive aspects of the interaction are pointed out.

What's the Theme?   Have parents talk about themes that have emerged in their children's play. Discuss what they may mean. Have parents read the following examples and guess what issues the children may be dealing with.

● ●

Johnny, 3 years old, had played out a theme frequently in which a robber was in trouble for stealing money from a bank. The robber was now sorry and wanted to give it back, said Johnny, but the judge still sentenced him to jail for 20 years in jail. "Until you can control yourself, you can't come out," said the judge to the robber.

Chaya, who was 5 years old, spent a great deal of time playing out family themes. One that she tended to repeat frequently involved a train that was going to Florida with a family on board. A little girl had been left behind—separated from her family who was on the train—and it repeatedly failed to stop to pick her up. The little girl then ran after the train "all the way to Florida." Chaya did not seem extremely anxious about the play, but certainly she was excited when the little girl rejoined the family.

SAMPLE HOMEWORK ACTIVITIES

Here are several homework activities that parents can do to enrich their abilities to play with and encourage their children to play.

1. Play with infants every day in ways that make them laugh as they interact with you.

2. Observe your child playing and write down prominent themes.

3. Get down on the floor with your toddler and play for at least 10 minutes, following his or her lead.

4. Read a story to your child and include opportunities for storytelling for the child.

5. For older children, ask another child over to play and see how they cooperate and help them to do so when necessary.

6. Look at the handout of the developmental sequence of play and observe your child to see where he fits.

7. Draw with your child. Record what they draw and what it reveals.

8. Observe and then describe the type of player you think your child is.

9. Write a "play" diary for the child's week.

BIBLIOGRAPHY

REFERENCES

Achenback, T.M., & Edelbrock, C. (1983). *Manual for the Child Behavior Checklist.* Burlington: University of Vermont Press.

Alessandri, S.M. (1991). Play and social behavior in maltreated preschoolers. *Development and Psychopathology, 3,* 191–205.

Alessandri, S.M. (1992). Mother-child interactional correlates of maltreated and nonmaltreated children's play behavior. *Development and Psychopathology, 4,* 257–270.

Barnett, L.A. (1985). Young children's free play and problem-solving ability. *Leisure Sciences, 7,* 25–46.

Belsky, J., Goode, M.K., & Most, R.K. (1980). Maternal stimulation and infant exploratory competence: Cross-sectional, correlational, and experimental analysis. *Child Development, 51,* 1168–1178.

Berlyne, D.E. (1969). Laughter, humor, and play. In G. Lindzey & E. Aronson (Eds.), *The handbook of social psychology (Vol. 3).* Reading, MA: Addison-Wesley.

Bettelheim, B. (1987, March). The importance of play. *Atlantic Monthly,* 35–46.

Bornstein, M.H., Haynes, O.M., O'Reilly, A.W., & Painter, K.M. (1996). Solitary and collaborative pretense play in early childhood: Sources of individual variation in the development of representational competence. *Child Development, 67,* 2910–2929.

Bornstein, M.H., Haynes, O.M., Pascual, L., Painter, K.M., & Galperin, C. (1999). Play in two societies: Pervasiveness of process, specificity of structure. *Child Development, 70,* 317–331.

Bruner, J.S. (1972). Nature and uses of immaturity. *American Psychologist, 27,* 687–708.

Bundy, A.C. (1988). The play of preschoolers: Its relationship to balance and motor proficiency and the effect of sensory integrative dysfunction. *Dissertation Abstracts International, 48* (7–B): 1945.

Carlsson-Paige, N., & Levin, D.E. (1987). *The war play dilemma: Balancing needs and values in the early childhood classroom.* New York: Teachers College Press.

Caruso, D. (1981). *Measuring individual differences in qualitative aspects of infants' exploratory behavior: Relationships to problem-solving behavior.* Unpublished manuscript, Cornell University, Ithaca, NY.

Christie, J.F. (1983). The effects of play tutoring on young children's cognitive performance. *Journal of Educational Research, 76,* 326–330.

Christie, J.F. (1985). Training of symbolic play. *Early Child Development and Care, 19,* 43–52.

Cicchetti, D., & Beeghly, M. (1987). Symbolic development in maltreated youngsters: An organizational perspective. *New Directions for Child Development, 36,* 47–68.

Connolly, J.A., & Doyle, A.-B. (1984). Relation of social fantasy play to social competence in preschoolers. *Developmental Psychology, 20,* 797–806.

254

Damast, A.M., Tamis-LeMonda, C.S., & Bornstein, M.H. (1996). Mother–child play: Sequential interactions and the relation between maternal beliefs and behaviors. *Child Development, 67,* 1752–1766.

Dansky, J. (1980). Cognitive consequences of sociodramatic play and exploration training for economically disadvantaged preschoolers. *Journal of Child Psychology and Psychiatry and Allied Disciplines, 21,* 47–58.

Dockett, S., & Smith, I. (1995, March). *Children's theories of mind and their involvement in complex shared pretense.* Poster presented at the biennial meeting of the Society for Research in Child Development, Indianapolis.

Doctoroff, S. (1997). Sociodramatic script training and peer role prompting: Two tactics to promote sociodramatic play and peer interaction. *Early Child Development and Care, 136,* 27–43.

Doyle, A.-B., Ceschin, F., Tessier, O., & Doehring, P. (1991). The relation of age and social class factors in children's social pretend play to cognitive and symbolic ability. *International Journal of Behavioral Development, 14,* 395–410.

Droege, K.L., & Howes, C. (1991). *The effect of toy structure and center location on preschoolers' pretend play.* Paper presented at the biennial meeting of the Society for Research in Child Development, Seattle, Washington.

Dunn, L., & Herwig, J.E. (1992). Play behaviors and convergent and divergent thinking skills of young children attending full-day preschool. *Child Study Journal, 22,* 23–38.

Dunn, J., & Wooding, C. (1977). Play in the home and its implications for learning. In B. Tizard & D. Harvey (Eds.), *The biology of play* (pp. 45–58). London: Spastics International Medical Publications, Heinemann Medical Books.

Eaton, W.O., & Enns, L.R. (1986). Sex differences in human motor activity level. *Psychological Bulletin, 100,* 19–28.

Elkind, D. (1981). *The hurried child: Growing up too fast too soon.* Reading, MA: Addison-Wesley.

Erikson, E.H. (1963). *Childhood and society.* New York: Norton.

Farver, J.M. (1993). Cultural differences in scaffolding and pretend play: A comparison of American and Mexican mother-child and sibling-child pairs. In K. MacDonald (Ed.), *Parent-child play: Descriptions and implications* (pp. 349–366). Albany: State University of New York Press.

Farver, J.M., & Howes, C. (1993). Cultural differences in American and Mexican mother-child pretend play. *Merrill-Palmer Quarterly, 39,* 344–358.

Farver, J.M., & Shin, Y.L. (1997). Social pretend play in Korean and Anglo-American preschoolers. *Child Development, 68,* 544–556.

Farver, J.M., & Wimbarti, S. (1995). Indonesian children's play with their mothers and older siblings: *Child Development, 66,* 1493–1503.

Fein, G.G. (1981). Pretend play in childhood: An integrative review. *Child Development, 52,* 1095–1118.

Fein, G.G. (1989). Mind, meaning and affect: Proposals for a theory of pretense. *Developmental Review, 9,* 345–363.

Fein, G.G., & Apfel, N. (1979). The development of play: Style, structure, and situations. *Genetic Psychology Monographs, 99,* 231–250.

Feuerstein, R. (1979). *The dynamic assessment of retarded performers: The learning potential assessment device, theory, instruments, and techniques.* Baltimore: University Park Press.

Fiese, B.H. (1990). Playful relationships: A contextual analysis of mother-toddler interaction and symbolic play. *Child Development, 61,* 1648–1656.

Freud, S. (1961). *Beyond the pleasure principle* (J. Strachey, Ed. and Trans.). New York: Norton.

Freyberg, J.T. (1973). Increasing the imaginative play of urban disadvantaged kindergarten children through systematic training. In J.L. Singer (Ed.), *The child's world of make-believe: Experimental studies of imaginative play* (pp. 129–154). San Diego: Academic Press.

Gardner, R.A. (1972). Mutual storytelling: A technique in child psychotherapy. *Acta Paedopsychiatrica, 38,* 253–262.

Garvey, C. (1990). *Play.* Cambridge, MA: Harvard University Press.

Gaskins, S. (1996). How Mayan parental theories come into play. In S. Harkness & C.M. Super (Eds.), *Parents' cultural belief systems: Their origins, expressions, and consequences* (pp. 345–363). New York: Guilford Press.

Golomb, C., & Cornelius, C.B. (1977). Symbolic play and its cognitive significance. *Developmental Psychology, 13,* 246–252.

Göncü, A. (1993). Development of intersubjectivity in social pretend play. Special Topic: New directions in studying pretend play. *Human Development, 36,* 185–198.

Goodwin, M.P., Sawyers, J.K., & Bailey, K. (1988). The effects of exploration on preschoolers' problem-solving ability. *Journal of Genetic Psychology, 149,* 317–333.

Gordon, D.E. (1993). The inhibition of pretend play and its implications for development. *Human Development, 36,* 215–234.

Griffing, P. (1974). Sociodramatic play among young black children. *Theory Into Practice, 13,* 257–265.

Harper, J. (1991). Children's play: The differential effects of intrafamilial physical and sexual abuse. *Child Abuse and Neglect, 15,* 89–98.

Harter, S., & Chao, C. (1992). The role of competence in children's creation of imaginary friends. *Merrill-Palmer Quarterly, 38,* 350–363.

Hobson, R.P. (1986). The autistic child's appraisal of expressions of emotion. *Journal of Child Psychology and Psychiatry and Allied Disciplines, 27,* 321–342.

Howard, A.C. (1986). Developmental play ages of physically abused and nonabused children. *American Journal of Occupational Therapy, 40,* 691–695.

Howes, C., & Matheson, C.C. (1992). Sequences in the development of competent play with peers: Social and social pretend play. *Developmental Psychology, 28,* 961–974.

Kerns, K.A., & Barth, J.M. (1995). Attachment and play: Convergence across components of parent-child relationships and their relations to peer competence. *Journal of Social and Personal Relationships, 12,* 243–260.

Lamb, M. (1977). Father-infant and mother-infant interaction in the first year of life. *Child Development, 48,* 167–181.

Landy, S., & Menna, R. (1997). Mother's reactions to the aggressive play of their aggressive and nonaggressive young children: Implications for caregivers. *Early Child Development and Care, 138,* 1–20.

Leslie, A.M. (1987). Pretense and representation: The origins of theory of mind. *Psychological Review, 94,* 412–426.

Leslie, A.M. (1988). Some implications of pretense for mechanisms underlying the child's theory of mind. In J.W. Astington, P.L. Harris, & D.R. Olson (Eds.), *Developing theories of mind* (pp. 19–46). New York: Cambridge University Press.

Levy, D. (1938). Release therapy in young children. *Psychiatry, 1,* 387–389.

Li, A.K.F. (1985). Correlates and effects of training in make-believe play in preschool children. *Alberta Journal of Educational Research, 31,* 70–79.

Lillard, A.S. (1993). Pretend play skills and the child's theory of mind. *Child Development, 64,* 348–371.

MacDonald, K., & Parke, R.D. (1984). Bridging the gap: Parent-child play interaction and peer interactive competence. *Child Development, 55,* 1265–1277.

McCall, R.B., Hogarty, P.S., & Hurlburt, N. (1972). Transitions in infant sensorimotor development and the prediction of childhood IQ. *American Psychologist, 27,* 728–748.

Melragon, B.D. (1973). *A comparison of the sociodramatic play of low socioeconomic status black second grade children and low socioeconomic status black kindergarten children.* Unpublished doctoral dissertation, Ohio State University: Columbus.

Montessori, M. (1973). *The Montessori method.* Cambridge, MA: Bentley.

Morrison, C.D., Bundy, A.C., & Fisher, A.G. (1991). The contribution of motor skills and playfulness to the play performance of preschoolers. *American Journal of Occupational Therapy, 45,* 687–694.

Murphy, C.B. (1972). Infants' play and cognitive development. In M.W. Piers (Ed.), *Play and development.* New York: Norton.

New, R.S. (1994). Child's play-una cosa naturale: An Italian perspective. In J.L. Roopnarine, J.E. Johnson, & F.H. Hooper (Eds.), *Children's play in diverse cultures* (pp. 123–147). Albany: State University of New York Press.

O'Connell, B., & Bretherton, I. (1984). Toddler's play, alone and with mother: The role of maternal guidance. In I. Bretherton (Ed.), *Symbolic play: The development of social understanding* (pp. 337–368). San Diego: Academic Press.

Parten, M. (1932). Social participation among preschool children. *Journal of Abnormal and Social Psychology, 27,* 243–269.

Pellegrini, A.D., & Smith, P.K. (1998). Physical activity play: The nature and function of a neglected aspect of playing. *Child Development, 69,* 577–598.

Petrakos, H., & Howe, N. (1996). The influence of the physical design of the dramatic play center on children's play. *Early Childhood Research Quarterly, 11,* 63–77.

Piaget, J. (1962). *Play, dreams and imitation in childhood.* New York: Norton.

Riblatt, S.N. (1995). *Theory of mind in preschoolers: False beliefs, deception and pretense.* Paper presented at the biennial meeting of the Society for Research in Child Development, Indianapolis.

Rosen, C.E. (1974). The effects of sociodramatic play on problem-solving behavior among culturally disadvantaged preschool children. *Child Development, 45,* 920–927.

Rosen, C.S., Schwebel, D.C., & Singer, J.L. (1997). Preschoolers' attributions of mental states in pretense. *Child Development, 68,* 1113–1142.

Rubin, K.H., Fein, G.G., & Vandenberg, B. (1983). Play. In P.H. Mussen (Series Ed.) & E.M. Hetherington (Vol. Ed.), *Handbook of child psychology: Vol. 4. Socialization, personality, and social development* (4th ed., pp. 693–774). New York: John Wiley & Sons.

Rubin, K.H., Maioni, T.L., & Hornung, M. (1976). Free play behaviors in middle- and lower-class preschoolers: Parten and Piaget revisited. *Child Development, 47,* 414–419.

Saltz, E., Dixon, D., & Johnson, J. (1977). Training disadvantaged preschoolers on various fantasy activities: Effects on cognitive functioning and impulse control. *Child Development, 48,* 367–380.

Santostefano, S. (1978). *A biodevelopmental approach to clinical child psychology: Cognitive controls and cognitive control therapy.* New York: John Wiley & Sons.

Sears, S. (1977). *The relationship between sociodramatic play and school achievement of second grade low socioeconomic status black children.* Unpublished doctoral dissertation. Ohio State University: Columbus.

Segal, M., Peck, J., Vega-Lahr, N., & Field, T. (1987). A medieval kingdom: Leader-follower styles of preschool play. *Journal of Applied Developmental Psychology, 8,* 79–95.

Shmukler, D. (1979). Imaginative play in pre-school children as an indicator of emotional and cognitive development. *South African Journal of Psychology, 9,* 37–41.

Shmukler, D. (1981). Mother-child interaction and its relationship to the predisposition of imaginative play. *Genetic Psychology Monographs, 104,* 215–235.

Shmukler, D., & Naveh, I. (1984–1985). Structured vs. unstructured play training with economically disadvantaged preschoolers. *Imagination, Cognition and Personality, 4,* 293–304.

Sigel, J.E. (1986). Early social experience and the development of representational competence. *New directions of child development* (No. 32, pp. 49–65). San Francisco: Jossey-Bass.

Sigman, M., & Mundy, P. (1987). Symbolic processes in young autistic children. *New directions in child development* (No. 36, pp. 31–46). San Francisco: Jossey-Bass.

Singer, D.G. (1997). Imaginative play and television: Factors in a child's development. In J.A. Jefferson & P. Salovey (Eds.), *At play in the fields of consciousness: Essays in honor of Jerome L. Singer* (pp. 303–326). Mahwah, NJ: Lawrence Erlbaum Associates.

Singer, D.G., & Singer, J.L. (1990). *The house of make-believe: Children's play and the developing imagination.* Cambridge, MA: Harvard University Press.

Singer, D.G., & Singer, J.L (Eds.) (2000). *Handbook of children and the media.* Thousand Oaks, CA: Sage Publications.

Singer, J.L. (1973). Some practical implications of make-believe play. In J.L. Singer (Ed.), *The child's world of make-believe: Experimental studies of imaginative play* (pp. 231–259). San Diego: Academic Press.

Singer, M.I., Slovak, K., Frierson, T., & York, P. (1998). Viewing preferences, symptoms of psychological trauma, and violent behavior of children who watch television. *Journal of the American Academy of Child and Adolescent Psychiatry, 37,* 1041–1048.

Smalley, S.L., & Asarnow, R.F. (1990). Cognitive subclinical markers in autism. *Journal of Autism and Developmental Disorders, 20,* 271–278.

Smilansky, S. (1968). *The effects of sociodramatic play on disadvantaged preschool children.* New York: John Wiley & Sons.

Smith, P.K., & Whitney, S. (1987). Play and associative fluency: Experimenter effects may be responsible for previous positive findings. *Developmental Psychology, 23,* 49–53.

Smith, P.S., & Dutton, S. (1979). Play and training in direct and innovative problem solving. *Child Development, 50,* 830–836.

Susa, A.M., & Benedict, J.O. (1994). The effects of playground design on pretend play and divergent thinking. *Environment and Behavior, 26,* 560–579.

Sutton-Smith, B. (1985, October). The child at play. *Psychology Today, 19*(64), 2.

Tamis-LeMonda, C.S., & Bornstein, M.H. (1991). Individual variation, correspondence, stability, and change in mother and toddler play. *Infant Behavior and Development, 14,* 143–162.

Taylor, M., & Carlson, S.M. (1997). The relation between individual differences in fantasy and theory of mind. *Child Development, 68,* 436–455.

Tigerman, E., & Primavera, L. (1981). Object manipulation: An interactional strategy with autistic children. *Journal of Autism and Developmental Disorders, 11,* 427–438.

Tower, R.B. (1980). *The influence of parents' values on preschool children's behavior.* Unpublished doctoral dissertation, Yale University, New Haven, CT.

Udwin, O. (1983). Imaginative play training as an intervention method with institutionalised preschool children. *British Journal of Educational Psychology, 53,* 32–39.

Udwin, O., & Shmukler, D. (1981). The influence of sociocultural economic and home background factors on children's ability to engage in imaginative play. *Developmental Psychology, 17,* 66–72.

Vygotsky, L.S. (1966). Play and its role in the mental development of the child. In J.S. Bruner, A. Jolly, & K. Sylva (Eds.), *Play: Its role in development and evolution* (pp. 537–554). New York: Basic Books.

Vygotsky, L.S. (1978). *Mind in society: The development of higher psychological processes.* Cambridge, MA: Harvard University Press.

Weinstein, C.S., & Pinciotti, P. (1988). Changing a schoolyard: Intentions, design decisions, and behavioral outcomes. *Environment and Behavior, 20,* 345–371.

Wing, L., & Attwood, A. (1987). Syndromes of autism and pervasive developmental disorders. In D.J. Cohen, A.M. Donnellan, & R. Paul (Eds.), *Handbook of autism and pervasive developmental disorders* (pp. 3–28). New York: John Wiley & Sons.

Wing, L., Gould, J., Yeates, S.R., & Brierly, L.M. (1977). Symbolic play in severely mentally retarded and in autistic children. *Journal of Child Psychology and Psychiatry and Allied Disciplines, 18,* 167–178.

Wodrich, D.L. (2000). *Attention-deficit/hyperactivity disorder: What every parent wants to know* (2nd ed.). Baltimore: Paul H. Brookes Publishing Co.

Wolf, D.P. & Gardner, H. (1979). Style and sequence in early symbolic play. In N.R. Smith & M.B. Franklin (Eds.), *Symbolic functioning in childhood* (pp. 117–138). Mahwah, NJ: Lawrence Erlbaum Associates.

Wolf, D.P., & Grollman, S.H. (1982). Ways of playing: Individual differences in imaginative style. In D.J. Pepler & K.H. Rubin (Eds.), *The play of children: Current theory and research* (pp. 46–63). Basel, Switzerland: Karger.

Wolfberg, P.J. (1995). Enhancing children's play. In K.A. Quill (Ed.), *Teaching children with autism.* New York: Delmar.

Yarrow, L.J., Rubenstein, J.L., & Pedersen, F.A. (1975). *Infant and environment: Early cognitive and motivational development.* Washington, DC: Hemisphere.

Youngblade, L.M., & Dunn, J. (1995). Individual differences in young children's pretend play with mother and sibling: Links to relationships and understanding of other people's feelings and beliefs. *Child Development, 66,* 1472–1492.

FURTHER READING ON THE TOPIC

Axline, V. (1981). *Play therapy.* New York: Ballantine Books.

Bettelheim, B. (1989). *The uses of enchantment: The meaning and importance of fairy tales.* New York: Vantage Books.

Bretherton, I. (Ed.). (1984). *Symbolic play: The development of social understanding.* San Diego: Academic Press.

Britton, L. (1992). *Montessori play and learn.* London: Random House.

Bruner, J.S., Jolly, A., & Sylva, K. (Eds.). (1976). *Play: Its role in development and evolution.* Middlesex, England: Penguin UK.

Burtt, K.G., & Kalkstein, K. (1981). *Smart toys for babies from birth to two.* New York: Harper & Row.

Butler, D. (1998). *Babies need books: Sharing the joy of books with your child from birth to six.* Portsmouth, NH: Heinemann.

Casby, M.W. (1991). Symbolic play I: A developmental framework. *Infant-Toddler Intervention, 1,* 219–231.

Casby, M.W. (1991). Symbolic play II: A unified model. *Infant-Toddler Intervention, 1,* 223–243.

Christie, J.F. (1982). Sociodramatic play training. *Young Children, 37,* 25–32.

Christie, J.F. (1985). Training of symbolic play. *Early Child Development and Care, 19,* 43–52.

DeMille, R. (1994). *Put your mother on the ceiling: Children's imagination games.* New York: Viking.

Engel, S. (1995). *The stories children tell: Making sense of the narratives of childhood.* New York: W.H. Freeman.

Fintushel, N. (1992, May). When it's work to play. *Parents Magazine, 67*(5), 93.

Fisher, J.J. (1986). *Toys to grow with: Infants and toddlers: Endless play ideas that make learning fun.* New York: Putnam.

Fisher, J.J. (1987). *More toys to grow with: Infants and toddlers: Unique ideas for making everyday routines fun.* New York: Putnam.

Gestwicki, C. (1999). *Developmentally appropriate practice: Curriculum and development in early education* (2nd ed.). New York: Delmar Publishers.

Gil, E. (1991). *The healing power of play: Working with abused children.* New York: Guilford Press.

Greenfield, P.M. (1984). *Mind and media: The effects of television, video games, and computers.* Cambridge, MA: Harvard University Press.

Gregg, E.M., & Boston Children's Medical Center (1968). *What to do when there's nothing to do: 601 tested play ideas for young children.* New York: Delacorte Press.

Gunsberg, A. (1991). Improvised musical play with delayed and nondelayed children. *Childhood Education, 67,* 223–226.

Hagstrom, J. (1986). *Games toddlers play.* New York: Pocket Books.

Hagstrom, J., & Morrill, J. (1984). *Games babies play: A handbook of games to play with infants.* New York: Pocket Books.

Hagstrom, J., & Morrill, J. (1985). *More games babies play: Fun with babies from birth through the first birthday.* New York: Pocket Books.

Hanna, S., & Wilford, S. (1990). *Floor time: Tuning in to each child* (includes videotape and booklet). New York: Scholastic.

Herron, R.E., & Sutton-Smith, B. (1971). *Child's play.* New York: John Wiley & Sons.

Hitz, R. (1987). Creative problem solving through music activities. *Young Children, 42,* 12–17.

Jenkins, P.D. (1993). *Art for the fun of it: A guide for teaching young children.* New York: Prentice Hall Press.

Kraft, A. (1973). *Are you listening to your child? How to bridge the communication gap through creative play sessions.* New York: Walker & Co.

Levine, J.B. (1988). Play in the context of the family. *Journal of Family Psychology, 2,* 164–187.

Levine, K. (1991, January). What's your child's play style? *Parents Magazine, 66*(5), 62.

Lowenfeld, M. (1987). *Play in childhood.* New York: Cambridge University Press.

MacDonald, K. (Ed.). (1993). *Parent-child play: Descriptions and implications.* Albany: State University of New York Press.

Martin, T. (1982). *The pre-school craft book: Activities for the 2 to 5s in kindergartens, groups, nursery schools, and at home.* Sydney, Australia: Reed.

McCaslin, N. (1984). *Creative drama in the classroom.* New York: Longman.

Millar, S. (1968). *The psychology of play.* Harmondsworth, England: Penguin.

Oaklander, V. (1989). *Windows to our children: A Gestalt therapy approach to children and adolescents.* New York: The Center for Gestalt Development.

Oppenheim, J.F. (1984). *Kids and play.* New York: Ballantine Books.

Piers, M. (1988). *The gift of play: And why some children cannot thrive without it.* New York: Walker & Co.

Pines, M. (1978, September). Invisible playmates. *Psychology Today, 38*–100.

Roopnarine, J.L., Johnson, J.E., & Hooper, F.H. (Eds.). (1994). *Children's play in diverse cultures.* Albany: State University of New York Press.

Rosenthal, A. (1988, May). How fantasy helps kids grow. *Parents Magazine, 63,* 90(5).

Rubin, J.A. (1984). *Child art therapy: Understanding and helping children grow through art.* New York: John Wiley & Sons.

Segal, M. (1991). *Your child at play: Birth to one year.* New York: Newmarket Press.

Segal, M., & Adcock, D. (1985). *Your child at play: Two to three years.* New York: Newmarket Press.

Segal, M., & Adcock, D. (1991). *Your child at play: One to two years.* New York: Newmarket Press.

Segal, M., & Adcock, D. (1991). *Your child at play: Three to five years.* New York: Newmarket Press.

Singer, D.G., & Singer, J.L. (1977). *Partners in play: A step-by-step guide to imaginative play in children.* New York: Harper & Row.

Solnit, A.J., Cohen, D.J., & Neubauer, P.B. (1993). *The many meanings of play: A psychoanalytic perspective.* New Haven, CT: Yale University Press.

Sparling, J., & Lewis, I. (1984). *Learning games for the first three years: A guide to parent-child play.* New York: Walker & Co.

Sparling, J., & Lewis, I. (1984). *Learning games for threes and fours.* New York: Berkeley Books.

Stallibrass, A. (1989). *The self-respecting child: Development through spontaneous play.* Reading, MA: Addison-Wesley.

Sutton-Smith, B. (1974). *How to play with your children (and when not to).* New York: Hawthorn Books.

Weissbourd, B. (1987, June). The great pretender. *Parents Magazine, 62*(1), 158.

Winnicott, D.W. (1982). *Playing and reality.* New York: Routledge.

CHILDREN'S BOOKS ABOUT PLAY AND IMAGINATION

Agee, J. (1990). *The incredible painting of Felix Clousseau.* New York: Sunburst.

Asch, F. (1984). *Goodnight horsey.* Englewood Cliffs, NJ: Simon & Schuster.

Browne, A. (1990). *Changes.* London: MacRae Books.

Burningham, J. (1978). *Time to get out of the bath, Shirley.* London: J. Cape.

Burningham, J. (1992). *Come away from the water, Shirley.* London: Red Fox.

Burningham, J. (1994). *Would you rather . . . .* London: Red Fox.

Carrick, C. (1983). *Patrick's dinosaurs.* New York: Houghton Mifflin.

Carrick, C. (1988). *What happened to Patrick's dinosaurs?* New York: Houghton Mifflin.

Chapman, K.W. (1976). *The magic hat.* Chapel Hill, NC: Lollipop Power.

Cohen, M. (1989). *Jim meets the Thing.* New York: Yearling Books.

Cooke, T. (1994). *So much.* Cambridge, MA: Candlewick Press.

Cooney, N.E. (1990). *Go away monsters, lickety split!* New York: Putnam.

Denton, K.M. (1995). *Would they love a lion?* New York: Kingfisher Books.

Emberley, E. (1992). *Go away, big green monster!* Boston: Little, Brown.

Gackenbach, D. (1984). *Harry and the terrible whatzit.* New York: Houghton Mifflin.

Gardner, R.A. (1978). *Dr. Gardner's fairy tales for today's children.* Cresskill, NJ: Creative Therapeutics.

Harrison, T. (1997). *Don't dig so deep, Nicholas!* Toronto: Owl Communications.

Johnson, C. (1999). *Harold and the purple crayon.* New York: Econo-Clad Books.

Jonas, A. (1989). *The trek.* New York: Mulberry Books.

Khalsa, D.K. (1990). *Cowboy dreams.* New York: Clarkson N. Potter.

Khalsa, D.K. (1997). *I want a dog.* Montreal, Canada: Tundra Books.

Lionni, L. (1990). *Frederick.* New York: Alfred A. Knopf.

Mayer, M. (1968). *There's a nightmare in my closet.* New York: Dial Press.

McConnachie, B. (1992). *Elmer and the chickens vs. the big league.* New York: Crown Publishers.

McLerran, A. (1991). *Roxaboxen.* New York: Lothrop, Lee & Shepard Books.

McPhail, D. (1985). *Pig Pig rides.* New York: Dutton Children's Books.

Russo, M. (1986). *The line up book.* New York: Greenwillow Books.

Sendak, M. (1988). *Where the wild things are.* New York: HarperCollins Children's Books.

Sendak, M. (1995). *In the night kitchen.* New York: HarperCollins Children's Books.

Seuss, Dr. (1975). *Oh, the thinks you can think!* New York: Random House.

Shaw, C.G. (1993). *It looked like spilt milk.* New York: HarperCollins Children's Books.

Shulevits, U. (1986). *One Monday morning.* New York: Aladdin Books.

Steig, W. (1988). *Sylvester and the magic pebble.* New York: Simon & Schuster Books for Young Readers.

Stinson, K. (1990). *The dressed up book.* Willowdale, Ontario: Annick Press.

Stone, K.G. (1990). *Good night Twinklegator.* New York: Scholastic.

Tafuri, N. (1988). *Junglewalk.* New York: Greenwillow Books.

APPENDIX: SELECTED ASSESSMENT INSTRUMENTS

Play observations are often used to assess children's developmental status as well as their emotional and social development. Many of these observations use videotaped sessions, and if the child is 1 year old or older the child's capacity for pretend play and language are considered. Sometimes observations are scored and researchers and clinicians use a variety of standardized scales to examine various dimensions of play behavior, described here:

Measures of Children's Play

Table A4.1 describes some commonly used instruments to assess children's play, while Table A4.2 describes assessments that study play interactions between parents and infants or children.

Table A4.1. Selected assessments of children's play

Tool/instrument	Age range	Items/administration time	General description
Children's Playfulness Scale (CPS) Barnett, L.A. (1991). The playful child: Measurement of a disposition to play. *Play and Culture, 4,* 51–74.	2–5 years	23 items, 10 minutes	The *Children's Playfulness Scale (CPS)* uses a response scale ranging from "sounds exactly like the child" to "doesn't sound at all like the child." It assesses a child on five playfulness dimensions: 1) physical spontaneity, 2) social spontaneity, 3) cognitive spontaneity, 4) manifest joy, and 5) sense of humor. In addition, a general playfulness factor is obtained. The questionnaire is completed by child care teachers who have been able to observe the child over time.
The Developmental Play Assessment (DPA) Lifter, K. (1999). Linking assessment to intervention for children with developmental disabilities or at-risk for developmental delays: The Developmental Play Assessment (DPA) instrument. In K. Gitlin-Werner, A. Sandgrund, & C. Shaefer, *Play assessment and diagnosis.* New York: John Wiley & Sons.	Late infancy–preschool years	30 minutes	The *Developmental Play Assessment (DPA)* assesses the play of children with developmental delays in order to design individualized programming for them. The DPA assesses the frequency and variety of activities within each play category based on a 30-minute sample of the child's naturally occurring, unstructured play activities.
MacArthur Story-Stem Battery Bretherton, I., Prentiss, C., & Ridgeway, D. (1990). Family relationships as represented in a story-completion task at 37 and 54 months of age. In I. Bretherton & M.W. Watson (Eds.), *Children's perspectives on the family* (pp. 85–106). San Francisco: Jossey-Bass.	3–7 years	12 items, 30 minutes	The *MacArthur Story-Stem Battery* uses a standardized set of story beginnings and asks children to finish the stories using dolls, toys, and play furniture. The stories cover a wide range of events that relate to family relationships, such as being separated from parents and moral dilemmas. Contents are coded for the emotions displayed, themes expressed in the play (e.g., aggression, personal injury, sadness, concern), and the way the child told the stories.
Play Observation Scale (POS) Rubin, K.H. (1989). Sociability and social withdrawal in childhood: Stability and outcomes. *Journal of Personality, 57,* 239–255.	2–6 years	5-minute observation of play	The *Play Observation Scale (POS)* is an observational system used for rating free play. It evaluates the child's social and cognitive play and nonplay behaviors. The child is observed for a 10-second interval and the next 5–10 minutes are used to code the predominant activity observed and to record it on the scoring sheet. Up to 5 minutes of behavior are recorded on a given day. Affective quality of the play with other children also is recorded.
Play Rating Scales (PRS) Saracho, O.N. (1984). Construction and validation of the play rating scale. *Early Child Care and Education, 17,* 229–236.	3–5 years	16 items, 10 minutes	The *Play Rating Scales (PRS)* are used to assess four different play behaviors within four different forms of educational play: 1) physical play, 2) block play, 3) manipulative play, and 4) dramatic play. The scales describe the frequency of play, ability, and creativity to communicate ideas and social levels of participation in their play. The PRS provides detailed instructions for recording the observations.
Symbolic Play Test (SPT) 2nd Edition Lowe, M., & Costello, A.J. (1976). *The Symbolic Play Test.* Berkshire, England: NFER Nelson Publishing.	1–3 years	Four situations used; 30 minutes	The *Symbolic Play Test (SPT)* has been developed to use with children who have not developed receptive or expressive language. The child is presented with four separate sets of toys that are used in order to elicit free play from the child. Only minimal verbal instructions are given. Responses are scored for their representation of the objects according to how they are played with.

Table A4.2. Measures to assess play interactions between parents and infants or children

Tool/instrument	Age range
Emotional Availability Scales Biringen, Z., Robinson, J.L., & Emde, R.N. (1993). *Manual for scoring the Emotional Availability Scales.* Boulder, CO: University of Colorado.	Infants to school age
Parent-Child Early Relational Assessment (ERA) Clark, R. (1985). *The Parent–Child Early Relational Assessment Manual and Instrument.* University of Wisconsin Medical School, Department of Psychiatry, Madison, WI.	2 months–5 years
Mother-Infant/Toddler Play Scale Chatoor, I., & Menvielle, E. (1986). *Manual of the Observational Scale for Mother-Infant Toddler Play.* Washington, DC: Children's National Medical Center.	Birth–3 years
Parent/Caregiver Involvement Scale (P/CIS) Farran, D.C. (1986). *Parent/Caregiver Involvement Scale Workbook.* School of Human Environmental Science, the University of North Carolina at Greensboro.	Birth–6 years

● ● ● 5

ENCOURAGING LANGUAGE AND COMMUNICATION

When a problem arises within an organization, a family, a marital relationship, or between parent and child or even two countries, most people believe that a communication breakdown has occurred. At the very least, people generally view a lack of communication as an important contributor to problems in any relationship.

Communication can become difficult for a number of reasons. Some of the problems may rest with the sender of the message, while some rest with the listener, and others may result from noise or situations that are occurring at the time of the communication. Obviously, when participating in communication, individuals usually alternate between communicator and listener as messages are sent, received, and returned. As is discussed in this chapter, messages can get "lost" or are misinterpreted for a number of reasons, particularly by caregivers as they communicate with children. Many of these misinterpretations can be eliminated or improved, however.

In today's society, communication in families and between parents and children is becoming increasingly difficult. Some of the reasons include the following:

- Children and/or parents watch television excessively.

- Children are very involved with video or computer games.

- Parents are working and have extremely busy lifestyles, with little time for conversation.

- Families use physical means for expressing feelings rather than talking about issues.

- Yelling has become a way of "communicating" because of the models parents have been exposed to and the stress of busy schedules.

Improving communication, negotiating, and talking together are usually identified as ways to help resolve the problem. Good communication skills are crucial and vitally important in order for an individual to succeed in school, work, and in relationships. Consequently, learning to communicate in childhood is an important skill and necessary for developing a number of the competencies talked about in this book. In spite of stresses and changes in today's families, it remains critical for children to feel listened to and for them to learn to communicate clearly to others.

DEFINITIONS OF LANGUAGE AND COMMUNICATION

Words such as *communication, speech,* and *language* are used by everyone, often without the understanding of the important differences between the terms. As well, the literature on speech and language often contains a vast number of complicated terms that can make reading about it extremely challenging. For this reason, a list of the commonly used terms is included here:

- *Communication* involves the transfer of information between people by verbal or nonverbal means. People communicate in various ways: through the spoken and written word, facial expressions, gestures and body language, and even by silence.

- *Language* can be made up of gestures, signs, or words that have agreed-to meanings. Words are put together in a certain order and obey certain rules, such as grammar or syntax, making them understandable by the receiver. Language is further divided into receptive language and expressive language. *Receptive* language refers to language that is understood, whether conveyed in words or gestures. Many children understand more than they can say and can follow instructions that contain words that they cannot say themselves. Others may have great difficulty decoding words and have limited receptive vocabularies. *Expressive* language is the use of a socially shared code or system to communicate. The expressive vocabulary of some children may be much smaller than their receptive vocabulary. Other children use a lot of words in a parrot-like fashion yet understand very little of what they have said.

- *Speech* refers to the movements of the vocal and articulation system and to the sounds that come out of our mouths in the form of words. Speech, unlike language, could be a set of nonsense words while language does not always have to involve spoken words and includes sign language used by the deaf. Table 5.1 defines a number of other terms related to language and speech.

THEORIES OF LANGUAGE AND COMMUNICATION

Theories of language and communication vary according to the extent to which they emphasize language acquisition as innate or influenced by the child's social environment and its language input. A number of theorists have considered the development of language, and particularly the developmental changes in other areas—such as cognition and emotions—that influence it (see Table 5.2).

As yet, no one theory is assumed to be *the* correct one, and each gives insight into the processes of language development and acquisition that need to be considered. It is unlikely

Table 5.1. Important definitions related to speech and language acquisition

Term	Definition
Babbling	Sounds that are repeated, involving at least one consonant and one vowel; usually used by infants between 6 months and 1 year (e.g., "baba," "da")
Conversation	Occurs when two people take turns as speaker and listener and do this smoothly and with consideration of the relationship between participants (e.g., Child: "Play with me." Parent: "Okay, what would you like to play?")
Cooing	An early stage of the prelinguistic period when vowels are repeated (e.g., "ah," "oo")
Echolalia	Sounds or words are repeated over and over again or the child repeats the words other people say to him
Grammar	The study of word structures and word sequences
Mean length of utterance (MLU)	The average number of words per sentence; includes each word and inflections such as "s" or "ed"
Morphemes	The smallest units that can help in understanding the meaning of a sentence (e.g., "dog," "swim," -s, -ing)
Morphology	The study of how morphemes are combined to form larger words
Parentese/Motherese/ Child-Directed Speech (CDS)	Particular pattern of speech used by adults with babies and young children; is higher pitched, simpler, and more repetitive than speech used with other adults
Phoneme	The smallest unit of sound in a word (e.g., /b/, /h/, /a/)
Phonetics	The characteristics of sounds and the movements of the mouth used to make the sounds (e.g., "b" and "p" made between the lips)
Phonology	The study of the production of sounds and understanding of sounds and the relationship between sounds and meanings (e.g., may say "dwink" for "drink" or "wed" for "red")
Pragmatics	The appropriate use of language in various situations, including certain rules that involve how language is used in social situations and fits with other aspects of functioning (e.g., "Can I play with you?")
Semantics	The meaning of speech (e.g., "push truck," means "Help me push my truck")
Syntax	The sequence or structure of words within sentences or speech (e.g., "After you tear them out, stick them on")
Telegraphic speech	Characteristic of children's early language in which everything but the crucial words are omitted, similar to a telegram (e.g., "milk all gone" means "My milk is all gone")

that any one point of view will be sufficient or that a consensus will be reached. Each can bring a special insight to the understanding of language and communication, and certain emerging theories described later in this chapter are evident.

THE IMPORTANCE OF LANGUAGE AND COMMUNICATION

Language is one of the most important aspects of development and enables both children and adults to communicate with each other. In fact, without it today's complex society and civilization probably could not exist. Language helps us think, problem-solve, learn, remember, and understand what we see. It helps people maintain friendships even at a distance. It helps us use a computer and enables government and organizations to respond to their members. In fact, its uses are too numerous to mention them all.

Language acquisition is one of a young child's most impressive achievements. Most young children go from no words in infancy to a productive vocabulary of at least 2,500 words by age 6. They have an understanding of as many as 14,000 words and the ability to use complex sen-

Table 5.2. Theories of language and communication

Theorist	Type of theory	Major constructs
Vygotsky (1962)	Social process theory	Children learn that words are used to communicate only through social interactions.
		Communication develops out of the adults' responses to the child's gestures and words.
		Without social experiences, advances in language would not occur.
McNeill (1966)	Universality of language	Every language uses the same basic syntactic categories and grammatical relationships between them.
		Child may be prewired to detect certain categories of speech, which McNeill has called a Language Acquisition Device (LAD). Children process speech and learn a set of rules about it (e.g., grammar).
Lenneberg (1967)	Critical period theory	A critical period exists (from early childhood to puberty) during which language must be learned if it is to fully develop. Beyond this period, acquiring a first language becomes far more difficult.
		Research that shows the age at which deaf individuals learn to sign significantly relates to their ability in processing of sign language as adults.
Chomsky (1986)	Nativist or innateness theory	Sees the capacity to develop language and general form of language as programmed into the brain.
		Describes sentences as existing at two levels. The meaning (i.e., what the person wants to say) is contained in *deep structure* while the sentence as spoken is the *surface structure*. Earliest sentences come out of this deep structure, and as language develops the child learns the rules to turn basic meaning into complex sentences.
Bloom (1991, 1993)	Cognitive and affective theory	Theory based on longitudinal study of children from different backgrounds who were followed from infancy to 3 years of age.
		Describes how affective and infants' cognitive development influences their acquisition of language.
		Posits that intentionality is central to the learning of language and includes the child's feelings, beliefs, and wants.
		Intersubjectivity—or being with another person—drives the development of intentionality.

tences. Research has identified a number of significant relationships between the level of language achieved or the ability to communicate and a variety of important aspects of development that continue to affect an individual well into adulthood. Some of these are described here.

Strengthening Peer Relationships

From the time a child has reached 2 years of age, the ability to talk becomes more and more central to his life. In order to gain acceptance and be allowed to join in the play of his or her peers, a child has to be able to say the right words in the right way. In fact, a child's communication skills have been found to relate significantly to his or her popularity and acceptability to other children. Talking is vital to play interactions, and children with speech problems may have difficulty understanding what is going on and in repeating phrases that are relevant to the

type of play in which children are engaged. Language is necessary in order to talk about plans and to build a friendship, and just to tell another person that he or she is your "best friend."

Communicating within the Family

Because communication relies on giving clear messages, children who have a great deal of difficulty with speech will be severely compromised in the ability to let family members know their feelings, needs, and desires. Sometimes a child who seems to be having difficulty with paying attention and being part of family discussions may actually be having problems understanding what is being said and responding appropriately.

Fostering School Achievement/Cognitive Ability

Although not all subjects in school are dependent on speech and language, many are (e.g., English, social studies, foreign languages, general science). Even with subjects that do not depend so much on language (e.g., mechanics, geometry, algebra), children still need to listen, read instructions, and communicate. Moreover, language skills are related to subsequent reading skills, a central tool in all formal instruction.

Avoiding Emotional or Behavioral Disorders

Recent research has shown that children with language delays and disorders are at risk for developing psychiatric, emotional, or behavioral disorders. In fact, as many as 45% of children with language impairments have various psychiatric disorders. Among preschool children with language impairments, the prevalence has been found to be as high as 49% (Beitchman et al., 1996). This co-occurrence of language disorders and emotional disorders in children occurred in at least three countries and in a variety of studies. The causal link between the two has not been determined; however, it is clear that children who have good auditory processing and language skills are better able to listen and to get their message across, and therefore they feel less frustrated and more understood. In fact, many parents are surprised to find that tantrums subside and behavior dramatically improves as children acquire enough language to allow them to use words and to talk about their anger, frustration, and unhappiness. This ability to talk about feelings and emotions can significantly enhance the child's capacity for self-control and reduce the incidence of acting-out behavior.

DEVELOPMENT OF LANGUAGE AND COMMUNICATION

Speech and language development go through significant changes in the first 3–6 years of life, which allows clear delineation into stages (see Table 5.3). These stages are usually referred to as the preverbal (or prespeech) stage; first words or beginnings of speech; first sentences; and grammatization, which goes with increased elaboration of language. The explosion of words occurring in the typically developing child at approximately 18 months of age and the beginning of the ability to use complex sentences, with correct grammar, in the third year are quite remarkable achievements and appear quite effortlessly.

Table 5.3. Development of language and communication through the stages of a child's life

Stage	Age	Receptive language/ listening/understanding	Expressive language/ talking	Discourse/communication
PREVERBAL	Birth	Listens to sounds Responds to speech by turning to voice Startles and cries at noises Awakens at loud noises	Coos and gurgles Cries with loud, clear voice	Facial expressions, body posture, as well as cries give a great deal of information to caregivers No intentional communication but emotions are conveyed to caregiver
	Birth–3 months	Tries to turn to someone who is speaking Smiles when spoken to Seems to recognize parent's or other familiar voice Stops playing, crying, or sucking and appears to listen to a sudden new sound or speech Can distinguish between sounds such as "ba" and "pa"	Babbles with some vowel sounds (e.g., "ba-ba-ba") Cries differently for different needs (e.g., pain, hunger) Laughs when happy Repeats the same sounds over and over again with intonation changes Smiles at people	Increased engagement with caregiver Action and language-based interactions with caregiver Familiar face may produce cooing Beginning of use of gestures such as hand waving, index finger pointing
	3–6 months	Enjoys a musical toy Is quieted by mother's voice and recognizes angry tone of voice or "No" Turns in general direction of a new or sudden sound Understands and quiets to facial expressions	Makes many different sounds (e.g., gurgling when alone) Makes babbling sounds like adult speech, only not clear Seems to enjoy making sounds with voice, such as "oh-oh," or "mama" Tries games such as Pat-a-Cake and waving "bye-bye"	Uses babbling and other sounds to get attention Reciprocal exchanges with imitation of cooing and babbling with caregiver
	6–9 months	Responds to "No" Turns head when name is called Looks directly at new sound or voice and listens Listens to people talking Responds to many cries and routines with ritualized language	Enjoys imitating sounds, particularly "ah" sound Uses voice to get attention, may whine Makes more and different sounds and jabbers Uses jargon (babbling that sounds like real speech) Engages in repeating sounds Shakes head to say "No" Likes music	Looks when caregiver points at something (i.e., joint attention) Enjoys engaging in "conversations" with turn-taking Adult intonations are imitated May grin at caregiver to get attention Uses a lot of gestures and facial expressions to communicate Enjoys games such as Peek-a-Boo

Stage	Age	Receptive language/ listening/understanding	Expressive language/ talking	Discourse/communication
FIRST WORDS	9–12 months	Understands own name Follows spoken directions Responds to verbal requests Appears to understand simple questions Responds to rhythmic music and moves hand or body in approximate time to the beat Understands several words or phrases Recognizes names of familiar people and actions Looks at Daddy in response to "Where's Daddy?" Understands 30 words, especially common ones such as "juice"	Use of consonants begins to exceed vowels Says two to three words with consistency (e.g., "Dada!" Mama!" "No!") Vocalizes to songs or nursery rhymes Tries to imitate new words Points to a few body parts Vowel sounds have adult form	Increasingly uses communicative signals intentionally to get caregiver's attention Waves "bye-bye" Reaches to be picked up Attracts attention and points to things in environment Coordinates objects and social scheme (e.g., if cannot reach something, will cry or signal by reaching towards it) Gesture and eye contact goes with vocalization Increase in sharing and protest gestures such as showing, giving, turning away
FIRST SENTENCES	12–18 months	Points to parts of body (e.g., nose, ear) Identifies object when named Appears to understand more new words each week Stops when told "No" Follows simple directions or questions (e.g., "Roll the ball," "Where is the doll?") Responds to name Understands 200 words	Says 10 meaningful words Uses words rather than pointing to express wants and needs Repeats words overheard in conversation May use two word utterances Uses intonation of questioning	Uses verbal and nonverbal ways to communicate Waits and fills turn in interactions and can engage in multiple turns Speech is now much more a social means of expression Imitates a few sounds such as clicking with tongue Uses back-and-forth touches Enjoys interactive games with words and actions Continues to integrate gestures with vocalizations
	18–24 months	Follows directions such as "Drink your juice" Points to more body parts Can follow two verbal commands (e.g., "Get the pencil and close the door.") Enjoys being read to Recognizes and identifies pictures of common objects Understands 500 words Comprehends more language than can say Understands prepositons (e.g., "in," "on") Understands simple questions	Has vocabulary "explosion" Has expressive vocabulary of 50–300 words, uses some verbs and adjectives Puts two words together Refers to self by name or third person (e.g., "me") Asks simple questions with correct intonation (e.g., "Where is my book?")	Engages in simple two-way conversations May get simultaneous vocalization at times and can be very joyful at moments Increasingly uses questions such as "What's that?"

(continued)

Table 5.3. *(continued)*

Stage	Age	Receptive language/ listening/understanding	Expressive language/ talking	Discourse/communication
GRAMMATIZATION AND INCREASED ELABORATION	24–36 months	Understands time concepts Understands verbs, adjectives, prepositions, and pronouns (e.g., "come/go," "big/little," "on/under," "me/you") Understands longer and more complex sentences and about 1,000 words Notices and locates a sound out of sight Makes eye contact Attends to other people's conversations Can understand language about past and future events Points to pictures in books when asked	Uses some complex sentences of three to five words, with correct organization of words Says at least 500 different words Uses correct grammatical inflections that increase in complexity Uses "and" Uses a few plurals and past tense Can communicate about future and past events Refers to self using "I" or "me"	Responds to questions Likes to listen in on conversations Carries on a conversation and understands most words Keeps conversation going by asking questions about "who," "what," and "where" Can manage turn-taking in dialogue and sustain longer interaction sequences with remarks relevant to other person's Learns ways to enter a peer group and what to say Can explain to someone what he wants and wishes to be
	3–4 years	Answers simple questions Carries out a sequence of two to three directions Understands conversation easily Hears when called from another room Hears television or radio at average loudness level Has receptive vocabulary of 1,500 words Can repeat 5- to 10-word sentence	Talk about things not present Uses connecting words such as "but" and "because" Gives a connected account of recent experiences; begins to refer to future Asks many questions and gives directions Says at least 600 different words Uses 4- to 6-word sentences Recites nursery rhymes and sings songs Uses all parts of speech Speech now more readily understood by people outside family	Can be understood by most people and knows how to get their attention Increasingly engages in conversations and keeps them going Can sustain conversations with peers Continues to ask questions.
	4–6 years	Hears and understands most speech in the home Hears and answers when first called Hears quiet speech Understands 2,000 words Can understand movies Recognizes familiar signs like a stop sign Begins to recognize letters and sounds they make	Says almost all sounds correctly Uses the same sentence structure as adults in the family Voice sounds clear Has 50% of language development Describes a picture or what a word means Uses pronouns correctly. Has vocabulary of 2,000 words at 4 years, 10,000–14,000 at 6 years Tells stories that were read to them before in a book Names four colors	Takes turns in conversation and consistently uses words rather than physical actions to express anger Is capable of mature conversations, listening to the others' point of view and responding appropriately Can resolve conflicts with words Uses speech to disagree with others as well as to link with them

Preverbal and First Words Stages

The first 9 months of a child's life is considered a time before speech. This stage can be further broken down into a number of stages.

Birth to Six Months The period from birth to 6 months is a preverbal or prelinguistic stage, and the infant does not have intentional communication with sounds until approximately 3 months. Nevertheless, even from birth the infant's hearing is exquisitely attuned to the human voice and can even distinguish a variety of sounds like "ba" and "pa," quite an amazing achievement in the first month of life. But it is not until the end of the first year that infants begin to be able to understand meaningful speech and the transition from prespeech to language becomes possible.

In the first 2 weeks of life, infant sounds are restricted primarily to crying. Until caregivers can begin to determine the meaning of their baby's cries, a baby that cries excessively can be quite overwhelming. Gradually, most parents begin to understand what the cries mean. They can discern whether the baby is hungry, bored, wants attention, needs his diaper changed, is in pain, or maybe just needs to "let off steam." Many babies have a particular time of day when crying occurs most frequently; many babies experience this fussiness at the time of the evening meal. By 6 weeks, the infant is communicating with responsive smiling and sometimes other facial expressions that convey disgust, surprise, frustration, and even anger.

Other sounds begin to be used by about 2–3 months, including laughing and cooing. By 3 months, many infants begin to play with speech sounds when they are alone and, in addition, begin to play vocal games and to repeat sounds that are imitated by their caregivers. By 5 months these sounds are often repeated over and over again with varying pitch and volume so that they sound like words or speech. At about the same time a baby uses the sounds rather than crying to get attention, which is a very important occurrence for parents. These sounds are a great substitute to the crying that the baby always used before. By 6 months, many babies can begin to use consonants in their repertoire, usually beginning with *m, h, k,* and *g.* They often combine them with a vowel sound to make something like a word; *ga, ma,* and *da.* By 6 months, some babies may already enjoy taking part in games with actions and words such as Pat-a-cake and This Little Piggy Went to Market.

From about 4 months on, infants often use gestures with vocalizations or to follow words. These gestures may include prepointing (in which the index finger is extended) and hand waving.

Six to Twelve Months During this stage, the baby's sounds take on the intonation or patterns of adult speech. This jargon may rise at the end of a string of sounds and use a speech-like rhythm, even though the child is still only making meaningless sounds. It is interesting to note that by the time the child is about 5–6 months old, sounds are becoming narrowed down to those of her language, and sounds not in the language are no longer used. This is an indication that her sounds are now being matched more closely to the sounds she is hearing in the environment. By this time, the infant is beginning to repeat sounds made by others as well as her own sounds. Much of this vocal play is still more feedback she is giving herself, rather than communication with others. Nevertheless, sounds are sometimes used to get attention, and infants continue to listen to people talking and are quieted by a caregiver's voice. During this period the changeover from babbling to first words takes place, almost as if the baby learned how to make the babbling sound like words before the actual words appear—but the process appears to be a continuous one from one to the other.

Between 9 and 12 months, enormous changes take place in the baby's communication and language skills. Perhaps most important, gestures, actions and beginning words start to be used with greater intentionality. Not only does the infant understand an increasing number of words and phrases and recognize some names of people, but also she begins to engage in episodes of joint attention. In these episodes she may draw attention to an object by pointing, may follow the pointing of a caregiver, or may reach for something out of reach. At other times she may not just show or point to an object but may actually give it as another way of sharing attention with a caregiver. She may reach to be picked up or tug at her mother's clothes for attention and wave to someone she knows. Apart from these exciting gains in the capacity for joint attention and intentionality in communicating, the first two or three words begin to be used consistently. Language is beginning.

The First Sentences

From the time a typically developing child has reached the age of 1, the exciting verbalization of language has begun.

Twelve to Eighteen Months The period from 12 to 18 months is primarily a time of gradual vocabulary growth. It would seem that once the first word is used, at least partly because of the reaction she receives, the toddler is motivated to repeat the words and to learn more. In this period, usually about 10 words are learned and one- or two-word utterances may begin to be used. Most gains are made in the area of receptive language, and by the end of this period the infant may understand more than 200 words. As well, she may be able to point to pictures when an object is named and can understand simple directives or instructions such as "no," "roll the ball," or "where is the doll?"

Eighteen to Twenty-Four Months When a child reaches the age of approximately 18 months, a rapid increase in vocabulary occurs, with a new word added every 3 days. During this stage, one word may apply to a number of different, largely unrelated things. Once the child starts to add words to his repertoire, a stage of rapid acquisition will occur during which he will gain from 50 to 300 words very quickly, gradually adding verbs and adjectives to the nouns and forming real, short sentences. These early sentences are usually "telegraphic," with many nonessential words left out (e.g., "cat jumps," "watch star," "daddy car shop").

Grammatization and Increased Elaboration

Now that the child can say words, sentences begin to form.

Twenty-Four to Thirty-Six Months From the time a typically developing child has reached 3 years of age, the number of words she uses increases to 500. She now uses more complex sentences of three to five words with correct organization of the words and grammatical inflection. The child now refers to herself as "I" or "me." She can also now talk about the past and the future and uses plurals. An amazing growth also occurs in understanding; she increasingly enjoys listening to conversations and can understand longer and more complex sentences. Not only does she like to listen to conversations, she likes to carry on real conversations herself and will keep them going by asking questions such as "who?", "what?", and "where?" She now understands about 1,000 words and some of the rules of grammar but may overgeneralize them at first. When she learns about the use of past tense -ed, for example, she may add it to several

words—often inappropriately—so she may say "seed," "gooded," or "ated." After the child begins to use sentences, a natural transition into using grammar and elaborating on ideas begins.

Three to Four Years   Language growth continues between the ages of 3 and 4, and by 4 years of age, the typically developing child can say at least 600 words and understand 1,500. In addition to this vocabulary, he uses four- to six-word sentences and can begin to give a connected account of recent experiences. He also can follow a sequence of two or three directions (e.g., "Find your toys, pick them up, and put them in the toy box"), and is now understood by most people outside of his home. During this time, children begin to ask more and more questions; often it would seem that they are doing this more in order to hear their voices and to remain connected than to get an answer.

Four to Six Years   By 4 years of age, most children have acquired all the basics of grammar and 50% of their vocabulary. They now have a vocabulary of 2,000 words, understanding 10,000–14,000 by age 6. Most children use rules of grammar, which now include rules surrounding the use of tenses, plurals, and prepositional phrases. The use of irregular verbs such as *sing, sang,* and *sung* comes next, then possessives such as "Daddy's shirt" and "Mommy's dress." After that they also acquire the articles *a* and *the.* With this larger vocabulary as well as a deeper understanding of a sophisticated language structure, a child can now communicate comfortably in a variety of settings.

IMPORTANT RESEARCH FINDINGS

Researchers studying language and communication have often used detailed recordings of the speech acquisition and the language patterns of individual children in order to understand the acquisition of language. This method has been an important source of knowledge in psycholinguistics. Approaches used to gather the data have included laboratory assessments, as well as longitudinal studies of a small number of children. Some of the important areas of research are as follows.

The Development of Language and Communication in Early Childhood

Much research has been done on the development of language and communication in early childhood and on the outcomes of early language delays.

The Prelinguistic Stage   Since the 1970s, research has demonstrated that infants are attracted to the human voice and particularly to adult speech that is modified to speak to them. "Child-Directed Speech" (CDS) has also been called *parentese* or *motherese.* This type of speech has a higher pitch and a simpler structure and is slower than adult-to-adult communication and is usually used by caregivers quite naturally without conscious adaptation (Cooper & Aslin, 1990; Fernald & Kuhl, 1987; Papoušek, Bornstein, Nuzzo, Papoušek, & Symmes, 1990). Infants are also more tuned in to their mother's voice, and in a laboratory situation in which sucking is followed by the sound of a voice will suck harder to elicit the sound of their mother's voice then they will to elicit a stranger's voice (DeCasper & Fifer, 1980). It is likely that the child responds this way because of hearing his mother's voice more frequently than other voices when he is in the womb. Research has also shown that children prefer nursery rhymes, music, or songs that were repeated prenatally (DeCasper & Spence, 1986; Panneton & DeCasper, 1986). Also remarkable is the finding that neonates can distinguish between the sounds of "ba" and "pa," suggesting that neonates are innately programmed to tune into speech sounds (Eimas, Siqueland, Jusczyk & Vigorito, 1971; Morse & Cowan, 1982).

The first communicative behaviors of the infant are affective, primarily, and include crying and smiling. Infants also display a variety of other emotions such as disgust, anger, and surprise. Papoušek (1989) showed that adults could identify the meaning of different types of their children's cries. In the first 3 months, the infant is intensely interested in his caregiver's face, and communication typically takes place in a one-to-one or face-to-face interaction. Quite early, infants use gestures to communicate and at as early as 2 months, infants have been observed to show hand-waving and to extend their index fingers in a prepointing gesture (Thelen & Fogel, 1986; Trevarthen, 1977). These early gestures are important precursors to language. At 2–3 months, cooing begins and the infant produces a number of vowel-like sounds and some soft consonants. At this age, the infant also engages in vocalization exchanges or *proto-conversations* with caregivers, with some of these initiated by the infant (Reddy, Hay, Murray, & Trevarthen, 1997), and with the infant acting as active participant (Kaye & Fogel, 1980).

By 6 months of age, infants become more interested in objects in the larger environment, and communication often takes place about objects and events. Caregivers now communicate to the infant about the world, and this is seen as a critically important step in the development of communication (Messer, 1994; Newson, 1979). Shared attention can be elicited by the caregiver's pointing, head turning, or gazing toward an object (e.g., Butterworth & Jarrett, 1991), although infants younger than 12 months do not look beyond their immediate visual field. Sometimes, infants elicit attention by pointing or gazing at objects. This joint eliciting of attention appears to be crucial for the later development of communication skills (Baron-Cohen, 1995) because it is within these kinds of interactions that caregivers name objects and events for the child. At this time, infants start to babble, producing sounds consisting of a consonant followed by a vowel such as "ba," which, when repeated, may sound like a word. Researchers believe that this babbling is a precursor of the first words, or that there is continuity from one to the other (Blake & De Boysson-Bardies, 1992; Stoel-Gammon & Cooper, 1984). During this time (at approximately 12–14 months), intentionality emerges and it becomes clear that the infant is purposely attracting the caregiver's attention and directing it toward an object or requesting something (Franco & Butterworth, 1988; Hobson, 1994).

Communicating with Words and Gestures   Children typically produce their first words around the end of the first or beginning of the second year (mean age 13 months) (Bloom, 1993). Research on the development of the MacArthur Communicative Development Inventories (CDI) with data from 1,000 children showed that by 10 months of age some children produced 12 words and understood 67 (Bates et al., 1994). In a number of longitudinal studies it has been found that children's intentional gestures, such as waving "bye-bye," waving an arm to indicate "no," dancing when music is put on, and making drinking gestures with an empty glass to indicate that a drink is wanted, generally appear at about the same time (Acredolo & Goodwyn, 1985, 1988; Butterworth & Morissette, 1996; Casadio & Caselli, 1989; Caselli, 1990; Werner & Kaplan, 1963). The first words are often "mama," "dada," and "baby," and these simple first sounds or words are common to children all over the world.

A number of researchers have noted that after children's first words are produced, the acquisition of the next words is gradual (Bates, O'Connell, & Shore, 1987). At approximately 18 months, when children usually have about 50 words, however, they acquire words rapidly for a period so that in a few weeks their vocabulary has increased to as many as 400 words (Bates et al., 1994; Bates, O'Connell, & Shore, 1987; Goldfield & Reznick, 1992; McCune-Nicolich, 1981). Some studies of English-speaking children support the idea that their first words are

predominantly nouns and the acquisition of verbs generally lags behind. Some crosslinguistic studies suggest that children learning languages other than English may have a larger number of verbs in their early vocabularies relative to English-learning children, however (Choi & Bowerman, 1997; Tardif, Shatz, & Naigles, 1997).

Acquisition of Grammar and Discourse   More has likely been written about grammar acquisition than other aspects of language development. There is broad agreement in the literature that children in their third year begin to employ grammatical categories. These include the use of singular and plural (Valian, 1991); nouns used with appropriate adjectives (Bloom, 1991); past tense (Bloom, 1973) and the use of verbs with appropriate endings (e.g., "he jumped," "she is jumping") (Perez-Pereira, 1989). Children usually acquire grammar skills in this order: 1) plurals (2 years), 2) verb endings (e.g., *-ing* and *-ed*), 3) the use of prepositions (e.g., "on," "in"), 4) irregular verbs (e.g., "sang," "sing," "sung"), 5) the use of the possessive (e.g., Dolly's dress), and 6) articles (e.g., "a" and "the") by 30 months. By 3 years, children are able to use verb forms such as "I walk, he walks, you walk" (Beck, 1979). By 3 years of age, the child is usually using four-word sentences that include these grammatical morphemes. Some writers question, however, whether the early emergence of these grammatical constructs is the result simply of imitation or if the children understand the use of the word as of a particular grammatical class.

Although young children acquire a considerable vocabulary and some rules of grammar, it takes far longer for them to acquire the capacity for extended conversations or discourse. In fact, development of this skill extends well into adulthood. From infancy, children learn to engage in turn-taking with their caregivers during feeding or face-to-face interactions (Kaye, 1977; Snow, 1977). Once children are beginning to use words, however, caregivers may facilitate the conversations and help them keep going by answering their own questions and speaking for the child when necessary. It takes some time before children can assume more responsibility in conversation and it is not until about 3 years of age that they are able to respond more frequently to their mothers' questions (Olsen-Fulero & Comforti, 1983).

Communicating with Peers   With peers, young children are rarely able to maintain a topic without the structuring of an adult (Blank & Franklin, 1980). Conversation requires participants who can understand the others' perspective and who can listen. They must have the ability to present their own perspective and to present personal narratives about events. Although these abilities are present in rudimentary forms at 4 years of age, most children are well into the elementary school grades before these skills can be used with any consistency (Dorval & Eckerman, 1984; Garvey, 1984). Once children go to school, their ability to use conversation, and particularly to understand what is going on before asking to enter a group, has been linked to a number of social behaviors and found to be one distinguishing characteristic that separates popular or unpopular children. (Corsaro, 1981; Putallaz & Gottman, 1981). Successful and popular children seem to be able to sum up what is going on and to make relevant remarks. They also are able to revise their requests and eventually get accepted by the group if initially rejected (Forbes, Katz, Paul, & Lubin, 1982).

The Outcomes of Early Language Delays

Although the development of language generally follows a relatively clear timetable, children differ in terms of the rate of language acquisition, the way in which aspects of language are acquired, and how words are used in sentences. Toddlers have been shown to vary significantly in whether they use more nouns or a more heterogeneous vocabulary, including some "words" that are rote or combinations of sounds (Nelson, 1973, 1981; Pine, Lieven, & Rowland, 1997). As well, a number of children fail to develop language at expected ages. For some, the reasons are obvious; it may be that the child has a hearing impairment, a cognitive disability, a pervasive developmental disorder (PDD), or identified brain damage. Other children also show delayed or untypical language but have none of these identifiable problems, however. This type of delay has been called specific language impairment (SLI), meaning that the only identified impairment is in language. Although methods used to identify these discrepancies vary, most clinicians use a cut-off of between the 10th and 16th percentile on tests of vocabulary and the mean length of utterance (MLU) as the measure of delays (Records & Tomblin, 1994). The differences in assessment tools used and aspects of language considered (e.g., expressive or expressive and receptive) has made it difficult to determine prevalence rates (which have varied from 12% to 31% depending on the study) (Tomblin, Records, Buckwater, Zhang, Smith, & O'Brien, 1997). In a study of 7,218 kindergarten children who were screened for language delays and then assessed if they failed the screening, a prevalence rate of 7.4% was found. Unexpectedly, there was little difference between boys and girls; the boys did not show more delays in speech acquisition than the girls as had been expected (Tomblin et al., 1997). Of concern was that only 29% of the children with delays had been previously diagnosed.

The outcome for children with SLI seems to be unpredictable because the type of impairment can change with age and developmental level (Bishop, 1997; Bishop & Edmundson, 1987). Since the early 1990s, there have been five major follow-up studies of late-talking toddlers (Ellis-Weismer, Murray-Branch, & Miller, 1994; Paul, 1993, 1996; Paul, Hernandez, Taylor, & Johnson, 1996; Rescorla, Roberts, & Dahlsgaard, 1997; Thal & Tobias, 1992). The findings of the studies indicate that some children were "late bloomers" and overcame their delays, but a significant percentage continued to have delays—especially in expressive language. Other studies have shown that not only are children with SLI at risk for continuing to have delays but also they are more likely to have psychiatric disorders and behavioral and emotional problems (Beitchman et al., 1996; Cohen, Davine, Horodezky, Lipsett, & Isaacson, 1993; Kotsopoulos & Boodoosingh, 1987). They also are more likely to have difficulties with academic and/or social development (Aram, Ekelman, & Nation, 1984). Given that without intervention a significant number of children with expressive delays in early childhood continue to have significant problems, speech and language treatment needs to be made available early, including focusing on improving caregiver-child interactions (Carson, Klee, Perry, Muskina, & Donaghy, 1998).

The Effect of the Environment, Especially Caregiver Interactions, on Language and Communication Development

The controversy still continues as to the *degree* to which speech and language is canalized or innately laid down in the child and to what degree input in the environment as compared to maturation influences eventual outcome. Regardless of the level of influence assigned to the environment, there is general agreement that it is critically important and a great deal of evidence exists that links certain interactional qualities of caregivers with enhanced language and communication skills in children.

Some studies have shown an association between security of attachment and language competence (Main, 1983; Meins, 1998). In a meta-analysis of 32 studies, van IJzendoorn, Dijkstra, and Bus found only a small combined-effect association between the two. Although they sug-

gested several possible reasons for the association, they conclude that "the studies fail to describe the process of parent-child interaction in enough detail to establish how important each of the hypothetical factors are, and how they interplay" (1995, p. 125).

Although the expected relationship between attachment and speech and language development has not always been found, interactional variables that are known to contribute to secure attachment have often been found to be related. Other researchers have failed to find expected relationships (Barwick, 1999; Bretherton, Bates, Benigni, Camaioni, & Volterra, 1979; Klann-Delius & Hofmeister, 1997). A number of recent studies have found that sensitive responsiveness or synchronized interactions are related to more advanced language development (Barwick, 1999; Landry, Smith, Miller-Loncar, & Swank, 1997; Rescorla & Fechnay, 1996).

Other studies that have examined the effects of maternal input on speech and language development have tended to consider variables that relate more directly to the amount and type of talking in which the parent engages. At a basic level, the studies have shown that the more parents talk to children, the faster they acquire vocabulary (Huttenlocher, Haight, Bryk, Seltzer, & Lyons, 1991). As well, the acquisition of different word types was related to the amount of use of these types of words by the mothers.

One study of the effect of early parent interactions on later language ability spanned 8 years and followed 42 families from different socioeconomic categories (Hart & Risley, 1995). Researchers observed families interacting with their children in their homes for 2½ years. Children were tested at 3 years and then later at 9–10 years of age. Researchers found that certain characteristics of the communication styles of parents made a difference to the development of language, namely

- Language diversity

- Feedback tone (i.e., the emotionality of the parent-child interactions)

- Symbolic emphasis (i.e., language that refers to *relations* between things and events)

- Guidance style (i.e., number of times a child is asked rather than told what to do)

- Responsiveness of the parent (i.e., child's experience with controlling the course of the interaction and of being listened to)

All of these together, in a multiple regression analysis, accounted for 60% of the variance of language accomplishments at age 3 and of language at age 9–10.

Other aspects of maternal interactions that have been found to be important by other researchers for enhancing language are

- Engaging in less controlling behavior with fewer commands and a more conversational style (Rescorla & Fechnay, 1996)

- Following the infant's attention (Akhtar, Dunham, & Dunham, 1991)

- Following the child's interest (Tomasello & Farrar, 1986)

- Stimulating the child's conversation rather than providing a "relentless barrage" of information (Levenstein & O'Hara, 1993)

- Having the capacity to match their vocalizations to the child's age and level of language development (Murray, Johnson, & Peters, 1990; Snow, 1999)

Those interactions in which the parents indicate interest in the child's direction of attention may be examples of shared attention and understanding that may lead to enhanced language development. Other aspects of the language environment that have been noted to be important in terms of language development are storybook reading and the use of sophisticated vocabulary at mealtimes, both examples of interactions that are common in a variety of households. Research on the effects of reading on young children has become increasingly popular. Without exception, studies have shown that reading to young children is efficacious in enhancing speech, language, and literacy development (Bus, van IJzendoorn, & Pellegrini, 1995; Cochran-Smith, 1984; Dickinson & Smith, 1994; Hewison, 1988; Neuman, 1996; Sénéchal, LeFevre, Hudson, & Lawson, 1996; Whitehurst, Arnold, Epstein, Angell, Smith, & Fischel, 1994). The focused interaction that occurs during reading, among other characteristics, allows opportunities for the child to acquire new information and to experience word repetition, which facilitates his or her learning. Similarly, families who share mealtime discussions provide their children with exposure to sophisticated vocabulary, which has been found to relate to growth of vocabulary over time (Beals & Tabors 1995; Davidson & Snow, 1998; Weizman, 1995).

Studies have found that the language development of twins is often delayed compared with singletons. A variety of reasons have been considered, including that twins have more perinatal complications or that they use a shared language. The strongest evidence suggests that the delays are caused by the parents' division of caregiving resources, however. Bornstein and Ruddy (1984) found that twins were encouraged to attend to objects and events half as much as singletons and had half the vocabulary of singletons at 12 months. Similar results were found at 15 and 21 months by Tomasello, Mannle, and Kruger (1986), who found that twins tended to receive less joint attention to the same object and extension of conversation by caregivers, which-in turn-was related to poorer language development.

A number of studies have examined interactional characteristics in families of different socioeconomic levels and have found significant differences between families—particularly at the extremes (Gottfried, 1984; Hart & Risley, 1992, 1995; Heath, 1989). As would be expected, outcomes on language measures are lower in children in economically disadvantaged situations and higher in higher income brackets.

In spite of these findings about the importance of the effects of parents' interactional styles on language acquisition, other studies of children who grow up in situations of extreme sensory deprivation, particularly of isolation or hearing loss, show that their language development is affected but can be rehabilitated to some degree as long as they are placed in supportive and stimulating environments. These findings support the view of the nativists that language acquisition takes place automatically as long as the child is exposed to sufficient language before puberty, thus suggesting that the critical time for language acquisition may be quite extended (Messer, 1994; Oller, Eilers, Basinger, Steffens, & Urbano, 1995).

Implications for Intervention Approaches

The identification of the characteristics of interactions or maternal speech that enhance the development of speech and language have made it more possible to design interventions for children with language delays or for those at risk for delays because of environmental reasons (Whitehurst & Fischel, 1994). The literature suggests that, as far as possible, intervention strategies should be integrated into naturally occurring interactions in daycare or at home. Some of the approaches that are being used include

- Integrating learning opportunities into naturally occurring interactions such as play, book reading, and caregiving activities (McLean & Cripe, 1997)

- Having the caregiver follow the child's initiation or lead and building on the child's attention or interest in the moment (Manolson, Ward, & Dodington, 1995)

- Encouraging the caregiver to notice what the child is doing, to be available to respond to what the child is trying to say, and to comment on what is going on (Manolson et al., 1995)

Some of the possible techniques that can be employed are outlined in a variety of curricula or models (McLean & Cripe, 1997):

- Showing how a word can represent a variety of similar types within a category (e.g., collies, springer spaniels, and poodles are all dogs; apples, peaches, and oranges are all fruits)

- Gradually moving the child's vocabulary from the simple to the more complex

- Repeating and enlarging on phrases in different contexts so that the child's vocabulary does not become context-bound (e.g., on a visit to the zoo, "Lions like to have an afternoon nap just like your little sister does")

These types of interventions will be explained in more detail under the section that outlines the Growth-Promoting Environment, Principle 1. See Table 5.4 for a listing of all of the principles described in this chapter.

THE GROWTH-PROMOTING ENVIRONMENT: PRINCIPLES OF ENHANCING LANGUAGE AND COMMUNICATION

Previously in this chapter, we outlined how language and communication unfold from birth through infancy, toddlerhood, and the preschool period. Much of this development takes place naturally. Particularly as children get older, the interactions of caregivers with their children,

Table 5.4. Principles for encouraging language and communication

Principle 1	Adopt strategies to encourage the child's speech and language development and communication skills.
Principle 2	Adopt strategies to ensure that the child receives and understands your communication.
Principle 3	Make conversation a two-way process of communication between you and the child.
Principle 4	Use special strategies to ensure conversation is not cut off and is kept going, so issues can be discussed and resolved.
Principle 5	Communicate acceptance and respect for the child, even when the content of the message may be difficult.
Principle 6	Create a language-rich environment and make conversation and discussion a valued part of the caregiving environment.
Principle 7	Help young children learn to communicate with their peers.

the conversational environment provided, and modeling provided to children through conversations increasingly affect the sophistication of children's language and their ability to communicate and converse with adults and peers in their lives.

PRINCIPLE 1: *Adopt strategies to encourage the child's speech and language development and communication skills.*

One of the most critical aspects of encouraging children to communicate is to foster their speech and language development. Caregivers can use a number of well-researched strategies and techniques. A list of the most important of these is outlined below, chronologically under various developmental stages.

Preverbal Stage (Birth to Twelve Months)   In the early stages of the development of communication, the lion's share of initiation and follow-through rests with the caregiver. Caregivers nurture the growth of language in a variety of important ways:

- With very young infants, caregivers use face-to-face interactions: They talk to the baby directly throughout the day during diaper changing, bathing, feeding, and special holding times. Through *parentese* and adult words, the infant is exposed to a lot of talk. In these interchanges, adults take turns, imitate sounds, and look to the baby for a response. These pauses may be punctuated with the caregiver gesturing, clapping the infant's hands, leaning towards the infant in anticipation, and encouraging the infant to respond.

- Although encouraging language is not all about reinforcement, responding to those first sounds when the baby coos and babbles can increase his earliest communication. This can be done by responding as you would if she was really speaking or by repeating the sounds that he is saying.

- Try and find out the kinds of speech an infant responds to best and use them frequently. Some infants, for example, prefer a high-pitched voice while others prefer lower pitched sounds. Remember that some infants can be hypersensitive to loud noises or to certain sounds and may prefer gentle, very modulated speech.

- When an infant or child is playing with or looking at something or when you are dressing or playing with him, saying the name of the object, using the word in a short sentence, or just using the word by itself will help him begin to associate words with objects (e.g., "Teddy, teddy, here's your teddy"). Be excited about, and talk about, the play the child is enjoying.

- Look for the child's body language cues and say what the child would say if she could.

- Sing and recite rhymes and introduce games with actions such as Peek-a-Boo, Pat-a-Cake, and The Itsy-Bitsy Spider. Linking the play, musical rhythm, action, and gestures can all enhance an infant's interest and focus on language.

- Showing baby how to use gestures or signs for "more" or "eat" instead of only crying may help baby to be more content. Some programs have been developed for encouraging this early sign language.

Say what the child would say if she could! (From Johnston, Lynn [1978]. *Do they ever grow up?* Meadow-brook Press, Minnetonka, MN; reprint granted with written permission of Lynn Johnston Productions, Inc.)

- Many research studies show that reading to babies from very early on gives them positive associations towards books and significantly enlarges their vocabulary. Having lots of simple books around and making others for the baby can really be helpful. These books can be made with pictures of objects that the baby knows from magazines or with photos of the baby and other people in the family.

- Following baby's cues and tuning in to what he is indicating he is interested in can be crucial. Following that pointed finger and giving him the object while naming it; taking the toy he gives you and talking about it; helping him get something he is reaching towards or trying to ask for and naming it as you get it for him can all encourage language.

Toddlerhood (Twelve to Thirty-Six Months)   This is the period when first words emerge, slowly at first and then much more rapidly during the third year of life. From the time these first words are said, caregivers need to notice them and encourage the child to say them. Caregivers who can listen to, watch, and tune into toddlers are able to understand what children enjoy. They are available to follow through with the ideas for modeling and expanding language listed below. There are a number of ways to enhance language at this developmental stage:

- Acknowledge and repeat first words. Sometimes it is very difficult to understand what the words mean but usually the child's gestures or the context can help you work it out. Respond by repeating them, replying to the constant "What's that," and gradually supplying the child with more and more labels and names for objects.

- Some children at this age say few nouns and instead use strings of sounds that do not appear to be specific words. It can be helpful with these children to speak frequently and clearly, giving them the names of objects around them.

- Gradually expand the early words into slightly longer phrases but avoid very complex, long sentences. Nevertheless, once the child can use two or three words together it is time to begin using some other parts of speech such as pronouns ("I," "you," "we") and joining words ("when," "because").

- Because the speech and language of young children unfolds best within a language-rich environment, it is critical to model clear speech with emphasis on important words, as well as using the words in short sentences. When words are pronounced wrong, caregivers should not correct the child, but simply repeat the word saying it slowly and clearly. Children do not respond to correction and attempts to do this will simply create frustration for both the child and adult. Again, when toddlers begin to use grammar they may overgeneralize and add "ed" to the wrong words or "s" when it does not apply. Again the mistake should not be directly pointed out but instead the sentence should be just repeated back in its correct form.

- Expand on what the toddler says by filling in the missing words of telegraphic speech offering more words and extending the ideas that children introduce themselves.

- Tune into the child's talk about what she is doing and what is happening. Questions can often help the child keep the conversation going, "Where is Teddy going? Is he going to a party?" These keep the child thinking about what is going on and trying to find more words.

- Use actions with the words, linking sounds with visual cues as a powerful way to help the child learn to say and remember the words.

- Use pretend play as a stage for the child to learn more words and to expand them into sentences. The chapter on play outlines how critically important make-believe is for a child's expanding intelligence. Expanding language by making sentences longer and using new words is critical.

- At this age children will love to dance and sing to music. Joining in with songs and actions and having fun with them while doing it is far more exciting for children than simply watching them on television. Not only is it more fun, the child will have more understanding of the words if actions and emotions are added to them.

- Continue to use nursery rhymes and action songs and to have books constantly available.

- Encourage toddlers to use language to get the things they want. Wait briefly to see if the toddler can ask for something using words and encourage him to do so by asking questions. If he uses a gesture because he does not know the word, accept this as an effort to communicate. It is important not to continually frustrate a child who is unable to speak or has forgotten a particular word by not letting him have what he wants until he can say the word. This will only make him very resistant and maybe even ashamed because he cannot produce the word that is obviously needed.

- There is often a period during toddlerhood, which may be quite brief, when a child is obviously enthralled with language and how it is produced. She will watch her caregiver's face

and mouth, attempt to imitate words, bringing toys for labeling and enjoying having care-givers give labels for all those pictures in her favorite book. Capitalize on this special time because it is likely to be the time the child's language is being expanded enormously and new words are being added to her vocabulary every day.

Preschoolers and Young Children (Three to Six Years) During this time the young child will acquire about 50% of his language, including words and grammar. By 6 years of age, young children have from 10,000 to 14,000 words and speak in sentences using the grammar rules of their language in all their complexity. They can also be understood by strangers who are not familiar with their speech. At this stage they continue to need continuing opportunities to speak and to listen to peers, parents, and other caregivers, rather than lessons or drills about language. Without pressuring the child to learn specific words, allow time to try out words in the context of play and listen and provide opportunities to try out language. Examples of ways to enhance language are outlined below.

- *Talk to the child:* Conversations become extremely important for children during this time, and these can be with adults or other children. In general, adults need to connect with children and to listen and respond to what they have to say and to keep conversations going by asking questions and talking about subjects the child expresses interest in. Notice very quiet children and make special efforts to encourage them to talk; if children are having trouble communicating with each other, caregivers may help out and make sure children listen to each other.

- *Avoid criticizing the child:* Caregivers need to avoid correcting children continually but should show approval of their attempts and gently clarify what the children are trying to say.

- *Continue to use books:* Children will soon begin to recognize words and that letters are associated with sounds. Opportunities to learn about the meaning and shape of words can begin to make this link. This can also happen by providing children with letters and words on the fridge, on the walls, and in their toy boxes. Providing children with opportunities to learn to draw, copy, and write by having a chalkboard, painting material, and lots of paper with markers, crayons, pencils, scissors, and staplers to make their own pictures and books can all help stimulate this link and interest.

- *Go on outings:* Visit exciting places in the community to help the child add new words to her vocabulary. Follow up by showing pictures or props of what was seen can also enlarge vocabularies.

- *Discuss past, present, and future:* Discuss the past and encourage children to talk about what happened to them today, yesterday, and during important past events like their birthday, or when they went on a holiday, or began daycare. They can also be involved in planning about the future and about what they will be doing later today, tomorrow, and at exciting new events.

- *Put language into gross motor activities:* What better way to teach "under" the table than by going there? Want the child to learn "up" and "down"? Try having her jump. Teach "around" through a game of Ring Around the Rosie. This is especially helpful for children who are kinesthetic learners.

Visits in the community to exciting places can enhance a child's vocabulary.

PRINCIPLE 2: *Adopt strategies to ensure that the child receives and understands your communication.*

The first step in helping babies to listen and to begin to understand words and what you are saying is to help them pay attention to sounds and discriminate between them. Consequently, activities that help young children listen closely to sounds can be helpful. This can include making animal sounds and sounds of other objects the child is interested in, such as car noises, the telephone ringing, monsters roaring, or a drum banging. Some sounds can be recorded on tapes and used later on.

When a child can understand words, it is crucial to adopt strategies to make sure that he is hearing, understanding, and accepting communication that is used with him. Many children, for a variety of reasons, have difficulty processing and comprehending language. In addition, children who are not listened to, or are constantly told what and how to do things and even yelled at, develop strategies to "turn off" or shut out what is being said. For children who have difficulties understanding or who do not listen, special efforts on the part of caregivers may be needed to reopen the channels of communication. Some examples are listed here.

- Get the child's attention before speaking to her. Call her name and make sure you only begin to talk when you have her attention.

- Lower your voice and adjust your tone to be warm and friendly. Do not yell or use a commanding tone. Communicate acceptance and use some kind words.

- Communicate at eye level by stooping down or sitting on the floor or at a table with the child. Establish eye contact. Do not stand over her in a menacing way or sit at the opposite end of the room and expect that the message will be received.

- It may be necessary to turn off the television or other distractions to make sure your words and messages are heard.

- Touching in a supportive way can help foster positive attention.

- Make your words and sentences simple enough for the child to follow. Be as clear and brief as possible. Remember that some children may have difficulty processing or remembering more than one instruction or idea. Consequently, when a caregiver only uses one brief idea at a time, this may be a helpful way to make sure that the child can process, comprehend, and remember what is said.

- Do not lecture. Stick to the point and don't ramble. Do not nag the child.

- If you want the child to do something or to stop doing something, avoid yelling—but rather—speak firmly and give a reason for the request. Try not to display anger or frustration but maintain warmth in your voice while making it very clear that the statement needs a response. Mean what you say, and follow through when the child makes a request.

PRINCIPLE 3: *Make conversation a two-way process of communication between you and the child.*

For a conversation to be truly shared between two people, each needs to be listened to and to be given an opportunity to respond and express himself. If you think about it, it is very rare to have someone really listen to you—and most important—make a real effort to understand what you really mean. Much of the communication that takes place between people is very superficial. People ask how you are but seldom really want to know, unless it is a pleasant, "I'm fine, how are you?" Conversations frequently consist of each person telling the other about what is going on in his or her life, not really listening to what the other person is saying while he or she prepares to tell about the next piece of personal news. The situation is even worse for children with limited conversational skills and ways to get attention. So one of the greatest gifts to give a child may be to really *listen* to him, *understand* his ideas and point of view, and show him *acceptance* of his feelings and opinions.

Many things can get in the way of our capacity to pay the proper attention to children, such as being too busy. Having several children can make it difficult to respond to one child without interruption. When you cannot really think about what the child is saying because you are preoccupied with your own thoughts, this can be another barrier. Often, the problem is more complicated than this, and you may find yourself becoming very angry or frustrated by what the child is saying or how he is saying it. When this happens, you may express your own feelings without really listening to the child's feelings, and understanding what he is trying to say.

Look at the responses to children's comments in Table 5.5 for some examples of how, on one hand, a child can be shut off and communication can be stopped so readily and, on the other hand, how a sensitive remark can open communication lines and encourage more sharing. Table 5.6 lists several suggestions for how parents and caregivers can demonstrate that they are really listening to a child.

Table 5.5. Examples of strategies to repair communication through listening and responding sensitively

Child's statement	Negative response that cuts off communication	Positive response that encourages communication
"I left my lunch at home today and didn't have any. I'm really hungry."	"I'm tired of hearing you say you forgot your lunch, you're always doing it, you'll have to go hungry."	"I'm sorry; it must have been really hard having nothing to eat at lunchtime. I was a bit rushed this morning."
"I hate Johnny. He's mean and nasty."	"Now you know, Johnny is your good friend. Just play nicely with him."	"Johnny upset you? What happened? Can we work it out?"
"I had a terrible time at Dad's house yesterday."	"Well, you'll have to talk to him about it yourself."	"What happened? Do you want to tell me about it?"
"My brother was mean to me again today."	"You'd better start not being mean to him, or else."	"I'm sorry you two didn't get along. What did he do?"

PRINCIPLE 4: *Use special strategies to ensure conversation is not cut off and is kept going, so issues can be discussed and resolved.*

Negative feelings, and particularly, comments that we perceive as rude or as criticism, especially when they are unreasonable and unkind, usually bring strong emotional reactions. It is often difficult not to respond to anger with anger and to be disappointed when a child is showing jealousy of a sibling or another child, for example. Criticism can activate our own critical voice inside and sometimes hearing about fearfulness or sadness can be particularly difficult for some caregivers. These reactions are usually related to our own histories and vulnerabilities.

● ●

Peta was attending a parenting group and frequently brought up how her son's whining and crying infuriated her. She explained that she found it much easier to deal with his anger, but for some reason that was not clear to her, his sadness was hard for her to bear. In fact, she often gave in to him; anything to avoid or stop his crying. As the group progressed, Peta talked about her past and how her mother had died when she was 4. An aunt had brought her up, and never let her talk about or mourn her mother. The unresolved grief, in some way, intruded on her ability to accept her son's sadness and made her insist he not complain, just as had been done to her.

———————————————

Linda also joined a parent group and constantly talked about her adopted daughter's behavior, which she saw as frequently escalating out of control. Whether the girl was laughing intensely, crying, or angry, Linda saw her behavior as causing problems. She described a sense of absolute panic in response to her daughter's intense emotions. Although strategies were suggested for her to contain her daughter, they did not help. What did occur was a realization of what was being triggered. In fact, Linda's mother had suffered from bipolar disorder and her manic phases had terrified young Linda, who realized her mother was unable to control her behavior.

Table 5.6. Suggestions for how to be an active listener

Try and stop whatever you are doing and listen to the child. Do not interrupt.

Do not pretend you are listening if you are not. If you are too busy to listen, tell the child, "I'm busy now—but let's talk about it later." Then, be sure to follow through.

Respond and reflect nonverbal (or body language) as well as verbal messages. This opens the door to talk more about the issue if the child wants to (e.g., "I can see that you're feeling kind of sad right now").

Do not correct grammatical errors; it may interrupt the message the child is trying to get across and frustrate him.

Reflect what you understand her to be saying: "So you tried hard, but the teacher was still mad."

Let the child know you understand her feelings: "My, you must have felt really sad."

Let the child know you appreciate her telling you about the incident or situation.

Avoid lecturing and give the child a chance to give his point of view.

Learning to understand where our own struggles and issues with certain emotions may originate can help us respond in new ways to children's comments. When we are triggered to respond negatively to children, it is critical to adopt ways to stop the cycle of destructive communication. If, as the caregiver, you can change your responses to the criticism or anger of a child, it can dramatically affect the communication patterns being established—and consequently, the behavior of the child.

Remember that nonverbal cues can be damaging for children and cut off communication. Some very negative examples are

- Touching roughly or avoiding touch

- Negative facial expressions, such as frowning

- Staying far away and not giving the child attention

- Avoiding eye contact and looking away

- Leaning away and holding body rigid

- Angry, tense gestures

Some examples of ways to turn negative patterns of communication into positives are presented in Table 5.7. In the negative examples, the caregiver responds to the child's expression of jealousy, sadness, anger, or frustration with immediate reactions of anger, denial of the child's feelings, blame, putting the child down, or calling him names. Typically, the child immediately takes the remark personally and gets defensive. In the positive examples in this table, the adult reacts very differently and keeps the communication going. As you will notice, some of the most important components of the positive exchanges are that the caregiver

- Acknowledges the child's feelings and gives them a name if possible

- Does not judge the feeling or use name calling

- Encourages the child to explain the feelings further

- Leaves the child with some ideas for solutions

- Reminds the child of some of her related strengths

- Tries to find some solutions within himself if the child has a legitimate complaint

Of course, it takes time and effort to adopt a new way of responding, but it is well worth the effort. The changes in the child's reaction can be very positive, however, and can really help mend a difficult relationship and last well into adolescence and beyond.

PRINCIPLE 5: *Communicate acceptance and respect for the child, even when the content of the message may be difficult.*

It is interesting how positive messages given by someone who means them can make a big difference to anyone's day. If we arrive at work and someone comments on how hard we worked the day before, or how nice our hair looks, it can really make us feel better all day. These small words can be even more important for children who depend so much on our approval. Just as positive words can make so much difference to us, negative words, and particularly threats, can quickly destroy a child's self-esteem and sense of well being. Imagine the impact of remarks such as, "I hate you and I wish you were never born," "You bug me all the time," "If you do that once more I'll send you to a foster home," or "You're hopeless and you can never do anything." In fact, those who have experienced these kind of cruel words frequently describe them as just as destructive as physical or sexual abuse. There seem to be two distinct styles: direct attacks like these and more indirect and subtle attacks, which can be just as painful. These can include teasing, using sarcasm, insulting nicknames, or subtle put-downs. Imagine the impact of remarks like "That's a good-looking jacket—for a clown," "What's the queen want this morning?", or "That painting looks like it was scribbled by a 2-year-old." Just like the more direct attack, these more subtle digs can leave the child feeling totally inadequate. This can lead gradually to erosion of confidence and a sense of shame. Many caregivers get caught up in giving these kinds of responses, or on some days they feel that they have done nothing but say "No," "Don't," or "Stop it" all day. This may make them feel guilty and worry about the impact it can have on the child.

Clearly, children must be disciplined and at times told that a certain behavior is not allowed. It is *how* the message is conveyed that can make it acceptable and more likely that a child will respond positively to it than resist it. There are two useful ways to overcome destructive ways of communicating with children:

Changing the "Don'ts" into "Do's"

Instead of saying "don't do this" and "don't do that" all day, caregivers can rephrase their requests for better behavior in a positive way. (See Table 5.8.)

Giving "I" Messages

Giving "I" messages means phrasing things in terms of what you want or feel instead of simply identifying a problem or accusing the child of something. The "I" messages are much less likely to bring on the child's resistance and anger and he is more likely to follow through with

Table 5.7. Turning negative communication habits into positive strategies.

Child's statement	Negative conversation	Positive conversation
"You like her better than me."	Child: "My sister gets everything and I get nothing." Adult: "Don't be silly, you get everything and more than your sister gets." Child: "I don't get anything at all; I never get anything new and she gets everything." Adult: "Remember, you got two new pairs of jeans last week." Child: "That's just clothes to wear for school. I never get anything I want or like." Adult: "You're very ungrateful."	Child: "My sister gets everything and I get nothing." Adult: "It sometimes feels as if it's always her turn and you're left out." Child: "Yes, sometimes I feel like you only like her and don't like me." Adult: "Remember, we had such fun together last week when we went to the grocery store." Child: "Yes that was fun—especially when you let me choose some of the meals." Adult: "We could have a special time together; would that help?" Child: "Yes, that would be great."
"I wish you didn't go to work."	Child: "I miss you when I'm at child care. Why do you have to work?" Adult: "Don't make me feel guilty. I work hard all day and the weekend to buy things for you." Child: "Sometimes I cry all day for you." Adult: "Well, I'm afraid that's too bad, all the other children manage and so will you."	Child: "I miss you when I'm at child care. Why do you have to work?" Adult: "It must be hard sometimes when I'm not there." Child: "Yes, sometimes it feels like you have been gone for days." Adult: "What would help? Could I leave you a photo or a toy you like?" Child: "It will help me remember you all day, so that would help." Adult: "I think about you all day, too."
"I hate doing chores."	Child: "I'm tired of taking the garbage out. You make me do everything!" Adult: "You lazy little thing, you never do anything around here—and don't answer me back." Child: "I'm like a slave. I have the worst job to do." Adult: "Do it or else there will be a lot of trouble!"	Child: "I'm tired of taking the garbage out. You make me do everything!" Adult: "You're tired of taking out the garbage." Child: "Yes. I've been doing it for a hundred years, it feels like." Adult: "Well maybe next time we assign chores you could change with John and you could do his dishes." Child: "Do you think he would change with me?" Adult: "Let's discuss it next time we're all together."
"Daddy's much more fun than you are."	Child: "Daddy's much more fun than you are. He takes me out a lot." Adult: "It's all very well for your father. Of course he is fun because he doesn't have to put up with you all day like I do." Child: "I hate being around you all day. You're boring." Adult: "You whine all day and I have to cook, clean, and discipline you. No wonder your father can be fun."	Child: "Daddy's much more fun than you are. He takes me out a lot." Adult: "You really have fun with your Dad, and enjoy him a lot." Child: "Yes, we really had fun when we went to the swimming pool, he almost taught me to swim." Adult: "Yes, he told me you had lots of fun together on Saturday."
"I hate going to Grandma's for Sunday dinner."	Child: "I hate going to Grandma's for Sunday dinner." Adult: "You ungrateful little thing. Grandma cooks all week for that dinner." Child: "Yes, and I hate her food and it drives me crazy sitting there all day." Adult: "Well, I don't care what you think—you're going anyway and you'd better behave."	Child: "I hate going to Grandma's for Sunday dinner." Adult: "You find it hard to have to go all the time." Child: "Yes. She expects me to sit there and be quiet while you talk about boring things." Adult: "Would it help if you brought someone?" Child: "Do you think she would let me bring someone?" Adult: "Let's ask Grandma and see what she says."

Table 5.8. Examples of changing "don't" statements into "do" statements

"Don't" statements	"Do" statements
"Don't drag your coat on the floor."	"Hold your coat off of the floor."
"Don't squeeze the kitten."	"Carry the kitten gently."
"Don't slam the door."	"Close the door gently, please."
"Don't draw on the table."	"You can color on the page."
"Don't look at me like that."	"How about a smile on your face."

the behavior that is requested. It is really helpful, too, if the negative behavior is pointed out and the kind of behavior needed is explained. Table 5.9 includes some helpful ways to turn negative messages into positive "I" messages.

Along with being careful with the words that you use, it is important to watch your body language and facial expressions. Saying the more positive messages while looking furious or shaking your fist will not soften the messages or help with fostering cooperation.

PRINCIPLE 6: *Create a language-rich environment and make conversation and discussion a valued part of the caregiving environment.*

Providing a language-rich environment and one in which conversation is valued can require time and effort, but it can open up and keep communication going between family members and children in group care. Talking calmly and listening are critical strategies to model because children soon adopt the same communication strategies as their caregivers. When you provide a communicative environment, you encourage language and provide opportunities for children and adults to get together to talk and to share experiences and ideas and to make decisions. It is important to have times when the family or daycare group joins in songs, rhymes, and games. Some suggestions for creating a conversational and language-rich environment are listed in Table 5.10.

PRINCIPLE 7: *Help young children learn to communicate with their peers.*

For some children who have delayed language skills or difficulty communicating, talking to peers can be difficult, and may have a negative impact on their capacity to socialize and make

Table 5.9. Examples of changing negative statements into positive "I" messages

Negative messages	"I messages"
"Don't hurt your little sister."	"When you hurt your little sister it makes me very upset to see her in pain. Please leave her alone so she is not hurt."
"Don't climb on the banister."	"When you climb on the banister, I worry that you will hurt yourself. Please be careful going up the stairs."
"Don't make a noise."	"Those loud noises upset me because they hurt my ears. Go upstairs if you need to make a noise."
"I've told you 20 times to close the door."	"When you leave the door open, it lets the cold come in and I freeze. Please shut the door when you come in."

Have times when the child can join in group songs, rhymes, and games.

friends with others. Some of the ways that children may create difficulties for themselves and ways to help them overcome them are set out in Table 5.11. It is very important to help the young child with these skills because a child's social reputation and communication skills are firmly established by 4–5 years of age and are much more difficult to change after that time.

SOME COMMONLY RAISED ISSUES AROUND LANGUAGE AND COMMUNICATION

Many issues are common to the development of language and communication in children.

Table 5.10. Some suggestions for creating a conversational and language-rich environment

Encourage children to make choices and get them to explain the reason for them.

Read to children and encourage them to "read" some pages too. Talk about the story.

Act out dramas with a child, taking different parts.

Give all members of the family a small say in decisions about holidays and outings; for example, let children decide about what to take and give some choices about places to visit.

Have times when all the family or group join in songs, rhymes, riddles, or other games.

Have an evening without television.

Watch television shows together and talk about them.

Have mealtimes together as often as possible and give everyone a chance to talk about his or her day.

Discuss each person's best and worst moment of the week.

Use bath time, meal preparation, and other household routines as times to encourage communication with young children.

Ask children about how their day went and really listen to their responses. Share your own experiences.

Make sure to respond to your child's questions as quickly and as honestly as you can.

Table 5.11.   Ways to help a child communicate better with other children

Negative communication strategies	Positive ways to help the child
On trying to enter a group, the child barges in, knocking toys down in an effort to get attention.	Help the child see the connection between his action and the other children's responses.
	Suggest some ways for the child to enter the group by joining the play, such as helping to build a fort or taking on a role in the drama.
Child does not understand that a peer is asking her to play or know how to accept the invitation.	Coach the child to respond to the invitation and help her join in the play that is in progress.
Child may stand on the sidelines of a group and not know how to approach the other children or talk to them.	Coach the child to use names when talking to other children to gain their attention and then to talk directly to them and to look at them. Model these skills while coaching the child.
Child is constantly asking questions or criticizing the play.	Show the child how to join in and play in the game as it is, to "go with the flow," to not be intrusive, and to accept the direction of the conversation.
If the child is rejected by the group, he gives up.	Encourage the child to retry in order to gain access to the group. Popular children have been found to get rejected too, but to keep trying again. Support the child to do this and if necessary, coach him to do so.
Child barges into a group without being aware of what they are doing.	Encourage the child to sum up what is going on before attempting to join in.
	Have the child make remarks that fit in with what is going on. For example, saying "I can be a sailor?" rather than "Can I play?"

Speech and Language Delays

Not all children develop language effortlessly; about 7% struggle to achieve the skills to communicate. As has been pointed out in other sections of this chapter, children with language delays that persist past the preschool years are at risk for academic difficulties, particularly in reading and writing. As well, having limited verbal skills has been associated with poor social skills and later on, with behavioral, emotional, and psychiatric disorders. It is critical, therefore, that delays are identified early and intervention provided as soon as possible.

Not only do children differ significantly in the pace of their language acquisition, but also they vary in other ways that can cause problems. Here are some common language acquisition problems:

- Comprehension is adequate but the child's speech is very difficult to understand

- Child mispronounces words, and speech lacks fluency

- Child is hard to understand because enunciation and pronunciation are problematic

- Speech and language use are bizarre, and the child has great difficulty with turn-taking or maintaining a conversation

- The child may repeat words but fails to understand their meaning and is unable to use them communicatively

- Child may stutter or stammer or have difficulties with other dysfluencies

- Child may have significant auditory processing, comprehension, or receptive language problems and yet speak fluently or have significant expressive language problems as well

- A child has a hearing impairment or frequent ear infections resulting in intermittent hearing loss and uneven acquiring of language

- Child understands well, but can only produce very short sentences with significant grammatical errors

With some children, the cause of these speech and language impairments is easy to determine. A significant number of children with language delays have a neurodevelopmental disorder. Some of the most commonly occurring ones are Down syndrome, Williams syndrome, and autism spectrum disorders. With the exception of autism, these disorders are usually identified at birth, and the pattern of language, although not the extent of the language delay, is relatively predictable. Infants with autism, however, are in striking contrast to the other children with atypical development. Although some show obvious deficits from birth, others apparently enjoy normal development in the first year or so before their deficits become apparent. In comparison to these disorders, there is far less predictability in the acquisition of language in other neurodevelopmental disorders, such as fragile X syndrome, hydrocephalus, or other types of brain insult or damage.

Another group of children who have language delays are those with sensory disabilities including children who are deaf, blind, or who have suffered extreme neglect or environmental deprivation. Again, for these children their ability to communicate can vary considerably as a result of their level of intellectual ability, as well as the timing and extent of intervention strategies to which they are exposed.

Although for many children the reasons for their language delays are clear, there is another group for whom there is no identifiable physical or psychological basis. The term SLI is used to refer to these impairments because the delays are specific to speech and language and are not associated with other identifiable delays or deficits. Researchers and specialists often differ about the exact criteria for a child to be diagnosed as having specific language impairment (SLI); however, some of the less controversial criteria appear to have universal acceptance. These are that the SLI child has a verbal IQ score or language age (combination of receptive and expressive) of at least 12 months below their chronological age, their Performance IQ score, or their mental age. The child's non-verbal or Performance IQ score must be within one standard deviation of the mean.

Discussion of the subtypes of SLI is beyond the scope of this chapter. It should be noted that the number is extensive, however. Included are such disorders as 1) verbal auditory agnosia/word deafness (i.e., inability to comprehend spoken language with speech often absent), 2) semantic-pragmatic deficit syndrome (i.e., language usage is strange, and child has difficulty with turn taking in conversation and maintaining a topic), and 3) phonological-syntactic deficit syndrome (i.e., child mispronounces words, and speech is disjointed and lacks fluency).

Clearly, the diagnosis and consequently, the remediation of speech and language delays is complex and difficult. It is critical, therefore, that children who are showing delays in speech or other language difficulties are assessed by a speech and language pathologist and an audiologist as soon as difficulties are identified so rehabilitation can begin as early as possible. Although

the success of intervention will vary significantly, it is still important that children with delays receive specialized help to alleviate delays as far as possible and the opportunity to learn compensatory skills when this is not possible.

Given the complexity of language impairments, it is useful to know some warning signs that indicate that a child needs referral for speech and language assessment:

- An infant or young child seems to have difficulty hearing sounds or words.

- An infant does not vocalize.

- A child's speech after 18 months is totally echolalic.

- After using words initially at the beginning of the first year, speech practically disappears by approximately 18–24 months.

- By age 24 months, a child has fewer than 50 words and/or is not producing two-word combinations (e.g., "throw ball," "red ball"), or is nearly unintelligible.

- A 2-year-old has difficulty pointing to named objects in pictures or never uses gestures to express himself.

- A child reverses "I" and "you" at 3 years of age.

- A preschool or older child has difficulty remembering words.

- A child does not establish eye contact or want to communicate.

- A child does not use words socially to convey meaning or to initiate communication.

- Speech has unusual tone, inflection, or rhythm.

If these signs are identified by parents or other caregivers, it is important to refer the child to a speech–language pathologist for a screening or further assessment, if necessary, in order to determine if the perceived delays are significant and if they require treatment or intervention. Unfortunately, many family physicians and even pediatricians do not identify delays, partly because they do not want to alarm parents or label children and they think the problem will resolve itself. Others may hesitate to refer parents to speech–language professionals because they do not believe suitable services are available even if a problem is identified.

Stuttering

Stuttering (or stammering) is speaking with disruptions or blocking of speech that is not under voluntary control. These may include long pauses in sentences, during which the child cannot seem to get the words out; stopping in the middle of a sentence and then starting all over again; or repeating sounds ("I wa-wa-wa-want to go") or words or phrases ("Give, give, give me it"). Stuttering is common in girls from about 2 to 3 years of age and in boys between 3 and 4 years of age and affects about 4% of children.

No one really knows why stuttering occurs, although there are a number of theories about its causes. Some people believe the causes are physiological; for instance, stuttering may be related to auditory interference (i.e., receiving misleading feedback from one's own speech, a lack

of development of cerebral dominance, or a genetic predisposition). Another theory is that the child's ideas or thinking is ahead of his ideas to express thoughts verbally. He is trying to express an idea or feeling but cannot come up with the right words. A parent or caregiver's unrealistic expectations or overconcern about a child's speech can cause stuttering, and if caregivers initially or continually overreact to a child's stuttering, problems may worsen. A variety of stressful situations can also lead to stuttering. Family arguments, tension or fatigue, or anxiety about having to speak in school may cause more stuttering.

Some children are fluent with friends or alone but stutter severely with other people, and most do not stutter when singing. Some stuttering is temporary and lasts for only a few months, while other stuttering is more serious, occurs more frequently, and is accompanied by facial grimacing, clenching teeth, facial tics, arm or leg movements, stamping feet, blinking, or irregular breathing.

When stuttering is mild, some management strategies should be tried, but when it is more serious the child should be referred to a speech–language pathologist for assessment. Some suggestions for helping the child who stutters include the following:

- Remain calm and concentrate on what the child is trying to say. Be a good listener.

- Try not to draw attention to the stuttering, and discourage friends and relatives from pointing it out.

- Reduce situations that are stressful for the child and seem to increase stuttering.

- Keep speech slow when you talk to the child.

- Encourage all the child's speech whether interrupted or not, and show pleasure in it.

- Keep stressful communication situations to a minimum, such as talking to a child in a noisy situation.

- Suggest to the child that he try again when he uses "bumpy" speech, making sure that this is done in a gentle and encouraging way.

For children with persistent, severe, and secondary stuttering, combining the more indirect approaches with a speech–language pathologist's more direct interventions may be necessary. Sometimes the speech–language pathologist will coach the parents so they can provide some of the training. Currently, few clinicians would advocate a "wait and see" approach and most believe that early treatment is important.

Ear Infections or Otitis Media

Otitis media is a middle ear infection that reduces the efficiency of sound transmission. Otitis media can cause hearing loss, although the degree is variable. Approximately 92% of children with otitis media have some temporary sound loss. This hearing loss varies considerably from the child hearing a muffling of sounds to more severe cases that result in the child only being able to hear very loud voices. About 90% of children get these infections at some time, and most children have approximately 6 ear infections by age 2. As would be expected, the earlier the infections occur and the more frequent and longer lasting the ear infections, the poorer the language development might be. Consequently, it is important to have ear infections attended to so that they do not last for a lengthy period.

The most common problems that may arise with otitis media are its effect on a child's ability to discriminate sounds and to develop narrative and attentional skills. Some research indicates that deficits are usually not as significant as would be expected, which points to the resilience and recovery of the language learning system. Otitis media is probably best considered to be a risk factor that becomes important if there are other factors present, and particularly if there are multiple episodes in the first year of life.

Bilingualism

The available research on children's bilingualism is fraught with methodological problems, so clear answers cannot be given on a number of questions about the process or consequences of learning two languages in the early years. One of the main confusions is that there are a number of ways in which a young child may be exposed to and acquire more than one language. For example a child may

- Be exposed to two languages from birth onward

- Be exposed to two languages not at birth, but within the first 3 years

- Be exposed to one language before the other

Because of the complexity of children's language backgrounds and the lack of research comparing these very different situations, it is very difficult to arrive at definitive answers about the advantages or disadvantages of learning two languages in the early years or about the best way for a child to learn them. As well, for linguistically competent children with good receptive and expressive language skills, it probably is not as critical, but for children with delays or auditory processing difficulties, exposure to multiple languages may impose significant challenges. In spite of the complexity of the research, however, there are a few conclusions that can be made:

- Bilingual children go through three stages. During Stage 1, they may use a few words from the two languages. In Stage 2, children continue to use words from both languages but begin to use them discriminately with different people and in different contexts. During Stage 3, the two languages are differentiated and used appropriately.

- Bilingual children often score below monolingual children on vocabulary development in one language well into the early school grades. If their score for vocabulary using both languages is assessed, they are likely to be average or above average, however.

- The quality and type of interaction patterns and the input between child and caregiver are important factors in learning language. The interactive styles of parents will influence the child's learning of two languages. If the child's emotional bond is stronger with one parent, the language that parent uses will develop more predominantly.

- For children who begin learning English, or the language of a dominant culture in which they live, as a second language when they go to school, the way and the speed at which they

learn the language will vary significantly. Although a child may master good conversational skills in about 2 years, it may take up to 5–7 years for the children to become proficient on written language and academic tasks.

- For children who have identified auditory processing difficulties and other learning disabilities, learning another language before they have mastered the first may be very confusing and challenging (Hemmersam-Wiig & Messing-Semel, 1980).

Perhaps the overall conclusion as stated by Romaine is that "there are many different ways and contexts in which children become bilingual, and not surprising, many different outcomes. It is too early to compare with any confidence the outcomes of monolingual and bilingual acquisition" (1999, p. 272).

DISCUSSION QUESTIONS TO USE IN TRAINING PROFESSIONALS

1. Why is it so difficult to make a clear statement about the effects of a child learning two languages on the child's language development?

2. Describe the difference between the terms *speech, language,* and *communication.*

3. Describe some of the things that can get in the way of good communication. Discuss some ways to overcome them.

4. How can poor language and communication affect a child's later development in other areas?

5. What effect do caregiver interactions have on language development?

6. Describe the major stages of speech and language development.

7. How can parents create a conversational environment?

8. What should parents be told about stuttering?

9. What are some of the things that affect how caregivers interact with infants and young children about language?

10. Why is it so important to really listen to a child?

Caregivers differ significantly in terms of the language environment and communication experiences they provide. Some parents may not provide the necessary language experiences for their children. The reasons for this vary and include some of the following:

- The parents' own level of ease and confidence in communicating is not very high, as well as their comfort with verbalizing and using language.

- Parent does not realize that the infant can hear and recognize sounds and thinks talking to an infant or young child is a waste of time.

- The kind of language environment the parent was exposed to was not conducive to family communication.

- The parents hold cultural beliefs and philosophies that view children who express their opinions as being rude and "bratty," and therefore they discourage this kind of verbal expression.

- The parents or caregivers provide few books, tapes, and music in the home that are used with their children.

- The type of language input provided for children tends to be more directive rather than following the child's lead in introducing words and sentences.

- The style of communicating that is used with children in the family is very negative and confrontational.

- The parents' knowledge of language development and awareness of speech and language delays and impairments is minimal, and they are not willing to seek assessment and intervention if they identify a delay.

- The language that is modeled within the home between parents and between parents and children is conflictual, with yelling and screaming or silence.

People vary considerably not only in the environment that they provide for their children but also in their belief about the importance and need to encourage children to talk and communicate. Caregivers have as much, if not more, impact on their children's development of language and communication than they do in practically any other area of development. As well, an adult's ability to communicate and to be understood by his or her use of language will influence his or her life in many areas, especially in the ability to get an education and a job, as well as in the ability to get on with others. As with other aspects of development, intergenerational repetition of optimal or compromised ability to use language and to communicate with others is quite likely.

In working with parents to help them to encourage their children's speech, language, and communication, it is important to emphasize the importance of language and the need to begin to encourage it from birth on. Some parents are not aware of this need for early input or about the quantity and quality of input that is helpful. Some of the important points to make when talking to parents about children's language development include the following:

- For optimal language development, it is necessary to provide a child with input from early on. This needs to be derived from the language of the community as well as the family.

Waiting until a few months before the child enters school is not soon enough. Input can be provided by parents if they speak the language or by another program or child care.

- Children learn language best when it is integrated into their activities and the everyday care that they receive. Language-rich environments include naturally occurring conversation, play with children, songs and rhymes, and caregivers who sometimes follow the child's lead.

- Television and videotapes alone cannot provide children with the language input they need, primarily because these media do not provide an interactive experience.

- Concentrating on having a child learn to read the letters of the alphabet and certain words is not the way to encourage the child to learn or to enjoy language.

- Children learn when they have a voice in the family and are allowed to express their opinions, as long as it is in a respectful manner.

- Familiarize parents with developmental milestones in speech and language and encourage them to seek help if they are concerned about their children's hearing or understanding of words, their expressive language, pronunciation, and/or the ability to have conversations.

Most parents are very aware of their children's language development and become concerned if it is delayed. Many realize that it is critically important for school success, so they often are keen to work with their child to enhance it. If this is not the case, it will be extremely important to listen to their point of view and show acceptance before any suggestions of possible ways to work with their children are given. This will be very important, as will integrating the parents' goals for their children's learning into the treatment plan, in order to avoid building resistance toward intervention.

GROUP EXERCISES FOR PARENTS TO HELP THEM ENCOURAGE A CHILD'S LANGUAGE AND COMMUNICATION

This section includes exercises that can be used with parents and other caregivers to encourage them to enhance children's language and communication skills.

Communication in My Family as I Was Growing Up

Ask parents to think about how communication took place in their families as they were growing up. Did people yell? Did parents listen to them? Did people sulk and refuse to talk if they were upset? Did people talk their problems through? Ask parents to identify what they liked and did not like about these communication patterns and how they hope to be different with their own children.

Using Feelings Cards to Recognize Nonverbal Communications

Prepare cards with situations or feelings written on them (see Figure 5.1). Have participants pick one at random. Divide the group into pairs and ask one from each pair to communicate one of the situations or feelings without using words, while the other one tries to guess what is

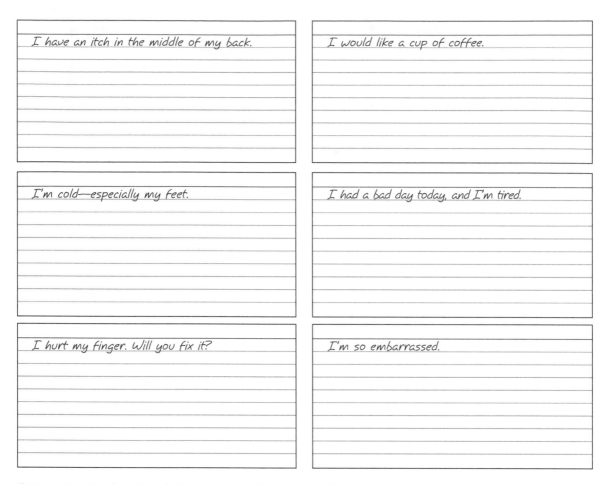

I have an itch in the middle of my back.

I would like a cup of coffee.

I'm cold—especially my feet.

I had a bad day today, and I'm tired.

I hurt my finger. Will you fix it?

I'm so embarrassed.

Figure 5.1. Examples of situation or feelings cards used to demonstrate the difficulty of expressing thoughts and emotions without words.

being communicated. Have volunteers demonstrate their best nonverbal communication. Point out that young children often try to communicate in this limited way when they cannot find or do not have the correct words. Point out how difficult it can be and how much they depend on the other person to understand them.

Changing Negative Statements to Positive Messages

Role Playing   Using examples from Principle 4, "Use special strategies to ensure conversation is not cut off . . . ," outline what caregivers need to do to change negative patterns of communication. Ask parents to volunteer for some role-playing episodes. Ask parents to play the role of their child and have them use statements made by their child that frustrate them and often trigger them to respond critically or negatively. Take the part of the parent through a negative interchange and follow it with a positive one. Ask parents to think about how the interchanges feel and discuss what is different about them.

What Were My Parents' Favorite Words to Describe Me?   Explain that messages we hear from our parents can stay with us for a lifetime and can transmit positive or negative ideals. Ask parents to share proverbs, sayings, or nicknames their parents used with them.

Instructions: Change the *don't* statements on the left into *do* statements on the right. For example: "Don't run like that" could be changed to "You can run outside if you want to."

Don'ts	Do's
"Don't color in a book." "Don't yell at me." "Don't jump on the furniture." "Don't touch."	

Figure 5.2.   Blank chart to record suggestions for turning "don't" statements into "do" statements.

Write them on a blackboard or on cards and have parents discuss how they felt about them and how they may have affected them. Have parents discuss better ways of communicating these messages if they were perceived negatively.

Translating "Don'ts" into "Do's"   Explain the principle of giving difficult information with as positive a message as possible. Give examples of how "don't" messages can be changed into "do's." Give parents a list of "don't" messages and have them change them into "do's." For example, "Don't run in the house" could be rephrased positively into "You can run outside if you want to" (see Figure 5.2).

Changing "You" Statements into "I" Statements   Discuss why "I" rather than "you" messages are helpful for children. Give some examples of changing "you" to "I" messages and give parents a list of "you" messages to change into "I" messages. For example, "You are a mean little brat to hurt your sister" is much more positive when stated as "It really upsets me when you hurt your sister" (see Figure 5.3).

Instructions: Change the *you* statements on the left into *I* statements on the right. For example: "You're a mean little brat to hurt your sister" could be changed to "It really upsets me when you hurt your sister."

"You" messages	"I" messages
"You're always late doing your homework." "You never finish your meals. Why are you such a picky eater?" "You're dumb." "You drive me crazy."	

Figure 5.3.   Blank chart to record suggestions for turning "you" messages into "I" messages.

Really Listening, Understanding, and Accepting What a Child Has to Say

Read the following vignette to parents and ask them to talk about the kind of response that Juanita needs. Brainstorm about the kind of response she should get and what they may have encountered in the same situation.

• •

Juanita was having a terrible day at the office. She arrived at work late after being up all night with the baby followed by a morning struggle getting her preschooler dressed and off to child care. When she arrived at work, she was greeted by an irate supervisor who asked her where the report was that she was supposed to have had the secretary photocopy and distribute. With rebukes of being disorganized and irresponsible ringing in her ears, she found out that the secretary was out sick and had not run off the report. After 10 phone calls with requests she did not have time for and more requests from her angry supervisor, she finally left the office an hour late, only to be confronted at home by the babysitter, who told her that the baby had a fever. As her husband arrived home, Juanita collapsed into sobs as she told him she hates her job and that she had had the worst day of her life.

Here are some possible examples of how Juanita's husband might respond to her need for support:

• A hug and expression of sympathy followed by listening to what happened and the offer of a cup of tea

• A comment indicating that if she were more organized and had gotten up earlier, she wouldn't have gotten into those difficulties

• Some generalized statement such as, "You're always in a muddle, why don't you organize yourself better?"

• Encouragement that they will sit down and find a solution together

• A suggestion to get up earlier and to talk to her boss about how he acted

Suggest that for most people in this situation, the immediate reaction they would need is a hug and an expression of sympathy, possibly when they were feeling calmer and more rested, and would be ready to try and find a solution to the situation. After this exercise, have parents think about some responses they have made to their children when they were in a similar state of distress and how they might have improved their interaction. Sum up by noting that children need to be listened to, nurtured if the situation calls for it, and allowed to have their point of view—even if they disagree with it. Have parents discuss ways to listen actively to their children and come up with some sensitive responses to the comments by children in Figure 5.4.

Learn to Respect Children

Read the "Etiquette Lesson" by Erma Bombeck (see Figure 5.5) to parents. This example is, of course, very humorous, but it does make us realize just how we talk to children and, at times,

Instructions: Read the comment on the left and respond on the right with an answer that indicates the speaker is responding sensitively. For example, if a child says, "I hate Johnny; he's mean and nasty," his caregiver could respond, "You say Johnny was mean. What happened?"	
Child's comments:	Your response
"I didn't bring any lunch today." "I had to go to the dentist yesterday, I hated it!" "I'm never coming here again, I hate you." "I had a terrible time at my father's yesterday." "Mummy, Mummy, the teacher was mean to me again today."	

Figure 5.4. Blank chart to record suggestions for listening actively.

forget to give them the respect they deserve. Have parents comment on how the example might apply to them.

Identify Miscommunications

Ask parents to think about any difficulties that they have in communicating with their children and things that they do that may get in the way or upset the child. Figure 5.6 includes a list of some communication problems from which the parent can choose to think about a solution. Brainstorm ways to improve the communication problems that are identified.

SAMPLE HOMEWORK ACTIVITIES

It is helpful to give parents who are attending a weekly parenting group some activities to try during the week that can be discussed at the next group meeting. Assign only a small number to each group participant or let him or her choose one or two the parent would like to do. Discuss how they worked out the next week.

1.   Ask parents to see how conversational their family environment is. Provide them with the list from Principle 6.

2.   Take one day and try saying only positive things to your child. Note the responses.

3.   Write a note to your child outlining some positive things and put it on her pillow or in her lunch box.

Etiquette Lesson

On TV, a child psychologist said parents should treat their children as they would treat their best friends—with courtesy, dignity and diplomacy. "I have never treated my children any other way," I told myself. But later that night, I thought about it. Suppose our good friends, Fred and Eleanor, came to dinner and . . .

"Well, it's about time you two got here! What have you been doing? Dawdling? Shut the door, Fred. Were you born in a barn? So, Eleanor, how have you been? I've been meaning to have you over for ages, Fred! Take it easy on the chip dip or you'll ruin your dinner."

"Heard from any of the gang lately? Got a card from the Martins—they're in Lauderdale again. What's the matter, Fred? You're fidgeting. It's down the hall, first door on the left. And I don't want to see a towel in the middle of the floor when you're finished. So, how are your children? If everybody's hungry, we'll go in to dinner. You all wash up, and I'll dish up the food. Don't tell me your hands are clean, Eleanor. I saw you playing with the dog."

"Fred, you sit there, and Eleanor you sit with the half glass of milk. You know you're all elbows when it comes to milk. Fred, I don't see any cauliflower on your plate. You don't like cauliflower? Have you ever tried it? Well, try a spoonful. If you don't like it, I won't make you finish it; but if you don't try it, you can forget dessert. Now, what were we talking about. Oh, yes, the Grubers. They sold their house, and took a beating, but—Eleanor, don't talk with food in your mouth. And use your napkin . . ."

At that moment in my fantasy, my son walked into the room. "How nice of you to come," I said pleasantly.

"Now what did I do?" he sighed.

Erma Bombeck
Publishers-Hall Syndicate

Figure 5.5. A humorous look at etiquette. (From Bombeck, E., Publishers-Hall Syndicate; reprinted by permission of the Aaron M. Priest Literary Agency).

4. Think about a positive message you want to give to your child. Say it.

5. Try really listening to your child. Let your child know you are aware of what he is saying.

6. Experiment with your child's ability to follow instructions. Try one, two, and three instructions. Note what he can understand and remember and use only that number of instructions at one time.

7. Try using the principles outlined in the role-playing examples when your child says something negative and upsetting. Write down what happened.

8. Keep a record for one day of the things you said to a child when he acted out. Bring the list for discussion next week.

Communication problem	Overcoming the problem
Child has difficulty processing the words.	
Child is not listening.	
Caregiver does not make sure child is listening.	
Child is upset and shuts out the words of the other person.	
Parent is angry and scares the receiver.	
Caregiver's words are too complicated.	
Words and emotions or body language do not match and child is confused (e.g., caregiver says how happy she is to see someone, while looking away).	
A "double-bind" message is given (e.g., telling a 4-year-old to be honest about something he did, and giving him a beating when he does).	

Figure 5.6. Blank chart to record strategies for overcoming communication problems.

BIBLIOGRAPHY

REFERENCES

Acredolo, L.P., & Goodwyn, S.W. (1985). Symbolic gesturing in language development: A case study. *Human Development, 28,* 40–49.

Acredolo, L.P., & Goodwyn, S.W. (1988). Symbolic gesturing in normal infants. *Child Development, 59,* 450–466.

Akhtar, N., Dunham, F., & Dunham, P.J. (1991). Directive interactions and early vocabulary development: The role of joint attentional focus. *Journal of Child Language, 18,* 41–49.

Amdur, J.R., Mainland, S.M.S., & Parker, K.C.H. (2001). *Diagnostic Inventory for Screening Children Manual.* Kitchener: Grand River Hospital.

Aram, D., Ekelman, B.L., & Nation, J.E. (1984). Preschoolers with language disorders: 10 years later. *Journal of Speech and Hearing Research, 27,* 232–244.

Baron-Cohen, S. (1995). The eye direction detector (EDD) and the shared attention mechanism (SAM): Two cases for evolutionary psychology. In C. Moore & P.J. Dunham (Eds.), *Joint attention: Its origins and role in development* (pp. 41–59). Mahwah, NJ: Lawrence Erlbaum Associates.

Barwick, M. (1999). Linking infants' attachment relationships with emerging communication and language. *IMPrint, 25,* 4–6.

Bates, E., Marchman, V., Thal, D., Fenson, L., Dale, P., Reznick, J.S., Reilly, J., & Hartung, J. (1994). Developmental and stylistic variation in the composition of early vocabulary. *Journal of Child Language, 21,* 85–123.

Bates, E., O'Connell, B., & Shore, C. (1987). Language and communication in infancy. In J. Osofsky (Ed.), *Handbook of infant development* (2nd ed., pp. 149–203). New York: John Wiley & Sons.

Beals, D.E., & Tabors, P.O. (1995). Arboretum, bureaucratic, and carbohydrates: Preschoolers' exposure to rare vocabulary at home. *First Language, 15,* 57–76.

Beck, M.S. (1979). *Baby talk: How your child learns to speak.* New York: New American Library.

Beitchman, J.H., Brownlie, E.B., Inglis, A., Wild, J., Ferguson, B., Schacter, D., Lancee, W., & Wilson, B. (1996). Seven-year follow-up of speech/language impaired and control children: Psychiatric outcome. *Journal of Child Psychology and Psychiatry and Allied Disciplines, 37,* 961–970.

Bishop, D.V.M. (1997). *Uncommon understanding: Development and disorders of language comprehension in children.* East Sussex, UK: Psychology Press.

Bishop, D.V.M., & Edmundson, A. (1987). Language impaired 4-year-olds: Distinguishing transient from persistent impairment. *Journal of Speech and Hearing Disorders, 52,* 156–173.

Blake, J., & De Boysson-Bardies, B. (1992). Patterns in babbling: A cross-linguistic study. *Journal of Child Language, 19,* 51–74.

Blank, M., & Franklin, E. (1980). Dialogue with preschoolers-a cognitively-based system of assessment. *Applied Psycholinguistics, 1,* 127–150.

Bloom, L. (1973). *One word at a time: The use of single word utterances before syntax.* The Hague: Mouton.

Bloom, L. (1991). *Language development from two to three.* Cambridge, UK: Cambridge University Press.

Bloom, L. (1993). *The transition from infancy to language: Acquiring the power of expression.* Cambridge, UK: Cambridge University Press.

Bloom, P. (1990). Subjectless sentences in child language. *Linguistic Inquiry, 21,* 491–504.

Bornstein, M.H., & Ruddy, M. (1984). Infant attention and maternal stimulation: Prediction of cognitive and linguistic development in singletons and twins. In H. Bouma & D.G. Bouwhuis (Eds.), *Attention and Performance: Control of language processes.* London: Lawrence Erlbaum Associates.

Bretherton, I., Bates, E., Benigni, L., Camaioni, L., & Volterra, V. (1979). Relationships between cognition, communication, and quality of attachment. In E. Bates (Ed.), *The emergence of symbols: Cognition and communication in infancy* (pp. 223–269). San Diego: Academic Press.

Bus, A.G., van IJzendoorn, M.H., & Pellegrini, A.D. (1995). Joint book reading makes for success in learning to read: A meta analysis on intergenerational transmission of literacy. *Review of Educational Research, 65,* 1–21.

Butterworth, G.E., & Jarrett, N. (1991). What minds have in common is space: Spatial mechanisms serving joint visual attention in infancy. *British Journal of Developmental Psychology, 9,* 55–72.

Butterworth, G.E., & Morissette, P. (1996). Onset of pointing and the acquisition of language in infancy. *Journal of Reproductive and Infant Psychology, 14,* 219–231.

Carson, D.K., Klee, T., Perry, C.K., Muskina, G., & Donaghy, T. (1998). Comparisons of children with delayed and normal language at 24 months of age on measures of behavioral difficulties, social and cognitive development. *Infant Mental Health Journal, 19,* 59–75.

Casadio, P., & Caselli, M.C. (1989). Early child's vocabulary: Gestures and words at the age of 14 months. *Età Evolutiva, 33,* 32–42.

Caselli, M.C. (1990). Communicative gestures and first words. In V. Volterra & C.J. Erting (Eds.), *From gesture to language in hearing and deaf children* (pp. 56–67). New York: Springer-Verlag.

Choi, S., & Bowerman, M. (1997). *Semantic categorization of spatial words: A developmental study of English and Korean.* Poster presented at the meeting for the Society for Research in Child Development meeting, Washington, DC.

Chomsky, N. (1986). *Knowledge of language: Its nature, origins, and use.* New York: Praeger.

Cochran-Smith, M. (1984). *The making of a reader.* Norwood, NJ: Ablex.

Cohen, N., Davine, M., Horodezky, N., Lipsett, L., & Isaacson, L. (1993). Unsuspected language impairment in psychiatrically disturbed children: Prevalence and language and behavioral characteristics. *Journal of the American Academy of Child and Adolescent Psychiatry, 32,* 595–603.

Cooper, R.P., & Aslin, R.N. (1990). Preference for infant directed speech in the first month after birth. *Child Development, 61,* 1584–1595.

Corsaro, W. (1981). Friendship in the nursery school. In S.R. Asher & J.M. Gottman (Eds.), *The development of children's friendships* (pp. 207–241). Cambridge, MA: Cambridge University Press.

Davidson, R., & Snow, C.E. (1998). *Social class differences in rare vocabulary.* Unpublished manuscript, Harvard Graduate School of Education, Cambridge, MA.

DeCasper, A.J., & Fifer, W.P. (1980). Of human bonding: Newborns prefer their mother's voice. *Science, 208,* 1174–1176.

DeCasper, A.J., & Spence, M.J. (1986). Prenatal maternal speech influences newborns' perception of speech sounds. *Infant Behavior and Development, 9,* 133–150.

Dickinson, D.K., & Smith, M.W. (1994). Long-term effects of preschool teachers' book readings on low-income children's vocabulary and story comprehension. *Reading Research Quarterly, 29,* 104–122.

Dorval, B., & Eckerman, C.O. (1984). Developmental trends in the quality of conversation achieved by small groups of acquainted peers. *Monographs of the Society for Research in Child Development, 49,* 1–72.

Eimas, P.D., Siqueland, E.R., Jusczyk, P., & Vigorito, J. (1971). Speech perception in infants. *Science, 171,* 303–306.

Ellis-Weismer, S., Murray-Branch, J., & Miller, J.F. (1994). A prospective longitudinal study of language development in late talkers. *Journal of Speech and Hearing Research, 37,* 852–867.

Fernald, A., & Kuhl, P.K. (1987). Acoustic determinants of infant preference for motherese speech. *Infant Behavior and Development, 10,* 279–293.

Forbes, D., Katz, M., Paul, B., & Lubin, D. (1982). Children's plans for joining play: An analysis of structure and function. *New Directions for Child Development, 18,* 61–79.

Franco, F., & Butterworth, G.E. (1988, September). *The social origins of pointing in human infancy.* Paper presented at the annual conference of the Developmental Section of the British Psychological Society, Coleg Harlech, Wales, United Kingdom.

Garvey, C. (1984). *Children's talk.* Cambridge, MA: Harvard University Press.

Goldfield, B.A., & Reznick, J.S. (1992). Rapid change in lexical development in comprehension and production. *Developmental Psychology, 28,* 406–413.

Gottfried, A.W. (1984). Home environment and early cognitive development. Integration, meta-analysis, and conclusions. In A.W. Gottfried (Ed.), *Home environment and early cognitive development: Longitudinal research* (pp. 329–342). Orlando, FL: Academic Press.

Hart, B., & Risley, T.R. (1992). American parenting of language-learning children: Persisting differences in family-child interactions observed in natural home environments. *Developmental Psychology, 28,* 1096–1105.

Hart, B., & Risley, T.R. (1995). *Meaningful differences in the everyday experience of young American children.* Baltimore: Paul H. Brookes Publishing Co.

Heath, S.B. (1989). Oral and literate traditions among Black Americans living in poverty. *American Psychologist, 44,* 367–373.

Hemmersam-Wiig, E., & Messing-Semel, E. (1980). Language demands of the curriculum content areas. In E. Hemmersam-Wiig & E. Messing-Semel, *Langauage assessment and intervention for the learning disabled.* Columbus, OH: Charles E. Merrill.

Hewison, J. (1988). The long term effectiveness of parental involvement in reading: A follow-up to the Haringey Reading project. *British Journal of Educational Psychology, 58,* 184–190.

Hobson, R.P. (1994). Perceiving attitudes, conceiving minds. In C. Lewis & P. Mitchell (Eds.), *Children's early understanding of mind: Origins and development* (pp. 71–93). Mahwah, NJ: Lawrence Erlbaum Associates.

Huttenlocher, J., Haight, W., Bryk, A., Seltzer, M., & Lyons, T. (1991). Early vocabulary growth: Relation to language input and gender. *Developmental Psychology, 27,* 236–248.

Kaye, K. (1977). Towards the origin of dialogue. In H.R. Schaffer (Ed.), *Studies in mother–infant interaction* (pp. 89–117). San Diego: Academic Press.

Kaye, K., & Fogel, A. (1980). The temporal structure of face-to-face communication between mothers and infants. *Developmental Psychology, 16,* 454–464.

Klann-Delius, G., & Hofmeister, C. (1997). The development of communicative competence of securely and insecurely attached children in interactions with their mothers. *Journal of Psycholinguistic Research, 26,* 69–88.

Kotsopoulos, A., & Boodoosingh, L. (1987). Language and speech disorders in children attending a day psychiatric programme. *British Journal of Disorders in Communication, 22,* 227–236.

Landry, S.H., Smith, K.E., Miller-Loncar, C.L., & Swank, P.R. (1997). Predicting cognitive-language and social growth curves from early maternal behaviors in children at varying degrees of biological risk. *Developmental Psychology, 33,* 1040–1053.

Lenneberg, E.H. (1967). *The biological foundations of language.* New York: John Wiley & Sons.

Levenstein, P., & O'Hara, J. (1993). The necessary lightness of mother-child play. In K. MacDonald (Ed.), *Parent-child play: Descriptions and implications. SUNY series, Children's play in society* (pp. 221–237). Albany: State University of New York Press.

Main, M. (1983). Exploration, play, and cognitive functioning related to infant-mother attachment. *Infant Behavior and Development, 6,* 167–174.

Manolson, A., Ward, B., & Dodington, N. (1995). *You make the difference in helping your child learn.* Toronto, Ontario: The Hanen Centre.

McCune-Nicolich, L. (1981). Toward symbolic functioning: Structure of early pretend games and potential parallels with language. *Child Development, 52,* 785–797.

McLean, L.K., & Cripe, J.W. (1997). The effectiveness of early intervention for children with communication disorders. In M.J. Guralnick (Ed.), *The effectiveness of early intervention* (pp. 349–428). Baltimore: Paul H. Brookes Publishing Co.

McNeill, D. (1966). Developmental psycholinguistics. In F. Smith & G.A. Miller (Eds.), *The genesis of language: A psycholinguistic approach.* Cambridge, MA: MIT Press.

Meins, E. (1998). The effects of security of attachment and maternal attribution of meaning on children's linguistic acquisitional style. *Infant Behavior and Development, 21,* 237–252.

Messer, D.J. (1994). *The development of communication: From social interaction to language.* New York: John Wiley & Sons.

Morse, P.A., & Cowan, N. (1982). Infant auditory and speech perception. In T.M. Field, A. Houston, H.C. Quay, L. Troll, & G.E. Finley (Eds.), *Review of Human Development.* New York: John Wiley & Sons.

Murray, A.D., Johnson, J., & Peters, J. (1990). Fine-tuning of utterance length to preverbal infants: Effects on later language development. *Journal of Child Language, 17,* 511–525.

Nelson, K. (1973). Structure and strategy in learning to talk. *Monographs of the Society for Research in Child Development, 38*(1) and (2).

Nelson, K. (1981). Individual differences in language development: Implications for development and language. *Developmental Psychology, 17,* 170–187.

Neuman, S.B. (1996). Children engaging in storybook reading: The influence of access to print resources, opportunity, and parental interaction. *Early Childhood Research Quarterly, 11,* 495–513.

Newborg, J., Stock, J., Wnek, L., Guidubaldi, J., & Svinicki, J. (1988). *Battelle Developmental Inventory (BDI).* Chicago: Riverside.

Newson, J. (1979). The growth of shared understanding between infant and caregiver. In M. Bullowa (Ed.), *Before speech: The beginning of interpersonal communication* (pp. 207–222). Cambridge, MA: Cambridge University Press.

Oller, D.K., Eilers, R.E., Basinger, D., Steffens, M.L., & Urbano, R. (1995). Extreme poverty and the development of precursors to the speech capacity. *First Language, 15,* 167–187.

Olsen-Fulero, L., & Comforti, J. (1983). Child responsiveness to mother's questions of varying type and presentation. *Journal of Child Language, 10,* 495–520.

Panneton, R.K., & DeCasper, A.J. (1986, April). *Newborns' postnatal preference for a prenatally experienced melody.* Paper presented at the International Conference on Infant Studies, Los Angeles.

Papoušek, M. (1989). Determinants of responsiveness to infant vocal expression of emotional state. *Infant Behavior and Development, 12,* 507–524.

Papoušek, M., Bornstein, M.H., Nuzzo, C., Papoušek, H., & Symmes, D. (1990). Infant responses to prototypical melodic contours in parental speech. *Infant Behavior and Development, 13,* 539–545.

Paul, R. (1993). Patterns of development in late talkers: Preschool years. *Journal of Childhood Communication Disorders, 15,* 7–14.

Paul, R. (1996). Clinical implications of the natural history of slow expressive language development. *American Journal of Speech Language Pathology, 5,* 5–21.

Paul, R., Hernandez, R., Taylor, L., & Johnson, K. (1996). Narrative development in late talkers: Early school age. *Journal of Speech and Hearing Research, 39,* 1295–1303.

Perez-Pereira, M. (1989). The acquisition of morphemes: Some evidence from Spanish. *Journal of Psycholinguistic Research, 18,* 289–312.

Pine, J.M., Lieven, E.V.M., & Rowland, C.F. (1997). Stylistic variation at the "single word" stage: Relations between maternal speech characteristics and children's vocabulary composition and usage. *Child Development, 68,* 807–819.

Putallaz, M., & Gottman, J. (1981). Social skills and group acceptance. In S.R. Asher & J.M. Gottman (Eds.), *The development of children's friendships* (pp. 116–149). Cambridge, MA: Cambridge University Press.

Records, N.L., & Tomblin, J.B. (1994). Clinical decision making: Describing the decision rules of practicing speech-language pathologists. *Journal of Speech and Hearing Research, 37,* 144–156.

Reddy, V., Hay, D., Murray, L., & Trevarthen, C. (1997, September). *Acting on attention: Towards an understanding of knowing in infancy.* Paper presented at the annual conference of the Developmental Section of the British Psychological Society, Strathclyde, Glascow.

Rescorla, L., & Fechnay, T. (1996). Mother-child synchrony and communicative reciprocity in late-talking toddlers. *Journal of Speech and Hearing Research, 39,* 200–208.

Rescorla, L., Roberts, J., & Dahlsgaard, K. (1997). Late talkers at 2: Outcome at age 3. *Journal of Speech, Language and Hearing Research, 40,* 556–566.

Romaine, S. (1999). Bilingual language development. In M. Barrett (Ed.), *The development of language* (pp. 251–275). East Sussex, UK: Psychology Press.

Sénéchal, M., LeFevre, J-A., Hudson, E., & Lawson, E.P. (1996). Knowledge of storybooks as a predictor of young children's vocabulary. *Journal of Educational Psychology, 88,* 520–536.

Snow, C.E. (1977). The development of conversation between mothers and babies. *Journal of Child Language, 4,* 1–22.

Snow, C.E. (1999). Social perspectives on the emergence of language. In B. MacWhinney (Ed.), *The emergence of language* (pp. 257–276). Mahwah, NJ: Lawrence Erlbaum Associates.

Sparrow, S., Balla, D., & Cicchetti, D. (1984). *Vineland Adaptive Behavior Scales (VABS).* Circle Pines, MN: American Guidance Service.

Stoel-Gammon, C., & Cooper, J.A. (1984). Patterns of early lexical and phonological development. *Journal of Child Language, 11,* 247–271.

Tardif, T., Shatz, M., & Naigles, L. (1997). Caregiver speech and children's use of nouns versus verbs: A comparison of English, Italian and Mandarin. *Journal of Child Language, 24,* 535–565.

Thal, D., & Tobias, S. (1992). Communicative gestures in children with delayed oral expressive vocabulary. *Journal of Speech and Hearing Research, 35,* 1281–1289.

Thelen, E., & Fogel, A. (1986). Toward an action-based theory of infant development. In J.J. Lockman & N.L. Hazen (Eds.), *Action in social context: Perspectives in developmental psychology* (pp. 23–63). New York: Plenum Press.

Tomasello, M., & Farrar, M.J. (1986). Joint attention and early language. *Child Development, 57,* 1454–1463.

Tomasello, M., Mannle, S., & Kruger, A.C. (1986). Linguistic environment of 1- to 2-year-old twins. *Developmental Psychology, 22,* 169–176.

Tomblin, J.B., Records, N.L., Buckwater, P., Zhang, X., Smith, E., & O'Brien, M. (1997). Prevalence of specific language impairment on kindergarten children. *Journal of Speech, Language, and Hearing Research, 40,* 1245–1260.

Trevarthen, C. (1977). Descriptive analysis of infant communicative behavior. In H.R. Schaffer (Ed.), *Studies in mother-infant interaction* (pp. 227–270). London: Academic Press.

Valian, V. (1991). Syntactic subjects in the early speech of American and Italian children. *Cognition, 40,* 21–81.

van IJzendoorn, M.H., Dijkstra, D., & Bus, A.G. (1995). Attachment, intelligence, and language: Meta-analysis. *Social Development, 4,* 115–128.

Vygotsky, L.S. (1962). *Thought and language.* NY: John Wiley & Sons.

Wechsler, D. (1989). *Wechsler Preschool and Primary Scale of Intelligence-Revised.* New York: The Psychological Corporation.

Weizman, Z.O. (1996). *Sophistication in maternal vocabulary input at home: Does it affect low-income children's vocabulary, literacy, and language success in school?* Unpublished doctoral dissertation. Cambridge, MA: Harvard Graduate School of Education.

Werner, H., & Kaplan, B. (1963). *Symbol formation: An organismic-developmental approach to language and the expression of thought.* New York: John Wiley & Sons.

Whitehurst, G.J., & Fischel, J.E. (1994). Early developmental language delay: What, if anything, should the clinician do about it? *Journal of Child Psychology and Psychiatry and Allied Disciplines, 35,* 613–648.

Whitehurst, G.J., Arnold, D.S., Epstein, J.N., Angell, A.L., Smith, M., & Fischel, J.E. (1994). A picture book reading intervention in day-care and home for children from low-income families. *Developmental Psychology, 30,* 679–689.

FURTHER READING ON THE TOPIC

Birdsong, B. (1983, March). Motherese. *Parents Magazine, 58,* 54–58, 61, 130–131.

Block, D., & Merrit, J. (1993). *Positive self-talk for children.* New York: Bantam Books.

Bolles, E.B. (1982). *So much to say: How to help your child learn to talk.* New York: St. Martin's Press.

Butler, D. (1998). *Babies need books: Sharing the joy of books with children from birth to six.* Portsmouth, NH: Heinemann.

Chapman, R.S. (1981). Exploring children's communicative intents: Experimental procedures. In J. Miller (Ed.), *Assessing language production in children* (pp. 111–136). Baltimore: University Park Press.

Cooke, J., & Williams, D. (1990). *Working with children's language.* Austin, TX: Communication Skill Builders.

de Villiers, P., & de Villiers, J. (1979). *Early language.* Cambridge, MA: Harvard University Press.

Defty, J. (1992). *Creative fingerplays and action rhymes: An index and guide to their use.* Westport, CT: Oryx Press.

Devine, M. (1990). *Growing together: Communication activities for infants and toddlers.* Tucson, AZ: Communication Skill Builders.

Dinkmeyer, D., & McKay, G. (1997). *Parenting young children.* New York: Random House.

Elgin, S.H. (1996). *The gentle art of communicating with kids.* New York: John Wiley & Sons.

Faber, A., & Mazlish, E. (1996). *How to talk so kids can learn.* New York: Simon and Shuster.

Faber, A., & Mazlish, E. (1999). *How to talk so kids will listen and listen so kids will talk.* New York: Avon Books.

Flodin, M. (1991). *Signing for kids: The fun way for anyone to learn American Sign Language.* New York: Putnam.

Fowler, W. (1990). *Talking from infancy: How to nurture and cultivate early language development.* Cambridge, MA: Brookline Books.

Gonzales-Mena, J., & Eyer, D.W. (1996). *Infants, toddlers and caregivers.* Mountain View, CA: Mayfield Publishing.

Goodman, S. (1988, December). Are you listening? *Parents Magazine, 63,* 89.

Goodwyn, S.W., Acredolo, L.P., & Brown, C.A. (2000). Impact of symbolic gesturing on early language development. *Journal of Nonverbal Behavior, 24,* 81–103.

Grayson, M. (1962). *Let's do fingerplays.* Washington, DC: R.B. Luce.

Hamaguchi, P.M. (1995). *Childhood, speech, language and listening problems.* New York: John Wiley & Sons.

Isaacs, S. (1987, December). Why everyone hates "friendly advice." *Parents Magazine, 62,*89.

Manolson, A. (1993). *It takes two to talk: A Hanen early language (Parent guide book),* 3rd Edition. Toronto, ON: The Hanen Centre.

McConkey, R., & Price, P. (1986). *Let's talk: Learning language in everyday settings.* London: Souvenir Press.

Mulvaney, A. (1991). *Look who's talking: How to help children with their communication skills.* New York: Simon & Schuster.

Musselwhite, C.R., & St. Louis, K.W. (1982). *Communication programming for the severely handicapped: Vocal and non-vocal strategies.* Houston, TX: College Hill Press.

Norton, G. (1984, July). Getting kids to listen: Here are twelve tips to make communicating with your children easier. *Parents Magazine, 59,* 52(5).

Rice, M.L., & Wilcox, K.A. (1995). *Building a language-focused curriculum for the preschool classroom.* Baltimore: Paul H. Brookes Publishing Co.

Roberts, J.E., & Crais, E.R. (1989). Assessing communication skills. In D.B. Bailey & M. Wolery (Eds.), *Assessing infants and preschoolers with handicaps.* Columbus, OH: Charles E. Merrill.

Rossetti, L. (1990). *Infant toddler assessment: An interdisciplinary approach.* Boston: Little, Brown.

Schrader, M. (1987). *Parent articles: Enhance parent involvement in language learning.* Tucson, AZ: Communication Skill Builders.

Schwartz, S., & Miller, J.E.H. (1996). *The new language of toys: Teaching communication skills to children with special needs. A guide for parents and teachers.* Bethesda, MD: Woodbine House.

Weitzman, E. (1992). *Learning language and loving it: A guide to promoting children's social and language development in early childhood settings.* Toronto, Ontario: Hanan Centre.

Wiener, H.S. (1988). *Talk with your child.* New York: Viking Press.

CHILDREN'S BOOKS ABOUT COMMUNICATION

Alexander, M.G. (1981). *Move over, Twerp.* New York: Dial Press.

Barrett, J. (1989). *Willie's not the hugging kind.* New York: HarperCollins Children's Books.

Carle, E. (1971). *Do you want to be my friend?* New York: HarperCollins Children's Books.

Havill, J., & O'Brien, A.S. (1993). *Jamaica and Brianna.* Boston: Houghton Mifflin.

Johnson, A. (1989). *Tell me a story, mama.* New York: Orchard Books.

Joosse, B.M. (1996). *I love you the purplest.* San Francisco: Chronicle Books.

Keats, E.J. (1999). *Maggie and the pirate.* New York: Econo-Clad Books.

Keats, E.J. (2001). *Louie.* New York: Greenwillow Books.

Keens-Douglas, R. (1996). *Grandpa's visit.* Toronto, Ontario: Annick Press.

McBratney, S. (2000). *Guess how much I love you.* Cambridge, MA: Walker Books.

Novak, M. (1994). *Mouse T.V.* New York: Orchard Books.

Polacco, P. (1996). *Aunt Chip and the great triple creek dam affair.* New York: Philomel Books.

Sharmat, M.W. (1980). *Sometimes mama and papa fight.* New York: Harper & Row.

Silsbe, B. (1995). *The watcher.* Toronto: Annick Press.

Wells, R. (1992). *Shy Charles.* New York: Puffin Books.

Wells, R. (2000). *Noisy Nora.* New York: Puffin Books.

Whitney, A.M. (1972). *Leave Herbert alone.* Reading, MA: Addison-Wesley.

Williams, S. (1997). *Library Lil.* New York: Dial Books for Young Readers.

Wood, A. (1984). *The napping house.* San Diego: Harcourt Brace.

Zolotow, C. (1980). *Say it!* New York: Greenwillow Books.

APPENDIX: SELECTED ASSESSMENT INSTRUMENTS

There are three major kinds of approaches and instruments most widely used to measure speech and language development in infants and young children: those that 1) record what children say, 2) directly test the child, or 3) ask teachers or parents to report about children's language.

Some assessments of speech and language are included in tests of intelligence or the developmental screening instruments listed in Chapter 1. These include the Diagnostic Inventory for Screening Children (DISC) (Amdur, Mainland, & Parker, 2000, Vineland Adaptive Behavior Scales (VABS) (Sparrow, Balla, & Cicchetti, 1984), Wechsler Preschool and Primary Scale of Intelligence-Revised (Wechsler, 1989), and Battelle Developmental Inventory (Newborg, Stock, Wnek, Guidubaldi, & Svnicki, 1988). Other assessment instruments are designed specifically to measure aspects of speech and language development in a number of areas or in specific areas such as receptive language, articulation, auditory comprehension, and early communication before language. Some of these assessment instruments are described in Tables A5.1–A5.4.

Table A5.1. Selected speech and language development assessments

Tool/instrument	Age range	Items/ administration time	General description
The Early Language Milestone Scale, 2nd Edition (ELM Scale–2) Coplan, J., & Gleason, J.R. (1990). Quantifying language development from birth to 3 years using the Early Language Milestone Scale. *Pediatrics, 86,* 963–971.	Birth to 3 years	43 items; 5–10 minutes	The *Early Language Milestone Scale, 2nd Edition* (ELM Scale–2) was developed as an early identification tool to identify language delays in children. It assesses language development from birth to 36 months, and intelligibility of speech from 18–48 months. The scale is divided into three skill categories: Auditory Expressive, Auditory Receptive, and Visual. Information on each item can be collected by the parent, by the parent providing a history of language development, by direct testing or by observation. The scale is a very useful instrument for routine developmental screening of very young children.
Expressive One-Word Picture Vocabulary Test– Revised (EOWPVT-R) Gardner, M.F. (1990). *Expressive One-Word Picture Vocabulary Test–Revised (EOWPVT-R).* Novate, CA: Academic Therapy Publications.	2–12 years	100 items; 15 minutes	The Expressive One-Word Picture Vocabulary Tests–Revised (EOWPVT-R) asks children to name items, usually with one word, illustrated in 100 pictures. This test assesses a child's speaking vocabulary and it can be used to screen children for preschool and kindergarten readiness. It can provide useful information about speech problems, learning disorders, and auditory processing.
Preschool Language Scale–3 (PLS–3) Zimmerman, I.L., Steiner, V.G., & Pond, R.E. (1992). *Preschool Language Scale–3.* San Antonio, TX: The Psychological Corporation.	Birth–6 years	96 items; 30 minutes	The Preschool Language Scale–3 (PLS–3) test has two subscales: Auditory Comprehension (AC) and Expressive Communication (EC). The test focuses on four language aspects: language precursors, semantics, structure, and integrative thinking skills. Standard scores and percentile rank equivalents for raw scores are provided.
Reynell-Zinkin Developmental Language Scales– 2nd Revision (RDLS) Reynell, J.K., & Gruber, C.P. (1990). *Reynell Developmental Language Scales–2.* Los Angeles: Western Psychological Services.	1–6 years	2–67 item scales; 30 minutes	The Reynell-Zinkin Developmental Language Scales (RDLS) consists of two scales: the Verbal Comprehension and the Expressive Language. Test stimuli consist of pictures and toy objects.
Test of Early Language Development, 2nd Edition (TELD-2) Hresko, W.P., Reid, D.K., & Hammill, D.D. (1991). *Test of Early Language Development (TELD–2).* Austin, TX: PRO-ED.	2–8 years	68 items; 15–40 minutes	The Test of Early Language Development, 2nd Edition (TELD-2), assesses the early development of oral language in the areas of receptive and expressive language, syntax, and semantics. It is easy to administer and is available in two parallel forms. The test yields a language quotient (LQ), a percentile rank, and an age-equivalent score.

Table A5.2. Assessments of receptive language and auditory processing

Tool/instrument	Age range	Items/ administration time	General description
Peabody Picture Vocabulary Test–Third Edition (PPVT-III) Dunn, L.M., & Dunn, L.M. (1997). *Peabody Picture Vocabulary Test–Third Edition (PPVT-III)*. Circle Pines, MN: American Guidance Service.	2.5 years–adult	175 items; 20 minutes	*The Peabody Picture Vocabulary Test–Third Edition (PPVT-III)* measures the child's receptive vocabulary and can provide a quick estimate of verbal ability or scholastic aptitude. The child is asked to point to the picture that best illustrates the meaning of a stimulus word. The test gives a mental age, intelligence quotient, and percentile rank so the child's score can be compared to that of the average child.

Other commonly used measures

Token Test for Children
Di Simoni, F. (1978). *The Token Test.* New York: Teaching Resources Corporation.

Test of Auditory Comprehension of Language (Revised Ed.)
Carrow-Woolfolk, E. (1985). *Test of Auditory Comprehension of Language (Revised Ed.).* Allen, TX: DLM Teaching Resources.

Goldman-Fristoe-Woodcock Test of Auditory Discrimination
Goldman, R.W., Fristoe, M., & Woodcock, R.W. (1970). *Goldman-Fristoe-Woodcock Test of Auditory Discrimination.* Circle Pines, MN: American Guidance Service.

Auditory Discrimination Test
Wepman, J.M. (1973). *Auditory Discrimination Test.* Chicago: Language Research Association.

Table A5.3. Articulation tests

Test Title	Age range	Items/administration time	General description
Photo Articulation Test (3rd Ed.) Lippke, B.A., Dickey, S.E., Selmar, J.W., & Soder, A.L. (1997). *Photo Articulation Test–3.* Danville, IL: The Interstate Printers and Publishers, Inc.	3–8 years	72 items; 5 minutes	The *Photo Articulation Test (3rd Ed.)* consists of 72 color photographs. The first 69 pictures test consonants and all but one vowel and a dipthong. The photographs stimulate interest and evoke spontaneous speech responses.
Picture Articulation and Language Screening Test Rodgers, W.C. (1976). *Picture articulation and language screening test.* Austin, TX: PRO-ED.			

Table A5.4. Tests of early communication

Test	Age range	Items/administration time	General description
Communication and Symbolic Behavior Scales (CSBS) Weitherby, A.M., & Prizant, B.M. (1993). *Communication and Symbolic Behavior Scales.* Baltimore: Paul H. Brookes Publishing Co.	9 months–2 years	20 items; 60 minutes	The *Communication and Symbolic Behavior Scales (CSBS)* examine the communicative, social, affective, and symbolic abilities of children whose functional communication age is between 9 months and 2 years. The scales are used to identify children with communication problems as early as possible and to devise intervention programs for them. The scales can be used with children who are not yet talking to examine their use of gestures and symbolic behaviors. The CSBS uses natural caregiver-child interactions and assesses behavior regulation, joint attention, social interactions, gestural communications, vocal and verbal communication, reciprocity, social-affective signalling, and symbolic behavior. The testing is videotaped for later analysis.

● ● ● **6**

LAYING A FOUNDATION
FOR POSITIVE SELF-ESTEEM

The importance of self-esteem in people's lives is a popular topic and has interested researchers, educators, parents, interventionists, policy makers, and even politicians. In fact, a 1986 task force (Promote Self-Esteem and Personal and Social Responsibility) was set up by the California Legislature because enhancing self-esteem was seen as an inoculation against social ills such as academic failure, dependence on welfare, and drug use. Many books and articles claim that how people feel about themselves is of central importance during childhood and adulthood. In 1989, Phillips and Bernstein wrote:

> *A great self-image is the single most important tool for successfully facing the problems, issues, and crises that arise in everyday life. Self-image is central to how your child learns, achieves, works, socializes, and loves. Self-image is the key to the way your child treats himself and is treated by others. (p. 7)*

Whether an individual's self-esteem is high or low has been linked with his or her sense of well-being, level of competence, and parenting effectiveness. Having a diminished sense of self-worth or low opinion of oneself has been found to be associated with behavioral problems and mental health difficulties, including anxiety and depression. "Self-esteem is essential for psychological survival. It is an emotional sine qua non—without some measure of self-worth life can be enormously painful, with many basic needs going unmet," wrote McKay and Fanning (1992, p. 1).

Despite the fact that an extraordinary number of writers and theorists have made the concept of self-esteem pivotal in their theories of human nature and personality development, we do not know as much about the topic as many popular articles have claimed. In fact, the relationship of self-esteem to other variables is much more complex than it may appear and relatively little is known about its development in early childhood.

Although a variety of programs are available that aim to develop self-esteem in children, they tend to be based on very simplistic meanings of the terms. Moreover, they have not taken into account a number of research findings that are important to consider in giving advice to parents about how to develop positive self-esteem in their children. These research findings include information about the possibly negative effects on behavior of grandiose self-esteem and the need instead for a realistic understanding of self. They usually do not include the importance of such tricky parental responsibilities as, for example, instilling a sense of right and wrong in children without shaming them. Such complex distinctions need to be considered and the subtleties integrated when developing strategies for developing optimal self-esteem in young children.

DEFINITIONS OF SELF-ESTEEM

Before defining self-esteem, it is important to consider the meaning of self. Coming up with a meaningful definition of self that describes a single concept that is constant across various cultures and societies is a task that has proved difficult. Even dictionary definitions are confusing; however, most people understand what is meant by *self* or *selfhood,* and would understand it as an individual's distinct personality or identity. Under this general definition, most writers have identified three main aspects that are central to this concept of selfhood: 1) the self that is aware of and evaluates the self (sometimes called the *reflective* self), 2) the self that relates to others, and 3) the self that determines what choices will be made and how they will be carried out. Although self-esteem is obviously influenced by all three aspects of this selfhood, it is primarily concerned with the reflective self or with evaluations of the self that are made by an individual of him- or herself.

Self-Esteem

Self-esteem is a significant component of the sense of self. Most theorists agree that it is the subjective evaluation (both cognitive and affective) that an individual holds about himself. Within that broad definition, various writers have disagreed about a number of issues. Although almost everyone agrees that self-esteem is multidimensional, the exact components that are attributed to the concept vary from theory to theory. Different models have considered various dimensions or domains of self-esteem, which have included a sense of competence in various aspects of functioning such as in physical and cognitive activities, worthiness, acceptance by others, and a sense of control over life. As noted, self-esteem also includes beliefs about how much we feel ourselves to be worthy of others' love, whether we believe we are "good" people, and how much we feel we can control events in our lives. In 1975, author D.C. Briggs wrote, "High self-esteem is not a noisy concert. It is a quiet sense of self-respect, a feeling of self-worth. When you have it deep inside, you're glad you're you" (p. 3).

Global self-esteem pertains to how an individual feels about him- or herself overall. This type of self-esteem is seen as dependent on two things: how important or significant a person's areas of competence are judged to be, and the discrepancy between the perceived self and the ideal self. For example, if someone is more successful in physical activities and sports than in tasks that involve the use of words or academic tasks but believes that only academic or school-related activities such as writing essays are worthwhile, he or she may have a low global self-

esteem. If he or she perceives physical activities and sports to be very important, however, the individual's global self-esteem may be very high. Similarly, how people believe they measure up to what they would like to be is also critical. If one's perceived successes are equal to or greater than one's expectations of success, high global self-esteem will result. Conversely, if things that are attempted are frequently experienced as less successful than expectations, low self-esteem results. Figure 6.1 depicts a formula for explaining positive and negative self-esteem as the balance between a person's ideal and perceived self (or how they see themselves).

As there are a number of ways to define and view self-esteem, there also are a number of related terms. Some of the most important ones are *internal representations, self-representations,* or *working models of self,* which refer to the beliefs, memories, and views that a person holds inside, consciously and unconsciously. These are used by the individual to assess new situations, to predict what will happen, and to plan behavior and actions.

Self-concept and *self-image* also refer to thoughts and feelings a person experiences when thinking about him- or herself that are not necessarily evaluative (e.g., "I am a person who likes to be with other people," "I am an athlete and enjoy running races").

Self-confidence and *self-efficacy* have been used to refer to the part of self-esteem that is about the sense that one is competent and able to achieve things (e.g., "Once I set my mind to doing something, I can usually get it done").

Although these terms refer to various types of a sense of self, the use of the term *self-esteem* is unique in that it includes an evaluative component and is about the individual's judgments about their self-worth.

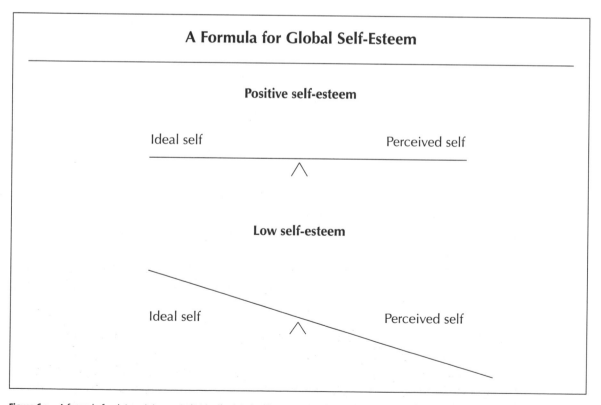

Figure 6.1. A formula for determining an individual's global self-esteem. Positive self-esteem occurs when there is a balance between the ideal self and the perceived self. Low self-esteem occurs when the perceived self is out of balance with the ideal self.

Parenting self-confidence refers to how parents view themselves as parents. Before they become parents, men and women have established a sense of self-esteem. The transition to parenthood always brings with it a number of new challenges, which in turn, result in a type of self-evaluation of parenting competence. Parenting self-confidence can, therefore, be defined as the belief that parents develop about their ability to care for and enhance the development of their child.

THEORIES OF SELF-ESTEEM

A number of writers and researchers have developed various approaches to self-esteem and its components that emphasize a different theoretical perspective of what it is and how it is developed. These ideas influence the way they assess self-esteem and propose enhancing it.

The study of self-esteem owes much to the legacy of William James, an American philosopher considered the founder of psychology who wrote about it in the late 1800s but whose work influenced such major modern theorists as Susan Harter. James first wrote about an *I-self.* He differentiated between the *material self,* the *social self,* and the *spiritual self.* Perhaps most important was his introduction of two main concepts, however, that 1) an individual possesses a global self-worth, which is determined by the ratio of how successful one is compared to how successful one believes one should be; and that 2) self-esteem is primarily formed out of this ratio, and it applies in areas that the individual values or considers important. The work of James primarily influenced the cognitive-analytic model of self-esteem, which Bednar, Wells, and Peterson (1995) and Epstein (1985) contributed to as well.

Cooley (1902) was also influential in developing another type of theory of self-esteem—the concept of the "looking-glass" or mirroring other people—and emphasized the importance of significant others and their attitudes toward a child on the development of self-esteem. He also singled out the effects of emotions, especially the self-conscious emotions of shame and pride that also arise out of the judgments of others, on self-esteem. These ideas gave rise to the social-cultural approach to self-esteem to which Sullivan (1947), Baldwin (1897), Rosenberg (1979), and Adler (1998) have also made enduring contributions.

A number of theorists have contributed significantly to our understanding of how the young child's first sense of self develops. For example, Piaget (1952) in his theory talked about how the child first develops a sense of competence or mastery by acting on the environment or by actually doing the actions in various activities. He also suggested that *disequilibrium,* or the experience of not being able to do something, motivates the individual to try again and to seek knowledge about how to do it. Winnicott (1971) stressed the importance of a social relationship (which he discussed in terms of the child's with the mother), or of *intersubjectivity* in relating with that person in developing or constructing one's self-concept. In other words, infants and young children develop their early sense of self from feedback from the mother or primary caregiver. He also stressed how important it is for the infant to be encouraged to develop a healthy sense of separateness from the mother so a clear sense of self can develop.

Stern has probably contributed the most to our understanding of the development of self in infants. In his book, *The Interpersonal World of the Infant: A View from Psychoanalysis and Developmental Psychology,* Stern (1985) explained how the child develops a sense of self as separate from the environment. He distinguished between the four senses of self: 1) the *emergent self* (birth–2 months); 2) the *core self* (2–6 months); 3) the *subjective self* (7–15 months); and 4) the *verbal self,* which forms later. He sees these senses of self all remaining functional throughout

life and "growing and coexisting." Unlike previous theorists, Stern does not believe that the infant, even at birth, experiences a symbiotic-like phase or a period of lack of differentiation between the self and other people. Also, unlike other psychoanalytic theorists, he does not see the period of 9–18 months as primarily one in which a child individuates from the primary caregiver but rather as a period in which the child seeks intersubjectivity or relationships in which thoughts and feelings are shared.

Other theoretical positions that have contributed significantly to our understanding of self-esteem include the psychodynamic view, the behavioral perspective, and humanistic and existential theories. While the social-cultural approach described above considers self-esteem as primarily externally driven, psychodynamic approaches have considered self-esteem more internally, or from the view of the individual. One of the first psychodynamic proponents was Robert White (1959), who talked about a drive toward achievement or motivation that could give rise to a sense of personal efficacy as long as the person receives affirmation from others. The more recent psychodynamic approach that has had a significant impact on our understanding of self-esteem, particularly on how it develops, is one that has been espoused by the attachment theorists. Many attachment theorists do not talk specifically about self-esteem but do emphasize the critical importance of internal working models of self and other. Attachment theorists who have talked specifically about the development of working models of attachment and their impact on behavior and development include John Bowlby, Mary Ainsworth, and Mary Main.

Theorists who consider self-esteem primarily from a learning and behavioral perspective have considered how children learn about themselves and have tended to emphasize the more behavioral aspects of parenting and its role in the development of self-esteem. Stanley Coopersmith and Albert Bandura have been significant contributors to this approach (Bandura, Barbaranelli, Caprara, & Pastorelli, 1996; Coopersmith, 1967). One group of theorists, humanistic and existential, has made major contributions to helping us understand that self-esteem is a central issue in people's lives. A number of writers can be considered under this category; Carl Rogers (1961), Karen Horney (1950), and Nathaniel Branden (1988, 1994) have each emphasized not only the importance of self-esteem but also that it can motivate people in a variety of positive or negative ways. Branden defined self-esteem as the following:

> *Self-esteem is 1) the confidence in our ability to think and to cope with the basic challenges of life (doing well), 2) confidence in our right to be happy, and 3) the feeling of being worthy, entitled to assert our needs and wants, and entitled to enjoy the fruits of our labors (feeling good). (1992, p. 3)*

Table 6.1 includes some of the major theorists on self-esteem and the main tenets of their approaches.

THE IMPORTANCE OF SELF-ESTEEM

It is clear from a theoretical and research perspective that having optimal self-esteem is important and can influence development in a positive way. The characteristics of optimal self-esteem are outlined here. Ideally, a person with good self-esteem has

- A global self-esteem or a basic core feeling of being worthy of love and respect and of being accepted by others

Table 6.1.   Theories of self-esteem

Theorist	Type of theory	Important principles
James (1890) Epstein (1985) Bednar, Wells, & Peterson (1995)	Cognitive-analytic model	The cognitions a person has about him- or herself are crucial and form the basis for self-esteem
		Examines different levels and domains of self-esteem that contribute to these cognitions
		Considers the information processing that contributes to cognitions of self-esteem
Cooley (1902) Sullivan (1947) Rosenberg (1979) Adler (1998)	Social–cultural approach	Emphasizes the importance of significant others in developing self-esteem
		Examines cultural or social characteristics and their role in shaping self-concept
		Looks at how a sense of being "good enough" or unworthy could come from socialization by parents
Horney (1950) Rogers (1961) Branden (1988, 1994)	Humanistic and existential theories	Considers self-esteem an inherent need
		Believes self-esteem can motivate an individual in positive or negative ways
		Emphasizes the crucial importance of "unconditional positive regard" and of approval and love for developing positive self-esteem
White (1959) Bowlby (1979) Ainsworth (1985) Main (1985)	Psychodynamic and attachment	Considers self-esteem from the "inside" or from the view of the person of himself
		Considers the effect of a sense of achievement and internal working models of self on development and behavior
		Has emphasized how feelings about oneself and not just cognitions influence self-esteem
Coopersmith (1967) Bandura, Barbaranelli, Caprara, & Pastorelli (1996)	Learning and behavioral perspective	Learning and behavioral principles such as modeling, and reinforcement are seen as central to the development of self-esteem
		Children learn about who they are from various aspects of how they are parented
		Positive reinforcement and consistent limits are seen as crucial for the development of self-esteem

- A basic core belief that he or she has the competence to survive and live a productive life and has a sense of control over life and sense of self-efficacy

- A realistic view of strengths and weaknesses in areas such as physical ability, intellectual capacity, moral worth, and view of others

- A sense of self that can adapt to and accommodate new information about self as it becomes available

- A sense that perfection is impossible. In other words, the person is not trying to live up to an ideal standard that is impossible to meet

The following vignettes illustrate the importance of positive self-esteem, especially when an individual is adjusting to new challenges.

• •

After giving birth to her third child, Mary experienced severe postpartum depression for many months. During that time, she often contemplated suicide, feeling so totally hopeless and unworthy that she believed that her husband and children would be better off without her. Although intellectually she knew her children were developing well and that she was intelligent and capable in a number of areas, she was still unable to overcome a feeling that she did not deserve love and respect from those around her. Mary's past history revealed that she had always felt rejected. Born to older parents who had not planned to have more children, she had always been told she was unwanted and made to feel incapable and unattractive. Consequently, she lacked a basic core feeling of being worthy of love and respect and tried to live up to an impossible standard she could never reach.

John, a thin and fretful baby, came to live with his current foster parents at 1 year of age after six previous unsuccessful placements. His new parents were determined to let John know that they cared about him "no matter what." Therefore, they accepted him unconditionally and let him know how worthwhile he was and how much they hoped he would stay with them. John gradually began to gain weight under the nurturing from his new parents. He was obviously secure in his relationship with them, and often let them know how happy he was to be their son. His parents realized that he would need to discuss his past and to reformulate his situation as he grew older and encouraged him to ask questions. They continued to let him know how competent they saw him to be. When John entered school it was obvious to everyone that he was confident and had a sense of being able to solve problems and of being accepted in the classroom.

These vignettes show how critical it is to be accepted warmly and unconditionally and how the way parents behave toward their children in the early years continues to affect self-esteem for years to come. These early models, once established, are not so stable that they cannot be changed, but they are stable enough that a great deal of persistence and considerable effort over a long time is needed to improve them. A child's level of self-esteem affects his functioning in a number of areas.

Cognition

Although self-esteem has not been shown to be directly related to intellectual functioning, children who feel good about themselves are much more able to persist at tasks even when they find them challenging, to problem-solve to come up with solutions and different ways to do things, and to ask for help if it is necessary. With these skills they often do well in school and are more likely to achieve academically at or above their intellectual level.

Social Competence

Children who feel good about themselves and who have positive self-esteem usually have more friends and have good social skills leading to popularity with peers. Children having positive

self-esteem are less likely to intrude on others or act out to get attention, or to hang back and avoid playing and joining in with groups of children. Of course, when children have problems socially their sense of not being worthwhile or loved is often intensified, as is their low self-esteem.

Emotional Development

Anxiety and depression have also been associated with low self-esteem in some studies. Feelings of lack of confidence, worthlessness, and hopelessness can lead to these conditions while positive self-esteem has been shown to be related to a sense of well-being, adaptation, and resilience.

Although self-esteem is not specifically linked to some areas of development such as gross and fine motor and language, a child who feels competent and good about herself is more likely to be interested in and excited about trying out activities and learning how to do things and is therefore more likely to do well in a range of areas of development.

THE DEVELOPMENT OF SELF-ESTEEM

Children do not really have the capacity to have a sense of self-esteem until about 8 years of age, because before that they do not have the cognitive capacity to engage in the self-appraisals that are necessary. Before this age, the development of self is proceeding, and children are developing a sense of separateness, self-efficacy, and self-recognition. By approximately age 8, a child is capable of having a conscious, verbalized concept of her *overall* worth as a person and to evaluate it negatively or positively, however. In this section the process of development of self is outlined, as well as some of the experiences that can lead to achievement of the positive self-esteem described. Table 6.2. provides a synopsis of how self-esteem develops throughout a typically developing child's various stages of life.

Birth to Three Months

During the first 3 months of life, infants gradually become more aware of the world and themselves as separate and apart from the primary caregiver. As the caregiver holds, rocks, talks, and sensitively responds to the infant, the baby experiences himself as separate and a physical sense of self is established. When someone comes when the infant is hungry, bored, overstimulated, or uncomfortable and comfort is given, the infant begins to experience himself as a person worthy of care and attention. Also, as the baby experiences making a mobile move or shaking a rattle, he realizes he can make things happen.

Four to Eight Months

From 4 to 8 months, the infant is increasingly aware of the animated world of people and the inanimate world of toys and other objects beyond the parent. Infants begin to learn more about cause and effect and making things happen. As they bang on a saucepan or pull a string to get something to move, they feel effective. Of course, the infant continues to want and need sensitive interactions with caregivers that are neither excessively stimulating nor under-stimulating.

Table 6.2. Development of self-esteem through the stages of a child's life

Age	Capacity
Birth–3 months	Begins to distinguish between self and other people Begins to recognize self as being able to "make things happen" Physical or sensorimotor sense of self laid down
4–8 months	Has increasing sense of self as being able to make things work Begins to understand cause and effect Interested in mirror image and will smile, vocalize to, pat, and play with it Still has more sustained interest and recognition of mother's image
9–18 months	Clearly differentiates between own and other reflection in mirror Develops capacity for intersubjectivity and interaffectivity (i.e., understanding thoughts and feelings of others) Still evaluates self in terms of what can achieve
19–24 months	Shows increasing awareness of self and for continuity of self Uses self pronouns "I" and "me" and pushes for "I want" or "mine" Sense of omnipotence and grandiose sense of self Shows pride in doing a task; is self-admiring to mirror image Can distinguish and name self in pictures Begins to show empathetic concern for others
2–3 years	Has ability to feel and express self-conscious emotions of pride, shame, and guilt Talks about self and actions: "I can build a tower," "I kicked the ball" May show shame at not being able to do a task Shows embarrassment at seeing something out of place on self (e.g., rouge on nose)
3–5 years	Can compare actions with another: "I did a good drawing; he did a poor one" Evaluates performance: "I built a tall tower" Shows pride in winning or doing well
5–8 years	Capable of communicating areas of personal success (e.g., "I'm good at sports") Continues to compare performance to that of others, especially as is more aware of the need to achieve abilities such as learning to read and write name By 8 years, is capable of evaluating self in a number of areas

By 6–8 months of age, the infant has often become more mobile and is able to sit alone to explore surrounding objects. Infants at this age are fascinated with the mirror image of themselves and other people. In fact, during this period they may be more excited about the reflection of their caregiver than themselves because they are more used to seeing that person. Nevertheless, there is an increasing interest in understanding humans, including themselves. The infant continues to need a caregiver who shows warmth and sensitivity as well as pleasure and interest in the infant's new explorations and achievements in the world. The infant's self-esteem also flourishes when caregivers do not overprotect but set up a safe environment for exploration.

Nine to Eighteen Months

The period from 9 to 18 months is a critical time in the development of self-esteem because the infant now has the capacity for intersubjectivity (i.e., the understanding of differences in individual minds) and for interaffectivity (i.e., the matching of feelings with those of the caregiver). A child's sense of responsiveness comes not only from toys and objects but also from ideas and emotions that people convey to toddlers about themselves. At this time a child experiences an increasing sense of differentiation between his and another's reflection in the mirror.

Though 4- to 8-month old infants are capable of exploring more, they continue to need sensitive interactions with caregivers.

Children continue to evaluate themselves in terms of immediate physical feedback derived from success or failure in achieving certain goals, however. Managing physical tasks becomes especially important.

Nineteen to Twenty-Four Months

During this toddler stage, the child becomes more aware of himself and demonstrates this with an increasing use of "I" and "me" and a push for what "I want" and for "mine." Along with this push for independence, the child also increasingly understands and wants to understand how other people feel and think about her. During the early part of this phase, a sense of omnipotence and grandiosity (i.e., "I can do anything") and of egocentricity (i.e., "I am the center of the universe") is usually at its height. Caregivers must not only provide admiration for the child's emerging autonomy and independence but also set firm and realistic limits. They must also ensure that the child does not lose every battle because the capacity for embarrassment at failure is emerging at this age. The child also enjoys meeting certain goals, and managing physical tasks.

Two to Three Years

During a child's third year of life, there is a tremendous leap forward and then a stabilization of the child's sense of self. He begins to talk about himself and his actions and to evaluate them with pride or shame. It is during this year that children show evidence that not only do they

Enable the growing toddler to succeed in achieving goals and managing physical tasks.

recognize their mirror image but also they notice it is different if it is violated by something being added. A child will show embarrassment about, for example, a smudge of dirt on his nose, so it is clear that the self-conscious emotions are possible which—if excessive—can negatively affect a child's self-esteem.

The child is much more capable now and needs the opportunity to take small responsibilities and to make decisions, for example, between certain clothes and certain foods. Having his opinion listened to and valued can make a tremendous difference for a child's growing self-esteem.

Three to Five Years

Between 3 and 5 years of age, the child's self-esteem is increasingly influenced by the world outside the home and how well she feels accepted by others (especially peers), in the school, child care, or other social situations. Many children at this time become able to compare themselves with what they could do when they were younger. They may make comparison statements such as "I'm doing much better now than I did before." As well, they begin to evaluate their performances and compare them to other children's. At the same time, the child will identify with the primary caregivers and may reflect their level of competence and strength. If a parent shows that he can handle situations without becoming overwhelmed, he will provide an excellent model for the child. By this age, the child's sense of self and view of the world is firmly established and influences how the child perceives, remembers, and acts in response to different situations. Although self-esteem is stable, it is also open to change.

Five to Eight Years

Between the ages of 5 and 8, the child gradually begins to be capable of evaluating himself in an area: "I'm good at sports," "I'm good at math." Consequently, children are more likely to become concerned if they realize they are having more difficulty than other children in learning to write their names or read some words. It is not until 8–10 years of age that the child is able to evaluate himself in a number of areas and to come up with an overall sense of self-esteem that considers the various areas of competence and integrates how other people view him, however.

IMPORTANT RESEARCH FINDINGS

Much of the research that has been carried out using self-esteem as a construct is fraught with difficulties. These problems are that the research

- Confuses the meaning and use of terms such as *self-concept* and *self-image* and how they relate to self-esteem, and consequently this lack of clarity can confuse the meaning of findings

- Defines low and high self-esteem differently, making it difficult to generalize across findings

- Tends to use survey instruments such as self-report questionnaires and large samples rather than direct observation and interviews with smaller samples. This makes it difficult to really understand what is behind these gross general statements.

- Often uses a retrospective approach in order to determine the contributors to self-esteem, risking contamination by intervening events and current views of self

- Primarily utilizes correlational methods that cannot be used to understand the direction of effects or the contribution of various factors over time

- Has not taken into account that self-esteem measures may not be able to determine what is an optimal level of self-esteem and cannot distinguish between positive self-esteem and grandiose views of self

In spite of these shortcomings, several cross-sectional research studies have consistently found certain variables to be associated with self-esteem. As well, studies with stronger methodology using path analytic models, which analyze data longitudinally or over time, looking for patterns in development and contributions to it, are beginning to demonstrate the mechanisms through which self-esteem affects a child's outcomes. This research review will consider some of the variables that are found to be associated with self-esteem and how self-esteem influences other areas of development. It will also consider the importance of parental self-confidence.

Variables Associated with Self-Esteem

Although some attempts have been made to find associations between various life stressors and environmental events and level of self-esteem, in general, relationships with other people, particularly parents, have been found to be more highly correlated with a child's self-esteem than

other variables (Barnes & Farrier, 1985; Luster & McAdoo, 1996). Among younger children, some researchers have studied the relationship between self-esteem and attachment classifications. In general, children with secure attachments, or more nurturing relationships with parents, have been found to have more optimal ratings of self-esteem (Cassidy, 1988; Verschueren, Marcoen, & Schoefs, 1996). These researchers noted that securely attached children may describe themselves positively but also are able to admit imperfections and to be more open to exploring both strong and weak aspects of self than are children with insecure attachment classifications.

Several studies have found that a variety of aspects of the parent–child interaction or relationship are related to a child's sense of self-worth. Perhaps one of the most well-known and frequently reported research studies was carried out by Stanley Coopersmith in 1967 in which a number of characteristics of parenting were found to be related to high self-esteem in 10-year-old boys. These qualities included parents having a close relationship with the children, being interested in their welfare, demanding standards of behavior, and being strict and consistent in enforcing rules. Although the study has been criticized, the findings have encouraged further research and have been supported by other findings. Other parental qualities that have been associated with high self-esteem include acceptance, warmth, the granting of autonomy, nurturance, and authoritative or democratic parenting styles (Burnett & Demnar, 1996; Kawash, Kerr, & Clewes, 1985; Litovsky & Dusek, 1985; McCormick & Kennedy, 1994; Pawlak & Klein, 1997; Rudolph, Hammen, & Burge, 1995). The research of Baumrind is described in more detail in Chapter 7; however, it is important to point out that she found that children who received authoritative or democratic parenting were more self-confident when assessed at 8 or 9 years of age (Baumrind, 1973).

Some studies have linked parents' unconditional positive regard with a child's high self-esteem (Forsman, 1989; Harter & Whitesell, 1996). Conversely, Harter, Marold, and Whitesell (1992) noted that parental support that is perceived as conditional has been found to be linked with low self-esteem.

Studies that have examined the extremes of negative parenting and child maltreatment have consistently found the expected links; for example, Kaufman and Cicchetti (1989) found that maltreated 8- to 11-year-old children had lower self-esteem than did matched children who had not been maltreated. In a review of the effects of sexual abuse on children, it was found that self-esteem in these children was consistently lower than it was in controls (Kendall-Tackett, Williams, & Finkelhor, 1993). In another study, the differences were found to persist even when family functioning and parental changes in abusive behavior were included in the analysis (Stern, Lynch, Oates, O'Toole, & Cooney, 1995). Other researchers have examined the representations of abused children of themselves and other people. In a study of 80 maltreated and 27 comparison children, Toth, Cicchetti, MacFie, and Emde (1997) found that maltreated children had more negative representations of themselves and their mothers. These models appeared to influence the children's interactions with the researcher, who was unfamiliar to them, and they were less friendly and more suspicious with the researcher than were control children. Other variables that have been linked to low self-esteem include parental favoritism to another child (Zervas & Sherman, 1994), interparental conflict (Pawlak & Klein, 1997), and sibling rivalry (Stocker, 1995). J.I. Clarke noted the importance of family on self-esteem:

> *Self-esteem is a family affair. Because the family is the first place we decide who we are and observe and practice how to be that way. To the extent that we decide that we are lovable, we build positive self-esteem. (1978, p. 4)*

Although parental and family variables have consistently been found to be related to self-esteem, in older children and adolescents, particularly those from less favorable family environments, friendships with peers may be critical for the development of self-esteem (Cramer, 1989; Gauze, Bukowski, Aquan-Assee, & Sippola, 1996; Rudolph et al., 1995). Harter and Whitesell (1996) found complex relationships among perceived competencies, peer relationships, and support from parents in a very interesting study of adolescents. For 91% of adolescents with low adjustment scores (low on self-worth, affect, and hope), perceptions of incompetence were not offset by positive relationships. Or as summarized by the researchers, "Support from either peers, parents or both . . . apparently does not offset the negative impact of these wide-ranging, negative self-perceptions" (Harter & Whitesell, 1996, p. 773). The results of this study suggest the importance of considering subgroups of children and adolescents with low self-esteem when considering both contributing variables and targeted interventions.

Self-Esteem and Its Effect on Development

Cross-sectional studies have found that high self-esteem is predictive of good adjustment, a lower incidence of behavior problems, fewer social difficulties, and fewer feelings of loneliness (Rudolph et al., 1995; Stocker, 1995). Depression has consistently been linked with low self-esteem (Burnett, 1995; Nielson & Metha, 1994; Oliver & Paull, 1995). Other authors have suggested that although there is this link, parental behaviors may mediate between the two. Garber, Robinson, and Valentiner (1997), for example, tested a path analytic model in which various parenting characteristics were expected to be mediated through the perception of self-worth of the child, which would result in symptoms of depression. The model was partially supported although parenting variables were found also to have direct effects on depression in children as well as the predicted indirect effects that were mediated through the children's perceptions of self-worth or self-esteem.

A few longitudinal studies have found that high self-esteem can act as a protective factor over time, particularly for children in high-risk situations. In a study that followed 15-year-olds for 6 years, for example, it was found that on the one hand, self-esteem was a mediator of depression regardless of family background. On the other hand, children (particularly boys) with low self-esteem were at greater risk for depression, irrespective of family background (Palosaari, Aro, & Laippala, 1996). Similarly, children who experienced divorce and who had high self-esteem were far less likely to become depressed than were children who experienced divorce and who had low self-esteem. In another study that followed 1,160 adolescents from sixth to tenth grade, consistently high or rising levels of self-esteem were related to higher school grades, less tolerance for deviance, and lower alcohol use over time (Zimmerman, Copeland, Shope, & Dielman, 1997). Jacobsen, Edelstein, and Hofmann (1994) followed 85 children and assessed two qualities: the children's attachment and self-confidence or trust in themselves at 7 years and their cognitive functioning at 7, 9, 12, 15, and 17 years. Self-confidence scores were based on behavioral observations of the children in three separate interviews. Children with secure attachments had the highest self-confidence, followed by the insecure-avoidant group. Children in the disorganized attachment group had the most negative feelings about themselves. It was found that securely attached children obtained higher scores on cog-

nitive tasks, and, in general, self-confidence had a strong independent, mediational influence on cognitive ability.

Self-Esteem and Continuity

A number of studies have found an individual's level of self-esteem to be fairly stable over time (Barnes & Farrier, 1985; Oates, O'Toole, Lynch, Stern, & Cooney, 1994). Other writers have noted that there are significant individual fluctuations in one's stability of self-esteem, however, and that large short-term fluctuations may represent fragility in self-representations. Children who experience these frequent changes may be especially sensitive to aversive events (Kernish & Waschull, 1996).

The Importance of Realistic Self-Evaluation

A few studies have explored the effects of having very high positive and unrealistic views of self. Some researchers have noted that, compared with nonagressive children, aggressive children are more likely to overestimate their competence (Hughes, Cavell, & Grossman, 1997; Hymel, Bowker, & Woody, 1993; Patterson, Kupersmidt, & Griester, 1990). Teenagers with psychiatric disturbances (Gralinski, Safyer, Hauser, & Allen, 1995) and children who are maltreated have also been found to inflate their abilities (Vondra, Barnett, & Cicchetti, 1990).

Some children with behavioral and emotional problems also have difficulty accepting and integrating negative feedback or more realistic estimates of competence into their sense of self. These inflated views of self are, therefore, subject to frequent disconfirmation when the child interacts with others, and aggression may result from these experiences. An individual's avoidance of realistic appraisals may, in fact, set up a self-perpetuating cycle of aggressive behavior. As pointed out by Baumeister, Boden, and Smart (1996) in an article on violent and aggressive adults, individuals' grandiose and inflated views of self or feelings of omnipotence may result in high scores on self-esteem scales, but when their self-esteem is threatened, they are likely to respond in irrational ways that can lead to destructive and violent behavior. As summed up by Patterson, Cohn, and Kao, "To the simple self-concept hypothesis, one might add a qualifier that high self-concepts mediate favorable development only if they are reasonably consistent with information from external sources" (1989, p. 34).

Parental Self-Confidence

Parental self-confidence can be defined as the perceptions that parents have of their ability to care for and understand their children. Gross and Rocissano have described it as the "necessary mediator between knowledge and action" (1988, p. 20). A relationship between parents' confidence and their self-esteem has been suggested and found by a number of writers (Brody, Stoneman, & McCoy, 1994; Mercer & Ferketich, 1995) and in this chapter the two concepts will be considered together. Much of the literature about parental self-confidence has been about mothers even though many fathers are actively involved with their children, particularly when mothers are employed (Lamb & Oppenheim, 1989).

A number of studies have considered the contribution of parental confidence to the adaptation to parenthood. Most researchers have found that a parent's adaptation to an infant is a complex physiological and psychosocial process (Palkovitz & Copes, 1988; Walker, Crain, & Thompson, 1986a, 1986b; Williams et al., 1987). Researchers have also found variables such as a parent's level of support, education level, and sense of internal control and mastery to be critical to the development of self-confidence in parenting (Dunst, Vance, & Cooper, 1986; Kinard, 1996; Mercer & Ferketich, 1994; Osofsky & Culp, 1993). Walker et al. noted that for first-time mothers, "forming the new relationship to their babies and gaining self-confidence in the parenting role appear interdependent" (1986a, p. 71).

Some researchers have explored various aspects of a mother's psychological functioning and various sociodemographic characteristics in order to determine their relative contributions to the mother's adjustment to her situation. In general, it has been found that only a minority of mothers experience serious psychological distress as a result of having a chronically ill child (Kazak, 1989; Patterson, 1991; Thompson, Gustafson, Hamlett, & Spock, 1992). In a study of 365 mothers of children with a chronic illness, personal psychological resources or self-esteem and self-efficacy of the mother were measured, along with an index of the child's functional impairment of their illness (Silver, Bauman, & Ireys, 1995). Mothers with more positive self-esteem who had a greater sense of having control over their lives suffered less psychological distress. In addition, the child's impairment as a result of the illness also contributed to the mother's adjustment. Having a child with a difficult temperament or behavioral problems has been found to be associated with low self-esteem for parents, however (Cutrona & Troutman, 1986; Finken & Amato, 1993; Mash & Johnston, 1983). Mash and Johnston (1983) found that mothers and fathers of children diagnosed as hyperactive rated themselves as less skilled and knowledgeable as parents.

Some studies have considered self-esteem and/or parental competence as contributors to parenting skills and child outcomes. In most studies that were reviewed that considered the effect of maternal self-confidence, it was found that low self-confidence was related to poor mother–infant interactions (Bohlin & Hagekull, 1986; Johnston, 1996; MacPhee, Fritz, & Miller-Heyl, 1996; Teti & Gelfand, 1991). Another study showed that low self-confidence was related to difficulties with prosocial capacity of the child (Brody et al., 1994). In a series of very interesting studies, Bugental and associates considered perceived parental control as a moderating variable that operates in situations in which the parent tries to discipline a difficult child. Mothers who attribute high control to the child and low control to themselves have been found to have caregiving problems sometimes as extreme as abuse (Bugental, 1992; Bugental & Shennum, 1984; Bugental, Blue, & Lewis, 1990). Although they attributed low control to themselves, they adopted very controlling approaches to disciplining their children but at the same time their messages were given less assertively and with unpleasant vocal intonation, both of which resulted in further acting out on the part of the children.

As with self-esteem, some researchers have suggested that the relationship between maternal self-confidence and parenting ability may be complex and curvilinear such that excessively high maternal self-confidence may not allow for acknowledging the complexity of parenting choices. In a study of 50 mothers and toddlers, it was found that the least knowledgeable and most confident mothers had less-positive interactions with their children than mothers who were less confident and had less knowledge (Conrad, Gross, Fogg, & Ruchala, 1992). The researchers suggested that these very confident mothers with low parental knowledge may be naïve about parenting but not open to the input of others, making intervention with these mothers very difficult.

Summary of Research

Although there is an extraordinary amount and great complexity of research findings on self-esteem and parental confidence, there are a few findings that would appear to be defensible, either because they have been repeated in a number of studies or they have been produced by sound and rigorous experimental designs. These include the following:

- The opinions of others are highly correlated to an individual's self-esteem. In early childhood, parent relationships are most important. As children get older and particularly in adolescence, the opinions of peers become very significant as well.

- A simplistic view of self-esteem as high or low does not reflect the subtleties of the construct or how it affects behavior. To those involved in intervention, the finding that "perfect" self-esteem is often a defensive idealization that closes an individual off to new information and can result in aggressive behavior, is an important one.

- Contributing parental factors to high self-esteem include warmth and closeness; interest in the child's welfare; strict, consistent rule enforcement; granting of autonomy for older children; and unconditional positive regard. When parenting is extremely negative, particularly if it is neglectful or abusive, children generally have low self-esteem.

- Depression is frequently associated with low self-esteem because it contributes to a sense of helplessness and lack of internal control.

- Realistic and positive self-esteem have been linked with adaptive functioning such as higher school grades and better cognitive functioning.

- Parental self-confidence seems to be linked more to levels of self-esteem and other psychological functioning than to difficulties with the child. Social support also contributes to the parent's sense of competence.

- High parental self-confidence without parenting knowledge may lead to less optimal parenting interactions and lack of openness to new information.

- A parent's sense of lack of control of the child may result in the parent adopting very controlling parenting strategies, but without demonstrating the confidence that the strategies will work.

THE GROWTH-PROMOTING ENVIRONMENT: PRINCIPLES OF DEVELOPING SELF-ESTEEM

This section presents a variety of principles that can guide caregivers in providing experiences for and interactions with children that encourage positive self-esteem (see Table 6.3). Ideas as to how the principles can be put into practice are given.

PRINCIPLE 1: *Show unconditional love, and let children know they are valued and accepted.*

Many writers have talked about the need for children to be given unconditional love. When caregivers convey this to a child they are letting him know that he is loved as he is and not be-

Table 6.3. Principles for encouraging self-esteem

Principle 1	Show unconditional love and let children know they are valued and accepted.
Principle 2	Acknowledge children's successes and abilities.
Principle 3	Structure situations to help children experience feelings of success.
Principle 4	Give children a feeling of reasonable control over their lives.
Principle 5	Value each child's uniqueness and tell the child about his or her special qualities.
Principle 6	Intervene when children put themselves down and express a sense of failure or hopelessness.
Principle 7	Establish a realistic view of self-esteem in children and help them cope with experiences of failure.
Principle 8	Model a sense of optimism and a positive view of yourself to the child.

cause of what he can or cannot do. The basic message is that the child is accepted "no matter what happens" and that the adult intends to always be there for the child.

Unconditional love can be shown in a variety of ways, from spending time with the child to using body language and facial expressions to show interest and joy in being with her. Positive times together can provide the child with warm memories that she can recall throughout a lifetime. When caregivers tell the child how special she is and notice her unique characteristics, this can also contribute to her sense of being valued and accepted. As the child matures, showing trust in her abilities, letting her know they trust in her capabilities, and noticing her ability to be self-sufficient can provide a sense of being loved and valued.

Conditional love, however, can leave a child feeling as if he can never be good enough to be accepted and will almost invariably result in poor self-esteem. Conditions that can be put on receiving love vary, but may include requiring that the child behaves well, stays quiet, or learns the alphabet quickly, for example.

PRINCIPLE 2: *Acknowledge children's successes and abilities.*

Children need to have their behavior acknowledged—particularly any efforts that they make to accomplish some desired task. Children do not need to be praised all of the time for completing activities and various tasks that they are *expected* to complete. In fact, when a child hears praise all the time it may lead to a number of unintended consequences:

- The child may come to rely on external praise in order to do something instead of doing it because of motivation from within.

- The praise may begin to seem insincere and empty, especially if it is used all of the time and even for things that should be done as a matter of course. Praising too frequently can lead the child to be passive and unenthusiastic about trying.

- It can encourage perfectionism, especially if the praise is reserved for a perfect, completed performance and is said with great enthusiasm. The child may feel that what he does is not acceptable unless it can be completed and be perfect.

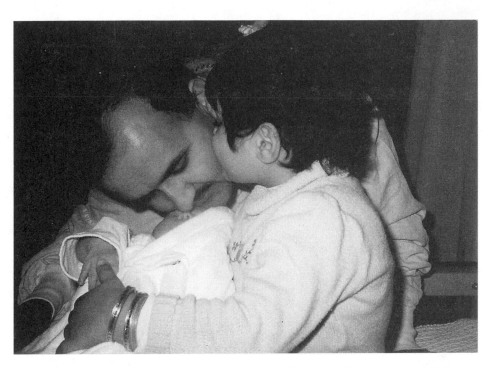

Showing unconditional love and letting children know they are valued and accepted is critical to their self-esteem.

• The child may only do things because caregivers notice and may begin to stop doing things he enjoys simply for the pleasure of doing them.

Many recommend providing encouragement on an ongoing basis rather than praise for task completion. Encouragement can take many forms. According to author Virginia Satir, "Every word, facial expression, gesture, or action on the part of the parent gives the child some message about his work" (1972, p. 4).

•••

Joan notices that her daughter Mary becomes upset easily if she is unable to complete a task. Joan does not have unreal expectations of Mary and certainly does not expect perfection. She does notice, however, that she waits for Mary to finish tasks and only then praises her with great enthusiasm like "That's terrific," "That's great," or "You did an amazing job." She realizes that perhaps Mary feels that her attempts are no good unless she receives this kind of response. Joan begins to encourage progress and notice small gains along the way. When Mary finishes her task, Joan tones down the strength of her praise for completing the task. As a result, Mary relaxes noticeably. Mary then begins to choose fun activities and to engage her mother's attention while she is doing an activity instead of striving for successful completion all of the time.

Giving children words to describe themselves can enable them to see themselves in a positive way. Here are some phrases or words that encourage positive self-esteem in children. Remember that the more specific the praise, the more valuable it will be to the child.

- That's really coming along well!

- You did it all yourself!

- I'm really proud of you for starting your homework before your television program.

- Thanks—when you set the table for dinner, that helped me a lot.

- I liked the way you did that.

- You must have really worked hard on this one.

- You are really improving with your reading.

- You have made so much progress this year.

- You are being very nice to your little sister.

- You really worked hard on that painting.

When children cannot manage an activity or experience failure, it is important to encourage them to talk about it and to help them try again. Sometimes providing children with some new strategies and being available to help if it becomes too difficult can be very helpful to overcome their feelings of low self-esteem that may otherwise result.

PRINCIPLE 3: *Structure situations to help children experience feelings of success.*

Although parents and caregivers cannot and should not try to protect children from all difficulties, having experiences of success can give children a positive sense of self that will allow them to face the larger difficulties they will inevitably be confronted with throughout their lives. When an infant is small, parents tend to do this all the time: We put a rattle close so the child can grab it; we hold the child's hands when they try those first steps. But as the child gets older we tend to allow things to get too difficult for her. For a young child, especially for one who has developmental delays, for example, what may seem to an adult like a simple task can be extremely challenging. Sometimes it can be helpful to break down what seems to be a relatively simple task (even cleaning teeth can be overwhelming for some children) into manageable steps and to notice the child's efforts along the way.

The following are other ways parents and caregivers can provide experiences of success:

- When a child is struggling to do something, assist but do not take over completely so that the child will experience the success of completion herself.

- Let children know that their efforts are noticed and appreciated.

- When children are upset because they cannot do the task, let them know it sometimes takes a long while to learn something and offer to help them learn it when they are ready.

- Let children make mistakes but notice the part of the project they did well and acknowledge this success.

- Provide tasks that can be accomplished initially quite easily and that gradually get harder.

When a child is struggling, allow her to experience the success of completion.

PRINCIPLE 4: *Give children a feeling of reasonable control over their lives.*

Children need rules and structure in their lives, and they need to know that certain rules are not to be negotiated or disputed. Small children can make some choices, however, that do not threaten their safety, their parents' morals, or anyone's health. Children must be encouraged to learn to do things and need to make choices such as which of two outfits to wear, the type of cereal they want for breakfast, and which play activities they would like during free time. These early, small choices can let children feel that they have a say in the family and that their ideas are valuable. This can help contribute to the development of a strong decision-maker in later life. Children who are given some control in their lives feel pride at a very early age, while children who are made to feel ineffective will quickly begin to experience shame and a sense of helplessness. This is particularly true if caregivers draw attention to a child's mistake and then make her feel ashamed about it. That is, instead of helping the child to make amends or to try again, she is made to feel as if she is useless, and in some cases, bad and incompetent.

PRINCIPLE 5: *Value each child's uniqueness and tell the child about his or her special qualities.*

On a daily basis, children can be made aware of their special qualities. These qualities may include personality traits, physical attributes, things the child does well, and positive behaviors. Children must be genuinely accepted as they are and be told how much they are valued for who they are. Do not compare children, but support each child's accomplishments independently.

Help children learn to evaluate their own performances so they are not dependent on adult evaluations. Ask them, for example, about their favorite stories or colors and encourage them to compare their own drawings over time.

While talking about the child's qualities, be careful not to label a child. The child who always hears that he is shy will continue to be shy; the child who hears that he is unkind will act unkind. Words and ideas will become part of the child's sense of self. Even positive labeling can cause pressure that children feel they must live up to. Children who are constantly told they are "very bright" may feel that they are failures for small missteps in school that do not fit with their self-image of always succeeding. Give children an opportunity to do things they are good at and do not push them to be something they are not. Of course, if it is something the child has to learn, such as speaking or walking, every effort will need to be made and opportunities provided for eventual success in achieving these abilities.

PRINCIPLE 6:   *Intervene when children put themselves down and express a sense of failure or hopelessness.*

During the preschool years, children are very sensitive to real or perceived rejection or failure. They display *splitting* (i.e., intense and sudden changes of feeling about others and themselves) because they cannot comprehend having mixed feelings but instead see things in black-or-white terms. When they are frustrated because they cannot do something or because someone sets strong limits, children find it hard to remember the good things and happy times. These mood changes occur more frequently if the child is tired, is not feeling well, or is having a generally stressful time. When the child is experiencing these "black" feelings, he really does view situations and people as bad and feels genuinely inadequate.

When this happens, caregivers need to avoid contradicting the child. Right or wrong, the way the child perceives the event influences how he or she feels, remembers, and acts upon the event. The child needs time to be understood and to experience support and understanding. After the feelings have been acknowledged, the child needs to be helped to remember some good times associated with the situation. The child may also need to be offered a solution or to be helped to find one.

Young children find it difficult to think about their own negative thoughts but can think through the same issues much better if they happen to a friend or fictional character. Playing with puppets or reading stories about troublesome issues can be effective in turning around a child's negative thoughts and encouraging a sense of optimism. Have children think of an upsetting situation and then imagine some effective ways to react. Then try some of them out. This will gradually help the child come up with solutions on his own.

PRINCIPLE 7:   *Establish a realistic view of self-esteem in children and help them cope with experiences of failure.*

When individuals talk and think about self-esteem, they only tend to think about ways to increase it. They do not always consider ways to encourage positive self-esteem that is also realistic and accurate. All children at approximately 1 or 2 years of age go through a stage of thinking they can do anything and that they are all-powerful (grandiosity and omnipotence), but when children continue to think this way it can become a significant problem. As a consequence, some children feel like failures if they cannot do things perfectly and without any ef-

fort, and become very upset when they have trouble and cannot do things as if by magic. The ways to prevent this from happening are twofold. The child needs to experience interest, support, concern, and affirmation of himself and what he does as well as firm and consistent limits on his behavior. Showing the child how to accomplish things by helping organize or structuring the activity along the way can also be helpful. Children must also experience support if they fail. It is also important to help children find a solution, a way to overcome obstacles, and ways to achieve some success the next time. In other words, to send this message: "You can do it, not by magic, but by trying hard and finding solutions to what is getting in the way." In essence, a balance needs to be provided in terms of

- Acknowledgment of efforts

- Support when things do not work out

- Encouragement to find new ways and a solution to problems

- An emphasis on worthwhile achievements requiring a lot of trying and effort before they are achieved

In this way, children can establish a sense of positive and realistic self-esteem and give up on their sense of grandiosity and omnipotence.

PRINCIPLE 8: *Model a sense of optimism and a positive view of yourself to the child.*

Between 3 and 5 years of age, children increasingly identify with their parents and begin to model themselves on the parents' sense of competence and strength. Well before this, however, the child has been matching his or her feelings with those of the parent. Of course, parents cannot, and should not, pretend to children that they are feeling differently from the way they truly are. If parents are frequently feeling very drained, depressed, pessimistic, or constantly angry with the child, it is important to try to find some ways to self-nurture, so that they can gradually become more positive and optimistic about their own ability and sense of control. As well, it is very important to give the child a sense that things will turn out all right generally and model ways of helping this happen. Finding positive models outside the home can be helpful, such as an individual from a service organization such as Big Brothers and Big Sisters. Books or movies can also provide children with models of people who have succeeded.

SOME COMMONLY RAISED ISSUES AROUND SELF-ESTEEM

Here are some commonly raised issues surrounding self-esteem.

What Can Be Done About Low Self-Esteem?

In considering whether a child has low self-esteem it can be helpful to try and determine in what areas the child seems to have low self-esteem and if there are some areas in which the child feels good about himself. It is also very important to see if the child's sense of self seems,

in some ways, to be realistic rather than just being low. This can be helpful in determining what can be done to help improve the child's level of self-esteem.

In considering low self-esteem, understanding how self-esteem is developed and how it changes over time can be helpful. We know that self-image and thus self-esteem gets formed out of experiences that the child has in the first 3 to 5 years of life. These experiences vary from child to child and family to family depending on many things:

- The characteristics and temperament of the child

- Parents' personality characteristics and their own experience of being parented

- The support the parents receive and the situation in which they live

- The interaction between parents and other caregivers and the child

If, for example, a child has physical or mental difficulties, or if the parent experienced severe trauma or lives in an extremely stressful situation currently, the child's early experience may be compromised. In these cases a high sense of self-esteem may be more difficult to establish.

A child's early daily experiences and interactions form memories or impressions of the outside world and of the self, including how worthy—how competent—and how acceptable the child is. Memories of small incidents gradually coalesce and affect how children perceive the world, how they remember events and, of course, how they respond to various situations. When children see the world as generally reliable and warm and themselves as worthy of positive attention, they will see situations as positive events, as "an adventure." When a child's experience is one of rejection, she is likely to perceive situations as hostile, people as angry and untrustworthy, and the self as unworthy and incompetent. These impressions influence current perceptions and behaviors and even future development, and can set in motion a cycle of inappropriate behavior and ongoing rejection (see Figure 6.2).

The following vignettes show how self-esteem influences the individual's subjective impressions and interpretations of current events and, consequently, the resulting behavior. The child's behavior, in turn, influences the behavior of others and can thus enhance or further destroy the child's self-esteem.

• •

Jim has lived in a family where there was never much time for him. He was told he was unwanted and a nuisance. When someone accidentally bumps him in the schoolyard, he immediately believes the person is out to hurt him. His impression or "internal representation" of the world as hostile makes him act in the same way and he hits back. After that, a fight usually results.

———————————————

Michael has always known he is loved and valued. When he is bumped in the schoolyard, he turns around to check out the situation. If it was an "accident," as he calls it, he usually calls out "watch out" and grins, which lets the person know he is not angry. Following this, play can resume without mishap.

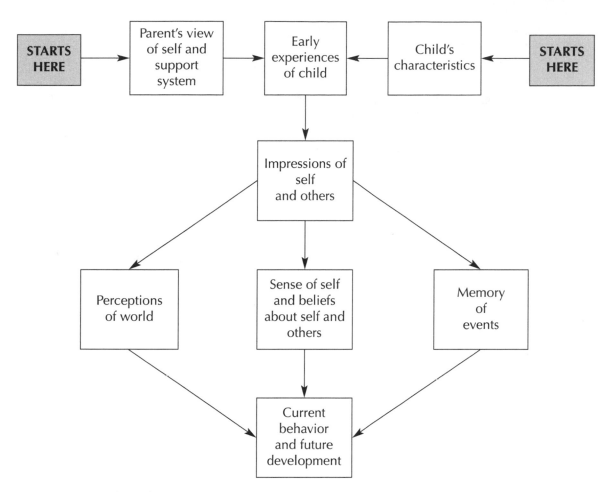

Figure 6.2. Flow chart showing how the parents' views of themselves and the support system they had as children, combined with the child's own characteristics, form a child's early experiences. These, in turn, contribute to a child's sense of self and beliefs about self and others.

Low self-esteem can arise out of a combination of difficulties the child may have that are due to genetic or biological predisposition and/or to experiences the child has in the first few years of life. Perhaps most destructive to a child's sense of self-esteem are physical or sexual abuse, neglect, or destructive comments. Many parents who have experienced very negative and ongoing criticisms express that they were as damaging as physical hurts to their sense of self-worth. When parents make comments such as "I wish you were never born," "I'm going to send you away (e.g., to a foster home)," "Why can't you be like your sister," "You're just like your stupid father," or "I should never have had you … you've ruined my life," the child's self-esteem is damaged. Children who continually hear such damaging comments soon come to believe them, and these comments become part of the child's sense of self. Other things can be more subtle and may involve harshness in discipline and nagging, blaming, criticizing, and shaming. All of these can be very destructive to children's belief in their own competence.

Some parents who try hard to make it clear that they are not criticizing the child but only his behavior can still affect his self-esteem if they correct the child too often or try to over-control him. A child who is constantly told to stop doing things or that the way he does things is not right can soon experience low self-esteem even when it is the behavior and not the child that is being criticized.

Sometimes a caregiver conveys to a child that he wants her to act smarter when she is having difficulty with learning or wants her to be more athletic when she has difficulty with coordination, for example. These types of comments can result in low self-esteem without the caregiver actually putting the child down.

It is also important to remember that if a child spends a lot of time in child care and with peers, these relationships and interactions can become very important contributors to the child's self-esteem as well. A child who is ridiculed, ostracized, or rejected by peers will soon develop low self-esteem. Sometimes, a sensitive child can quickly pick up signs that a teacher does not like her or a friend does not want her around any more. These can be devastating occurrences that can also lead to low self-esteem.

Once a sense of self is laid down by approximately 3–5 years of age, it influences what children perceive, how they react, and what they remember, which makes it very difficult to change their level of self-esteem. For example, if a child has a poor sense of self at this point he will perceive events to fit with that perception. Moreover, it will now feel comfortable when comments and events fit with that sense of self and uncomfortable when they do not. This explains why telling a child she's done well or noticing good things cannot immediately be integrated into a new sense of self and can take a long while to be accepted or believed.

Self-Concept and Children with Physical or Intellectual Challenges

Children who have various disabilities usually begin to develop a self-concept and self-esteem at the age expected according to their developmental level. In other words, the course of their development, including of self-esteem, and the sequences and stages they go through, for most of these children, is similar to that of individuals without disabilities as over time the children acquire increasingly complex skills. This is not true for children such as those with autism spectrum disorder who have more difficulty developing a distinction between self and other and possibly for children with Tourette syndrome, who have chronic and multiple tics that they cannot control. As a consequence, these children may have difficulty developing a sense of competence.

Although most children with disabilities go through the same stages of development of self and self-esteem, in many cases the quality of their self-esteem may be different than that of children without these challenges. This can be due to a number of issues:

- They have a great deal of difficulty controlling parts of their bodies and doing certain tasks or activities.

- Reactions of other people, particular other children, may draw attention to their disability and others may tease them about it.

- Being with children without disabilities in integrated settings may make the children with disabilities more aware of their difficulties in doing certain things.

- In some cases temperamental issues or their biochemical make-up may make them more easily frustrated or upset.

- They have difficulty keeping up with other children in the same group environment.

- Various medical interventions may contribute to the child's sense of having a "damaged" body self and may create a sense of people in the outside world as physically hurtful.

- The children may have experienced periods of relative isolation from other children due to illness or hospitalization.

- Caregivers may either expect too much or too little of these children.

Parents often make the observation that their children with disabilities had high self-esteem before they went to school. The reason(s) for this can be myriad, including some of the reasons just mentioned. The reason may be developmental, however, as these children may not be able to evaluate themselves, either in terms of how well they are doing over time or in comparison to other children, until they are approximately 7–8 years of age. When they reach the ages of 7–8, however, they may be capable of exactly the types of self-evaluation that can negatively affect their self-esteem.

When children with disabilities do seem to be developing poor self-esteem, it is important to encourage parents and caregivers to practice these four strategies:

- Listen to what the child is saying about how he is feeling and what he identifies as the situations that make him feel incompetent or negative about himself.

- Observe the child with other children individually and in groups to identify interactions or situations that may be contributing to his low self-esteem.

- Consider situations or tasks that may be particularly distressing or difficult for the child.

- Identify areas of competence.

Some ideas for caregivers to use for improving the self-esteem of children with intellectual or physical challenges are set out below:

- Provide the child with social experiences with children who share similar difficulties and challenges. Self-help groups for adults, parenting groups, and social skills groups for children have clearly shown how helpful it can be to spend time with others who face the same challenges.

- Intervene in order to stop any criticism or other type of rejection of the child.

- Make sure the child is provided with a lot of support and nurturing before, during, and after a significant and/or painful medical procedure or hospitalization. The use of play therapy before or after the procedure to help the child deal with the pain and anxiety may be helpful.

- Make sure adults who look after or interact with the child know as much about the child's special needs as possible. This information needs to include strengths as well as difficulties. Nevertheless, accommodations may need to be made for a child's exceptionalities in order to adapt to her unique makeup.

- Arrange for the child to have a "buddy" who is of similar age or a bit older who regularly spends time with her, is able to adapt to her special requirements, and enjoys the experi-

ence. An older mentor who has a similar disability to the child and provides a model of a positive, active person who is happy and managing well may also be helpful.

- Make sure any talents and abilities are nurtured and opportunities provided for the child to participate in any activities related to them. As well, give the child some special responsibility such as feeding the pets, which she can get some acknowledgment for.

- Set up activities whenever possible in which the child can feel some success during and upon completing it herself. A caregiver should also provide any special equipment that can increase the child's independence and self-care.

- Make sure that the child is provided with opportunities for emotionally positive, fun, and happy times.

- Emphasize building the child's sense of being able to cope by teaching specific strategies for dealing with the situations that the child finds difficult.

- Remember that providing limits and expectations within the child's abilities is crucial. In this way, the child can gradually learn self-discipline and feel more in control of his own behavior.

- Make sure the child is not overindulged and spoiled. Limits are very important to give the child a sense of competence.

- Provide information to other parents about the child's disability, making sure that a philosophy of acceptance is fostered and that they can use the information to encourage the child to be the best he can be.

- Remind parents and caregivers that nurturing themselves is critical as well and that developing a support system of family, friends, and professionals is crucial.

Remind parents and caregivers that it is important to seek professional help if the child is showing signs of depression or withdrawal.

THE ROLE OF PARENTS IN SELF-ESTEEM

People vary in their level of self-esteem and how confident they feel about parenting. As in other areas, it is important that they remain open to new information about child development and parenting and that they believe in their ability to parent a particular child. Many parents do not have a sense of confidence in their ability to parent, which can be related to a number of factors:

- Having experienced aversive, abusive, or neglectful parenting during childhood or other types of trauma or loss. These experiences may impact on a parent's ability to be sensitive to a child and to provide appropriate discipline.

- Expecting to be "perfect" parents and finding it difficult to accept that they feel angry and frustrated at times.

- Having low self-esteem and a sense of being worthless and/or having no control over life.

- Lack of support and/or recent life stresses such as divorce, a death, or job loss.

- Poor health or emotional difficulties.

- Overcompensating for the negative patterns of parenting that they received. This can result in a parent's failing to discipline or in giving a child everything he wants.

Caring for children can be stressful, and parents can experience burnout whether they are working outside of or in the home. Many people working in the human services area experience burnout for many of the same reasons that parents do: They can feel unappreciated and unsupported in their role. Strategies to get out of this rut are much the same as with other types of burnout. They include nurturing oneself, overcoming the belief that one must be the perfect parent or caregiver, accepting mistakes, learning to handle criticism, and finding a supportive network of people.

DISCUSSION QUESTIONS TO USE IN TRAINING PROFESSIONALS

1. Define what self-esteem means and describe some characteristics of it.

2. Based on your experience of working with children and families, list at least six factors that can contribute to a child's development of self-esteem.

3. Inflated self-esteem can be a problem. Describe someone you know or who is in public life who has an unrealistically inflated view of him or herself.

4. List some reasons children and adults may develop an inflated sense of themselves.

5. List events or experiences that children need in the first 5 years of life in order to develop sound self-esteem.

6. What effect does a child's level of self-esteem have on her behavior and personality?

7. List the reasons that having good self-esteem is so important for children.

8. What are the important components of parental burnout and how can they be overcome?

WORKING WITH PARENTS:
GROUP EXERCISES AND SAMPLE HOMEWORK ACTIVITIES

As has been explained in this chapter, how parents and other caregivers feel about themselves and their ability to care for young children can influence how they interact with their children. This can, in turn, influence how their children feel about themselves. Consequently, some of the important ways to work with parents and caregivers in improving children's self-esteem are set out in this section.

Most parents are aware of the importance of their child feeling good about him- or herself, but they may be less clear about how to achieve that. Sometimes their own experience growing up can make them emphasize one aspect of parenting over others. For example, the parent who remembers too much criticism and strict discipline may decide to provide too little structure, an approach that can actually undermine his or her child's self-esteem. Sometimes, a parent who believes that too little was expected of them may have very high expectations of his or her child instead. In these cases, it is important to affirm the positive aspects of the parenting that are being provided but to remind the parent of the child's other needs.

When parents are too intrusive, overprotective, or restrictive of their children, professionals can suggest that they need to allow their children to have a little more responsibility and to make a few decisions. They need to be told that this will send a message to children that they are capable of doing things on their own and can do them well. If parents spend too little time encouraging children, however, suggesting that they spend time on activities with them and showing them how to set situations up for success can be very useful.

Some parents find the concept of unconditional love hard to understand, and it is helpful to let them know that there are many things they probably do naturally that provide this experience. Having them think about their own experience growing up may help them identify experiences they felt provided them with a sense of this and any that did not. Thinking about this will probably help them decide on any changes they would like to make in order to enhance a sense of this kind of love for their child.

For parents who do not feel very competent about themselves in their parenting role, being around other parents in parenting groups can be very helpful. There is nothing like finding out that other children do the same sort of things as yours do and that other parents are unsure about their parenting ability and sometimes do things they wish they had not done with their children, to make parents feel better about themselves. Then assuring them that one cannot be or should not try to be the "perfect" parent, just a "good enough" parent, can be very affirming and encouraging.

Other ways to help parents enhance their children's self-esteem have been included in other parts of this chapter and in other chapters in this book. They include trying to adapt the environment to their child's special temperament so he can experience success; listening to him and giving him a chance to be heard; and being there when he is upset, hurt, or frustrated.

GROUP EXERCISES TO HELP PARENTS ENCOURAGE SELF-ESTEEM

These group activities will help parents and caregivers enhance their children's sense of self-esteem, increase their own sense of competence in caregiving, and overcome burnout.

What are some ideas for showing unconditional love?	List special times you can share together.	List positive words to describe your child.

Figure 6.3. A blank chart for parents to list some ways to express unconditional love for a child.

Showing Unconditional Love

Introduce the concept of unconditional love and have parents discuss how they provide it and in what circumstances it is more difficult. Ask parents to think about whether or not they practice these behaviors (see Figure 6.3):

- Let the child know that although you may disapprove of a behavior, you love the child "no matter what."

- Use positive words to describe your child.

- Spend some time with your child when you can give him your exclusive attention.

A parent's unconditional love for his children is often obvious to others. (From Johnston, Lynn [1978]. *Do they ever grow up?* Minnetonka, MN: Meadowbrook Press; reprint granted with written permission of Lynn Johnston Productions, Inc.)

- Tell the child often how much you love her and that you are glad she is your child.

- Smile at the child. Remember, seeing a smiling, approving face can make anyone's day a little better—especially a child's.

Review the chart in Figure 6.3, and have the group complete it.

Assessing Issues a Child is Facing

Changing a child's low self-esteem to a belief in his competence can best be dealt with by going through the checklist of possible issues that the child may be experiencing (see Figure 6.4) and trying to determine from it what can be changed.

Instructions: Read the following list and check off any items that pertain to you.

____ My expectations of the child may be too high.

____ I lose my temper with the child too quickly and frequently.

____ I am often depressed or convey a sense of hopelessness to the child.

____ The child is often rejected by other children.

____ The child has a physical or intellectual challenge of which he is aware and that upsets him.

____ I seem to be constantly saying "no" to the child.

____ I shame and embarrass the child.

____ I constantly praise the child but only when she completes something.

____ I threaten my child that I will go away or leave her.

____ The child has experienced or is experiencing some kind of abuse.

____ My partner and I fight or yell at one another.

____ I feel challenged as the children can do more now and do not need my help as much. Sometimes I may hold them back and do things for them that they should be encouraged to do themselves.

____ I resent having to help the child all the time and complain about it a lot.

____ The child's daycare provider is very negative with her.

____ I do not provide much structure and do not make sure the children are given help in order for them to complete something.

____ Tasks the child is expected to do are unrealistic given her ability level.

____ Activities are too easy and the child is not challenged enough given her ability level.

Figure 6.4. Checklist of parental behaviors and issues that foster poor self-esteem in children.

When difficulties are identified, new strategies should be chosen from the principles in this chapter and tried over time until the child can gradually integrate these new self-concepts into her sense of self.

Setting Up Situations for Children to Feel Success

Explain to parents that small children may need help getting started and staying focused on a task. This can be done by breaking tasks down for the child such as tying shoes or brushing teeth so they do not seem so overwhelming, and encouraging the child along the way. Have parents complete the steps for the tasks in Figure 6.5.

Encouraging Children to Be Involved in Decision and Rule Making

Suggest to parents and caregivers some decisions a child can be encouraged to make, such as choosing an outfit for the day. Suggest some decisions a child cannot be allowed to make such as when she must go to bed every night. Discuss the difference between absolute rules, such as not hurting others or running on the road, and structures and limits in which some flexibility can be allowed. It is expected that children will come to the table and eat for a certain time, for example, but some flexibility may be allowed in terms of the vegetable they choose to eat and

Instructions: Think of a task a child will learn at each stage such as tying shoes or brushing teeth. Suggest ways to help him learn it. Break it down into tasks involved. For young children, make pictures of each task.

Age	Task	Steps to complete the task
Birth–12 months	(e.g., banging objects together)	
1–2 years	(e.g., building a tower of blocks)	
2–3 years	(e.g., doing a puzzle)	
3–4 years	(e.g., singing a song and doing actions)	
4–6 years	(e.g., writing the letters of the alphabet)	

Figure 6.5. Blank chart that parents and caregivers can use to practice helping children break tasks down into steps involved.

Table 6.4. Ways to express encouragement for a child who is having difficulty completing a task

Difficulty	Words of encouragement
Trying to complete a puzzle	"You're almost done."
Remembering to do homework	"When you've finished, you can play until bedtime."
Sitting still	"I'm sure you can sit still for a little while; let's see how long."
Brushing hair	"Your hair looks so shiny when you brush it."
Losing things	"It's hard when we lose something we like. I wonder how you could remind yourself about it next time."

when they may be excused from the table (within reason, such as when a certain amount of food has been eaten).

Helping Children Deal with Difficult Tasks

Ask parents to suggest strategies that have worked for them to encourage children to do tasks that may be causing them difficulty. Table 6.4 includes some examples of words of encouragement when a child is having difficulty.

Role Playing to Intervene When Children Express Low Self-Esteem

Demonstrate how to intervene when children put themselves down and express a sense of failure and hopelessness by role playing. Encourage parents to role-play the kind of experiences their children seem to be having and have them try ways to help children feel better. Table 6.5 includes role-playing examples that elicit negative and positive results.

Add other role plays, with parents taking roles in situations that are familiar but difficult for them. Point out that what is important in each example is that the following occurs:

- The child's discouragement and frustration is heard, acknowledged, and understood.

- The child is reminded of a time when the situation had worked out or was positive.

- Some ways to overcome the difficulty are suggested. (Make sure to follow through with the suggestion.)

Table 6.5. Role plays demonstrating negative and positive results

Role-play demonstration: Negative result		Role-play demonstration: Positive result	
Child:	Johnny hit me; everyone hurts me.	Child:	Johnny hit me; everyone hurts me.
Parent:	Don't be silly; everyone is nice to you.	Parent:	What Johnny did makes you feel sad? You wish he would stop doing that?
Child:	No they're not. And you hurt me too.	Child:	Yes! He did it yesterday, too!
Parent:	I'm always doing things for you!	Parent:	Didn't you two have fun together the other day in the water?
Child:	You never listen, you don't understand. [Slams out of room].	Child:	Yes. Johnny can be nice, too.
Parent:	You rude little thing; come here!	Parent:	Perhaps you could ask him over to play in the water again one day.

Overcoming a Tendency to Expect Perfection in Parenting

Explain how expecting to be perfect can really make parents feel inadequate, because no parent can be perfect. Have parents discuss what realistic expectations are. It is important for parents to acknowledge the reality that all parents at times feel they have failed their children.

Parents need to be encouraged to change the "shoulds" to "I will try" or "I will not expect this of myself or my child right now." They need to learn to try to rewrite perfectionist or impossible scripts with scripts that are gentler, kinder, and perhaps more age-appropriate for their child and thus more attainable. To get practice in this, have parents list some expectations for themselves and their children that are unrealistic and have them change them to more realistic expectations for themselves (see Figure 6.6 for an example).

Instructions: Look at some of the examples of unrealistic expectations in the column on the left. On the right, come up with some expectations that are more realistic and some strategies to reach them. Two examples are given.

The "shoulds": What I expect of myself and my child	"I will try to": What is realistic
My children should always be polite.	I will encourage my children to be polite by noticing the good manners and accepting that small children are still learning.
My child will always behave well when we go shopping.	I will help my child feel better about shopping by keeping it short and involving her in the shopping if possible.

Figure 6.6. Blank chart that parents and caregivers can use to list some of the expectations for themselves and their children that are unrealistic and those that are more attainable and strategies to attain realistic expectations.

Enhancing Self-Confidence and Self-Esteem by Identifying Triggers

All people experience fluctuations in terms of how they feel about themselves from day to day. It is helpful for parents to be aware of the triggers that can make them feel low, depressed, or unworthy and what can cheer them up. Some of the triggers that may cause the drop in self-esteem include being criticized, ignoring the positive, jumping to conclusions too quickly, believing that they can be perfect, being too sensitive or taking things personally, or exaggerating a problem. Parents will benefit from a discussion of how these triggers might be dealt with or avoided. Figure 6.7 provides a chart that can be used to help parents identify these triggers, times that these happened, and ways to improve or change these tendencies.

Enhancing a Feeling of Worthiness

Ask parents to write down 14 positive qualities or attributes about themselves, and then to read the list aloud to the other group members. These need not be significant achievements but can be little things they do well, such as being cheerful in the morning, baking great pies,

Trigger: What made me feel down?	When has this happened?	What could I have done or do in the future to make the outcome better?
Someone criticized me.	My spouse told me I was lazy.	I could have explained all of the things I had done that day.

Figure 6.7. Blank chart that parents and caregivers can use to identify triggers that make them depressed and what can be done about them.

and so forth. Parents may then be asked to read the list in the morning and evening throughout the week after the group session.

Identifying Things I Would Like To do Better

In this exercise, give each participant a 3" x 5" card or piece of paper. Ask them to list three faults or parenting responses to their children's behavior that they would like to improve. Then have the group leader collect the cards and shuffle and redistribute them to everyone, so no one knows which belongs to whom. If someone in the group receives his or her own card, ignore this and continue the process in the same way. Have each parent in turn read the faults or parenting responses. Then have the group brainstorm possible solutions. Ask the group leader to also write all the identified faults on the blackboard. People can thus notice similarities to their own problems and see the range of concerns that have been shared. The group leader will comment on solutions as well as suggest some parenting techniques that may be helpful.

Overcoming the Experience of Burnout

The statements shown in Figure 6.8 can be used by parents to assess themselves in terms of their degree of burnout. Parents can be asked to circle the number of items that apply to them.

Instructions: Are you experiencing burnout? Circle the numbers that apply to you.	
1. Feeling exhausted, drained, and sometimes depressed, and having little energy or motivation to do things	7. Feeling drained because everyone is dependent on you and makes demands on you all the time
2. Feeling angry and often losing control and yelling or hitting your child or others	8. Constantly resenting and disliking your child for getting in the way of your own life
3. Feeling inadequate and a bad parent compared to other parents	9. Forgetting things and feeling disorganized all the time
4. Not wanting to get up in the morning to deal with your child	10. Blaming self or family for feeling so drained and exhausted and for not helping.
5. Feeling a sense of helplessness and of lacking control of your child and how he or she behaves	11. Feeling your child should be more mature and not understanding that he or she is only a child
6. Feeling tired all the time and experiencing physical symptoms such as headaches, pains, and getting ill frequently	**Total circled =**

Figure 6.8. Questionnaire to determine if a parent or caregiver is experiencing burnout. (*Key:* Anyone with four or more of these difficulties could benefit from talking to their physician or other professional.)

Table 6.6. Ways to avoid or lessen parental burnout

Find someone you can really talk to and who listens without judging. This could be a friend, partner, or a counselor.

Try and arrange time for yourself only, at least once a week, and nurture yourself. Do something you enjoy.

Watch television.

Have a massage.

Allow yourself to take up a hobby or a course in an area in which you do well and enjoy.

Make sure you get enough rest and sleep.

Include exercise in your day.

Find a parent support group.

Allow yourself to feel anger toward those who may have hurt you in your past. Repressed anger can cause exhaustion and depression.

Learn relaxation and breathing techniques to help you calm down.

Use visualization techniques to "go to" a relaxing place that allows you to "let go" of a current stress (e.g., a special room, a place in the outdoors, the beach). Relaxation, breathing, and visualization techniques can be especially helpful because they can be carried out at home and at a suitable time. This may be crucial for parents with young children who find it difficult to get out. Having a person with expertise demonstrate the techniques may be very helpful for parenting groups.

Have parents discuss the results. Parents need to know that everyone feels burned out sometimes, but that if they feel this way all the time they should take some action. Parents who check four or more of the statements as applying to them should look for ways to overcome burnout. Discuss ways to overcome burnout and provide parents with some suggestions to try, such as those listed in Table 6.6. What people do about burnout varies according to what people enjoy and what makes them feel relaxed and fulfilled.

SAMPLE HOMEWORK ACTIVITIES

Parents in group situations will find the concepts easier to put into practice if they are given simple activities or other ideas to try with their children at home. The results can then be discussed with the support of the group. Assign only one or two of the suggested tasks.

1. Ask parents to avoid saying negative things to their children for a week.

2. Have parents write down labels they use with their children during the week, both positive and negative.

3. Have parents teach their child a simple task by breaking it down into component parts. Have them encourage their children along the way.

4. Suggest that parents do one thing just for themselves.

5. Ask parents to make a note of positive behaviors their children display during the week.

6. Have parents write an advertisement for themselves listing their good points.

7. Have parents read their "positive features" list each morning and evening throughout the week.

BIBLIOGRAPHY

REFERENCES

Adler, A. (1998). *Understanding human nature.* Center City, MN: Hazelden.

Ainsworth, M.D. (1985). Patterns of infant–mother attachment: Antecedents and effects on development. *Bulletin of the New York Academy of Medicine, 61,* 771–791.

Baldwin, J.M. (1897). *Social and ethical interpretations in mental development: A study in social psychology.* New York: MacMillan.

Bandura, A., Barbaranelli, C., Caprara, V., & Pastorelli, C. (1996). Multifaceted impact of self-efficacy beliefs on academic functioning. *Child Development, 67,* 1206–1222.

Barnes, M.E., & Farrier, S.C. (1985). A longitudinal study of the self-concept of low-income youth. *Adolescence, 20,* 199–205.

Baumeister, R.F., Boden, J.M., & Smart, L. (1996). Relation of threatened egotism to violence and aggression: The dark side of high self-esteem. *Psychological Review, 103,* 5–33.

Baumrind, D. (1973). The development of instrumental competence through socialization. In A.D. Pick (Ed.), *Minnesota symposium on child psychology* (Vol. 7, pp. 3–46). Minneapolis: University of Minnesota Press.

Bednar, R.L., Wells, M.G., & Peterson, S.R. (1995). *Self-esteem: Paradoxes and innovations in clinical theory and practice.* Washington, DC: American Psychological Association.

Bohlin, G., & Hagekull, B. (1986). "Good mothering": Maternal attitudes and mother–infant interaction. *Infant Mental Health Journal, 8,* 352–363.

Bowlby, J. (1979). *The making and breaking of affectional bonds.* London: Routledge, Capman and Hall.

Branden, N. (1988). *How to raise your self-esteem.* New York: Bantam Books.

Branden, N. (1992). *The power of self-esteem.* Deerfield Beach, FL: Health Communications.

Branden, N. (1994). *The six pillars of self-esteem.* New York: Bantam Books.

Briggs, D.C. (1975) *Your child's self-esteem: The key to life.* New York: Doubleday.

Brody, G.H., Stoneman, Z., & McCoy, J.K. (1994). Contributions of protective and risk factors to literacy and socioemotional competency in former head start children attending kindergarten. *Early Childhood Research Quarterly, 9,* 407–425.

Bugental, D.B. (1992). Affective and cognitive processes within threat-oriented family systems. In I.E. Sigel, A.V. McGillicuddy-Delisi, & J.J. Goodnow, *Parental belief systems: The psychological consequences for children.* Mahwah, NJ: Lawrence Erlbaum Associates.

Bugental, D.B., Blue, J., & Lewis, J. (1990). Caregiver beliefs and dysphoric affect directed to difficult children. *Developmental Psychology, 26,* 631–638.

Bugental, D.B., & Shennum, W.A. (1984). "Difficult" children as elicitors and targets of adult communication patterns: An attributional–behavioral transactional analysis. *Monographs of the Society for Research in Child Development,* 49(1, Serial No. 205).

Burnett, P.C. (1995). Irrational beliefs and self-esteem: Predictors of depressive symptoms in children? *Journal of Rational-Emotive & Cognitive-Behavior Therapy, 13,*193–201.

Burnett, P.C., & Demnar, W.J. (1996). The relationship between closeness to significant others and self-esteem. *Journal of Family Studies, 2,* 121–129.

Cassidy, J. (1988). Child–mother attachment and the self in six-year olds. *Child Development, 59,* 121–134.

Cassidy, J. (1990). Theoretical and methodological considerations in the study of attachment and the self in young children. In M.T. Greenberg, D. Cicchetti, & E.M. Cummings. *Attachment in the preschool years: theory, research and intervention* (pp. 87–120) Chicago: The University of Chicago Press.

Clarke J.I. (1978). *Self-esteem: A family affair.* New York: Harper & Row Publications.

Conrad, B., Gross, D., Fogg, L., & Ruchala, P. (1992). Maternal confidence, knowledge, and quality of mother–toddler interactions: A preliminary study. *Infant Mental Health Journal, 13,* 353–362.

Cooley, C.H. (1902). *Human nature and the social order.* New York: Scribner.

Coopersmith, S. (1967). *The antecedents of self-esteem.* San Francisco: Freeman.

Cramer, D. (1989). Self-esteem and the facilitativeness of parents and close friends. *Person-Centered Review, 4,* 61–76.

Cutrona, C.E., & Troutman, B.R. (1986). Social support, infant temperament, and parenting self-efficacy: A mediational model of postpartum depression. *Child Development, 57,* 1507–1518.

Dunst, C.J., Vance, S.D., & Cooper, C.S. (1986). A social systems perspective of adolescent pregnancy: Determinants of parent and parent–child behavior. *Infant Mental Health Journal, 7,* 34–48.

Epstein, S. (1980). The self-concept: A review and proposal of an integrated theory of personality. In E. Staub (Ed.), *Personality: Basic aspects and current research* (pp. 83–131). Englewood Cliffs, NJ: Prentice Hall.

Epstein, S. (1985). The implications of cognitive-experiential self-theory for research in social psychology and personality. *Journal for the Theory of Social Behavior, 15,* 283–310.

Finken, L.L., & Amato, P.R. (1993). Parental self-esteem and behavior problems in children: Similarities between mothers and fathers. *Sex Roles, 28,* 569–582.

Forsman, L. (1989). Parent–child gender interaction in the relation between retrospective self-reports on parental love and current self-esteem. *Scandinavian Journal of Psychology, 30,* 275–283.

Garber, J., Robinson, N.S., & Valentiner, D. (1997). The relation between parenting and adolescent depression: Self-worth as a mediator. *Journal of Adolescent Research, 12,* 12–33.

Gauze, C., Bukowski, W.M., Aquan-Assee, J., & Sippola, L.K. (1996). Interactions between family environment and friendship and associations with self-perceived well-being during early adolescence. *Child Development, 67,* 2201–2216.

Gralinski, J.H., Safyer, A.W., Hauser, S.T., & Allen, J.P. (1995). Self-cognitions and expressed negative emotions during midadolescence: Contributions to young adult psychological adjustment. *Development and Psychopathology, 7,* 193–216.

Gross, D., & Rocissano, L. (1988). Maternal confidence in toddlerhood: Its measurement for clinical practice and research. *Nurse Practitioner, 13,* 19–22, 25, 28–29.

Harter, S., Marold, D.B., & Whitesell, N.R. (1992). A model of psychosocial risk factors leading to suicidal ideation in young adolescents. *Development and Psychopathology, 4,* 167–188.

Harter, S., & Whitesell, N.R. (1996). Multiple pathways to self-reported depression and psychological adjustment among adolescents. *Development and Psychopathology, 8,* 761–777.

Horney, K. (1950). *Neurosis and human growth: The struggle toward self-realization.* New York: Norton.

Hughes, J.N., Cavell, T.A., & Grossman, P.B. (1997). A positive view of self: Risk or protection for aggressive children? *Development and Psychopathology, 9,* 75–94.

Hymel, S., Bowker, A., & Woody, E. (1993). Aggressive versus withdrawn unpopular children: Variations in peer and self-perceptions in multiple domains. *Child Development, 64,* 879–896.

Jacobsen, T., Edelstein, W., & Hofmann, V. (1994). A longitudinal study of the relation between representations of attachment in childhood and cognitive functioning in childhood and adolescence. *Developmental Psychology, 30,* 112–124.

James, W. (1890). *The principles of psychology.* Chicago: Encyclopedia Britannica.

Johnston, C. (1996). Parent characteristics and parent–child interactions in families of nonproblem children and ADHD children with higher and lower levels of oppositional-defiant behavior. *Journal of Abnormal Child Psychology, 24,* 85–104.

Kaufman, J., & Cicchetti, D. (1989). Effects of maltreatment on school-age children's socioemotional development: Assessments in a day-camp setting. *Developmental Psychology, 25,* 516–524.

Kawash, G.F., Kerr, E.N., & Clewes, J.L. (1985). Self-esteem in children as a function of perceived parental behavior. *The Journal of Psychology, 119,* 235–242.

Kazak, A.E. (1989). Families of chronically ill children: A systems and social-ecological model of adaptation and change. *Journal of Consulting and Clinical Psychology, 57,* 25–30.

Kendall-Tackett, K.A., Williams, L.M., & Finkelhor, D. (1993). Impact of sexual abuse on children: A review and synthesis of recent empirical studies. *Psychological Bulletin, 113,* 164–180.

Kernish, M.H., & Waschull, S.B. (1996). The interactive roles of stability and level of self-esteem: Research and theory. In M.P. Zanna (Ed.), *Advances in experimental social psychology* (Vol. 27, pp. 93–141). San Diego: Academic Press.

Kinard, E.M. (1996). Social support, competence and depression in mothers of abused children. *American Journal of Orthopsychiatry, 66,* 449–462.

Lamb, M.E., & Oppenheim, D. (1989). Fatherhood and father–child relationships: Five years of research. In S.H. Cath, A. Gurwitt, & L. Gunsberg (Eds.), *Fathers and their families* (pp. 11–26). Hillsdale, NJ: Analytic Press.

Litovsky, V.G., & Dusek, J.B. (1985). Perceptions of child rearing and self-concept development during the early adolescent years. *Journal of Youth and Adolescence, 14,* 373–387.

Luster, T., & McAdoo, H.P. (1996). Factors related to self-esteem among African American youths: A secondary analysis of the High/Scope Perry preschool data. *Journal of Research on Adolescence, 5,* 451–467.

MacPhee, D., Fritz, J., & Miller-Heyl, J. (1996). Ethnic variations in personal social networks and parenting. *Child Development, 67,* 3278–3295.

Main, M. (1985, April). Adult mental organization with respect to attachment: Related to infant Strange Situation attachment status. In M. Main (Chair), *Attachment: A move to the level of representation.* Symposium conducted at the meeting of the Society for Research in Child Development, Toronto.

Mash, E.J., & Johnston, C. (1983). Parental perceptions of child behavior problems, parenting self-esteem, and mothers' reported stress in younger and older hyperactive and normal children. *Journal of Consulting and Clinical Psychology, 51,* 86–99.

McKay & Fanning, P. (1992). *Self-esteem: A proven program of cognitive techniques for assessing, improving, and maintaining your self-esteem.* Oakland, CA: New Harbinger Pub.

McCormick, C.B., & Kennedy, J.H. (1994). Parent–child attachment working models and self-esteem in adolescence. *Journal of Youth and Adolescence, 23,* 1–18.

Mercer, R.T., & Ferketich, S.L. (1994). Predictors of maternal role competence by risk status. *Nursing Research, 43,* 38–43.

Mercer, R.T., & Ferketich, S.L. (1995). Experienced and inexperienced mothers' maternal competence during infancy. *Research in Nursing & Health, 18,* 333–343.

Nielsen, D.M., & Metha, A. (1994). Parental behavior and adolescent self-esteem in clinical and nonclinical samples. *Adolescence, 29,* 525–542.

Oates, R.K., O'Toole, B.I., Lynch, D.L., Stern, A., & Cooney, G. (1994). Stability and change in outcomes for sexually abused children. *Journal of the American Academy of Child and Adolescent Psychiatry, 33,* 945–953.

Oliver, J.M., & Paull, J.C. (1995). Self-esteem and self-efficacy: Perceived parenting and family climate; and depression in university students. *Journal of Clinical Psychology, 51,* 467–481.

Osofsky, J.D., & Culp, R. (1993). A relationship perspective on the transition to parenthood. In G.H. Pollock & S.I. Greenspan (Eds.), *The course of life: Vol 5. Early adulthood* (pp. 75–98). Madison, CT: International Universities Press.

Palkovitz, R., & Copes, M. (1988). Changes in attitudes, beliefs and expectations associated with the transition to parenthood. *Marriage and Family Review, 12,* 183–199.

Palosaari, U., Aro, H., & Laippala, P. (1996). Parental divorce and depression in young adulthood: Adolescents' closeness to parents and self-esteem as mediating factors. *Acta Psychiatrica Scandinavica, 93,* 20–26.

Patterson, C.J., Cohn, D.A., & Kao, B.T. (1989). Maternal warmth as a protective factor against risks associated with peer rejection among children. *Development and Psychopathology, 1,* 21–38.

Patterson, C.J., Kupersmidt, J.B., & Griester, P.C. (1990). Children's perceptions of self and of relationships with others as a function of sociometric status. *Child Development, 61,* 1335–1349.

Patterson, J.M. (1991). Family resilience to the challenge of a child's disability. *Pediatric Annals, 20,* 491–499.

Pawlak, J.L., & Klein, H.A. (1997). Parental conflict and self-esteem: The rest of the story. *The Journal of Genetic Psychology, 158,* 303–313.

Phillips, D., & Bernstein, F.A. (1989). *How to give your child a great self-image.* New York: Random House.

Piaget, J. (1952). *The origins of intelligence in children.* New York: International Universities Press.

Rogers, C. (1961). *On becoming a person: A therapist's view of psychotherapy.* Boston: Houghton Mifflin.

Rosenberg, M. (1965). *Society and the adolescent self-image.* Princeton, NJ: Princeton University Press.

Rosenberg, M. (1979). *Conceiving the self.* New York: Basic Books.

Rudolph, K.D., Hammen, C., & Burge, D. (1995). Cognitive representations of self, family, and peers in school-age children: Links with social competence and sociometric status. *Child Development, 66,* 1385–1402.

Satir, V (1972). *Peoplemaking.* Palo Alto, CA: Science and Behavioral Books.

Silver, E.J., Bauman, L.J., & Ireys, H.T. (1995). Relationships of self-esteem and efficacy to psychological distress in mothers of children with chronic physical illnesses. *Health Psychology, 14,* 333–340.

Stern, A.E., Lynch, D.L., Oates, R.K., O'Toole, B.I., & Cooney, G. (1995). Self-esteem, depression, behavior and family functioning in sexually abused children. *Journal of Child Psychology and Psychiatry and Allied Disciplines, 36,* 1077–1089.

Stern, D.N. (1985). *The interpersonal world of the infant: A view from psychoanalysis and developmental psychology.* New York: Basic Books.

Stocker, C.M. (1995). Children's perceptions of relationships with siblings, friends, and mothers: Compensatory processes and links with adjustment. *Journal of Child Psychology and Psychiatry and Allied Disciplines, 35,* 1447–1459.

Sullivan, H.S. (1947). *Conceptions of modern psychiatry.* New York: W.W. Norton.

Teti, D.M., & Gelfand, D.M. (1991). Behavioral competence among mothers of infants in the first year: The mediational role of maternal self-efficacy. *Child Development, 62,* 918–929.

Thompson, R.J., Gustafson, K.E., Hamlett, K.W., & Spock, A. (1992). Stress, coping, and family functioning in the psychological adjustment of mothers of children and adolescents with cystic fibrosis. *Journal of Pediatric Psychology, 17,* 573–585.

Toth, S.L., Cicchetti, D., MacFie, J., & Emde, R.N. (1997). Representations of self and other in the narratives of neglected, physically abused, and sexually abused preschoolers. *Development and Psychopathology, 9,* 781–796.

Verschueren, K., Marcoen, A., & Schoefs, V. (1996). The internal working model of the self, attachment, and competence in five-year-olds. *Child Development, 67,* 2493–2511.

Vondra, J.I., Barnett, D., & Cicchetti, D. (1990). Self-concept, motivation, and competence among preschoolers from maltreating and comparison families. *Child Abuse & Neglect, 14,* 525–540.

Walker, L.O., Crain, H., & Thompson, E. (1986a). Maternal role attainment and identity in the postpartum period: Stability and change. *Nursing Research, 35,* 68–71.

Walker, L.O., Crain, H., & Thompson, E. (1986b). Mothering behavior and maternal role attainment during the postpartum period. *Nursing Research, 35,* 352–355.

White, R.W. (1959). Motivation reconsidered: The concept of competence. *Psychological Review, 66,* 297–333.

Williams, T.M., Joy, L.A., Travis, L., Gotowrec, A., Blum-Steele, M., Aiken, L.S., Painter, S.L., & Davidson, S.M. (1987). Transition to motherhood: A longitudinal study. *Infant Mental Health Journal, 8,* 251–265.

Winnicott, D.W. (1971). *Playing and reality.* New York: Basic Books.

Zervas, L.J., & Sherman, M.F. (1994). The relationship between perceived parental favoritism and self-esteem. *The Journal of Genetic Psychology, 155,* 25–33.

Zimmerman, M.A., Copeland, L.A., Shope, J.T., & Dielman, T.E. (1997). A longitudinal study of self-esteem: Implications for adolescent development. *Journal of Youth and Adolescence, 26,* 117–141.

FURTHER READING ON THE TOPIC

Anderson, E., Redman, G., & Rogers, C. (1984). *Self-esteem for tots to teens: Five principles for raising confident children.* New York: Meadowbrook.

Andrew, C., & Tracy, N. (1996). First steps toward competence: Promoting self-esteem and confidence in young children with disabilities. In L.E. Powers, G.H.S. Singer, & J.A. Sowers (Eds.), *On the road to autonomy: Promoting self-competence in children and youth with disabilities* (pp. 373–387). Baltimore: Paul H. Brookes Publishing Co.

Barba, M. (1989). *Esteem builders.* Carson, CA: Jalmar Press.

Baumeister, R. (Ed.). (1993). *Self-esteem: The puzzle of low self-regard.* New York: Plenum Press.

Bjorklund, D.F., & Bjorklund, B.R. (1991, February). "I can do it, mom!" *Parents Magazine, 66(5),* 92.

Brazelton, B. (1987, March). How to raise your child's self-esteem. *Family Circle,* 37–42.

Briggs, D.C. (1975). *Your child's self-esteem.* New York: Doubleday.

Comer, J.P. (1987, February). Encouraging self-esteem. *Parents Magazine, 62(1),* 162.

Curry, N.E., & Johnson, C.N. (1990). *Beyond self-esteem: Developing a genuine sense of human value.* Washington, D.C.: National Association for the Education of Young Children.

Damon, W., & Hart, D. (1988). *Self-understanding in childhood and adolescence.* New York: Cambridge University Press.

Fleming, R.A. (1979). Developing a child's self-esteem. *Pediatric Nursing, 5,* 58–60.

Harter, S. (1999). *The construction of the self: A developmental perspective.* New York: Guilford Press.

Hitz, R., & Driscoll, A. (1988). Praise or encouragement? New insights into praise: Implications for early childhood teachers. *Young Children, 43,* 6–13.

Isaacs, S. (1989, February). "You can do it!" *Parents Magazine, 64(5),* 114.

Kostelnik, M.J., Stein, L.C., & Whiren, A.P. (1988). Children's self-esteem: The verbal environment. *Childhood Education, 65,* 29–32.

Loomans, D., & Loomans, J. (1994). *Full esteem ahead: 100 ways to teach values and build self-esteem for all ages.* Tiburon, CA: Kramer.

Mack, J.E., & Ablon, S.L. (1983). *The development and sustenance of self-esteem in childhood: From the study group of the Division of Child Psychiatry of the Harvard Medical School, and the Cambridge-Somerville Mental Health and Retardation Center.* New York: International Universities Press.

Marshall, H.H. (1989). The development of self-concept. *Young Children, 44,* 44–51.

McKay, M., & Fanning, P. (1997). *Self-esteem.* Oakland, CA: New Harbinger.

Mecca, A.M., Smelser, N.J., & Vasconcellos, J. (Eds.). (1989). *The social importance of self-esteem.* Berkeley, CA: University of California Press.

Mruk, C.J. (1995). *Self-esteem: Research, theory and practice.* New York: Springer Publishing.

Phillips, D. (1991). *How to give your child a great self-image.* New York: Penguin.

Pomeranz, V.E., & Schultz, D. (1985, June). A sense of self. *Parents Magazine, 60(1),* 128.

Pope, A.W., McHale, S.M., & Craighead, W.E. (1988). *Self-esteem enhancement with children and adolescents.* New York: Pergamon Press.

Price, A.H., & Parry, J.A. (1982). *101 ways to boost your child's self-esteem.* Wauwatosa, WI: American Baby Books.

Segal, J. (1996, May). "You're the Greatest!", *Parents Magazine, 71,* 84–88.

Weissbourd, B. (1986, March). Help your child feel great: Improving your child's self-image. *Parents Magazine, 61(1),*174.

Weissbourd, B. (1990, October). Building your toddler's self-esteem. *Parents Magazine, 65(1),* 204.

Wells, L.E., & Marwell, G. (1976). *Self-esteem: Its conceptualization and measurement.* Beverley Hills: Sage.

White, M. (1989, April). "My son needed to feel needed." *Parents Magazine, 64(4),* 84.

Wylie, R. (1974). *The self-concept.* Lincoln: University of Nebraska Press.

Yoder, J., & Proctor, W. (1988). *The self-confident child.* New York: Facts on File.

Youngs, B.B. (1993). *How to develop self-esteem in your child: 6 vital ingredients.* New York: Fawcett Columbine.

CHILDREN'S BOOKS ABOUT SELF-ESTEEM

Ashley, B. (1995). *Cleversticks.* New York: Random House.

Bannatyne-Cugnet, J. (1993). *Estelle and the self-esteem machine.* Red Deer, Canada: College Press.

Barrett, J.D. (1989). *Willie's not the hugging kind.* New York: HarperCollins Children's Books Group.

Carlson, N. (1985). *Louanne pig in the talent show.* New York: Carolrhoda Books.

Carlson, N. (1990). *I like me!* London: Puffin Books.

Carlson, N. (1997). *ABC, I like me!* New York: Viking Children's Books.

Charlip, R. (1996). *Hooray for me!* Berkeley, CA: Tricycle Press.

Cohen, M. (1980). *No good in art.* New York: Greenwillow Books.

Cohen, M. (1998). *So what?* New York: Yearling.

Falconer, I. (2000). *Olivia.* New York: Atheneum Books for Young Readers.

Herron, C. (1997). *Nappy hair.* Toronto: Random House of Canada.

Hoffman, M. (1991). *Amazing Grace.* London: Frances Lincoln.

Howe, J. (1987). *I wish I were a butterfly.* San Diego: Harcourt Brace.

Hru, D. (1993). *Joshua's Masai mask.* New York: Lee & Low.

Liddell, S. (1994). *Being big.* Toronto: Second Story Press.

Medearis, A.S. (1994). *Annie's gifts.* Orange, NJ: Just Us Books.

Prater, J. (1997). *The greatest show on earth.* Cambridge, MA: Candlewick Press.

Wells, R. (1981). *Timothy goes to school.* New York: Dial Books for Young Readers.

Wilhelm, H. (1990). *A cool kid—like me!* New York: Crown.

APPENDIX: SELECTED ASSESSMENT INSTRUMENTS

ASSESSING SELF-ESTEEM AND PARENTAL CONFIDENCE

Lack of clarity regarding the definition and theoretical basis of the concept of self-esteem has resulted in difficulties and hindered the development of adequate measuring instruments. With adults, self-esteem has primarily been measured using self-report measures that require verbal reasoning and the ability to consider a variety of possible responses. Young children, of course, do not have these abilities. For this reason, other methods have been adopted such as asking them to tell stories about pictures or observing their behavior and inferring from it their beliefs about themselves. Because of the growing understanding of the importance of parenting self-confidence in enhancing parent–child interactions and relationships, a few measures of this characteristic have been included. As will be noticed, some of these measures have been developed to assess maternal self-confidence, and tests that can be used with fathers are scarce. The following assessment tools for both adults and children may be useful to help program leaders assess the success of interventions by using them for pre- and post-measures.

Table A6.1 includes some measures for assessing self-esteem in children, and Table A6.2 includes a list of self-esteem measures for adolescents and adults.

Table A6.1. Selected self-esteem measures for children

Instrument	Age range	Items/administration time	General description
Internal Working Model of Self–Puppet Interview Cassidy, J. (1990). Theoretical and methodological considerations in the study of attachment and the self in young children. In M.T. Greenberg, D. Cicchetti, & E.M. Cummings. *Attachment in the preschool years: Theory, research and intervention* (pp. 87–120). Chicago: The University of Chicago Press.	3–6 years	20 questions are asked about the child, using a puppet; 10 minutes	The *Internal Working Model of Self–Puppet Interview* assesses the child's self-representation and consists of an interview carried out with a large hand puppet. The interviewer questions the child, who operates the puppet. The interviewer might ask: "Do you like [child's name] the way he is, or do you want to make him better? How?" "Do you think [child's name] is important or not important? It is expected that the interview will reveal the way the child imagines that others view him or her.
The Joseph Preschool and Primary Self-Concept Screening Test (JPPSST) Wylie, R.C. (1989). *Measures of self concept.* Lincoln, NB: University of Nebraska Press. Joseph, J. (1979). *Joseph Preschool and Primary Self-Concept Screening Test.* Wood Dale, IL: Stoelting Company.	3–9 years	15 items; 5–7 minutes	The *Joseph Preschool and Primary Self-Concept Screening Test (JPPSST)* uses stimulus cards that present the child with pictures of two children at the desirable and undesirable end of a behavior or characteristic (e.g., clean–dirty; winner–loser). The child is asked to choose "Which one is most like you?" Each item is scored from 1–2 and a maximum score is 30. Children in the high-risk category are usually referred for further testing.
The Pictorial Scale of Perceived Competence and Social Acceptance for Young Children (PSPCSA) Harter, S., & Pike, R. (1984). The Pictorial Scale of Perceived Competence and Social Acceptance for Young Children. *Child Development,* 55. 1969–1982.	4–7 years	24 items; 20 minutes	These *PSPCA* scales are designed to measure perceived competence and social acceptance. They yield four subscale scores for Cognitive Competence, Physical Competence, Social Acceptance by Peers, and Maternal Acceptance. The test does not provide a single or global measure of self-esteem but rather an assessment and profile of self-judgements in the domains mentioned above. The test consists of a booklet with pictures of children and descriptions from which the examiner reads to the child, for example, "This child is good at doing puzzles and this child isn't very good."
Self-Perception Profile for Children (SPPC) Harter, S. (1985). *Self-Perception Profile for Children.* Denver, CO: University of Denver Press.	8 years or older; however, the global scale consisting of 7 items has been used for children as young as 6 years of age.	7 items for global scale; 5 minutes	The *Self-Perception Profile for Children (SPPC)* instrument is designed to measure perceptions of competence. There are six subscales, with five designed to assess specific domains (Scholastic Competence, Social Acceptance, Athletic Competence, Physical Appearance and Behavioral Conduct) and one intended to measure global self-worth.

Table A6.2. Selected self-esteem measures for adults

Type of measure	Instrument	Age range	Items/ administration time	General description
Assessing self-confidence of adolescents and adults	*Multidimensional Self-Esteem Inventory (MSEI)* Epstein, S. (1980). The self-concept: A review and proposal of an integrated theory of personality. In E. Staub (Ed.), *Personality: Basic aspects and current research* (pp. 83–131). Upper Saddle River, NJ: Prentice Hall.	Adolescents and adults	116 items; 15–20 minutes	The *Multidimensional Self-Esteem Inventory (MSEI)* is interpreted according to 11 scales. These are Global Self-Esteem, Competence, Lovability, Likability, Personal Power, Self-Control, Moral Self-Approval, Body Appearance, Identity Integration, Defensive Self-Esteem Enhancement, and Body Functioning. The strengths of the instrument are that it is grounded in a theory of self-esteem, and the scale of global self-esteem is defined as a generalized summary of feelings of worthiness.
	Pearlin Sense of Mastery Scale Pearlin, L.L., & Schooler, C. (1978). The structure of coping. *Journal of Health and Social Behavior, 19,* 2–2².	Adolescents and adults	7 items; 5 minutes	The *Pearlin Sense of Mastery Scale* is a brief measure which can assess the extent to which an individual feels in control of life as opposed to feeling ruled by fate. There are 7 items with a 4-point rating from "strongly agree" to "strongly disagree." "Scores are additive and higher scores indicate greater control.
	Rosenberg Self-Esteem Scale (RSES) Rosenberg, M. (1965). *Society and the adolescent self-image.* Princeton, N.J.: Princeton University Press. Rosenberg, M. (1979). *Conceiving the self.* New York: Basic Books.	For adolescents, grade levels 9–12 and adults, although Rosenberg has recently used it with grade-school children.	10- and 7-item versions available; 5 minutes	The *Rosenberg Self-Esteem Scale (RSES)* is a multidimensional measure of self-esteem that assesses an individual's sense of acceptance and self-worth. This widely used measure addresses global positive or negative attitudes toward the self. Items are of the following type: "I feel that I have a number of good qualities"; "All in all, I am inclined to feel I am a failure." Subjects are asked to rate on a 5-point scale the extent to which each statement is felt or experienced by them. The possible scores on self-acceptance and self-worth range from 1 (low self-esteem) to 4 (high self-esteem). High self-esteem signifies the individual respects him or herself as worthy; low self-esteem reflects both lack of self-respect and feelings of inadequacy.

(continued)

365

Table A6.2 *(continued)*

Type of measure	Instrument	Age range	Items/ administration time	General description
	Tennessee Self Concept Scale (TSCS) Walsh, J., Wilson, G., & McLellarn, R. (1989). A confirmatory factor analysis of the Tennessee Self-Concept Scale. *Criminal Justice and Behavior, 16 (4),* 465–472.	12 years or older	100 self-admin-istered items; 10–20 minutes	The *Tennessee Self-Concept Scale (TSCS)* assesses the following dimensions of self-esteem: Identity, Moral-Ethical Self, Self-satisfaction, Personal Self, Behavior, Family Self, Physical Self, and Social Self. There is also a Total Scale Score based on the subscales.
Assessing par-enting self-confidence	*The Maternal Self-Report Inventory (MSI)* Shea, E., & Tronick, E.Z. (1988). The Maternal Self-Report Inventory. In H.E. Fitzgerald, B.M. Lester, & M.W. Yogman. *Theory and research in behavioral pediatrics (Vol. 4),* pp. 100–139.	Any mother regardless of age	100 items; short form of 26 items; 10 min-utes for short version	The *Maternal Self-Report Inventory (MSI)* measures dimensions of perceived areas including Caretaking Ability, General Ability and Preparedness for Mothering Role, Acceptance of Baby, Expected Relationship with Baby, Parental Acceptance, Body Image and Health, and Feelings Concerning Pregnancy, Labor, and Delivery.
	Parenting Sense of Competence Scale (PSOC) Johnston, C., & Mash, E.J. (1989). A measure of parenting satisfaction and efficacy. *Journal of Clinical Child Psychology, 18,*167–175.	Any parent regardless of age who has a toddler	17 items; 5 minutes	The *Parenting Sense of Competence Scale (PSOC)* has parents rate themselves on a 5-point scale on items designed to measure parents' ability to meet demands of parenting situations. The scale taps two aspects of parenting: 1) satisfaction with parent-ing, including frustration and anxiety; and 2) efficacy, reflecting competence, problem-solving ability, and capability in the par-enting role. It can be used with parents with infants and chil-dren of all ages.
	Toddler Care Questionnaire (TCQ) Gross, D., & Rocissano, L. (1988). Maternal confidence in toddlerhood: Its measurement in clinical practice and research. *Nurse Practitioner, 13,* 19–29.	Any mother regardless of age	36 items; 5 minutes	The *Toddler Care Questionnaire (TCQ)* measures "maternal confi-dence," which is defined as the mother's perception of her effec-tiveness in managing a series of tasks or situations relevant to raising her toddler. Mothers rate their confidence in their ability to perform parenting tasks specific to their children. Ratings range on a 5-point scale from very little confidence to quite a lot of confidence. The items are summed to obtain a total score. Higher scores indicate greater maternal confidence.

● ● ● 7

DISCIPLINING TO ENCOURAGE
SELF-REGULATION, MORALITY,
AND A SENSE OF CONSCIENCE

Of all of the topics discussed in this book, discipline is one of the most talked about by caregivers. Moreover, a large percentage of parenting books are about disciplining techniques for children, and in parenting groups discipline is usually the first topic that caregivers want to discuss. Typically, they want to find the ideal solution or a discipline technique that can solve any behavioral problem.

For parents of toddlers and preschoolers these concerns are not surprising, as acting-out episodes with toddlers can occur at home at least as often as every 10 minutes. Outside the home, especially in the grocery store, negative behavior can occur far more often, sometimes as often as every minute! Unfortunately, although most children become more amenable to discipline by 3 or 4 years of age, a small but significant number of children develop severe behavioral difficulties that can become chronic, leading to serious consequences as these children become adolescents and adults.

One of the things we know about discipline is that if it is incorporated into the child's daily routine from very early on it is relatively easy to make it a natural part of the child's life. Once a child has developed behavior problems it becomes much more challenging to establish good behavior, however, and parents need enormous energy and commitment to establish positive discipline strategies that work. Gaining back control and setting up a discipline schedule can still be done, but many battles may have to be fought before the plan becomes effective.

Many parenting books and articles are quite limited in their advice about discipline. Most people concentrate only on behavioral methods and do not consider or integrate into their suggestions the significant number of research findings on the topic. Areas of develop-

ment other than self-control are often not considered in the advice given. Parents and other caregivers need to be provided with a full understanding of how discipline relates to all aspects of child development. As well, they need to understand why it is so important to provide both control and an atmosphere of warmth and caring when dealing with discipline issues. In other words, while children should not be allowed to win all the battles, they also should not be made to feel that they lose them all. The following vignettes show how the extremes of permissiveness and harshness in child rearing can affect children.

● ●

Michael's parents sought help from a therapist because Michael was "out of control." His pediatrician had diagnosed him as having attention-deficit/hyperactivity disorder (ADHD), which his parents did not agree with. When Michael was observed with his siblings and parents, the therapist saw a child whose every whim was responded to. His mother, Ann, seemed exhausted from running after him, keeping him happy, and providing lengthy explanations for every limit she tried to impose on him. Michael presented as a very anxious, bright, and friendly child—but at the same time he could be defiant and demanding.

Mimi brought her 4-year-old daughter Laura for psychological treatment because of her "anger and rudeness." Laura swore, hit, and refused to do anything for her mother. Interaction between the two revealed extreme hostility on the part of Mimi, who continually imposed harsh limits. For example, Mimi talked about how sleeping was no longer a problem after she had left Laura to cry for 3 hours a night for several nights. She was unable to see the obvious sadness and sense of despair under Laura's defiant exterior.

Both mothers described in the vignettes had experienced significant abuse (verbal and physical) from their parents. For Ann, this had resulted in an urgent determination to avoid being punitive at all costs. For Mimi, the result was a reenactment of her feelings of hostility toward her mother on Laura, whom she saw as embodying all of the negative characteristics she remembered in her mother.

Parents use a variety of strategies to discipline young children, including spanking, time-outs, natural consequences, ignoring, positive reinforcement, distraction, and other variations of these. Some are too lax, some are too strict, and others alternate between the two. A fortunate few are able to set up a cooperative environment where conflicts are minimal and the child can learn to internalize values and to eventually control his impulses.

Parents discipline in a particular way for all sorts of reasons, some of which will be explored in later sections of this chapter. Whatever the type of discipline or the reason behind it, it is clear that there are some basic principles of discipline that must be in place for children to gradually gain sufficient self-control and a sense of morality.

DEFINITIONS OF SELF-REGULATION, MORALITY, AND CONSCIENCE

Although the terms used in this chapter are words that are used in everyday language, there is a great deal of confusion about what they actually mean. In some cases the words can evoke strong feelings and intense debate.

The word *discipline* is seen by some as a synonym for punishment. In fact, the word *discipline* comes from the word *disciple,* which means to lead and teach. Discipline is less about controlling a child and much more about helping children learn to gain self-control, to gradually know right from wrong, and to care and respect the rights and feelings of others.

Self-regulation—or *self-control*—refers to the child's ability to contain and manage his own behavior without relying on caregivers to guide him. Gaining self-control is a long process and depends on the child gradually internalizing an understanding of what behaviors are acceptable and not acceptable, distinguishing right from wrong, and meeting the requirements and standards of society. At first, for the young child this will mean learning such things as not to break toys or hit or bite another child; it may even mean something that should be done, such as comforting a crying baby. As the child grows, it can be about not stealing or telling lies and helping a sick or elderly person.

Compliance is about a child's ability and willingness to modulate her behavior to meet the expectations and limits expected by caregivers. A child is behaving in a compliant manner when he follows a caregiver's request or direction. These requests are "don't" requests when the child is told not to do something, and "do" requests when the child is told to do something. Following through on the "do" demands is harder for children and takes longer to develop (Kochanska, Coy, & Murray, 2001). This seems to be because it is harder to maintain a committed compliance to a more difficult task. Optimal compliance is achieved within a parent–child relationship that is loving and cooperative and in which the parent allows the child some autonomy so that there is, at least for part of the time, an eagerness to comply with the parent's agenda. It is a phrase that may also suggest that a child is being made to conform and, as a consequence, loses the ability to be self-reliant, self-motivated, and independent. Indeed, children with parents who demand unquestioning obedience and absolute compliance at all times may pay a price in terms of children's lower levels of spontaneity, creativity, and self-esteem. On one hand, if the parent is physically or verbally punishing or excessively harsh and angry, the child may become constantly vigilant and fearful. On the other hand, the child who becomes constantly noncompliant, defiant, and oppositional also pays a price—usually in terms of having few friends or having difficulty adjusting to child care and school. This constant defiance often sets up coercive cycles of acting out and being punished, all of which are harmful to the child.

Conscience is a term that is rarely used in parenting books. Yet, developing a conscience may be the most critical component of achieving self-control, following rules, and adhering to a set of moral values. Conscience is the internal voice or the internal system of moral values that not only allows a person to judge whether certain acts are right or wrong, but makes him feel guilty or uncomfortable if he does not live up to the moral code. Conscience is not something the child is born with but something that is built gradually from the relationships the child has with those around him. It depends on the internalizing of standards of behavior that are taught by caregivers. Most theorists believe that the process happens primarily because the child wants to please his parents, identifies with them, and wants to be like them. Their values then become part of his beliefs.

Moral development refers to a process whereby the norms, rules, and values of the family and society become part of an internal motive system and guide behavior even in the absence of external authority. Morality refers to two main characteristics of an individual: 1) meeting the standards of society and 2) concern for the welfare of others and the ability to express it through acts of caring and kindness. In this chapter the first of these characteristics will be the primary focus and the other will be considered in more detail in Chapter 10.

THEORIES RELATED TO DISCIPLINE, MORALITY, AND SELF-REGULATION

Many of the beliefs and practices of discipline and child rearing of previous generations are now seen as cruel and inhumane, and even today many different beliefs and theories exist about how best to discipline and how a child develops morality and self-regulation. This section discusses theories that have been particularly influential on current thinking.

One of the major differences between theories relates to their emphasis on various ways to encourage compliance in children. Behavioral and social interactional theories, for example, emphasize how caregivers may actually train a child to be compliant or noncompliant by modeling and reinforcement. More psychodynamic and attachment-related theorists focus instead on the *representations of self and other* that the child develops through interactions with primary caregivers and how these in turn influence how the child behaves and relates to others.

Theories of discipline also vary in terms of how much emphasis they place on the behavioral or interactional patterns that develop between parents and children compared with the emotional quality of the parent–child relationship. Patterson (1976, 1982) has identified, for example, coercive cycles in which parents reinforce noxious behaviors, thus "training" the child to increase the rate and intensity of the behavior. Attachment and psychodynamically oriented theorists look more at the affective tone of interactions and the ongoing quality of the parent–child relationship as most important in developing compliance, morality, and self-regulation. Similarly, attribution theorists have emphasized the caregiver's subjective view of the infant or young child as central to how a caregiver behaves with and disciplines a child, while in many other theories this has been ignored—or at least has not been central in any discussions of discipline. Some major contemporary theories are outlined in Table 7.1.

THE IMPORTANCE OF SELF-REGULATION AND MORALITY

Achieving adequate self-regulation or self-control and moral development are two of the most important and fundamental capacities of child development. Without self-control, the young child will constantly challenge parents and other caregivers, may upset or even harm peers, and will eventually become overwhelmed with feelings of lack of control and, consequently, low self-esteem. Children without a sense of morality can be destructive in relationships with others. Self-control can influence a number of other areas of development, as outlined in the following sections.

Concentration and Attention

The capacities of concentration and attention will be explained in more detail in Chapter 9; however, without self-control children may find it difficult to concentrate on a specific task

Table 7.1.   Theories of development of self-regulation, morality, and a sense of conscience

Theorist	Type of theory	Major constructs
Freud (1959)	Psychoanalytic theory	Children internalize their parents' values, which form a superego or conscience. This occurs during the first 5 years
		Incestuous wishes toward opposite-sex parent at about 5 years of age create anxiety that he or she will lose the love of the same-sex parent. Instead, the child relinquishes desires in favor of identification with same-sex parent
		Through this identification, the child adopts the behaviors and values of the parent
		Parents are the most important socializing agents
Kohlberg (1969)	Cognitive-developmental theory	A stage theory of moral development that is based on—but is more comprehensive than—Piaget's cognitive theory
		Proposes six stages that are ordered under three levels of moral orientation: 1) premoral, 2) morality of conventional role-conformity, and 3) morality of self-accepted moral principles. Children up to age 6 are seen as premoral
		Proposes two processes involved in the individual's progress through the stages: cognitive disequilibrium and role taking
Smetana (1983) Turiel (1983)	Social interactional theory	Proposes that morality and conventional obligation are two different areas of development
		Both are present universally and are differentiated very early in child hood, with children understanding the difference between them and acting differently as a consequence
		Children learn to distinguish these two aspects of self-regulation through social interactions and experience with both
Bandura (1991)	Social cognitive theory	Describes behavior as regulated by two major mechanisms: social control and self-regulation
		Individual's perception of his ability to achieve personal control plays an important role
		Whether a person acts morally is determined reciprocally by thoughts and perceptions, behavior, and a series of social influences.
		Series of cognitions can determine how a person behaves antisocially, including dehumanizing the victim, distortion of consequences of behavior, and displacing responsibility
		Sees imitation of models as critical in the development of moral attitudes, values, and standards
Hoffman (1991)	Moral socialization theory	Emphasizes society's transmission of moral norms through internalization and development of conscience
		Appropriate types of discipline are seen as leading to acceptance of standards and moral norms
		Success of internalization depends on the development of empathy within the child
		Empathic affect reliably predisposes people to consider the needs of others
Bugental (1992) Dix (1993)	Attribution theory	Emphasizes the importance of parents' view, or attributions and expectations of the child on parent behavior and child development
		Parental beliefs are seen as acting to filter the child's behavioral acts, to determine their meaning for the caregiver, and to influence how the parent reacts
		When a parent believes she has little power or competence and cannot control a child, her discipline becomes ineffective

and instead react to everything that is going on around them. They may be unable to delay immediate gratification or to follow through on instructions and requests of caregivers. This, in turn, will quickly affect academic achievement and learning ability.

Peer Relationships

Children who have no sense of right and wrong and little self-control are not well liked or accepted by others. By age 4 or 5, most young children have a clear picture of rules and can be very frustrated by another child who does not follow the rules of games, child care, or school and what they perceive as family rules.

Behavior

One of the areas in which failure to have self-control and to follow rules will be most likely to show will be in the development of behavior problems and oppositional defiant disorder (ODD), often with excessive aggression. As explained in Chapter 1, contributions to this disorder come from a variety of sources, both within the child and the environment. Unfortunately, up to 50% of children who develop these problems in the early years will continue to display them and may develop conduct disorders later.

THE DEVELOPMENT OF SELF-REGULATION, MORALITY, AND CONSCIENCE

Psychoanalytic and Piagetian theorists did not believe that infants and young children are capable of understanding moral rules until 4 or 5 years of age; however, research beginning in the 1990s has demonstrated that children can show concern for others at an earlier age. For example, young children have been shown to understand the difference between behaviors that go against rules and those that are a violation of a moral principle. Through a great deal of naturalistic research, there is a coherent and consistent picture now of when children begin to develop self-control and compliance. This research has shown that self-regulation is not a capacity that appears suddenly, but that there is a gradual development from early infancy to 5 or 6 years of age. There is also a gradual change from externally controlled behavior to behavior that is under the control of internal factors. Not only is development of a conscience slow, at times children may seem to stand still or even regress in their compliance, especially if their lives are disrupted by family events such as a move, the birth of a sibling, hospitalization, death, or other separations. With consistent and caring discipline, most children by 5 years of age are quite strict about following rules and directions at home and at school, however, and have internalized most of the important rules and standards of home, school, and society. Table 7.2 illustrates how the development of self-regulation and morality changes over the course of a child's early life.

Birth to Twelve Months

In the first year of life, children are not expected to understand about safety or any other rules. By the end of the first year, however, children may occasionally show that they expect to be re-

Table 7.2. The development of self-regulation, morality, and a sense of conscience

Age	Self-regulation	Morality
Birth–12 months	Begins to be able to calm self for brief periods by sucking, staring at an object, and so forth By 3 months, will have begun to establish a routine with more predictable sleep–wake cycles and a feeding schedule By the end of the first year, a child may begin to develop an expectation of being stopped if he gets into a dangerous situation Continually needs to stay away from danger	Early face-to-face interactions provide internalized rules about reciprocity, turn taking and discourse May sometimes show signs of "global empathy" and get upset when someone else is upset Monitors mother's emotional expressions in situations of uncertainty
12–24 months	Begins to express desire for individuality "No" saying and tantrums are frequent expressions of desire to be independent Only follows "the rules" or complies about 45% of time Shows concern about broken toys or damaged goods that do not conform to an expected standard May show signs of pride if, for example, he cleans up a mess Some rudimentary self-control sometimes demonstrated when stops himself doing something, but still unreliable	Shows genuine concern for another's distress Empathetic behavior may be a projection of child's own needs on the other Begins to understand that sharing is important Still likely to take another child's toys and possessions
24–36 months	Begins to be able to follow internalized rules part of the time Uses social referencing (checking out emotional response of another) to regulate behavior Often pretends to discipline dolls during play, showing understanding of rules Still has difficulty transferring rules across time and settings Still relies on caregivers to follow rules and to contain impulses some of the time and may act out if no one is in the room Prefer undamaged to damaged objects Guilt behavior may occur May be able to generalize about objects he cannot touch	Has more understanding and perspective of the needs of others Realizes others' needs may be different from his own Aware has done wrong and anticipates feelings of others Aware of difference between moral and social-conventional violations and respond by telling other child about the effect of his behavior May confess and offer reparation if he hurts another child Shows signs that he may feel guilt if he hurts another child
3–4 years	Has internalized rules involving "do's" and "don'ts" May argue with caregiver about what he is supposed to do Will use private or inner speech to help remember rules and standards for behavior Negativism wanes and child complies about 80% of the time	More likely to experience guilt when he hits another child, breaks toy, or makes parent sad Some self-criticism, shame, and guilt if he misbehaves Sharing is much more consistent and seen as an obligation by the child Can struggle with and resolve a moral dilemma that they are asked about
4–6 years	Develops a sense of conscience that is quite strict and rule bound Continues to add, modify, and revise values and behavioral standards Noncompliance and defiance are generally rare although may still argue and try and negotiate the rules	Has well-developed sense of fairness Can present narratives that show understanding of moral rules May want to help the poor, etc. Strongly identifies with and imitates moral models of caregivers Internalize rules of family, school, and society

moved or distracted from certain situations and may not protest the action. Although the infant cannot control his behavior, he is becoming able to regulate his frustration, at least for a short period of time. He can suck on a pacifier or a thumb, fixate his gaze on an object, or play with an object alone for brief periods of time. By 3–6 months, most babies also acquire some predictability in their eating and sleeping patterns, another sign that self-regulation is being established. Along with these signs of self-regulation, infants in the first year of life are learning about reciprocity, turn taking, and discourse through face-to-face interactions with caregivers, as evidenced by their growing ability to cooperate in simple games with adults (e.g., Peek-a-Boo). Most remarkable, babies show signs of monitoring and mirroring the emotions of others and may imitate or mirror their intense emotions.

Twelve to Twenty-Four Months

During this next stage from 12–24 months, children are often at their most noncompliant, sometimes needing to be told 20 times a day not to behave in a particular way. In fact, although they have some understanding of what is expected of them, at 14 months, children are only capable of following the rules about 45% of the time for "don't" requests, and 14% of the time for "do" requests (Kochanska et al., 2001). There are two main reasons for this: 1) this second year of life is characterized by a push to independence (or to individuation); and 2) the young child has limited language, either to express herself or sometimes to understand the directives that are being given to her. This can lead to added frustration as well as confusion about what the child is supposed to do. Some children may comply somewhat with rules when the caregiver is around and then behave as they want to or disobey rules when the caregiver leaves the room.

A number of researchers have found that young children of this age become concerned about toys or photos of people that are broken or distorted. At the same time, they seem consistently drawn to examine the broken objects, suggesting that they already have some internalized standard of how things are supposed to be and are checking to see if they meet the standards. The child now has a rudimentary understanding of values and also shows genuine distress about another person who is upset. Although, when children play together there are many fights over possession of objects, young children at this stage are beginning to learn to be able to share their toys or other possessions.

Twenty-Four to Thirty-Six Months

Children begin to internalize rules between the ages of 24 and 36 months, but behaving still depends very much on the physical presence of the caregiver.

Children often use social referencing at this time and check their caregivers' facial expressions to see if a behavior is approved or disapproved of. One of the first signs that a child understands the rules may be observed when she is playing and is heard telling her dolls, animals, or friends to stop doing something. It may often sound as though a child is mimicking her parents' voices. This evidence that a child remembers the rules is encouraging, because as yet the rules are rarely consistently followed. Children may also have a great deal of difficulty transferring rules across situations. For example, a child may leave a vase alone at home but grab at it in another setting.

When the child is alone, prohibited things can be far too tempting!

At this stage, perhaps the most gains are made in children's capacity to begin to understand how others feel. Related to this emerging empathy, a child may feel considerable guilt if he hurts another child, and he may make efforts to make things better.

Three to Four Years

In this stage, the extreme negativism of the previous period is usually reduced and the child will comply when asked about 85% of the time for "don't" requests, but still only 30% of the time for "do" requests (Kochanska et al., 2001). As well, some internalized rules of what the child can and cannot do are in place so he can contain his desire to do certain prohibited actions even when the caregiver is out of the room—at least some of the time. The capacity for shame (i.e., feeling unworthy because of not behaving or not measuring up in some way) and guilt (i.e., feeling bad because of a certain act and wanting to make it right) are in place and the child may feel either in certain situations. Sometimes a child may use private or inner speech to help stop himself from doing something he should not do. Sharing is now much more consistent, and is seen as an obligation. Children are also able to decide about moral themes in stories and about what is right and wrong and what should be done about it.

Some children can frustrate parents at this age because they insist on arguing and trying to negotiate everything, especially about following through on the requests of caregivers. It is very important for caregivers to continue setting limits but to allow negotiation about some of them. Discussing a limit as a way to give different perspectives on the issue can be helpful for encouraging cooperation.

Four to Six Years

During this period, the child develops a sense of conscience, which at first tends to be quite strict and extreme. If friends visit, children are often very rigid and demand that the visitors follow the rules of the house. They are also demanding of themselves and may have a sense of guilt if they break a rule, regardless of whether anyone sees them. Children at about 5 years of age are very strict about rules of behavior and also insist on rules in games and in other interactions with peers.

Children often identify with parents at this time and want to be just like them, including dressing alike and carrying out chores. When noncompliance does occur, it is generally within the context of an attempt to reason or negotiate to get their own way.

IMPORTANT RESEARCH FINDINGS

Much of the advice in parenting books about discipline is not necessarily based on sound research. This may be because the research on discipline is confusing and often does not provide clear ideas or directions about how parents should react to children or on the best ways to encourage compliance, self-control, and moral development. Nevertheless, a number of studies are beginning to clarify what is critically important in parenting for children to gain self-regulation. This section will consider the following areas of research:

- Types of discipline strategies and their effect on behavioral outcomes

- The effects of various parenting environments or other contexts on development

Four- to 6-year-old children identify closely with parents.

- Influences on the development of parenting styles

- The effect of parent education on children and parenting

- New directions for research

Types of Discipline Strategies and Their Effect on Behavioral Outcomes

Parenting techniques take prominence in the majority of studies on discipline, and particularly in considering ways to assist children with developmental and/or behavior problems. Often, the techniques are investigated one dimension at a time. Some discipline strategies that have been researched include time-out, physical punishment, induction (i.e., "other-oriented" explanations or reasoning), and use of natural or logical consequences.

Time-out, a brief period during which a child is removed from other people, is one of the most popular and frequently used discipline procedures with young children; it is also one of the most written about. Roberts and colleagues have both carried out a number of experiments using time-out and have reviewed literature on its success. They conclude that in general the technique, when used as a consequence for negative behavior, can significantly reduce noncompliance in young children (Roberts, 1982, 1988; Roberts & Powers, 1990). Other researchers have also found positive effects for use of the strategy (Patterson, Chamberlain, & Reid, 1982; Webster-Stratton & Hammond, 1990). Suggestions as to how best to use time-out are outlined starting on page 393.

According to a number of parent polls, corporal punishment such as spanking, slapping, grabbing, and shoving is used with more than 90% of children in the United States and is most commonly used with very young children. Some children are hit on a daily basis, and in a recent longitudinal study, 60% had been spanked in the last week (Giles-Sims, Straus, & Sugarman, 1995; Yankelovich, 2000). Most parents believe that corporal punishment is the only method that immediately stops bad behavior and that produces good long-term effects (Giles-Sims et al., 1995; Strassberg, Dodge, Pettit, & Bates, 1994; Straus & Donnelly, 1994).

These statistics are staggering given strong evidence that the use of physical force actually increases the incidence of aggression and defiance in children (Deater-Deckard, Dodge, Bates, & Pettit, 1996; Lefkowitz, Eron, Walder, & Huesmann, 1977). As well, physical punishment has been associated with a variety of other negative outcomes including delayed impulse control, impaired psychological adjustment, and abusive parenting (Patterson, 1982; Power & Chapieski, 1986; Weiss, Dodge, Bates, & Pettit, 1992). Baumrind (2001) has stated that when parents who frequently use physical punishment with at least some intensity were removed from a study she conducted, the researchers did not find that spanking was related to child outcomes. She concluded, however, that she is not an advocate of spanking and that it may be traumatic for fearful children. On a larger societal level, there is less violence and lower crime rates in cultures such as Sweden, where the use of corporal punishment has been banned (Deley, 1988).

The effects of positive versus negative discipline strategies have also been explored, including the use of "do" requests compared with "don't" commands. Two studies demonstrated that using "do" commands led to increased compliance, while the "don't" instructions tended to increase rates of inappropriate behavior (Houlihan & Jones, 1990; Neef, Shafer, Egel, Cataldo, & Parrish, 1983). Houlihan and Jones suggested that the reason for the difference may be that saying "don't" with some difficult children may act as a reinforcer of negative behavior if the behavior does not stop after it has been used, thus setting up "coercive chains" of negative behavior. These coercive cycles begin with poor parenting practices such as lack of monitoring, criticism and harshness, and inconsistent discipline. In turn, the child responds with demanding and coercive or controlling behavior. The parent may give in and allow the child to "win." The child, as a consequence, continues to engage in these behaviors and the parent continues with the ineffective discipline, often escalating with angry and hostile responses. In this way, the child never learns skills to improve her behavior responses and also feels increasingly rejected and unsupported (Dishion, French, & Patterson, 1995; Patterson, 1982).

In his theory of moral socialization, Hoffman (1983, 1988) discussed several types of discipline. He proposed that most important for the development of conscience was the use of induction techniques in which the parent explains to the child the effect of his behavior on others. Hoffman maintained that induction does not produce high levels of anger or anxiety in the child, thus allowing the child to be open for optimal learning (Hoffman, 1970, 1983, 1991). When the child becomes capable of having a conscience at about age 5, the practice of using induction will usually result in feelings of guilt and thus provide motivation for good behavior. A few researchers have been able to demonstrate the relevance of this theory and to show how the use of induction can enhance prosocial development (Brody & Shaffer, 1982; Radke-Yarrow, Zahn-Waxler, & Chapman, 1983; Zahn-Waxler, Radke-Yarrow, & King, 1979).

Very few studies have considered the importance of the child's individuality in influencing the success of discipline strategies. In one series of studies that did consider a child's individuality, however, Kochanska considered the discipline that works best for fearful and more fearless children. She concluded that gentle discipline based on reasoning and explanation and de-emphasizing of power methods works best with children whose temperament is somewhat fearful. For more fearless and uninhibited children, methods based on induction and power assertion are less effective because these children are not motivated by a desire to avoid anxiety. For these children, discipline needs to be built on a secure, cooperative relationship with the parent and parental responsiveness in order to be effective. In this way, the child does what is asked because of a desire to be like or to identify with the emotionally available parent (Kochanska, 1995, 1997; Kochanska & Thompson, 1997).

The Effects of the Parenting Environment or Context on Development of Self-Regulation

A number of studies have shown that parental warmth, high parental responsiveness, and synchrony are related to current and later compliance (Parpal & Maccoby, 1985; Rocissano, Slade, & Lynch, 1987; Rothbaum & Weisz, 1994). With younger and older children alike an atmosphere of warmth, empathy, and supportiveness has been found to be related to the child's later capacity for empathy, negotiation, social competence, and prosocial behavior (Maccoby & Martin, 1983; McFarlane, Bellissimo, & Norman, 1995; Parker, 1983; Pettit, Bates, & Dodge, 1997; Travillion & Snyder, 1993; Trommsdorff, 1991). Conversely, hostile and conflictual interactions have been found to result in defiance, extreme disobedience, and conduct problems (Keenan & Shaw, 1995; Pfiffner & O'Leary, 1989; Rueter & Conger, 1995).

Attachment researchers have also demonstrated that children with secure attachments, who have experienced sensitive and responsive caregiving, are more compliant and cooperative as preschoolers than children with insecure attachments (Erickson, Egeland, & Pianta, 1989; Erickson, Sroufe, & Egeland, 1985; Sroufe, 1983).

In a series of classic studies, Baumrind and associates followed preschoolers into middle childhood and adolescence and linked components of family interactions and discipline style to a number of developmental outcomes (Baumrind, 1971, 1973; Baumrind & Black, 1967). Three primary types of discipline were identified: authoritarian, authoritative, and permissive. The authoritarian pattern is high in parent demandingness and low in responsiveness to the child's needs. Authoritative parenting includes enforcement of rules and standards, open discussion between parents and children, and encouragement of the child's individuality. With permissive parenting, parents make few demands and have few expectations of the child and allow or expect the child to self-regulate (Baumrind, 1971, 1973).

In her original study, Baumrind found that by 8 or 9 years of age, children who had received the different kinds of discipline outlined above showed very different response styles (Baumrind, 1971, 1973). The children in the authoritative families were more competent (achievement-oriented and independent) and socially responsive (interpersonally cooperative and friendly) than those in the other two types, who had lower social and cognitive competence. Another study found that authoritarian and permissive styles were related to low school grades in adolescence, while authoritative parenting was associated with high grades (Dornbusch, Ritter, Leiderman, Roberts, & Fraleigh, 1987).

A number of researchers have tried to further examine and analyze these parts into more global constructs. Specifically, in looking at authoritative parenting they have examined the differential contribution of parental warmth and acceptance, behavioral control, parental involvement, and the encouragement of psychological autonomy or democracy to adolescent outcomes (Steinberg, Lamborn, Darling, Mounts, & Dornbusch, 1994; Steinberg, Lamborn, Dornbusch, & Darling, 1992; Steinberg, Mounts, Lamborn, & Dornbusch, 1991). Steinberg et al. (1992) found that each of these aspects of parenting contributed to the outcomes of school achievement and overall school success.

Lamborn, Mounts, Steinberg, and Dornbusch (1991) distinguished two very different kinds of permissive parenting. One was described as "neglectful" and disengaged and the other as more laissez-faire or indulgent, which was often accompanied by a philosophy or belief in providing a certain kind of parenting. There was a great deal of difference between these types of permissive parents in the amount of love and hostility that was present. The neglectful parents tended to be extremely hostile and to show little caring or love, while the indulgent parents were often very loving and caring toward their children. On one hand, children of neglectful parents fared worse than those in any of the groups on indexes of competence, self-perceptions, and misbehavior; and had the highest levels of antisocial and impulsive behavior, delinquency, alcohol and drug use, and sexual promiscuity. On the other hand, adolescents of indulgent parents scored among the highest on measures of social competence and self-confidence but were also likely to have relatively high levels of delinquent behavior and alcohol and drug use.

Other researchers have examined such dimensions as parental involvement and parental encouragement and have considered how a general atmosphere of parental encouragement is distinguished from more specific hands-on parental involvement. For example, some parents may be involved only at one level or only involved in one domain of child functioning such as in school or social events, academic functioning, limit-setting, and so forth. A study that examined parent involvement with the school (attending school programs, monitoring and encouraging school success and progress) and its relationship to the adolescent's school success found that direct involvement made a significant contribution to school success. Encouragement did not contribute to the outcome directly, however (Steinberg et al., 1994).

External Influences on Parenting Practices   A number of cultural, peer, neighborhood, and community differences affect the parenting context and practices. One of the most interesting findings has been that in studies of discipline styles, in Caucasian and Hispanic populations, high levels of authoritative parenting styles or context are associated with greater competence, but this is not always the case for Asian American and African American children. This unexpected finding may be related to the interpretation given to certain parenting practices in some cultures, with Asian American and African American cultures seeing stricter, more authoritarian discipline as a sign of concern on the part of parents.

Similarly, authoritarian styles seem to be more successful for some cultures than others (Baumrind, 1997; Steinberg, Dornbusch, & Brown, 1992). Steinberg, Dornbusch, et al. (1992) suggested that for Asian American youth, strong peer support may substitute for or ameliorate the effects of authoritarian parenting or may train them to be part of a philosophy of care or concern for other children. For African American children, mild physical discipline may be interpreted as a sign of caring and concern of parents. It may also be that to keep children safe in dangerous, violent neighborhoods and communities, very strict enforcement of rules and expectation for unquestioning obedience may be required (Baldwin, Baldwin, & Cole, 1990; Baumrind, 1997).

Influences on the Development of Parenting Styles

Because the influence of parental discipline strategies is so critical in determining child development outcomes, it is important to consider factors that contribute to their presence. Level of parental education has frequently been found to be related to discipline techniques, with parents with lower education tending to be more prohibitive and intrusive than college-educated parents (Kelley, Power, & Wimbush, 1992).

Other variables found to be frequently associated with parenting style include income level (Dodge, Pettit, & Bates, 1994) and social support or networks (Crittenden, 1985; Jennings, Stagg, & Connors, 1991; Pascoe, Loda, Jeffries, & Earp, 1981). When income is low or supports less available, parents tend to have less optimal parenting behavior and to use harsh discipline, to show lack of warmth, and to use aggressive methods. Crittenden (1985) cautioned that, in considering the relevance of the findings about social support, in some families, frequent contact with network members can be a source of stress and can drain resources rather than provide support. A related variable implicated in many studies is parenting stress, with high stress contributing to use of stricter discipline techniques (Creasey & Jarvis, 1994).

One of the most important contributing factors is the parents' experience of being parented. Evidence from intergenerational studies of attachment classifications shows that children tend to have the same attachment classifications as their parents and grandparents. This shows clear evidence of intergenerational transmission through parenting interactions (e.g., Benoit & Parker, 1994; Grossman, Fremmer-Bombik, Rudolph, & Grossman, 1988; Main & Goldwin, 1984; Main, Kaplan, & Cassidy, 1985; Zeanah, Benoit, Barton, Regan, Hirschberg, & Lipsitt, 1993). Studies that have directly examined the use of discipline strategies across generations have found evidence of similarity in the tendency to use punishment and rewards (Covell, Grusec, & King, 1995; Ringwalt, Browne, Rosenblum, Evans, & Kotch, 1989).

Among the most interesting contributors to parenting styles and to choice of discipline techniques are the parents' beliefs, cognitions, or attributions of their child's personality and their capacity to discipline them (Applegate, Burleson, & Delia, 1992; Bugental, 1992; Dix & Grusec, 1992). Holden and Miller (1999) found that in two-parent families, parents often use

the same discipline strategies and share similar beliefs about child rearing. In a number of studies, Bugental and colleagues have shown that parents who believe they have little power or lack sufficient competence to be able to manage a child's behavior will behave in ways that maintain the child's difficult behavior. They will also behave in ways that perpetuate their own beliefs about their lack of parenting competence (Bugental, 1985; Bugental & Shennum, 1984). In extreme cases, parents may see their child's behavior as a threat and uncontrollable. Parents like this have been found to exhibit significant caregiving problems, including the use of physical abuse (Bugental, Blue, & Cruzcosa, 1989).

Other researchers have studied the beliefs and attributions of parents of preschoolers presenting with behavior problems (Dix & Lochman, 1990; Mills & Rubin, 1990; Rubin & Mills, 1990). Parents of children with behavior problems have been found to be more likely to see their children's behavior as either intentional or due to their child's personality. They also perceive themselves as having lost control of their children, and the children's behavior as uncontrollable (Alexander, Waldron, Barton, & Mas, 1989; Baden & Howe, 1992; Sagatum, 1991).

Other researchers have emphasized the necessity to consider how the child's behavior and temperament contribute to parent disciplinary strategies. Temperament researchers such as Thomas and Chess (1985) and Bates (1989) have identified a number of child characteristics that can make parenting extremely challenging. These include irritability, intensity of reaction, poor concentration, and lack of adaptability. It is obvious that these kinds of temperament can contribute to difficulties in parent–child interactions.

The Effect of Parent Training on Children and Parents

Parent training based on principles of operant reinforcement and punishment, until very recently, has been the most frequently used and evaluated type of parent intervention, particularly with parents whose children have behavior difficulties (Patterson, 1976). These types of parenting groups have primarily focused on improving parent–child interactions and particularly on teaching parents to use strategies such as negative and positive reinforcements (e.g., Forehand & McMahon, 1981; Kazdin, 1985). Although initial results were very encouraging for short-term improvements (Moreland, Schwebel, Beck, & Wells, 1982), further studies have shown that long-term results are often not as positive and have not easily generalized in other settings (Forehand & Long, 1988). Moreover, a large proportion of the more high-risk clients drop out of the programs before completion (Holden, Lavigne, & Cameron, 1990).

Given these mixed results and subsequent developmental research and understanding, a few researchers and clinicians have added aspects to parent training that have gone beyond the enforcement of parenting techniques or surface structures alone. They have instead included strategies to enhance parent–child relationships and the emotional development of the child. Attachment theory has often been used as the framework for these new models of parent training (Speltz, 1990; Webster-Stratten & Hammond, 1990). Some training models view parenting or discipline techniques not as isolated but as aspects of a relationship between parent and child. This newer emphasis, then, is on a more contextual approach, which views discipline as only one aspect of a broader parenting approach.

Some training models have, for example, incorporated child-directed play activities into the course and have trained parents on how to react to the child's play (Eyberg & Robinson, 1982; Forehand, 1977), while other researchers have emphasized the effect of the play on the parent–child relationship and the child's self-esteem (Hembree-Kigin & McNeil, 1995; Speltz, 1990).

New Directions for Research

Some writers have criticized the research that has been carried out and have suggested a variety of new directions for studying how parents contribute to children's acquisition of self-regulation and morality or values (Cummings, Davies, & Campbell, 2000; Grusec, Goodnow, & Kuczynski, 2000). Some of the areas that have been suggested for further research include

- Giving greater consideration to the different types of discipline and parenting that are required at different developmental stages (Cummings et al., 2000; Holden & Miller, 1999)

- Studying the impact of individual characteristics of the child, such as temperament, on the effects of different discipline styles and techniques (Grusec & Goodnow, 1994)

- Taking into account the influence of the class, culture, neighborhood, community, child care, and school, and peer interactions on parenting beliefs and practices (Chao, 1994; Deater-Deckard & Dodge, 1997)

- Studying the "bidirectionality" of parent–child interactions and the degree to which parents' understanding of the child and their adaptation to the child's negotiation and actions contribute to positive or negative outcomes (Dix, 1992; Grusec et al., 2000)

- Exploring the importance of parent–child relationships for the development of self-regulation. This does not revolve solely around attachment-related dimensions such as how parents respond to distress but is also a function, for example, of how parents assist the child in various situations and how they teach the child about a number of rules and values. (See Chapter 1 for an outline of these various roles.) It will be important for new research to examine how these different aspects of parenting individually and collectively contribute to the development of self-regulation and morality (Grusec et al., 2000).

Summary of Research Findings

Shifts in parent training somewhat mirror the growth in understanding of the need to consider more than discipline techniques and strategies as important for child development. Research overall has shown that the affective tone of parent–child interactions and the emotional family climate are major contributors to positive child development. As well, it has been found that positive and cooperative parent–child relationships—combined with firm control and encouragement of independence—are most predictive of a number of positive developmental outcomes.

THE GROWTH-PROMOTING ENVIRONMENT: PRINCIPLES OF ENHANCING SELF-REGULATION AND MORALITY

A child acquires compliance, self-regulation, and morality through a complex process that depends very much on the interaction between caregivers and the child over time. Finding the right way to discipline can be quite difficult, and may need to be adjusted frequently according to the child's age or temperament or because a technique has stopped working. Principles for enhancing these capacities are set out here and in Table 7.3:

Table 7.3. Principles for encouraging self-regulation, conscience, and morality

Principle 1	Set up a warm, reciprocal and responsive caregiving environment within which limits and standards are firmly enforced, so that children want to be cooperative with most of the requests made.
Principle 2	Be clear about who is in charge. Do not try to be an equal and a friend to children in your care.
Principle 3	Present a united front with other caregivers. Keep channels of communication open so any differences can be identified and discussed.
Principle 4	Draw up a list of absolute rules and standards to which children must adhere. Communicate them clearly to children and be consistent in enforcing them.
Principle 5	Explain the reasons for certain behaviors that are expected and requested.
Principle 6	Decide on areas in which there can be some flexibility and let children express their point of view around these issues.
Principle 7	Select consequences for not complying with rules and let children know ahead of time what they will be.
Principle 8	Make sure that good behavior is noticed and acknowledged and that negative behavior is stopped.
Principle 9	Use problem-solving strategies to find solutions to discipline difficulties.

PRINCIPLE 1: *Set up a warm, reciprocal, and responsive caregiving environment within which limits and standards are firmly enforced, so that children want to be cooperative with most of the requests made.*

Research has shown that it is the emotional "climate" within a home and family that sets the stage, as it were, for the gradual internalization of values and a smooth, cooperative following of standards and rules. This has sometimes been called flexibility within clear boundaries. This climate allows children to know what is acceptable and what is not, to feel secure about this, but at the same time to feel encouraged to be independent and to have some say in what goes on in the family.

Although the details of disciplining can be confusing and frustrating for parents, a large body of research has continued to support the findings of the original research of Dianne Baumrind in the 1970s about the type of parenting style that results in the best outcomes for children. Provoked by arguments for extreme permissiveness in childrearing in the 1940s and 1950s, Baumrind began a program of research to determine the parenting atmosphere of a home that has the most positive effects and enhances the development of competence in children. This led to her definitions of permissive, authoritarian, and authoritative parenting (see Table 7.4 for details of these parenting patterns or styles).

After extensive studies and follow-up of children, Baumrind was able to conclude that authoritative parents were more likely to have competent children who were more capable of responsible behavior. The children of authoritative parents were found to be more self-confident, self-controlled, and assertive, and obtained higher grades in high school. Children of authoritarian parents, however, were discontent, submissive, whiny, distrustful, withdrawn, and often

Table 7.4. Characteristics of permissive, authoritarian, and authoritative parenting styles

Permissive	Authoritarian	Authoritative
Discipline style lacks rules and structure and parents have high tolerance for disruptive behavior	Parents enforce an absolute set of standards to shape and control children	Parents set clear rules, routines, and standards
Critical points in the day (e.g., bedtime, meal times) are often chaotic and children make their own decisions about when and how they happen	Parents rigidly enforce rules without explanations or discussion of reasons for rules	Parents firmly enforce rules and standards with consequences when necessary
Parents provide few consequences for actions	Parents emphasize obedience, respect for authority, punctuality, work, and order	Child's independence and individuality are encouraged and mature behavior is expected
Parents allow child a great deal of choices and freedom beyond those that the child can manage	Assertion of individuality by child is met with swift and severe punishment	Child and parent rights and needs are respected
Whatever the child wants he or she gets even when it is at the expense of the parents' own needs	Parents discourage verbal give-and-take with children	Parents encourage open communication and verbal give-and-take with children
Parents accept and tolerate nearly every behavior of their children	Parental responsiveness to children is low and love is conditional	Consequences for irresponsible behavior are natural or reasonable
When the parent is frustrated about the child's behavior, he may revert to the strict discipline he may have received as a child	Parents often use humiliation, threats, and bribes to instill obedience	Love is unconditional and a high degree of warmth and acceptance is present
	Parental style is detached, lacks warmth, and discourages autonomy	Children are taught how to think and problem-solve
		Parents allow flexibility in some areas and children can express their points of view in these
		Parents notice, acknowledge, and encourage good behavior
		Parents explain the reasons for certain behaviors that they expect

aggressive. Permissive parents produced children who were immature and lacking in self-reliance and self-control, while children with either authoritarian and permissive parents had lower grades than those who experienced authoritative parenting. Consequently, it is important to encourage a style of parenting that is firm with clear boundaries but that encourages children's independence and individuality.

PRINCIPLE 2: *Be clear about who is in charge. Do not try to be an equal and a friend to children in your care.*

Many parents who want to maintain open communication with their children or perhaps had very little closeness or openness with their own parents want to be a friend to their child. Consequently, they may fail to give a clear message to the child that they are in control and in charge, and that they will keep them safe. This lack of clarity is very frightening for children who can feel that there is no one there to take care of them and that they must therefore look after themselves. Such a situation can also lead to severe difficulties with controlling children as they become teenagers and demand to be allowed to do exactly as they want. Although children need and deserve attention and respect, they do not need another friend. Instead, they need parents (natural, adoptive, or foster) to provide the kind of love and concern for their welfare that can come from no one else.

• •

Faye had felt very unloved by her mother and decided that more than anything else, she would be a best friend to her daughter, Julie. As Julie became old enough to understand a conversation, Faye shared everything that was going on in her life with her. When Faye's marriage broke up, the situation became even more exaggerated and Julie was encouraged to sleep with her, to discuss the details of the separation, and to share leisure time activities. Faye proudly told everyone that they were "best friends" and could tell each other everything.

This kind of closeness between parent and child can lead to role reversal and the child's feeling as if she is taking care of the parent. This can also lead the child to expect that she is equally in charge and responsible for her own life, which is too overwhelming at this stage of development.

PRINCIPLE 3: *Present a united front with other caregivers. Keep channels of communication open so any differences can be identified and discussed.*

Differences of opinion about ways to parent can be very sensitive, particularly between couples, between separated parents when the child spends time with both, between parents and child-care workers or teachers, and between parents and grandparents. Again, if rules and expectations are very different and other caregivers provide a lot of the care for a child, not following similar rules can be very confusing and will result in a lack of consistency across situations and in various contexts. Therefore, it is extremely important for caregivers to support one another in imposing discipline and to prevent a child playing one caregiver against the other.

Parents may disagree with each other and with their own parents over some of the following issues:

- Whether a crying baby should be picked up, and whether this is spoiling her

- Whether children should be spanked for misbehaving

- Whether children should be allowed to express their opinion about instructions or rules

- When weaning, toilet training, or chores should be introduced

Ways to encourage a united front or agreement on rules might include

- Meeting with caregivers and drawing up a list of rules that everyone can agree with

- Letting other caregivers know the areas and aspects of your child's upbringing that are not negotiable (e.g., not spanking, not letting the child stay up too late, not swearing)

- Keeping communication open and allowing time to discuss what went on when your child was in someone else's care

- Having a book that goes back and forth between parents and teacher that outlines things each wants the other to know. Scheduling extra parent–teacher conferences when parents are concerned can also be helpful.

Remember that it may not be possible to have this kind of comfortable sharing of ideas and acceptance of other points of view in every situation. In these cases, you may need to make a decision about whether you want to continue having your child cared for by the other person. If you do or if you have no choice in the matter, maintain your same rules in the home and continue to enforce them because children can adapt to differences and learn what is expected in different situations. Remember to listen to the point of view of others and make sure your point of view is sound.

PRINCIPLE 4: *Draw up a list of absolute rules and standards to which children must adhere. Communicate them clearly to children and be consistent in enforcing them.*

Children need to have some rules that are nonnegotiable. Remember to keep the list to a minimum, otherwise you will find yourself saying "no" or "don't" all day and will leave yourself exhausted and your child extremely resentful.

The nonnegotiable rules you decide on will fall into three general areas: safety, morality, and social-conventional, which deals more with structures and routines in the caregiving environment. Interestingly, children typically learn about these from caregivers using different parenting strategies, and by 2–3 years of age children are able to understand the differences. Examples of these different types of rules are set out in Table 7.5.

It is critical that children understand the rules and why they are important. The reasons for safety and social-conventional rules should not be repeated constantly. Around issues of morality, particularly for each situation in which the child is not being kind or is being hurtful to others, the child should hear the reasons for the discipline and how the behavior hurt the other person.

Sometimes it is difficult for children to remember the rules, especially if their language comprehension is limited. In such cases, it is sometimes helpful for parents and caregivers to draw pictures and write the rules down in an age-appropriate way. Once the rules are explained and understood, it is critical that they be enforced consistently. Consistency allows children to know what to expect, and consequently, to be able to trust their environments.

PRINCIPLE 5: *Explain the reasons for certain behaviors that are expected and requested.*

In a variety of research studies it has been found that morality does not develop in children by using power assertion methods alone, but that it depends on using inductive methods and explanations and reasoning as well. In other words, if children are to learn rules and values and to internalize them they will need to hear why it is important to share, how other people feel when they say mean things, and why certain rules and laws are needed. The child does not learn these values by being sent to his room or by being counted out. Instead, these values develop out of discussions, explanations, and sharing of emotional responses.

The other important characteristic for encouraging moral behavior is showing affection frequently in non-discipline situations. Other actions that can be helpful for the development of conscience and moral behavior are modeling caring behavior; discussing the reason for rules; reading stories about brave, concerned people; and explaining how the other person feels. In summary, the child not only needs to experience the consequences for misbehavior but also needs to experience these types of reasoning and explanations as well.

Table 7.5. Sample of nonnegotiable rules

Physical safety	Morality	Social/conventional
Do not run across the road without looking.	There is no violence (hitting, biting) in the home.	Children must adhere to a bedtime routine.
No climbing on the stove.	No one in the home is to be verbally abused.	The family will follow a mealtime schedule.
Do not go near water without an adult.	Other people's property is to be respected.	It is important to be up on time and follow a routine throughout the day.
Do not talk to or get into a car with a stranger.	Helping and showing concern for others is important.	Everyone will pick up their own toys and things.

PRINCIPLE 6: *Decide on areas in which there can be some flexibility, and let children express their point of view around these issues.*

Although you may keep your list of rules to a minimum, it can still be quite large and cover a number of areas in your child's life. Because you may have several rules it will be important to allow some flexibility on certain issues and decisions. Children can also grow in responsibility if they are allowed to contribute their ideas to the development of certain family rules.

If, for example, the rule is that children come to the table at meal times, a child might be given a choice about which vegetable they eat and how soon they leave the table after eating some food and being excused. At bedtime children must get into bed on time but could choose the story. Other examples of choices are set out in Chapter 6.

PRINCIPLE 7: *Select consequences for not complying with rules and let children know ahead of time what they will be.*

It is clear that methods used to discipline children will change as they get older. For example, in a child's first 2 years, methods of discipline will rely more on removing the child from certain situations and distracting her and will continually require the physical presence of the caregiver to carry them out. For children between the ages of 2 and 6 years, it is helpful to have many strategies rely primarily on various kinds of consequences and methods of induction to explain the reasons behind the discipline. In the middle years of childhood (7–12 years), having consequences but increasingly using reasons and explanations and expecting that rules have been internalized will be important. Later, in adolescence, a balance of still maintaining rules and standards and monitoring the young person, while allowing more discussion of decisions and some of the rules, will be crucial. Whatever the young person's age, there are some fundamentals about discipline that can make it work:

- Caregivers need to be consistent because even occasionally failing to enforce rules will keep a behavior going indefinitely.

- Basic rules must be enforced in public places and in other people's homes, as well as at home.

- A way of disciplining that worked for a time may not work forever, so it is important to be flexible and to employ different methods when needed.

- When rules are changed, improvements may take a long time if a child is very noncompliant, so it is necessary to stay with the new strategies for several weeks before determining that they do not work.

- There is no point in arguing and giving reasons and explanations when a child already understands why a rule is in place.

- Some reasoning and explanations are necessary around certain limits (such as not hurting or being mean to others) to encourage the child to internalize these limits and rules and to develop a conscience.

- It is critical to notice a child's positive behaviors and efforts towards improvement.

- Consistently lecturing can turn children off listening.

- Believe in and respect yourself and your child.

- Provide a structure that is firm, fair, and flexible.

Various discipline strategies are outlined later in this book and can be used in the ways that are described and for the age groups suggested.

PRINCIPLE 8: *Make sure that good behavior is noticed and acknowledged and that negative behavior is stopped.*

If a child gets attention or responses only for negative or bad behavior, she may soon give up on trying or being involved in positive interactions and efforts. It is critical to notice and acknowledge positive behaviors to let the child know that efforts to behave, cooperate, and show caring behavior are appreciated. Noticing positives after you have to correct negative behavior can be very valuable for bolstering self-esteem and increasing positive behavior.

Another approach to decreasing negative behavior and increasing positive behavior is positive reinforcement. This involves providing the child with an incentive to stop negative behavior as well as to increase positive behavior. One way is to provide a child with a tangible way of collecting awards for good behavior, such as a "star chart," a marble jar, or a bank with tokens or chips. In all cases the child receives an immediate reward and can also accumulate the rewards over time to "cash in" for an outing; time with the caregiver; or a small, appropriate gift. Being noticed for good behavior and the immediacy of the reward can sometimes break a cycle of rejection and provide the incentive to turn a situation around. The reward should be immediate, consistent, and relevant. It is also important to remember that only one behavior that caregivers want to eliminate should be worked on at a time.

PRINCIPLE 9: *Use problem-solving strategies to find solutions to discipline difficulties.*

When a caregiver is continually confronted by the same behavior problem with a child, it can often be helpful to step back and calmly examine the difficulty in order to come up with possible solutions. This self-reflection often allows the caregiver to discover ways that his reactions may be keeping the behavior going. Here are some steps to problem-solving with a child:

1. *Define the problem behaviorally:* Observe what is really going on and, if possible, determine what is provoking the difficulty. Rephrase the problem in positive terms.

2. *Decide who owns the problem:* Decide whose needs are not being met. Needs can be either those of the caregiver or the child. The choice of the solution will depend on who owns the problem. If it is the child's problem, he should be helped to find a solution, if it is the caregiver's problem, he or she may need to modify his or her behavior or the environment and also, identify things in the environment that may be causing the problem. Could it be a recent move, a developmental change, stress in the home, or a new sibling?

3. *Generate possible solutions:* Generating possible solutions can be done alone or with other people giving input, such as in a parenting group, and suggesting ideas that have worked for them. At this point, do not evaluate the ideas—just generate them.

4. *Evaluate the ideas and choose one:* Evaluate the ideas and choose the one that is the most feasible and fits your and your child's needs.

5. *Evaluate the solution:* Try out the chosen solution over a reasonable period of time. Go back and problem-solve again and try another solution if the first one is not successful.

Table 7.6 summarizes 10 of the best discipline tips. Inherent in all of these rules is a reminder for parents and caregivers to be firm, but not to expect too much.

SOME COMMONLY RAISED ISSUES AROUND DISCIPLINE, SELF-REGULATION, AND BEHAVIOR PROBLEMS

Here are some of the most commonly raised issues around discipline.

Discipline Techniques for Avoiding Problems

There is no one most-effective disciplinary method. The most effective ways to discipline will depend on the age of the child, and some methods will work better in some situations than others.

Table 7.6. The 10 best discipline tips

1. Express love and caring toward the child.
2. Be predictable in providing structures and setting up consequences for disobeying rules.
3. Set up reasonable limits and expectations that relate to the child's age and temperament.
4. Notice good behavior and efforts to make things work.
5. Do not overreact by being too emotional with the child and do not use force, but lead and teach.
6. Avoid problems by planning ahead, supervising, and stepping in before situations escalate out of control.
7. Teach your child gradually to self-regulate, problem-solve, and negotiate. Let him or her learn from the consequences.
8. Communicate rules and limits clearly and listen to children's reasons for their behavior. Explain the reasons for the rules.
9. Model problem-solving and understanding of others, as well as the behaviors you want your child to have.
10. Respect and show your respect for your child and yourself.

Preparation   Preparation can be used when you have to take the child to the grocery store or doctor or you are changing from one place or situation to another (e.g., leaving the park to go home), a transition that is difficult for many children. Establishing a routine for preparing for this can be very helpful. New places or situations that are overstimulating can be very difficult for some children or when a child is tired or not feeling well.

For these situations, allow plenty of time, prepare the child ahead of time for what to expect, and most important, try and choose a time of day that your child is less tired. Try and make some preparations for situations that are difficult, such as shopping or a long trip in the car, by planning to have something for him to do. Some ideas are set out below:

- Prepare the child for change or outings well ahead of time.

- Give up to three warnings that it is time to get ready.

- Explain what will happen and for how long.

- If possible, let the child have a role in the event (e.g., finding some things at the grocery store).

- Remember to keep the outing manageable and vary it according to the child's level of coping.

- If appropriate, compensate in some small way for good behavior.

- Choose the best time of day for the outing, when your child is likely to be at her best.

Other transitions are also very difficult, such as leaving home in the morning, returning home at the end of the day, and bedtime. Most of the previous ideas are helpful, and, remember, it is especially important to prepare your child ahead of time.

• •

Three-year-old Jonathan had been a very sensitive and slow-to-warm-up child since infancy. As a consequence, he found outings where there were several people around very difficult. Maria and Tom, his parents, knew this, and found that letting him know about the outing at least a day in advance was especially helpful. They would talk with him about what he would like to take with him to do during the outing and how long it was likely to be. If it was to be an especially challenging event for him, they often spent time with him, acting out with his pretend family and other little people what it might be like. Prepared like this, Jonathan was usually able to remain calm.

Some ideas to help prepare children for transitions include the following:

- Make some rituals the whole family follows (e.g., get dressed before coming down for breakfast, set a bedtime routine).

- Give small children time to finish activities. Use a timer to give them a warning.

- Lay out clothes the night before.

- Give the child an alarm clock for getting up in the morning.

- Give advance warning about schedules. Explain the meaning of "before" and "after."

- Allow the child some times during the week that she does not need to rush and be scheduled.

Distraction   Distraction is a great method for younger children and can even work for children well into elementary school if a situation has changed, such as the birth of a sibling. With infants, just removing an object from their immediate vicinity can be an adequate distraction. For older children it can be used to avoid difficulties developing when it looks as if siblings are going to fight or a child is getting bored or overexcited. Distraction can change sad and angry feelings back to positive ones, or divert attention away from a problem once it has been initiated. The following vignettes illustrate how distraction can be helpful in preventing discipline problems from occurring.

* *

Louise could tell that her 2- and 4-year-olds were getting tired and irritable. She quickly changed the pace, suggesting a snack, a rest, and a trip to the park. After a few protests the children happily complied and the day progressed without major problems.

———————————————

Phyllis heard screams from the family room and found her 5- and 7-year olds, Pierre and Michael, fighting over a television program. She turned the television set off, saying it was time for playing outside. After a walk to the park to play on the swings, the boys were in a more positive mood and returned home in much better humor with each other.

Changing the don'ts to do's can increase compliance: "Gently, gently, stroke the kitty gently."

Table 7.7. Changing "don'ts" to "do's"

"Don't" or "No" statement	Alternative	Benefit to child
"No, you can't have a cookie."	"Yes, you can have a cookie after supper."	The child is encouraged to wait and to build inner controls.
"Don't carry on like that at the dinner table."	"You can either sit nicely and eat your supper or get down and not eat until snack time."	The child feels that he or she has a choice and some control but meal-time rules are maintained.
"Don't squeeze the baby like that; that's bad."	"I understand you want to look after your little brother; let's be gentle."	Even if this comment ignores the anger it does help the child to begin to be a big brother or sister.

Alternatives to a Straight "No"   Parents and caregivers will feel better, as will the child, if they can avoid saying "no" or "don't" all day.

Using "do" instead of "don't" can often, in the long run, increase compliance. When we cut off requests and activities with continual "no's," we add to the child's sense of helplessness. There are a number of ways to make the child feel more in control while at the same time enforcing necessary limits and structures. Some ways to allow some options and choices by changing "don'ts" to "do's" are outlined in Table 7.7.

• •

Marlene had been attending a parenting group and had heard about trying to change the "don'ts" to "do's." She decided to follow through on the suggested home-work activities of tape-recording what went on during hectic mornings when 2-year-old Aidan and 3-year-old Hope were supposed to be eating breakfast with them before they raced off to work. She also recorded bedtimes. After listening to the tapes, Marlene and Myles were horrified to find out how many "no's and "don'ts" they typically said in the relatively short but intense transitions. Together they resolved to change their language and their tone of voice to be more positive. In a month, they were thrilled to find that when they listened to new recordings of what went on at the same times, the tapes revealed a much more positive morning and evening for them all. Much to their surprise, their children were more willing to follow through with expected routines.

Humor   Humor can be used occasionally as a way to bring a negative situation back to positive. Subjecting a child to teasing, laughing, and cruel joking is destructive and demeaning. Kind imitation of a child or making light of a situation, if done sensitively, may help a child see the funny side of what he is doing and turn a situation back to positive.

• •

Like her parents, 3-year-old Emma had quite a sense of humor, so when she was getting oppositional, she could often be brought around to cooperate if her father started making up simple rhymes about the situation. This was one of her favorite rhymes:

Poor little Emma is angry
She's mad as a person can be
But out popped a wonderful monster
And danced with her until she was free!

Emma's parents would sing these poems to her and dance around with her, and usually she was quickly changed back to her happy self, laughing hysterically. What's more, she was much more amenable to undertake the task that had to be done.

Discipline Techniques for Dealing with Negative Behavior

However hard you try, there will always be times that a child does transgress or misbehave. Parents and caregivers need to have several strategies that let their child know the behavior was not acceptable. Following are a few suggestions.

Time-Out   Time-out is probably the most commonly used method to discipline young children. Used appropriately, it can be an excellent strategy as long as it is not used to shame the child (as did the old "sit in the corner" strategy). As expert Otto Weininger (1998) said, time-out works if "time in" is positive. Tips to remember about how and when to use time-out are outlined here.

- Time-out is not a punishment but a way to encourage a child and caregiver to calm down.

- In order to encourage self-regulation, tell the child he can come out when he can behave.

- The time-out is best done away from other things that are going on. A time-out may be given in the child's room or just away from others.

- Do not isolate the child for more than 1 or 2 minutes for every year of age.

- Do not keep nagging once the time-out is over, and praise the child for calming down.

Instructions for time-out:

- Give time-out instructions in a simple, direct way.

- Ignore all promises, arguments, and pleas from the child.

- Stay in the room to make sure he follows through and calms down.

- Give the time-out where there are no play materials or television.

- Praise any display of self-control.

- Make the child stay for 1–2 minutes for each year of the child's age or until the child calms down.

- Encourage the child to let you know when he has calmed down.

Remember, time-out can give both child and caregiver time to cool off and should not be made into a rigid punishment, but instead, a method to teach a child a way to get control of his *own* behavior.

• •

Margaret found that she and her 4-year-old daughter Pia would both get very upset when Pia refused to do as she was told. Sometimes Pia would scream at her mother, using rude words that really upset Margaret and made her furious. Margaret found that Pia responded well to being put in her room until she calmed down. It also prevented the two of them from ending up in a screaming match and let Margaret calm down and get the situation into perspective. Often, the 4- to 10-minute break was enough for Pia to agree to follow through with her mother's request.

Counting to Three   Some parents find it helpful to use the "counting to three" strategy to deal with difficult situations. In this strategy the parent or caregiver counts to three, at which point the child is expected to comply. As the author Thomas W. Phelan (1995) suggested, it can be very helpful to deal with behavior parents want to stop and can avoid them getting into ongoing, repetitive nagging that just goes over rules that children already know about. As long as it is used along with other, more positive approaches, it can be a helpful strategy.

Natural and Logical Consequences   Allowing children to experience the natural and logical consequences of their actions helps children understand the reasons for limits that are imposed. The effectiveness of this strategy comes from the fact that motivation for good behavior comes from the child's personal experience. Natural consequences are those that follow naturally from certain behavior. For example, the consequence of not eating lunch may be that the child feels hungry until the next meal. If the child dawdles in getting ready to go the park, a natural consequence is that there is not enough time to go. Obviously, in many instances, the child must be protected from the natural consequences of the action, such as running across the street or climbing on the stove.

When natural consequences cannot be applied, logical consequences can be used instead. Logical consequences are established by the caregiver and are a direct and logical consequence of the child's behavior. A child who runs outside without permission has to stay inside for the rest of the day. A child who refuses to pick up toys has the toys removed out of reach for a period of time. It is important for the child to see some link between the consequence and the behavior, making the consequence and the rule and limit seem more acceptable and understandable.

• •

Maluna, age 3, repeatedly got into fights with her friend Jo when she and her mother Kaye went to visit Jo and her mother Molly. Kaye watched carefully and found that most of the time Maluna was instigating the fights. After warning Maluna of the consequences, the next time a fight occurred Kaye calmly told Maluna that she could not play any more that day and took her home for a nap instead. As she tucked her into bed, Kaye told her that if she could not stop fighting with Jo she could not go visiting her and would have to stay home. Because Maluna loved being around her friend Jo, at the next visit she played happily with her. Kaye and Molly made sure that the children remained calm and encouraged them when they played cooperatively.

Spanking: Why It's a Bad Idea

Physical punishment of children in the United States is a nearly universal phenomenon, with as many as 90% of children receiving spankings occasionally in their childhood (Straus & Donnelly, 1994). Some parents believe that it is irresponsible not to spank children and believe that "to spare the rod is to spoil the child." Spanking can range from an occasional tap on the bottom all the way to severe whippings and beatings. Parents who advocate spanking usually argue that it is the way to get quick, effective control of their children. Physical punishment is actually ineffective over time for a number of reasons, however. Hitting may be effective—in the short term, but ultimately it backfires for the following reasons:

- It creates feelings of resentment, anger, humiliation, and fear in the child; deep down it may leave the caregiver feeling defeated and humiliated, too.

- It does not teach children anything about better ways to behave and resolve conflict.

- If the child does not immediately stop the negative behavior, it can escalate into more abusive punishments such as thrashing, beating, or using the strap or belt.

- It teaches a child to fear, hate, and mistrust you. It injures the relationship.

- It can damage a child emotionally.

- Young children may become excessively compliant, extremely angry, or very dishonest and sneaky.

Corporal punishment may leave a caregiver feeling defeated and humiliated, too. (From Johnston, Lynn [1978]. *Do they ever grow up?* Minnetonka, MN: Meadowbrook Press; reprint granted with written permission of Lynn Johnston Productions, Inc.)

- Child may hit back and the episode can degenerate into a violent interchange as a result.

- Hitting models one of the things you probably want children to stop doing.

- Children who are smacked have been shown to be more aggressive than those who are not.

•••

Reg seemed a somewhat unwilling participant in the parent group and had been told he must attend by a child protection agency. When types of discipline were being discussed he indicated that hitting was the only thing that works with his 4- and 5-year-old children, and that it hadn't hurt him when he was a child. When the group leader asked him gently how he had felt when he was hit, he was able to say that he often felt sad, upset, and angry all at once. Gradually, during subsequent group meetings, Reg shared more about the physical punishment he had received and his anger and hurt about it and he became open to learning more effective strategies to use with his children.

Some Common Misbehaviors and How to Cope with Them

The following are some common behaviors that most children exhibit from time to time.

Lying   Lying is one common children's behavior that most parents believe requires disciplinary action. Young children lie for three main reasons:

1. *The child has mixed fantasy with reality and may really believe the invented events that she is telling:* By age 3 or 4, most children have the ability to differentiate actual and imagined events. This ability is usually not complete until 6 or 7 years of age, however. An example of such a story would be the little girl who looked out the back window and came running in to her parents insisting there is an elephant out there sitting at the picnic table.

2. *The child has regressed to a type of wishful thinking because he is dealing with an intolerable reality:* The child who has been abandoned by a parent, for example, may invent stories about the parent as being unable to reach a phone or not knowing his phone number. Sometimes a child may wish for something so much that he begins to believe the fantasy. "I wish I could get a dog" may come out as "I'm getting a dog for my birthday."

3. *The child is telling a lie to escape criticism or punishment:* The child may know that what he is saying is not the truth at first, but may begin to really believe some parts of the story. The child is protecting himself from punishment—a display of pragmatism that is part of the normal development of children. Sometimes, the more intelligent and more capable the child, the more likely that he will lie about doing something wrong. An example of this type of lie would be when a child firmly denies pulling the flowers out of the flowerbed but has been seen in the act and the flowers are in his room.

In order to determine why a child is lying, it is helpful to know something about the child's background, whether she is facing a particular trauma, or if her parents are very punitive with discipline. These kinds of circumstances can certainly lead a child to a greater tendency toward lying.

In dealing with lying in young children, it is important to remain calm and avoid immediately labeling the child as a liar. A good way to do this may be to think of some of the small lies we often tell to protect others from what we are really thinking; for example, not telling someone you think a new dress or hairstyle is unsuitable.

It is important to try and determine what kind of lie the child is telling. If it is a fantasy lie it is best to help the child distinguish between what is real and imagined and not to make the child feel as if she did anything wrong. If the child is reacting to difficult circumstances and creating a happier reality, respect this but encourage the child to express feelings about what is going on instead and to try and find some solutions together. If the lie is primarily to get away with doing something that the child knows is wrong, it is better to talk to the child about what was wrong and why, rather than getting too perturbed about the lie. Praise the child when he does own up and be encouraging about being honest. If a child lies often, is very withdrawn from other people, or reports seeing or hearing things, it is important to seek professional help.

Swearing, Using "Bad" Language, and Answering Back

All small children at one time or another will swear and answer back to caregivers. Sometimes they use hurtful words, such as saying someone else is stupid or ugly. With younger children, bathroom or toilet words like "poo-poo head" and "kaka face" are usually favorites, while the 5- or 6-year-old may use sexual words or sexual talk. Children are more likely to use "swear" words when they are at school age. In all cases, they reflect to a certain extent issues that the child is concerned with and interested in. If use of profanities becomes an ongoing and intense problem, it is important to step back and try and determine where the behavior came from and what is keeping it going.

The obvious reasons for swearing are that the child is hearing swearing at home or elsewhere or that when he uses the words caregivers get very upset and he gets exciting attention for his behavior. Caregivers sometimes overreact because the words trigger unhappy memories or have very aggressive or sexual connotations they find uncomfortable.

Most experts agree that keeping your cool and ignoring the words and making sure they are eliminated from the children's environment will usually work best. The first time the unacceptable words are used, it is a good idea to ask if the child knows what the word means. If the child can define it, explain that the word is not one to be used in the home. If the behavior persists it should be dealt with in exactly the same ways as other negative behaviors—by time-out or the logical consequence of being ignored—until he can use a more appropriate word or express his feelings in a clearer way. Giving the child some words to express frustration can also help.

Answering back is often a way of refusing to comply and may be one indication of a developmental stage in which the child is stubbornly exerting her individuality. Sometimes stubbornness can be a way to exert power when a child is feeling overwhelmed. This kind of behavior can be a frequent reaction to stressful changes such as starting in a new school or moving to a new home. Young children can become overloaded by hectic schedules and unrealistic expectations and they just shut down. Again, the same firm discipline techniques should be used. Remember though, that children between the ages of 3 and 6 years need to exert their sense of self; they need to be listened to, and to have an opportunity to express their opinion without being seen as rude. Also, consider your expectations of the child and make sure the child is not being uncooperative because her schedule or your expectations are beyond the child's capacity.

Stealing

Most young children up to 3 years of age do not really understand the moral implications of stealing, and it will take at least another year until they understand that there are things that are "my" things and "your" things. If a child steals, remember the following:

- Do not overreact.

- Let the child know that he cannot take something that belongs to someone else.

- Let the child know that the person the object belongs to will be sad and upset about losing it.

- Make sure the child gives the thing back to the owner and apologizes.

- Remember, although they may know it is wrong because they have been told it is, most children—until the age of 6 or 7—may not understand clearly why stealing is wrong or what the consequences are, or feel guilty about it.

If stealing becomes chronic, the problem should be checked out. Parents may want to confer with a guidance counselor or therapist. Sometimes children steal because they try and fill an emotional need that is not being met by people in their lives.

Misbehavior in Public Places   Taking young children out in public places can be an embarrassing experience when they act out, and most parents find trying to discipline with strangers watching a challenge and a strain. There are some rules that can help the outings to be more likely to succeed, however.

- Try to make the trip as short and calm as possible. Half an hour is as much shopping as a young child can handle.

- Let the child know important rules ahead of time such as not running away and not picking things off the shelves.

- It is also helpful to let the child know ahead of time if she will not be bought anything.

- Notice efforts to do well.

- Allow the child to participate in the outing in some way such as picking out some items on the shelves at the grocery store from *his* grocery list.

- If necessary, apply the same rules in public as you would at home. This could include taking an acting-out child home; or time-out *with you* in a washroom, the car, or a far corner of the store. Remember, it is crucial that you remain with the child and stay as calm as possible, just letting him know you will wait until he calms down or you will be taking him home.

- If a child does behave, reward the behavior by acknowledging it. Sometimes purchasing a small item may keep good behavior going. It is important, however, not to always be buying gifts as a bribe.

Solutions for other discipline problems are discussed in the next chapter, including dealing with tantrums; aggression, including hitting and biting; and sibling fights.

THE ROLE OF PARENTS IN DISCIPLINE

For parents who received good discipline when they were children, providing helpful and appropriate discipline may come very naturally. For most parents, some of the discipline they received may not have been appropriate and they may decide to do at least some things differ-

ently. When this happens, parents may overcompensate and they may become too lenient because they were too strictly disciplined, or give reasons and choices for everything because they never felt really listened to. Other reasons for failing to provide appropriate structures and limits include

- Lacking parenting or developmental information and expecting too much from a child

- Not knowing what limits are appropriate and realistic for the age of the child

- Avoiding imposing limits because they believe they will destroy their child's creativity or injure his self-esteem

- Being afraid that limits will make their child not love them

- Having little confidence in their ability to have children behave

- Being concerned that they will abuse the child if they set limits

- Believing that "sparing the rod will spoil the child," so they hit the child frequently

- Seeing their child as a "monster" or totally out of control and believing that he cannot be controlled; sometimes even being frightened by the child's behavior

- Feeling that nothing works so they give up

- Being at work all day and feeling guilty about imposing limits at the end of the day

DISCUSSION QUESTIONS TO USE IN TRAINING PROFESSIONALS

1. How do children develop self-regulation and morality? Make a list that could be used with parents.

2. How may temperament make a difference in the development of self-regulation?

3. Discuss Baumrind's three discipline styles and how they may lead to the child outcomes that research has shown.

4. When do you think reasoning and explaining are helpful? When and why should you sometimes not use induction?

5. How would you help a resistant parent deal with a child's severe behavior problem?

6. How would you define "discipline," and why?

7. What is compliance and why is it important?

8. Discuss some of the major theories of discipline. How are they the same and how do they differ?

9. How may guilt and shame affect a child? What are they and how are they similar and different?

10. What are parental attributions and why are they so influential on how a parent disciplines?

11. If you could tell a parent one thing about disciplining a child, what would it be?

WORKING WITH PARENTS: GROUP EXERCISES AND SAMPLE HOMEWORK ACTIVITIES

When parents are interested in improving a child's behavior and are willing to try out new ways and suggestions for discipline, working with parents can be relatively straightforward and can bring changes quite rapidly. Some parents can present very difficult challenges for the following reasons, however:

- Parent has strong cultural or religious beliefs that hitting and rigid discipline are the only way to instill obedience in a child.

- Parent refuses to consider that he or she could learn anything about parenting.

- Parent is convinced the child is bad and that nothing can be done to change the child.

- Parent believes that just loving a child will be enough to have the child develop compliance. This is sometimes due to a belief in the absolute goodness of people.

- Parent is too preoccupied to bother with disciplining the child.

- Parent has great deal of difficulty controlling her anger and frequently ends up hitting the child and screaming and yelling.

Here are a few strategies professionals can use that can help parents to try new solutions.

Most important is to listen to the frustration the parent may be experiencing with the child and to show real concern and understanding about the situation. This nurturing of the parent is likely to allow the parent, in turn, to be available to nurture the child. It is very important to ally with the parent and create a partnership to find effective strategies to work with the child.

Giving the parent a new, more positive view of the child can also be helpful. This can be done by noticing positive things the child does or by speaking for the child so the parent understands what is going on developmentally. For example, when a child is crying, say, "Oh dear; she's crying because she misses you, she loves you so much."

One way to encourage a parent to see herself parenting and how the child reacts to the parenting is to videotape and play the tape back to the parent for discussion. Having the parent observe the child and talking about what she notices can also be helpful. Other ways to help may be by modeling appropriate discipline techniques or offering parenting groups where information is provided and problems discussed. Sometimes, working with parents to decide one behavior they would like to work on (e.g., bedtime) and giving them strategies can be helpful because focusing in this way is likely to be successful and to encourage parents to try with other aspects of their child's behavior. The support of other parents may be crucial. When it is clear that the parent's history is getting in the way of his ability to discipline appropriately, it may be important to ask the parent about how he was parented, how it made him feel, and how he would like to have been treated differently. This can lead to discussions of how parents would like to change their discipline style and how they could learn to react differently.

GROUP EXERCISES TO HELP PARENTS ENCOURAGE SELF-REGULATION, MORALITY, AND A SENSE OF CONSCIENCE

This section includes exercises that can be used with groups of parents and other caregivers to encourage them to enhance self-regulation, morality, and a sense of conscience in children.

400

How I Would Like to Be Disciplined

Ask parents to list five positive characteristics and five negative characteristics they have experienced with supervisors. Parents will probably list fairness, respect, listening, clear rules, firmness, and modeling as desirable characteristics and being too strict, playing favorites, not appreciating work, knowing little about supervising, and unpredictability as some negative characteristics. Have parents discuss how the positive qualities they identify may relate to good parenting techniques.

How Was I Disciplined?

Ask parents to think back to the way they were disciplined and to list what they liked (and would like to continue) and what they did not like (and would like to change). Discuss how they feel they are doing with their children.

Working on Ongoing Problem Behaviors

Have parents volunteer to discuss their children's ongoing behavior problems. Use Figure 7.1 and have the group problem-solve around the problem. First, have them define the problem

Define the problem behaviorally.
Decide who owns the problem.
Generate possible solutions.
Evaluate the ideas; choose and implement one.
Evaluate the solutions.

Figure 7.1. Blank chart for finding solutions to ongoing discipline problems.

behaviorally. Then have them determine who "owns" the problem. Allow all group participants to come up with solutions but have the parents who volunteered the problem choose a solution they feel could work for them. Ask parents to use the solution consistently for a week and to report on what happened next week.

Making a List of Bottom-Line Rules

Ask parents to come up with a list of rules that will be enforced at all times. Point out that the more they have, the greater the effort needed to enforce them. Have the group list the behaviors under the categories of safety, morality, and social-conventional rules. After the listing of the rules, talk about how to make them clear to children with written instructions and pictures. Add any essential ones that seem to have been left out.

How My Parents' Disciplinary Style Might Have Affected My Own

To help parents see the relationship between their own style of discipline and their parents', have them identify words that describe their own way of setting limits and then words describing how their parents set limits (see Figure 7.2). After the exercise, have parents discuss similarities and how they are different from their parents in disciplining.

How Do I Overcome Poor Discipline Practices?

Have parents discuss the poor discipline practices with which they struggle. Use the chart in Figure 7.3 and brainstorm about ways to overcome them.

Identifying My Style of Parenting

Ask parents to complete the questionnaire given in Figure 7.4. Those who check several "B's" tend to be permissive, "A's" are more punitive and authoritarian, and "C's" are more democratic or authoritative. Ask parents why they think "C" answers are more helpful for the child.

Instructions: Circle characteristics in disciplining young children that apply to you. Double circle those that apply to your parents, too.

Inconsistent	Firm	Confusing/unclear
Expectations too high	Patient	Indecisive
Protective	Harsh	Distant
Loving	Consistent	Avoiding
Persistent	Avoids conflicts	Easy to win over

Figure 7.2. Worksheet for determining disciplining characteristics that apply to you and to your parent(s).

Instructions: Look at the poor discipline practice listed on the left and list some suggestions to overcome the problem on the right. For example, for "Always sending a child to time-out without an explanation," you might write "Tell the child why he is in time out, how long he must remain there, and what kind of behavior specific to the situation is expected in the future."

Poor discipline practice	Suggestions to overcome the problem
Always sending a child to time-out without any explanation.	
Becoming very upset and screaming when child misbehaves.	
Hitting or biting back when a child hits or bites.	
Providing no routines and structures.	
Consistently giving reasons and explanations without acting.	
Being inconsistent.	
Ignoring rather than acting when action is called for.	
Other:	
Other:	

Figure 7.3. Blank worksheet for suggesting ways to overcome poor disciplining practices.

Where Do My Expectations for My Child Come From?

Sometimes our expectations for our children can be unrealistic. It is often important to see where our expectations are coming from and to check them against what developmental theory can tell us about them. Have parents list some of their expectations for their children and what aspects in the environment or their own backgrounds are influencing these expectations (see Figure 7.5). Parents might list what friends or relatives say about their children when they act out, for example, as influencing their own expectations.

Instructions: Read the following situation and circle the answer under each number that best describes the kind of discipline you provide.

1. **You have asked several times for your child to clean up her toys but she refuses. What do you do?**

   a) Scream at her.

   b) Clean it up myself.

   c) Make sure she does it, but help a little.

2. **You are at the store and your child starts screaming halfway through the grocery shopping. Do you . . .**

   a) Buy him candy and continue on.

   b) Drop everything and go home.

   c) Explain that the shopping has to be done but express empathy for the ways he feels about shopping.

3. **Your child has been whining all day. Do you . . .**

   a) Spank him in frustration.

   b) Give him what he wants.

   c) Spend some time with him and then try and get him to have a rest.

4. **Your child brings over a book for you to read to her just as you are going to have a few moments to yourself. Do you . . .**

   a) Tell her to go away because you're busy.

   b) Go ahead and read to her.

   c) Invite her to join you and tell her you will read to her later.

Figure 7.4. Questionnaire for determining what kind of discipline you provide. (*Key:* Mostly "A's": Punitive and authoritarian; mostly "B's": Permissive; mostly "C's": Democratic or authoritative.)

What About Spanking?

Parents are asked to discuss their ideas about spanking. Ask them to discuss why it is inappropriate and to come up with some alternatives for various situations.

SAMPLE HOMEWORK ACTIVITIES

In order to encourage parents to try out some of the new discipline ideas discussed in the group meetings, it is helpful if parents can be given some homework tasks to do between sessions. The results can then be discussed the next week with the support of the group. Assign one or two of the suggested activities:

1. Jot down the number of times you say "no" to your child in a day.

Instructions: In the left-hand column, write some expectations you know you have for your child. In the middle column, think of some things other people say that influence that particular expectation. In the right-hand column, write something from your past that probably fostered that expectation in you. For example, if you list "My child will be polite at all times," you might list "My neighbors get upset if my child grabs things" under "What others say." Under "What my background says," you might write "My mother always insisted on politeness."

My expectation	What others say	What my background says

Figure 7.5. Blank worksheet for understanding how others' expectations and our backgrounds affect our own expectations.

2. Write down information about a particular behavior of your child that bothers you. Problem-solve for solutions and share ideas with the group next week.

3. Decide on common rules with your child's other caregivers. Discuss topics that might be causing disagreement and conflict.

4. Make sure you comment on your child's positive behavior every day.

5. Try and get through a whole day without saying "no" or "don't" but set the limits at the same time. Use as many "do's" as possible.

6. Troubleshoot ahead of time before going on an errand and see if it can be successful in avoiding problems.

7. If your parents criticize your child-rearing practices, try and come up with new ways to deal with the criticism and reasons for your own strategies.

8. Make a sign using words and pictures that list family rules.

9. Make a tape recording of yourself with your children in the morning and at night. Listen and note the negative and positive comments and strategies that are used. Bring it for discussion next week.

10. Make a star chart to use to eliminate one difficult behavior.

BIBLIOGRAPHY

REFERENCES

Alexander, J.F., Waldron, H.B., Barton, C., & Mas, C.H. (1989). The minimizing of blaming attributions and behaviors in delinquent families. *Journal of Consulting and Clinical Psychology, 57,* 19–24.

Applegate, J.L., Burleson, B.R., & Delia, J.G. (1992). Reflection-enhancing parenting as an antecedent to children's social-cognitive and communicative development. In J.E. Sigel, A.V. McGillicuddy-DeLisi, & J.J. Goodnew (Eds.), *Parental belief systems: The psychological consequences for children* (2nd edition, pp. 3–39). Mahwah, NJ: Lawrence Erlbaum Associates.

Baden, A.D., & Howe, G.W. (1992). Mothers' attributions and expectancies regarding their conduct-disordered children. *Journal of Abnormal Child Psychology, 20,* 467–485.

Baldwin, A.L., Baldwin, C., & Cole, R.E. (1990). Stress-resistant families and stress-resistant children. In J.E. Rolf, A.S. Masten, D. Cicchetti, K.H. Nuechterlein, & S. Weintraub (Eds.), *Risk and protective factors in the development of psychopathology* (pp. 257–280). New York: Cambridge University Press.

Bandura, A. (1991). Social cognitive theory of moral thought and action. In W.M. Kurtines & J.L. Gewirtz, *Handbook of moral behavior and development: Vol. 1. Theory* (pp. 45–103). Mahwah, NJ: Lawrence Erlbaum Associates.

Bates, J.E. (1989). Concepts and measures of temperament. In G.A. Kohnstamm, J.A. Bates, & M.K. Rothbart (Eds.), *Temperament in childhood* (pp. 3–26). New York: John Wiley & Sons.

Baumrind, D. (1971). Current patterns of parental authority. *Developmental Psychology, 4,* 1–103.

Baumrind, D. (1973). The development of instrumental competence through socialization. In A.D. Pick (Ed.), *Minnesota symposium on child psychology* (Vol. 7, pp. 3–46). Minneapolis: University of Minnesota Press.

Baumrind, D. (1997). Necessary distinctions. *Psychological Inquiry, 8,* 176–182.

Baumrind, D. (2001). *Does causally relevant research support a blanket injunction against disciplinary spanking by parents?* Invited address at the 109th annual convention of the American Psychological Association.

Baumrind, D., & Black, A.E. (1967). Socialization practices associated with dimensions of competence in preschool boys and girls. *Child Development, 38,* 291–327.

Benoit, D., & Parker, K.C.H. (1994). Stability and transmission of attachment across three generations. *Child Development, 65,* 1444–1456.

Brody, G.H., & Shaffer, D.R. (1982). Contributions of parents and peers to children's moral socialization. *Developmental Review, 2,* 31–75.

Bugental, D.B. (1985). Unresponsive children and powerless adults: Cocreators of affectively uncertain caregiving environments. In M. Lewis & C. Saarni (Eds.), *The socialization of emotions* (pp. 239–261). New York: Plenum Press.

Bugental, D.B. (1992). Affective and cognitive processes within threat-oriented family systems. In I.E. Sigel, A.V. McGillicuddy-DeLisi, & J.J. Goodnow (Eds.), *Parental belief systems: The psychological consequences for children* (2nd ed., pp. 219–248). Mahwah, NJ: Lawrence Erlbaum Associates.

Bugental, D.B., Blue, J., & Cruzcosa, M. (1989). Perceived control over caregiving outcomes: Implications for child abuse. *Developmental Psychology, 25,* 532–539.

Bugental, D.B., & Shennum, W.A. (1984). "Difficult" children as elicitors and targets of adult communication patterns: An attribution-behavioral transactional analysis. *Monographs of the Society for Research in Child Development, 49*(1, Serial No. 205).

Chao, R.K. (1994). Beyond parental control and authoritarian parenting style: Understanding Chinese parenting through the cultural notion of training. *Child Development, 65,* 1111–1119.

Covell, K., Grusec, J., & King, G. (1995). The intergenerational transmission of maternal discipline and standards for behavior. *Social Development, 4,* 32–43.

Creasey, K.L., & Jarvis, P.A. (1994). Relationships between parenting stress and developmental functioning among 2-year-olds. *Infant Behavior and Development, 17,* 423–429.

Crittenden, P.M. (1985). Social networks, quality of child rearing and child development. *Child Development, 56,* 1299–1313.

Cummings, E.M., Davies, P.T., & Campbell, S.B. (2000). New directions in the study of parenting. In E.M. Cummings, P.T. Davies, & S.B. Campbell, *Developmental psychopathology and family process: Theory, research, and clinical implications* (pp. 200–250). New York: Guilford Press.

Deater-Deckard, K., & Dodge, K.A. (1997). Externalizing behavior problems and discipline revisited: Nonlinear effects and variation by culture, context, and gender. *Psychological Inquiry, 8,* 161–175.

Deater-Deckard, K., Dodge, K.A., Bates, J.E., & Pettit, G.S. (1996). Physical discipline among African American and European American mothers: Links to children's externalizing behaviors. *Developmental Psychology, 32,* 1065–1072.

Deley, W.W. (1988). Physical punishment of children: Sweden and the U.S.A. *Journal of Comparative Family Studies, 19,* 419–431.

Dishion, T.J., French, D.C., & Patterson, G.R. (1995). The development and ecology of antisocial behavior. In D. Cicchetti & D.J. Cohen (Eds.), *Developmental psychopathology: Vol. 2. Risk, disorder, and adaptation* (pp. 421–471). New York: John Wiley & Sons.

Dix, T.H. (1992). Parenting on behalf of the child: Empathic goals in the regulation of responsive parenting. In E. Sigel, A.V. McGillicuddy-DeLisi, & J.J. Goodnow (Eds.), *Parental belief systems: The psychological consequences for children* (2nd ed., pp. 319–346). Mahwah, NJ: Lawrence Erlbaum Associates.

Dix, T.H. (1993). Attributing dispositions to children: An interactional analysis of attribution in socialization. *Personality and Social Psychology Bulletin, 19,* 633–643.

Dix, T.H., & Grusec, J.A. (1992). Parent attribution processes in the socialization of children. In I.E. Sigel, A.V. McGillicuddy-DeLisi, & J.J. Goodnow (Eds.), *Parental belief systems: The psychological consequences for children* (2nd ed., pp. 201–233). Mahwah, NJ: Lawrence Erlbaum Associates.

Dix, T.H., & Lochman, J.E. (1990). Social cognition and negative reactions to children: A comparison of mothers of aggressive and nonaggressive boys. *Journal of Social and Clinical Psychology, 9,* 418–438.

Dodge, K.A., Pettit, G.A., & Bates, J.E. (1994). Socialization mediators of the relation between socioeconomic status and child conduct problems. *Child Development, 65,* 649–665.

Dornbusch, S.M., Ritter, P.L., Leiderman, P.H., Roberts, D.F., & Fraleigh, M.J. (1987). The relation of parenting style to adolescent school performance. *Child Development, 58,* 1244–1257.

Erickson, M.F., Egeland, B., & Pianta, R. (1989). The effects of maltreatment on the development of young children. In D. Cicchetti & V. Carlson (Eds.), *Child maltreatment: Theory and research on the causes and consequences of child abuse and neglect* (pp. 647–684). New York: Cambridge University Press.

Erickson, M.F., Sroufe, L.A., & Egeland, B. (1985). The relationship between quality of attachment and behavior problems in preschool in a high-risk sample. *Monographs of the Society for Research in Child Development, 50*(1–2, Serial No. 209).

Eyberg, S.M., & Robinson, E.A. (1982). Parent-child interaction training: Effects on family functioning. *Journal of Clinical Child Psychology, 11,* 130–137.

Forehand, R. (1977). Child noncompliance to parent commands: Behavioral analysis and treatment. In M. Hersen, R.M. Eisler, & P.M. Miller (Eds.), *Progress in behavior modification* (Vol. 5, pp. 111–147). San Diego: Academic Press.

Forehand, R., & Long, N. (1988). Outpatient treatment of the acting-out child: Procedures, long term follow-up data, and clinical problems. *Advances in Behavior Research and Therapy, 10,* 129–177.

Forehand, R.L., & McMahon, R.J. (1981). *Helping the noncompliant child: A clinician's guide to parent training.* New York: Guilford Press.

Freud, S. (1959). *The passing of the Oedipus complex: Collected papers* (Vol. 11). New York: Basic Books (Original work published 1924).

Giles-Sims, J., Straus, M.A., & Sugarman, D.B. (1995). Child, maternal and family characteristics associated with spanking. *Family Relations: Journal of Applied Family and Child Studies, 44,* 170–176.

Grossman, K., Fremmer-Bombik, E., Rudolph, J., & Grossman, K. (1988). Maternal attachment representations are related to patterns of infant–mother attachment and maternal care during the first year. In R.A. Hinde & J. Stevenson-Hinde (Eds.), *Relationships within families: Mutual influences* (pp. 241–260). Oxford, England: Clarendon Press.

Grusec, J.E., & Goodnow, J.J. (1994). The impact of parental discipline methods on the child's internalization of values: A reconceptualization of current points of view. *Developmental Psychology, 30,* 4–19.

Grusec, J.E., Goodnow, J.J., & Kuczynski, L. (2000). New directions in analyses of parenting contributions to children's acquisition of values. *Child Development, 71,* 205–211.

Hembree-Kigin, T.L., & McNeil, C.B. (1995). *Parent–child interaction therapy.* New York: Plenum Press.

Hoffman, M.L. (1970). Moral development. In P.H. Mussen (Ed.), *Carmichael's manual of child psychology* (Vol. 2, pp. 261–360). New York: John Wiley & Sons.

Hoffman, M.L. (1983). Affective and cognitive processes in moral internalization. In E.T. Higgins, D.N. Ruble, & W.W. Hartup (Eds.), *Social cognition and social development: A sociocultural perspective* (pp. 236–274). Cambridge: Cambridge University Press.

Hoffman, M.L. (1988). Moral development. In M. Bornstein & M. Lamb (Eds.), *Developmental psychology: An advanced textbook* (pp. 497–548). Mahwah, NJ: Lawrence Erlbaum Associates.

Hoffman, M.L. (1991). Empathy, social cognition and moral action. In W.M. Kurtines & J.L. Gewirtz, *Handbook of moral behavior and development: Vol. 1. Theory* (pp. 275–301). Mahwah, NJ: Lawrence Erlbaum Associates.

Holden, G., Lavigne, V.V., & Cameron, A.M. (1990). Probing the continuum of effectiveness in parent training: Characteristics of parents and preschoolers. *Journal of Clinical Child Psychology, 19,* 2–8.

Holden, G.W., & Miller, P.C. (1999). Enduring and different: A meta-analysis of the similarities in parents' child rearing. *Psychological Bulletin, 125,* 223–254.

Houlihan, D., & Jones, R.N. (1990). Exploring the reinforcement of compliance with "do" and "don't" requests and the side effects: A partial replication and extension. *Psychological Reports, 67,* 439–448.

Jennings, K.D., Stagg, V., & Connors, R.E. (1991). Social networks and mothers' interactions with their preschool children. *Child Development, 62,* 966–978.

Kazdin, A.E. (1985). *Treatment of antisocial behavior in children and adolescents.* Homewood, IL: Dorsey Press.

Keenan, K., & Shaw, D.S. (1995). The development of coercive family processes: The interaction between aversive toddler behavior and parenting factors. In J. McCord (Ed.), *Coercion and punishment in long-term perspectives* (pp. 165–180). New York: Cambridge University Press.

Kelley, M.L., Power, T.G., & Wimbush, D.D. (1992). Determinants of disciplinary practices in low-income black mothers. *Child Development, 63,* 573–582.

Kochanska, G. (1995). Children's temperament, mothers' discipline, and security of attachment: Multiple pathways to emerging internalization. *Child Development, 66,* 597–615.

Kochanska, G. (1997). Mutually responsive orientation between mothers and their young children: Implications for early socialization. *Child Development, 68,* 94–112.

Kochanska, G., Coy, K.C., & Murray, K.T. (2001). The development of self-regularion in the first four years of life. *Child Development, 72,* 1091–1111.

Kochanska, G., & Thompson, R.A. (1997). The emergence and development of conscience in toddlerhood and early childhood. In J.E. Grusec & L. Kuczynski (Eds.), *Parenting and children's internalization of values: A handbook of contemporary theory* (pp. 53–77). New York: John Wiley & Sons.

Kohlberg, L. (1969). Stage and sequence: The cognitive-developmental approach to socialization. In D.A. Goslin (Ed.), *Handbook of socialization theory and research* (pp. 347–480). Chicago: Rand McNally.

Lamborn, S.D., Mounts, N.S., Steinberg, L., & Dornbusch, S.M. (1991). Patterns of competence and adjustment among adolescents from authoritative, authoritarian, indulgent, and neglectful families. *Child Development, 62,* 1049–1065.

Lefkowitz, L., Eron, L., Walder, L., & Huesmann, L. (1977). *Growing up to be violent: A longitudinal study of the development of aggression.* New York: Pergamon.

Maccoby, E., & Martin, J. (1983). Socialization in the context of the family: Parent–child interaction. In P.H. Mussen (Series Ed.) & E.M. Hetherington (Vol. Ed.), *Handbook of child psychology: Vol. 4. Socialization, personality, and social development* (pp. 1–101). New York: John Wiley & Sons.

Main, M., & Goldwyn, R. (1984). Predicting rejection of her infant from mother's representations of her own experiences: Implications for the abused-abusing intergenerational cycle. *Child Abuse and Neglect, 8,* 203–217.

Main, M., Kaplan, N., & Cassidy, J. (1985). Security in infancy, childhood and adulthood: A move to the level of representation. *Monographs of the Society for Research in Child Development, 50* (1, Serial No. 209).

McFarlane, A.H., Bellissimo, A., & Norman, G.R. (1995). Family structure, family functioning and adolescent well-being: The transcendent influence of parental style. *Journal of Child Psychology and Psychiatry and Allied Disciplines, 36,* 847–864.

Mills, R.S.L., & Rubin, K. (1990). Parental beliefs about problematic social behaviors in early childhood. *Child Development, 61,* 138–151.

Moreland, J.R., Schwebel, A.I., Beck, S., & Wells, R. (1982). Parents as therapists: A review of the behavior therapy parent training literature—1975–1981. *Behavior Modification, 6,* 250–276.

Neef, N.A., Shafer, M.S., Egel, A.I., Cataldo, M.F., & Parrish, J.M. (1983). The class specific effects of compliance training with "do" and "don't" requests: Analogue analysis and classroom application. *Journal of Applied Behavior Analysis, 16,* 81–99.

Parker, G. (1983). Parental 'affectionless control' as an antecedent to adult depression: A risk factor delineated. *Archives of General Psychiatry, 40,* 956–960.

Parpal, M., & Maccoby, E.E. (1985). Maternal responsiveness and subsequent child compliance. *Child Development, 56,* 1326–1334.

Pascoe, J.M., Loda, F.A., Jeffries, V., & Earp, J.A. (1981). The association between mothers' social support and provision of stimulation to their children. *Journal of Developmental and Behavioral Pediatrics, 2,* 15–19.

Patterson, G.R. (1976). The aggressive child: Victim and architect of a coercive system. In E.J. Mash, A. Hamerlynck, & L.C. Handy (Eds.), *Behavioral modification and families: Theory and research* (pp. 267–315). New York: Brunner/Mazel.

Patterson, G.R. (1982). *Coercive family process.* Eugene, OR: Castalia.

Patterson, G.R., Chamberlain, P., & Reid, J.B. (1982). A comparative evaluation of a parent–training program. *Behavior Therapy, 13,* 638–650.

Pettit, G.S., Bates, J.E., & Dodge, K.A. (1997). Supportive parenting, ecological context, and children's adjustment: A seven-year longitudinal study. *Child Development, 68,* 908–923.

Pfiffner, L.J., & O'Leary, S.G. (1989). Effects of maternal discipline and nurturance on toddlers' behaviour and affect. *Journal of Abnormal Child Psychology, 17,* 527–540.

Phelan, T.W. (1995). *1–2–3 Magic: Training your children to do what you want!* (Book and video). Glen Ellyn, IL: Child Management Inc.

Power, T.G., & Chapieski, M.L. (1986). Childrearing and impulse control in toddlers: A naturalistic investigation. *Developmental Psychology, 22,* 271–275.

Radke-Yarrow, M., Zahn-Waxler, C., & Chapman, M. (1983). Prosocial dispositions and behaviour. In P.H. Mussen (Series Ed.) & E.M. Hetherington (Vol. Ed.), *Handbook of child psychology: Vol. 4. Socialization, personality, and social development* (pp. 469–545). New York: John Wiley & Sons.

Ringwalt, C.L., Browne, D.C., Rosenblum, L.B., Evans, G.A., & Kotch, J.B. (1989). Predicting adult approval of corporal punishment from childhood parenting experiences. *Journal of Family Violence, 4,* 339–351.

Roberts, M.W. (1982). The effects of warned versus unwarned timeout procedures on child noncompliance. *Child and Family Behavior, 4,* 37–53.

Roberts, M.W. (1988). Enforcing chair timeouts with room timeouts. *Behavior Modification, 12,* 353–370.

Roberts, M.W., & Powers, S.W. (1990). Adjusting chair timeout enforcement procedures for oppositional children. *Behavior Therapy, 21,* 257–271.

Rocissano, L., Slade, A., & Lynch, V. (1987). Dyadic synchrony and toddler compliance. *Developmental Psychology, 23,* 698–704.

Rothbaum, F., & Weisz, J.R. (1994). Parental caregiving and child externalizing behavior in non-clinical samples: A meta-analysis. *Psychological Bulletin, 116,* 55–74.

Rubin, K.H., & Mills, R.S. (1990). Maternal beliefs about adaptive and maladaptive social behaviors in normal, aggressive, and withdrawn preschoolers. *Journal of Abnormal Child Psychology, 18,* 419–435.

Rueter, M.A., & Conger, R.A. (1995). Antecedents of parent-adolescent disagreements. *Journal of Marriage and the Family, 57,* 435–448.

Sagatum, I.J. (1991). Attributions of delinquency by delinquent minors, their families, and probation officers. *Journal of Offender Rehabilitation, 16,* 43–56.

Smetana, J.G. (1983). Social cognitive development: Domain distinctions and coordinations. *Developmental Review, 3,* 131–147.

Speltz, M.L. (1990). The treatment of preschool conduct problems: An integration of behavioral and attachment concepts. In M.T. Greenberg, D. Cicchetti, & E.M. Cummings (Eds.), *Attachment in the preschool years: Theory, research and intervention* (pp. 399–426). Chicago: University of Chicago Press.

Sroufe, L.A. (1983). Infant-caregiver attachment and patterns of adaptation in preschool: The roots of maladaptation and competence. In M. Perlmutter (Ed.), *Minnesota symposium in child psychology: Vol. 16. Development and policy concerning children with special needs* (pp. 41–48). Mahwah, NJ: Lawrence Erlbaum Associates.

Steinberg, L., Dornbusch, S.M., & Brown, B.B. (1992). Ethnic differences in adolescent achievement: An ecological perspective. *American Psychologist, 47,* 723–729.

Steinberg, L., Lamborn, S.D., Darling, N., Mounts, N.S., & Dornbusch, S.M. (1994). Impact of parenting on adolescent achievement: Authoritative parenting, school involvement, and encouragement to succeed. *Child Development, 65,* 754–770.

Steinberg, L., Lamborn, S.D., Dornbusch, S.M., & Darling, N. (1992). Impact of parenting, school involvement, and encouragement to succeed. *Child Development, 63,* 1266–1281.

Steinberg, L., Mounts, N.S., Lamborn, S.D., & Dornbusch, S.M. (1991). Authoritative parenting and adolescent adjustment across varied ecological niches. *Journal of Research on Adolescence, 1,* 19–36.

Strassberg, Z., Dodge, K.A., Pettit, G.S., & Bates, J.E. (1994). Spanking in the home and children's subsequent aggression toward kindergarten peers. *Development and Psychopathology, 6,* 445–461.

Straus, M.A., & Donnelly, D.A. (1994). *Beating the devil out of them: Corporal punishment in American families.* New York: Maxwell Macmillan International.

Thomas, A., & Chess, S. (1985). Genesis and evolution of behavioral disorders: From infancy to early adult life. *Annual Progress in Child Psychiatry and Child Development,* 140–158.

Travillion, K., & Snyder, J. (1993). The role of maternal discipline and involvement in peer rejection and neglect. *Journal of Applied Developmental Psychology, 14,* 37–57.

Trommsdorff, G. (1991). Child-rearing and children's empathy. *Perceptual and Motor Skills, 72,* 387–390.

Turiel, E. (1983). *The development of social knowledge: Morality and convention.* New York: Cambridge University Press.

Webster-Stratton, C., & Hammond, M. (1990). Predictors of treatment outcome in parent-training for families and conduct problem children. *Behavior Therapy, 21,* 319–337.

Weininger, O. (1998). *T.I.P.S.: Time-in parenting strategies.* Binghamton, NY: ESF Publishers.

Weiss, B., Dodge, K.A., Bates, J.E., & Pettit, G.S. (1992). Some consequences of early harsh discipline. Child aggression and a maladaptive social information processing style. *Child Development, 63,* 1321–1335.

Yankelovich, D. (2000). *What grownups understand about child development: A national benchmark survey.* CIVITAS initiative, Brio Corporation, researched by Dyg, Inc.

Zahn-Waxler, C., Radke-Yarrow, M., & King, R.A. (1979). Child rearing and children's prosocial initiations towards victims of distress. *Child Development, 50,* 319–330.

Zeanah, C., Benoit, D., Barton, M., Regan, C., Hirschberg, L.M., & Lipsitt, L.P. (1993). Representations of attachment in mothers, and their one-year-old infants. *Journal of the American Academy of Child and Adolescent Psychiatry, 32,* 278–286.

FURTHER READING ON THE TOPIC

Barkely, R.A. (1997). *Defiant children.* New York: Guilford Press.

Barrett, K.C., & Campos, J.J. (1987). Perspectives on emotional development II: A functionalist approach to emotions. In J.D. Osofsky (Ed.), *Handbook of infant development* (2nd ed., pp. 555–578). New York: John Wiley & Sons.

Bjorklund, B.R., & Bjorklund, D.F. (1990, August). Setting limits: Disciplining techniques for preschoolers. *Parents Magazine, 65(4),* 69.

Bjorklund, B.R., & Bjorklund, D.F. (1999). *Parents' book of discipline.* New York: Ballantine Books.

Brenner, B. (1983). *Love and discipline.* New York: Ballantine Books.

Coloroso, B. (2000). *Kids are worth it.* Toronto: Penguin.

Crary, E. (1990). *Pick up your socks—and other skills growing children need!* Seattle, WA: Parenting Press.

Crary, E. (1993). *Without spanking or spoiling.* Seattle, WA: Parenting Press.

Damon, W. (1990). *The moral child: Nurturing children's natural moral growth.* New York: Free Press.

Dinkmeyer, D., McKay, G.D., & Dinkmeyer, J.S. (1990). *Parenting young children.* New York: Random House.

Dorr, D., Zaz, M., & Bonner, J. (1983). *The psychology of discipline.* New York: International Universities Press.

Dunn, J. (1990). The beginning of moral understanding: Development in the second year. In J. Kagan & S. Lamb (Eds.), *The emergence of morality in young children* (pp. 91–112). Chicago: University of Chicago Press.

Emde, R.N., & Buchsbaum, H.K. (1990). "Didn't you hear my mommy?" Autonomy with connectedness in moral self-emergence. In D. Cicchetti & M. Beeghly (Eds.), *The self in transition: Infancy to childhood* (pp. 35–60). Chicago: University of Chicago Press.

Emde, R.N., Johnson, W.F., & Easterbrooks, A. (1990). The do's and don'ts of early moral development: Psychoanalytic tradition and current research. In J. Kagan & S. Lamb (Eds.), *The emergence of morality in young children* (pp. 245–376). Chicago: University of Chicago Press.

Eyre, L., & Eyre, R. (1993). *Teaching your children values.* New York: Simon & Schuster.

Fitzpatrick, J.G. (1995, June). Teaching values. *Parents Magazine, 70(4),* 34.

Friedman, M., & Weiss, E. (1992, October). How to handle a biter. *Parents Magazine, 67(4),* 128.

Gadlin, H. (1978). Child discipline and the pursuit of self: An historical perspective. In H.W. Reese & L.P. Lipsitt (Eds.), *Advances in child development and behavior* (Vol. 12, pp. 231–265). San Diego: Academic Press.

Golant, M., & Golant, S.K. (1997). *Disciplining your preschooler.* Los Angeles: Lowell House.

Green, C. (1998). *Toddler taming: A survival guide for parents.* New York: Fawcett Columbine.

Harris, T. (1989, August). The 12 building blocks of discipline. *Parents Magazine, 64,* 76–82.

Hoffman, M.L. (1977). Moral internalization: Current theory and research. In L. Berkowitz (Ed.), *Advances in experimental social psychology* (pp. 85–133). San Diego: Academic Press.

Hyde, C. (1988, August). The spoiling zone. *Parents Magazine, 63,* 95(5).

Kagan, J., & Lamb, S. (1990). *The emergence of morality in young children.* Chicago: University of Chicago Press.

Kersey, K. (1995). *The art of sensitive parenting.* New York: Berkley Books.

Kilpatrick, W. (1993). *Why Johnny can't tell right from wrong.* New York: Distican.

Kurshan, N. (1987). *Raising your child to be a mensch.* New York: Atheneum.

La Farge, P. (1993, February). Team up with your caregiver. *Parents Magazine, 68(4),* 87.

Le Shan, E. (1988, March). The best kept secret about discipline. *Parents Magazine, 63(3),* 102.

MacKenzie, R.J. (1998). *Setting limits: How to raise responsible, independent children by providing clear boundaries.* Roclin, CA: Prima Publishing.

Marion, M. (1995). *Guidance of young children.* Englewood Cliffs, NJ: Merrill.

McCall, R.B. (1987, October). Dads who hit. *Parents Magazine, 62(1),* 242.

Millar, T.P. (1989). *The omnipotent child: How to mold, strengthen and perfect the developing child.* Vancouver, British Columbia: Palmer Press.

Miller, C.S. (1984). Building self control: Discipline for young children. *Young Children, 40,* 15–19.

Mitchell, G. (1982). *A very practical guide to discipline with young children.* New York: Monarch.

Nechas, E., & Foley, D. (1992). *What do I do now?* New York: Simon & Schuster.

Nelsen, J., Erwin, C., & Duffy, R. (1998). *Positive discipline for preschoolers.* Rocklin, CA: Prima Publishing.

Nelson, G.E. (1984). *The one-minute scolding: The amazingly effective new approach to child discipline.* New York: Shambhala.

Provence, S. (1992). Helping young children channel their aggressive energies. *Zero to Three, 5,* 13–16.

Rosenberg, M. (1989, January). "No, I won't!" *Parents Magazine, 64(4),* 68.

Salmon, D.K. (1992, February). Making time-out work. *Parents Magazine, 67(3),* 98.

Samalin, N. (1998). *Loving your child is not enough.* New York: Penguin.

Schwartzman, M. (1992). *The anxious parent: Freeing yourself from the fears and stresses of parenting.* New York: Simon & Schuster.

Siberman, M., & Wheelan, S. (1981). *How to discipline without feeling guilty.* Champaign, IL: Research Press.

Taffel, R. & Blau, M. (1993). *Parenting by heart: How to be in charge, stay connected, and instill your values, when it feels like you've got only 15 minutes a day.* Reading, MA: Addison-Wesley.

Theroux, P. (1989, June). Children without limits: Setting firm boundaries can give a child a sense of proportion. *Parents Magazine, 64(3),* 62.

Varni, J.W., & Corwin, D. (1991). *Time-out for toddlers: Positive solutions to typical problems in children.* New York: Be Jo Sales.

Welch, M.G. (1989). *Holding time: How to eliminate conflict, temper tantrums and sibling rivalry and raise happy, loving successful children.* New York: Distican.

Weston, D.C., & Weston, M.S. (1993). *Playful parenting: Turning the dilemma of discipline into fun and games.* New York: J.P. Tarcher.

Whitman, C. (1991). *Win the whining war and other skirmishes.* Los Angeles: Perspective Publishing.

Wyckoff, J., & Unell, B. (1984). *Discipline without shouting and spanking.* New York: Meadowbrook Books.

CHILDREN'S BOOKS ABOUT COMPLIANCE AND MORALS

Aesop. (1991). *Androcles and the lion.* New York: Holiday House.

Alexander, M.G. (2001). *I sure am glad to see you, blackboard bear.* New York: Candlewick.

Allard, H. (1977). *Miss Nelson is missing!* Boston: Houghton Mifflin.

Arnold, T. (1997). *The signmaker's assistant.* New York: Puffin.

Berenstain, S., & Berenstain, J. (1988). *The Berenstain Bears and the truth.* New York: Random House.

Berenstain, S., & Berenstain, J. (1988). *The Berenstain Bears get the gimmies.* New York: Random House.

Berry, J.W. (2000). Series of books, *Let's Talk About ... ,* on various behavioral issues such as showing off, teasing, swearing, etc. New York: Goldstar.

Cohen, M. (1995). *Liar, liar, pants on fire!* New York: Yearling.

Cummings, P. (1991). *Clean your room, Harvey Moon!* Toronto: Simon and Schuster Children's Publishing.

Gretz, S. (1990). *Roger takes charge!* London: Dial Books.

Henkes, K. (1986). *A weekend with Wendell.* New York: William Morrow.

Henkes, K. (1988). *Chester's way.* New York: Greenwillow Books.

Hutchins, P. (1989). *The doorbell rang.* New York: Mulberry Books.

Hutchins, P. (1995). *Tidy Titch.* New York: Morrow Avon.

Lindgren, B. (1988). *Sam's car.* New York: William Morrow.

Lindgren, B. (1988). *Sam's cookie.* New York: William Morrow.

Lionni, L. (1996). *It's mine!* New York: Turtleback Books.

Merriam, E. (1992). *Fighting words.* New York: Morrow Junior Books.

Moss, M. (1989). *Who was it?* Boston: Houghton Mifflin.

Naylor, P.R. (1991). *King of the playground.* New York: Atheneum Books.

Numeroff, L.J. (2000). *If you give a mouse a cookie.* New York: HarperCollins Children's Books.

Sendak, M. (1988). *Where the wild things are.* New York: HarperCollins Children's Books.

Silverstein, S. (1986). *The giving tree.* New York: HarperCollins Juvenile Books.

Steptoe, J. (1987). *Mufaro's beautiful daughters: An African tale.* New York: Lothrop, Lee & Shepard Books.

Wells, R. (1973). *Noisy Nora.* New York: Dial Books for Young Readers.

Zion, G. (1956). *Harry the dirty dog.* New York: HarperCollins Children's Books.

Zolotow, C. (1975). *The unfriendly book.* New York: HarperCollins Children's Books.

Zolotow, C. (1982). *The quarreling book.* New York: Trophy.

Zolotow, C. (1989). *The hating book.* New York: Trophy.

APPENDIX: SELECTED ASSESSMENT INSTRUMENTS

● ● ●

ASSESSING SELF-REGULATION, COMPLIANCE, CONSCIENCE, AND MORAL DEVELOPMENT OF YOUNG CHILDREN AND THE DISCIPLINE STRATEGIES OF PARENTS

Three main strategies are used for assessing the compliance, conscience, and moral development of young children. The choice of method will vary according to the purpose for which the data is being collected. The main methods are

1. Observation of the child with parents or other caregivers in the home, child care environment, or in the research environment. Parents are instructed to have their child carry out a task such as cleaning up toys or helping out in some way. Usually, a specially designed rating system will be used.

2. A situation is created in the research environment to test the child's capacity to delay gratification and to obey instructions (e.g., the child is told not to touch a toy or peep inside a parcel). How long the child can wait and the strategies used to do this are then recorded.

3. Parents or other caregivers are asked to rate children on their behavior and response to instructions. Rating of parenting capacity or strategies can also be carried out in a similar way.

   • Parent and child are observed in the home or laboratory and the parent is rated on the type of strategies used to get the child to clean up or conform to another task.

   • Parent-report measures are used to rate the parent's parenting knowledge and discipline strategies.

Tests to Assess Children's Self-Regulation, Compliance, Conscience, and Morality

Table A7.1 includes frequently used tests to assess children's self-regulation, compliance, conscience, and morality.

Assessments of Parenting Measures

Table A7.2 includes assessments of parenting skills and styles related to discipline.

Table A7.1. Selected assessments of children's self-regulation, compliance, conscience, and morality

Title	Age range	Items/administration time	General description
Burks Behavior Rating Scales: Preschool and Kindergarten Edition (BBRS) Burks, H.F. (1977). *Burks Behavior Rating Scales: Preschool and Kindergarten Version-manual.* Los Angeles, CA: Western Psychological Services.	3–6 years	105 items; 30 minutes	The *Burks Behavior Rating Scales (BBRS)* are designed to identify children with problems with noncompliance and impulse control. The test can be completed by parents or teachers and provides a profile of the severity of the child's inappropriate behavior in 19 categories. Examples of some of the categories are poor impulse control, excessive aggressiveness, excessive resistance, and poor attention.
Child Behavior Checklist (CBCL) Achenbach, T.M. & Edelbrock, C.S. (1983). *Manual for the Child Behavior Checklist.* Burlington: Department of Psychiatry, University of Vermont	2–16 years (separate versions for 2–4 and 4–16 years)	100 items; 20 minutes	Two versions of the *Child Behavior Checklist (CBCL)* are available: a parent's and a teacher's version. Responses to the checklists provide accurate and comprehensive descriptions of children's behavior that distinguish between children who are typical and those having significant behavioral disturbances. The items cluster into behavioral syndromes that are similar to syndromes in the *Diagnostic and Statistical Manual of the American Psychiatric Association, Text Revised Fourth Edition (DSM-IV-TR)*. The scale isolates two main syndrome characteristics: Internalizing and Externalizing, as well as a number of specific syndromes, including hyperactive, aggressive, and delinquent. It is a sophisticated and widely used measure.
Conners' Rating Scales (CPTRS) Conners, C.K. (1982). Parent and teacher rating forms for the assessment of hyperkinesis in children. In P.A. Keller & L.G. Ritte (Eds.), *Innovations in clinical practice: A source book.* Sarasota, FL: Professional Research Exchange.	3–17 years	Parent Scales (48 or 93) and Teacher Scales (28 or 39); time varies	The instrument consists of two forms: teacher rating scales and parent rating scales. Both have dimensions regarding hyperactivity and conduct problems. It is mainly used to screen children for possible behavior problems and to evaluate the results of medication.
Eyberg Child Behavior Inventory (ECBI) Robinson, E.A., Eyberg, S.M., & Ross, A.W. (1980). The standardization of an inventory of child conduct problem behavior. *Journal of Clinical Child Psychology, 9,* 22–29.	2–16 years	36 items; 10 minutes	The *Eyberg Child Behavior Inventory (ECBI)* is used to get ratings of conduct problems and acting out behavior for children. It identifies problems indicative of aggression, impulsivity, and hyperactivity. The scale is completed by parents. The scale is useful as it taps into a wide range of behaviors and can provide information that can enable their prioritization. It is easy to administer and score.
Preschool Behavior Questionnaire (PBQ) Behar, L., & Stringfield, S. (1974). *Manual for the Preschool Behavior Questionnaire.* Durham, NC: Learning Institute of North Carolina.	3–6 years	30 items; 5 minutes	The *Preschool Behavior Questionnaire (PBQ)* questionnaire is designed as a screening tool to identify emotional/behavioral problems in children. It can be completed by parents or teachers and provides scores for Hostile–Aggressive, Anxious–Fearful, Poor Attention Span, and a Total Score.

Other commonly used measures

Title	Age range		
The Conscience Measure Kochanska, G. (1994). Maternal reports of conscience and temperament in children. *Child Development, 65,* 852–868.	2–6 years		
The Compliance Test Roberts, M.W., & Powers, S.W. (1988). The Compliance Test. *Behavior Therapy, 9,* 793–798.	2–6 years		

416

Table A7.2. Selected parenting measures

Title	Age range	Items/ administration time	General description
Child Rearing Practices Report Q Sort (CRPR) Block, J.H. (1981). *The Child Rearing Practice Report (CRPR): A set of Q items for the description of parental socialization attitudes and values.* Unpublished manuscript, Institute of Human Development, University of California, Berkeley.	Adults with children	91 items; 60 minutes (shorter versions of 40 or 29 items have been used by some researchers)	The *Child Rearing Practices Report Q Sort (CRPR)* is designed to identify child-rearing attitudes and values. The report may be completed by the parent to describe his or her own child-rearing behavior or by the child to describe the child-rearing orientations of his or her parents. Parents sort the cards into seven piles (13 cards each) categorized from "most descriptive" to "least descriptive." Parental scores on the Authoritarian and Authoritative scales of the CRPR have been found to relate to parental behavior in interaction with a child.
Dyadic Parent–Child Interaction Coding System (DPICS) Eyberg, S.M., & Robinson, E.A. (1983). *Dyadic Parent-Child Interaction Coding System: A Manual. Psychological Documents, 13,* 24. MS #2582.	2–10 years	72 items; 15 minutes	The *Dyadic Parent–Child Interaction Coding System (DPICS)* is a direct observation procedure for assessing the quality of interactions between parents and children. It was designed for use in place of a full psychological assessment of childhood behavior problems and parenting skills. Some of the parent behaviors that are coded are Direct Command, Physical Positive, Physical Negative, Labeled and Unlabeled Praise, Responds to or Ignores Deviant Behavior. The DPICS has been used with a variety of populations including abusive and neglectful mothers, behavior problem children, and children in preschools.
Home Observation for Measurement of the Environment (HOME) Caldwell, B.M., & Bradley, R.H. (1984). *Home Observation for the Measurement of the Environment.* Little Rock, University of Arkansas.	0–6 years	45–55 items; 60 minutes	The *Home Observation for Measurement of the Environment (HOME)* was developed to assess the quality of the child's environment, which includes a number of items that consider how the parent interacts with the child. The inventory is administered by a person who goes into the home when the child is awake and can observe the normal routine of the home and how the parent interacts with the child. About a third of the items are parent report, which are asked to get information on issues not likely to occur between parent and child at the time of the home visit. Subscales measure caregiver emotional and verbal responsivity, avoidance of restriction and punishment, organization of environment, provision of appropriate play materials, caregiver involvement with child, and variety of daily stimulation. Items are scored "yes" or "no." The HOME can identify a child's risk for developmental delays due to insufficient environmental support and can be used in planning of appropriate interventions as well as for research purposes.
Iowa Parent Behavior Inventory Crase, S.J., Clark, S., & Pease, D. (1978). *Iowa Parent Behavior Manual.* Ames, IA: Iowa State University Foundation.	2–16 years	36 items; 10 minutes	The *Iowa Parent Behavior Inventory* was designed to assess the behaviors of parents with their children. It is a parent-report instrument that rates parents on parental involvement, limit setting, responsiveness, reasoning/guidance, free expression, and intimacy. There is a separate inventory for fathers. The inventory looks at actual behaviors, not attitudes. A five-point scale is used to score the items.

(continued)

Table A7.2. (continued)

Title	Age range	Items/administration time	General description
The Knowledge of Infant/Child Development Inventories (KIDI) MacPhee, D. (1981). *Manual: Knowledge of Infant Development Inventory.* Unpublished manuscript, University of North Carolina. (1974).	Birth–6 years (Two versions: Birth–3 and 3–6 years)	75 items; 20 minutes	The *The Knowledge of Infant/Child Development Inventories* (KIDI) was developed to assess parents' knowledge of child development and parental practices. Subscores are obtained for norms and milestones, principles, parenting health, and safety. Parents are asked whether they agree or disagree with or are not sure about each of the first 48 statements (e.g., "You must stay in the bathroom when your baby is in the tub").
Parenting Practices Scale Strayhorn, J.M., & Weidman, C.S. (1988). A Parent Practices Scale and its relation to parent and child mental health. *Journal of the American Academy of Child and Adolescent Psychiatry, 27,* 613–618.	Preschool children	34 items; 15 minutes	The *Parenting Practices Scale* assesses the favorableness of parenting practices with preschool children. The 34 items relate to cognitions of practices of parenting which were selected as effecting the quality of the parent–child relationship. Items are scored from 0–6. The scale has been used for clinical and/or research purposes.

Other commonly used measures

Title	Age range	Items/administration time	General description
Parent Behavior Rating Scales: Mother and Father Scales Baumrind, D. (1971). Current patterns of parental authority. *Developmental Psychology,* 1–103.	Adults		
The Parenting Scale Arnold, D.S., O'Leary, S.G., Wolf, L.S., & Acker, M.M. (1993). The Parenting Scale: A measure of dysfunctional parenting in discipline situations. *Psychological Assessment, 5*(2), 137–144.	Adults with children up to 4 years		
Ideas About Parenting (IAP) Scale Heming, G., Cowan, P.C., & Cowan, C.P. (1990). Ideas About Parenting. In J. Touliatos, P.F. Perlmutter, & M.A. Straus (Eds.), *Handbook of family measurement techniques* (pp. 362–363). Thousand Oaks, CA: Sage.	Adults		

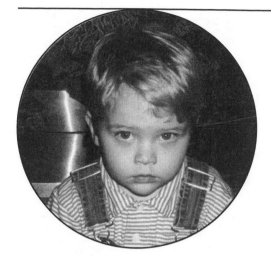

●●● 8

ENCOURAGING EMOTION REGULATION

Throughout a typical day, young children experience all sorts of emotions. At times, they may overwhelm children. Following are examples of three of the types of emotions—sadness, anger and frustration, and joy—that young children may experience in a day.

●●

Two-year-old Aimée has only been coming to child care for about a week. Today, she is recovering from a cold and does not want to come, which she demonstrates by loudly protesting all the way in the car. On arrival at child care, she clings to her mother desperately and cries inconsolably. The child-care provider gently takes her from her mother and calms her by taking her over to her favorite play area. Nevertheless, Aimée continues to sob and is not interested in her favorite toys.

As she has done many times before, Sushila tells 3-year-old Anat that he cannot have a chocolate bar at the grocery store checkout. Today, Anat becomes furious—stamping his feet, screaming that his mother is mean, and throwing himself on the floor, kicking. Sushila, surprised at this unexpected outburst, calms him as best she can, sure that the whole store population is witnessing this scene and suspecting her of bad mothering. She gets through the line as quickly as possible and hurries home, explaining to Anat why he cannot always have a chocolate bar while shopping.

Paul, father of 6-month-old Elisa, tickles his daughter. She shrieks with delight and laughs loudly. She seems to enjoy this game, but at one point the intensity of her laughter seems to become overwhelming, and she pushes her father away and looks toward a toy in her crib as a way of calming down. Her father then begins to talk to her gently, realizing the tickling has become too much for Elisa.

In these examples, all three children are overcome with their emotions and need their caregivers to help them calm down before their own coping skills can be reinstated. The last example illustrates how even when a child is experiencing a positive emotion initially, she can become overwhelmed if the emotion becomes too intense.

Given the degree of children's emotional reactions and how frequently they can occur on a daily basis, it is amazing that in the 1940s and 1950s some writers in psychology and child development called for abandoning the consideration of emotions in personality development. At that time, the theory of behaviorism was in vogue. Behavior was explained in terms of stimulus and response (Skinner, 1953; Watson, 1966). Emotions, if considered at all, were relegated to a role as intervening variables between the stimulus (input) and response (outcome).

Later, researchers began to realize that human behavior is more complex than a series of stimuli and responses and that people behave differently in similar circumstances because of the way they perceive a particular situation. Consequently, in the 1960s and 1970s, cognitive views such as those of Bandura and Piaget began to dominate and behavior was seen as influenced by observational learning and subjective attributions or understanding of events or conditions of life. Both of these theorists saw learning as reciprocal and that it resulted from interactions between the child and his environment (Bandura, 1992; Piaget, 1959). The following vignette shows how differently young children can interpret the same event.

• •

On the way home from sledding, Sunil's car has a flat tire. His daughter Rhea sobs, believing she will never get home, while his son Andreas has fun picking up some snow and making snowballs. Each child interprets the meaning of the situation from a very different emotional perspective.

The role of emotions as motivators, activators, and organizers of behavior has become increasingly understood. It is now obvious that emotion regulation is critical for preventing stressful levels of negative emotions and maladaptive behavior and that most behavioral and emotional problems involve emotion regulation—or more frequently—dysregulation. Clearly, young children such as the ones in the examples experience very strong emotions just like adults do. It is also obvious that individual differences in the way the emotions are experienced and in the ways their caregivers handle them make a tremendous difference to children's current and future adjustment.

DEFINITIONS OF EMOTIONS AND EMOTION REGULATION

Although it is relatively easy for everyone to list a number of emotions and to know how these emotions feel and look in themselves and others, finding a definition of emotion that fits all of

them is more difficult. Consequently, many writers have developed definitions to fit their own theoretical biases about the essence or core of emotions. For this chapter, emotions are defined as Kagan (1994, p. 75) described them: 1) "the acute changes in physiology, cognition, and action that occur in response to novelty, challenge, loss, attack, or frustration"; and 2) "longer lasting affect states created by experiences over months or years."

Scientists such as Ekman, Izard, and Tomkins have identified a set of eight basic emotions: joy, sadness, fear, anger, disgust, interest, surprise, and excitement (Ekman, 1984; Izard, 1971; Tomkins, 1984), although it is obvious that children experience several more such as jealousy, shame, pride, and contentment. When an emotion is intense, it involves three systems or sets of processes: physiological, cognitive, and response actions. For example, if someone is in the house alone and hears noises and is not expecting anyone, she is likely to experience the following in rapid succession:

- *Physiological reactions* that include autonomic nervous system activity that is not under voluntary control, such as the activity of the heart, blood vessels, stomach and intestines, brain activity, and hormonal secretions. For a person lying awake listening to strange noises, these reactions can include increased heart rate, sweating, and tightness of muscles. Some people may become so overwhelmed by this panic state that they cannot move into the next stages.

- *Cognitions* or *subjective experiences* of the emotional response, which in this example may be thinking through possible explanations for the noises and considering various courses of action.

- *Action responses*, in which the individual would probably exhibit the facial expression of fear or possibly anger, and would make motor responses such as going to look for an intruder or perhaps hiding or seeking help by telephoning 911.

Longer lasting emotional states build up over time and are created by hundreds of different experiences. These emotional states can become chronic moods and are usually accompanied by different physiological states and cognitions than the more immediate emotional reactions discussed above. Some of the better known ones are *anxiety states,* where a person is in an ongoing state of feeling generalized anxiety; and *depression,* when a person may be overwhelmed with ongoing feelings of sadness, apathy, and hopelessness.

Emotion regulation, sometimes called *affect regulation,* refers to the process by which people control or self-regulate internal reactions to emotions as well as their outward expression. For infants and very young children, much of the necessary regulation is provided by caregivers who soothe the child or adjust the environment so he is not overwhelmed by excessive stimulation. Gradually, the infant and young child become more and more able to control their own emotional responses even when these involve very intense feelings and emotions. The methods used by children and caregivers to assist in emotion regulation are outlined in later sections of the chapter.

THEORIES OF EMOTION AND EMOTION REGULATION

As mentioned, many theories of human behavior before the 1960s ignored the importance of emotions. Perhaps the theories that paid the most attention to them were the psychoanalytic theories of Freud, Erikson, and Mahler. Freud referred to uncontrolled emotional behavior with little ability to delay gratification of the feelings as *primary process functioning* and the part of the

individual's personality ruled by these primary processes as the *id* (Freud, 1953). An individual's id was thought to be gradually brought under control by the *ego* (which maintains contact with reality and helps the person cope with the world) and *superego* (which, like conscience, assures that behavior meets moral and social standards). Although modern psychoanalytic theorists do not emphasize the role of the id, ego, and superego, the role of the defense or coping mechanisms of the ego in response to anxiety continue to be seen as crucial by many psychoanalytic theorists and clinicians (e.g., Bucci, 1997, Kernberg, 1990). These emotional coping skills include projection of evil onto others, reaction formation, sublimation, splitting, and denial of reality.

Erikson expanded on Freud's theory to include external social factors along with psychological factors as important forces in determining personality development. In his stage theory he emphasized a number of emotions that could result depending on how the stage was resolved. These included *trust versus mistrust, autonomy versus shame and doubt, initiative versus guilt,* and *industry versus role confusion.* Erikson considered that the conflicts of these stages were never totally resolved and that conflicts from earlier stages could continue to affect later development (Erikson, 1950).

Margaret Mahler emphasized the developmental period between approximately 14 and 24 months, when she believed the child goes through a stage in which an initial psychological separation takes place. In talking about this stage, she noted the importance of emotions, with the child described as elated during the early toddler stage when beginning to walk, then anxious at the separation and frustrated by not being able to do things independently. This transition from elation to frustration often seems to happen in quick succession (Mahler, Pine, & Bergman, 1975).

Almost all modern theorists integrate the role of emotions into their theories; however, we are left with a confusing array of theories that vary in terms of their positions on such aspects as

- How emotions are displayed and experienced

- The role of emotions in development

- The importance of the environment in influencing emotional expression

- The role of genetics in shaping emotional/temperament traits

Some of the different ways theorists have considered emotions are outlined in Table 8.1. It is noteworthy that few of the theories specifically address the role of emotion regulation but instead are more concerned with understanding the emotions.

THE IMPORTANCE OF EMOTION REGULATION

The importance of emotion regulation to children's and adults' functioning cannot be emphasized enough. In order to deal with the normal frustrations of the day and other intense emotions it is crucial that the individual learns a number of coping strategies to deal with them. It is also important that the individual develops a strong sense of self to serve as a foundation for dealing with frustrations and intense emotions. In fact, many writers and researchers believe that failure to gain adequate regulation of affect is largely responsible for the development of

Table 8.1. Theories of emotion regulation

Theorist	Type of theory	Major constructs
Tomkins (1962, 1963, 1984)	Affect socialization	Two of the most important human goals are increasing positive affect and decreasing negative affect
		Outlines ways in which parents minimize negative affect
		Outlines ways in which parents can maximize positive affect
		Theory of affective organization and its socialization
Izard (1971) Ekman (1984) Tomkins (1984)	Discrete emotion	There is an innate set of independent basic emotions including interest, fear, anger, sadness, joy, surprise, excitement, and disgust
		Each basic emotion has a characteristic facial expression that is universal across cultures
		Each emotion is accompanied by a different motivational intent (e.g., anger motivates people to try a situation)
		Children gradually develop ability to self-regulate emotions
		Later on the basic emotions become more complicated and can be "mixed" and people learn to disguise their feelings if necessary
Lewis & Michalson (1983) Lutz (1988) Fogel et al. (1992)	Sociocultural and social constructionist views	Social and cultural influences are critical to the formation and functions of emotions
		Emotions undergo development according to the social rules and their meanings that an individual believes in rather than just innate bodily states
		Social context exerts a direct influence on any emotional reaction
		Similar emotional reactions serve different functions in different relationships and environments
		Processing of information (cognition) is linked with emotional response to stimulus
Campos & Barrett (1985) Barrett & Campos (1987) Barrett (1998)	Functionalist	Emotions allow the individual to adapt to the environment by providing motivation to act in functional ways
		Emotions are linked not only to facial expressions but also to movements, vocalizations, and cognitions that are associated with each emotion
		Neurophysiological processes underlie emotions, which vary across situations and individuals
		Great importance is given to the role of social influences on emotions
Lazarus (1990, 1991)	Relational	Describes emotions as psychophysiological reactions to ongoing "relationships with the person-environment"
		The experience of each emotion concerns what is happening in a core relational theme and the coping or resources available to deal with it
		Describes emotion as based on these "appraisals" or cognitions but also sees it as including physiological reactions, motivations, and impulses to action
		Development enhances the integration of cognition, emotion, and motivation
Sroufe (1996)	Structural-developmental	Emotions and their regulation undergo a series of changes from simple and more global forms to more complex and mature forms
		Each emotion system is differentiated from the other
		Emotion is connected to cognition and physiological responsiveness but with different organizations at different ages in childhood
		Emotions are seen as adaptive in facilitating responses in emergencies and promoting mastery over situations

behavior problems and can lead to a variety of serious psychopathologies. Some examples of these and the impact of emotion dysregulation are listed below:

- *Character disorders:* Often, individuals with character disorders experience intense rage and failure to regulate emotions.

- *Anxieties and phobias* (e.g., agoraphobia, a fear of open spaces or of being outside the house): Individuals experience anxieties and fear that seriously limit their coping. Symptoms of rapid heart rate, sweating, and even blacking out may occur in panic attacks.

- *Psychotic symptoms:* Individuals exhibit blunted affect and failure to contain affect arousal. Information processing deficits, as well, may be demonstrated.

- *Depression:* Individuals express intense sadness and feelings of hopelessness and worthlessness. They may also demonstrate a lack of energy and masked anger.

- *Bipolar disorder:* Individuals exhibit total dysregulation, with intense happiness and activity alternating with intense sadness and depression.

- *Conduct disorder with aggression:* Individuals respond with immediate anger and aggression to frustrating and frequently ambivalent situations. Co-occurrence with depression is often found.

- *Drug and alcohol abusers:* People use drugs and alcohol to overcome feelings of anxiety and worthlessness.

- *Obsessive-compulsive disorder (OCD):* Individuals exhibit marked anxiety about negative feelings and rigidity and avoidance of them. They tend to use "magical solutions" in order to find relief.

- *Alexithymia:* Individuals demonstrate a lack of ability to identify and name emotions or to use them as signals of internal changes. Consequently, intense rage reactions are common.

In addition to these serious conditions, other, more common difficulties such as behavior problems, internalizing problems of highly fearful and anxious children, and attention-deficit/hyperactivity disorder (ADHD) may be related to an individual's failure to develop adequate strategies to cope with intense, especially negative, emotions.

The incidence in young children with difficulties with affect regulation is very high. In a survey of parents of 3-year-olds carried out in a rural area by the present author, it was found that 25% rated their children as hostile-aggressive, 17% as anxious-withdrawn, and 11% as hyperactive. After the children entered school, teachers rated them with a similar questionnaire. The teachers came up with almost identical percentages. These statistics from a very stable community tell us that emotion regulation difficulties are prevalent in young children and should not be ignored (Landy & Peters, 1992). A child who is overwhelmed by or acts out his emotions continuously is compromised in many aspects of his development as well as with peers, family, and teachers. Some of the areas that are significantly affected by young children's capacity for emotion regulation are outlined in the following sections.

Social Relatedness   Children who have good emotion regulation get along better with and are more accepted by their peers. Some of the mechanisms for this appear to be their

greater friendliness in interactions, their ability to deal with conflicts without becoming overwhelmed, and their ability to hear and accept others' perspectives. They are also less likely to use aggression and venting in social situations and can focus away from an emotionally arousing stimulus and move situations to more positive aspects. Sometimes introducing a game, reminding other children that something fun will be happening later, or telling a joke may do this.

Empathy and Caring Behavior   Children with adequate emotion regulation have good perspective-taking skills and can differentiate their own emotions from those of others. Consequently, they do not become overwhelmed in emotion-arousing situations. They are able to use energy to problem-solve and to show caring behavior toward others. There is a clear developmental progression from being totally overwhelmed by, for example, a peer or caregiver crying and being able to control one's own emotions and help the other person by showing caring behavior.

Problem-Solving and Cognition   Theory clearly demonstrates that emotion and cognition are significantly related. For example, children may fail to concentrate if they are overwhelmed emotionally by stressful situations. They are likely to have difficulty with concentrating, problem-solving, and cognitive flexibility. Memory capacity can also be affected. Children with good emotion regulation are more likely to be able to shift attention and to focus on the problem at hand, thus enhancing cognitive ability.

Coping and Resilience   Some researchers are now talking about emotional IQ in addition to intellectual IQ. Emotional competence refers to capacities that have been listed under emotion regulation, including awareness of ones' emotions and the emotions of others, keeping disruptive emotions and impulses in check, and exhibiting empathy and social skills. These capacities have all been related to coping and long-term resilience even in situations of great adversity. Although children need the support of a caring adult, coping skills can, nevertheless, enable them to be far more in control and flexible in adapting, even when confronted by significant problems and the need to deal with changing or difficult life circumstances.

DEVELOPMENT OF EMOTION REGULATION

For some children, the development of emotions and emotion regulation shows a gradual and predictable pattern of growth. It is clear that infants have few capacities to soothe themselves and that they have quite intense emotions and global responses to these emotions. By the ages of 4 or 5, preschoolers experience fewer fluctuations in emotions and have usually developed a number of focused strategies to enable them to regulate their emotions themselves. More than in most other areas of development, for some children, emotion regulation does not move forward smoothly and may not show continual gains during the early years of life. For these children, progressions are followed by plateaus and sometimes they experience regressions and loss of capacities as new developmental phases are encountered or disruptive events (e.g., the birth of a sibling) occur. Such difficulties are most obvious during the toddler period when increasing independence and a push towards separation bring added caregiver prohibitions that can result in increased temper tantrums and fluctuating emotions. Sleeping and eating may also be disrupted as a result. The sequence of stages at which typically developing children acquire these abilities is set out in Table 8.2.

Table 8.2. The development of emotions and emotion regulation

Age	Emotional expression	Emotion regulation
Birth–11 months	Newborns display at least three emotions at birth: rage-anger, sadness-distress, and pleasure-joy Smiles as a way to express pleasure in place by 2–3 months Affect expression is at first very global and then becomes more refined and differentiated Fear, shyness, and disgust emerge at about 9–12 months Wariness of heights is strong from about 7 months and stranger and separation anxiety develop There is usually an increase in positive emotions as the infant becomes able to laugh at about 7 months Surprise also emerges between 8 and 12 months	Physiological regulation of eating and sleeping generally is achieved At 1 month, inborn stimulus barrier disappears and infant may have more difficulty modulating affect Self-regulation of tension begins and the infant can sometimes spontaneously calm with thumb sucking or visually concentrating on an object Can gradually be calmed by seeing caregiver and hearing her voice as well as by being held and rocked Secure attachment can enable child to be more modulated with affect
12–24 months	At 12 months, infants often show a predominance of elation. This generally lasts until about 18 months At 18 months, there is often an increase in angry responses such as tantrums Increasing ability to store memories of others helps allay fear of being alone Increase in capacity for fear reactions as well as depression if the child experiences loss At 18 months, jealousy is shown, especially toward siblings or peers At approximately 18–24 months the self-conscious emotions emerge: pride, shame, and very rudimentary feelings of guilt Cannot conceive of mixed emotions, so "splitting" predominates	Toddler approaches a variety of objects and uses them to distract himself from becoming distressed Child commonly uses transitional objects (e.g., blankets, stuffed animals) to self-regulate Child can use cues to signal caregiver that a certain kind of assistance is needed Child uses social referencing (e.g., expression on parent's face) to get clues about the importance of his emotions and how to behave
24–36 months	At this age a full range of emotions becomes possible Child is better able to distinguish happy emotions than negative ones At age 30 months, tantrums and aggression are at their height and conflicts may increase Many children experience a lot of fears, which may be expressed through nightmares and difficulty sleeping Child becomes aware of self as object as well as the causes of emotional distress Although tantrums reach their height during this age period, toward the end of the third year they begin to reduce and the child may be able to recover from them spontaneously	Child becomes able to talk about emotions and the situations that elicit them Child is more able to decode the emotions of others Child becomes increasingly able to solicit help from caregivers when he or she comes up against a barrier Pretend play is increasingly used to play out negative feelings and as a framework to talk about them

Age	Emotional expression	Emotion regulation
3–6 years	Become more aware of situations that would evoke pride, worry, and jealousy Child becomes capable of empathy Other social emotions such as jealousy, pride, shame, and guilt become more common By 6 years, child is beginning to understand that someone can have mixed emotions about the same situation Can still be overwhelmed by conflicting emotions	Play with peers continues to be used as a context for understanding emotions Child can now regulate intense emotions without external controls Understanding another's perspective brings aggression under control Emotion and cognition are well-integrated and are expressed in an organized way The child is more able to use an increasing number of response strategies in frustrating or emotion-arousing situations Increasing capacity to use distraction, focusing attention, talking self through situations and perspective taking to self-calm in difficult situations Capacity to display emotions other than the one felt underneath (e.g., smile when receiving a gift one does not like) By 6 years, a child is beginning to be able to recognize that a person may have a positive and negative emotions in the same situations

Birth to Twelve Months

Although there is some disagreement about the exact emotions that newborns display, there is ample evidence that the infant displays various reactions to discomfort such as anger and distress. Soon, by 6 weeks or even earlier, the infant begins to smile and coo and show pleasure at being touched and interacted with by loving caregivers. The experience of joy seems to increase as the child is less overwhelmed by hunger and becomes capable of real laughter. Fear and shyness arrive between the ages of 9 and 12 months in the form of stranger and separation anxiety. At first, reactions tend to be quite global and occur in response to a variety of situations. These reactions gradually become less intense and occur in response to fewer events. Even at this age, infants have some capacity for regulating their emotions and use self-calming (e.g., thumb or pacifier sucking, rocking, concentrating on an object) in order to calm down. Of course, a caregiver's soothing and calming is essential if a baby becomes very upset.

Twelve to Twenty-Four Months

During the first half of the second year of life, as the toddler gains locomotion skills, a state of elation often predominates. Not only can the infant walk, with increasing skill she can now manipulate objects, plan actions, and make things happen. Between the ages of 16 and 19 months, however, the child becomes more aware of the minds and thoughts of others. This elicits fear in the child who now believes that the caregiver can leave without her and not come back. At this point this wariness may result in the toddler "shadowing" or following the caregiver and becoming very demanding and whiny. It may also result in an increased fear reaction and even depression as a result of a temporary sense of loss of feelings of elation and security.

During this year, the child can employ a variety of ways to help regulate his emotions. These include distracting himself through toy play and exploring parts of his body in order to self-soothe. Transitional objects (e.g., blankets, stuffed toys) become important and they can substitute for caregivers in children's efforts to calm down. Children also interact socially and signal caregivers to ask for very specific assistance; for example, when a stranger is around, the child may tug at the caregiver or ask to be held.

Children look for and then use the emotional expressions of caregivers (i.e., social referencing) to determine if a situation is safe or dangerous, exciting or depressing. If the caregiver smiles the baby is encouraged to try the situation, such as moving toward a scary looking toy. If the caregiver looks afraid, the baby will withdraw.

Twenty-Four to Thirty-Six Months

At this age, children are at the height of temper tantrums, with the incidence falling off by about 30 months of age. Children can only control their emotions about 45% of the time. In addition to the more basic emotions, shame and embarrassment become more common as self-awareness and self-consciousness grow. Children at this stage have an increasing understanding of what they want and what is required of them. At the same time, they realize that they can alter the causes of their own discomfort. Perhaps most useful, children gain the ability to solicit help from caregivers and to be able to talk about their feelings and those of others instead of physically acting them out all the time. A child's use of pretend play and ability to talk about feelings while doing so is crucial at this time. As children increasingly understand what they should do and not do, they become better able to hold back from acting in unacceptable ways. They may feel pride when they manage to do this and distress or even shame when they do not. While they have greater capacity to control their emotions, they continue to need the caregiver's help to maintain control when tired, frustrated, and stressed.

Three to Six Years

During the period between 3 and 6 years of age, tantrums and fears begin to subside. A full range of emotions continues to be expressed including guilt, shame, and embarrassment. New fears may result as the child becomes more aware of situations around him. As a consequence, fears may arise such as fear of going to school, of death, of kidnappers, or of storms. During this period, the child becomes capable of controlling his actions and feeling guilt if he fails to do so. In the context of play with other children and using language, peer interactions provide a powerful context for emotion regulation. In general, language, in conjunction with cognitive processing skills used to understand situations, gradually enables the child to develop more tools to self-regulate. Because of these growing cognitive competencies, children can acquire a basic knowledge of themselves, their families, peers, social events, and social expectations. These expectations help with emotion regulation and encourage an increasing ability for perspective taking and empathy. At this time, the child begins to be able to experiment with alternative strategies to regulate emotions and to use the most effective ones. By age 5 or 6, children begin to be able to recognize that it is possible to feel two opposite emotions about the same situation. For example, a child may understand that she can love her sibling and want him around but also be very jealous of the attention he receives from their parents. Emotions also become more "socialized" and children can fake emotions when appropriate, such as pretending they like a present when they don't.

IMPORTANT RESEARCH FINDINGS

One of the most striking developments in contemporary psychological theory has been the resurgence of interest in human emotions and their regulation. Lewis (1985) pointed out that even as late as 1979, only about 8% of pages in child psychology textbooks were devoted to topics of emotional development (e.g., Mussen, 1970; Osofsky, 1987). Up to that time behaviorism and cognitive theory had dominated the interest of researchers.

There has been not only a significant increase in the amount of research carried out on emotion regulation but also a change in understanding of the manner in which it occurs. There is an increasing acceptance that emotions are important motivators of human behavior and that with adequate regulation they can serve adaptive functions in the expression of individual and interpersonal behavior. Following are reviews of three relevant areas of research on emotion regulation, including 1) how it develops, 2) what contributes to it, and 3) what are the individual differences and failures related to it.

Research on the Development of Emotion Regulation

Over an individual's first 5 years of life, strategies used for emotion regulation show a gradual change. The child changes from primarily relying on a caregiver or external support for much of the modulation and regulation of intense emotions to the child's learning to control or manage his emotions himself.

As mentioned, at birth infants display at least three emotions: anger, pleasure, and sadness, and even at this age infants show some fleeting capacity for self-comforting. In the newborn, discomfort relates to disturbances of physiological functioning associated with hunger, extreme temperature, pain, and tiredness. In the first days of life these distressing states are altered by activation of reflex patterns of behavior. These include sucking on a thumb or pacifier, "shutting down" and falling asleep, and staring at an object in the environment (Brown, 1993; Campos, Campos, & Barrett, 1989; Kopp, 1989). Periods of alert inactivity are brief in the first month but while they are occurring the infant is in an optimum state to be able to take in sensory information and interact playfully. By the fourth week, the baby can turn her head toward specific objects in the environment and can actively look for new objects and experiences (Stechler & Carpenter, 1967). The caregiver's role is, of course, critical as she uses a variety of soothing methods and provides the infant with a rich assortment of sensory experiences through touch, voice, rocking, and eye-to-eye contact (Stern, 1985). By 2–3 months of age, maturation allows the infant more control of the level of stimulation and he actively seeks familiar and unfamiliar stimuli. His capacity to use gaze aversion in face-to-face interactions increases (Banks & Salapatek, 1983; Stifter & Moyer, 1991). In addition, by the third month infants enjoy viewing and waving their own arms and hands and reaching for objects. This capacity further allows them to self-distract and to alleviate distress while they concentrate on interesting objects (Demos, 1986). Nevertheless, it is clear that there are still major constraints on the young infant's ability to manage discomfort on his own. Consequently, caregivers continue to need to soothe and calm upset infants during this stage (Als, 1978; Lewis & Michalson, 1983). Between 3 and 7 months of age, elementary emotion regulation strategies emerge in the infant that now allow him to use various organized behaviors to calm himself and settle. The infant now exhibits a social smile to draw other people to himself but also at a physiological level this action results in heart rate deceleration and regulation of arousal (Brazelton,

Koslowski, & Main, 1974; Field, 1981). As mentioned, caregivers are still critical, and infants now become much more able to communicate or to signal their needs, for example, for feeding, changing, or attention. The "still face" paradigm (i.e., instructing mothers to remain quiet and immobile) has been used in split screen video research to show how upset infants are when they are not able to get responses to their social initiations. The infant quickly becomes overwhelmed and his behavior becomes disorganized (Tronick, 1989; Weinberg & Tronick, 1996).

On their own initiative, infants continue to use self-soothing strategies such as sucking and focusing on objects to contain their overwhelming emotions (Mangelsdorf, Shapiro, & Marzolf, 1995). At this time infants become far more competent in distracting themselves using new visual-motor and cognitive skills as they can increasingly use toy play, reaching, grasping, and moving about to relieve their distress when caregivers are not available. If frequently ignored, a baby may self-stimulate through body rocking compulsively or by using mouthing motions. By 1 year of age, infants have much more awareness of their other emotions such as fear and excitement, rather than primarily of discomfort. The study of social referencing has shown that infants as young as 10 months old regard the emotional expression of significant others prior to determining their own resulting behavior. In an experiment that created the illusion of a drop, or "visual cliff," for example, it was demonstrated that infants who are shown an encouraging face are likely to advance over the "cliff" while those who see a fearful expression are far more likely to pull back (Mumme, Fernald, & Herrera, 1996; Sorce, Emde, Campos, & Klinnert, 1985; Walden, 1991).

Between the ages of 18 and 24 months, infants become increasingly autonomous and concerned with issues of control and may use control of activities as one way to lower levels of negative emotionality (Parritz, 1996; Parritz, Mangelsdorf, & Gunnar, 1992). The ability to walk can expose children to increases in pain-eliciting stimuli and frustrating situations; however, this and the beginning of the ability to verbalize can also open up another range of possibilities for being able to modulate their own affects (Biringen, Emde, Campos, & Appelbaum, 1995).

For most infants, walking and verbalizing also promote the use of cues to signal caregivers about their needs. Most common are infants' efforts to get close to their caregiver when a stranger approaches (Grolnick, Bridges, & Connell, 1996), to cry to signal personal needs, and to get attention and calming from others (Demos, 1986; Grolnick et al., 1996).

During a child's second year, he uses transitional or attachment objects (such as blankets and soft toys) to calm his fears about separation (Lehman, Denham, Moser, & Reeves, 1992). Children seem to become much more able to determine the cause and even the significance and potency of a difficulty and to seek out help more quickly and with more determination. Growth in the capacity to use words and particularly to talk about emotions between 18–30 months becomes a very powerful tool for expressing their emotions and being able to gain greater control of them (Barden, Zelko, Duncan, & Masters, 1980; Bretherton, Fritz, Zahn-Waxler, & Ridgeway, 1986; Terwogt & Olthof, 1991). At this stage, children begin pretend play and to use language about feelings that goes along with the pretend play in order to work out their understanding about emotions and how to control them (Gottman, 1986; Harris, 1989). Over the next several years, verbal interactions with caregivers, siblings, and peers frequently help preschoolers to understand, express, and modulate emotions better (Brown & Dunn, 1991, 1996; Manstead & Edwards, 1992).

A major shift takes place at approximately 3 years of age when children become aware that others may have feelings and thoughts different from their own about the same situation; in other words, they have achieved a *theory of mind* (Astington, Harris, & Olson, 1988; Harris, Johnson, Hutton, Andrews, & Cooke, 1989; Hughes & Dunn, 1998). This cognitive shift and

an increase in attentional control allows for a number of new emotion regulation strategies to emerge. These include the ability to divert attention from a negative situation, to choose social contexts that maximize positive affect and are more satisfying, to "talk oneself through" a frustrating or difficult task or situation, and to rephrase a situation in more positive terms. Although younger children may need assistance to use these strategies, when they are successful they have been shown to dramatically improve the capacity to modulate and regulate a child's negative feelings (Aldwin, 1994; Saarni, 1997, 1999; Schibuk, Bond, & Bouffard, 1989; Wolchik & Sandler, 1997). Some of these strategies are discussed in more detail in the next chapter. Nevertheless, in spite of having acquired these coping strategies, children remain vulnerable to being overwhelmed with emotions. This can often be due to their inability to understand and to integrate mixed emotions (both their own and others) and their tendency to split or see things from a black-and-white perspective. This often makes it difficult to identify, name, talk about, and most important, to understand their own and other people's emotions. In fact, children do not acknowledge mixed feelings until late in childhood, so up to approximately 6 years of age they lack understanding of the complexity of situations. They also have a tendency to become overwhelmed by the confusing feelings they experience at times (Harter & Buddin, 1987; Meerum Terwogt, Koops, Oosterhoff, & Olthof, 1986; Peng, Johnson, Pollock, Glasspool, & Harris, 1992).

Contributors to Emotion Regulation

In order to encourage affect regulation in infancy, mothers and infants appear to need to be attuned or synchronized, or to be coordinated behaviorally and/or physiologically (Robinson, Little, & Biringen, 1993). This can also be described as the need to adjust to the rhythm of the infant (Biringen & Robinson, 1991; Field, 1994; Stern, 1983). Researchers have examined the effects of this attunement on the infant's behavior and physiological stress reaction. When researchers observed mothers and infants of 3, 6, and 9 months of age at play, significant relationships between maternal sensitivity or responsivity to the infant's distress and behavioral organization were found at all three ages. Higher levels of the stress hormone cortisol were found in the saliva of the children with insensitive mothers who tended not to comfort their infants (Spangler, Schieche, Ilg, Maier, & Ackermann, 1994). Also, children raised in Romanian orphanages—where they were severely deprived of loving, warm, and responsive care—showed rising cortisol levels throughout the day (Gunnar, 1998). Longitudinal studies have demonstrated a relationship between early maternal responsiveness and emotional synchrony and subsequent development of social and cognitive skills related to emotion regulation. Egeland and Erickson (1987) found a relationship between psychological unavailability of the mother in the first year and excessive anger and negative mood in preschoolers. The preschool children also showed lower compliance and creativity in problem solving.

Toddlers are influenced and guided in their behavior and emotions by the facial expressions of their caregivers (Sorce et al., 1985). It has also been shown that when a mother is present but emotionally unavailable in an unpredictable situation, infants show less pleasure and exploration than when the mother is responsive (Sorce & Emde, 1981; see Chapter 3). A clear relationship has also been found between attachment security and emotion regulation. In other words, securely attached children who have been responded to consistently are able to accept and understand positive and negative affects, while insecure children frequently exhibit limited or heightened negative affect and have difficulty in modulating emotions (Cassidy, 1994;

Denham, Mitchell-Copeland, Strandberg, Auerbach, & Blair, 1997; Laible & Thompson, 1998; Malastesta-Magai, Leak, Tesman, Shepard, Culver, & Smaggia, 1994).

Another important aspect of interaction is the amount and nature of parents' discourse about feelings with their children (Denham & Auerbach, 1995; Dunn & Brown, 1994; Dunn, Bretherton, & Munn, 1987). For example, it has been found that families that frequently discuss their feelings about events and encourage this in their children enhance their children's capacity for self-regulation of emotions. In one study, it was found that 6-year-old children who had grown up in families in which feeling-state talk was frequent were better at making judgments about the emotions of unfamiliar adults in a conversation than were children who had not been exposed to feeling-state talk as frequently (Dunn, Brown, & Beardsall, 1991). Children whose mothers explained emotions to their children in experimental situations were less sad in preschool (Denham, Cook, & Zoller, 1992). Strategies that are very helpful in encouraging emotion regulation include discussing the causes and consequences of emotions with children to encourage perspective taking (Denham, 1989; Denham & Grout, 1993), and apologizing to children for acting angrily toward them (Denham & Grout, 1993; El-Sheikh, Cummings, & Reiter, 1996).

The emotional climate within a family has been related to the child's capacity for affect regulation. Parents socialize their children's display of emotions through modeling emotion containment and through their own displays of emotions, such as by being generally positive rather than providing a constant example of anger, anxiety, or depression (Barrett & Campos, 1991). They also demonstrate their own ways of coping and dealing with emotional situations. Positive emotions seem to be contagious. When parents respond warmly and supportively to their children's emotions, their children cope better in their absence and are happier with other children (Davies & Cummings, 1995; Denham, 1989, 1993; Roberts & Strayer, 1987). Conversely, punitive socialization, when there is dismissing or punishing of emotions and high levels of parental anger, results in children feeling more sadness and exhibiting poorer emotional understanding (Denham, 1989; Denham & Grout, 1993). Radke-Yarrow, Richters, and Wilson (1988) found that children who had experienced high levels of negative affect such as fear, anger, sadness, and anxiety from caregivers had fewer coping strategies at 6 years of age.

The effects of extremes in negativity in the emotional climate of families or abuse and neglect on children are clearly significant and can lead to emotion dysregulation (e.g., Aber & Allen, 1987; Shields, Cicchetti, & Ryan, 1994). Recently, the significance of fighting between couples and violence in the family on children's emotion regulation has been more fully documented. Statistics show that 40%–50% of children who are exposed to severe marital hostility and violence exhibit extreme behavior problems (Wolfe, Jaffe, Wilson, & Zak, 1985) or withdrawal and inhibition (Cummings & Davies, 1994; Davies & Cummings, 1994, 1995; Johnston, Gonzales, & Campbell, 1987). The effects of emotion dysregulation in parents on their children's emotion regulation is well known as well. The effect of maternal depression and other psychopathology has been related to children's poor social skills, lack of coping strategies, failure in self-recognition, excessive negativity, developmental difficulties, behavior disorders, and excessive anxiety and withdrawal, for example (Ciccheti, Rogosch, Toth, & Spagnola, 1997; Clark, 1986; Dodge, 1990; Fendrich, Warner, & Weissman, 1990; Field, 1992; Goodman, Brogan, Lynch, & Fielding, 1993).

The effects of discipline strategies on the development of noncompliance and behavior problems are well documented (Patterson, 1982). In some families, coercive child behaviors such as yelling, noncompliance, and destructiveness are reinforced rather than positive models of coping strategies. Bates and Bayles (1988) found that lower levels of affection and play and

higher restrictive control of 2-year-olds predicted maternal ratings of externalizing behavior problems in the children when they were 6 years old. Other researchers have found similar results, for example, that educational and containing exchanges between mothers and their 4-year-old children were strongly related to absence of aggressive behavior problems (Gardner, 1989; Pettit & Bates, 1989). Hinde and colleagues (1993) found that mothers who showed a balance of warmth and structure had children with less aggression and acting-out behavior than mothers who were low in warmth and high in control or low in both (Hinde, Tamplin, & Barrett, 1993). Gottman, Katz, and Hooven (1997) drew attention to the importance of *meta-emotion* in socializing children and consequently on the development of emotion regulation. They define meta-emotion as "emotion about emotion," and believe that how parents feel about a certain emotion is crucial and significantly affects how they react to their children's emotional displays. For example, because of their own early experiences some parents may find anger, sadness, or other emotions hard to accept. Consequently, these reactions need to be considered in any assessment of parent–child interactions or in parenting interventions.

Although we have emphasized parental contributions on children's emotion regulation in this section, it is clear that other caregivers, such as child care providers, have a significant impact. How they relate to young children's emotions can also influence how the children cope with them (Denham & Burton, 1996; Hyson & Lee, 1996). Peers and siblings also elicit intense emotions, and frequent exposure to negative emotions and conflicts in these relationships can add to children's sadness, anger, and fear. Indeed, these relationships are significant sources of learning about emotions (Brown & Dunn, 1992; Calkins & Johnson, 1998; Dunn, Brown, Slomkowski, Tesla, & Youngblade, 1991; Howe, 1991).

Individual Differences and Failures of Emotion Regulation

Much of the research on individual differences in emotion regulation has focused on the neuro-physiological, endocrinological, and other biological bases of children with temperamental differences. As pointed out in Chapter 1, many temperament theories have considered emotionality and emotion regulation as key components of temperamental differences (Goldsmith, Buss, Plomin, Rothbart, Thomas, Chess, Hinde, & McCall, 1987; Rothbart & Derryberry, 1987).

A number of researchers have looked for individual differences in physiological reactivity and their possible relationship to differences in children's emotion regulation. For example, in longitudinal studies of fearful and inhibited children, Kagan and associates have found that these children have a lower threshold of reactivity in their limbic systems, resulting in higher heart rate, salivary cortisol, and urinary epinephrine levels than other children (Kagan, Reznick, & Snidman, 1988). Children who cry more when separated from their mothers tend to have greater activation in the right frontal area of the brain (Davidson & Fox, 1982; Dawson, 1994; Fox, 1989; Kagan & Snidman, 1991). Another physiological reaction that has been implicated in emotion regulation difficulties is low heart rate variability (HRV). Children with this type of reaction are more likely to become dysregulated and distressed and to show avoidant or aggressive coping responses to a crying baby, for example (Eisenberg & Fabes, 1992; Fabes, Eisenberg, Karbon, Bernzweig, Speer, & Carlo, 1994; Radke-Yarrow & Zahn-Waxler, 1982). On one hand, early tendencies for hypersensitivity to sensory stimulation (Fish & Dixon, 1978; Walker & Emory, 1983); early difficulties in regulation of negative affects (De-Gangi, Porges, Sickel, & Greenspan, 1993); and early distractibility and difficult temperament (Barron & Earls, 1984; Himmelfarb, Hock, & Wenar, 1985; Sroufe, Fox, & Pancake, 1983)

have all been found to be related to a higher incidence of behavioral disturbance, attention deficit disorders, cognitive delays, and severe emotional disturbances in later years. On the other hand, an individual's ability to engage in attentional or orienting behavior has been found to be related to his or her ability to gain control over emotional states (Eisenberg, Fabes, Nyman, Bernzweig, & Pinuelas, 1994).

In summary, a clear timetable exists for the acquisition of different emotions and capacities for regulating these emotions. The course of acquiring them and the types of strategies used, however, vary significantly in individual children. These differences appear to be related both to individual differences in reactivity and coping as well as to the parenting and emotional climate to which infants and young children are exposed. Further research is likely to be able to more clearly identify the strength and contribution of these different factors.

THE GROWTH-PROMOTING ENVIRONMENT: PRINCIPLES OF DEVELOPING EMOTION REGULATION

Table 8.3 outlines the major principles of developing emotion regulation.

PRINCIPLE 1:   *Structure environments to provide a level of stimulation, frustration, and soothing that is appropriate for the child's age and reactivity.*

Infants and young children can become overwhelmed with stimulation that they find excessive and with intense—particularly negative—emotions. Young children cannot be protected from all frustrations, however, and in fact need to experience them within reason in order to realize that they *can* deal with them and to learn some strategies to manage them better.

Some children are more hypersensitive and easily overstimulated than others. For these children, it is important to try and make their environments as relaxed and calming as pos-

Table 8.3.   Principles of encouraging emotion regulation

Principle 1	Structure environments to provide a level of stimulation, frustration, and soothing that is appropriate for the child's age and reactivity.
Principle 2	Accept children's emotions and do not deny, punish, or withdraw from them for having emotions. Communicate acceptance of the feelings to children.
Principle 3	Teach children appropriate strategies or outlets to help them learn to cope with their strong emotions.
Principle 4	Provide children with frequent experiences that are happy, pleasant and, at times, joyful.
Principle 5	If caregivers lose control, they should talk about the feelings naturally and apologize to the child if their behavior was inappropriate.
Principle 6	Provide a context or environment in which emotions are discussed and included when talking about people and situations.
Principle 7	Avoid presenting children with an overwhelming diet of anger, fear, or depression. Seek help if necessary.
Principle 8	Adopt strategies to help children deal with intense negative emotions such as fear, anger, jealousy, and sadness.

sible. Obviously, infants and children cannot and should not be protected from all excessive stimulation. But if a child is constantly upset and overwrought it is important to examine the environment and the daily routine to see if any changes are needed. Some children are extroverts, for example, and love having people around. Introverts, on the other hand, need time alone and have a strong need for personal space, finding too much chattering and company very upsetting. Before making any adaptations to the environment, it is important to observe children and think about each child's personality. Encourage parents to talk to older children about what makes them feel good, afraid, and angry and include this information in your decisions. Some aspects of the environment that need to be considered are the following:

- *The noise level in the home:* Are people yelling and shouting frequently or do they talk at an appropriate noise level? Is the television, radio, or stereo constantly on, especially at a very high noise level? Noise should be reduced whenever possible and children who get upset very easily should be talked to calmly and quietly. Soft music can be used at times to provide a calming background.

- *The level of visual stimulation:* Young children do better in a relatively uncluttered environment in which there are only a few toys for them to play with. Babies can only attend to one object at a time but do enjoy different ones provided over time. Children can become overwhelmed with too many toys or books—especially if no one plays with the toys with them. Going through the toy box or shelf where the toys are and putting away toys that are too young or too old for the child can be helpful. A few should be left out and rotated so children have "new" toys regularly. Showing children how to use toys can be useful. Also notice if a child is overwhelmed with very bright lights or sunlight and if necessary, provide shielding from them.

- *Degree of touch and movement:* Some infants and young children are tactile defensive and very sensitive to certain kinds of soft touch; they may also find too much movement aversive. When light touch seems to be upsetting, trying firm touch is useful. Gentle rocking and avoiding too much rough housing may be necessary. Holding a child and providing massage may help her reduce muscle tension. If labels or rough materials in her clothes upset a child, try and accommodate her needs for smoother textures as much as possible.

The daily routine should be kept as calm and unhurried as possible. Caregivers can make mornings as calm as possible by preparing ahead and setting up a strict routine (e.g., the child must come to breakfast dressed). It is a good idea to allow time to talk after a child is picked up from child care, but not to force conversation. Providing a soothing and regular bedtime routine is essential. If a child seems to be overstimulated, provide a very relaxing weekend, let him stay home from lessons or activities if he wants to, and provide calm times to help settle him down. The whole family may benefit from not forcing children into unnecessary weekend activities when they have been overstimulated during the week.

PRINCIPLE 2: *Accept children's emotions and do not deny, punish, or withdraw from them for having emotions. Communicate acceptance of the feelings to children.*

Children need to know that their emotions are real and acceptable, and they need to be shown a variety of ways to deal with them in socially appropriate ways (see Principle 3). When infants and young children experience intense, negative emotions they may feel terrified and out of control. Calm containment is critical at these times and it is important that caregivers neither withdraw from nor punish the emotions. If children experience either punishment or lack of acceptance of their emotions, they may feel rejected and temporarily try to contain and inhibit the response. This may result in the child's eventually becoming more hostile and angry, sad, or fearful over time because repressed emotions do not go away. The child whose feelings are accepted and who is shown ways of coping and dealing with them, however, will gradually learn ways to both regulate them and express them in useful ways. It is also important to help children deal with and sort out mixed emotions. This can also help children feel less confused and upset.

As noted in Principle 1, a certain percentage of children need a great deal of care, nurturance, and extra containment because of their susceptibility to experiencing greater intensity of emotions, low adaptability to change, and more negative affect. These children often elicit more negative responses from caregivers but may actually need more attention in positive ways. Everyone has more difficulty with certain emotions than with others. This will depend a lot on our history of being parented and our experiences in other relationships.

• •

Mirvana had been physically abused as a child and had also been involved in two abusive relationships. When her son Ricki started to have temper tantrums, his anger and the anger she felt towards him were overwhelming and she sometimes ended up punishing him or locking herself away, frightened that she would harm him. Ricki's outbursts escalated.

―――――――――――――

Parames had always been a difficult and irritable infant, but as a toddler her whining escalated and she frequently cried inconsolably. Marguerite, her mother, found her daughter's sadness unacceptable and was not able to provide the comforting her daughter needed. In talking to Marguerite about her childhood, she remembered that her own mother had experienced bouts of depression and melancholia and how difficult she had found this growing up.

―――――――――――――

Heather could not understand why her daughter Felicity's extreme emotions made her feel panicky and out of control, especially because she would feel this way even when Felicity was very excited and happy. Heather was very open about her background and her mother's psychiatric history of having bipolar disorder. While she was growing up Heather would have to go and stay with another family member when her mother had one of her episodes. Heather's panic about even extreme happiness in her children seemed to be triggered by re-experiencing her mother's out-of-control excitement and happiness during periods of mania.

Helping caregivers understand these links with the past and offering counseling to deal with the issues that are raised can foster better ways to deal with emotions in their children.

PRINCIPLE 3: *Teach children appropriate strategies or outlets to help them learn to cope with their strong emotions.*

Strategies for teaching emotion regulation in infants, toddlers, and preschoolers differ significantly, partly because of children's different predominant moods and also because their cognitive and emotional capacities vary significantly. The following are some helpful tips to pass along to parents and other caregivers:

Birth to Three Months

- Infants need to be physically soothed and calmed and to receive necessary caregiving when they become upset.

- Infants must experience consistency and predictability and need to experience periods of quiet alertness between sleeping times. These times of alertness are the early beginnings of focusing on people and objects that can be increasingly used as an emotion regulation strategy in the years to come.

- If an infant wakes before naptime or nighttime is over and is not too upset, wait a few minutes to see if he can resettle so he learns some strategies to self-soothe. Never leave him too long or let him become really overwhelmed with crying. Remember, babies do not always want to be fed when they cry. They may be feeling discomfort from gas or be bored, tired, or even too hot or too cold; or they may be seeking the close contact and warmth of a caregiver.

- Attractive toys such as mobiles and musical boxes can help babies calm, too, as their attention is focused on them. Such toys become sights and sounds that babies associate with calm, interesting, and pleasant episodes.

Three to Twelve Months

During this period, babies still need to be soothed and calmed frequently. They are often able to amuse themselves for longer periods and will have developed a number of self-calming efforts such as fixating their attention on objects, sucking their fist, thumb, or a pacifier, and possibly rocking themselves.

- In addition to holding and rocking an infant to calm him, a caregiver may talk to him in a soothing voice to help him feel calmer and more able to calm himself.

- Remember that when children smile they are changing their moods and calming, so caregivers should smile and talk to them often.

- Attractive toys that infants can activate can help them calm down because the concentration needed to make them "work" can help them focus away from other needs.

- When a baby can move around freely and safely, this will help him self-regulate because he can seek out interesting objects and toys in the environment.

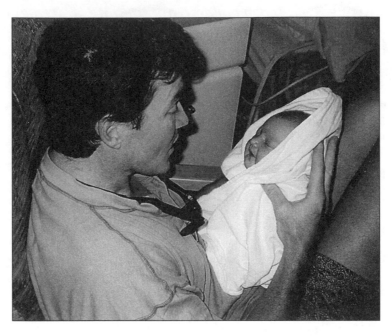

An infant needs to be soothed and calmed when she becomes upset.

- Remember that strangers and even brief separations can be scary for a baby, so he will need calming and attention during these times. Toward the end of this stage a special blanket or cuddly toy can work wonders to calm a baby or to substitute for caregivers—especially in the night.

Twelve to Twenty-Four Months

Toddlers will probably be quite exhilarated by the experience of walking and for a while may seem somewhat impervious to bumps and scrapes.

- As the child begins to use words, a caregiver can include feeling words such as *happy, sad, mad/angry,* and *afraid* in their exchanges so that the child begins to get used to the words for emotions. Use pictures of faces and play a game of naming the feelings (see Figure 8.1). As she begins to be able to identify these emotions in the pictures, gradually add others such as jealous, surprised, and disgusted.

- Talk with the child about what might have happened for someone to be feeling a particular emotion. Ask her when she might feel that way, e.g., "I feel sad when _____"; "I feel mad when _____." Ask children to guess how other people are feeling in the family. Have the person tell them how they feel.

- Remember, when a toddler is overwhelmed, calm and console him, and verbalize his emotions so the feeling words become very familiar and meaningful.

HAPPY   SAD   AFRAID

MIXED-UP   ANGRY

Figure 8.1. Have children name the feelings in pictures such as these to help them identify emotions. Drawing by Catherine Christie; reprinted by permission.)

- Tantrums will probably be at their height as the toddler exerts her independence—and becomes frustrated every time she does not get her way. Strategies to deal with these are included under Principle 8.

- Toddlers usually begin to enjoy pretend play, especially when they are with other children. Help children play out their anger, fears, and sadness through their pretend play. (See the section in Chapter 4 on pretend play.)

Two to Four Years

During these years from 2 to 4, the strategies outlined above can continue to be used with somewhat more sophistication.

- Cut out pictures from magazines and talk about how the people in them may be feeling about the situations.

- Introduce some books that talk about emotions and how children feel about difficult situations. Examples of specific books are provided in the Bibliography. These can be about situations that are going on in the child's life such as a move, a new sibling, and so forth. When reading these and other books, stop occasionally and ask the child to guess how someone in the story is feeling.

- When children face a frustrating situation or are struggling to complete a task, support them and verbalize their frustration but show them how to cope with it.

When a toddler is overwhelmed, calm and console him and verbalize his emotions.

- As a child becomes able to draw, help him draw simple faces with different emotions (e.g., happy, sad, angry).

- While giving children permission to share emotions with you when they are very upset and perhaps angry about a situation, gently remind them about some things that are going well and shift their attention to things they can look forward to. Rephrase the situation in a more positive way. Perhaps a child has just not been able to write his name like the other children. Acknowledge how disappointed or angry he must be but remind him of how well he did with his skating or remind him of something he is looking forward to in the next couple of days. Laugh together about something that happened so he can move away from his current negativity.

- Using puppets can be a wonderful way for children to talk about emotions and to learn about another person's feelings and point of view. The playing out of different experiences becomes a very real way for children to understand their own emotions and those of other people better. Role playing with different characters, sometimes reversing them, can also help them experience how others feel.

- Ask children to name three things that make them happy, sad, mad, jealous, and so forth.

- Sing songs about emotions.

- Teach children to understand and use words such as *some* and *all, now* and *later,* and *before* and *after.* Words such as *some* and *all* help children distinguish between an "all or none" or "black and white" perspective and a more even view of things. Words such as *now* and *later* and *before* and *after* provide a time frame that can help children get over wanting things im-

mediately. Knowing and understanding these words can help children learn to consider and think their problems through.

• Provide children with physical outlets, such as running, jumping, and yelling outside, and remove children from upsetting situations.

Four to Six Years

At this stage, children are aware of most of the emotions and are beginning, by 6 years of age, to understand about mixed emotions and feigning emotions in certain situations.

Caregivers will probably notice by now that when a child is obviously very upset, asking him about what happened may immediately close down any communication and discussion. Sometimes when a caregiver just acknowledges that she can see he is upset or that it looks like he had a tough day, it can be extremely helpful in having him open up. This may not happen right away, but he will appreciate your understanding of his painful feelings and that he does not feel able to talk about it right away.

By 6 years of age, children are beginning to understand that people can feel opposite emotions about the same situation. For example, they could feel excited about going to an amusement park while feeling afraid of some of the rides. Learning that they can feel more than one way about something can gradually help children accept having opposite feelings about the same person (e.g., "I'm mad at Mom because she won't let me go outside in the mud but I still love her because she's nice and helps me, too"). This is still difficult for children even into early adolescence, but nevertheless talking about these opposite feelings will help children understand and deal with them better.

As we get older, it is often necessary to cover our true feelings and feign others. Young children can be extremely honest and blunt about their emotions. Although we do not want them to deny or be dishonest about their emotions, it is important to teach children how to avoid hurting others with somewhat cruel comments. Telling the waitress that her uniform makes her look fat is not acceptable, while a quiet comment that her uniform is a pretty color may be.

In certain situations it is very important to give older children information about how and when to get help if they are afraid, sad, or angry so that they can feel some sense of control. Having phone numbers handy, explaining how to phone 911, having someone in the area they can call if they need to, and encouraging them to talk to the teacher if there is bullying going on are all useful strategies to provide to children.

Children need to be able to integrate their life stories into a coherent narrative, so talking to them about important past events and about their related feelings can be very helpful. Discussions about daily events can also be very helpful.

PRINCIPLE 4: *Provide children with frequent experiences that are happy, pleasant and, at times, joyful.*

Happiness is contagious, just as are, unfortunately, depression and sadness. Infants of depressed mothers actually develop a depressive style of interaction too, and are at increased risk for developing depression and anxiety themselves later on. Those positive, fun activities that caregivers have with children are critically important. Some suggestions are set out in Chapters 2 and 4 so will not be repeated here in detail. Other suggestions for caregivers include the following:

- *Smile and laugh:* When a child sees happiness in the caregiver's face, this is a critically important way for the caregiver to demonstrate how she feels about the child. It also reinforces how the child feels about himself.

- *Get out and about:* It's wonderful when caregivers participate in fun, spontaneous activities with children. Try rolling in the leaves, jumping in puddles, and rough-and-tumble games.

- *Play games and dance around and sing:* Play games such as hide-and-seek and musical chairs. Play creative games that produce unpredictable results and stimulate the senses, such as blowing bubbles, finger painting, or playing in water.

- *Slow it down:* Provide time for calm activities such as going for a walk, reading, driving, or cuddling.

Remember, choose things that you and the child enjoy and are comfortable with, or the joy will be lost.

PRINCIPLE 5: *If caregivers lose control, they should talk about their feelings naturally and apologize to the child if their behavior was inappropriate.*

Research actually shows that repairing the relationship if you lose control and scream or yell at a child is helpful, and can help the child be more able to talk about her emotions and regulate them. This does not mean saying that the child was in the right and you are a terrible person. But it is helpful to say, "I can be angry without yelling," "I wish I hadn't talked that way," "what can I do to help you stop behaving that way?" Mending things with a reassuring hug can make an extraordinary difference for a child's self-esteem and for the caregiver–child relationship. Some possible strategies that caregivers can use when they become angry with children have been talked about in previous chapters and include

- Using words that express the feelings without criticizing, blaming, or shaming the child

- Using brief, strong statements about the behavior without screaming, yelling, or hitting

- Taking a time-out in order to calm down

- Redirecting the situation or activity, or changing the environment by going somewhere different

PRINCIPLE 6: *Provide a context or environment in which emotions are discussed and included when talking about people and situations.*

When families talk about emotions and children have access to a caregiver who is interested in their feelings, they are more likely to understand their feelings and the feelings of others. Later on (usually by 6 years of age), this understanding has been found to relate to children's social sensitivity and the development of empathy and remorse (Hubbard & Cole, 1994; Zahn-Waxler, Radke-Yarrow, & King, 1979).

● ●

Dad had a terrible day and was feeling irritated and upset. By the look on 4-year-old Gabriella's face, she was not doing well either. The family of four came together for supper, and Dad asked everyone how their day had been. He also shared how difficult his day had been. At work, a number of people he supervised had been complaining and he had felt quite angry and overwhelmed. He also let his family know how good it was to be home and to talk about what had gone on. Quickly, Gabriella told about how her friend had been mean to her at child care and how sad she had felt. All members of the families sympathized about the bad parts of the day and felt comfortable that if things were still bad for them later on, they could talk about it again.

PRINCIPLE 7: *Avoid presenting children with an overwhelming diet of anger, fear, or depression. Seek help if necessary.*

Children are negatively affected if constantly exposed to parental depression; severe anxiety; yelling and screaming; family violence; continual criticism; and physical, emotional, or sexual abuse. If parents or other caregivers reach this level of burnout or despair, it is crucial that they find support to help them to stop displaying these scary emotions too frequently. Remember, too, that excessive conflict between siblings can be equally damaging, particularly to the victimized child. Seek professional help if feelings and reactions to children are escalating out of control and if exchanges often end up with severe and continual punishing of the child.

PRINCIPLE 8: *Adopt strategies to help children deal with intense negative emotions such as fear, anger, jealousy, and sadness.*

In the course of normal development, children display fears or anxieties, anger (temper tantrums or aggression), jealousy (particularly sibling rivalry) or sadness (whining). Sometimes, these may be signs of stressful situations that the child is facing or signs of new cognitive gains that the child has made. In either case, caregivers need to adopt strategies to assure that such emotional struggles are satisfactorily negotiated and exaggerated emotional reactions do not become a permanent part of the child's personality. Some general strategies that can be used for all emotional lessons include the following:

- Examine what has been going on for the child and see if there are ways to reduce stress.

- Spend some extra time with the child and really tune into his emotions and use emotional moments when the child is not out of control to get close to the child.

- Encourage the child to express his feelings in socially appropriate ways and before they escalate out of control.

- When he does lose control assure him that you will not let him hurt himself or anyone else and use the strategies suggested above so he can learn to problem-solve and control his own emotions.

- If he does lose control help him afterwards to see how the situation might be avoided again (e.g., not building a block tower where the baby is crawling) or dealt with differently.

Dealing with Fears and Anxieties

Almost all children go through periods during which fears increase and their sleep is disturbed by nightmares. The peak for fears is usually about 3 years of age and drops off after that. Some children seem to have more fears than others and may experience heightened anxiety when they face certain events and new situations and experiences. Fear and anxiety occur when a child feels helpless in the face of something experienced as dangerous. Table 8.4 includes a list of some fears that are quite predictable and the ages at which they tend to occur.

The object of children's fears changes as they get older and are capable of new kinds of reasoning and understanding of potential threats. For example, children do not fear separation from their caregivers until they have a true sense of themselves as separate and are capable of object permanence, or know that when a caregiver leaves the room he still exists. Chil-

Table 8.4. The occurrence of fears throughout different stages of childhood

Age	Fears/anxieties
Birth to 12 months	Strangers
	Separation
	Loud noises like sirens or vacuum cleaners
	Heights
	Loss of support when being held
12–24 months	Strange people and situations
	Bath and the drain
	Water
	Fear of falling at heights
	The toilet
2–3 years	The dark
	Doctors and dentists
	Monsters
	Ghosts
	Snakes
	Animals
	Bugs and large insects
3–5 years	School phobia
	Storms, thunder and lightening
	Imaginary animals
	Blood
	Death of loved ones or loss of their love
	Loss or damage to a part of their body
	Kidnappers
	Airplane flying
	Moving
	Going to a new school
	Fires

dren without the capacity for imagination are unlikely to be afraid of monsters or ghosts. As a consequence, as children mature and are capable of greater understanding of their world, the variety of fears they have often expands. Some suggestions for ways to deal with fears are listed here:

- For infants, the game of Peek-a-Boo can let them experience "separations" in a fun and controllable situation.

- For children who fear loud noises like vacuum cleaners or sirens, it is helpful to calm them when unexpected loud noises appear and to provide comfort and holding. It can also be helpful to anticipate these frightening situations and avoid them if possible until the child has learned to deal with them.

- Do not try to turn a child who needs to take his time getting familiar with something new into a "plunger." Let a shy or anxious child cling to you until he feels comfortable enough to join in. Be supportive and encouraging.

- When introducing a child to something new, such as wading in the ocean, let him take his time and stay close until he's ready to try it out.

- For children who fear the bath drain or the toilet, demonstrate that large things like them cannot go down. Assure them they are safe. Stay with them when they are in the bath if they continue to fear the drain, or flush the toilet after they are out of the room until they become more comfortable.

When introducing a child to something new, let him take his time and stay close until he's ready to try it out.

- If children develop fears about monsters, ghosts, and imaginary animals in their rooms respect the fear and avoid laughing, ignoring, or ridiculing. Look in the closet and cupboards with the child to reassure her that no monsters are lurking there. Offer reassurance that you are close by and will keep her safe. Be sure to be cheerful and matter-of-fact because being too serious may make the child more anxious.

- Read books about how other children have overcome their fears.

- Listen to the child's fears. Encourage the child to talk about them. Assure her that you are confident she will be able to handle them but you are there for her. Help her come up with ways to deal with them.

- Assure the child it is normal to have fears and that even grown-ups get afraid sometimes. Let her know she will get over her fears, too. Use examples of her recovery from certain fears as a sign that she can get over them.

- If a child has suddenly become more fearful and this continues, talk to the child and check out the situation at school or child care as well as home and think about what may be triggering the fears.

- Avoid reading scary books or letting the child watch upsetting movies, especially before bedtime.

- Play out frightening situations with small toys. Offer resolutions. Go over an upcoming situation in advance to help the child confront the situation later.

- Do not be overprotective or overpermissive. The former can rob the child of her independence, and the latter of her sense of structure and safety.

- Let children talk about fear of injury and death, and reassure them that you intend to be around to take care of them for a long time.

- Avoid stopping a child's aggressive pretend play or verbal expressions of anger. Excessive repression of a child's anger may lead to angry thoughts, fears of reprisal, and even more generalized anxiety.

- When a child fears an object, try to introduce it very gradually. Begin with very slight exposure through books and pretend play, then try the real experience while you hold the child close and reassure her. This very gradual approach, stopping the process if the child becomes upset, may enable the child to deal with the object alone next time and will eventually desensitize the child to the fear.

- Give children responses to follow if something scary happens. Avoid overburdening with all sorts of scenarios, but some simple instructions and strategies can be reassuring.

Dealing with Anger

There is no question that tantrums or expressions of frustration, anger, and being overwhelmed are a normal part of growing up. Children have tantrums for different reasons, however, and they may need to be dealt with somewhat differently at different times.

Tantrums   Several situations usually lead to temper tantrums:

- The child is totally exhausted or sick and feels a sense of confusion, helplessness, and even terror because of all the overwhelming feelings. He screams because he can no longer control the intense feelings.

- The child is expressing a sense of independence and is infuriated because your refusal to give him what he wants makes him feel small and inadequate. He is determined to get his own way, and screams with anger and frustration when you say "No," and expresses real hatred at that moment.

- The child feels left out, ignored or lonely and is seeking attention.

Regardless of the cause of temper tantrums, there are a few simple rules about what to do:

- Never lose your temper and scream at, hit, or throw things at the child. This is only modeling the very thing you are trying to stop.

- Do not give the child what he is throwing a tantrum for. Learning theory tells us that even if you give in once or twice, the child will continue to have tantrums in subsequent situations in an attempt to get his own way.

- Try to soothe, calm, and talk to the child after removing him from the situation. If this is not successful let him cry it out and then calm him later. Once the child will allow it, gentle holding, talking, calming, and reassurance may be very helpful. Help him verbalize his anger.

- Let the child know you do not accept tantrums, although you understand his frustration. Encourage the child to talk about his feelings instead. Let the child know you will stop him hurting himself and you because you love him and do not want him to hurt anyone or to get hurt.

If your child is frequently losing control, try and find out what is triggering the tantrums. If it is a push for independence, make sure he is allowed to make some simple decisions; if it seems to be a desire for attention, try and provide for a little more time alone with the child and give the child attention during quiet, calm moments. Although tantrums are quite normal, if the child shows excessive and frequent tantrums that include hurting others this is not average behavior and the child may need special help to deal with it.

Aggression   Aggression includes physical aggression (e.g., hitting, biting, kicking, shoving) and verbal aggression (e.g., swearing, name calling, belittling). It is important to remember that verbal aggression such as screaming at others, using cruel words, and putting others down is as upsetting as physical aggression to the victim and needs to be stopped.

Aggression usually does not get excessive until some time during the second year. At that point the child is just beginning to understand about cause and effect to understand the consequences of her action. Toddlers do not "know better" than to hit or bite. What toddlers understand is not that they have hurt someone but that their parents are upset about what they did. Ways to calm and channel children's aggression are set out next:

- Never attempt to teach a child not to be aggressive by acting aggressively towards the child so he can "know how it feels."

- Try to figure out why the child is being aggressive. For example, is this a bid for more attention, is she being given a model of anger as a way to deal with things, or is she just not able to cope yet with extreme emotions?

- When a child is playing with other children, try and keep an eye on them and be ready to head off problems if necessary, but let the children sort out the problems on their own if they can. Usually, children younger than 3 years old will need some help.

- Set limits on aggressive behavior; make it clear that children may not hurt themselves or others. These rules must be consistently enforced and reasons for them repeated.

- Stop aggressive behavior and give the child something else to do. Offer some materials for children to use that allow them to divert their anger and energy into some socially acceptable outlets. Maybe using punching bag, pounding boards, or going outdoors where she can kick, stomp, and run can help.

- Separate her from the other children if necessary. Also, show her other ways to deal with the anger like using words instead.

- If the child is old enough, encourage her to talk about her feelings of anger and hurt and help her begin to think of a solution.

• •

John has hit someone at his child care for the second time in one day and his teacher can see that something is bothering him. She knows that his mother has been ill and in the hospital.

Teacher: [Stops John hurting Mary.] "John, you seem pretty upset today. Anything you'd like to tell me about?"

John: "My mom's away in the hospital."

Teacher: "That must be very hard for you."

John: "Yes, my dad's at the hospital all the time too, and my grandma hates me and only likes my sister. She's mean."

Teacher: "So you really feel left out and miss your mom."

John: "I want to see my mom."

Teacher: "Can you talk to her on the telephone, or send her a picture you drew?"

John: [Looking brighter.] "Yes, I could; she's coming home next week."

Teacher: "Well let's draw a nice picture for her." [They draw a picture together and the teacher helps him choose a happy and fun time to draw about.]

Sometimes aggression becomes so intense and frequent that it goes beyond what is normal at a particular age. Guidelines of when to seek help for a child's aggression are outlined in Table 8.5.

Table 8.5. When to seek help for aggression

1. When intensity increases to become dangerous to self and/or others.
2. When it is so frequent it is habitual.
3. When a child seems to find pleasure in hurting others.
4. When it includes fire setting or other destructive behaviors.
5. When it goes beyond an occasional outburst with a sibling.
6. When it is planned and malicious.
7. When the child has no empathy for the victim or remorse for her actions.
8. When the child hurts animals.
9. When you fear for your or other people's safety.

Dealing with Jealousy and Sibling Rivalry

Perhaps the most common problem that caregivers face is sibling rivalry. Although sibling fights are universal, they may cause more concern and frustration for parents than anyone else. Caregivers are often confused about the intensity of the jealousy that is expressed and the pain and hurt that siblings often seem to want to inflict on one another.

Although many books advise leaving brothers and sisters alone and letting them argue and fight it out, in fact some adults report that they were hurt, even abused by a sibling without their parents doing anything about it. As a result many adults still carry intense feelings of anger toward siblings and many refuse to be in contact with them. Given these possible extremes in behavior between siblings, it is critical that caregivers remain aware of what is going on between them and monitor their interactions regularly. Sibling rivalry is normal to a degree, but can advance to an unhealthy level. Here are some suggestions for dealing with sibling rivalry and fights:

- It is critical to make sure that no child is getting hit or verbally or even sexually abused by a sibling. Enforce a rule in the home that does not allow violence of any kind or between any members of the family.

- Do not always decide squabbles or step in to stop them. Sometimes they can be avoided before they get out of hand.

- Avoid labeling children even with good labels as this can set up rivalries. Labels can be difficult for a child to live up to if they are good, and self-fulfilling prophecies or calls to action if they are bad (e.g., "Emma is the best girl in the whole-wide world," "Cameron is such a handful").

- Try not to have favorites. Value each child for his unique characteristics and let him know about them. Do not compare children in unfavorable ways.

- Avoid giving the children exactly the same thing all the time. Allow each child a turn at having a treat or the new piece of clothing. Assure the other children it will be their turn next time. This will avoid the insistence that everything must be the same.

- Accept that it is normal that siblings have angry feelings toward each other and remember that most siblings will often support each other against other people outside the family.

- Do not constantly play referee. Do not reward tattling or always take one child's side. If you see play beginning to become fighting, step in and divert the children's attention to something else.

What to Do When Fights Occur

- Let children work it out themselves if possible.

- Intervene if one or both children are getting very upset or combative.

- Separate the children and comfort a child who is very hurt and upset.

- Do not take sides unless you saw what happened.

- Encourage both children to talk about their feelings and about what happened and ask them to come up with solutions to the conflict. Practice will encourage them to do this on their own. This kind of negotiation and problem solving will be dealt with in greater detail in the next chapter.

Dealing with Sadness and Depression

Unfortunately, a number of young children become sad and depressed. Children become depressed most frequently because they are missing someone or something. Children who have been hospitalized, who lose parents or caregivers, or even who move away may experience real sadness. Other children can become depressed because of threats of loss of love or because they face a situation they find overwhelming or too difficult; if they become discouraged because they hear too much criticism; or if they experience a sense of rejection or abandonment. Children may also get depressed if they are dealing with parental separation or divorce and one parent has left the house.

Again, it is critical to let the child know you understand and empathize with his feelings. Encourage him to talk about the sadness and any anger that may be present. Let the child know you are there for him by holding him and showing warmth and protection. Provide extra comforting for the child such as a warm drink, bath, or a special treat. Make sure the child knows that if a person has gone away (died or separated) that it was not their fault. Encourage him to talk about the person or place he is missing. Try and find things the child enjoys and does well and reassure him about his competence.

As Martin Seligman (1995) in *The Optimistic Child* explained, the secret of raising optimistic children is encouraging them to use certain ways to think about events that happen to them. One way is to help the child to think about how he can change an event or feel better about it. Caregivers can teach children about finding solutions by

- Using an optimistic explanatory style, only addressing the changeable aspect of the problem

- Listening to what the child is most concerned about and helping him find something controllable he can do

- Making adjustments in the family environment if the sadness appears to be coming from something the caregiver is doing such as being too angry, critical, rejecting, or overwhelming

- Reassuring the child that he is wanted and will always be taken care of

If children are having severe problems with these emotions and if the symptoms last for more than a few weeks without improving, it is important to seek help from a mental health professional.

THE ROLE OF PARENTS IN EMOTION REGULATION

One of the most frequent concerns of parents is losing control when they become angry at their young children's crying or acting-out behavior. Many parents think that they should not *feel* angry when confronted by their children's negative behavior. It is clear that young children, particularly if they are our own, raise intense emotions of caring and love in us, but also at times, intense anger and frustration. Most parents of young children will find themselves suddenly feeling furious and tempted to yell, scream, and even hit their children. A number of things can trigger these intense feelings of anger:

Immediate Triggers:

- Events unrelated to the child such as pressures at work or worries over money and other issues that can reduce our patience with a child

- Pressure that has been building from other behaviors the child has been engaging in throughout the day, which can blow when the child does just one more thing

- Exhaustion from lack of sleep or just trying to do too much every day without enough support

- Embarrassment in public by a child's behavior

- Frustration because the parent tried so hard to reason and be fair and the child responded with a negative emotion and irrationality anyway

- Rejection by the child. The child may say something such as "I hate you," "You're a lousy [mother/father]."

- The child put herself or someone else at risk and the parent's fear escalates into anger

Long-Term Issues:

- Something said or done by the child triggers something from the past when the parent was treated unkindly or even cruelly, and the parent strikes out.

- A strong tendency to be very explosive and hostile in many situations

Although we try to not repeat patterns from the past, most of which we are not aware, in certain emotionally laden situations the negative patterns of how we were parented may surface. Certain people are more susceptible to explosive outbursts and have more difficulty staying calm in stressful situations. The reasons for these reactions are not always clear, but in many cases early childhood experiences, including traumatic experiences, can play a role. For some people who have experienced traumas early or later in life, the memory of the trauma may persist as intrusive and repetitive thoughts or nightmares about the events. As well, they may experience heightened arousal to certain triggers that are similar to the event. They become in a state of chronic hyperarousal and cannot recognize normal emotional signals. As a result, they are not alerted to what is happening and do not take action to adjust situations to avoid a problem. Instead, they go immediately into a fight-or-flight reaction without the cognitive process that would help them problem solve and calm down in between. This often leads to an explosive rage in response to a small incident. Moreover, these individuals' hyperarousal often continues to generalize beyond the trauma that triggered it originally; for example, to include being yelled at, a rejecting word, a child waving his arms, or simply feeling out of control. For parents who frequently experience these kinds of reactions, it is important for them to seek professional help.

Parents may dismiss some emotions in their children. They ignore and deny certain emotions because to deal with them seems overwhelming. Parents like this often do anything to distract the child away from the emotion, to punish it, or withdraw from the child. They may insist on a happy child, a spunky child, or a compliant child and refuse to allow one or more negative emotions. This can result in the development of a "false" self or a person who is constantly "sweet and nice," although the anger underneath may be obvious. Sometimes, parents show contempt and disapproval of an emotion through criticizing, ridiculing, punishing, or laughing at the child. Children are then deprived of the opportunity to learn acceptance of the emotion and to learn how to modulate it. The denied emotion can, as a consequence, continually intrude and result in a variety of symptoms perhaps more direct such as anger and hostility or in psychosomatic symptoms or excessive anxiety, even phobias. Again, if families have adopted these kinds of reactions to emotions it will be important to provide them with parent or family counseling to help them deal with their deeper issues.

DISCUSSION QUESTIONS FOR TRAINING PROFESSIONALS

- Why is emotion regulation so crucial in combination with adequate discipline?

- Discuss examples of adults who may have extreme reactions to their children because of traumatic stress reactions.

- What may be the most difficult developmental stage for parents of young children in terms of emotion regulation?

- Why may parents dismiss or punish a certain emotion?

- How may both cognitive and emotion theoretical perspectives be important and how can they both be useful?

- How does emotion regulation change from infancy to early childhood? Give some examples.

- Why may sibling rivalry be one of the most important issues for parents to deal with?

- Why are mixed emotions difficult for young children to interpret and deal with?

- What are the most important messages to give parents about emotion regulation?

- Why do many parents and other caregivers get so upset about young children's aggression?

- Why is psychoanalytic theory no longer accepted as a complete explanation of the development of emotion regulation or of failure to achieve it?

It is crucial that parents understand that their children need to learn to regulate and deal with their emotions and that they as parents have a critical role to play in this. Make it clear that what has been called emotional intelligence quotient (EQ) is just as important as an IQ and that EQ will influence a number of areas of their child's development including success in school, getting along with others, and coping, to name a few.

Some parents have somewhat extreme reactions to their children's emotional displays, but others simply do not know how important their reactions to their children's emotions are, not just to their behavior but also to their feelings of emotional well being. When this is explained to caregivers and they are provided with some strategies, as outlined in the previous principles, this can often be sufficient for them to be able to begin to help their children with their emotions in more positive ways. These are some of the most important principles that need to be communicated:

- It is crucial to notice, acknowledge, and encourage young children to talk about their emotions. Also let parents know that a wide array of emotions is normal, but that it is what one does with them that is important.

- Times when the child is out of control are not the best times to talk about emotions.

- Wait until feelings are less intense.

- Help the child label the feeling if she cannot and teach her names of emotions, what they feel like, and when they occur. For example, explore with the child the feelings she feels if someone is mean to her and how they may include anger and sadness. Set limits on the acting out of intense emotions so that the child feels safe.

- Teach the child strategies to use to modulate his emotions and encourage him to come up with ideas himself.

In order to help parents deal with their own intense negative emotions (especially anger) toward their children, some strategies are

- Help parents identify which emotions they have the most difficulty dealing with in their children (e.g., anger, jealousy, whining, fear, anxiety, affection, excitement).

- Review a particular incident when their children's emotions were hard to deal with. Discuss how they felt and what they might have thought before, during, and after the incident.

- Praise parents for anything they might have done well in the situation with their child or in reviewing the situation with you.

- Problem-solve with them about other ways they might deal with a similar situation in the future and positive ways they might think about themselves and their children during such situations.

- Suggest some ways to calm down. Leaving the room, letting the child know they are leaving the room to calm down, and reassuring the child they will return can be helpful. Encourage parents to use ways to calm down such as taking several deep, slow breaths and counting slowly to 10; visualizing a calm and relaxed place; or doing something pleasurable (see Eastman, 1997). Writing or remembering an inspirational poem such as the one provided in Figure 8.2 is another helpful way for parents to keep positive.

453

The Best Is Yet to Come

At times like these when it seems like the worst is happening
There are things that I must remember
I must remember to be strong
To be the best that I can be
Take one day at a time
Just live life as it comes to me

At times like these when it feels like the sun isn't going to come up tomorrow
I have to remember that it came up today
And there will be lots of times when all that I want to do is cry
Times when I'm not sure what to do
Times when it seems like the worst is happening
But also that the best is yet to come

Figure 8.2. Writing or memorizing poems such as this can provide inspiration and encouragement to parents and caregivers in difficult times. (From "The Best Is Yet to Come," by Amber Patterson, 2001; reprinted by permission.)

GROUP EXERCISES TO HELP PARENTS ENCOURAGE EMOTION REGULATION

The following exercises can be used in parenting groups. Not all should or need to be used, but appropriate ones can be selected depending on the composition of the group.

As I Was Growing Up . . .

Ask parents to identify, from the ways of dealing with emotions given in Figure 8.3, how feelings were dealt with at home as they were growing up. Ask parents to describe how they would like things to be the same or different in their present family.

What Emotions Are Difficult For Me

Everyone is more comfortable with some emotions than others. Ask parents to identify which emotions they have the most difficulty dealing with in their children (e.g., anger, jealousy, sadness and whining, fear and anxiety, intense happiness, affection). In the discussion, ask parents to

- Describe a situation in which their child's emotion triggered difficult feelings

- Try and identify what is triggered in them by the emotion

- Imagine what they think contributed to them being triggered by the emotion

Instructions: Check each of the following statements that describe the emotional climate of your home when you were growing up.

____ Feelings were demonstrated through positive actions (e.g., hugs, kisses).

____ Feelings were demonstrated through negative actions (e.g., yelling, hitting).

____ Feelings were largely ignored and rarely talked about.

____ Children were taught to repress negative emotions.

____ Parents were emotionally available and noticed and understood my feelings.

____ Everyone yelled and screamed at one another.

____ People complained about each other all the time but never found a solution.

____ Our family talked about feelings and tried to find positive, constructive solutions.

____ I was expected to be an emotional caregiver to one of my parents.

____ There was a lot of silence in my home.

____ There was a lot of slamming of doors in my house.

Figure 8.3. Blank worksheet for assessing the emotional climate in which a parent or caregiver was raised.

- Identify whether they deny or punish their own children's emotions
- Think of ways to overcome the difficulty

Point out that continuously denying certain emotions can create a child who does not feel "real" or a child who continuously displays another emotion other than the real one in an effort to remain feeling accepted and connected. This has been called creating an unreal or false self in the child.

Seeing the Grays

This exercise can be presented as a game for caregivers to try with children, but it can also be helpful to modify parents' extreme feelings. Sometimes people get upset, angry, or elated because they react to a situation without really examining it or understanding it. Often it is difficult to retain the understanding that people (children and parents) are a mixture of strengths and weaknesses and to remember positive things about situations when one is emotionally aroused.

To do the exercise, put words on a blackboard or a flipchart, placing a word at either end representing the extremes of a concept (see Figure 8.4). Have parents name examples of things that fall at either end and at various points in-between. This process will help parents realize about the "grays" or "in-betweens" of people, their behavior, and their emotional reactions.

Continuum of Extremes				
1	**3**	**5**	**7**	**10**
Cowardly (e.g., someone who ignores a child who is drowning)	.... (e.g., someone who calls 911)...............			**Brave** (e.g., throwing something into the water to rescue the child by pulling them to safety)
Bad	....			**Good**
Lazy	....			**Industrious**
Unkind	....			**Kind**
Ugly	....			**Attractive**

Figure 8.4. Diagram for teaching caregivers to see the "gray" areas between extremes of thought about labels.

Acceptable Ways to Express Anger

Explain to parents that anger toward children is inevitable and normal. In other words, we must accept that we have these emotions and find ways to express them in a helpful way. Ask parents to discuss ways that they believe are acceptable ways to express anger towards children. After discussion it is important that the following ways of expressing anger are highlighted:

• Let the child know in controlled words that you are angry and that you understand their feelings but cannot accept and will not let them hurt another person or themselves.

• Remember to apologize if you became very upset and said or did hurtful things.

• Let children know you need some time-out to calm down. Express your feelings and exit, letting them know you will come back soon.

• Note other useful ideas parent may have. Point out that sending the child to his room for long periods, criticizing and putting the child down, screaming and yelling, threatening to send him away or leaving, and laughing at the child are not acceptable.

Table 8.6. Strategies to bring anger under control

1. **Detect early warning signs.** Become aware of the thoughts, feelings, and physiological reactions that seem to precede an outburst. Write them down. Try and avoid any escalation by changing the "scene" or exiting.

2. **Reason with self.** Instead of exploding, talk to yourself about the situation and try and talk yourself out of being upset. This may mean running through a brief problem-solving sequence in your head. Review how you may be affecting the child and the message he is getting from you.

3. **Stop hostile thoughts and feelings.** Shout "Stop" to yourself in your head or distract yourself with a soothing activity such as listening to music, looking at a magazine, or daydreaming. Increase positive, calming, and coping thoughts (e.g., "This isn't the end of the world," "I did well with her whining today").

4. **Explain your feelings and exit.** If no attempts to stop your hostility have worked, explain your feelings to your child (e.g., "I will leave until I am calmer") and go somewhere else in the house. Lock yourself in bathroom or in bedroom with earphones for a few minutes.

5. **Nurture and calm yourself.** Use calming methods such as 10 minutes of meditation, or nurture yourself.

6. **Use strong discipline methods.** Some parents reach a stage when they believe they cannot manage a young child. You have to believe you can get back in control.

7. **Learn to listen.** Listen to what your child is communicating through paying attention to what he is saying and his body language.

8. **Trust your child.** Give your child some small control in his life and allow yourself not to have to control everything in his life.

Strategies to Bring Anger Under Control

Explain that what is most important is to resume thinking rationally as soon as possible. Suggest that talking themselves through the steps may also be helpful. Explain each of these strategies given in Table 8.6. Role-play some of the strategies. Ask parents to experiment with the strategies during the week.

Testing Your Emotional Intelligence

Have parents answer the emotional intelligence test provided in Figure 8.5 and discuss how they did, or ask them to do it for homework and have their partner do it too. It can be important to encourage partners to act in a similar and, thus, less confusing way.

SAMPLE HOMEWORK ACTIVITIES

Choose some of the following as homework activities. Have parents record their reactions to discuss in the group next week.

1. Tape-record yourself at times when you lose control and after listening to the tape-recording, problem-solve around new strategies.

2. Keep a hostility log. List all the triggers and your thoughts, feelings, and actions.

Testing Your Emotional Intelligence (EQ)

Instructions: Picture yourself in the following scenarios and circle the answer that best matches the response you would make.

1. **As usual, your friend shows up 15 minutes late for lunch and you are going to be late in returning to work. What's your response?**
   A. Tell her, as calmly as possible, that it is very inconvenient when she's late and ask her to be on time next time.
   B. Greet her without saying anything.
   C. Fly into a rage, and scream at her for being late.

2. **Someone in front of you at the checkout counter is taking forever asking about the cost of her purchases. What do you do?**
   A. Wait and tell yourself she will get through soon and watch to see if another checkout is free.
   B. Tap your feet impatiently.
   C. Angrily tell the shop assistant to hurry it up.

3. **Your children are fighting about who will get to choose the television show. How do you handle it?**
   A. Help them to problem-solve about who's turn it is.
   B. Ignore it. It's just sibling rivalry.
   C. Scream at them and send them to their rooms.

4. **Every time you visit your mother, she criticizes your parenting skills and tells you what to do instead. What do you do?**
   A. Let her know it bothers you and get her to understand your position.
   B. Gather up the children and leave.
   C. Scream at her and tell her you won't come back again.

5. **Your best friend asks you to babysit for her 4-year-old for the afternoon so she can get some rest after being ill. Her daughter doesn't stop crying. What do you do?**
   A. Try to find ways to calm her down such as playing a game or going to the park.
   B. Scream at the child and tell her to stop acting spoiled and then try to ignore the crying.
   C. Call your friend and tell her to come and get her child because you can't stand it anymore. You also angrily tell her that her daughter is spoiled.

6. **You've given your daughter several hints about what you'd like for your birthday. Instead, she gets you something for the house you don't want. What do you do?**
   A. Let her know you're disappointed and ask if you could go together and exchange it.
   B. Thank her, say nothing about your disappointment, but feel hurt and annoyed.
   C. Get very angry, accusing her of being thoughtless, and refuse to accept it.

What's Your Score?

Give yourself 3 points for each A, 2 points for each B, and 1 point for each C.

If you scored 15–18 points	If you scored 11–14 points	If you scored 6–10 points
You try to consider and understand your own feelings and the feelings of those around you and to do something about their cause.	Although you control yourself, you tend to avoid dealing with issues you find troubling.	Sometimes you let your emotions get the better of you. Often you lose control and do not consider the feelings of others. This can be very hard for children.

Figure 8.5. Questionnaire: What is your emotional intelligence quotient (EQ)?

3. Step back and listen to your child when he is angry and upset. Acknowledge the anger. Do the same when he is whining or sad.

4. Try being assertive once and list what you said and how it worked.

5. Remember a funny incident with your child and record it. List times you had fun with your child.

6. Write down some things that you would like to tell your parents about how they solved conflict.

7. Once during the week forgive someone for negative behavior.

8. Complete the "Testing Your Emotional Intelligence (EQ)" questionnaire (see Figure 8.5) and consider your score. If it is low, check some of the strategies in the principles.

9. If you lose control, apologize to your child.

10. If you find yourself beginning to lose control, take a time-out and try and calm yourself down.

BIBLIOGRAPHY

REFERENCES

Aber, J.L., & Allen, J.P. (1987). Effects of maltreatment on young children's socioemotional development: An attachment theory perspective. *Developmental Psychology, 23,* 406–414.

Aldwin, C. (1994). *Stress, coping and development: An integrative perspective.* New York: Guilford Press.

Als, H. (1978). Assessing an assessment: Conceptual considerations, methodological issues, and a perspective on the future of the Neonatal Behavioral Assessment Scale. In A.J. Sameroff (Ed.), *Organization and stability of neonatal behavior: A commentary on the Brazelton Neonatal Behavioral Assessment Scale. Monographs of the Society for Research in Child Development, 43* (5-6, Serial No. 177).

Astington, J., Harris, P.L., & Olson, D.R. (Eds.). (1988). *Developing theories of mind.* Cambridge, UK: Cambridge University Press.

Bandura, A. (1992). Social cognitive theory. In R. Vasta (Ed.), *Annals of child development: Six theories of child development: Revised formulations and current issues* (pp. 1–60). Bristol, PA: Jessica Kingsley Publishers.

Banks, M., & Salapatek, P. (1983). Infant visual perception. In P.H. Mussen (Series Ed.) & M.M. Haith & J.J. Campos (Vol. Eds.), *Handbook of child psychology: Vol. 2. Infancy and developmental psychobiology* (4th ed., pp. 435–572). New York: John Wiley & Sons.

Barden, R.C., Zelko, F.A., Duncan, S.W., & Masters, J.C. (1980). Children's consensual knowledge about the experimental determinants of emotion. *Journal of Personality and Social Psychology, 39,* 968–976.

Barrett, K.C. (1998). A functionalist perspective to the development of emotions. In M.F. Mascolo & S. Griffin (Eds.), *What develops in emotional development? Emotions, personality and psychotherapy* (pp. 109–133). New York: Plenum Press.

Barrett, K.C., & Campos, J.J. (1987). Perspectives on emotional development II: A functionalist approach to emotions. In J.D. Osofsky (Ed.), *Handbook of infant development* (2nd ed., pp. 555–578). New York: John Wiley & Sons.

Barrett, K.C., & Campos, J.J. (1991). A diacritical function approach to emotions and coping. In E.M. Cummings, A.L. Greene, & K.H. Karraker (Eds.), *Lifespan developmental psychology: Perspectives on stress and coping* (pp. 21–41). Mahwah, NJ: Lawrence Erlbaum Associates.

Barron, A.P., & Earls, F. (1984). The relation of temperament and social factors of behavior problems in three-year-old children. *Journal of Child Psychology and Psychiatry and Allied Disciplines, 25,* 23–33.

Bates, J.E., & Bayles, K. (1988). Attachment and the development of behavior problems. In J. Belsky & T. Nezworski (Eds.), *Clinical implication of attachment* (pp. 253–299). Mahwah, NJ: Lawrence Erlbaum Associates.

Biringen, Z., Emde, R.N., Campos, J.J., & Appelbaum, M.I. (1995). Affective reorganization in the infant, the mother, and the dyad: The role of upright locomotion and its timing. *Child Development, 66,* 499–514.

Biringen, Z., & Robinson, J.L. (1991). Emotional availability in mother–child interactions: A reconceptualization for research. *American Journal of Orthopsychiatry, 61,* 258–271.

460

Brazelton., T.B., Koslowski, B., & Main, M. (1974). The origins of reciprocity: The early mother–infant interaction. In M. Lewis & L.A. Rosenblum (Eds.), *The effect of the infant on its caregiver* (pp. 49–76). New York: John Wiley & Sons.

Bretherton, I., Fritz, J., Zahn-Waxler, C., & Ridgeway, D. (1986). Learning to talk about emotions: A functionalist perspective. *Child Development, 57,* 529–548.

Brown, D. (1993). Affective development, psychopathology, and adaptation. In S.L. Ablon, D. Brown, E.J. Khantzian, & J.E. Mack (Eds.), *Human feelings: Explorations in affect development and meaning* (pp. 5–66). Hillsdale, NJ: Analytic Press.

Brown, J.R., & Dunn, J. (1991). "You can cry mum": The social and developmental implications of talk about internal states. *British Journal of Developmental Psychology, 9,* 237–256.

Brown, J.R., & Dunn, J. (1992). Talk with your mother or your sibling? Developmental changes in early family conversations about feelings. *Child Development, 63,* 336–349.

Brown, J.R., & Dunn, J. (1996). Continuities in emotion understanding from three to six years. *Child Development, 67,* 789–802.

Bucci, W. (1997). The emotion schemas and their vicissitudes. In W. Bucci, *Psychoanalysis and cognitive science: A multiple code theory* (pp. 195–213). New York: Guilford Press.

Calkins, S.D., & Johnson, M.C. (1998). Toddler regulation of distress to frustrating events: Temperamental and maternal correlates. *Infant Behavior and Development, 21,* 379–395.

Campos, J.J., & Barrett, K.C. (1985). Toward a new understanding of emotions and their development. In C.E. Izard, J. Kagan, & R.B. Zajonc (Eds.), *Emotions, cognition and behavior* (pp. 229–263). New York: Cambridge University Press.

Campos, J.J., Campos, R.G., & Barrett, K.C. (1989). Emergent themes in the study of emotional development and emotion regulation. *Developmental Psychology, 25,* 394–402.

Cassidy, J. (1994). Emotion regulation: Influences of attachment relationships. *Monographs of the Society for Research in Child Development, 59,* 228–249.

Cicchetti, D., Rogosch, F.A., Toth, S.L., & Spagnola, M. (1997). Affect, cognition, and the emergence of self-knowledge in the toddler offspring of depressed mothers. *Journal of Experimental Child Psychology, 67,* 338–362.

Clark, R. (1986, April). *Maternal affective disturbance and child competence.* Paper presented at the International Conference on Infant Studies, Los Angeles.

Cummings, E.M., & Davies, P. (1994). *Children and marital conflict: The impact of family dispute and resolution.* New York: Guilford Press.

Davidson, R.T., & Fox, N.A. (1982). Asymmetrical brain activity discriminates between positive and negative affective stimuli in human infants. *Science, 218,* 1235–1237.

Davies, P.T., & Cummings, E.M. (1994). Marital conflict and child adjustment: An emotional security hypothesis. *Psychological Bulletin, 116,* 387–411.

Davies, P.T., & Cummings, E.M. (1995). Children's emotions as organizers of their reactions to inter adult anger: A functionalist perspective. *Developmental Psychology, 31,* 677–684.

Dawson, G. (1994). Frontal electroencephalographic correlates of individual differences in emotion expression in infants: A brain systems perspective on emotion. *Monographs for the Society for Research in Child Development, 59,* 135–151.

DeGangi, G.A., Porges, S.W., Sickel, R.Z., & Greenspan, S.I. (1993). Four-year follow-up of a sample of regulatory disordered infants. *Infant Mental Health Journal, 14,* 330–343.

Demos, V. (1986). Crying in early infancy: An illustration of the motivational function of affect. In T.B. Brazelton & M.W. Yogman (Eds.), *Affective development in infancy* (pp. 39–73). Norwood, NJ: Ablex.

Denham, S.A. (1989). Maternal affect and toddlers' social-emotional competence. *American Journal of Orthopsychiatry, 59,* 368–376.

Denham, S.A. (1993). Maternal emotional responsiveness and toddlers' social-emotional competence. *Journal of Child Psychology and Psychiatry and Allied Disciplines, 34,* 715–728.

Denham, S.A., & Auerbach, S. (1995). Mother–child dialogue about emotions and preschoolers' emotional competence. *Genetic, Social and General Psychology Monographs, 121,* 313–337.

Denham, S.A., & Burton, R. (1996). A social-emotional intervention for at risk four-year-olds. *Journal of School Psychology, 34,* 225–245.

Denham, S.A., Cook, M.C., & Zoller, D. (1992). "Baby looks very sad": Implications of conversations about feelings between mother and preschooler. *British Journal of Developmental Psychology, 10,* 301–315.

Denham, S.A., & Grout, L. (1993). Socialization of emotion: Pathway to preschoolers' emotional and social competence. *Journal of Nonverbal Behavior, 17,* 205–227.

Denham, S.A., Mitchell-Copeland, J., Strandberg, K., Auerbach, S., & Blair, K. (1997). Parental contributions to preschoolers' emotional competence: Direct and indirect effects. *Motivation and Emotion, 21,* 65–86.

Dodge, K.A. (1990). Developmental psychopathology in children of depressed mothers. *Developmental Psychology, 26,* 3–6.

Dunn, J., Bretherton, I., & Munn, P. (1987). Conversations about feeling states between mothers and their young children. *Developmental Psychology, 23,* 132–139.

Dunn, J., & Brown, J. (1994). Affect expression in the family, children's understanding of emotions and their interactions with others. *Merrill-Palmer Quarterly, 40,* 120–137.

Dunn, J., Brown, J., & Beardsall, L. (1991). Family talk about feeling states and children's later understanding of others' emotions. *Developmental Psychology, 27,* 448–455.

Dunn, J., Brown, J., Slomkowski, C., Tesla, C., & Youngblade, L. (1991). Young children's understanding of other people's feelings and beliefs: Individual differences and their antecedents. *Child Development, 62,* 1352–1366.

Eastman, M. (1997). *Taming the dragon in your child.* New York: John Wiley & Sons.

Egeland, B., & Erickson, M.F. (1987). Psychologically unavailable caregiving. In M.R. Brassard, R. Germain, & S.N. Hart (Eds.), *Psychological maltreatment of children and youth* (pp. 110–120). New York: Pergamon Press.

Eisenberg, N., & Fabes, R.A. (1992). Emotion, self–regulation, and the development of social competence. In M.S. Clark (Ed.), *Review of personality and social psychology* (Vol. 14, pp. 119–150). Thousand Oaks, CA: Sage.

Eisenberg, N., Fabes, R.A., Nyman, M., Bernzweig, J., & Pinuelas, A. (1994). The relations of emotionality and regulation to children's anger-related reactions. *Child Development, 65,* 109–128.

Ekman, P. (1984). Expression and the nature of emotion. In K.R. Scherer & P. Ekman (Eds.), *Approaches to emotion* (pp. 319–343). Mahwah, NJ: Lawrence Erlbaum Associates.

El-Sheikh, M., Cummings, E.M., & Reiter, S. (1996). Preschoolers' responses to ongoing interadult conflict: The role of prior exposure to resolved versus unresolved arguments. *Journal of Abnormal Child Psychology, 24,* 665–679.

Erikson, E. (1950). *Childhood and society.* New York: Norton.

Fabes, R.A., Eisenberg, W., Karbon, M., Bernzwerg, J., Speer, A.L., & Carlo, G. (1994). Socialization of children's vicarious emotional responding and prosocial behavior: Relations with mothers' perceptions of children's emotional reactivity. *Developmental Psychology, 30,* 44–55.

Fendrich, M., Warner, V., & Weissman, M.M. (1990). Family risk factors, parental depression, and psychopathology in offspring. *Developmental Psychology, 26,* 40–50.

Field, T. (1994). The effects of mother's physical and emotional unavailability on emotion regulation. *Monographs for the Society for Research in Child Development, 59,* 208–227.

Field, T.M. (1981). Infant gaze aversion and heart rate during face-to-face interactions. *Infant Behavior and Development, 4,* 307–315.

Field, T.M. (1992). Infants of depressed mothers. *Development and Psychopathology, 4,* 49–66.

Fish, B., & Dixon, W.J. (1978). Vestibular hyporeactivity in infants at risk for schizophrenia: Association with critical developmental disorders. *Archives of General Psychiatry, 35,* 963–971.

Fogel, A., Nwokah, E., Dedo, J.Y., Messinger, D., Dickson, K.L., Matusov, E., & Holt, S.A. (1992). Social process theory of emotion: A dynamic systems approach. *Social Development, 1,* 122–142.

Fox, N.A. (1989). Psychophysiological correlates of emotional reactivity during the first year of life. *Developmental Psychology, 25,* 364–372.

Freud, S. (1953). Three essays on the theory of sexuality. In J. Strachey (Ed. and Trans.), *The standard edition of the complete psychological works of Sigmund Freud* (Vol. 7). London: Hogarth Press. (Original work published 1903.)

Gardner, F.E.M. (1989). Inconsistent parenting: Is there evidence for a link with children's conduct problems? *Journal of Abnormal Child Psychology, 17,* 223–233.

Goldsmith, H., Buss, A., Plomin, R., Rothbart, M., Thomas, A., Chess, S., Hinde, R., & McCall, R. (1987). What is temperament? Four Approaches. *Child Development, 58,* 505–529.

Goodman, S.H., Brogan, D., Lynch, M.E., & Fielding, B. (1993). Social and emotional competence in children of depressed mothers. *Child Development, 64,* 516–531.

Gottman, J.M. (1986). The observation of social process. In J.M. Gottman & J.G. Parker (Eds.), *Conversation of friends: Speculations on affective development. Studies in emotion and social interaction* (pp. 5–100). Cambridge: Cambridge University Press.

Gottman, J.M., Katz, L.F., & Hooven, C. (1997). *Meta-emotion: How families communicate emotionally.* Mahwah, NJ: Lawrence Erlbaum Associates.

Grolnick, W.S., Bridges, L.J., & Connell, J.P. (1996). Emotion regulation in two-year-olds: Strategies and emotional expression in four contexts. *Child Development, 67,* 928–941.

Gunnar, M. (1998). Quality of care and the buffering of stress physiology: Its potential role in protecting the developing brain. *IMPrint, 21,* 4–7.

Harris, P.L. (1989). *Children and emotion: The development of psychological understanding.* Oxford, UK: Basil Blackwell.

Harris, P.L., Johnson, C., Hutton, D., Andrews, G., & Cooke, T. (1989). Young children's theory of mind and emotion. *Cognition and Emotion, 3,* 379–400.

Harter, S., & Buddin, B.J. (1987). Children's understanding of the simultaneity of two emotions: A five-stage developmental acquisition sequence. *Developmental Psychology, 23,* 388–399.

Himmelfarb, S., Hock, E., & Wenar, C. (1985). Infant temperament and noncompliant behavior at four years. A longitudinal study. *Genetic, Social and General Psychology Monographs, 111,* 7–21.

Hinde, R.A., Tamplin, A., & Barrett, J. (1993). Home correlates of aggression in preschool. *Aggressive Behavior, 19,* 85–105.

Howe, N. (1991). Sibling-directed internal state language, perspective-taking, and affective behavior. *Child Development, 62,* 1503–1512.

Hubbard, J.A., & Cole, J.D. (1994). Emotional correlates of social competence in children's peer relationships. *Merrill-Palmer Quarterly, 40,* 1–20.

Hughes, C., & Dunn, J. (1998). Understanding mind and emotion: Longitudinal associations with mental-state talk between friends. *Developmental Psychology, 34,* 1026–1037.

Hyson, M.C., & Lee, K.M. (1996). Assessing early childhood teachers' beliefs about emotions: Content, contexts, and implications for practice. *Early Education and Development, 7,* 59–78.

Izard, C.E. (1971). *The face of emotion.* New York: Appleton-Century-Crofts.

Johnston, J.R., Gonzales, R., & Campbell, L.E. (1987). Ongoing post-divorce conflict and child disturbance. *Journal of Abnormal Child Psychology, 15,* 493–509.

Kagan, J. (1994). Distinctions among emotions, moods and temperamental qualities. In P. Ekman & R.J. Davidson (Eds.), *The nature of emotion: Fundamental questions* (pp. 74–78). New York: Oxford University Press.

Kagan, J., Reznick, J.S., & Snidman, N. (1988). Biological bases of childhood shyness. *Science, 240,* 167–171.

Kagan, J., & Snidman, N. (1991). Infant predictors of inhibited and uninhibited profiles. *Psychological Science, 2,* 40–44.

Kernberg, O. (1990). New perspectives in psychoanalytic affect theory. In R. Plutchik & H. Kellerman (Eds.), *Emotions: Theory, research, and experience* (pp. 115–131). San Diego: Academic Press.

Kopp, C.B. (1989). Regulation of distress and negative emotions: A developmental view. *Developmental Psychology, 25,* 343–354.

Laible, D.J., & Thompson, R.A. (1998). Attachment and emotional understanding in preschool children. *Developmental Psychology, 34,* 1038–1045.

Landy, S., & Peters, R. DeV. (1992). *The incidence of preschool behavior problems identified in a tracking system at school entry.* Paper presented at the World Infant Psychiatry Conference, Chicago.

Lazarus, R.S. (1990). Constructs of the mind in adaptation. In N.L. Stein, B. Leventhal, & T. Trabasso (Eds.), *Psychological and biological approaches to emotions* (pp. 3–19). Mahwah, NJ: Lawrence Erlbaum Associates.

Lazarus, R.S. (1991). *Emotion and adaptation.* New York: Oxford University Press.

Lehman, E.B., Denham, S.A., Moser, M.H., & Reeves, S.L. (1992). Soft object and pacifier attachments in young children: The role of security of attachment to the mother. *Journal of Child Psychology and Psychiatry and Allied Disciplines, 33,* 1205–1215.

Lewis, M. (1985). The role of emotion in development. *Journal of Children in Contemporary Society, 17,* 7–22.

Lewis, M., & Michalson, L. (1983). *Children's emotions and moods: Developmental theory and measurement.* New York: Plenum Press.

Lutz, C.A. (1988). *Unnatural emotions: Everyday sentiments on a Micronesian atoll and their challenge to Western theory.* Chicago: University of Chicago Press.

Mahler, M., Pine, F., & Bergman, A. (1975). *The psychological birth of the human infant: Symbiosis and individuation.* New York: Basic Books.

Malastesta-Magai, C., Leak, S., Tesman, J., Shepard, B., Culver, C., & Smaggia, B. (1994). Profiles of emotional development: Individual differences in facial and vocal expression of emotion during the second and third years of life. *International Journal of Behavioral Development, 17,* 239–269.

Mangelsdorf, S.C., Shapiro, J.R., & Marzolf, D. (1995). Developmental and temperamental differences in emotion regulation in infancy. *Child Development, 66,* 1817–1828.

Manstead, A.S.R., & Edwards, R. (1992). Communicative aspects of children's emotional competence. In K.T. Strongman (Ed.), *International review of studies on emotion* (Vol. 2, pp. 167–195). New York: John Wiley & Sons.

Meerum Terwogt, M., Koops, W., Oosterhoff, T., & Olthof, T. (1986). Development in processing multiple emotional situations. *Journal of General Psychology, 11,* 109–119.

Mumme, D.L., Fernald, A., & Herrera, C. (1996). Infant's responses to facial and vocal emotional signals in a social referencing paradigm. *Child Development, 67,* 3219–3237.

Mussen, P.H. (Ed.). (1970). *Carmichael's manual of child psychology: Vol. 18, 2.* (3rd ed.). New York: John Wiley & Sons.

Osofsky, J.D. (Ed.). (1987). *Handbook of infant development* (2nd Ed.). New York: John Wiley & Sons.

Parritz, R.H. (1996). A descriptive analysis of toddler coping in challenging situations. *Infant Behavior and Development, 19,* 171–180.

Parritz, R.H., Mangelsdorf, S., & Gunnar, M.R. (1992). Control, social referencing and infants' appraisal of threat. In S. Feinman (Ed.), *Social referencing and the social construction of reality in infancy* (pp. 209–228). New York: Plenum Press.

Patterson, G.R. (1982). *A social learning approach to family intervention: III. Coercive family process.* Eugene, OR: Castalia.

Peng, M., Johnson, C., Pollock, J., Glasspool, R., & Harris, P. (1992). Training young children to acknowledge mixed emotions. *Cognition and Emotion, 6,* 387–401.

Pettit, G.S., & Bates, J.E. (1989). Family interaction patterns and children's behavior problems from infancy to 4 years. *Developmental Psychology, 25,* 413–420.

Piaget, S. (1959). *The language and thought of the child* (Gabain, Trans.). London: Routledge & Kegan Paul.

Radke-Yarrow, M., Richters, J., & Wilson, E. (1988). Child development in a network of relationships. In R.A. Hinde & J. Stevenson-Hinde (Eds.), *Relationships within families: Mutual influences* (pp. 48–67). Oxford, UK: Oxford University Press.

Radke-Yarrow, M., & Zahn-Waxler, C. (1982). Roots, motives and patterns in children's prosocial behavior. In J. Reykowski, J. Karylowski, D. Bartal, & E. Staub (Eds.), *Origins and maintenance of prosocial behavior.* New York: Plenum Press.

Roberts, W., & Strayer, J. (1987). Parents' responses to the emotional distress of their children: Relations with children's competence. *Developmental Psychology, 23,* 415–422.

Robinson, J., Little, C., & Biringen, Z. (1993). Emotional communication in mother-toddler relationships: Evidence for early gender differentiation. *Merrill-Palmer Quarterly, 39,* 496–517.

Rothbart, M.K., & Derryberry, D. (1987). Development of individual differences in temperament. In M.E. Lamb & A.L. Brown (Eds.), *Advances in Developmental Psychology, Vol. 1* (pp. 37–86). Mahwah, NJ: Lawrence Erlbaum Associates.

Saarni, C. (1997). Coping with aversive feelings. *Motivation and Emotion, 21,* 45–63.

Saarni, C. (1999). *The development of emotional competence.* New York: Guilford Press.

Schibuk, M., Bond, M., & Bouffard, R. (1989). The development of defenses in childhood. *Canadian Journal of Psychiatry, 34,* 581–588.

Seligman, M.H. (1995). *The optimistic child: A revolutionary program that safeguards children against depression and builds lifelong resilience.* New York: Houghton Mifflin.

Shields, A.M., Cicchetti, D., & Ryan, R.M. (1994). The development of emotional and behavioral self-regulation and social competence among maltreated school-age children. *Development and Psychopathology, 6,* 57–76.

Skinner, B.F. (1953). *Science and human behavior.* New York: Macmillan.

Sorce, J.F., & Emde, R. (1981). Mother's presence is not enough: Effect of emotional availability on infant exploration. *Developmental Psychology, 17,* 737–745.

Sorce, J.F., Emde, R., Campos, J., & Klinnert, M. (1985). Maternal emotional signaling: Its effect on the visual cliff behavior of 1-year-olds. *Developmental Psychology, 21,* 195–200.

Spangler, G., Schieche, M., Ilg, U., Maier, U., & Ackermann, C. (1994). Maternal sensitivity as an external organizer for biobehavioral regulation in infancy. *Developmental Psychobiology, 27,* 425–437.

Sroufe, L.A. (1996). *Emotional development: The organization of emotional life in the early years.* New York: Cambridge University Press.

Sroufe, L.A., Fox, N.E., & Pancake, V.R. (1983). Attachment and dependency in developmental perspective. *Child Development, 54,* 1615–1627.

Stechler, G., & Carpenter, G. (1967). A viewpoint on early affective development. In J. Hellmath (Ed.), *The exceptional infant* (pp. 163–189). Seattle: Special Child Publications.

Stern, D.N. (1983). *The role and nature of empathy in mother–infant interaction.* Paper presented at the Second World Congress of Infant Psychiatry, Cannes, France.

Stern, D.N. (1985). *The interpersonal world of the infant: A view from psychoanalysis and developmental psychology.* New York: Basic Books.

Stifter, C.A., & Moyer, D. (1991). The regulation of positive affect: Gaze aversion activity during mother–infant interaction. *Infant Behavior and Development, 14,* 111–123.

Terwogt, M.M., & Olthof, T. (1991). Awareness and self-regulation of emotion in young children. In C. Saarni & P.L. Harris (Eds.), *Children's understanding of emotion.* New York: Cambridge University Press.

Tomkins, S.S. (1962). *Affect, imagery, consciousness: Vol. 1. The positive affects.* New York: Springer.

Tomkins, S.S. (1963). *Affect, imagery, consciousness: Vol. 2. The negative affects.* New York: Springer.

Tomkins, S.S. (1984). Affect theory. In K.R. Scherer & P. Ekman (Eds.), *Approaches to emotion* (pp. 163–196). Mahwah, NJ: Lawrence Erlbaum Associates.

Tronick, E.Z. (1989). Emotions and emotional communication in infants. *American Psychologist, 44,* 112–119.

Walden, T. (1991). Infant social referencing. In J. Garber & K. Dodge (Eds.), *The development of emotion regulation and dysregulation* (pp. 69–88). New York: Cambridge University Press.

Walker, E., & Emory, E. (1983). Infants at risk for psychopathology: Offspring of schizophrenic parents. *Child Development, 54,* 1269–1285.

Watson, J.S. (1966). The development and generalization of "contingency awareness" in early infancy: Some hypotheses. *Merrill-Palmer Quarterly, 12,* 123–135.

Weinberg, M.K., & Tronick, E.Z. (1996). Infant affective reactions to the resumption of maternal interaction after the still-face. *Child Development, 67,* 905–914.

Wolchik, S., & Sandler, I. (Eds.). (1997). *Handbook of children's coping: Linking theory with intervention.* New York: Plenum Press.

Wolfe, D.A., Jaffe, P., Wilson, S.K., & Zak, L. (1985). Children of battered women: The relation of child behavior to family violence and maternal stress. *Journal of Consulting and Clinical Psychology, 53,* 657–665.

Zahn-Waxler, C., Radke-Yarrow, M., & King, R.A. (1979). Child-rearing and children's prosocial initiations toward victims of distress. *Child Development, 50,* 319–330.

FURTHER READING ON THE TOPIC

Costello, J. (1985, February). Handling feelings. *Parents Magazine, 60*(1), 140.

Dodge, K., & Garber, J. (Eds.). (1991). *The development of emotion regulation and dysregulation.* New York: Cambridge University Press.

Dunn, J. (1977). *Distress and comfort.* Cambridge, MA: Harvard University Press.

Eyre, L. (1994). *Teaching your children joy.* New York: Fireside.

Faber, A., & Mazlish, E. (1987). *Siblings without rivalry: How to help your children live together so you can live too.* New York: Avon Books.

Garber, S., Daniels, M., & Spizman, R. (1993). *Monsters under the bed and other childhood fears: Helping your child overcome anxieties, fears and phobias.* New York: Willard.

Gaylin, W. (1989). *The rage within: Anger in modern life.* New York: Penguin Books.

Goleman, D. (1997). *Emotional intelligence.* New York: Bantam Books.

Gottman, J.M. (with J. DeClaire). (1997). *The heart of parenting.* New York: Simon & Schuster.

Greenspan, S.I., & Greenspan, N.T. (1989). *The essential partnership: How parents and children can meet the emotional challenges of infancy and childhood.* New York: Viking.

Greenspan, S.I., & Greenspan, N.T. (1994). *First feelings: Milestones in the emotional development of your baby and child.* New York: Penguin.

Katz, L.G. (1990, June). When your child is angry. *Parents Magazine, 65*(1), 178.

Kellerman, J. (1981). *Helping the fearful child: A parent's guide to everyday and problem anxieties.* New York: Norton.

Kopp, C. (1982). Antecedents of self-regulation: A developmental perspective. *Developmental Psychology, 18,* 199–214.

Landy, S., & Peters, R. DeV. (1992). Toward an understanding of a developmental paradigm for aggressive conduct problems during the preschool years. In R. DeV. Peters, R.J. McMahon, & V.L. Quinsey (Eds.), *Aggression and violence throughout the life span* (pp. 1–30). Beverly Hills: Sage Publications.

Lerner, H.G. (1988). *The dance of anger.* New York: Harper & Row.

LeShan, E. (1985). *When your child drives you crazy.* New York: St. Martin's Press.

Lewis, M., & Saarni, C. (1985). *The socialization of emotions.* New York: Plenum Press.

Marzollo, J., Prentice, S., & McCall, R.B. (1986, January). "Mommy, I'm scared!" *Parents Magazine, 61*(6), 67.

McKay, M., Roger, P.D., & McKay, J. (1989). *When anger hurts: Quieting the storm within.* Oakland, CA: New Harbinger.

Parens, H. (1987). *Anger in our children: Coping with it constructively.* Northvale, NJ: Jason Aronson.

Saarni, C. (1999). *The development of emotional competence.* New York: Guilford Press.

Saarni, C., & Harris, P. (1989). *Children's understanding of emotions.* Cambridge, UK: Cambridge University Press.

Samalin, N., & Whitney, C. (1995). *Love and anger: The parental dilemma.* New York: Penguin Books.

Sammons, W.A.H. (1991). *The self-calmed baby: A liberating new approach to parenting your infant.* New York: St. Martin's Paperbacks.

Schwartzman, M. (1992). *The anxious parent: Freeing yourself from the fears and stresses of parenting.* New York: Fireside Books.

Segal, J. (1988, August). "I'm so angry!" *Parents Magazine, 63*(5), 106.

Shure, M.B., & Di Geronimo, T.F. (1994). *Raising a thinking child.* New York: Henry, Holt and Company.

Tavris, C. (1989). *Anger: The misunderstood emotion.* New York: Touchstone Books.

Williams, R., & Williams, V. (1998). *Anger kills: Seventeen strategies for controlling the hostility that can harm your health.* New York: Harper Perennial.

Wolman, B. (1978). *Children's fears.* New York: Grosset & Dunlap.

CHILDREN'S BOOKS ABOUT EMOTIONS

Alder, K., & McBride, R. (1986). *For sale: One sister—cheap!* Chicago: Children's Press.

Aliki. (1984). *Feelings.* New York: Greenwillow Books.

Anholt, C. & Anholt, L. (1996). *What makes me happy?* Cambridge, MA: Candlewick Press.

Blegvad, L. (1985). *Anna banana and me.* New York: Atheneum Books.

Bourgeois, P. (1987). *Franklin in the dark.* Toronto: Scholastic.

Bourgeois, P. (1989). *Grandma's secret.* Toronto: Kids Can Press.

Brandenberg, F. (1976). *I wish I was sick, too!* New York: Greenwillow Books.

Cain, B.S., & Patterson, A. (2000). *Double dip feelings: A book to help children understand emotions.* New York: Magination.

Carlson, N. (1985). *Witch lady.* Minneapolis, MN: Carolrhoda Books.

Carlson, N. (1992). *What if it never stops raining?* New York: Viking Children's Books.

Cohen, M. (1989). *Jim meets the thing.* New York: Yearling Books.

Cohen, M. (1990). *The real-skin rubber monster mask.* New York: Greenwillow.

Cooney, N.E. (1990). *Go away monsters, lickety split!* New York: G.P. Putnam's.

Crowe, R. L. (1993). *Clyde monster.* New York: Puffin Books.

Cutler, J. (1993). *Darcy and Gran don't like babies.* New York: Scholastic.

Denton, K.M. (1988). *Granny is a darling.* London: Walker Books.

Drescher, H. (1999). *Simon's book.* New York: Econo-Clad Books.

Drescher, J.E. (1993). *The birth-order blues.* New York: Viking Children's Books.

Edwards, F.B. (1991). *Melody Mooner stayed up all night.* Newburgh, Ontario, Canada: Firefly Books.

Emberley, E. (1993). *Go away, big green monster!* Boston: Ladybird Books.

Gackenback, D. (1979). *Harry and the terrible whatzit.* New York: Houghton Mifflin.

Gliori, D. (1992). *My little brother.* Cambridge, MA: Candlewick Press.

Goode, D. (1993). *I hear a noise.* New York: Unicorn Paperbacks.

Green, J.F., & Hendry, L. (1987). *There's a dragon in my closet.* Toronto: North Winds Press.

Grifalconi, A. (1987). *Darkness and the butterfly.* Boston: Little, Brown.

Havill, J. (1993). *Jamaica and Brianna.* Boston: Houghton Mifflin.

Hazen, B.S. (1990). *Wally the worry-warthog.* New York: Clarion Books.

Henkes, K. (2000). *Lilly's purple plastic purse.* New York: Live Oak Media.

Hines, A.G. (1986). *Don't worry, I'll find you.* New York: Dutton Children's Books.

Hoban, R. (1993). *A baby sister for Frances.* New York: HarperCollins Children's Books.

Hoban, R. (1994). *A birthday for Frances.* New York: HarperCollins Children's Books.

Hoban, R. (1995). *Bedtime for Frances.* New York: HarperCollins Children's Books.

Hoellwarth, C.C. (1990). *The underbed.* Intercourse, PA: Good Books.

Howe, J. (1987). *I wish I were a butterfly.* New York: Gulliver Books.

Keller, H. (1987). *Lizzie's invitation.* New York: Greenwillow Books.

Kraus, R., Arugeo, J., & Arugeo, D.A. (1989). *Where are you going, little mouse?* New York: Mulberry Books.

Lasky, K. (1993). *The tantrum.* Toronto: Maxwell Macmillan Canada.

Mayer, M. (1987). *There's an alligator under my bed.* New York: Dutton.

Mayer, M. (1992). *There's a nightmare in my closet.* New York: Dutton.

Mayer, M. (1999). *There's something in my attic.* New York: Econo-Clad Books.

Moses, B. (1994). *I feel angry.* Hove, England: Wayland.

Moses, B. (1994). *I feel frightened.* Hove, England: Wayland.

Moses, B. (1994). *I feel jealous.* Hove, England: Wayland.

Moses, B. (1994). *I feel sad.* Hove, England: Wayland.

Murphy, J.B. (1985). *Feelings.* New York: Firefly Books.

Polacco, P. (1997). *Thunder Cake.* New York: Paper Star.

Preston, E.M. (1976). *The temper tantrum book.* New York: Puffin Books.

Rockwell, A.F. (1995). *No! No! No!* New York: Simon and Schuster.

Sharmat, M.W. (1978). *Thornton, the worrier.* New York: Holiday House.

Smith, W. (1988). *The lonely, only mouse.* London: Puffin Books.

Zolotow, C. (1982). *The quarreling book.* New York: Trophy.

Zolotow, C. (1989). *The hating book.* New York: Trophy.

APPENDIX: SELECTED ASSESSMENT INSTRUMENTS

ASSESSING EMOTION REGULATION

A child's level of emotion recognition and regulation can be measured in a variety of ways, and many research studies use multiple measures:

- Having parents, child care workers, or teachers complete questionnaires about children's behavior (e.g., temperament questionnaires) and comparing the responses to norms of the way children of the same age would behave. These are subjective views.

- Observing children in natural settings and recording how they respond to frustration and the strategies they show

- Setting up laboratory situations of children in frustrating situations and observing their behavior

- Analyzing the responses children make to pictures, videotapes, or live situations staged for the assessment

- Observing parents and children interacting in play, during teaching, after separation (e.g., Strange Situation)

- Using noninvasive psychophysiological procedures for measuring certain phenomenon (e.g., heart rate and vagal tone, adrenocortical activity [cortisol levels], brain electrical activity [EEG and hemispheric specialization])

The tests outlined below do not include psychophysiological procedures and only include laboratory measures when they have been standardized and made widely available.

Some tests discussed in other chapters (particularly the chapters on development and temperament and self-regulation) may be applicable here too. These include

- Child Behavior Checklist (CBCL)

- Preschool Behavior Questionnaire (PBQ)

- Eyberg Child Behavior Inventory (ECBI)

- Burke Behavior Rating Scales

- Various temperament measures

Tests to Assess Children's and Parents' Emotion Regulation and Interaction

Table A8.1 includes tests to assess aspects of children's emotion regulation, while parent interactional measures of emotion regulation are described in Table A8.2.

Table A8.1. Selected assessments of children's emotion regulation

Title	Age range	Items/administration time	General description
Ages & Stages Questionnaires: Social-Emotional (ASQ:SE) Squires, J., Bricker, D., & Twombly, E. with Yockelson, S., Davis, M.S., & Kim, Y. (2001). *Ages & Stages Questionnaires: Social-Emotional (ASQ:SE): A parent-completed, child-monitoring system for social-emotional behaviors.* Baltimore: Paul H. Brookes Publishing Co.	6–60 months	8 questionnaires	The *Ages & Stages Questionnaires: Social-Emotional* assist with the monitoring of the social and emotional development of children from birth through the preschool years. Parents answer questions in seven key areas: self-regulation, compliance, communication, adaptive functioning, autonomy, affect, and interaction with people. Professionals evaluate scores, then compare them with empirically derived cutoff points.
The IFEEL Pictures Emde, R.N., Osofsky, J.D., & Butterfield, P.M. (1993). The IFEEL Pictures: A new instrument for interpreting emotions. *Clinical Infant Reports, 5.* Madison, CT: International Universities Press.	2–3 years to adults	20 pictures; 10 minutes	The *IFEEL Pictures* test consists of 30 pictures of 1-year-olds displaying varying emotions. Subjects are asked to name the "strongest and clearest feeling" the baby is showing and to write them on a scoring sheet. A profile of the responses is then developed. Responses are scored according to categories of emotions, arousal level of the emotions, and the number of positive and negative emotions identified.
Infant-Toddler Social and Emotional Assessment (ITSEA) Briggs-Gowan, M.J., & Carter, A.S. (1998). Preliminary acceptability and psychometrics of the Infant-Toddler Social and Emotional Assessment (ITSEA): A new adult-report questionnaire. *Infant Mental Health Journal, 19,* 422–445.	12–36 months	40 items; 40 minutes	The *Infant-Toddler Social and Emotional Assessment (ITSEA)* evaluates social-emotional competence in a variety of areas including four problem areas (externalizing, internalizing, dysregulation and maladaptive behaviors). Each item is rated on a 3-point scale from *not true/rarely* to *very true/often.* Items were chosen by a panel of experts in the fields of infant mental health and child development. A "no opportunity" code can also be used if there has been no opportunity to observe the behavior.
MacArthur Story-Stem Battery (MSSB) Bretherton, I., Oppenheim, D., Buchsbaum, H., Emde, R.N., & The MacArthur Narrative Group (1990). *MacArthur Story-Stem Battery.* Unpublished manual.	Preschoolers	12 story items; 40 minutes	The *MacArthur Story-Stem Battery (MSSB)* test involves 12 story items that describe emotionally laden, conflictual family interactions and children are asked to finish the story. The items are presented and acted out with toys, and the child is asked to "show me and tell me what happens next." The stories are coded for content themes (e.g., empathy, affection), coherence, investment in performance and interaction with the examiner.
Minnesota Preschool Affect Rating Scales (MN-PARS) McPhee, J.T., & Shapiro, E.G. (1993). *Revised Manual for the Minnesota Preschool Affect Rating Scales.* Minneapolis: Division of Pediatric Neurology, University of Minnesota.	8–36 months	Rating of videotape of 24 minutes of child and parent play interaction, 15 scales assessed; 30 minutes	The *Minnesota Preschool Affect Rating Scales (MN-PARS)* assesses behavior in three general areas: expressed emotion, parent–child communication, and arousal/self modulation. Five scales assess aspects of emotions expressed during play. Provides clinical researchers with a way to study the effects of medical and neurological conditions on self-regulation in children.

| Test of Early Socioemotional Development (TOESD) | 3–7 years | 30–36 items; 10 minutes | The *Test of Early Socioemotional Development (TOESD)* examines behavioral perceptions at home, school, and in interpersonal relationships. Children complete a set of three behavior-rating scales, and there is also a sociogram of peer perceptions of the child. Low scores are seen as evidence of problematic behavior. Because positive behaviors are not included, the test is better at identifying problematic behavior than measuring socioemotional competence. |

Hresko, W.P., & Brown, L. (1984). Manual for the Test of Early Socioemotional Development (TOESD). Austin, TX: PRO-ED.

Other commonly used measures

Preschool Socioaffective Profile (PSP)
La Frenière, P.J., Dumas, J.E., Capuano, F., & Dubeau, D. (1993). Development and validation of the preschool socioaffective profile. *Annual Progress in Child Psychiatry and Child Development*, 104–122.

Minnesota Preschool Affect Checklist (MPAC)
Schork, E., & Sroufe, L.A. (1984). The Minnesota Preschool Affect Checklist. Unpublished manuscript. Minneapolis: University of Minnesota.

A System for Identifying Affect Expressions by Holistic Judgments (Affect)
Izard, C.E., Dougherty, L.M. & Hembree, E.A. (1983). *A system for identifying affect expressions by holistic judgments (affect)* (Rev. Ed.). Newark: University of Delaware Instructional Resources Center.

Self-Regulatory Behavior Scoring System
Gianino, A. (1985). *Individual differences in infant response to an interpersonal stress at 6 months.* Unpublished doctoral dissertation, University of Massachusetts, Amherst.

Table A8.2. Selected assessments of parents' emotion regulation

Title	Age range	Items/ administration time	General description
The Emotional Availability Scales (EAS) Infancy and Early Childhood Version Biringen, Z., Robinson, J.L., & Emde, R.N. (1988/1993). *Manual for scoring the Emotional Availability Scales.* Unpublished document. University of Colorado.	Mothers; children from birth to 6 years	Five dimensions, scored on 10 minutes of free play	The *Emotional Availability Scales (EAS)* were developed to measure maternal sensitivity and other interactional characteristics in shorter observations than those used by Mary Ainsworth. Both versions (used at different ages) are global scales of sensitivity focusing on behavioral style rather than discrete behaviors. The EAS examines five relationship dimensions: maternal sensitivity, maternal structuring/intrusiveness, maternal overt and covert hostility, child responsivity to mother, and child involvement with mother.
Parent-Child Early Relational Assessment (ERA) Clarke, R. (1986). *The Parent-Child Early Relational Assessment: Manual and Instrument.* Unpublished manuscript, University of Wisconsin Medical School.	Parents; children from 2 months to 5 years	Videotaped interactions of four 10-minute episodes. Scoring extensive and time consuming	*Parent-Child Early Relational Assessment (ERA)* was developed as a measure of both affective and behavioral aspects of the early parent–child relationship. The measure is intended to measure maternal affect as a regulatory or organizing function for the infant. Dyads can be observed during free play, a structured teaching task, a feeding, and a separation and reunion. The mother is rated on her tone of voice, overall need, expressed affect, attitude toward the child, affective and behavioral involvement, and parental style. The child is rated on expressed affect and overall mood, behavior and adaptive abilities, activity level, and communication.

Other commonly used measures

Emotional Availability Observation Scales
Osofsky, J., Culp, A., Hann, D., & Eberhart-Wright, J. (1990). *Emotional Availability Observation Scales.* Unpublished manuscript, Louisiana State University Medical Center, New Orleans.

Family Expressiveness Questionnaire (FEQ)
Halberstadt, A.G. (1986). Family socialization of emotional expressiveness styles and nonverbal communication skills. *Journal of Personality and Social Psychology, 51,* 827–836.

● ● ● 9

ENCOURAGING CONCENTRATION, PLANNING, AND PROBLEM-SOLVING

In the preschool room, the children are busily engaged in a variety of activities. In one corner, children are involved in acting out a complex story about a sea adventure with monsters and villains, while in another area, children are painting or drawing. In the corner with large blocks, Malgorzata, Tim, and Marion are working together solving a problem—how to make a bridge wide enough for the large fire engine to go under to reach the burning house. Although they use some trial-and-error, if watched closely, it is clear that some of the "experimentation" is taking place in their heads. If you listen carefully you can hear Marion talking aloud about the plans and encouraging herself to keep trying. In fact, these young children are concentrating and engaging in planning and problem-solving as they work out how to build the bridge and make it work.

Although this kind of planning and problem-solving forms the basis for cognitive and intellectual development, it is crucial for emotional and social development, as well. Problem-solving is present in rudimentary form in toddlers, but it is not until children are approximately 4 or 5 years of age that these capacities are fully established. In fact, these abilities of concentration, planning, and problem-solving are absolutely crucial for a child's adjustment to school. Children who have difficulty with these functions, who act impulsively instead of planning, who flit from one activity to another without spending time and concentrating on one, or who give up instead of trying to find a solution, often have difficulty learning and dealing with the other inevitable frustrations and challenges that they encounter everyday in school, at home, and in everyday life.

Views differ as to the best way to stimulate a child's intellectual development and problem-solving in difficult situations in the early years. Numerous articles address the importance of experience on brain development and the need for "quality" time between parents and children. Parents often see it as essential that children are exposed to learning their colors, numbers, and

letters as early as possible. They may think that by doing this they can create a "Superbaby" who will be able to read and do math by 3 or 4 years of age. Because they are aware of the importance of education, they may worry that unless the child is learning these school activities very early they will be surpassed by other children. In fact, there is no evidence that exposing children to flash cards in infancy or intensive educational programs in preschool makes children more intelligent or successful. Providing early stimulation for children with delays has been found to be effective, however. Some psychologists such as David Elkind (1987) have warned parents not to "push" or "hurry" their child and rather to let their children learn by giving them appropriate toys and activities and letting them play. As with most debates, both points of view have their merits.

It is clear that children learn best when the activity is one in which they are interested and that they find challenging. Effective learning takes place when caregivers build on children's natural curiosity and interest and their inborn passion for learning and discovery. This chapter discusses ways to encourage children's ability to concentrate, plan, and problem-solve and describes the development of these capacities.

DEFINITIONS OF CONCENTRATION, PLANNING, AND PROBLEM-SOLVING

Concentration, planning, and problem-solving are familiar words but for clarification, their use in the research literature and in describing children's behavior will be described.

Concentration and the related term *attention* actually refer to several aspects of functioning, and consequently are defined somewhat differently by various writers. The two major behaviors that the words have been used to describe are 1) focusing or "tuning in" on certain stimuli from among the wide range of information available, and 2) information processing or acting on the information that takes place during the time that the stimulus is being focused on. It is clear that children who are able to concentrate are less distracted by other things that are going on and are thus more likely to successfully problem-solve and complete tasks.

Planning involves thinking about a desired outcome before acting and deciding on the actions that need to be taken before taking them. Planning is an important part of problem-solving, but occurs before an act happens. Planning requires some understanding of past, present, and future and for older preschoolers, thinking about an event in another setting and at a different time, and being able to transfer information across situations.

Problem-solving is what children do when they have a goal in mind but are encountering an obstacle to reaching the goal and do not know how to achieve it. Part of the challenge of problem-solving is being able to understand what causes what, believing that making it happen is possible, and choosing a solution that relates to what is going on and is not closed to all sorts of possible options. For example, a child is having a problem fitting in at school, and he is willing to explore with his parents the reasons that he is having these problems. Together, the child and the parents decide on some new ways to approach the other children. By doing so, the child is not totally blaming the other children and is leaving the situation open to being solved.

Some terms that are used in the literature to describe other aspects of these abilities are defined next.

Self-talk (i.e., *private speech*) is "communication with the self," unlike social speech. It is used by preschool-age children as a mediating tool during problem-solving to guide and direct their activity. It also serves a self-regulating function and can be helpful to encourage young children to keep trying and not to give up.

Theory of mind, as mentioned in other chapters, refers to a crucial accomplishment of childhood that occurs at approximately 4 years of age when children become aware of other people's thoughts, beliefs, and desires, and how they differ from their own. These aspects of an individual's mental world are, of course, different from the physical and factual worlds, and thus young children also are gradually acquiring the ability to distinguish between reality (i.e., the way things actually are) and appearance (i.e., the way they are perceived as being).

Executive functioning, a somewhat strange phrase to use to describe a capacity when it relates to early childhood, refers to a set of abilities that are used to problem-solve in order to attain a goal. These abilities are separate from language, perception, and memory; they instead include inhibition of attending to irrelevant stimuli, planning, and forming a mental representation of the task. Some researchers have referred to these functions as capacities of the prefrontal cortex (PFC), although it is also recognized that other brain regions may play a role.

THEORIES OF CONCENTRATION, PLANNING, AND PROBLEM-SOLVING

A number of theories have considered the nature of intelligence, with the most influential being that of Jean Piaget (1963). Piaget's theory is outlined in Chapter 1, however, it should be pointed out that his research has significantly contributed to our understanding of children's thinking and problem-solving. He described how young children adapt existing schemas (i.e., ways of thinking) to accommodate new ideas and situations, a process he called *adaptation.* Piaget saw cognitive development occurring through direct experiences of learning, social contact with and observation of others, and maturation or biological development.

While research has supported a number of Piaget's views, some of them have been found not to be applicable and have ignored the socioemotional aspects of children's functioning that significantly influence their thinking. Since Piaget's pioneer work, a number of theorists have continued to further describe the nature of intelligence, as well as how it can best be enhanced. These theorists include Gardner (1983), Hunt (1965), Sternberg (1988), Vygotsky (1962), and White (1959). Recently, a number of developmentalists and researchers have considered essential aspects of information processing, and particularly those that relate to attention and concentration, planning and executive functioning, and short-term memory as the basis for cognitive development. Researchers have considered the growth of the child's theory of mind, which has resulted in a number of studies of how a child acquires the capacity to understand other people's minds and then to take on a variety of new cognitive capacities, especially representational thought. They have also considered how theory of mind relates to executive functioning. Specific theories are outlined in Table 9.1.

THE IMPORTANCE OF CONCENTRATION, PLANNING, AND PROBLEM-SOLVING

The abilities to concentrate, to plan cognitive strategies, and to problem-solve are crucial for human learning and cognitive functioning. In other words, without these abilities children are compromised in their capacity to use language, to remember, and to think. Difficulties with concentration, planning, and problem-solving can affect children's behavior as well. Children without these abilities will have significant difficulty coping with new situations and modifying their behavior to deal with frustrating events. Consequently, it is crucial that children acquire these abilities in order to succeed in school, and deficits in any of these processes can re-

Table 9.1. Theories of concentration, planning, and problem-solving

Theorist	Type of theory	Major constructs
White (1959) Hunt (1965)	Mastery and competence	Infants are born with an intrinsic motivation to explore their environment, which results in independent and persistent task-directed behavior in problem-solving situations
		Mastery efforts of children believed to be predictive of later cognitive competence
		Children's *approach* to learning, not just the content, believed to be critical in later development
		Response from people in the environment is crucial to maintain mastery efforts
Vygotsky (1962)	Social constructivism	Saw higher mental functions as operating first on a social level and then on an individual level
		Speech seen as a uniquely human capacity that allows children to control their behavior
		The "zone of proximal development" described as the developmental level at which children can best learn
		Children learn self-regulation by being led through a task by an adult, preferably in their "zone of proximal development"
Gardner (1983)	Multiple intelligences	Described intelligence not as a single entity but as many types of intelligent behavior
		Described certain fundamental intellectual abilities, including linguistic, musical, spatial, and logical-mathematical
		Each individual has different competencies in the areas and needs a different educational program
Fagan (1984) Zelazo (1988) Bornstein & Mayes (1991) Colombo (1993) McCall (1994)	Infant attention and development	Emphasized that tests of development administered in the first 2 years of life do not predict later IQ score
		Considered infant attention, habituation, and recognition memory as possible predictors of later intelligence
		Looked for an "underlying mechanism" as predictive of later intelligence; for example, the ability to "inhibit" attending to other stimuli in order to concentrate on one particular stimulus or problem and/or the speed of processing information
Sternberg (1988)	"Triarchic" theory of intelligence	Examined three different kinds of intelligence or mental abilities: information processing, ability to deal with novel problems, and practical intelligence
		Information processing components include planning and reasoning
Perner (1991) Wellman (1992) Astington (1993) Baron-Cohen (1994)	Theory of mind	Children's understanding of their own and others' mental states seen as a crucial aspect of development
		Having a theory of mind has been linked to the capacity for metarepresentational thought, executive functioning, and pretense
		Children acquire an understanding of theory of mind at 4 years of age, although modification of the context in which testing takes place can sometimes place it earlier
		Theory of mind seen as influencing both cognitive capacity and social abilities
Bransford & Stein (1993) Butterfield, Albertson, & Johnston (1995)	Information processing/ executive functioning	Focused on developing models of information processing, thinking, and problem-solving
		Discussed the role of various kinds of memory in receiving and storing information
		Looked at developmental changes in the acquisition of various control processes and changes in knowledge base as the child builds knowledge and skills in various areas of expertise
		Examined components of problem-solving such as problem identification and definition, selecting approaches, and trying them out

476

sult in school failure. These abilities affect functioning in the areas of development listed subsequently.

School Achievement/Cognitive Ability   A child's ability to set other activities aside in order to concentrate on school assignments and to plan and problem-solve about the best ways to complete them is crucial for school success. Even children with high intelligence who are unable to use these abilities may fail to learn relevant material or to acquire basic skills in reading and mathematics, which compromises their success in school and later in the workforce.

Interpersonal Relationships   The aspect of intellectual development that has been most clearly linked to interpersonal relationships has been the acquiring of a theory of mind. This is because this capacity increases the child's potential for perspective-taking, and empathy and consequently for good peer interactions and popularity. Children who are impulsive and have little frustration tolerance often have difficulty in being accepted by peers because they frequently lose control during play interactions and do not have the patience or skills to join in reciprocal and cooperative interactions.

Self-Control   Children who have adequate executive functioning skills have longer attention spans and better self-control. They can keep future goals in mind and delay immediate gratification in order to achieve them. As a result they are more likely to complete tasks on time, to follow rules, and to meet the requirements of others.

Self-Esteem   Children who can complete tasks on time, follow rules, and make their own decisions usually feel in control and good about themselves. This, in part, is because their behavior generally brings positive reactions from parents, teachers, and peers, making them feel competent and accepted and reinforcing their positive behaviors. Children with difficulties concentrating and problem-solving often feel confused, out of control, and rejected, which can significantly affect their self-esteem and cause them to exhibit more behavior problems.

THE DEVELOPMENT OF CONCENTRATION, PLANNING, AND PROBLEM-SOLVING

The full capacity for planning and problem-solving is not present at birth, shows rapid and very substantial changes between birth and 6 years of life, and continues to develop gradually throughout life. Significant gains are made at about 4 years of age when a theory of mind is achieved, metacognition is possible, and analogical thinking allows transfer of problem-solving rules across situations. Cognitive abilities that facilitate concentration, planning and problem-solving include the following:

- Understanding how to make things happen and the consequences of actions

- Capacity for purposeful experimentation and trying out different solutions or actions

- Using language and pretend play to transport experience across time and space

- Being aware of other people's feelings, thoughts, beliefs and desires

- Using self talk and private speech to self regulate and problem-solve

- Categorizing objects into classes

- Playing cooperatively around a common theme

- Integrating "good" and "bad" views of self and others

- Changing magical thinking into an understanding of what has to be done to achieve an event

- Understanding the difference between appearance (i.e., how something may look or seem) and reality (i.e., how it actually is)

- Understanding and respecting rules

- Delaying gratification in order to find a solution

- Having a concept of yesterday, today, and tomorrow or a time sense

Some of the capacities that children develop in various stages from birth to 6 years of age are set out in Table 9.2 and described in the following sections.

Birth to Six Months

Infants start out life with a basic problem-solving strategy. In other words, they have goals and use different kinds of actions in order to achieve them. They can persist in order to achieve these goals and self-correct their actions when they are not working. Even newborns often get their thumb or fist to their mouth in order to suck and can imitate an adult sticking out their tongue, for example. Infants also kick and activate a mobile and seem to increase their kicking to get it to move more. Also, infants cry in order to have someone come to comfort and feed them. From birth, infants can concentrate on certain stimuli and will turn to different visual and auditory stimuli that interest them. The length of fixation or concentration on visual stimuli (especially the human face) increases over the first 6 weeks of life. Gradually, babies also begin to be able to concentrate for increasing periods of time on toys and to persist in order to achieve goals.

Six to Twelve Months

By 6 months, babies correct actions that do not work and may begin to do other things such as climbing on a chair or using a stick in order to reach or achieve a goal. This has been called the development of means–end behavior. By about 7 months, babies will achieve object permanence and will search for hidden objects and over the next few months increase the number of screens they will pull away in order to search underneath for the object. At this time, this behavior no longer happens by chance and is now far more intentional. This problem-solving primarily uses trial-and-error and exploration of toys or barriers but nevertheless, is quite purposeful. Now babies can imitate adults, not just doing one action, but a sequence of simple actions. During this stage, concentration improves as babies spend increasing periods of time exploring objects by manipulating, examining, shaking, hitting, or banging them. By 12 months, the baby has a mental picture of an object that does not depend on his immediate perceptions and will persist and look for objects that he does not see being hidden. There is now a real push toward independence, and the toddler in the next stage will often insist that he do things himself.

Table 9.2. The development of concentration, planning, and problem-solving

Age	Concentration, planning, and problem-solving skills
Birth–6 months	Intentionally gets fist or thumb to mouth
	Concentrates on visual and auditory stimulation
	Learns about some behavioral contingencies (e.g., if she cries, someone comes)
	Reaches to get things and persists if not successful first time
	Kicks to activate a mobile
	Problem-solving is done by trial and error (e.g., tries to reach a toy by moving or signaling to caregiver)
6–12 months	Understands means–end actions and consequences of actions
	Engages in goal-directed behavior
	Shows persistence and intention in getting a desired object
	Establishes object permanence, and search behavior is more deliberate and persistent
	Problem-solving consists of exploration and trial-and-error learning with objects
12–24 months	Focuses attention for longer periods of time on toys
	Shows increase in purposeful experimentation. Child tries out different solutions or actions
	Decentration takes place and child understands objects as independent of his own action schemas
	Represents objects and events in thoughts by symbols and acts on the basis of the symbols
	Child sets standards for herself and works on problems to meet them
	Can concentrate for long periods in pretend play or if an object interests her
	Begins to be able to plan and monitor actions in problem-solving situations
	Seeks help from adults to solve problems
	Uses pretend play to begin to substitute objects for other things
2–3 years	Language is increasingly critical to transport experience across time and space
	Can be very persistent in trying to reach goal and removes objects to do so
	May be able to count up to 10
	Can see how one thing may lead to something else
	May use private speech to control and to help with problem-solving
	Is increasingly able to memorize and to integrate information from multiple sources for problem-solving
	Increase in pretend play allows the child to play out the events of tomorrow and yesterday and gain ability to plan
	Through pretend play, child tries out different roles and begins to understand mental states of others
3–4 years	Can transfer knowledge of rules from one situation to another
	Becomes increasingly aware of another's point of view
	Verbal self-talk changes to internal dialogue
	Can categorize objects into classes with ease
	Gains understanding of differences between appearance and reality
	Gains understanding of time and space. Can plan ahead to carry out an activity
	Can identify rules for problem-solving or use analogical reasoning
	Increase in frustration tolerance and impulse control
4–6 years	Has theory of mind or understands that other people do not think, believe, or feel as they do
	Can complete appearance–reality and false belief tasks
	Can now understand the difference between inanimate and living objects
	Learns more about categories and can refine and correct them
	Understands and enjoys games with rules
	Begins to understand the concept of numbers

Twelve to Twenty-Four Months

During the stage between 1 and 2 years of age, children make tremendous gains in a number of cognitive areas that affect their ability to problem-solve. During this year, children are increasingly determined to do things themselves and may persist on tasks beyond their capabilities in order to try and complete them. This behavior will increase their ability to concentrate and attend to tasks or problems. Children also make major gains in the use of words to get what they want and in the ability to use pretend play and symbolization to problem-solve and plan. As a consequence, children in some instances substitute trial-and-error problem-solving for thinking ahead and imagining solving a problem in their head before they actually do it. In other words, toddlers now pause and think about an action before they carry it out and may not need to physically try it out first. Solutions are now found mentally and actions can therefore be transferred across time and situations. Because the toddler now has standards for her behavior and wants to see something completed, she will work hard in order to accomplish it. Imitation is now used frequently as toddlers can imitate actions they have not seen before; they can wrinkle their noses, wave good-bye, blow out a candle, and imitate a scene they saw a day or two earlier, for example.

Two to Three Years

During the period between 2 and 3 years of age, attention span increases quite dramatically and children spend longer periods of time watching a television program or following through in order to complete a task. At about this age, children begin to use private speech to help them during problem-solving. This implies that the child is gradually beginning to rely on his own ability to self-regulate rather than on someone else to help him through tasks all the time. As well, increasingly complex forms of pretending appear and play sequences can be quite long and involved. These play scenes reproduce reality at the beginning but then change and often represent wishes and dreams about how the world might be. Now social problems can be worked on and little ones explore how other people in their world think, believe, and feel. Children begin to work out what works in different situations and to use the information from multiple situations in order to problem-solve. Nevertheless, children still cannot plan a course of action for solving a problem in advance and will need some help structuring the task in order to do so.

Three to Four Years

During the year between ages 3 and 4, children begin to be much more reasonable. More advanced speech and a capacity for internal dialogue help the child become more and more able to think symbolically and to plan ahead in order to solve problems. Some new conceptual abilities also facilitate the ability to problem-solve and plan. These include the ability to categorize objects into classes; so, for example, dogs, cats, and alligators are now understood as animals and dresses and shorts as types of clothes. The young child becomes somewhat more able to distinguish between appearance and reality, in other words, she knows that things may not always be what they appear to be. Children also begin to have more control over their attention and can stop and try out one or two possible solutions before getting frustrated. Increased

understanding of time and space usually helps this consolidation. During this stage, children become capable of understanding rules for problem-solving (analogical reasoning) and can transfer these rules across situations and time.

Four to Six Years

During this period, much of what happens is a stabilization or consolidation of what has happened in the previous stages. Some new gains that affect other areas of development are made that help children to problem-solve in new ways, however. These include change from *animism* (i.e., thinking that inanimate objects have intentions) to understanding the difference between man-made objects and living objects. Children now understand that the cloud does not move because it wants to. With the acquiring of a theory of mind, children are no longer totally egocentric in their thinking. They understand that—not only do other people have beliefs and desires—but also they have emotions, such as fear and anger, which all influence the way they behave. More important, they now understand that these can be very different from their own. Children's ability to classify now includes shapes, colors, and size and they have more of an idea about the concept of numbers. Their understanding of rules is now used to follow games and to be more understanding and accepting of the rules of their home or school.

IMPORTANT RESEARCH FINDINGS

This summary of research focuses on two areas: 1) precursors of adequate concentration, planning, and problem-solving in young children; and 2) caregiver interactions that can enhance concentration, planning, and problem-solving.

Precursors of Adequate Concentration, Planning, and Problem-solving in Young Children

Studying the development of attention, concentration, planning, and problem-solving has often been challenging, especially as it relates to planning skills.

Attention and Concentration in Infancy and Early Childhood   A number of early reviews of studies of the predictive validity of a variety of developmental tests used during infancy found age-to-age correlations to be disappointing (Lewis & Brooks-Gunn, 1981; McCall, 1972; McCall, 1976; McCall, 1979a, 1979b), although it has been found that prediction improves considerably if tests are administered in the second rather than the first year of life. From these studies, a number of researchers concluded that infant developmental tests were measuring the wrong things and began searching for other infant characteristics that might be more predictive. This resulted in a large body of research on infant attention and concentration in an effort to identify a better predictor of intelligence.

Much of this more recent research has studied visual attention and selective looking in infants as possible predictors of later intelligence. Specifically, researchers have examined visual habituation (i.e., how quickly an infant's attention declines when presented repeatedly with the same stimulus); response to novel stimuli (preference for a new stimulus compared to one that has been seen before); and processing speed (the duration of time that an infant fixates on

a visual stimulus) (Berthenthal, Haith, & Campos, 1983; Bornstein, 1985; Colombo, 1993). Recent studies have, in fact, found that these early measures of visual processing are related to later cognitive abilities (for reviews see Bornstein & Sigman, 1986; Colombo & Mitchell, 1990; Fagan & Singer, 1983; McCall & Carriger, 1993; Rose, 1993; Slater, 1995). In other words, infants who habituate quickly, recognize and respond to new stimuli, and process information rapidly tend to perform better on assessments of various cognitive abilities at later ages. As pointed out by McCall, however, although the associations are higher than between standardized infant tests and later IQ scores, they are "still too modest for the diagnosis of individuals, and the correlation is not higher than for parental socio-economic status (SES)" (1994, p. 108). It has also been pointed out that it is important to better understand the neural systems that are responsible for attentional control (Colombo, 1995; McCall, 1994).

Precursors of later cognitive ability have also been considered in slightly older children by a number of researchers using a variety of measures of attending and concentrating. A number of researchers have found that the ability to sustain attention, not attending to irrelevant objects, and persistence on difficult tasks predicted later cognitive abilities and continuing ability to concentrate (Kagan, McCall, Repucci, Jordan, Levine, & Minton, 1971; Kopp & Vaughn, 1982; Messer, McCarthy, McQuiston, MacTurk, Yarrow, & Vietze, 1986; Power, Chapieski, & McGrath, 1985; Ruff & Lawson, 1988, 1990; Ruff, Lawson, Parinello, & Weissberg, 1990; Ruff, McCarton, Kurtzberg, & Vaughn, 1984; Willatts, 1989; Yarrow, McQuiston, MacTurk, McCarthy, Klein, & Vietze, 1983).

Other researchers have explored whether persistence displayed on certain specific tasks is predictive of later cognitive abilities (Messer et al., 1986). In one study, 6-month-olds' early persistence in trying to reach a toy was found to correlate significantly with later success at completing tasks on the Bayley test and during play (Yarrow et al., 1983).

Self-Talk or Private Speech   Private speech develops in the preschool years and is typically used by children during problem-solving. A child typically uses private speech between 3 and 4 years of age, and this practice peaks between 5 and 6 years. It is an important way in which children organize, understand, and gain control over tasks; in fact, some researchers have shown that children who are good problem-solvers actually use more private speech (Azmita, 1992; Bivens & Berk, 1990; Gaskill & Diaz, 1991; Goodman, 1981). The research has been criticized for methodological problems, however, because some researchers have found negative correlations or nonsignificant ones between the use or private speech and problem-solving success (Berk, 1986; Frauenglass & Diaz, 1985; Goudena, 1987). Diaz (1992) explained this discrepancy by pointing out that the specific relationship between private speech and cognitive performance may depend on how difficult a task is for a particular child and their level of competence. A child who is presented with a very simple task may not need to use private speech to solve it, and similarly a child who has reached a certain level of general competence may no longer use private speech because it may have been replaced by automatic and silent problem-solving.

Private speech has also been researched as a predictor of creativity in young children. For example, Daugherty and colleagues (1994, 1996) examined the relationship between private speech and measures of creativity and found that private speech that was used as a way of coping with and reinforcing problem-solving was related to creativity (Daugherty & Logan, 1996; Daugherty, White, & Manning, 1994). Finally, private speech has also been found to be associated with IQ, with bright children using more and internalizing private speech earlier than children with average IQ scores (Berk, 1986; Kohlberg, Yaeger, & Hjertholm, 1968).

Planning Behavior   Since the mid-1980s, researchers have begun to study planning behavior in young children, although as yet surprisingly little is known about the way children acquire planning skills and how these skills develop during early childhood. In infancy, most of the research on planning has been in the context of infants' ability to solve means–end problems. A series of studies have shown that infants as young as 9–18 months can plan and monitor their actions in problem-solving contexts (Willatts, 1984; Willatts & Rosie, 1989). Over a course of repeated trials, children at 18 months could plan actions on a task that required a three-step procedure in order to retrieve a toy. During the trials they became increasingly successful at planning and solving the problem (Chen, Sanchez, & Campbell, 1997; Willatts & Fabricius, 1993). Similarly, on tasks that required the children to solve novel problems that required planning of a number of steps, Bauer, Schwade, WeWerka and Delaney found that between 20 and 27 months there were significant gains in the capacity to "plan, monitor, and execute a course of action" (1999, p. 1335).

Even 3-year-olds have difficulty planning ahead, however, especially if the task has a number of steps (Pea & Hawkins, 1987; Welsh, 1991). While 4- and 5-year-olds can plan ahead, the development of flexible planning adapted to complex task circumstances does not develop until much later (Gardner & Rogoff, 1990; Welsh, 1991). Researchers have found somewhat differing results in terms of the level of performance children are capable of at various ages, however. It has been concluded that differences in terms of the support given to children may have influenced the results (Borys, Spitz, & Dorans, 1982; Klahr & Robinson, 1981; Spitz, Minsky, & Bessellieu, 1985).

Other researchers have examined children's ability to create goals and plans through their story narratives about the past and future (DeLoache, Cassidy, & Carpenter, 1987; Hudson & Shapiro, 1991; Seidman, Nelson, & Gruendel, 1986; Stein, 1988; Trabasso, Stein, Rodkin, Munger, & Baughn, 1992). Studies of this capacity in young children have shown that 3- to 4-year-old children differ from older children as their descriptions of events and planning focus on describing isolated events and external actions rather than considering more complex situations and the underlying goals and plans that motivate the actions. The researchers note that certain experimental conditions enhanced the performance of these younger children, such as having access to pictures of the stories and responding to questions asked about the story. It is likely, however, that more advanced language development as well as planning ability influence the growth in ability to use increasing narrative complexity and coherence.

Without a doubt, concentration and planning are interwoven, as are capacities of self-regulation such as impulse control, frustration tolerance, and delay of gratification. As outlined in Chapter 7, self-regulatory capacities are present in rudimentary form in the latter part of the second year but flexible monitoring or self-control does not develop until the third or fourth year of life (Kopp, 1982; Vaughn, Kopp, & Krakow, 1984). It is important to note that various aspects contribute to the gaining of these capacities, particularly early parent–child interactions and cognitive abilities (Olson, Bates, & Bayles, 1990).

In examining the strategies that young children use to delay gratification, "high control" children use techniques to distract themselves from the wanted object, while "low control" children tend to focus much more on the desired gift (Cournoyer & Trudel, 1991; Vaughn, Kopp, Krakow, Johnson, & Schwartz, 1986).

The capacity for impulse control in children shows consistency across situations by 2 years of age, and individual differences have been found (Jacobvitz & Sroufe, 1987; Silverman & Ragusa, 1990). A young child's ability to self-regulate or delay immediate gratification has been found to be predictive of being less hostile and hyperactive at age 5 years (Zahn-Waxler, Schmitz,

Fulker, Robinson, & Emde, 1996) and in adolescence of being "able to cope and deal with stress more maturely and [be] . . . more self-assured" (Mischel, Shoda, & Peake, 1988, p. 693).

Other researchers have related the ability for self-regulation to interactions with parents, noting that when mothers are overcontrolling and exert excessive pressure to gain compliance, children are less likely to develop self-regulating ability (Jacobvitz & Sroufe, 1987; Silverman & Ragusa, 1990).

Problem-Solving Strategies   A number of problem-solving strategies have been identified as important for optimal cognitive development. It is important to point out that the type of problem and its familiarity influences their use significantly, however (Gelman, 1978).

One of the most common strategies used by young children is *trial-and-error and exploration*. Infants' exploratory behavior has been related to measures of cognitive functioning. For example, studies have found play scores to be related to Bayley Mental Development Index (MDI) scores (Hrncir, Speller, & West, 1985). Caruso (1993) discovered that the more interested the infant is in exploration and the more strategies he engages in, the more success and cognitive sophistication he is likely to have in problem-solving. Other studies have found a similar relationship between exploration and problem-solving success (Barnett, 1985; Sylva, Bruner, & Genova, 1976). Barnett (1985) found that when children 3.5–5 years were allowed to explore toys in order to solve a problem, they were able to complete the task in the same amount of time and with as little assistance as children who were given a physical or video-taped demonstration of the assembly. They were also more enthusiastic about the task, suggesting that they were motivated by an intrinsic rather than an extrinsic source to complete it.

Another kind of problem-solving that young children engage in from a very young age is that of planned *means–end behavior*. Hood and Willatts (1986) found that 5-month-old infants showed intention and persistence in getting an attractive object. As well, infants as young as 3 months will kick to activate a mobile (Rovee-Collier, 1983). The most familiar kind of means-end behavior is the search behavior that infants display by 7 or 8 months in looking for a hidden object (Willatts, 1985, 1989). In their second year, children improve this type of behavior and become far more effective at solving problems by using tools and discovering new actions to use (Goldfield, 1983; McCrickard, 1982; Mounoud & Hauert, 1982). For problem-solving to become more successful, children need to be able to remember the parts of their efforts that were successful in solving the problem. By 2 years of age, a child's skill in transferring strategies across situations appears to improve.

As children get somewhat older, they are able to conceptualize rules for transfer of knowledge across situations, also known as *analogical thinking*. In this kind of problem-solving, the child has to construct a representation or schema of the problem situations and this abstract schema allows the transfer to happen. For the problem to be solved, the important similarities between the two situations have to be identified and the irrelevant ignored. The child also needs to be able to see beyond surface features and to identify the causal structures that are common to situations (Chen, 1996). In a study of 32-month-old children, Zelazo, Reznick, and Pinon (1995) found that the children had trouble using rules and tended instead to perseverate using similar behaviors. However, by 3–4 years, children have been shown to be able to transfer knowledge across situations or to demonstrate analogical reasoning. A number of other researchers have found that the ability to abstract and generalize solutions from one situation to another increases with age and IQ and have usually placed the ability to begin to do this at 3 to 4 years of age (Brown, Kane, & Echols, 1986; Holyoak, Junn, & Billman, 1984; Kanevsky, 1990).

By the end of the second year of life, children have begun to show awareness of their abilities and their competencies in reaching certain goals. By *seeking help from adults* and receiving assistance, children learn to manage their own problem-solving and to develop knowledge about their own thinking and the strategies they use for thinking. Help-seeking has, therefore, been seen as an important problem-solving strategy that emerges out of children's self-evaluative awareness in relation to goals (Stipek, Recchia, & McClintic, 1992). In fact, while dependency may decline with age, help-seeking may increase (DeCooke & Brownell, 1995; Nelson-Le Gall & Glor-Scheib, 1985). As such, it enables children to remain involved with difficult tasks and enhances opportunities for learning.

Theory of Mind The capacity for having a theory of mind is present in very rudimentary form in children as young as 2 years of age. In other words, children at this age understand what other people are doing and what they want. Children continue to increase their understanding of others' minds as they get older in order to make sense of social situations. A 3-year-old child understands and reports on how an object looks (appearance) but has difficulty understanding how another person sees it. By 4 years of age, researchers have found that children understand that other people have different beliefs, wishes, feelings, and intentions from their own and can make a judgment from another person's perspective (Astington, 1993; Astington & Olson, 1995; Mitchell, 1997).

Although cognitive shifts contribute to the acquiring of a theory of mind, some researchers have examined the contribution of caregivers and family background to its acquisition. Some researchers have found an association between family measures (e.g., *talk about feelings* and *number of children in the family*) and false belief tasks (Dunn, Brown, Slomkowski, Tesla, & Youngblade, 1991; Jenkins & Astington, 1996; Perner, Ruffman, & Leekam, 1994).

Caregiver Interactions that Enhance Concentration, Planning, and Problem-solving

In general, interactions with caregivers and parents that encourage a sense of competence, self-efficacy, and problem-solving in children are those in which they are shown more warmth, acceptance, responsiveness, and delight in their achievements (Dumas & LaFreniere, 1993; Mondell & Tyler, 1981; Skinner, 1986). Similarly, it has been found that mothers of securely attached children are more in touch with their children's level of performance and give more appropriate assistance and support than mothers of insecure children (Frankel & Bates, 1990; Moss, Gosselin, Parent, Rousseau, & Dumont, 1997).

Researchers have evaluated the usefulness of a number of strategies used by caregivers to encourage concentration, planning, and problem-solving. Some of these that were found to be useful with young children are

- *Scaffolding:* Scaffolding means providing a supportive context in which children are able to explore new responses as their mastery expands. During scaffolding, caregivers set things up for the activity, simplify tasks for success, and provide structure for children's attempts. Sometimes a strategy of jointly completing a task is used. In one experiment it was found that these scaffolding behaviors made it easier for infants and toddlers to participate in social games; however, they did not correlate with the child's language development (Rome-Flanders, Cronk, & Gourde, 1995).

- *Selecting learning tasks that are within the "zone of proximal development":* This implies that the tasks are at a level of functioning between the child's actual level of performance and the level that he is capable of through the collaboration of a more competent other. This is usually an adult but can be a more competent peer. Freund (1990) found that when a task was used that included familiar objects and in a situation that had meaning to the child and mother, this led to more improvement in the child's ability to perform the task independently than when the task was challenging, as well as unfamiliar to the child.

- *Helping the child to stay on task and giving feedback about the success or failure of their task behaviors:* Freund (1990), in the same series of experiments, found that when mothers exhibited this type of behavior, along with choosing appropriate tasks, this helped the child become more independent in carrying out later tasks.

Other strategies that have been observed when parents are assisting young children with tasks include breaking a task down into manageable steps and reminding the child about the next step (Kontos, 1983), giving more indirect suggestions and fewer commands or solutions (Moss & Strayer, 1990), helping the child focus on essential aspects of the task by labeling them and cueing the child about them (Moss & Strayer, 1990), and modeling until the child takes over the task himself (Gallimore & Tharp, 1990). These strategies have not been evaluated individually but do seem to collectively improve performance.

THE GROWTH-PROMOTING ENVIRONMENT: PRINCIPLES OF ENHANCING CONCENTRATION, PLANNING, AND PROLEM-SOLVING

The course of the development and enhancement of these capacities is complex and is outlined in the following principles, listed in Table 9.3.

PRINCIPLE 1: *Show the world to the child and celebrate it with him. Allow the child to lead and nurture his curiosity and interests.*

Table 9.3. Principles of encouraging concentration, planning, and problem-solving

Principle 1	Show the world to the child and celebrate it with him. Allow the child to lead and nurture his curiosity and interests.
Principle 2	Use scaffolding to help the child learn during problem-solving. Encourage the child to concentrate.
Principle 3	Encourage the use of self-talk or private speech during problem-solving.
Principle 4	Teach the child strategies to solve problems.
Principle 5	Help the child learn about the sequences of events and routines. Teach about the past, present, and future.
Principle 6	Encourage perspective taking. Give children a voice and an opinion about the solution to a problem.
Principle 7	Allow the child to experience the consequences of her actions unless to do so would be dangerous. Then, explain what happened and why.

The fun of discovery can be shared in all sorts of situations, such as on a walk.

Research has shown that children who are shown more about the world by caregivers in the early months tend to have higher scores on tests of mental and verbal abilities as well as interest in exploration than those who did not receive this stimulation (Belsky, Goode, & Most, 1980). The fun of discovery can be shared in all sorts of situations: on a walk, at the library, in the park, fishing, at a museum, and of course, at home or in child care.

Homes that are safety-proofed and are set up so the child does not have to be constantly told "don't do this" and "don't touch that" are more conducive to exploring and learning. A home that is full of "don't touch" objects is certainly not one that encourages a sense of wonder, fun, or curiosity.

The philosophy of Maria Montessori (1964) and the important research of Burton White (1995) have fostered the idea of the "teachable moment" and "teaching on the fly." These concepts imply attending to a child when he has a question, becomes frustrated with a task, or just wants to share a triumph, rather than imposing teaching on a child who is not interested at the time.

Parents who do this well are not necessarily involved with children over longer periods than other parents, but their interest in the child's actions *at the time* and their use of small, everyday opportunities to expand knowledge seems to be what is most crucial. This "teaching" can take place during unremarkable events or quite naturally as children and caregivers go about their day. It is also clear that caregivers who intrude on and "overload" infants and young children during interactions discourage them from learning, problem-solving, and initiating their own activities. Pushing children beyond their capabilities without being aware of what the child is capable of can also turn the child off from a love of learning. Consequently, providing play spaces and toys that can accommodate a child's interests, attention span, and intellectual level is also important.

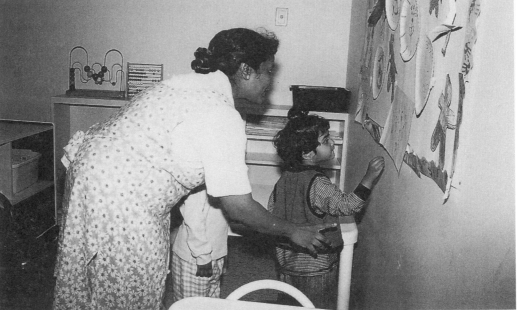

Attend when a child has a question—and provide interest in the child's action at the time.

PRINCIPLE 2: *Use scaffolding to help the child learn during problem-solving. Encourage the child to concentrate.*

Scaffolding, as defined previously, is structuring or tutoring used by parents and caregivers during children's problem-solving efforts. Paul Trad (1990), has talked about "infant previewing," which is an activity most parents engage in quite naturally. It refers to the way that parents encourage their child to acquire his next developmental stage. For example, caregivers naturally help infants try out their legs to learn to walk. What is important, however, is that the caregiver does not force the child beyond his capabilities and allows him to return to his current level of functioning when he is tired. Other examples of this kind of previewing or scaffolding include expanding sentences for a child who is still talking in one- or two-word sentences, encouraging the child to use a spoon but letting him use his fingers when it becomes too tiring or difficult, and using gradual integration in child care as a rehearsal for all-day separations. Scaffolding is actually something that many caregivers do quite naturally. Sometimes it has to be learned, however. Caregivers may be too intrusive or challenging in their expectations of what the child can do or they may ignore the child or expect him to play alone all the time. During scaffolding, a caregiver may set up the situation or just be available to interact at an appropriate time. Typical scaffolding strategies include

- Being aware of and responsive to the child's level of functioning so that the activity is at a manageable level of difficulty

- Structuring the situation to support the child to solve the problem. This might involve, for example, putting two puzzle pieces close to where they go so the child can fit them in

- Structuring the situation to fit with the child's motivation and enthusiasm at a particular time

- Allowing the child to take the lead whenever possible but staying close if he becomes bored or discouraged, and structuring the event to meet those needs

- Encouraging the child during problem-solving by noticing small successes and commenting on them, "Good for you," or "That's great"

- Enabling the child to keep trying if the problem is seen as being too difficult or is close to being solved

PRINCIPLE 3: *Encourage the use of self-talk or private speech during problem-solving.*

The development of private speech is positively related to the scaffolding that is provided to the child during problem-solving and particularly to what is said to the child to help her to stay involved. Children, it appears, hear the speech of their caregivers, internalize it, and transform it into private speech. For that reason, talking about consequences, explaining tasks, and talking about events are crucial. The following example of a child's internal dialogue shows how private speech can help keep the child from getting too anxious about a task.

• •

Six-year-old Daniel is having an internal dialogue with himself in order to work out a problem he is having with reading a book chapter: "I really can't do this; it's much too hard. I wish I could go home. Mommy and Daddy said I should try, though. First of all, I'll read the next chapter and see if I understand it. It's about dogs; I like dogs. It seems

Structure the situation to support the child to solve the problem.

Encourage the child during problem-solving by noticing small successes and commenting on them.

to be a nice story, but I'll bet I don't know the answers. No, the story is really good and they explain all the things that happen in it. I think I'll be able to answer the questions after all. I must remember what happened. John wanted a dog and he got one. It ran away and the police found it. They put it in a kennel. Now I can do this and answer the questions."

In this example, Daniel is remembering things that his parents have said and uses them in order to stay focused and to concentrate on the story. In the same way, private speech can be used when a child is in a situation that produces fear or anger as a response. As self-talk comes out of things that have been said to a child, it is clear that words and phrases that are encouraging and positive can be containing and motivating for the child later. Think of the effect of having words in your head internalized from caregivers, such as "You can do it"; "Good try"; "You can mange it, I know you can"; "You have what it takes to do it," when a problem or a challenge presents itself.

PRINCIPLE 4: *Teach the child strategies to solve problems.*

Children can be taught problem-solving strategies when they face a real-life situation or a homework task. Some of the ways this can be done are the following:

- Ask questions that can help children consider alternatives to the solution they are trying to find.

- Help them remember things that worked another day, and notice the differences between situations. Some researchers have noted that questions can be used to help children dis-

tance themselves in time and space from what they are doing, so they can imagine things differently or consider new solutions.

- Provide hints on how to do things and stay involved so the child does not become discouraged. Make suggestions as to how things might work better. Give open-ended responses that are not intrusive but allow the child to remain focused.

- Model parts of how to do the task so that the child can imitate and do them herself. Sometimes join in a task such as building, and do a piece while the child does another piece.

- Give instructions with words, pictures, or actions when the child is doing something wrong or is really stuck. Help the child focus on aspects of a task by labeling things and cueing the child when her attention lags.

- Help the child with planning by verbalizing ahead what needs to be done first and later. Make sure the necessary materials and tools are available to complete the task. Break the task down into small component parts and make sure they are ordered so the child can be successful.

For some children who consistently have difficulty managing homework or other tasks, it can be helpful to give them some steps to follow:

1. Decide what is supposed to be done: "What do you have to do?" "This is what it says you have to do."

2. Examine ways the task could be done: "Do you know how to do it?" "Could you do it this way?"

3. Focus and concentrate on the task: "Spend time thinking about it and then begin." "Keep trying and don't give up."

4. Find an answer or a strategy: "That looks like a good answer." "That worked."

5. Check out the answer: "Is this the right answer?" "Is this the best way?"

The first few times these strategies are used, parents can scaffold them by being available, asking questions, and supporting the child to do the task. As the child gets more confident, he will be able to take over the steps himself. Sometimes writing the steps on a piece of cardboard that the child keeps available can be helpful.

PRINCIPLE 5: *Help the child learn about the sequences of events and routines. Teach about the past, present, and future.*

Teaching about sequencing and time usually happens naturally as children and caregivers go through the routine of the day. The first requirement is to make sure that a structure and routine is in place. Using language to describe the routines and sequences of the day are excellent ways to introduce children to the concept of time and order. It is also important to make children aware of impending events naturally throughout the day and to prepare them ahead for changes when possible (e.g., "When you get dressed we will go out for a walk," "When you have your bath it will be bedtime"). Gradually increase the time between discussing the event and when it actually happens.

Scaffold by being available and supporting the child to do the task.

It is important to be aware that some children have a great deal of difficulty learning about time and the sequencing of events. It may be that remembering the sequence is difficult, that holding more than one idea in mind at a time is challenging, or that she cannot visualize events that are not happening. For these children, visual cues—in addition to telling them about sequences—may be very important. Other activities and ideas to help teach about sequencing are listed below.

Watching For the Bus   If there is a bus stop near your window, as the bus comes and goes, provide the child with a running commentary: "It's coming—now it's stopping. Now it's stopped; the door is opening and some people are getting off. One, two, three people. Some more are getting on—one, two. The door closes. Creak! It's closed. They put their money in and off it goes. Bye, bye bus." This shows the child the orderly sequence of what happens and can be backed up by an actual trip on the bus.

The Mistake Game   Teach sequencing by pretending to do something in the wrong order. Making a cake or a salad or doing the washing might be used. Pretend to forget how to do the job and have the child help you with doing something that they know how to do. For example, say "I'm not sure how to make a cake. Let's see. Spread the butter on the counter." The child will interrupt and tell you it needs to be in the cake tin. "Now I'll put the eggs and milk in" (e.g., putting the eggs in without breaking them). The child will show you how to break the eggs. "Now I have to mix it up. I'll use a knife." The child will show you how to use an eggbeater. Then forget to add any flour and have the child show you how to add it. Leave it on the counter to cook and let the child tell you to put it in the oven.

Planning Events   Help the child plan future events. Talking about what is going to happen in the future can help the child put events in sequence and help them plan an event.

Make lists of the plan and what has to be done. Planning his birthday party or a family outing can be great examples of doing this.

Using a Calendar   Marking future events on a calendar can also be helpful for children to understand how things happen and helps them prepare for a future event.

Sequence of Events   Emphasize the sequence of events at different times of the day from getting up in the morning to going to bed at night. Discuss and remind him of things you did earlier in the day, yesterday, or last weekend. Tell him about events that will take place tonight or tomorrow. Stress words like *before, after, now, soon, today,* and *yesterday.*

Singing Songs   Sing songs like "The Farmer in the Dell" and "The House that Jack Built," which talk about a sequence of events.

Understanding the Past   Take your child to museums and exhibits so she can see things such as an antique fire engine and a knight in armor, and explain these were used "long, long ago." This can give her an idea of the past.

Ordinary Daily Activities   Clip photographs from magazines that represent ordinary daily activities such as getting out of bed in the morning, washing and brushing teeth, having breakfast, going to child care, playing with toys, going on outings, reading a book, taking a bath, going to bed, and sleeping. Add others that apply to your routine. Mount them on cardboard and discuss them with your child and arrange them in order. Let her put them in the correct order for the day.

Remembering the Past   Having some memory of what went on in the past may be very important for children and having them contribute to the narrative is helpful. To do this,

- Ask the child if he can remember a certain trip.

- Elaborate on how he got there, and what he did.

- Ask for elaboration: "What was most fun about that?", "What did you wear?"

- Prompt the child's memory and remind him of the sequence of events.

This prompting can be used to help the child remember happy or difficult events and to avoid repressing or distorting memories.

PRINCIPLE 6:   *Encourage perspective-taking. Give children a voice and an opinion about the solution to a problem.*

Because children up to 3 or 4 years of age tend to be egocentric, it is very important to encourage them to understand the point of view of others. Two great ways to encourage perspective-taking are through role-playing and the use of puppets. In role-playing, the child will play the role of another person. As she enacts another person, a parent, teacher, or another child, she understands more about that person's needs, feelings, and goals and this will encourage the development of a theory of mind. It will also help her feel empathy towards the other person. Acting out conflict situations can also be helpful as long as it is done with humor. Switching roles and rehearsing real conflicts can help bring insight.

If role-playing is something with which the child is not comfortable, puppets can allow the child a little more distance and may encourage discussion of situations the child will not talk about naturally. Other ways to encourage perspective-taking can include discussion of television shows, especially about how the characters feel; and telling stories together, taking turns and taking the part of different characters.

Perspective-taking can also be encouraged in real-life situations by having the child participate in family discussions about solutions to problems. Being a part of the process will teach him there are different perspectives to every issue and that there is not only one way to do anything. He will quickly learn he cannot always get his way, although sometimes he will have his solution chosen.

PRINCIPLE 7: *Allow the child to experience the consequences of her actions unless to do so would be dangerous. Then, explain what happened and why.*

Children can only really find out what will happen when they do certain things if adults let them experience the consequences of what they have done. Obviously, this cannot apply to situations when the child would be placed in danger, such as when the child is trying to run on the road or touch something hot. If he has been told a toy will be taken away if he fights over it or he will miss dessert if he does not eat dinner, however, the consequences must be imposed in a way that he learns that "if I do that, this will happen." Make sure that the reasons for the consequences are clear and explain what happened and why. In fact, clinical information suggests that parents who are excessively permissive and who constantly bail their children out and do not allow them to get into trouble when they deserve it from school or police officials, may contribute to the development of delinquency in children (Lambourn, Mounts, Steinberg, & Dornbusch, 1991).

SOME COMMONLY RAISED ISSUES AROUND CONCENTRATION, PLANNING, AND PROBLEM-SOLVING

Parents are often concerned about young children they perceive as unable to play on their own, or who are very active or impulsive. In this section, problems like these are discussed and suggestions given for parents in order to help children with these issues.

Children Who Have a Short Attention Span and Are Distractible

Children vary in terms of the length of time that they are able to concentrate on an activity. Distractible children seem to be drawn to other activities, stimulation, or personal feelings and do not focus on the task at hand. Children like this flit from one toy or activity to another and do not settle for any length of time on one task. Consequently, they seldom finish anything and fail to attend to relevant information in order to do so.

Differences in the ability to concentrate are often apparent from early infancy, and distractibility is seen as a temperament characteristic that can persist into adulthood. As a general

rule, 2-year-olds should be able to concentrate for at least 7 minutes, 4-years-olds for 12 minutes, and 5-year-olds for 15 minutes. Parents sometimes note, however, that children can attend to certain tasks or toys that they like to play with but flit between others that they do not like. Parents can help children concentrate better by using some of the following strategies:

- Select activities and tasks for your child that he enjoys and can complete. Praise task completion.

- Notice and praise persistence, focused attention, and trying.

- Help the child structure the task, break it up into smaller pieces, and talk to the child about each part.

- Minimize distractions, have the television off, and insist that the child spend a few minutes with you once a day doing some activity. Use a timer to indicate the end of the activity period and gradually increase the time.

- Keep the child's work table uncluttered and organized.

- Help the child plan how to carry out the problem and have everything available he will need. Work together to complete the activity.

- Give all instructions very clearly and one at a time, making sure he listened and understood them. Use very short phrases and explanations.

- If a child appears to be very tense or anxious about the activity, encourage him to relax and talk in a very calm way to him.

Children Who are Very Impulsive and Do Not Plan

Impulsive children do not plan an activity but act in unpredictable ways without thinking and have very little frustration tolerance. Many impulsive children are also aggressive. These children are often unable to delay gratification and demand things immediately. They may be very egocentric and self-centered and want things their own way all the time.

Impulsive children must be told that they cannot have things immediately. It is critical that they not be given what they want if it is unreasonable to do so, even though they may whine and complain about having to wait. Ways to help the impulsive child wait for things and plan are the following:

- Teach the child to use private speech by talking him through a waiting period or a task.

- Provide a structure and calm routine to which the child must adhere.

- Teach a child to use fantasy or pleasant thoughts to wait. Have him distract himself away from what he wants immediately by imagining something else or focusing his attention on another object.

- Teach turn taking.

- Encourage pretend play and help the child expand play themes.

- Teach about cause and effect: "If you hit Johnny, he will be very upset."

- Ask children to come up with several solutions to problems; for example, if the child is building a tower with blocks, ask him how he could build it higher and still have it stand. Listen for answers such as, "I could try it this way," or "I could get a bigger block that fits in," or "I could balance it with this piece of wood."

- Sometimes using signs or cards with instructions can help a child go through the stages of problem-solving.

- Notice times the child does wait for a few minutes. Let him know you that have noticed and give him positive feedback.

- Teach the child ways to calm down, such as using deep breathing, taking a time out, or, if they are old enough, thinking about something more pleasant.

Children with Attention-Deficit/Hyperactivity Disorder (ADHD)

Children who have a great deal of difficulty with concentrating, planning, and problem-solving and are hyperactive are often diagnosed with attention-deficit/hyperactivity disorder (ADHD). Children with ADHD have difficulty with short-term memory and with filtering out irrelevant stimulation and instead attend to extraneous things in the environment. Parents are very confused about ADHD, and many people are concerned about the apparent increase in its incidence. It is believed to affect 3%–5% of school-age children (Wodrich, 2000), but in some surveys as many as 20% of children are said to have the disorder (Shaywitz & Shaywitz, 1992). It is more common in boys than in girls, with ratios estimated from 2 to 1 to as high as 10 to 1 (Wodrich, 2000). In fact ADHD is one of the most common conditions seen in various clinics and treatment centers for children. As Barkley (2000) pointed out, the difficulties of children with ADHD are common at one time or another with all toddlers and preschoolers, but children with ADHD have extreme difficulties and often have behavioral difficulties as well. Sometimes it is hard to distinguish between what is a typical behavior and what is a symptom of an actual disorder. As well, children may present with these symptoms when they are under stress such as after the birth of a sibling, parents' separation, or a move. Sometimes the symptoms may disappear when the situation returns to normal. Because diagnosing is complex, it is important that it be done by a professional, preferably with some specialization in the disorder. For children who have an accurate diagnosis of ADHD, 71% do not outgrow the symptoms in adolescence (Barkley, Fischer, Edelbrock, & Smallish, 1990), and 66% still have some of the symptoms as adults (Weiss & Hechtman, 1993).

The condition is often not diagnosed or identified until children go to school and are expected to be able to concentrate and complete various activities and tasks. ADHD probably begins in infancy or the toddler period and may be exhibited by impulsivity, noncompliance, and difficulty concentrating on certain tasks and playing alone. ADHD is believed to have a mixed etiology; causes may vary from child to child and include

- Neurobiological factors, including differences in brain activity and neurosubstrates, or brain chemistry

- Heredity, with children with ADHD often having relatives with similar difficulties

- Parent–child interactions and attitudes towards the child. Some parents of children with ADHD have been found to be more negative, directive, and less responsive with their children than parents of children who are not diagnosed with the disorder

Some of the less obvious symptoms of ADHD, underneath the poor attention, excessive activity, and impulsivity, include the following:

- Marked cognitive impairments that include various executive functions, especially in response inhibition (Barkley, 1997, 1998), verbal working memory (Schweitzer, Faber, Grafton, Tune, Hoffman, & Kilts, 2000), and nonverbal working memory (Barnett et al., 2001; Kempton, Vance, Maruff, Luk, Costin, & Pantolis, 1999).

- Learning disabilities leading to academic difficulties (children are usually higher functioning in some areas than in others)

- Difficult temperaments and hypersensitivities and regulatory disorders in infancy and early childhood (DeGangi, 2000)

Some children with ADHD are treated with medication. It can be very successful in helping the child settle and concentrate better without being distracted by everything around him. Medication needs to be given on a trial basis, carefully monitored by a health professional for side effects, and tracked to see if it results in the expected improvements.

Parents often benefit from attending parenting classes that help them deal with the difficult behavior these children often display (Cunningham, 1999). More recent research, however, is recognizing the primary importance of deficits in working memory and recommend that interventions need to not only concentrate on improving behavior, but also on instruction and strategies that can improve the cognitive difficulties associated with the disorder (Tannack & Martinussen, 2001). Most parents of young children prefer to manage the child's ADHD without medication, especially when he is young and when his symptoms are relatively mild. It is important, however, to try and deal with cognitive difficulties early. Some of the ways of helping the young child with ADHD include

- Making sure the child has regular routines, rules, and structures and enforcing them consistently

- Giving the child as much positive feedback as possible. It is crucial to try and help the child maintain an adequate level of self-esteem

- Helping the child concentrate, plan, and problem-solve and helping structure his learning situations for optimal achievement; remembering to model, repeat, define the task, elaborate, and scaffold frequently

- Noticing any efforts made to concentrate, follow-through, and complete an activity or task and giving acknowledgment for them

- Emphasizing the child's social skills as elaborated in the next chapter on social competence

- Providing mnemonics (or tricks to remember things). Use rhymes and pictures to enhance memory of things and ways to carry out tasks.

- Other suggestions given under the Principles 2, 3, and 4 in this chapter can be particularly helpful.

THE ROLE OF PARENTS IN HELPING
CHILDREN CONCENTRATE, PLAN, AND PROBLEM-SOLVE

Parents vary significantly in terms of how much scaffolding and assistance they give to children. Some parents do not assist their children at all and expect that they will be able to play alone and complete tasks with little or no help. They may have very unrealistic ideas of what a child should be able to do, choose toys or activities that are too easy or too difficult, and get frustrated that the child will not play alone at all. At the other extreme, there are parents who are determined that their children will learn things very quickly and they consequently spend a lot of time with them trying to improve their cognitive abilities. They insist on teaching them letters, numbers, shapes, colors, and so forth regardless of whether the child is interested. In either case, the child may lose her sense of competence and desire to learn new things and this can lead to significant difficulties with concentrating, planning, problem-solving, and emotional development, as well as negatively affect the parent–child relationship and the child's ability to do well in school.

Caregivers also differ significantly in their problem-solving methods. Everyone encounters a certain level of stress in their lives, but this can be especially difficult to deal with for parents who have experienced a lot of previous trauma or who have few supportive people or support systems in their lives. Some of the things that affect how parents deal with crises include

- Whether they believe they have some control over events in their lives

- How effective a support system they have in terms of partner's extended family, friends or religious community, and helping professionals

- The problem-solving strategies that the person has that can help her plan a way to deal with the situation and solve the problem

- Whether the person can keep his or her negative thoughts and anger from becoming overwhelming

Apart from these more personal characteristics, the ability of the individual to problem-solve will vary according to the intensity of the difficulty, whether it is ongoing or intermittent, its controllability, and the personal meaning it may have for an individual. The following two women have very different problem-solving strategies:

● ●

Peta was devastated when her husband left her soon after their baby was born. She was enraged and overwhelmed with intense emotions and had few resources to deal with her baby. She was full of feelings of abandonment yet did nothing to make arrangements with a lawyer about custody arrangements or maintenance. Eighteen months after the separation, she remained angry and overwhelmed. She talked constantly about her situation, yet made no efforts to move on with her life.

Marjorie was also devastated when her husband left her soon after their baby was born. Although she was angry, she could see the earlier signs of her husband's lack of support and realized she must try and remain emotionally available for her infant. She sought advice from a lawyer and support from family and friends and began looking for a job. Despite her bitter feelings, she made a conscious effort to think ahead and plan for the future. She even allowed herself to consider the possibility of eventually beginning a new relationship.

In these two examples, the women coped in very different ways and began to have very different emotions and experiences related to the event soon after it occurred. Although Marjorie was initially as angry and upset as Peta, she was gradually able to see hope in her future and to change her interpretation of the event to one of an opportunity for a new life. Peta, on the other hand, continued to feel victimized and abandoned. It is not uncommon to see reactions such as Peta's continuing years after the event has occurred.

DISCUSSION QUESTIONS TO USE IN TRAINING PROFESSIONALS

1. What may be some alternatives for infant developmental tests and why?

2. Discuss why there seem to be so many more children diagnosed with ADHD than there were 20 years ago.

3. When and why do children use private speech?

4. What are some strategies children can use to help them concentrate on a task?

5. What is analogical thinking and when do children learn to use it?

6. What is a theory of mind and why is it important for children to develop it?

7. How can pretend play help children with concentration and problem-solving?

8. Why is scaffolding so important for a child to help him problem-solve?

9. How can talking about a past event help a child learn to problem-solve?

10. What are some of the reasons why children may vary significantly in their ability to concentrate, plan, and problem-solve?

11. How would you help a parent whose child is having a problem with concentrating or is impulsive and has little frustration tolerance?

12. How would having difficulties with concentrating, planning, or problem-solving affect a child's development?

WORKING WITH PARENTS:
GROUP EXERCISES AND SAMPLE HOMEWORK ACTIVITIES

When parents are having difficulty with helping their young children concentrate, plan, or problem-solve or are having difficulty with these strategies in their own lives, it is likely that they will be feeling very stressed or their children will be having symptoms of stress or experiencing difficulties.

It is critical to teach parents the most appropriate ways to work with their children to help them complete tasks and problem-solve if their children are having difficulties with attentional problems or with cognitive tasks. Whether the parent is being intrusive or is ignoring the child, they are likely to be concerned if the child is having difficulty at child care and will be open to ideas to help the child concentrate and problem-solve. Some of the strategies in the listed principles can be explained to parents as suggestions for them to use.

When parents have difficulty problem-solving themselves, it is important to support them to come up with solutions that can help them with problems they have with their children. Strategizing with them around issues with their children and things going on in their lives can be very useful.

GROUP EXERCISES TO HELP PARENTS ENCOURAGE CHILDREN'S ABILITY TO CONCENTRATE, PLAN, AND PROBLEM-SOLVE

This section includes exercises that can be used with parents and other caregivers to help them learn to encourage children's concentration, planning, and problem-solving.

How Problems Were Solved in My Family as I Was Growing Up

The way that parents saw problems solved in their families may influence how they solve difficulties in their own lives. Have parents in the group answer the following questions:

1. Did my parents fight physically or scream or yell at each other?

2. Did my parents lose control when they were angry?

3. Did they have ways to resolve conflicts?

4. Did they punish each other by sulking or withdrawal?

5. Were problems or conflicts talked about and solutions found?

6. Did I get to give an opinion about solutions to problems and conflicts?

Discuss the parents' answers as well as how they manage problems in their own families and what they would like to do the same or differently.

My Problem

Each participant is asked to describe in writing (without signing their name) a problem that they have had in their lives. The problem cards are collected and redistributed at random and a blank sheet is given out at the same time. Group members are asked to write down their suggestions for the anonymous problem. Parents then read the problems and their solutions and group members are encouraged to offer additional solutions.

500

A Challenging Journey

Parents are introduced to the exercise by the group leader acknowledging how difficult it can be to reach life goals and how obstacles may result in these goals needing to be modified. Participants are asked to think about a goal they set up for themselves that was hard to reach. Ask them to write the fears, self-doubt, or conflicts they experienced before it was reached. Group members are invited to talk about their experience of setting the goal, what motivated them, if they had to adjust their goals, what happened before they achieved it, and how they felt. The discussion can emphasize the importance of planning and adjusting plans, and staying focused on the final product.

Changing Negative Thoughts to Positive Ones

We may often feel overwhelmed in certain situations because memories are triggered that can lead to negative, self-critical, and upsetting thoughts. These thoughts can make problem-solving and action difficult. Making an effort to change these thoughts to constructive, positive, and encouraging ones can help eliminate these negative feelings and help us to begin the problem-solving process (See Table 9.4).

Some of the positive thoughts that people come up with may involve actual problem-solving but they are intended to reflect a sense of optimism and some understanding of why a child is acting up.

Exploring Your Family Problem-Solving Style

It is critically important that families work out ways to solve problems and to model these to their children. In order for parents to determine how well their family is doing, have them complete the questionnaire given in Figure 9.1. The group can discuss their answers and some strategies that might help solve problems better.

Table 9.4. Examples of ways to change negative thoughts to positive ones

Situation	Negative thoughts	Positive thoughts
You are in the grocery store and your 3-year-old throws a tantrum.	"Everyone is thinking I'm the worst mother." "He's doing this to make me feel embarrassed."	"This happens to all children and parents." "I'm sure everyone understands." "I'll stay calm and we'll have a talk afterward."
You get a call from the teacher to tell you your 4-year-old is hitting other children.	"He is just getting worse and worse." "He's getting out-of-control."	"It will be important to see what actually happened." "I'll have to think about what might be upsetting him."
Your 2-year-old insists on interrupting when you are on an important phone call.	"I never get a minute to myself." "She's so spoiled; it's all my fault."	"She really finds it hard to not have my attention." "I'm really important to her." "I must make sure to have some interesting toys available."

	Yes	No
Instructions: Place a check mark under the Yes or No column for each item describing how your current family solves problems.		
1. Is there a place to air complaints and concerns?		
2. Are issues talked about?		
3. Is a decision-making process clear and organized?		
4. Do family members listen to and respect feelings in each other?		
5. Do we tend to blame one another or other people?		
6. Do we avoid blaming and look for how to correct problems instead?		

Figure 9.1. Questionnaire: How does our family solve problems?

What Coping Strategies Do I Use?

When faced with stressful situations and problems, people adopt different "coping" strategies that can include avoiding the problem, blaming other people, depending on others to solve the problem, refusing to accept help or expertise, failing to consider options and acting impulsively, or starting to plan a way to cope with the situation. Parents are asked to think of a stressful situation they face or have faced and to think of problem-solving or coping strategies. Have parents brainstorm around the situations and complete the worksheet provided in Figure 9.2.

SAMPLE HOMEWORK ACTIVITIES

To strengthen the concepts and skills broached in the group meetings, it is helpful if parents can be given some homework tasks to do between sessions. The results can then be discussed the next week with the support of the group. Assign one or two of the suggested activities:

1. Keep a diary of issues and conflicts that arise during the week with your child. Find solutions.

2. If your child has a problem, help him come up with a strategy to solve it.

3. Spend some time getting down on the floor with your child and follow his lead with an activity.

4. Go on an outing and explore something with your child. Observe some plants or birds on a walk or a display at a museum.

Instructions: Suggest some ways that parents of young children may encounter stress and conflict. Identify possible coping strategies. For example, for the stressful situation of "Dealing with conflicting views of parenting between parents (e.g., spoiling a baby, discipline methods) you might brainstorm and write the strategy "Attending a parenting class together."

Situations of stress and conflict	Possible coping strategies

Figure 9.2. Blank worksheet: Creating coping strategies to deal with stress and conflict.

5. Read one of the following books by Jon Kabat-Zinn: *Wherever You Go, There You Are* and *Full Catastrophe Living.*

6. Change a negative thought to a positive one. Start a journal of positive thoughts.

7. Spend some time helping your child complete a task using scaffolding.

8. Have a family meeting to plan an outing or upcoming holidays. Make a calendar so your child can see when the event is coming up. Let children discuss the plans.

9. Think about some activities that would be in your child's "zone of proximal development" or something that he has nearly mastered.

10. Talk about a past event with your child, about what happened, how it happened, and her memory of it.

BIBLIOGRAPHY

REFERENCES

Astington, J.W. (1993). *The child's discovery of the mind.* Cambridge, MA: Harvard University Press.

Astington, J.W., & Olson, D.R. (1995). The cognitive revolution in children's understanding of mind. *Human Development, 38,* 179–189.

Azmita, M. (1992). Expertise, private speech and the development of self-regulation. In R.M. Diaz & L.E. Berk (Eds.), *Private speech: From social interaction to self-regulation* (pp. 101–122). Mahwah, NJ: Lawrence Erlbaum Associates.

Barkley, R.A. (1997). Attention deficit hyperactivity disorder, self-regulation, and time: Toward a more comprehensive theory. *Journal of Developmental Behavioral Pediatrics, 18,* 271–279.

Barkley, R.A. (1998). Attention deficit hyperactivity disorder. *Scientific American, 279,* 66–71.

Barkley, R.A. (2000). *Taking charge of ADHD: The complete, authoritative guide for parents.* New York: Guilford Press.

Barkley, R.A., Fischer, M., Edelbrock, C.S., & Smallish, L. (1990). The adolescent outcome of hyperactive children diagnosed by research criteria: An eight-year prospective follow-up study. *Journal of the American Academy of Child and Adolescent Psychiatry, 20,* 546–557.

Barnett, L.A. (1985). Young children's free play and problem-solving ability. *Leisure Sciences, 7,* 25–46.

Barnett, R., Maruff, P., Vance, A., Luk, E.S., Costin, J., Wood, C., Pantel, S.C. (2001). Abnormal executive function in attention deficit hyperactivity disorder: The effect of stimulant medication and age on spatial working memory. *Psychological Medicine, 31,* 1107–1115.

Baron-Cohen, S. (1994). From attention-goal psychology to belief-desire psychology: The development of a theory of mind, and its dysfunction. In S. Baron-Cohen, H. Tager-Flusberg, & D.J. Cohen (Eds.), *Understanding other minds: Perspectives from autism* (pp. 59–82). Oxford, UK: Oxford University Press.

Bauer, P.J., Schwade, J.A., WeWerka, S.S., & Delaney, K. (1999). Planning ahead: Goal-directed problem-solving by 2-year-olds. *Developmental Psychology, 35,* 1321–1337.

Belsky, J., Goode, M.K., & Most, R.K. (1980). Maternal stimulation and infant exploratory competence: Cross-sectional, correlational, and experimental analyses. *Child Development, 51,* 1168–1178.

Berk, L.E. (1986). Relationship of elementary school children's private speech to behavioral accompaniment to task, attention, and task performance. *Developmental Psychology, 22,* 671–680.

Berthenthal, B.I., Haith, M.M., & Campos, J.J. (1983). The partial-lag design: A method for controlling spontaneous regression in the infant-control habituation paradigm. *Infant Behavior and Development, 6,* 331–338.

Bivens, J.A., & Berk, L.E. (1990). A longitudinal study of the development of elementary school children's private speech. *Merrill-Palmer Quarterly, 36,* 443–463.

Bornstein, M.H. (1985). Habituation of attention as a measure of visual information processing in human infants: Summary, systematization, and synthesis. In G. Gottlieb & N.A. Krasnegor (Eds.),

Measurement of audition and vision in the first year of postnatal life: A methodological overview (pp. 253–300). Norwood, NJ: Ablex.

Bornstein, M.H., & Mayes, L. (1991). Taking the measure of infant mind. In F.S. Kessel & M.H. Bornstein (Eds.), *Contemporary constructions of the child: Essays in honor of William Kessen* (pp. 45–55). Mahwah, NJ: Lawrence Erlbaum Associates.

Bornstein, M.H., & Sigman, M. (1986). Continuity in mental development from infancy. *Child Development, 57,* 251–274.

Borys, S.V., Spitz, H.H., & Dorans, B.A. (1982). Tower of Hanoi performance of retarded young adults and nonretarded children as a function of solution length and goal state. *Journal of Experimental Child Psychology, 33,* 87–110.

Bransford, J.D., & Stein, B.S. (1993). *The ideal problem-solver: A guide for improving thinking, learning, and creativity.* New York: W.H. Freeman.

Brown, A.L., Kane, M.J., & Echols, C.H. (1986). Young children's mental models determine analogical problems with a common goal structure. *Cognitive Development, 1,* 103–121.

Butterfield, E.C., Albertson, L.R., & Johnston, J.C. (1995). On making cognitive theory more general and developmentally pertinent. In F.E. Weinert & W. Schneider (Eds.), *Memory performance and competencies: Issues in growth and development* (pp. 181–205). Mahwah, NJ: Lawrence Erlbaum Associates.

Caruso, D.A. (1993). Dimensions of quality in infants' exploratory behavior: Relationships to problem-solving ability. *Infant Behavior and Development, 16,* 441–454.

Chen, A., Sanchez, R., & Campbell, T. (1997). From beyond to within their grasp: The rudiments of analogical problem-solving in 10- and 13-month-olds. *Developmental Psychology, 33,* 790–801.

Chen, Z. (1996). Children's analogical problem-solving: The effects of superficial, structural and procedural similarity. *Journal of Experimental Child Psychology, 62,* 410–431.

Colombo, J. (1993). *Infant cognition: Predicting later intellectual functioning.* Newbury Park, CA: Sage.

Colombo, J. (1995). On the neural mechanisms underlying developmental and individual differences in visual fixation in infancy: Two hypotheses. *Developmental Review, 15,* 97–135.

Colombo, J., & Mitchell, D.W. (1990). Individual differences in early visual attention: Fixation time and information processing. In J. Colombo & J. Fagan (Eds.), *Individual differences in infancy: Reliability, stability, prediction.* Mahwah, NJ: Lawrence Erlbaum Associates.

Cournoyer, M., & Trudel, M. (1991). Behavioral correlates of self-control at 33 months. *Infant Behavior and Development, 14,* 497–503.

Cunningham, C.E. (1999). In the wake of the MTA: Charting a new course for the study and treatment of children with attention deficit hyperactivity disorder. *Canadian Journal of Psychiatry, 44,* 999–1005.

Daugherty, M., & Logan, J. (1996). Private speech assessment: A medium for studying the cognitive processes of young creative children. *Early Child Development and Care, 115,* 7–17.

Daugherty, M., White, C.S., & Manning, B.H. (1994). Relationships among private speech and creativity measures of young children. *Gifted Child Quarterly, 38,* 21–26.

DeCooke, P., & Brownell, C. (1995). Young children's help-seeking in mastery-oriented contexts. *Merrill-Palmer Quarterly, 41,* 229–246.

DeGangi, G. (2000). *Pediatric disorders of regulation in affect and behavior: A therapist's guide to assessment and treatment.* San Diego: Academic Press.

DeLoache, J.S., Cassidy, D.J., & Carpenter, C.J. (1987). The three bears are all boys: Mothers' gender labeling of neutral picture book characters. *Sex Roles, 17,* 163–178.

Diaz, R.M. (1992). Methodological concerns in the study of private speech. In R.M. Diaz & L.E. Berk (Eds.), *Private speech from social interaction to self-regulation* (pp. 55–81). Mahwah, NJ: Lawrence Erlbaum Associates.

Dumas, J.E., & LaFrenière, P.J. (1993). Mother child relationships as sources of support or stress: A comparison of competent, average, aggressive, and anxious dyads. *Child Development, 64,* 1732–1754.

Dunn, J., Brown, J., Slomkowski, C., Tesla, C., & Youngblade, L. (1991). Young children's understanding of other people's feelings and beliefs: Individual differences and their antecedents. *Child Development, 62,* 1352–1366.

Elkind, D. (1987). *Miseducation: Preschoolers at risk.* New York: Alfred A. Knopf.

Fagan, J.F. (1984). The relationship of novelty preferences in infancy to later intelligence and recognition memory. *Intelligence, 8,* 339–346.

Fagan, J.F., & Singer, L.T. (1983). Infant recognition memory as a measure of intelligence. In L.P. Lipsitt, & C.K. Rovee-Collier (Eds.), *Advances in infancy research* (Vol. 2, pp. 31–78). Norwood, NJ: Ablex.

Frankel, K.A., & Bates, J.E. (1990). Mother–toddler problem-solving: Antecedents in attachment, home behavior, and temperament. *Child Development, 61,* 810–819.

Frauenglass, M.H., & Diaz, R.M. (1985). Self-regulatory functions of children's private speech: A critical analysis of recent challenges to Vygotsky's theory. *Developmental Psychology, 21,* 357–364.

Freund, L.S. (1990). Maternal regulation of children's problem-solving behavior and its impact on children's performance. *Child Development, 61,* 113–126.

Gallimore, R., & Tharp, R. (1990). Teaching mind in society: Teaching, schooling, and literature discourse. In L.C. Moll (Ed.), *Vygotsky and education: Instructional implications and applications of sociohistorical psychology* (pp. 175–205). New York: Cambridge University Press.

Gardner, H. (1983). *Frames of mind: The theory of multiple intelligences.* New York: Basic Books.

Gardner, W., & Rogoff, B. (1990). Children's deliberateness of planning according to task circumstances. *Developmental Psychology, 26,* 480–487.

Gaskill, M.N., & Diaz, R.M. (1991). The relation between private speech and cognitive performance. *Infancia y Aprendizaje, 53,* 45–58.

Gelman, R. (1978). Cognitive development. *Annual Review of Psychology, 29,* 297–332.

Goldfield, E.C. (1983). The development of control over complementary systems during the second year. *Infant Behavior and Development, 6,* 257–262.

Goodman, S. (1981). The integration of verbal and motor behavior in preschool children. *Child Development, 52,* 280–289.

Goudena, P.P. (1987). The social nature of private speech of preschoolers during problem-solving. *International Journal of Behavioral Development, 10,* 187–206.

Holyoak, K.J., Junn, E.N., & Billman, D.O. (1984). Development of analogical problem-solving skills. *Child Development, 55,* 2042–2055.

Hood, B., & Willatts, P. (1986). Reaching in the dark to an object's remembered position: Evidence for object permanence in 5-month-old infants. *British Journal of Developmental Psychology, 4,* 57–65.

Hrncir, E.J., Speller, G.M., & West, M. (1985). What are we testing? *Developmental Psychology, 21,* 226–236.

Hudson, J.A., & Shapiro, L.R. (1991). From knowing to telling: The development of children's scripts, stories and personal narratives. In A. McCabe & C. Peterson (Eds.), *Developing narrative structure* (pp. 89–136). Mahwah, NJ: Lawrence Erlbaum Associates.

Hunt, J. McV. (1965). Intrinsic motivation and its role in psychological development. In D. Levine (Ed.), *Nebraska symposium on motivation* (pp. 189–282). Lincoln: University of Nebraska Press.

Jacobvitz, D., & Sroufe, L.A. (1987). The early caregiver–child relationship and attention deficit disorder with hyperactivity in kindergarten: A prospective study. *Child Development, 58,* 1496–1504.

Jenkins, J.M., & Astington, J.W. (1996). Cognitive factors and family structure associated with theory of mind development in young children. *Developmental Psychology, 32,* 70–78.

Kagan, J., McCall, R.B., Repucci, N.D., Jordan, J., Levine, J., & Minton, C. (1971). *Change and continuity in infancy.* New York: John Wiley & Sons.

Kanevsky, L. (1990). Pursuing qualitative differences in the flexible use of problem-solving strategy by young children. *Journal of the Education of the Gifted, 13,* 115–140.

Kempton, S., Vance, A., Maruff, P., Luk, E, Costin, S., & Pantolis, C. (1999). Executive function and attention deficit hyperactivity disorder: Stimulant medication and better executive function performance in children. *Psychological Medicine, 29,* 527–538.

Klahr, D., & Robinson, M. (1981). Formal assessment of problem-solving and planning processes in preschool children. *Cognitive Psychology, 13,* 113–148.

Kohlberg, L., Yaeger, J., & Hjertholm, E. (1968). Private speech: Four studies and a review of theories. *Child Development, 39,* 691–736.

Kontos, S. (1983). Adult-child interaction and the origins of meta cognition. *Journal of Educational Research, 77,* 43–54.

Kopp, C.B. (1982). The antecedents of self-regulation: A developmental perspective. *Developmental Psychology, 18,* 199–214.

Kopp, C.B., & Vaughn, B.E. (1982). Sustained attention during exploratory manipulation as a predictor of cognitive competence in preterm infants. *Child Development, 53,* 174–182.

Lambourn, S.D., Mounts, N.S., Steinberg, L, & Dornbusch, S.M. (1991). Patterns of competence and adjustment among adolescents from authoritative, authoritarian, indulgent, and neglectful families. *Child Development, 62,* 1049–1065.

Lewis, M., & Brooks-Gunn, J. (1981). Visual attention at three months as a predictor of cognitive functioning at two years of age. *Intelligence, 5,* 131–140.

McCall, R.B. (1972). Similarity in developmental profile among related pairs of human infants. *Science, 178,* 1004–1007.

McCall, R.B. (1976). Towards an epigenetic conception of mental development. In M. Lewis (Ed.), *Origins of intelligence: Infancy and early childhood* (pp. 97–122). New York: Plenum Press.

McCall, R.B. (1979a). Qualitative transitions in behavioral development in the first two years of life. In M.H. Bornstein & W. Kessen (Eds.), *Psychological development from infancy: Image to intention* (pp. 183–224). Mahwah, NJ: Lawrence Erlbaum Associates.

McCall, R.B. (1979b). The development of intellectual functioning in infancy and the prediction of later IQ. In J.D. Osofsky (Ed.), *Handbook of infant development* (pp. 707–741). New York: John Wiley & Sons.

McCall, R.B. (1994). What process mediates predictions of childhood IQ from infant habituation and recognition memory? Speculations on the roles of inhibition and rate of information processing. *Intelligence, 18,* 107–125.

McCall, R.B., & Carriger, M.S. (1993). A meta-analysis of infant habituation and recognition memory performance as predictors of later IQ. *Child Development, 64,* 57–79.

McCrickard, D. (1982). *Some aspects of tool use in infancy.* Unpublished master's thesis, University of Dundee, Scotland.

Messer, D.J., McCarthy, M.E., McQuiston, S., MacTurk, R.H., Yarrow, L.J., & Vietze, P.M. (1986). Relation between mastery behavior in infancy and competence in early childhood. *Developmental Psychology, 22,* 366–372.

Mischel, W., Shoda, Y., & Peake, P.K. (1988). The nature of adolescent competencies predicted by preschool delay of gratification. *Journal of Personality and Social Psychology, 54,* 687–696.

Mitchell, P. (1997). *Acquiring a conception of mind: A review of psychological research and theory.* Hove, UK: Psychology Press.

Mondell, S., & Tyler, F.B. (1981). Parental competence and styles of problem-solving/play behavior with children. *Developmental Psychology, 17,* 73–78.

Montessori, M. (1964). *The Montessori method.* New York: Schocken Books.

Moss, E., Gosselin, C., Parent, S., Rousseau, D., & Dumont, M. (1997). Attachment and joint problem-solving experiences in the preschool period. *Social Development, 6,* 1–17.

Moss, E., & Strayer, F.F. (1990). Interactive problem-solving of gifted and non-gifted preschoolers with their mothers. *International Journal of Behavioral Development, 13,* 177–197.

Mounoud, P., & Hauert, L.A. (1982). Development of sensorimotor organization in young children: Grasping and lifting objects. In G.E. Forman (Ed.), *Action and thought: From sensorimotor schemes to symbolic operations* (pp. 3–35). San Diego: Academic Press.

Nelson-Le Gall, S.I., & Glor-Scheib, S. (1985). Help-seeking in elementary classrooms. An observational study. *Contemporary Educational Psychology, 10,* 58–71.

Olson, S.L., Bates, J.E., & Bayles, K. (1990). Early antecedents of childhood impulsivity: The role of parent-child interaction, cognitive competence, and temperament. *Journal of Abnormal Child Psychology, 18,* 317–334.

Pea, R.D., & Hawkins, J. (1987). Planning as a chore-scheduling task. In S.L. Friedman, E.K. Schol-nick, & R.R. Cocking (Eds.), *Blueprints for thinking: The role of planning in cognitive development* (pp. 273–302). Cambridge, England: Cambridge University Press.

Perner, J. (1991). *Understanding the representational mind.* Cambridge, MA: The MIT Press.

Perner, J., Ruffman, T., & Leekam, S.R. (1994). Theory of mind is contagious: You catch it from your sibs. *Child Development, 65,* 1228–1238.

Piaget, J. (1963). *The origins of intelligence in children.* New York: Norton.

Power, T.G., Chapieski, M.L., & McGrath, M.P. (1985). Assessment of individual differences in infant exploration and play. *Developmental Psychology, 21,* 974–981.

Rome-Flanders, T., Cronk, C., & Gourde, C. (1995). Maternal scaffolding in mother–infant games and its relationship to language development: A longitudinal study. *First Language, 15,* 339–355.

Rose, S.A. (1993). Infant information processing and later intelligence. In D.K. Detterman (Ed.), *Individual differences and cognition: Current topics in human intelligence* (Vol. 3, pp. 31–54). Norwood, NJ: Ablex.

Rovee-Collier, C.K. (1983). Infants as problem-solvers: A psychological perspective. In M.D. Zeiler & P. Harzen (Eds.), *Advances in analysis of behavior* (Vol. 3, pp. 63–101). London: John Wiley & Sons.

Ruff, H.A., & Lawson, K.R. (1988, April). *Development and individuality in sustained attention.* Paper presented at the International Conference on Infant Studies, Washington, DC.

Ruff, H.A., & Lawson, K.R. (1990). Development of sustained, focused attention in young children during free play. *Developmental Psychology, 26,* 85–93.

Ruff, H.A., Lawson, K.R., Parinello, R., & Weissberg, R. (1990). Long term stability of individual differences in sustained attention in the early years. *Child Development, 61,* 60–75.

Ruff, H.A., McCarton, C., Kurtzberg, D., & Vaughn, H.G. (1984). Preterm infants' manipulative exploration of objects. *Child Development, 55,* 1166–1173.

Schweitzer, J.B., Faber, T.L., Grafton, S.T., Tune, L.E., Hoffman, J.M., & Kilts, C.C. (2000). Alterations in the functional anatomy of working memory in adult attention deficit hyperactivity disorder. *American Journal of Psychiatry, 57,,* 278–280.

Seidman, S., Nelson, K., & Gruendel, J. (1986). Make-believe scripts: The transformation of ERS in fantasy. In K. Nelson (Ed.), *Event knowledge: Structure and function in development.* Mahwah, NJ: Lawrence Erlbaum Associates.

Silverman, I.W., & Ragusa, D.M. (1990). Child and maternal correlates of impulse control in 24-month-old children. *Genetic, Social and General Psychology Monographs, 116,* 435–473.

Shaywitz, S.E., & Shaywitz, B.A. (1992). *Attention-deficit disorder comes of age.* Austin, TX: PRO-ED.

Skinner, E.A. (1986). The origins of young children's perceived control: Mother contingent and sensitive behavior. *International Journal of Behavioral Development, 9,* 359–382.

Slater, A. (1995). Individual differences in infancy and later IQ. *Journal of Child Psychology and Psychiatry and Allied Disciplines, 36,* 69–112.

Spitz, H.H., Minsky, S.K., & Bessellieu, C.L. (1985). Influence of planning time and first move strategy on Tower of Hanoi problem-solving performance of mentally retarded young adults and nonretarded children. *American Journal of Mental Deficiency, 90,* 46–56.

Stein, N.L. (1988). The development of children's storytelling skill. In M.B. Franklin & S. Barten (Eds.), *Child language: A reader* (pp. 282–297). New York: Oxford University Press.

Sternberg, R.J. (1988). Intelligence. In R.J. Sternberg & E.E. Smith (Eds.), *The psychology of human thought* (pp. 267–308). New York: Cambridge University Press.

Stipek, D., Recchia, S., & McClintic, S. (1992). Self-evaluation in young children. *Monographs of the Society for Research in Child Development, 57*(1, Serial No. 226).

Sylva, K.J., Bruner, J., & Genova, P. (1976). The role of play in the problem-solving of children 3–5 years old. In J.S. Bruner, A. Jolly, & K. Sylva (Eds.), *Play: Its role in development and evolution* (pp. 244–260). New York: Basic Books.

Tannack, R., & Martinussen, R. (2001). Reconceptualizing ADHD. *Educational Leadership, 59,* 1–7.

Trabasso, T., Stein, N.L., Rodkin, P.C., Munger, M.P., & Baughn, C.R. (1992). Knowledge of goals and plans in the on-line narration of events. *Cognitive Development, 7,*133–170.

Trad, P.V. (1990). *Infant previewing: Predicting and sharing interpersonal outcome.* New York: Springer-Verlag.

Vaughn, B.E., Kopp, C.B., & Krakow, J.B. (1984). The emergence and consolidation of self-control from eighteen to thirty months of age: Normative trends and individual differences. *Child Development, 55,* 990–1004.

Vaughn, B.E., Kopp, C.B., Krakow, J.B., Johnson, K., & Schwartz, S.S. (1986). Process analyses of the behavior of very young children in delay tasks. *Developmental Psychology, 22,* 752–759.

Vygotsky, L.S. (1962). *Thought and language.* Cambridge, MA: MIT Press.

Weiss, G., & Hechtman, L.T., (1993). *Hyperactive children grown up (2nd ed.).* New York: Guilford Press.

Wellman, H.M. (1992). *The child's theory of mind.* Cambridge: MIT Press.

Welsh, M.C. (1991). Rule-guided behavior and self-monitoring on the Tower of Hanoi disk-transfer task. *Cognitive Development, 6,* 59–76.

White, B. (1995). *The first three years of life.* New York: Fireside.

White, R.W. (1959). Motivation reconsidered: The concept of competence. *Psychological Review, 66,* 297–333.

Willatts, P. (1984). The Stage-IV infant's solution of problems requiring the use of supports. *Infant Behavior and Development, 7,* 125–134.

Willatts, P. (1985). Adjustment of means–end coordination and the representation of spatial relations in the production of search errors by infants. *British Journal of Developmental Psychology, 3,* 259–272.

Willatts, P. (1989). Development of problem-solving in infancy. In A. Slater & G. Bremner (Eds.), *Infant development* (pp. 143–182). Mahwah, NJ: Lawrence Erlbaum Associates.

Willatts, P., & Fabricius, W.V. (1993, April). *The towers of Hanoi: The origin of forward search planning in infancy.* Paper presented at the biennial meeting of the Society for Research in Child Development, New Orleans.

Willatts, P., & Rosie, K. (1989, April). *Planning by 12-month-old infants.* Paper presented at the biennial meeting of the Society for Research in Child Development, Kansas City, MO.

Wodrich, D.L. (2000). *Attention-deficit/hyperactivity disorder: What every parent wants to know* (2nd ed.). Baltimore: Paul H. Brookes Publishing Co.

Yarrow, L.J., McQuiston, S., MacTurk, R.H., McCarthy, M.E., Klein, R.P., & Vietze, P.M. (1983). Assessment of mastery motivation during the first year of life: Contemporaneous and cross-age relationships. *Developmental Psychology, 19,* 159–171.

Zahn-Waxler, C., Schmitz, S., Fulker, D., Robinson, J., & Emde, R. (1996). Behavior problems in 5-year-old monozygotic and dizygotic twins: Genetic and environmental influences, patterns of regulation, and internalization of control. *Development and Psychopathology, 8,* 103–122.

Zelazo, P.R. (1988). Infant habituation, cognitive activity and the development of mental representation. *Current Psychology of Cognition, 8,* 649–654.

Zelazo, P.D., Reznick, J.S., & Pinon, D.E. (1995). Response control and the execution of verbal rules. *Developmental Psychology, 31,* 508–517.

FURTHER READING ON THE TOPIC

Armstrong, T. (1991). *Awakening your child's natural genius: Enhancing curiosity, creativity, and learning ability.* Los Angeles: Tarcher.

Astington, J.W. (1993). *The child's discovery of the mind.* Cambridge, MA: Harvard University Press.

Astington, J.W., Harris, P.L., & Olson, D.R. (Eds.). (1988). *Developing theories of mind.* Cambridge, UK: Cambridge University Press.

Bjorklund, D.F. (Ed.). (1990). *Children's strategies: Contemporary views of cognitive development.* Mahwah, NJ: Lawrence Erlbaum Associates.

Bloch, D. (1993). *Positive self-talk for children.* New York: Bantam Books.

Bos, B. (1990). *Together we're better.* Roseville, CA: Turn the Page Press.

Burack, J.A., & Enns, J.T. (Eds.). (1997). *Attention, development, and psychopathology.* New York: Guilford Press.

Colombo, J., & Fagen, J. (Eds.). (1990). *Individual differences in infancy: Reliability, stability, prediction.* Mahwah, NJ: Lawrence Erlbaum Associates.

Diaz, R.M., & Berk, L.E. (1992). *Private speech: From social interaction to self-regulation.* Mahwah, NJ: Lawrence Erlbaum Associates.

Forman, S.G. (1993). *Coping skills interventions for children and adolescents.* San Francisco: Jossey-Bass.

Goswami, U. (1992). *Analogical reasoning in children.* Hove, England: Lawrence Erlbaum Associates.

Jacob, S.H. (1992). *Your baby's mind.* Holbrook, MA: Bob Adams.

Kendall, P.C., & Braswell, L. (1984). *Cognitive-behavioral self control therapy for children.* New York: Guilford Press.

Kersey, K. (1986). *Helping your child handle stress: The parent's guide to recognizing and solving childhood problems.* Washington, DC: Acropolis Books.

Lyon, G.R., & Krasnegor, N.A. (Eds.). (1996). *Attention, memory, and executive function.* Baltimore, MD: Paul H. Brookes Publishing Co.

Marks, J. (1987, September). There's got to be a better way. *Parents Magazine, 62,* 106(5).

Rosenbaum, M. (Ed.). (1990). *Learned resourcefulness: On coping skills, self-control, and adaptive behavior.* New York: Springer.

Schmidt, F. (1986). *Creative problem-solving for kids.* G.C.A. Conflict Project.

Schulman, M. (1991). *The passionate mind: Bringing up an intelligent and creative child.* New York: The Free Press.

Shapiro, L.E. (1997). *How to raise a child with a high EQ: A parents' guide to emotional intelligence.* New York: Harper Collins.

Shure, M. (1992). *I can problem-solve: An interpersonal cognitive problem-solving program—Preschool.* Champagne, IL: Research Press.

Strayhorn, J.M. (1988). *The competent child: An approach to psychotherapy and preventive mental health.* New York: Guilford Press.

Thornton, S. (1995). *Children solving problems.* Cambridge, MA: Harvard University Press.

Zeitlin, S., & Williamson, G.G. (1994). *Coping in young children: Early intervention practices to enhance adaptive behavior and resilience.* Baltimore: Paul H. Brookes Publishing Co.

CHILDREN'S BOOKS ON CONCENTRATION, PLANNING, AND PROBLEM-SOLVING

Bourgeois, P. (1993). *Franklin is bossy.* Toronto: Kids Can Press.

Crary, E. (1996). *I want it.* Seattle: Parenting Press.

Fowler, S.G. (1994). *I'll see you when the moon is full.* New York: Greenwillow Books.

Henkes, K. (2000). *Lilly's purple plastic purse.* New York: Live Oak Media.

Hoban, R. (1993). *Bread and jam for Frances.* New York: HarperCollins Juvenile Books.

Hutchins, P. (1989). *The doorbell rang.* New York: Mulberry Books.

Hutchins, P. (1990). *What game shall we play?* New York: Greenwillow Books.

Turner, A. (1991). *Stars for Sarah.* New York: HarperCollins Children's Books.

APPENDIX: SELECTED ASSESSMENT INSTRUMENTS

● ● ●

ASSESSING CONCENTRATION, PLANNING, AND PROBLEM-SOLVING

Testing of the capacities talked about in this chapter is complex and often varies from one laboratory to another. Some researchers observe children in naturally occurring situations; others set up a waiting task or other situations, and sometimes standardized testing of children or questionnaires completed by parents or teachers are used. In this section, tests are listed under different aspects of the abilities needed for problem-solving such as theory of mind, attention, concentration, and planning. Some assessments of these abilities are included in various tests of intelligence or developmental screening instruments listed in Chapter 1. These include the Wechsler Preschool and Primary Scale of Intelligence–Revised (Wechsler, 1989) and the Kaufman Assessment Battery for Children (K-ABC) (Kaufman, 1983).

Attention, Concentration, and Planning

Table A9.1 includes tests of children's abilities in attention, concentration, and planning. Table A9.2 includes some measures of parental problem-solving and mastery.

Theory of Mind Tests

Appearance and reality tasks usually ask children to name, for example, a rock that looks like a sponge, then to feel and explore it and name it again. Children who are unable to pass the test will continue to call the object a sponge even after exploration. Another version is the Smarties Box, which contains crayons. After inspection, some children will still say the box contains Smarties (a type of small round candy) instead of crayons.

False belief tasks can be of various kinds but, in general, in the task, the child discovers something that another person would not know. Children are asked what the other person would think. Those who fail the test would answer it as they now understand the facts to be instead of realizing that the other person would think about it as they had originally thought about it or believed the situation to be. For example, the child is shown a cartoon in which Harry has a chocolate in a box. He goes outside and someone steals it. The child, of course, now knows that the chocolate is missing. They are then asked what Harry would do if he comes inside and wants to eat the chocolate. Those without the theory of mind would expect Harry to know the chocolate would not be there, as they do. Those with theory of mind understand that Harry would look for the chocolate in the same place as it was before he went outside.

Table A9.1. Selected assessments of children's attention, concentration, planning, and problem-solving

Topic	Title	Age range	Items/ administration time	General description
Attention, concentration, and planning	*The Goodman Lock Box* Goodman, J.F., Fox, A.A., & Glutting, J.J. (1986). Contributions of the Lock Box to preschool assessment. *Journal of Psychoeducational Assessment, 4,* 131–144.	2–5 years	10 items; 6 minutes	*The Goodman Lock Box* test was designed to evaluate young children's response to a novel problem-solving situation. It is used to identify children's problems with attention and concentration and to observe their approach to problem-solving. The Lock Box is a wooden container with 10 compartments, accessible from one side and with small, locked doors on each. Each of the latches differ (e.g., padlock, leather strap) Each compartment has a different toy in it and children are asked to find the toys. Scores are assigned in three areas: Competence, Organization, and Aimless Actions. Competence is the number of locks opened successfully.
	Kansas Reflection Impulsivity Scale for Preschoolers (KRISP) Wright, J., Gaughan, D., & McClanahan, R. (1978). *The KRISP: A narrative evaluation.* Unpublished manuscript, Kansas Center for Research in Early Childhood Education, University of Kansas. Salkind, N., & Wright, J. (1977). The development of reflection-impulsivity and cognitive efficiency: An integrated mode. *Human Development, 20,* 377–387.	3–5.5 years	15 items; 10 minutes	The *Kansas Reflection Impulsivity Scale for Preschoolers (KRISP)* is designed to distinguish between children who are unusually reflective or impulsive in their cognitive style or tempo. The child matches a drawing of a figure to the exact copy of the figure from a number of other figure drawings. The child's total errors and mean time to first response on each of the items is recorded as his or her score.
	Matching Familiar Figures Test (MFFT) Kagan, J., & Messer, J.B. (1975). The Matching Familiar Figures Test as a measure of reflection-impulsivity. *Developmental Psychology, 11,* 244–248.	2–12 years	12 items; 10 minutes	The *Matching Familiar Figures Test (MFFT)* test measures reflection-impulsivity or the ability to evaluate several possible problem solutions. From sets of pictures of familiar objects consisting of a standard picture and six similar pictures (with only one being identical), the child is asked to identify the one that is the same as the one in the original set. Children are rated as reflective or impulsive according to whether they are above or below a median score for their age.
Competence, coping, and resiliency	*The California Child Q Set (CCQ)* Block, J.H., & Block, J. (1980). The role of ego-control and ego-resiliency in the organization of behavior. In W.A. Collins (Ed.), *Minnesota symposia on child psychology* (Vol. 13, pp. 39–101). Mahwah, NJ: Lawrence Erlbaum Associates. Block, J.H., & Block, J. (1980). *The California Child Q-Set.* Palo Alto, CA: Consulting Psychologist Press, Inc.	2–5 years	100 items; 20–40 minutes	The *California Child Q Set (CCQ)* consists of 100 personality descriptions of children, each printed on a separate card. Respondents sort the cards into nine piles that range from Most Descriptive to Least Descriptive. Adults such as parents, researchers, and therapists who have had the opportunity to observe the child over a period of time complete the sort. The items result in an estimate of ego-control (i.e., ability to modulate impulses and delay gratification) and ego-resiliency (i.e, ability to adjust one's level of self-control to changing situational demands).

(continued)

Table A9.1. *(continued)*

Topic	Title	Age range	Items/administration time	General description
	Early Coping Inventory and the *Coping Inventory for Children and Youth* Zeitlin, S., Williamson, G.G., & Szczepanski, M. (1988). *Early Coping Inventory.* Bensenville, IL: Scholastic Testing Service. Zeitlin, S. (1985). *Coping Inventory.* Bensenville, IL: Scholastic Testing Service.	*Early Coping Inventory:* 4 months– 3 years *Coping Inventory for Children and Youth:* 3–16 years	*Early Coping Inventory:* 48 items; scoring about 30 minutes *Coping Inventory for Children and Youth:* 48 items; scoring about 30 minutes	The *Early Coping Inventory* and the *Coping Inventory for Children and Youth* tests are criterion-reference tests designed for use in observations of infants and children. Information used on the tests is collected over a period of time from observing the child in a variety of situations. The *Early Coping Inventory* yields three types of information: an Adaptive Behavior Index, a Coping Profile, and a list of the Most and Least Adaptive Coping Behaviors. For the *Coping Inventory for Children and Youth* two categories are assessed: Coping with Self and Coping with the Environment.
Problem-Solving and executive functioning	*Tower of Hanoi Disk Transfer Task* Simon, H.A. (1975). The functional equivalence of problem-solving skills. *Cognitive Psychology, 7,* 268–288.	3–12 years	Varies	The *Tower of Hanoi Disk Transfer Task* consists of disks placed in a particular pattern on three pegs and the goal is to have children create a tower pattern on one of the three pegs. The task requires future-oriented planning to be completed.

Other commonly used measures

Rapid-Alternating-Stimulus-Naming Test
Wolf, M. (1986). Rapid alternating stimulus naming in the developmental dyslexias. *Brain and Language, 27,* 360–379.

Tapping Test
Becker, M.G., Isaac, W., & Hynd, G.W. (1987). Neuropsychological development of nonverbal behaviors attributed to frontal lobe functioning. *Developmental Neuropsychology, 3,* 275–298.

Visual Search Test
Plude, D.J., & Doussard-Roosevelt, J.A. (1989). Aging, selective attention, and feature integration. *Psychology and Aging, 4,* 98–105.

513

Table A9.2. Selected parent tests of problem-solving and mastery

Title	Age range	Items/ administration time	General description
Parent Means–End Problem-Solving Instrument (PPSI) Wasik, B.H., Bryant, D., & Eishbein, J. (1980). *Assessing parent problem-solving skills.* Paper presented at the 15th Annual Conference on Advanced Behavior Therapy, Toronto, Canada.	Adult	10 items; 30 minutes	In the *Parent Means–End Problem-Solving Instrument (PPSI)*, parents are read the beginning and the end of a "story"/situation that is com-monly faced by par-ents of young children. Following each reading, the parent is asked to make up the "middle" of the story. The stories are scored on five dimensions: 1) total number of items on which relevant solutions were given; 2) total number of items on which relevant solutions; 3) total number of items on which elaboration occurs; 4) total number of solutions on which elaboration does not occur; 5) total number of content areas in all the stories.

Other commonly used measures

Pearlin Sense of Mastery Scale Pearlin, L.L., & Schooler, C. (1978). The structure of coping. *Journal of Health and Social Behavior, 19,* 2–21.			See Chapter 6 appendix for a description of the scale.
Internal-External Locus of Control Scale Rotter, J.B. (1966). Generalized expectancies for internal versus external control of reinforcement. *Psychological Monographs, 80,* 1–25.			

● ● ● 10

ENCOURAGING SOCIAL COMPETENCE, EMPATHY, AND CARING BEHAVIOR

Our society is becoming increasingly aware of and concerned about human cruelty, crime, and violence. Every day, in newspapers, on television, and on the radio there are new stories of conflicts taking place across the world. We are deluged with accounts and stories of inhumanity—of racial brutality, war crimes, terrorist attacks, torture, child abuse, and injustice. We are concerned about keeping children safe in this kind of world. These influences have led to an increasing interest in the academic community in combating these trends by discovering how to develop social competence and caring behavior in children.

In spite of this very negative picture, examples abound of individuals and groups who display caring toward others. Some individuals do put their own lives on the line to help others; organizations and churches devote themselves to helping the poor, and individuals give extraordinary amounts of energy and compassion to helping a family member who is ill or has a developmental disability. It is clear, therefore, that many people are both socially competent and caring, and the challenge is to find ways to enhance social competencies in young children.

Perhaps most gratifying is how much research about social behavior has burgeoned since the 1980s. As well, ways to help develop empathy and helping behavior in young children are better understood and can be used by parents and caregivers in the home as well as in child cares and schools. There has also been an increasing understanding and acknowledgment of how socialization outside the immediate parent–child interaction and the family by peers, teachers, and others is extremely influential. This is particularly important because increasing numbers of infants and young children are spending large amounts of time in child care or other care outside the immediate family.

DEFINITIONS OF SOCIAL COMPETENCE, EMPATHY, AND PROSOCIAL BEHAVIOR

Social competence in children is reflected in their successful social functioning with peers and adults. It involves the social skills that allow children to succeed in achieving certain social goals. These goals include being liked and accepted, having friends, and engaging in rewarding and reciprocal interactions with others. *Empathy* involves recognizing another person's emotional state and responding with the identical or a very similar emotion to the one that the other person is experiencing. *Sympathy* results from empathy, is other-oriented, and involves feeling concern or sadness for the situation or emotional state that the other person is experiencing.

Although both empathy and sympathy can be linked to positive behavior toward others, in some cases empathy may result only in personal distress or a self-focused reaction because the person is not able to differentiate his own emotions from those of the other person. In these cases, empathy may occur, but without being accompanied by sympathy or true concern for the other person's well being.

Prosocial behavior includes cooperation and caring behaviors such as sharing, helping, or comforting another person as well as responding with concern to the distress of someone else. These acts are voluntary and are intended to help others; however, they can be motivated by more selfish reasons such as wanting to be noticed or to get a reward. In other cases, these acts may occur because the person is really concerned about the other individual or a group of people.

Altruism refers to prosocial behavior that is motivated from within and does not involve personal gain. Individuals who carry out altruistic acts may suffer guilt or feel unworthy if they do not carry them out and experience feelings of pride and self-esteem if they do. They do not depend on acknowledgment and rewards from outside, however.

Young children may not be able to differentiate their emotions from others. (From Johnston, Lynn [1978]. *Do they ever grow up?* Minnetonka, MN: Meadowbrook Press; reprint granted with written permission of Lynn Johnston Productions, Inc.)

THEORIES OF SOCIAL COMPETENCE, EMPATHY, AND CARING BEHAVIOR

Although social competence and prosocial behavior have been of interest to many theorists of personality and development, they have not been core issues of most psychological theories. Table 10.1 includes only those theories that focus on social behavior. In addition, some major researchers in the area and the focus of their research have been included. Other theories that are not included but that have relevance for social development (e.g., theories of moral development, ethological theory, theory of mind) are discussed in previous chapters.

Some of the earlier theorists were interested in how social competence was fostered in the family. Their theories also emphasized how adults who had experienced a lack of nurturance could be helped to overcome the results of this background within a healing, therapeutic relationship (see "object relations" and "self-actualization" theories). Other theorists have been interested in discovering, by observation and research, when the capacities develop in children and how they can be encouraged both within and outside of the family (i.e., social-developmental). Also very influential in understanding how social development takes place are those researchers who have considered how behaviors are learned and which information-processing mechanisms children use that influence their social interactions (i.e., social learning and social–cognitive). Together, these researchers and theorists have provided us with an increasingly clear picture and understanding of how social competence develops, how it can be enhanced, and how it can get delayed or distorted.

THE IMPORTANCE OF SOCIAL COMPETENCE, EMPATHY, AND CARING BEHAVIOR

Many aspects of development contribute to social competence and can lead to the child's acceptance, popularity, and capacity to have close friendships. These developmental areas include

- Language and communication (particularly the capacity for reciprocal communication)

- Emotion regulation and self-regulation of negative behaviors

- The ability to engage in pretend play and to assume various roles

- Moral development

- A secure attachment

As well, social competence and the capacity for empathy and caring behavior contribute to and affect children's ability to cope in a number of settings. As social competence or difficulties tend to be relatively stable, this is particularly important. Children who do not develop social competence often show excessive amounts of externalizing behavior (e.g., aggression) or internalizing behavior (e.g., shyness, withdrawal from others). Social competence, therefore, can contribute to the areas of development noted in the following sections.

Academic Success and School Achievement Children who are unpopular and have few friends are far more likely later to be truant, to have discipline problems, and to drop out of school. Difficulties in school occur from three to five times more often for children with social difficulties, and although the social problems have not been proved to be causative, they

Table 10.1. Theories of social competence, empathy, and caring behavior

Theorist	Type of theory	Major constructs
Kohut (1959, 1984) Sullivan (1962) Kernberg (1980) Schultz & Selman (1989)	Object relations	Saw psychopathology mainly as the result of interpersonal difficulties such as being socially disengaged and having difficulty with trusting people. Believed that this occurs as a result of lack of mirroring and empathy in early relationships with parents Therapy or treatment seen as providing a reparative relationship by providing mirroring and empathy for the client Therapeutic relationship seen as providing a new and positive view of others that can be internalized Considered the nature of the representation of self and others formed in the early years as crucial in determining an individual's social interactions
Rogers (1959, 1975)	Self-actualization	Believed that the positive forces or growth in personality development could be distorted by the negative input of significant others Saw growth as being brought about by unconditional positive regard and empathy Rogerian therapy provided an atmosphere of acceptance, positive regard, and empathy, which were believed to play a key role in producing positive personality change Empathy training programs in schools and for adults seen as helpful to make societal change
Hartup (1970) MacDonald & Parke (1984) Radke-Yarrow & Zahn-Waxler (1984) Howes (1987, 1988) Eisenberg (1992) Putallaz & Sheppard (1992) Dunn (1993)	Social developmental	Considered the cognitive, affective, and motivational factors that are important in the development of social competence Considered factors beyond the individual and family such as the influence of peers, friends, siblings, teachers, child cares, and so forth Interested in when capacities for social competence are developed
Selman (1980, 1981) Dodge (1986)	Social cognitive	Stressed the importance of various aspects of information processing that occur in social interaction Considered individual differences in these processes in different groups of children who were having difficulties with socialization, such as aggressive and shy and withdrawn children Considered the sequential processes of information processing involved in social interactions, including encoding stimuli, interpreting them, deciding on a response, and acting on the selected response Looked at the use of this information in conflict situations
Bandura (1986)	Social learning	Considered that social behavior is learned and shaped by the experiences or environmental events to which the child is exposed Considered how children become socialized through, for example, modeling, social referencing, and direct reinforcement Conditioning and learning concepts were used to explain the development of empathy and prosocial behavior. Considered modeling and imitating of models as ways that children can develop social competence.

are certainly frequently linked. Conversely, children who are rated as more popular by peers are more likely to adjust well, to enjoy going to, and to complete school.

Self-Esteem   Shyness and aggression have been found to be associated with low self-esteem, especially in middle childhood. In early childhood, self-esteem is largely determined by what is experienced in the home and in relationships with parents and other family members. As children enter school, their self-esteem is increasingly affected by how well-liked they are by peers and how easily they can form friendships.

Emotional Development   Difficulties with social relatedness and empathy and caring can contribute to a number of behavioral and emotional disorders, including conduct disorder (particularly with aggression), anxiety disorders, and even depression. Socially competent children with a number of friends are more likely to experience support outside the family and are less likely to develop disorders. They are, therefore, more likely to cope and to show resiliency when they encounter traumas or difficult situations.

THE DEVELOPMENT OF SOCIAL COMPETENCE, EMPATHY, AND CARING BEHAVIOR

Although researchers are finding social or interactive behaviors in children at earlier and earlier ages, it is important to point out that these often represent only a very small proportion of the behaviors that are happening in a social setting and that there are vast individual differences in children's social competence. So, for example, while some 1-year-olds may be capable of giving objects to one another and comforting another child, these behaviors only represent about 30% of what goes on and some children may not be able to demonstrate the behaviors at all. Table 10.2 shows how the capacities of social competence develop throughout the various stages of a child's early life.

Birth to Twelve Months

From the very beginning, infants demonstrate interest in other people. From birth, they are more attracted to the human face than to objects and seek out eye-to-eye contact with others. They enjoy interactions with caregivers from a very early age as long as they can respond at their own pace and are allowed to back off when they wish to. In the first few months of life, babies smile at other people, indiscriminately at first, and enjoy cooing in response to caregivers talking to them. As attachment to their caregivers is established, they show preference for them and may become upset and afraid in the company of strangers.

By about 6 months of age, infants respond to other infants and may direct smiles and vocalizations toward them. These interactions are as yet not truly cooperative, but they certainly show interest in infants and in their behaviors. A 6- to 9-month-old infant may even touch another person if he is close enough.

Signs of empathy and caring behavior are evident quite early. Even newborns may cry if other babies (or adults) cry and show different responses to and reflect the emotions of friendly and unfriendly faces. By the end of the first year, they may begin to offer objects and food to other babies.

Table 10.2. The development of social competence, empathy, and caring behavior

Age	Social competence	Empathy and caring behavior
Birth–12 months	Reacts to the human face more than to objects Enjoys face-to-face interaction and social interchange with adults very early Shows fear of strangers and preference for familiar caregivers Attachment to primary caregivers established Engages in turn-taking with adults Some parallel play evident; may look towards peers and direct smiles and vocalization toward them	Sensitive to emotions and activities of others Responds differently to friendly and unfriendly faces Cries when other people (especially other babies) cry Offers objects and food to others
12–24 months	Enjoys parallel play but can cooperate for brief periods of time Imitates others; begins to play follow-the-leader games Still seeks out the secure base of the caregiver Interactions with peers often become struggles over possessions Still frequently engages in solitary play 60%–80% of play is very object-centered	Increasingly uses social referencing or responding to and using emotions of another person to guide behavior Will try and comfort another person who is upset Increasingly shares things with others, helps others, "cares" for baby siblings
2–3 years	Friendships more stable Demonstrates cooperation with peers in problem-solving Imitates social interactions more Is able to resolve conflicts and work collaboratively toward a goal with friends and peers Consistently plays more cooperatively and interactively Shared themes in play are possible	Begins to be concerned about standards of social behavior (e.g., broken toys, missing buttons) Tries various methods to comfort others Realizes others have inner states, thoughts, and perceptions
3–4 years	Cooperates with peers to achieve common goals Spends more time interacting with other children Acts out complementary roles in complex social pretend games Can maintain cooperative play for longer periods of times Is better able to work out conflicts	Sympathetic reactions to other children become common Increased ability to listen to others Theory of mind established and more able to understand others' perspectives and feelings Shows increased ability to respond to the feelings of others by comforting Sometimes helping behavior drops off a little because teachers are seen as the ones to do the work.
4–6 years	Enjoys interactive games with rules Identifies with people in and outside the family Plans games with other children, and can think before acting Can exhibit quite sophisticated problem-solving ability around social issues	Can integrate mixed emotions, so less likely to suddenly become extremely angry Is capable of concern for future welfare of others

From the beginning, an infant demonstrates interest in other people.

One to Two Years

From the first to the second year of life, toddlers enjoy being around other children and like to play close to them. Solitary play is still common and interactions with peers often involve struggles over possessions as toddlers tend to jealously guard their space and toys. The play between toddlers that does occur is mostly object-centered, and cooperation is only possible for very brief periods of time. Toddlers still need the secure base of their caregivers; though they may run off to join other children, they tend to come back to caregivers for "refueling."

In spite of the infrequency of cooperative play, 1-year-olds increasingly respond to and copy the emotions of others. This includes comforting another child or adult who is upset. Parents report that their children respond with stroking and other signs of concern when they are upset. Of course, not all children exhibit these behaviors. Some even become upset when others cry and may actually hit them in an attempt to make the crying stop. In this year there is an increase in sharing things that can be divided, such as food and parts of games. Many of these behaviors are more likely to occur when supported by adults.

Two to Three Years

From the ages of 2 to 3, a child experiences a significant increase in her ability to cooperate in games with peers and is far more likely to directly initiate interactions with others. Pretend play, in which common themes are used and social roles are played out, increases as well. This facilitates true cooperative play and an increase in understanding of others' perspectives. There is also a noticeable gain in a child's ability to jointly problem-solve, work collaboratively toward a goal, and resolve conflicts. Of course, conflicts are common and many need the inter-

At 6–9 months, an infant may touch another person if close enough.

vention of an adult in order to be resolved, but there is a marked increase in children's willingness and ability to do this.

In this year of life, children become somewhat more able to understand another person's emotions without feeling the same ones themselves. Children try out various methods to comfort others. At the same time, children become more aware and concerned about standards of social behavior and may get very upset if these rules are violated. This can include, for example, when they break toys or have missing buttons on their clothes.

Three to Four Years

During this year, friendships become more stable. Friends can become significant attachment figures, and children can become upset if they go away. Social skills are more available to children and significantly more time is spent in cooperative play in which more conflicts can be solved between children.

By the end of this stage, children gain a "theory of mind" and become much better about taking the perspective of others and understanding that others' thoughts, ideas, and feelings are different from their own. As a consequence, they are more able to listen to others' points of views and sympathetic and helping responses to other children usually become more common. In other words, by this time a child's responses are less related to how being upset makes him feel but more related to how he believes the other child feels.

Four to Six Years

Although pretend play is still common, children now cooperate around games with rules, although they still sometimes change the rules to suit the situation. Sometimes games are planned ahead of time and children problem-solve around resolving conflicts and social issues.

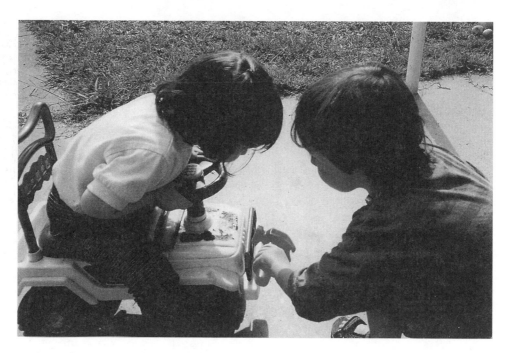

At 2–3 years there is a significant increase in the ability to cooperate in games with peers.

Children now identify with a number of people inside and outside the family and may pretend to be—and take roles and imagine themselves to be—just like them. Of course, they like to imagine themselves as superheroes or other characters as well.

Children can now integrate mixed emotions so they can understand the feelings of others with greater clarity. They are also less likely to be overwhelmed with other people's emotions and respond with appropriate affect to them. Now children can feel guilty if they do not respond by helping and can be concerned about the future welfare of others.

IMPORTANT RESEARCH FINDINGS

Since the 1970s there has been a significant increase in research focused on understanding the development of and contributors to social competence, empathy, and prosocial behavior. Some of this has arisen out of concerns about various forms of violence in today's society and the lack of caring toward others less fortunate. There has also been increasing realization that, although children's social development is deeply affected by early relationships with parents, other social relationships are very important as well. This summary of the research focuses on the following:

- The influence of age, gender, and culture on social competence, empathy, and prosocial behavior

- Socialization within the family

- Socialization outside the family

- The importance and effect of emotional and cognitive factors within the child

The Influence of Age, Gender, and Culture on Social Competence, Empathy, and Prosocial Behavior

Much research has been done on the influence of age, gender, and culture on social competence, empathy, and caring behavior.

Age   Research that has been carried out in order to identify early social behaviors has typically used case studies of a small number of children; sociometric methods; observations of children in the laboratory, home, or social settings; or questionnaires or ratings. The latter are given to peers, parents, and teachers, and ask about the incidences of various social behaviors. Some researchers have also used a technique in which parents are placed in the role of observer and are asked to record their children's social behaviors over a period of time. The use of a variety of methods has sometimes produced differing results; however, clear trends—and in some cases, conclusions—have been found.

From studies that have been carried out with infants and young children, various social behaviors have tended to be identified much earlier than had previously been considered. The actual timetable for the development of social competence is set out in the previous section, so only some findings of particular significance are included here.

Research conducted in the early 1990s has put the beginnings of interest in peers as early as 2 months, when infants exhibit high rates of looking at one another (Brownell & Brown, 1992). Relatively little interaction or engagement is seen until children are 6–9 months old, when infants may directly smile at each other or try and touch if close enough (Brownell & Brown, 1992; Howes & Matheson, 1992). By the end of the first year, infants have a number of ways of directing attention to each other, although they lack the skills to engage in true interactive social play. Especially after 18 months, peer play can be maintained for longer and is more coordinated between the participants. Much of the play is still centered around objects, however, and many attempts to play by one of the participants will be ignored by the other (Brownell & Brown, 1992; Hanna & Meltzoff, 1993; Howes & Matheson, 1992). Between 24 and 36 months, there is a marked change in social play, and interactions include more social games and joint pretend play, where themes are shared and behavior is coordinated with one another rather than simply being imitative as it was before (Camaioni, Baumgartner, & Perucchini, 1991).

In this period, children have the necessary social and cognitive abilities to cooperate, assume different roles, engage in turn-taking, and work to achieve a goal collaboratively (Brownell & Carriger, 1990; Eckerman & Whitehead, 1999; Howes & Matheson, 1992; Schaffer, 1991).

From the time a child is 3 to 4 years of age and older, most of the play that occurs is cooperative, often occurring in the context of pretend play (Göncü, 1993). During this period children become increasingly able to resolve conflicts and to work out conciliatory ends to disputes (Caplan, Vespo, Pederson, & Hay, 1991; Dunn, 1995; Dunn & Herrera, 1997). In a study of preschoolers ages 3–6 years of age, Rourke, Wozniak, and Cassidy (1999) found that conflicts were frequent and that children used yielding to one another, disengagement, and negotiation to resolve conflicts. Sophistication of interactions increased with age, as did the children's tendency to use negotiation. Although friendships have been common previously, they become far more stable during this period and become an important way in which to learn about cooperating and resolving conflicts (Dunn, 1993; Dunn & McGuire, 1992; Gottman, 1983, 1986; Howes, Unger, & Matheson, 1992).

As with social relatedness, research has tended to show that the beginnings of empathy and prosocial behavior occur much earlier than had previously been considered possible. At

a very early age, infants show a primitive form of empathy, and cry when other infants cry (Hay, 1994). By 6 months, they may try and comfort a crying baby, motivated primarily by emotional contagion and their own personal distress, it would appear (Eisenberg, 1986, 1992; Eisenberg & Mussen, 1989; Hay, Nash, & Pedersen, 1981). Toward the end of the first year, toddlers will share by offering objects to others and putting the objects in the other child's hands (Brownell & Brown, 1992; Hay et al., 1981). In the second and third year of life, children's prosocial activities become much more elaborate and common and occur in about a third of possibilities (Sharron, 1991). Children help each other and "care" for their baby siblings, although these behaviors are more common and sophisticated when scaffolded by adults (Eisenberg, 1992; Lamb & Zakhireh, 1997; Radke-Yarrow, Zahn-Waxler, Richardson, Susman, & Martinez, 1994). By now, many children make concerted efforts to interact with other children who are in distress by patting and touching (Kitwood, 1990; Radke-Yarrow & Zahn-Waxler, 1984).

Although prosocial behaviors are seen in toddlers, young children often ignore another child's distress or even behave aggressively toward them (Dunn, 1988; Howes & Farver, 1987; Zahn-Waxler & Radke-Yarrow, 1982). From 2 to 3 years of age, there is an increase in frequency of comforting behaviors, but some researchers have actually noted a decline in prosocial behavior in the preschool years, with an increase occurring again in the years from 6 to 12 (Gottman & Parkhurst, 1980; Hay, 1994). This dropping off in helping behavior in the preschool years has been difficult to explain, but it has been suggested that by this age it is no longer expected by peers or needed to keep interactions going. It may also be because preschoolers see teachers as the ones who should assume the role of helping (Caplan & Hay, 1989; Dunn, 1988; Hay, 1994; Hay, Caplan, Castle, & Stimson, 1991).

Gender   Few differences have been identified between the genders in social competence; however, by the preschool years gender segregation begins to be evident (Johnson, Ironsmith, Witcher, Poteat, Snow, & Mumford, 1997). Researchers have noted that the types of social play that boys and girls engage in is often quite different (Alexander & Hines, 1994; Maccoby, 1990). Boys prefer play that is characterized by a rough-and-tumble style, competition, and dominance, while girls prefer play that is less aggressive and more cooperative. Children from either gender can be unpopular or ostracized, however. Researchers, therefore, suggest that the gender segregation or the preference or tendency for children in preschool and elementary school to play with their own gender may be based more on the sharing of similar play interests than on merely being of the same gender (Alexander & Hines, 1994).

Studies of the incidence of empathy and prosocial behavior have varied in whether they have found gender differences in terms of degree of showing these behaviors. When gender differences have been found they have tended to slightly favor girls on scores involving expression of empathy (Eisenberg & Mussen, 1989; Radke-Yarrow, Zahn-Waxler, & Chapman, 1983). In a more recent study, Zahn-Waxler, Radke-Yarrow, Wagner, and Chapman (1992) found that 1- to 2-year-old girls showed more concern when another child was distressed than boys, but not more actual prosocial or helping behavior. In a study of twins in the second year of life, girls also scored higher on measures of empathy (Zahn-Waxler, Robinson, & Emde, 1992), although Howes and Farver (1987) found that for 16- to 33-month-olds, boys actually responded more and showed more prosocial behavior. In a review of studies, Eisenberg and Lennon (1983) concluded that boys show similar physiological responses to the distress of others, but less facial or verbal reactions. Consequently, their responses to the upset of others may be misinterpreted unless changes in physiological reactions are measured and their actual helping behavior is recorded.

Culture   In some cultures prosocial behavior, cooperation, and social responsibility are predominant, while in others much more egocentric and individualistic reactions are common. Probably most interesting is that the values of the society are passed down as they are emphasized and modeled by parents and taught in schools and other group situations (Eisenberg & Mussen, 1989). These differences can be based on tradition and the norms and values of the culture as well as determined by whether the society is more or less industrialized.

Socialization within the Family

Significant individual differences have been found between children in their social competence and empathy and helping behavior. Consequently, a great deal of research has been directed toward identifying contributors to these differences. A focus of some of this research has been to consider the interactions of parents with infants and young children, their discipline styles, and the family context. Research has found a number of relationships between these variables and children's social competence (Austin & Lindauer, 1990).

Parents' Relationships with Their Children   Some researchers have found that young children's early attachment classification affects some aspects of their interactions with others or their social competence (Elicker, Englund, & Sroufe, 1992). On one hand, securely attached children show better interpersonal problem-solving and social engagement with peers compared with insecurely attached children (Rose-Krasnor, Rubin, Booth, & Coplan, 1996). They also exhibit more empathy and concern for others (LaFrenière & Sroufe, 1985; Londerville & Main, 1981; Park & Waters, 1989; Sroufe, 1983; Waters, Wippman, & Sroufe, 1979; Weston & Main, 1980). On the other hand, Rose-Krasnor and colleagues (1996) found that insecurely attached children used more aggressive strategies in interactions with peers. Another study found a very strong relationship between avoidant attachment and later behavior problems (Vondra, Shaw, Swearingen, Cohen, & Owens, 1999). Other researchers have found that anxiously attached children (both avoidant and resistant) are more likely to have their social overtures rejected and to have negative and asynchronous interactions with peers than securely attached children (Fagot, 1997; Youngblade & Belsky, 1992).

The way parents think about their children has been shown to influence their interactions with them. For example, Cohen (1989) found that the more mothers believe they can affect the sociability of their children or that the fault does not lie solely with the child when things do not work out, the more likely they are to be involved in making sure their children have opportunities for relationships with their peers. In other studies it has been found that parents who generally view their children's behavior positively and expect positive outcomes have more socially competent children (Dix & Grusec, 1985); while parents who expect negative behavior and who think their children are to blame for negative outcomes have children who do not demonstrate competence (Hastings & Rubin, 1999; Rubin, Mills, & Rose-Krasnor, 1989). Similarly, Rubin and Mills (1990) found that mothers who believed their children were responsible for social difficulties placed more importance on directly or intrusively teaching social skills and had preschoolers who showed more aggressive or withdrawn behaviors. In other words, parents who believe the social behavior of their children to be more determined by internal factors of the child or who blame their children for peer difficulties tend to be more angry and directive with their children and to have more socially incompetent children.

Parents' Interactions with Children

Other researchers have been more interested in the actual behavioral exchanges that take place between parents and children than in the internal representations that are formed as a consequence (e.g., MacDonald & Parke, 1984; Putallaz, 1987). For example, a number of researchers have found that parents who initiate more social contacts for their children, who coach or scaffold and give more adequate advice about peer interactions, or who encourage appropriate social skills have more socially competent children (e.g., Ladd & Hart, 1992; Mize & Pettit, 1997; Profilet & Ladd, 1994). Kerns, Cole, and Andrews (1998) found the relationship only held for girls, however.

A number of other researchers have examined the relationship between parents' emotional displays and their regulation of their children's emotions and later social competence. For example, Denham and Grout (1993) found that, in general, preschoolers' social competence as evaluated by teachers was associated with maternal happiness during interactions. In a related study that considered maternal and paternal play interactions with 4- and 5-year-olds, fathers' rather than mothers' interactions were found to be related to children's social competence. Children of fathers who responded to their negative affect displays with negative displays of their own were more likely to be verbally aggressive, to share less, and to avoid others. The researchers noted that mothers may be less likely to engage in physical play, which might account for the lack of association of mothers' interactions with children's social competence (Carson & Parke, 1996). Similar findings were reported for kindergarten children by Isley, O'Neil, and Parke (1996) but not by Garner, Jones, and Miner (1994). Roberts (1999) reported correlations between mothers' encouragement of emotional control and tolerance of expression of emotional distress in their 4-year-olds and the children's prosocial behavior and resourcefulness at 7 years.

Parents' Discipline Practices and the Family Milieu

Parents' discipline practices have also been studied for their relationship to later social competence of children. In a study of preschoolers' sociometric status or popularity that examined the relationship of a number of parenting variables, Peery, Jensen, and Adams (1985) found that the use of structure and discipline combined with high praise was positively related to children's popularity. Rubin (1995) found "high power" or very directive control to be associated with aggressive and disruptive behavior in children, although he pointed out that the parents' behavior may result from the child's behavior rather than the other way around. Caregiver modeling of empathetic, warm interactions has been found to be associated with prosocial behaviors toward peers in distress (Zahn-Waxler, Radke-Yarrow, & King, 1979). In addition to modeling, explaining, and teaching with words about social interactions, especially when the effects of helping are explained, have been found to encourage children to help other children (Clary & Miller, 1986; Moore & Eisenberg, 1984). Inductive disciplinary techniques—which call attention to a victim's distress and encourage perspective-taking—also have been found to promote moral development and prosocial behavior (Eisenberg-Berg & Geisheker, 1979; Howard & Barnett, 1981; Miller, 1984).

Instead of looking at specific interactions and discipline techniques, a number of researchers have considered broad aspects of the family milieu and parent–child relationship issues that contribute to social competence. Some researchers, instead of considering single dimensions of parenting, have looked at styles and patterns. The most often considered study is that of Baumrind (1967, 1973, 1988) who compared authoritative, permissive, and authoritarian parents and their relationships to long-term outcomes including social competence and social responsibility (or prosocial behavior). Her findings showed that authoritative parenting, (i.e., when parents are warm, loving, responsive, and supportive and combine this with firm limits) is more likely to produce socially competent children. Dekovic and Janssens (1992) also found similar links with 6- to 12-year-old children's sociometric status and authoritative parenting.

Sibling Influences　　More than 80% of American children have one or more siblings, and apart from the influence of parents, interactions with siblings have been shown to have the most effect on children's social competence. Sibling relationships provide intense emotional interactions, and children display a great deal of conflict as well as nurturing behavior with their siblings (Dunn & Munn, 1986). Thus, social skills may be developed in sibling relationships, and siblings can support each other in times of stress. Siblings who show high levels of sharing, helping, and cooperating toward each other are more cooperative later with peers than siblings who do not act in this way toward each other (Dunn & Munn, 1986). In a study that examined the social behavior of 7-year-old children from the Colorado Adoption Study, Stocker and Dunn (1990) found that children behaved similarly with siblings and peers; however, they noted that the relationships were complex and influenced by child temperament, gender, and adoptive status as well.

Socialization Outside of the Family

In today's society many young children are in child care from quite early on and exposed to the influence of people outside the home including peers and teachers. These people can have a significant effect on the socialization of children. When children first began attending child care in large numbers there were a number of concerns that children would be adversely affected, especially their social and emotional development. In fact, although children who attend child care may initially be somewhat more aggressive than those who do not, in general, access to other children and the opportunity to learn from them has enriched children's lives and enabled them to learn to interact better with others and to learn prosocial behaviors (DiLalla, 1998).

Teachers can be powerful models of prosocial behavior (Mitchell-Copeland, Denham, & DeMulder, 1997) and schools have often been the site of a number of organized programs that have successfully taught whole classrooms of children to show more empathy and caring behavior toward each other (Feshbach, Feshbach, Fauvre, & Ballard-Campbell, 1983; Hertz-Lazarowitz & Sharan, 1984; Spivak & Shure, 1989).

Children's peers and friends act as socializers for one another. They can serve as models of aggression, of sociability, or of withdrawal. Peers can also model caring behaviors, such as sharing, helping others, expressing sympathy, and being generous. Children whose peers expose them to these types of behavior are more likely to act the same way themselves. In fact, peers can be as strong an influence on children's behavior as parents. Also, peers provide different experiences, with more reciprocity and cooperation between equals (Eisenberg-Berg, Cameron, Tryon, & Dodez, 1981; Zahn-Waxler, Iannotti, & Chapman, 1982).

Children's friendships, even in the early years, are also important contexts for socialization and provide resources for having fun and learning about solving conflicts (Costin & Jones, 1992; Hartup, 1992). Friends can show sharing, understanding, and loyalty toward each other and children can also learn in that context that conflicts can be solved and friendships preserved (Gottman & Parker, 1986; Hartup, Laursen, Stewart, & Eastenson, 1988; Vespo & Caplan, 1993). Although friendships may not be essential for children, they can certainly provide

advantages and be a source of support to those who have them (Hartup & Sancillio, 1986; Walden, Lemerise, & Smith, 1999). Children with emotional and behavioral difficulties often have more difficulties in maintaining friendships and children without friends are often very unhappy and lonely (Cassidy & Asher, 1992). Also, children who lose friends because they move away may show a decline in social competence for a significant time period, showing how important the support provided by friends can be (Field, 1984; Howes, 1987, 1988).

The Importance and Effect of Emotional and Cognitive Factors Within the Child

Temperamental factors within the child can contribute to styles of social relatedness in young children. For example, slow-to-warm-up and inhibited children may have more difficulties relating to peers, while very irritable and intense children may be more aggressive (see Chapter 1). It is important to note, however, that physiological differences have been found to relate to prosocial behavior, with children who become severely dysregulated as measured by skin conductance less likely to respond prosocially (Fabes, Eisenberg, Karbon, Bernsweig, Speer, & Carlo, 1994).

Research has shown that two aspects of emotional functioning are particularly important in the development of social competence. These are 1) the understanding of and regulation of emotions and 2) positivity of emotional response in interactions with other children (Raver, Blackburn, Bancroft, & Torp, 1999; Roberts & Strayer, 1996). Also, children who have learned to discuss emotions and to follow expected rules are more popular (Hubbard & Cole, 1994). Alessandri (1991), in comparing maltreated preschoolers and matched controls, found that the maltreated children were less socially competent and had difficulty with self-regulation, which resulted in aggressive and disruptive behavior.

Perhaps one of the areas that has been most researched, especially in relation to children who have significant difficulties with socialization, has been social information processing (Akhtar & Bradley, 1991; Dodge & Price, 1994). Dodge and colleagues have identified five steps that children go though in responding to social interactions:

1. Encoding of social stimuli and cues (registering what other children are doing)

2. Interpreting this information, or what the other child(ren) is doing

3. Thinking about a number of possible responses to the situation (response search)

4. Choosing the appropriate response for the situation

5. Carrying out the response and evaluating its success

Children who rate high in social competence do better in all these steps. The first steps are particularly important, because if the situation is misunderstood and misinterpreted from the beginning, the response chosen may fail to take into account the perspective of others and the group's frame of reference, which can lead to rejection from the peer group. Dodge and colleagues have found that aggressive children, for example, are far more likely to attribute hostile intent to peers' intention (whether it was benign or ambiguous) and to act accordingly. They are also more likely to attend to and remember aggressive cues than they are to remember positive ones. These researchers have also found that these information-processing variables are significantly correlated with peer and teachers' evaluations of social competence (Dodge, 1980, 1986; Dodge & Coie, 1987).

Another area of research has been how children's ability to resolve conflicts relates to social competence. Undoubtedly, conflicts in young children's play are common and the ability to resolve them without dissolution of interactions and friendships is crucial (Shantz, 1987). Dunn, Slomkowski, Donelan, and Herrera (1995) found that children's strategies varied with friends, siblings, and their mother, with children using more other-oriented arguments with friends and more self-oriented strategies with siblings and mothers. They also found little carry-over between what happened in the family and outside the home. Other researchers have noted that conflict-resolution ability matures with age and relates to increased perspective-taking, successful peer group entry, negotiation skills, and the ability to make friends (Iskandar, Laursen, Finkelstein, & Frederickson, 1995). Rourke, Wozniak, and Cassidy (1999) found that children between 4 and 6 years of age gained more ability to resolve conflicts with age and that they were also more likely than younger children to negotiate and to use power assertion as opposed to using disengagement, giving up, or seeking adult intervention or help.

In conclusion, a number of research studies have demonstrated that children's social competence, empathy, and caring behavior are influenced by a variety of factors. They have also shown that changes can occur in children's level of social competence by enhancing parent–child interactions, intervening in schools, encouraging appropriate peer interactions, and enhancing the emotional and cognitive aspects of young children's development.

THE GROWTH-PROMOTING ENVIRONMENT: PRINCIPLES OF ENCOURAGING SOCIAL COMPETENCE, EMPATHY, AND CARING BEHAVIOR

This section explores a number of principles for encouraging social competence, empathy, and caring behavior in young children in the home and in group settings (see Table 10.3).

PRINCIPLE 1: *Model caring behavior toward the child and others. Show caring behavior toward the less fortunate. Reinforce and encourage caring behavior.*

The adage that children do as you do and not as you say is very true. In fact, no principle of child rearing is more powerful in instilling a social and caring conscience in children than providing a good example. Children, almost from birth, love to imitate and are surrounded by

Table 10.3. Principles for encouraging social competence, empathy, and caring behavior

Principle 1	Model caring behavior toward the child and others. Show caring behavior toward the less fortunate. Reinforce and encourage caring behavior.
Principle 2	Help children see the effect of their behavior on others. Encourage role-taking and perspective-taking.
Principle 3	Encourage responsibility by having children do chores.
Principle 4	Expose children to contacts with peers and teach them social skills and strategies for positive social interactions with others.
Principle 5	Teach conflict resolution and interpersonal negotiation skills to children.

Caring needs to be woven into the fabric of the home environment.

positive and negative influences and models from which to draw their impressions. Nevertheless, the way the caregiver responds to the child is the most important and most crucial model.

Children can learn to care by seeing parents show interest and caring about what they say and do and by experiencing comforting when they feel upset and in danger. Modeling prosocial behavior or altruistic attitudes such as not putting others down and respecting the other person's point of view can be a powerful example for children to follow. Also showing responsible behavior toward the family, in the workplace, and in other activities can be excellent models. In other words, caring must be woven into the fabric of the home environment. The child who feels loved and valued will have the energy and security to be able to notice and respond lovingly to others.

Clearly, it is difficult and inappropriate to expose young children to a full understanding of the problems people in the world face. It *is* important to provide opportunities for demonstrating caring and altruistic behavior toward the less fortunate, however. In other words, it can be very helpful for children to gradually see that the family has a commitment to some larger goal or tradition beyond self-interest. Although children do not understand societal values, they can be involved in caring activities such as donating toys and clothes to charity, taking food to the food bank, helping the homeless, and participating in a walkathon.

Parents can also notice children's spontaneous helping behavior and let them know how pleasing it is. Young children often show caring behavior in a number of ways: protecting a sibling, comforting a friend, feeding a pet, or sharing a treat with another. There are usually a variety of small instances of this kind of behavior that happen every day, all of which provide excellent opportunities to let children know that their efforts are noticed and appreciated. Children need to be told frequently about the pleasure and pride they cause when they help others. In other words, it is as important to notice acts of kindness as it is to respond to demonstrations of competence.

Playing cooperative games with young children can be fun and encourages caring behavior instead of competition. In these games, each child takes a turn, but may have a task of helping another rather than trying to get to a certain place first.

PRINCIPLE 2:   *Help children see the effect of their behavior on others. Encourage role-taking and perspective-taking.*

Research clearly shows that in order to be sociable and empathetic, children must be able to understand the point of view of the other person. In order to do this, a number of role-playing or perspective-taking activities can be helpful. Many of these have been talked about in other chapters, especially Chapter 4 on play, and include interactive story-telling, doing short skits or plays, pretend play, and using puppets and reversing roles. Another game that children love is the detective game. In this game, people and characters that the child knows and likes are chosen. Children are then asked to figure out what makes the people or characters happy or unhappy, what they like or dislike, and what makes them mad or afraid. The children are asked to think what they could do to make the person feel happy, and charts of their responses can be made. The child can be helped to do this if it is reasonable. For example, Aunt Lillian may like flowers, so the child could plant some seeds or buy a rose to take on the next visit.

Simply telling a child it is not nice to be unkind or punishing the child for hitting or teasing another child will not teach about the value of caring for others. If a child is unkind to someone else, refuses to share, or will not play with another child, be very clear that you are upset, unhappy, and angry about her insensitivity. Ask her to think about how she would feel and how she thinks the other child feels. In other words, it is crucial that she learns about other people's perspectives, feelings, and point of view so she can feel for them or have sympathy. Without this, caring behavior will not be learned and internalized for the future.

PRINCIPLE 3:   *Encourage responsibility by having children do chores.*

In an increasing number of families today there is a tendency to ignore the need to teach children responsibility. Even young children need to share responsibilities within the family, however. Along with the good feelings of helping, children can gain a sense of their own competence. One way of encouraging responsibility is to have children involved in the management of the home and responsible for certain chores. If presented in a positive and cheerful way, caregivers can provide children with a greater sense of usefulness and belonging. Even young children like to feel they are contributing.

Just as with any kind of routine, doing chores has to be reinforced, and time should be taken to monitor that they are being done. As children get a little older it can be helpful to have them involved in planning what needs to be done and who will do what. Some suggestions for chores that young children could manage are set out in Table 10.4.

PRINCIPLE 4:   *Expose children to contacts with peers and teach them social skills and strategies for positive social interactions with others.*

Most young children love to be around other children. Although some children seem to find playing with other children and developing friendships natural and easy, others have a great deal of difficulty learning to relate to other children and may need to be taught some of the

Letting a child help with simple chores can enhance his sense of competence and responsibility.

necessary skills. It is critical for children to have friends and to be accepted by other children because being rejected can make them feel sad, anxious, angry, and worthless. With these types of feelings, socializing can get more and more difficult. Obviously, just teaching social skills without laying a foundation for the child to feel competent, respected, and listened to is not helpful. There are a number of skills that that caregivers can foster in children.

Research has shown that it is crucial that young children have the opportunity to be around other children, either in an organized program (e.g., child care, nursery school) or in

Table 10.4. Examples of suitable chores for different ages

Age range	Chore
2–3 years	Get own drink of water
	Put dirty diapers in pail or garbage
	Put spoons in the dishwasher
	Pick up toys
3–4 years	Help set the table (e.g., by putting out some utensils)
	Fill pet dishes with water and dry food
	Help with shopping
	Get the mail
4–5 years	Pour milk or juice
	Water plants
	Make bed
	Answer telephone
6 years	Rake leaves
	Put plates in the dishwasher
	Put dirty clothes in hamper
	Assist with grocery shopping

Young children love to be around other children.

more casual settings (e.g., the park, a drop-in center, at family gatherings). If a child is having social difficulties, it is important to invite one child over that the child plays well with and to observe and intervene if necessary to ensure that the visit goes well. Keeping the visit short at first and making sure interesting toys and activities are available can help the visit go smoothly. Some skills that children need to learn are set out in Table 10.5.

Teaching Skills for Entering a Group of Children

During the toddler and preschool years, children go from more uncoordinated play and tentative peer contacts to being able to sustain quite long and complex interactions with each other and being able to make friends. In order for this to happen, children need a number of social skills—particularly the ability to enter an ongoing interaction between groups of peers or to accept being approached by other children. This can be very difficult, as interactions in preschool settings can be quite brief, so children have to constantly be renegotiating entry into groups of peers. Also, once children are already playing with each other they tend to protect their interactive space and sometimes as many as 60% of entry attempts are rejected by the other children.

In trying to enter groups and initiate contact, children use a number of strategies that can range from quite passive and just hovering on the edge to insisting on entering the group. The types of strategies children use are related to how successful they will be in gaining entry to the group. Success in entry attempts appears to be related to three main elements. First, children who observe the play that is going on and adapt and contribute to that are more likely to be accepted and integrated into the play. Second, it is important that the child make a bid for entry

Table 10.5. Social skills that can help children better interact with peers and others

Skills for joining a group of children	Skills for keeping play going and making friends	Skills for cooperating and sharing
Establishing eye contact, and asking to play in a pleasant tone of voice	Avoiding biting, yelling at, or in any way hurting others	Sharing toys with others
Listening and observing what is going on before entering and then fitting in with the play	Standing up for oneself and not accepting being bullied	Helping out another child
Using polite statements (e.g., "Please" "Thank you" "Excuse me")	Listening to other children and being able to have a conversation	Playing games that can be enjoyed as a group
Watching children's play and choosing an appropriate role and time to join in and blending into the play	Learning to negotiate and resolve conflicts	Helping, for example, by building part of a building made of blocks
	Understanding the emotions of other children and containing their own.	Taking part in turn-taking games or interactive/pretend play such as playing doctors or teachers
	May need to agree with other children at times to keep the interaction going	Physical types of play such as playing chasing games together
		Games with rules as children get older

if it seems that he could be accepted. Third, the manner in which the approach is made can be critical, too; a bid is far more likely to be accepted if the child makes his approach in a confident and positive way; children who are perceived as whiny or aggressive are far more likely to have their requests for entry rejected.

If a child is having difficulty entering play groups, it can be necessary to both coach the child and to encourage the other children to allow him to enter the group. If possible, setting up activities for more interactive and cooperative play in terms of the toys available and scaffolding the choice of play can be helpful. Although constantly organizing and hovering over play is not helpful in the long term, it may be necessary in the beginning to help the child experience some success in entering a group so he can begin to feel more positive about the experience and to build his self-esteem. Some suggestions for helping with group entry are the following:

- Have toys such as blocks and pretend play materials available that can encourage collaboration.

- Make sure enough toys are available, but not too many as to be overwhelming. Have duplicates of some very popular toys, especially if they can only be used by one child at a time or if having two can encourage interactive play (e.g., two telephones so that children can hold a pretend telephone conversation). If toys can be on shelves and relatively uncluttered, this can also encourage their appropriate use and cooperative play.

- Choose children who can play together or just one playmate who the child likes to encourage a child's ability to join in. Join the group yourself and make sure all or both of the children can take part. Sometimes it may be necessary to choose the activity and to select the toys to assure success. Once things are going well, remain available on the "sidelines," but do not be too intrusive or overbearing.

- Help a child who is having difficulties, observe what is going on, talk about this with her, and suggest things she could say or do to enter the group. If the children are playing tea party, for example, suggest she take a cup and ask for some tea, or that she offer to help with pouring or doing the dishes. Suggest alternative ways to ask to join in such as, "Can I play? That looks like fun."

- In large groups of children it may be necessary to comfort those who are upset because of being rejected. Offer suggestions to children who are having difficulty playing together and praise children who are cooperating well together.

- Because many frequently rejected children misread social cues and tend to think children are rejecting them or are hostile toward them, it is important to intervene when this happens and to reinterpret the intentions of the other child immediately. Quickly asking what has happened and correcting any misconceptions can help a child to ignore the event and keep the play going without acting out aggressively. This strategy, over time, can help a child find new ways to process information.

- Sometimes a more competent or older child can be recruited to help a child who is having difficulty entering a group.

- Draw a child's attention to efforts other children may be making to communicate with her and help her make her own communication to others clearer.

- Encourage children to participate in pretend play, plays, or puppet shows to enable passive children to try out more assertive roles and aggressive children to act out more cooperative roles.

- Read children's stories about rejection and cooperation so children can learn to understand how other children feel about relationships and how they can work (see the children's books at the end of this chapter for some examples).

- Activities that teach social problem-solving and negotiation, as discussed under Principle 4, can also be helpful.

Teaching Skills for Keeping Play Going and Making Friends

Once a child has gained entry into a group he needs to be able to keep the play going. The level of social participation may shift during an interaction between quite intense communication and interactive play and more parallel play. Interactive play can become interrupted if children become bored with an activity or because one or more children interrupt the play. Play can be kept going when children engage in conversations and when they listen to each other, so encouraging communication skills can be crucial. It may also be important to interpret another child's feelings for the child and to encourage him to talk about his feelings. Gaining control of emotional outbursts is crucial for a child to be accepted in a group and to allow interactions to continue. Remember that children who are more cheerful and positive with others are more likely to be popular and accepted, so give children an opportunity to discuss negative feelings but make an effort to help them bring them back to positive. Encourage pretend play, as much of the successful interactions that take place in preschool settings involve pretending. Join the child yourself in these games so he or she can learn about how such interactions can take place.

Skills for Cooperating and Sharing

For preschool children, learning to share is a difficult process and one that does not happen without a lot of coaching. This is primarily because young children have an egocentric view of the world and "It's mine" and "Gimme" feature significantly in their vocabulary. Another reason is that young children often equate sharing with giving something away completely. Possessions for the young child are seen as extensions of themselves and more fights occur over possessions than over anything else. Moreover, children cannot see that if they share a toy now, someone may share with them later. When a child grabs a toy from another child and refuses to share, making another child cry, the immediate reaction needs to be to restore calm and to help the crying child. It is also helpful to ask the child who grabbed the toy why she did that, as it is likely she does not realize that she will have a turn later. Staying close and asking the child to share something with reassurances that she will get it back later can also help. Other ideas to encourage cooperation include

- Play turn-taking games children can enjoy in a group.

- Have toys that really encourage sharing, such as blocks, as well as pretend-play and imaginative toys such as Playdoh and Plasticine.

- Help a child to build something if she is having difficulties.

- Encourage interactive play such as "doctor and patient," "school," or "tea party."

- With a group of children, dance to music and change between different partners. Dance in a circle.

- Provide opportunities for children to help and cooperate in cleaning up.

PRINCIPLE 5: *Teach conflict resolution and interpersonal negotiation skills to children.*

Conflicts occur all the time when toddlers and preschoolers play together. In fact, they have been seen to occur up to 23 times an hour in some groups. Conflicts can be frustrating, of course, but they can play an important role in children's social development by forcing children to learn about other people's perspectives. Children must learn neither to act aggressively nor to use physical force but instead to use more indirect methods to resolve the conflicts.

Children are able to settle most conflicts by themselves, with one child submitting to or cooperating with the other and with no adult intervention. Adults need to help children learn effective conflict-resolution skills, and children frequently provide caregivers with excellent exchanges for teaching conflict resolution when they get into fights with peers or siblings. The skills are best taught on the spot as the conflict happens and before the caregiver or children are too worked up. Learning to resolve conflicts can involve two major strategies: 1) helping children learn to process and interpret the social cues or reactions of the other child, and 2) learning actual conflict-resolution skills. As noted previously, some children continually misinterpret what the other child is doing or saying as rejection or aggression, and some conflicts can be stopped from escalating by explaining to the child what was actually meant and having the other child tell him he did not mean to hurt him. When a conflict cannot be avoided in this way, however, it can be helpful to go through the steps given in Table 10.6 with the children involved.

Many parents are very surprised how well this method can work—even with children as young as 3 years of age—and how quickly children can learn to use it in situations that have

Table 10.6. The steps of conflict resolution

1. Ask each child to define the problem. Let each speak and express the problem while the other listens. Allow emotions to be expressed but not by swearing, shouting, or hitting. Insist they "use their words."
2. Ask some open ended questions and reflect what is being said. "I guess you both want to play with _____." "You need _____."
3. Brainstorm for different solutions. Generate ideas yourself. Be receptive to ideas from the children and write them down. Do not judge their quality and praise the children for their suggestions.
4. Select a solution that satisfies both sides. Get the children to see both perspectives. Agree to try the solution for a week.
5. Put the solution or plan in writing or pictures. Review it in a week to see how it is working. Adjust what is not working.

not yet escalated out of control. If children have become extremely upset and angry, tears and anger must be brought under control before using it. Once children have calmed down, however, the conflict can be discussed. If necessary, of course, providing children with good problem-solving skills and conversational abilities can support their ability to use these strategies.

Although talking through conflicts is helpful and should be used when possible, it may take too much time. If this is the case, the object that the children are fighting about should be removed, and the children separated and distracted with another activity.

SOME COMMONLY RAISED ISSUES AROUND SOCIAL COMPETENCE, EMPATHY, AND CARING BEHAVIOR

The following are some commonly raised issues around social competence, empathy, and caring behavior.

The Effect of Television and Videotapes on Empathy and Caring Behavior

The effects of television and videotapes on play have already been discussed in Chapter 4; however, television is an important socializer of children and parents worry about its effect on their children's social interactions and altruistic behavior. As some young children watch several hours of television a week, it can have a major influence on them (Huston, Wright, Marquis, & Green, 1999; Woodard, 2000). Television can influence even young children and pervasive messages about behaviors, values, attitudes, and social norms are modeled through characters. As children get older, rock stars, soap opera characters, and other media stars can become powerful models.

A number of studies and real-life examples indicate that watching violent television, especially if it is frequent and over many years, has a causal effect on aggressive behavior in children and adolescents (Bryant, 1990; Desmond, Singer, & Singer, 1990; Singer & Singer, 2000; Singer & Singer, 1986). Other studies suggest that watching certain television shows may provide a "dulling" effect, so that cruelty or another person's pain is no longer upsetting or significant. This may result in actual dulling of physiological arousal mechanisms to scenes of violence. The effect of watching sexually explicit acts may have a similarly devastating effect.

Also, for younger children, television viewing can replace warm social interactions and play with toys and consequently, affect development (Anderson & Evans, 2001). As much as children can learn negative behaviors and attitudes from television shows, however, television can be used to foster positive learning. The positive effects of television can include the following:

- Because children associate television with pleasure and recreation, it can be an excellent teaching tool.

- Some shows can teach socially desirable behaviors, empathy, and prosocial behaviors.

- Some shows can take children to places and situations they would never experience otherwise.

- Some shows can provide opportunities for families to be together.

- Some shows can stimulate imagination and give children people to identify with and things to dream about.

- Some shows can provide positive role models.

Parents can use different ways to control television in their homes and to turn it into a more positive influence for children. Some ideas are set out in Table 10.7.

Keeping Children Safe in an Unpredictable World

As people hear about terrifying crimes against children and the significant incidence of sexual abuse, there is a natural tendency to develop strategies to keep children safe or to street proof them. Consequently, many young children are given a variety of rules and information about the world so they can keep themselves safe. Although this is understandable, it is also clear that protecting a small child is an adult's responsibility and that expecting the child to assume that responsibility is likely to cause significant emotional damage. Young children must learn to trust and to feel safe in order to be able to develop an inner sense of security and competence and a belief in their own ability to solve problems and manage the world. The following vignettes illustrate some of these ideas.

Table 10.7. Strategies for getting control of television and making television viewing positive

Strategies for getting control of television viewing	Strategies for making television viewing positive
Limit the time children watch television.	Discuss shows with children, for example, about characters, the plot and ending, and so forth.
Turn off television and do other family activities.	
Have a timetable of acceptable shows.	Use shows that teach prosocial messages and teach about self-control.
Put the television in an out-of-the-way place; this is especially helpful with young children.	Encourage children to create their own versions of the program by providing props and allowing space to use them.
Record shows that are acceptable or have videos that have positive themes and encourage children to watch these.	Talk about the values and the difficult issues dealt with in some television shows or movies.
Have watching television or a video be a family event or something special.	Consider how characters feel, which enhances perspective-taking.

• •

Mia had been raped by her grandfather and continued to struggle with feelings of helplessness and anger. In order to protect her own daughter, Tammy, she began at a very young age to warn her about the dangers of strangers, male relatives, and walking outside. She also asked her daughter, every night, if any men had touched her or talked to her. By 5 years of age Tammy was terrified of men, running away if a male teacher talked to her or tried to help her.

Enrique came from a country in which a civil war raged and it was difficult to trust anyone. When his son Christopher was 3 years old, he decided it was time to teach him that he could trust no one. He took him to the playground, had him climb to the top of the slide, and encouraged him to jump down into his arms. At the last minute he moved away, letting the child fall and break his arm. This experience, Enrique believed, would teach him that nobody can be trusted and would consequently make the child fit to survive in a cruel, unhelpful world. Christopher presented at school as an isolated, angry boy.

Mary had moved with her husband from a small town where she knew everyone to a large city. At first, she felt overwhelmed and lonely, especially after her baby was born and she was home on maternity leave. At this point she decided to make a conscious effort to get to know people in the community and to make sure her son, Thomas, had other children to play with. When Thomas was a preschooler, Mary told him and showed him many exciting things he could do in the city. While she taught him about how strangers could be dangerous, she also made sure he knew that not all people are bad and that there are people close to home who can help him if he needs it.

The first two vignettes are extreme, but they illustrate the way in which excessive emphasis on the dangers of the world can cause emotional and social difficulties. The presentation of these kinds of models of the world leaves little opportunity for the children to find positive models to identify with in schools or other organizations to which they are exposed, while the model Mary gave Thomas was that there are many exciting places and kind people around him that he can enjoy.

It is, therefore, critical that caregivers come up with a system that will establish guidelines and keep children safe but will not flood small children with facts and thoughts that they cannot handle and that will damage their sense of trust in the world. In other words, protecting a small child is the responsibility of *adults.*

The ideas presented in Table 10.8 can help parents find a balance between the need to keep children safe and the need to tell them about the potential dangers in the world. With this kind of balance, young children are not flooded with information about terrible people and awful events that can heighten anxiety and create unnecessary fears. We cannot expect children

Table 10.8. Absolute rules for keeping children safe

What the adult must do	What to tell children
Teach children rules of social conduct (e.g., it is acceptable to say "I don't like to be picked up and hugged.").	Tell children it is an absolute rule they cannot wander away. Check with them so they show they remember the rule.
Check out in detail anyone (especially caregivers) who will be alone with a child.	Teach children about people they can turn to in emergencies (e.g., policeman, neighbors, teachers).
Teach children their address and telephone number.	Teach children they must never go in a car with anyone they do not know or accept gifts from strangers.
Encourage open communication so the child will tell caregivers about problems.	Tell children to let you know if anyone or anyone's behavior makes them uncomfortable.
Make sure the child is never alone on the way to and from school or in a mall.	

to go to child care or school excited about learning if they are constantly vigilant. Nor can we expect them to trust, respect, and be friendly with sitters and other reliable people if we tell them people cannot be trusted.

What To Do About Bullying

Bullying among children is not a new phenomenon, and many adults have had personal experiences of being bullied in their childhood. Our awareness of the extent of the problem and its negative effect on children who are victimized is growing, however. Research now indicates that preschoolers are particularly at risk for being victimized compared with older children and that it often remains an ongoing and chronic problem if not dealt with, making it even more significant. Children who are teased, threatened, or physically attacked by peers may develop very negative feelings toward school and may resist going. They are lonelier, more depressed, anxious, and less liked than children who are not bullied and may believe negative things that are said about them such as "You are clumsy" or "You are stupid."

Kochenderfer and Ladd (1996) identified two types of victimized children; those who are sometimes quite provoking and are aggressive and hot tempered and those who are passive and insecure. Some of the passive children become very upset and cry when they are victimized and make no effort to stop the attacks. They are often cautious, sensitive, and quiet children who look upon themselves as failures or exhibit behaviors that make them appear different or vulnerable to peers. Parents of children who are being victimized can help their children by

- Talking to personnel at the child care or preschool and alert them to the child's difficulties

- Asking that the teacher make every effort to keep the child safe from verbal or physical attacks or teasing

- Letting the child know that they will keep him safe and encouraging him to talk about what is going on at school and how he feels about it

- Not being too overprotective of the child. Make sure he gets opportunities to play with other children and encourage him to enter groups and to develop some of the interpersonal skills outlined previously

- Encouraging the child in any way possible to make small decisions and use every opportunity to give him a feeling of competence; for example, give the child a chance to take the

lead in conversations and pretend play and do not be too demanding of the child in interactions; show interest and respond to any initiations the child makes

- Bringing any aggression under control (as outlined in Chapter 8)

- Stopping children in exclusive groups from victimizing others and encouraging children to accept the victimized children into their play

Overcoming Grandiosity and Self-Centered Behavior

A number of children at 4, 5, and 6 years of age continue to show behaviors and attitudes that are typical of much younger children. They are self-centered to a degree that they do not understand and are not even interested in the perspective of others, and they have a fragile grandiosity about things they can do and their control over other people. When these children find that they cannot do something, however, they get very anxious and often refuse to participate in learning the skills necessary to be successful. Without a capacity to see others' point of view, they show little concern for the welfare of peers or adults and seem to lack the capacity for empathy or for helping others. These children are often lonely and unpopular and frequently antagonize peers and adults alike.

The reasons for this developmental failure are not always clear. It could be contributed to by the child having a difficult temperament or attention-deficit/hyperactivity disorder (ADHD); however, certain parenting reactions and styles of parenting may contribute. It is, therefore, very important that certain approaches be used to help these children move beyond their egocentricity and self-centeredness to be able to show empathy and concern for others. Strategies include the following:

- Set effective limits so that the child learns that his caregivers can control his aggressive impulses and keep him safe. He also learns that other people's needs must be taken into account.

- Do not allow the child to take control and to try and overpower the caregivers.

- Be responsive to the child's needs for interest and affection so that the child no longer has an intense need for control and becomes much more trusting of the world.

- Do not give reasons and explanations for everything the child is asked to do so that he learns that parents are in charge. When a child hurts someone else, he must be told how this makes the other child feel, however.

- Show the child that learning to do things takes time and that he cannot expect to do things without effort. In other words, things cannot be done as if by magic by anyone.

- Stop aggression and encourage interactive play instead.

- Make an effort to help the child understand and accept the point of view and needs of others. Children must learn about how their behavior hurts others and receive consequences for it.

- Pretend play and role playing can be excellent ways to teach perspective-taking.

- Sometimes spending more time with the child can be helpful, especially if concern for her is shown and nurturing and caring is modeled.

Autism Spectrum Disorders

Children with autism are primarily characterized by social isolation, as well as speech deficits and stereotypic and ritualistic behavior. Children with autism rarely play with other children and prefer to play alone. They do not develop the ability to understand the perspective of others or a theory of mind and can act without concern for other people because of this. Since Leo Kanner first described autism in the 1940s, research has escalated. It has now been established that autism is organically or biologically—rather than psychologically—based and that autism is not caused by parental behavior or family dysfunction as was first thought. In cases of extreme deprivation or abuse, however, some children may present with some of the symptoms of autism because they have lacked the nurturing needed to develop adequate language and socialization.

Autism is usually diagnosed by 3 years of age by direct observations of the child's behavior and the use of various assessment tools. Autism affects about 5–15 of every 10,000 children, regardless of culture, socioeconomic status, or family or parent characteristics. It is more prevalent in boys than in girls. About 75%–80% of children with autism have mental retardation of varying degrees as well, making it even more difficult for them to learn and play with other children of similar age.

When a child is diagnosed with autism, various therapies may be suggested that include sensorimotor interventions, psychotherapies, biological treatments, and behavior interventions. Some of these are briefly described in the following section and the common elements noted.

Speech and Language Interventions   *Facilitated communication* is a relatively recent addition to the range of treatments for autism. It is based on the idea that children with autism can understand spoken and written language but that a deficit prevents them from expressing themselves. A facilitator holds the child's hands, wrists, or arms and helps him type out messages on the keyboard. Although it was very popular in the early 1990s, research has since suggested that the facilitators unintentionally created the messages. A debate about the treatment's efficacy and validity still continues (Bebco, Perry, & Bryson, 1996; Bomba, O'Donnell, Markowitz, & Holmes, 1996). Other speech and language interventions include reinforcement of any communication efforts (Lovass, 1977).

Sensorimotor Intervention   *Sensory integration therapy* has been used with children with autism because they often have difficulty processing sensory input from the environment. This problem accounts for some of the ritualistic behaviors such as rocking, finger flicking, sniffing objects, or repetitive touching. Sensory integration therapy is described in Chapter 2, and includes body massaging, swinging and rocking, or spinning on special chairs. It has shown few effects on language acquisition or in reducing ritualistic or self-injurious behavior (Ayers, 1979; DeGangi & Greenspan, 1997; Fisher, Murray, & Bundy, 1991).

Psychotherapies   The following psychotherapies have been used with children with autism. *Play therapy* has been used with children with autism as a way to encourage the child's capacity for pretend play and communication. Greenspan used play with a parent present to help improve contact with the child, to enable the parent to follow the child's lead, and to extend play themes within the child's choice of play (Greenspan, 1997; Greenspan, Kalmanson, Shahmoon Shanok, Wieder, Williamson, & Anzalone, 1997). For high-functioning children with autism, this approach has been useful as one of a range of treatments.

Music therapy has also been used with children with autism and has provided them with a channel of communication that is usually easier than communicating with language. Sometimes music and play therapy are used together and center around playing with the child and a musician who uses music to help structure the interaction. Again, the parent is usually included in the intervention sessions.

A program has been developed in which children are taught to *mind-read* by expressing emotions and understanding the perspectives of others (Howlin, Baron-Cohen, & Hadwin, 1999). Early outcome results show that this can be very effective.

Biological Treatments   *Biological treatments* have included use of medications to reduce aggression and ritualized behaviors. So far, medications have only been found to be helpful for reducing acting-out behaviors but not for increasing adaptive behaviors such as play and language. Vitamins and minerals (especially B_6 and magnesium) and special diets (such as gluten-free diets and those that eliminate such foods as sugar, eggs, corn, chocolate, preservatives, and food coloring) have also been used, but findings on their usefulness have been mixed and there is little evidence that they are effective (Campbell, 1989; Crook, 1987).

Behavior Interventions   Behavior interventions aim to teach the children skills that can help them adapt to the environment and decrease inappropriate behavior. Applied behavior analysis (ABA) is one of the most widely used methods. It uses reinforcement, by shaping (this is used to teach a new behavior my modifying an existing behavior through reinforcing small changes to it until it is like the desired behavior), fading, extinction, and so forth to teach the child. Tasks are broken into small steps and each is taught by giving consistent cues that are gradually faded out. The child is rewarded with acceptable reinforcers such as food and toys. It is usually used in child care, school, and at home so that the reinforcement is given consistently. ABA has been shown to have very positive results (Schopler, Mesibov, & Hearsey, 1995). Often, a range of treatments can be most useful, including speech and language therapy, behavioral treatments, occupational therapy, and play and music therapy. Occupational therapy can be used to improve fine motor and gross motor development and behavior therapy can be used to improve eye contact, language, and task completion. It can also be used to reduce undesirable behaviors. Other methods can be used to enhance the child's motivation and pleasure in interaction and social relatedness. These include music, deep touch, use of play, and engaging the child through very animated and focused interactions such as using rhymes and finger plays. Some other principles of treatment need to be considered when working with children with autism in child-care centers and other settings. These include the following:

- It is essential to start treatments as early as possible because early treatment can greatly improve a child's capacities.

- Treatment strategies need to be adapted to various characteristics of the child. These include his cognitive ability, whether he has language, the level of ritualistic or stereotyped behaviors, and whether he engages in self-injurious or aggressive behavior. The type of reinforcers and punishments used also need to be adapted to the interests of the child.

- Intensity of intervention is crucial and needs to be provided both in the home and in the child care or school placement.

- Support for parents and parent relief are crucial, especially when children have more difficult behaviors.

THE ROLE OF PARENTS IN ENCOURAGING SOCIAL COMPETENCE, EMPATHY, AND CARING BEHAVIOR

Adults and their behavior and beliefs about socialization have significant effects on various aspects of children's social competence. Adults vary significantly in a number of aspects of socialization, which include their

- Comfort level with amount of socialization and closeness with others

- Ease in interacting with others and their temperament style

- Beliefs in the trustworthiness and safety of other people

- Interest in and involvement with extended family, the school, church, recreation center, and other sources of support and social contact

- Beliefs about the poor and disenfranchised of society

- Ability to be sensitive to and empathetic toward others

- Ways of dealing with conflict situations

- Interest in and ability to understand and discuss feelings about self and others

These differences are influenced by temperament and inborn dispositions, cultural beliefs, and the type of parenting they experienced.

As explained in Chapter 1, some children are born more shy and inhibited and these tendencies may continue into adulthood. For example, parents who are very shy may choose not to go out much so their child can be around other children. Instead, they may prefer to spend a lot of time at home alone with their child.

As well, parents who experienced early trauma may be overprotective and become very anxious if their child is away from them at child care. This can create a belief in the child that the world must be a threatening place. Individual difference may also be related to early experiences with caregivers and later experiences with partners, friends, and exposure to trauma and loss. Some parents who have experienced cumulative negative events may have little energy and few models to follow in order to teach their children strategies to encourage social competence. In addition, parents who were not nurtured themselves may find it hard to model for children the caring behavior they need to learn.

DISCUSSION QUESTIONS TO USE IN TRAINING PROFESSIONALS

1. What are the differences between empathy and sympathy, and how can the ability to show them affect social competence?

2. What gender differences are found in social competence?

3. Can parents encourage their children's social competence?

4. How can a child care environment be set up to encourage empathy and caring behavior?

5. How can influences outside the family help children's social competence?

6. Why are some children more aggressive than others?

7. Why do some children become victims and get bullied in school and what can be done about it?

8. How soon do children show the ability to play with other children, share, and show concern for others?

9. What cognitive factors influence social competence in children?

10. Do you think aspects of social competence are genetic?

11. How may cultural differences affect social competence and socialization practices?

WORKING WITH PARENTS:
GROUP EXERCISES AND SAMPLE HOMEWORK ACTIVITIES

Much of the emphasis of enhancing children's development in the early years has been on the importance of their relationship with their parents. While this is crucial, parents need to be informed about the important influence of children's interactions with their peers. Also, it is important that caregivers understand that children who are socially competent and popular at school usually do well academically and those who are unpopular and rejected feel lonely and are far more likely to drop out of school later. Although the importance of peers and their influence on development has been emphasized for teenagers, up until recently their importance for young children's development was not as well understood and appreciated.

Parents who have their children in group care need to be encouraged to make sure that their children are accepted by the other children and that they are not experiencing too much rejection. For children who are not in group care, parents need to make sure that their children get opportunities to be around other young children. Parents also need to make sure that young children fit in well and enjoy the interactions, and are able to enter groups and to sustain interactions.

As developing caring and empathy in children is best done by modeling caring and concern toward the child, parents who have difficulty doing this may need special help. Some of the types of strategies that have been used include

- Providing information about child development and temperament in a dyadic model

- Encouraging them to join parent groups that suggest various strategies of parenting or parent techniques that encourage parents to relate in new ways with their children

- Providing supportive therapy in which parents are given strategies for getting practical help with housing, food, and other basic necessities

- Providing interactional coaching/guidance during which the interviewer watches or joins a parent–child interaction and speaks for the child or models different ways to interact

- Providing psychotherapy, during which the parent recalls past trauma and loss, begins to associate events with feelings, and links the past with the present

- Encouraging caregivers to learn to talk about how they feel in relation to their children and helping them to see the situation from the child's point of view

- Encouraging self-reflectivity and empathy through viewing videotapes of parents' interactions with their children. During playback of the interactions, parents can be asked to comment on what and how they think their child was thinking about and feeling at certain times and how they think their interactions worked. Strengths can also be identified and reinforced.

GROUP ACTIVITIES FOR PARENTS TO ENCOURAGE THEIR CHILDREN'S SOCIAL COMPETENCE, EMPATHY, AND CARING BEHAVIORS

This section includes exercises that can be used with parents and other caregivers to help them to encourage children's social competence, empathy, and caring behaviors.

Encouraging Perspective-Taking and Understanding the Child

Ask parents to think about and discuss any information that they found out recently that has allowed them to understand their child's point of view differently, feel more sympathy toward the child, or adapt their parenting to accommodate their child.

Ways I Show Concern for My Child

Ask parents to prepare a list of ways they think they show empathy and concern for their child. Put the examples on the blackboard and provide it as a list of ways to show concern. Some common examples are provided in Figure 10.1 to get parents started. Ask parents if they think that their children understand how much they care about them and make a list of ways they can let their children know how much they are loved.

A Balance Between Appropriate Guilt and Shame

In teaching children about right and wrong and caring for others, we need to promote a balance between feelings of responsibility if they do not follow rules (or an internal feeling of having done wrong) and shame (a feeling of worthlessness and despair about the act). With guilt, the child is left with feelings that there is something she can do about what she did. She can make the situation better or do it better next time. With feelings of shame, the child is left feeling flawed and diminished and that there is nothing to do about it. Shame can be present in a child as early as 2 or 3 years of age.

My Caring List

1. I make sure my child is safe at all times.

2. I spend time talking and listening to my child every day.

3. I make sure my child has food and clothing.

4. I make sure he has some fun times, such as going to the park on weekends.

5. When my child breaks a rule, I listen to his explanation even though I am angry sometimes.

Figure 10.1. Example of "My Caring List" exercise. Participants can write such a list on a blackboard or piece of paper to facilitate their discussion on ways they show caring, empathy, and sympathy toward children.

This balance is a fine line at times. In order to help parents better understand the difference, have them think about remarks that promote one or the other (see Table 10.9). Obviously, the first type of remark can only lead to low self-esteem and resentment while the second insists that the child take action and makes it clear that there is a way to be responsible. Ask parents to think of examples of remarks their parents used which encouraged responsibility and those that made them feel ashamed. Also, have them think of remarks to promote responsibility with their own children.

How You Were Taught Empathy and Caring

Ask parents to think about positive and negative examples from their childhoods of when they were taught empathy and caring. Was there a lot of sharing? Did parents model caring and empathy?

Today's World

Ask parents to talk about concerns they may have about society today. Do they feel it is a less-caring community? Then ask parents to come up with ideas of what people can do about the problems (i.e., too much violence, lack of concern by government).

What Would Life Be Like?

Ask parents to describe someone they know in a difficult situation and to explain how they feel about it, including what kind of emotions it arouses in them (see Figure 10.2). Make a list on the blackboard. Discuss how group members felt, if it was similar or different.

What a Child Feels Like

Have parents in a group use toys, Plasticine, finger paints, and other activities. Ask them to describe how it felt to do those activities. Note observations they may have had. Suggest that it is fun sometimes to put themselves in their child's place and to understand their feelings. This could be a great way to introduce the last session of a parenting group.

Table 10.9. Encouraging responsibility without shame by turning negative messages into positive ones

Messages that encourage feelings of shame	Messages that encourage feelings of responsibility for a wrongdoing
"You are so stupid; how could you fail again?"	"I noticed you failed your math. Perhaps you need to study more tonight."
"You are a lazy, messy slob."	"I had to clear the table last night. It is your responsibility to do it tonight."
"You are unkind and cruel. You'll end up in jail."	"It really hurts me when I see you treat your brother that way. It's important that you treat him better."

Instructions: In the left-hand column below, write about a difficult situation faced by someone you know. In the middle column, discuss how it probably makes that person feel. In the right-hand column, write how the situation makes you feel. One example is provided.

The situation	How it made the person feel	How it made me feel
Example: *A neighbor whose husband just left her with three small children*	*She is devastated and feels helpless.*	*I feel very sad for her and angry at her husband.*

Figure 10.2. Example of brainstorming to gain a better understanding of someone else's situation. This type of exercise fosters empathy and sympathy.

SAMPLE HOMEWORK TASKS

To strengthen the concepts and skills broached in the group meetings, it is helpful if parents can be given some homework tasks to do between sessions. The results can then be discussed the next week with the support of the group. Assign one or two of the suggested activities:

1. Record any example of empathy and prosocial behavior you see from your child during the week. Record what led up to the incident and what happened and make sure your child is acknowledged for the behavior.

2. Start a "helping tree," or a big picture of a tree without leaves. Anytime your child helps or shows concern, add a leaf or a fruit to the tree.

3. Keep a television diary of what your child watches. Record any examples of discussions you have about the shows.

4. Have children do one act of kindness during the week. This can be with the whole family or with one child.

5. Try a role-playing game or act out a story or game with your child. Discuss the feelings of the characters.

6. Think about your family's schedule and see how opportunities could be provided to share time and activities together.

7. Have a friend over for your child to play with and ensure that it is a cooperative time between them. Provide toys and a snack and encourage sharing.

8. Check toys and see that there are some available that can encourage sharing.

9. Try using the suggested conflict resolution skills with two children present and notice how it works.

10. Watch your child entering a group and coach him if he seems to have problems.

BIBLIOGRAPHY

REFERENCES

Akhtar, N., & Bradley, E.J. (1991). Social information processing deficits of aggressive children: Present findings and implications for social skills training. *Clinical Psychology Review, 11,* 621–644.

Alessandri, S.M. (1991). Play and social behaviour in maltreated preschoolers. *Development and Psychopathology, 3,* 191–205.

Alexander, G.M., & Hines, M. (1994). Gender labels and play styles: Their relative contribution to children's selection of playmates. *Child Development, 65,* 869–879.

Anderson, D.R., & Evans, M.K. (2001). Peril and potential of media for infants and toddlers. *Zero to Three, 22,* 10–16.

Austin, A.M.B., & Lindauer, S.L.K. (1990). Parent–child conversation of more-liked and less-liked children. *The Journal of Genetic Psychology, 151,* 5–23.

Ayres, A.J. (1979). *Sensory integration and the child.* Los Angeles: Western Psychological Association.

Bandura, A. (1986). *Social foundations of thought and action: A social cognitive theory.* Upper Saddle River, NJ: Prentice-Hall.

Baumrind, D. (1967). Child care practices anteceding three patterns of preschool behaviour. *Genetic Psychological Monographs, 75,* 43–88.

Baumrind, D. (1973). The development of instrumental competence through socialization. In A.D. Pick (Ed.), *Minnesota symposium on child psychology* (Vol. 7, pp. 3–46). Minneapolis: University of Minnesota Press.

Baumrind, D. (1988). *Familial antecedents of social competence in middle childhood.* Unpublished manuscript.

Bebco, J.M., Perry, A., & Bryson, S. (1996). Multiple method validation study of Facilitated Communication: II. *Journal of Autism and Developmental Disorders, 26,* 19–42.

Bomba, C., O'Donnell, C., Markowitz, C., & Holmes, D.L. (1996). Evaluating the impact of facilitated communication on communicative competence of 14 students with autism. *Journal of Autism and Developmental Disorders, 26,* 43–58.

Brownell, C.A., & Brown, E. (1992). Peers and play in infants and toddlers. In V.B. Van Hasselt & M. Hersen (Eds.), *Handbook of social development: A life-span perspective. Perspectives in developmental psychology* (pp. 183–200). New York: Plenum Press.

Brownell, C.A., & Carriger, M.S. (1990). Changes in cooperation and self-other differentiation during the second year. *Child Development, 61,* 1164–1174.

Bryant, J. (1990). *Television and the American family: Communication.* Mahwah, NJ: Lawrence Erlbaum Associates.

Camaioni, L., Baumgartner, E., & Perucchini, P. (1991). Content and structure in toddlers' social competence with peers from 12 to 36 months of age. *Early Child Development and Care, 67,* 17–27.

Campbell, M. (1989). Pharmacotherapy in autism: An overview. In C. Gillberg (Ed.), *Diagnosis and treatment of autism* (pp. 203–217). New York: Plenum Press.

Caplan, M., Vespo, J., Pederson, J., & Hay, D.F. (1991). Conflict and its resolution in small groups of one- and two-year-olds. *Child Development, 62,* 1513–1524.

Caplan, M.Z., & Hay, D.F. (1989). Preschoolers' responses to peers' distress and beliefs about bystander intervention. *Journal of Child Psychology and Psychiatry and Allied Disciplines, 30,* 231–242.

Carson, J.L., & Parke, R.D. (1996). Reciprocal negative affect in parent–child interactions and children's peer competency. *Child Development, 67,* 2217–2226.

Cassidy, J., & Asher, S.R. (1992). Loneliness and peer relations in young children. *Child Development, 63,* 350–365.

Clary, E.G., & Miller, J. (1986). Socialization and situational influences on sustained altruism. *Child Development, 57,* 1358–1369.

Cohen, J.S. (1989). *Maternal involvement in children's peer relationships during middle childhood.* Unpublished doctoral dissertation, University of Waterloo, Ontario.

Costin, S.E., & Jones, D.C. (1992). Friendship as a facilitator of emotional responsiveness and prosocial interventions among young children. *Developmental Psychology, 28,* 941–947.

Crook, W.G. (1987). Nutrition, food allergies, and environmental toxins. *Journal of Learning Disabilites, 20,* 260–265.

DeGangi, G., & Greenspan, S.I. (1997). The effectiveness of short-term interventions in treatment of inattention and irritability in toddlers. *Journal of Developmental and Learning Disorders, 1,* 277–298.

Dekovic, M., & Janssens, J.M. (1992). Parents' child-rearing style and child's sociometric status. *Developmental Psychology, 28,* 925–932.

Denham, S.A., & Grout, L. (1993). Socialization of emotion: Pathway to preschoolers' emotional and social competence. *Journal of Nonverbal Behaviour, 17,* 205–227.

Desmond, R.T., Singer, J.L., & Singer, D.G. (1990). Family mediation: Parental communication patterns and the influences of television on children. In J. Bryant (Ed.), *Television and the American family: Communication* (pp. 293–309). Mahwah, NJ: Lawrence Erlbaum Associates.

DiLalla, L.F. (1998). Daycare, child, and family influences on preschoolers' social behaviors in a peer play setting. *Child Study Journal, 28,* 223–244.

Dix, T.H., & Grusec, J.E. (1985). Parent attribution processes in the socialization of children. In I.E. Sigel (Ed.), *Parental belief systems: The psychological consequences for children* (pp. 201–233). Mahwah, NJ: Lawrence Erlbaum Associates.

Dodge, K.A. (1980). Social cognition and children's aggressive behavior. *Child Development, 51,* 162–170.

Dodge, K.A. (1986). A social information processing model of social competence in children. In M. Perlmutter (Ed.), *Eighteenth Minnesota symposium on child psychology* (pp. 77–125). Mahwah, NJ: Lawrence Erlbaum Associates.

Dodge, K.A., & Coic, J.D. (1987). Social-information-processing factors in reactive and proactive aggression in children's peer groups. *Journal of Personality and Social Psychology, 53,* 1146–1158.

Dodge, K.A., & Price, J.M. (1994). On the relation between social information processing and socially competent behavior in early school-aged children. *Child Development, 65,* 1385–1397.

Dunn, J. (1988). *The beginnings of social understanding.* Cambridge, MA: Harvard University Press.

Dunn, J. (1993). Young children's close relationships: Beyond attachment. *Individual Differences and Development Series, 4.* Beverly Hills: Sage Publications.

Dunn, J. (1995). Children as psychologists: The later correlates of individual differences in understanding of emotions and other minds. *Cognition and Emotion, 9,* 187–201.

Dunn, J., & Herrera, C. (1997). Conflict resolution with friends, siblings, and mothers: A developmental perspective. *Aggressive Behavior, 23,* 343–357.

Dunn, J., & McGuire, S. (1992). Sibling and peer relationships in childhood. *Journal of Child Psychology and Psychiatry and Allied Disciplines, 33,* 67–105.

Dunn, J., & Munn, P. (1986). Siblings and the development of prosocial behaviour. *International Journal of Behavioral Development, 9,* 265–284.

Dunn, J., Slomkowski, C., Donelan, N., & Herrera, C. (1995). Conflict, understanding and relationships: Developments and differences in the preschool years. *Early Education and Development, 6,* 303–316.

Eckerman, C.O., & Whitehead, H. (1999). How toddler peers generate coordinated action: A cross-cultural exploration. *Early Education and Development, 10,* 241–266.

Eisenberg, N. (1986). *Altruistic emotion, cognition, and behaviour.* Mahwah, NJ: Lawrence Erlbaum Associates.

Eisenberg, N. (1992). *The caring child.* Cambridge, MA: Harvard University Press.

Eisenberg, N., & Lennon, R. (1983). Sex differences in empathy and related capacities. *Psychological Bulletin, 94,* 100–131.

Eisenberg, N., & Mussen, P.H. (1989). *The roots of prosocial behavior in children.* New York: Cambridge University Press.

Eisenberg-Berg, N., Cameron, E., Tryon, K., & Dodez, R. (1981). Socialization of prosocial behavior in the preschool classroom. *Developmental Psychology, 17,* 773–782.

Eisenberg-Berg, N., & Geisheker, E. (1979). Content of preachings and power of the model/preacher: The effect on children's generosity. *Developmental Psychology, 15,* 168–175.

Elicker, J., Englund, M., & Sroufe, L.A. (1992). Predicting peer competence and peer relationships in childhood from early parent–child relationships. In R.D. Parke & G.W. Ladd (Eds.), *Family–peer relationships: Modes of linkage* (pp. 77–106). Mahwah, NJ: Lawrence Erlbaum Associates.

Fabes, R.A., Eisenberg, N., Karbon, M., Bernzweig, J., Speer, A.L., & Carlo, G. (1994). Socialization of children's vicarious emotional responding and prosocial behavior: Relations with mothers' perceptions of children's emotional reactivity. *Developmental Psychology, 30,* 44–55.

Fagot, B.I. (1997). Attachment, parenting, and peer interactions of toddler children. *Developmental Psychology, 33,* 489–499.

Feshbach, N.D., Feshbach, M., Fauvre, M., & Ballard-Campbell, M. (1983). *Learning to care: Classroom activities for social and affective development.* Glenview, IL: Scott, Foresman.

Field, T. (1984). Separation stress of young children transferring to new schools. *Developmental Psychology, 20,* 786–792.

Fisher, A.G., Murray, E.A., & Bundy, A.C. (1991). *Sensory integration, theory, and practice.* Philadelphia: F.A. Davis.

Garner, P.W., Jones, D.C., & Miner, J.L. (1994). Social competence among low-income preschoolers: Emotion socialization practices and social cognitive correlates. *Child Development, 65,* 622–637.

Göncü, A. (1993). Development of intersubjectivity in the dyadic play of preschoolers. *Early Childhood Research Quarterly, 8,* 99–116.

Gottman, J.M. (1983). How children become friends. *Monographs of the Society for Research in Child Development, 48* (3, Serial No. 201).

Gottman, J.M. (1986). The observation of social process. In J.M. Gottman & J.G. Parker (Eds.), *Conversations of friends: Speculations on affective development. Studies in emotion and social interaction* (pp. 51–100). New York: Cambridge University Press.

Gottman, J.M., & Parker, J.G. (Eds.). (1986). *Conversations of friends: Speculations of affective development.* New York: Cambridge University Press.

Gottman, J.M., & Parkhurst, J.T. (1980). A developmental theory of friendship and acquaintanceship processes. In A. Collins (Ed.), *Development of cognition, affect, and social relations. The Minnesota symposium on child psychology* (Vol. 13, pp. 197–253). Mahwah, NJ: Lawrence Erlbaum Associates.

Greenspan, S.I. (1997). *Developmentally based psychotherapy.* Madison, CT: International Universities Press.

Greenspan, S.I., Kalmanson, B., Shahmoon Shanok, R., Wieder, S., Williamson, G.G., & Anzalone, M. (1997). Assessing and treating infants and young children with severe difficulties in relating and communicating. *Zero to Three, 17,* 5–64.

Hanna, E., & Meltzoff, A.N. (1993). Peer imitation by toddlers in laboratory, home, and day-care contexts: Implications for social learning and memory. *Developmental Psychology, 29,* 701–710.

Hartup, W.W. (1970). Peer interaction and social organization. In P.H. Mussen (Ed.), *Carmichael's manual of child psychology* (Vol. 11, pp. 361–456). New York: John Wiley & Sons.

Hartup, W.W. (1992). Peer relations in early and middle childhood. In V.B. Van Hasselt & M. Hersen (Eds.), *Handbook of social development: A lifespan perspective* (pp. 257–281). New York: Plenum Press.

Hartup, W.W., & Sancillio, M.E. (1986). Children's friendships. In E. Schopler & G.B. Mesibov (Eds.), *Social behavior in autism* (pp. 61–79). New York: Plenum Press.

Hartup, W.W., Laursen, B., Stewart, M.A., & Eastenson, A. (1988). Conflict and the friendship relations of young children. *Child Development, 59,* 1590–1600.

Hastings, P.D., & Rubin, K.H. (1999). Predicting mothers' beliefs about preschool-aged children's social behavior: Evidence for maternal attitudes moderating child effects. *Child Development, 70,* 722–741.

Hay, D.F. (1994). Prosocial development. *Journal of Child Psychology and Psychiatry, 35,* 29–71.

Hay, D.F., Caplan, M., Castle, J., & Stimson, C.A. (1991). Does sharing become increasingly "rational" in the second year of life? *Developmental Psychology, 27,* 987–993.

Hay, D.F., Nash, A., & Pedersen, J. (1981). Responses of six-month-olds to the distress of their peers. *Child Development, 52,* 1071–1075.

Hertz-Lazarowitz, R., & Sharan, S. (1984). Enhancing prosocial behaviour through cooperative learning in the classroom. In E. Staub, D. Bar-Tal, J. Karylowski, & J. Reykowski (Eds.), *The development and maintenance of prosocial behavior: International perspectives on positive morality* (pp. 423–443). New York: Plenum Press.

Howard, J.A., & Barnett, M.A. (1981). Arousal of empathy and subsequent generosity in young children. *Journal of Genetic Psychology, 138,* 307–308.

Howes, C. (1987). Social competence with peers in young children: Developmental sequences. *Developmental Review, 7,* 252–272.

Howes, C. (1988). Peer interaction of young children. *Monographs of the Society for Research in Child Development, 53* (1, Serial No. 217).

Howes, C., & Farver, J. (1987). Toddlers' responses to the distress of their peers. *Journal of Applied Developmental Psychology, 8,* 441–452.

Howes, C., & Matheson, C.C. (1992). Sequences in the development of competent play with peers: Social and social pretend play. *Developmental Psychology, 28,* 961–974.

Howes, C., Unger, O., & Matheson, C. (1992). *The collaborative construction of pretend: Social pretend play functions.* Albany: State University of New York Press.

Howlin, P., Baron-Cohen, S., & Hadwin, J. (1999). *Teaching children with autism to mind-read: A practical guide.* Chichester, Sussex: John Wiley & Sons.

Hubbard, J.A., & Cole, J.D. (1994). Emotional correlates of social competence in children's peer relationships. *Merrill-Palmer Quarterly, 40,* 1–20.

Huston, A., Wright, J., Marquis, J., & Green, S. (1999). How young children spend their time: Television and other activities. *Developmental Psychology, 35,* 912–925.

Iskandar, N., Laursen, B., Finkelstein, B., & Frederickson, L. (1995). Conflict resolution among preschool children: The appeal of negotiation in hypothetical disputes. *Early Education and Development, 6,* 359–376.

Isley, S., O'Neil, R., & Parke, R.D. (1996). The relation of parental affect and control behaviors to children's classroom acceptance: A concurrent and predictive analysis. *Early Education and Development, 7,* 7–23.

Johnson, J.C., Ironsmith, M., Witcher, A.L., Poteat, G.M., Snow, C.W., & Mumford, S. (1997). The development of social networks in preschool children. *Early Education and Development, 8,* 389–405.

Kernberg, O.F. (1980). Some implications of object relations theory for psychoanalytic technique. In H.P. Blum (Ed.), *Psychoanalytic explorations of technique* (pp. 207–239). New York: International Universities Press.

Kerns, K.A., Cole, A.K., & Andrews, P.B. (1998). Attachment security, parent–peer management practices, and peer relationships in preschoolers. *Merrill-Palmer Quarterly, 44,* 504–522.

Kitwood, T. (1990). *Concern for others: A new psychology of conscience and morality.* London: Routledge.

Kochenderfer, B.J., & Ladd, G.W. (1996). Peer victimization: Manifestations and relations to school adjustment in kindergarten. *Journal of School Psychology, 34,* 267–283.

Kohut, H. (1959). Introspection, empathy, and psychoanalysis: An examination of the relationship between mode and observation and theory. *Journal of the American Psychoanalytic Association, 7,* 459–483.

Kohut, H. (1984). Introspection, empathy, and the semicircle of mental health. In J. Lichtenberg, M. Bornstein, & D. Silver (Eds.), *Empathy* (Vol. 1, pp. 81–100). Mahwah, NJ: Lawrence Erlbaum Associates.

Ladd, G.W., & Hart, C.H. (1992). Creating informal play opportunities: Are parents and preschoolers' initiations related to children's competence with peers? *Developmental Psychology, 28,* 1179–1187.

LaFrenière, P.J., & Sroufe, L.A. (1985). Profiles of peer competence in the preschool: Interrelations between measures, influence of social ecology, and relation to attachment history. *Developmental Psychology, 21,* 56–69.

Lamb, S., & Zakhireh, B. (1997). Toddlers' attention to the distress of peers in a day care setting. *Early Education and Development, 8,* 105–118.

Londerville, S., & Main, M. (1981). Security of attachment, compliance, and maternal training methods in the second year of life. *Developmental Psychology, 17,* 298–299.

Lovass, O.I. (1977). *The autistic child: Language development through behavior modification.* New York: Irvington.

Maccoby, E.E. (1990). Gender and relationships. A developmental account. *American Psychologist, 45,* 513–520.

MacDonald, K., & Parke, R.D. (1984). Bridging the gap: Parent–child play interactions and peer interactive competence. *Child Development, 55,* 1265–1277.

Miller, P.A. (1984). *Maternal child rearing practices and daughters' empathic response to peer distress.* Unpublished doctoral dissertation, University of Texas, Austin.

Mitchell-Copeland, J., Denham, S.A., & DeMulder, E.K. (1997). Q-sort assessment of child–teacher attachment relationships and social competence in the preschool. *Early Education and Development, 8,* 27–39.

Mize, J., & Pettit, G.S. (1997). Mothers' social coaching, mother–child relationship style and children's peer competence: Is the medium the message? *Child Development, 68,* 312–332.

Moore, B.S., & Eisenberg, N. (1984). The development of altruism. In G. Whitehurst (Ed.), *Annals of child development* (pp. 107–174). Greenwich, CT: JAI Press.

Park, K.A., & Waters, E. (1989). Security of attachment and preschool friendships. *Child Development, 60,* 1076–1081.

Peery, J.C., Jensen, L., & Adams, G.R. (1985). The relationship between parents' attitudes towards child rearing and the sociometric status of their preschool children. *The Journal of Psychology, 119,* 567–574.

Profilet, S.M., & Ladd, G.W. (1994). Do mothers' perceptions and concerns about preschoolers' peer competence predict their peer management practices? *Social Development, 3,* 205–221.

Putallaz, M. (1987). Maternal behavior and children's sociometric status. *Child Development, 58,* 324–340.

Putallaz, M., & Sheppard, B.H. (1992). Conflict management and social competence. In C.U. Shantz & W.W. Hartup (Eds.), *Conflict in child and adolescent development* (pp. 330–355). New York: Cambridge University Press.

Radke-Yarrow, M., & Zahn-Waxler, C. (1984). Roots, motives, and patterns in children's prosocial behaviour. In E. Staub, D. Bar-Tal, J. Karylowski, & J. Reykowski (Eds.), *The development and maintenance of prosocial behavior: International perspectives on positive morality* (pp. 81–99). New York: Plenum Press.

Radke-Yarrow, M., Zahn-Waxler, C., & Chapman, M. (1983). Children's prosocial dispositions and behaviour. In P. Mussen (Ed.), *Manual of child psychology: Vol. 4. Socialization, personality, and social development* (4th ed., pp. 469–545). New York: John Wiley & Sons.

Radke-Yarrow, M., Zahn-Waxler, C., Richardson, D.T., Susman, A., & Martinez, P. (1994). Caring behaviour in children of clinically depressed and well mothers. *Child Development, 65,* 1405–1414.

Raver, C.C., Blackburn, E.K., Bancroft, M., & Torp, N. (1999). Relations between effective emotional self-regulation, attentional control, and low-income preschoolers' social competence with peers. *Early Education and Development, 10,* 333–350.

Roberts, W., & Strayer, J. (1996). Empathy, emotional expressiveness, and prosocial behavior. *Child Development, 67,* 449–470.

Roberts, W.L. (1999). The socialization of emotional expression: Relations with prosocial behavior and competence in five samples. *Canadian Journal of Behavioural Science, 31,* 72–85.

Rogers, C. (1959). A theory of therapy, personality, and interpersonal relationships as developed in the client-centered framework. In J.S. Koch (Ed.), *Psychology: A study of science. Vol. 3. Formulations of the person in the social context* (pp. 184–256). New York: McGraw-Hill.

Rogers, C. (1975). Empathic: An unappreciated way of being. *Counselling Psychologist, 5,* 2–10.

Rose-Krasnor, L., Rubin, K.H., Booth, C.L., & Coplan, R. (1996). The relation of maternal directiveness and child attachment security to social competence in preschoolers. *International Journal of Behavioral Development, 19,* 309–325.

Rourke, M.T., Wozniak, R.H., & Cassidy, K.W. (1999). The social sensitivity of preschoolers in peer conflicts: Do children act differently with different peers? *Early Education and Development, 10,* 209–227.

Rubin, K.H. (1995). Parents of aggressive and withdrawn children. In M.H. Bornstein (Ed.), *Handbook of parenting: Vol. 1. Children and parenting* (pp. 255–284). Mahwah, NJ: Lawrence Erlbaum Associates.

Rubin, K.H., & Mills, R.S.L. (1990). Maternal beliefs about adaptive and maladaptive social behaviors in normal, aggressive and withdrawn preschoolers. *Journal of Abnormal Child Psychology, 18,* 419–435.

Rubin, K.H., Mills, R.S.L., & Rose-Krasnor, L. (1989). Maternal beliefs and children's competence. In B.H. Schneider, G. Attili, J. Nadel, & R.P. Weissberg (Eds.), *Social competence in developmental perspective* (Vol. 51, pp. 313–331). Dordrecht, Netherlands: Kluwer.

Schaffer, R. (1991). Early social development. In M. Woodhead, R. Carr, & P. Light (Eds.), *Child development in social context: Vol. 1. Becoming a person* (pp. 5–29). London, England: Routledge.

Schopler, E., Mesibov, G.B., & Hearsey, K. (1995). Structured teaching in the TEACCH system. In E. Schopler & G.B. Mesibov (Eds.), *Learning and cognition in autism* (pp. 243–267). New York: Plenum Press.

Schultz, L.H., & Selman, R.L. (1989). Bridging the gap between interpersonal thought and action in early adolescence: The role of psychodynamic processes. *Development and Psychopathology, 1,* 133–152.

Selman, R.L. (1980). *The growth of interpersonal understanding: Developmental and clinical analyses.* New York: Academic Press.

Selman, R.L. (1981). The development of interpersonal competence: The role of understanding in conduct. *Developmental Review, 1,* 401–422.

Shantz, C. (1987). Conflicts between children. *Child Development, 58,* 283–305.

Sharron, L. (1991). First moral sense: Aspects of and contributors to a beginning morality in the second year of life. In W.M. Kurtines & J.L. Gewirtz (Eds.), *Handbook of moral behavior and development: Vol. 1. Theory* (pp. 171–189). Mahwah, NJ: Lawrence Erlbaum Associates.

Singer, D.G., & Singer, J.L. (Eds.). (2000). *Handbook of children and the media.* Beverly Hills: Sage Publications.

Singer, J.L., & Singer, D.G. (1986). Family experiences and television viewing as predictors of children's imagination, restlessness, and aggression. *Journal of Social Issues, 42,* 107–124.

Spivak, G., & Shure, M. (1989). Interpersonal cognitive problem solving (ICPS): A competence-building primary prevention program. *Prevention in Human Services, 6,* 151–178.

Sroufe, A. (1983). Infant caregiver attachment and patterns of adaptation in preschool: The roots of maladaptation and competence. In M. Perimutter (Ed.), *Minnesota symposium on child psychology* (Vol. 16, pp. 41–79). Mahwah, NJ: Lawrence Erlbaum Associates.

Stocker, C., & Dunn, J. (1990). Sibling relationships in childhood: Links with friendships and peer relationships. *British Journal of Developmental Psychology, 8,* 227–244.

Sullivan, H.S. (1962). *Schizophrenia as a human process.* New York: W.W. Norton.

Vespo, J.E., & Caplan, M. (1993). Preschoolers' differential conflict behavior with friends and acquaintances. *Early Education and Development, 4,* 45–53.

Vondra, J.I., Shaw, D.S., Swearingen, L., Cohen, M., & Owens, E.B. (1999). Early relationship quality from home to school: A longitudinal study. *Early Education and Development, 10,* 163–190.

Walden, T., Lemerise, E., & Smith, M.C. (1999). Friendship and popularity in preschool classrooms. *Early Education and Development, 10,* 351–371.

Waters, E., Wippman, J., & Sroufe, L.A. (1979). Attachment, positive affect, and competence in the peer group: Two studies in construct validation. *Child Development, 50,* 821–829.

Weston, D.R., & Main, M. (1980, April). *Infant responses to the crying of an adult actor in the laboratory: Stability and correlates of "concerned attention."* Paper presented at the Second International Conference on Infant Studies, New Haven, CT.

Woodard, E. (2000). *Media in the home 2000: The fifth annual survey of parents and children.* Survey No. 7. Philadelphia: The Annenberg Public Policy Center of the University of Pennsylvania.

Youngblade, L.M., & Belsky, J. (1992). Parent–child antecedents of 5-year-olds' close friendships: A longitudinal analysis. *Developmental Psychology, 28,* 700–713.

Zahn-Waxler, C., Iannotti, R., & Chapman, M. (1982). Peers and prosocial development. In K.H. Rubin & H.S. Ross (Eds.), *Peer relationships and social skills in childhood* (pp. 133–162). New York: Springer-Verlag.

Zahn-Waxler, C., & Radke-Yarrow, M. (1982). The development of altruism: Alternate research strategies. In N. Eisenberg, *The development of prosocial behavior* (pp. 109–137). San Diego: Academic Press.

Zahn-Waxler, C., Radke-Yarrow, M., & King, R.A. (1979). Child rearing and children's prosocial initiations towards victims of distress. *Child Development, 50,* 319–330.

Zahn-Waxler, C., Radke-Yarrow, M., Wagner, E., & Chapman, M. (1992). Development of concern for others. *Developmental Psychology, 28,* 126–136.

Zahn-Waxler, C., Robinson, J.L., & Emde, R.N. (1992). The development of empathy in twins. *Developmental Psychology, 28,* 1038–1047.

FURTHER READING ON THE TOPIC

Begun, R.W. (Ed.). (1996). *Social skills lessons and activities for grades Pre-k.* New York: The Center for Applied Research in Education.

Bos, B. (1990). *Together we're better: Establishing a coactive learning environment.* Roseville, CA: Turn the Page Press.

Dodge, K.A., Pettit, G.S., McClasky, C.L., & Brown, M.M. (1986). Social competence in children. *Monographs of the Society for Research in Child Development, 51* (25, Serial No. 213).

Eisenberg, N. (1986). *Altruistic emotion, cognition, and behavior.* Mahwah, NJ: Lawrence Erlbaum Associates.

Eisenberg, N. (1992). *The caring child.* Cambridge, MA: Harvard University Press.

Eisenberg, N., & Strayer, J. (Eds.). (1987). *Empathy and its development.* New York: Cambridge University Press.

Eyre, L., & Eyre, R.M. (1995). *Teaching children sensitivity.* New York: Simon and Schuster.

Feshbach, N., & Roe, K. (1982). The measurement of empathy. In C.E. Izard (Ed.), *Measuring emotions in infants and children* (pp. 279–296). New York: Cambridge University Press.

Hoffman, M.L. (1982). Development of prosocial motivation: Empathy and guilt. In N. Eisenberg (Ed.), *The development of prosocial behavior* (pp. 281–313). San Diego: Academic Press.

Luke, C. (1988). *Television and your child: A guide for concerned parents.* Toronto: Kagan and Woo.

Rubin, Z. (1980). *Children's friendships.* Cambridge, MA: Harvard University Press.

Shantz, C.U., & Hartup, W.W. (Eds.). (1992). *Conflict in child and adolescent development.* New York: Cambridge University Press.

Shulman, S. (1995). Close relationships and socioemotional development. *Human Development* (Vol. 7). Stamford, CT: Ablex.

Singer, J.L., & Singer, D.G. (1983). Implications of television viewing for cognition, imagination and emotion. In J. Bryant & D.R. Anderson (Eds.), *Children's understanding of television: Research on attention and comprehension.* San Diego: Academic Press.

Trovato, C.A. (1987). *Teaching kids to care: 150 activities to help young children cooperate, share and learn together.* Cleveland, OH: Instructor Books.

Winn, M. (1985). *The plug-in drug: Television, children and the family.* London: Viking Press.

Zahn-Waxler, C., Cummings, F.M., & Iannotti, R. (1986). *Altruism and aggression: Biological and social origins.* Cambridge: Cambridge University Press.

CHILDREN'S BOOKS ABOUT SOCIAL COMPETENCE, EMPATHY, AND CARING BEHAVIOR

Allison, B. (1999). *Effie.* Richmond Hill, Ontario: Scholastic Canada.

Andersen, H.C. (1987). *The little match girl.* New York: Putnam.

Andersen, H.C. (1988). *The steadfast tin soldier.* New York: Magna Books.

Berry, J.W. (1984). *Let's talk about being selfish.* Chicago: Children's Press.

Carle, E. (1971). *Do you want to be my friend?* New York: HarperCollins Children's Books.

Casely, J. (1991). *Harry and Willy and Carrothead.* New York: Greenwillow Books.

Cohen, M. (1967). *Will I have a friend?* New York: Macmillan.

Cohen, M. (1989). *Best friends.* New York: Aladdin Books.

Crary, E. (1996). *I want it.* Seattle: Parenting Press.

DiSalvo-Ryan, D. (1997). *Uncle Willie and the soup kitchen.* New York: Mulberry Books.

Havill, J. (1993). *Jamaica and Brianna.* Boston: Houghton Mifflin.

Heath, A. (1992). *Sophie's role.* New York: Four Winds Press.

Henkes, K. (1988). *Chester's way.* New York: Greenwillow Books.

Henkes, K. (1991). *Chrysanthemum.* New York: Greenwillow Books.

Hoban, R. (1969). *Best friends for Frances.* New York: HarperCollins Children's Books.

Hoban, R. (1999). *A bargain for Frances.* New York: Harper Festival.

Hutchins, P. (1989). *The doorbell rang.* New York: Mulberry Books.

Joyce, W. (1985). *George shrinks.* New York: HarperCollins Children's Books.

Keats, E.J. (1998). *Peter's chair.* London: New York: Viking.

Keller, H. (1987). *Lizzie's invitation.* New York: Greenwillow Books.

Lester, H. (1992). *Me first.* Boston: Houghton Mifflin.

Lindgren, B. (1988). *Sam's car.* New York: William Morrow.

Lobel, A. (1970). *Frog and toad are friends.* New York: HarperCollins Children's Books.

MacDonald, A. & Fox-Davies, S. (1990). *Little beaver and the echo.* London: Putnam.

Marshall, J. (1974). *George and Martha.* Boston: Houghton Mifflin.

Naylor, P.R. (1991). *King of the playground.* New York: Atheneum Books.

Numeroff, L.J. (2000). *If you give a mouse a cookie.* New York: HarperCollins Children's Books.

Rogers, F. (1996). *Making friends.* New York: Putnam.

Schwartz, A. (1994). *Bea and Mr. Jones.* Scarsdale, NY: Aladdin Paperbacks.

Stevenson, J. (1995). *The worst person in the world.* New York: Mulberry Books.

Viorst, J. (1972). *Alexander and the terrible, horrible, no good, very bad day.* New York: Atheneum Books.

Yashima, T. (1976). *Crow boy.* New York: Penguin.

APPENDIX: SELECTED
ASSESSMENT INSTRUMENTS

ASSESSING SOCIAL COMPETENCE

A variety of methods have been used to assess the social competence of young children, including

- Teacher and parent ratings of various social behaviors

- Sociometric ratings by peers of their classmates

- Observational methods in both a laboratory and naturalistic setting

Each of the techniques generates useful but somewhat different information about children's social competence. Because the information provided by each technique is so different, many researchers use multimethods and collect information from different sources and in various settings, instead of relying on a single assessment approach.

Some assessment tools already discussed in other chapters of this book have a social development scale as one of a number of other scales. These include: Child Behavior Checklist (CBCL) (Achenbach, 1981), Vineland Adaptive Behavior Scales (Sparrow, Balla, & Cicchetti, 1984), and the Diagnostic Inventory for Screening Children (DISC) (Amdur, Mainland, & Parker, 1984). Other tests that have been developed specifically to test social competence are outlined in Table A10.1.

Cognitive Interpersonal Problem-Solving

Because social information processing has been found to be so important for determining social competence in children, measures of the cognitive aspects of social functioning are often used. Some of the more commonly used measures are listed in Table A10.2.

Assessing Empathy and Prosocial Behavior

A number of methods have been used in order to assess empathy and prosocial behavior in young children. These are the following:

- Asking children how they would feel in certain situations using written vignettes or pictures

- Showing pictures of children exhibiting different feelings and asking children to identify the emotions

- Showing children slides or having researchers act out specific situations, watching their reactions, and asking them how they feel after they watch the drama

- Observing children's interactions at home, child care, or in other groups of children and marking instances of empathy or rating the child on certain scales related to caring behaviors

- Rating scales that ask parents to rate children in their everyday lives on certain characteristics related to empathy

Table A10.3 and Table 10.4 list some specific tests to measure these abilities in children and parents.

Table A10.1. Selected assessments of children's social competence

Tool/instrument	Age range	Items/ administration time	General description
California Preschool Social Competence Scale (CPSCS) Levine, S., Elzey, F.F., & Lewis, M. (1969). *California Preschool Social Competence Scale Manual.* Palo Alto, CA: Consulting Psychologists Press.	3–6 years	30 items; 10 minutes.	The *California Preschool Social Competence Scale (CPSCS)* includes parent and teacher rating scales. The items contain four descriptions of children that detail varying degrees of competence relative to the behaviors being measured.
Kohn Social Competence Scale Kohn, M., & Resman, B.L. (1972). A Social Competence Scale and Symptom Checklist for the Preschool Child: Factor dimensions, their cross instrument generality, and longitudinal persistence. *Developmental Psychology, 6,* 430–444.	3–6 years	73 items for children in full-day programs and 64 for children in half-day programs; 10–15 minutes	The *Kohn Social Competence Scale* is a teacher rating instrument used to assess a child's social competence in a child care, preschool or kindergarten environment. The scale measures two bipolar dimensions of social functioning: Interest Participation versus Apathy–Withdrawal and Cooperation–Compliance versus Anger–Defiance. There is a scoring key that takes about 3 minutes to complete.
A Measure of Peer Sociometric Ratings Asher, S.R., Singleton, L.C., Tinsley, B.R., & Hymel, S. (1979). A reliable sociometric measure for preschool children. *Developmental Psychology, 15,* 443–444.	3–6 years	Varies according to size of class	In this method, children are individually shown pictures of the other children in the class and asked to place the pictures on either a happy, neutral, or sad face to indicate whether they liked, neither liked nor disliked, or disliked a classmate. Scores are then summarized across the responses to give a summary score for each child in the class. The scores can be used to identify popular, rejected, or neglected (neither liked or disliked children).
Social Competence and Behavior Evaluation: Preschool Edition (SCBE) LaFrenière, J.P., & Dumas, J.E. (1995). *Social Competence and Behavior Evaluation, Preschool Edition (SCBE).* Los Angeles: Western Psychological Services.	2–6 years	80 items; 15 minutes	The *Social Competence and Behavior Evaluation: Preschool Edition (SCBE)* is a teacher rating scale that measures the social competence, emotional expression, and adjustment of young children. The items address behaviors commonly observed among preschoolers and measure social competence, emotional expression, and adjustment. The obtained scores can be used to design classroom interventions that can focus on the child's strengths and weaknesses.

(continued)

Table A10.1 *(continued)*

Tool/instrument	Age range	Items/ administration time	General description
Social Skills Rating System (Parent and Teacher Forms) (SSRS–P) Gresham, F.M., & Elliott, S.N. (1990). *Social Skills Rating System Manual.* Circle Pines, MN: American Guidance Service.	3–5 years (preschool level); 6–12 years (elementary school level)	38 items; 10 minutes	The *Social Skills Rating System (SSRS-P)* evaluates social skills and problem behaviors. Each behavior is rated as to how frequently it occurs and how important it is perceived to be. The system measures cooperation, assertion, responsibility, empathy, and self-control. It can be used to design interventions.

Other commonly used measures

Baumrind Preschool Behavior Q-Sort (BQS)
Baumrind, D. (1968). *Manual for the Preschool Behavior Q-Sort.* Berkeley, CA: University of California.

Baumrind, D. (1971). Current patterns of parental authority. *Developmental Psychology Monographs, 4* (1, Part 2), 1–103.

Matson's Evaluation of Social Skills with Youngsters (MESSY)
Matson, J.L., Rotatori, A.F., & Helshel, W.J. (1983). Development of a rating scale to measure social skills in children: The Matson Evaluation of Social Skills with Youngsters (MESSY). *Behavior Research and Therapy, 21,* 335–340.

Preschool and Kindergarten Behavior Scales (PKBS)
Merrell, K.W. (1996). Social-emotional assessment in early childhood: The Preschool and Kindergarten Behavior Scales. *Journal of Early Intervention, 20,* 132–145.

Table A10.2. Selected assessments to measure cognitive interpersonal problem-solving

Tool/instrument	Age range	Items/administration time	General description
Attributional Biases and Response Styles Dodge, K.A., & Frame, C. (1982). Social cognitive biases and deficits in aggressive boys. *Child Development, 53,* 620–635.	3–6 years	10 stories; 20 minutes	Hypothetical stories with pictures are used to measure children's social skills and biases in interpreting peers' intentions. The stories depict children in situations in which they try to enter a group and are rejected by a peer or a peer ridiculed or bumped them, for example. The stories are scored for hostile intent.
The Preschool Interpersonal Problem Solving Test (PIPS) Shure, M.B., & Spivack, G. (1974). *Preschool Interpersonal Problem Solving (PIPS) Test Manual.* Philadelphia: Department of Health Sciences, Hahnemann Community Mental Health Center.	4–5 years	7–10 peer problem situations and 5–10 mother problem situation; 30 minutes	The *Preschool Interpersonal Problem Solving Test (PIPS)* assesses preschoolers' ability to consider alternative solutions to interpersonal problems and has them identify a preferred solution to peer and mother problem situations (e.g., wanting a toy another child has; damaging something that belongs to the mother). The score for each item is the number of possible solutions that are generated. The items are administered using pictures of the situations and toys.
The What Happens Next Game (WHNG) Shure, M.B. (1990). *The What Happens Next Game (WHNG) Manual.* Department of Mental Health Sciences, Hahnemann University, Philadelphia, PA.	4–5 years	12–20 items; 30 minutes	The *What Happens Next Game (WHNG)* measures the child's ability to conceptualize different consequences to two interpersonal acts: 1) grabbing a toy from a peer, and 2) taking something from an adult without asking. The procedure is similar to the PIPS test and uses pictures and stick figures. A child's score consists of the total number of different relevant consequences of both types of interpersonal situations.

564

Table A10.3. Selected assessments to measure empathy and prosocial behavior

Test/instrument	Age range	Items/administration time	General description
Borke Test of Interpersonal Awareness Borke, H. (1971). Interpersonal perception of young children: Egocentrism or empathy. *Developmental Psychology, 5*, 203–269.	3 years and up	21 items; 10 minutes	The *Borke Test of Interpersonal Awareness* was originally designed by Helen Borke to show that young children are aware of the feelings of others and that they try to understand them. Part 1 uses stories describing general situations that might make a child feel happy, sad, afraid, or mad. The child is asked to complete the picture by choosing from pictures of happy, sad, afraid, or mad faces, the face that best shows how the child in the story feels. Part 2 asks children to describe the subject as behaving toward another child in ways that might make the other child feel happy, afraid, sad, or mad. Children receive one point for each emotion that they identify correctly. The number obtained can be compared to norms in the child's age group.
Bryant Index of Empathy Bryant, B.K. (1982). An index of empathy for children and adolescents. *Child Development, 53*, 413–425.	5 years and up	22 items; 10 minutes	The *Bryant Index of Empathy* asks children to answer "yes" or "no" to test statements or items (e.g., "Sometimes I cry when I watch television"). In this way, the test emphasizes the experience of sharing feelings.
Prosocial Behavior Questionnaire Weir, K., Stevenson, J., & Graham, P. (1980). Behavioral deviance and teacher ratings of prosocial behavior. *Journal of the American Academy of Child Psychiatry, 19*, 68–77. Weir, K., & Duveen, G. (1981). Further development and validation of Prosocial Behavior Questionnaire for use by teachers. *Journal of Child Psychology and Psychiatry, 22*, 357–374.	3–6 years	20 items; 10 minutes	The *Prosocial Behavior Questionnaire* is a teacher report questionnaire consisting of items that are rated on a 5-point scale according to how descriptive each item is of a particular child. The items include a number of interpersonal behaviors such as helping, sharing, cooperating, and responding to distress.

Other commonly used measures

Early Childhood Measure of Empathy
Feshbach, N., & Roe, K. (1968). Empathy in six- and seven-year-olds. *Child Development, 39*, . 133–145

Prosocial Scale for the Preschool Behavior Questionnaire
Tremblay, R.E., Vitaro, F., & Gagnon, C. (1992). A Prosocial Scale for the Preschool Behavior Questionnaire: Concurrent and Predictive Correlates. *International Journal of Behavioral Development, 15*, 227–245.

The Young Children's Empathy Measure
Poresky, R.H. (1990). The Young Children's Empathy Measure: Reliability, validity and effects of companion animal bonding. *Psychological Reports, 66*, 931–936.

Table A10.4. Test of parent's social competence

Test/instrument	Items	General description
Interpersonal Competence Questionnaire (ICQ) Buhrmester, D., Furman, W., Wittenberg, M.T., & Teis, H.T. (1988). Five domains of interpersonal competence in peer relationships. *Journal of Personality and Social Psychology, 55,* 991–1008.	40 items	The *Interpersonal Competence Questionnaire* (ICQ) includes measured on a 5-point Likert scale ranging from 1 (*I am very poor at this*) to 5 (*I'm extremely good at this*). The scores are then summed and result in five subscales: Initiation of Interactions and Relationships; Assertion of Personal Rights; Self-Disclosure of Personal Information; Emotional Support of Others; and Conflict Management.

EPILOGUE:
PUTTING THE PIECES TOGETHER

Pathways to Competence: Encouraging Healthy Social and Emotional Development in Young Children describes a number of young children's capacities and competencies and suggests many strategies caregivers can employ to enhance them. The competencies are described individually, but together they lay the foundation for resilience and coping throughout an individual's lifetime. These capacities and competencies develop in succession, appear at different times during a child's first 6 years, and then strengthen until they are fully developed (see Figure E.1). After 6 years of age, adjustments and gains will continue. Once these competencies are established in the early years, however, other developmental achievements or qualitative shifts become more readily attained later.

A great deal of development takes place in the first year of life that lays the foundation for a child's sound sense of body schema and body image. Later in the first year and into the beginning of the second year, a child forms attachments with primary caregivers, and if these attachments are secure, they can become a major positive organizer for later development.

During the second year and at the beginning of the third year of a child's life, the capacity for play is established and strengthened—particularly the ability to engage in and enjoy pretend play. At approximately the same time, language expands enormously and becomes a child's major means of communicating and relating to others.

During the third year, a child's language development makes a tremendous leap forward in ability and complexity, and the child's sense of a positive self is stabilized as a foundation for a belief in his sense of competence. By 3 years of age, a child is willing and able to follow caregivers' requests for certain behaviors and is far less likely to ignore directives; however, it takes longer for a conscience to be internalized. By 4 years of age, a child is better able to modulate and regulate her emotions without relying on people from the outside. At first, this ability to regulate emotions remains fragile under stress, particularly when conflicting emotions are involved.

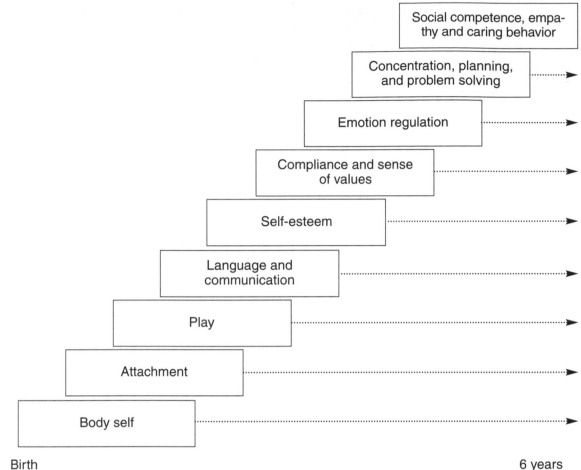

Figure E.1. A child's capacities and competencies develop in succession, build on each other during the first 6 years, and then strengthen until they are fully developed.

Although children quite early on can use basic problem-solving strategies, concentration, planning, and complex problem-solving abilities do not become possible until ages 3–4 years, when they begin to understand the underlying rules for problem-solving that can be transferred across time and context. At about 4 years of age, children develop a *theory of mind,* which enables them to understand how other people think, feel, and believe. This capacity prepares them for the final achievement of true caring behavior and helping others without concern for a reward or for being noticed, which may have motivated these behaviors previously. As well, the ability to cooperate with adults and other children is fully established.

The pathway to healthy social and emotional development a child follows is complex. To achieve both a sense of competence and control it is important to establish all of the abilities, for if one is missing, the absence seriously affects other areas. As explained in Chapter 8 in the discussion of emotional intelligence, although intellectual development is important, having the capacities described in this book can make an enormous difference in coping and having a successful life. Thus, children and adults so equipped are likely to better manage the stresses, both significant and insignificant, and to have satisfying relationships, families, and careers.

Although the emphasis in this book has been on describing the areas of development separately, it is obvious that they are all intricately related and affect one another. Gains in one area can influence development in other aspects and problems in one aspect can reverberate in many other areas of development. The examples are numerous.

● ●

Two-year old Samina has just learned to talk, and her mother is delighted to find that Samina's frequent temper tantrums seem to be decreasing a little. Also, she now seems to be able to engage in pretend play with other children over extended periods. In fact, she engages in lengthy conversations in which she discusses the theme of the play and seems to help keep the play coordinated.

———————————————

Until a few months ago, 3-year-old Juan was constantly getting frustrated over little things when he played with other children. Lately, however, he seems to be gaining much more control of his anger, and talks about it and walks away if he gets angry. He is now much more accepted by peers and is settling much better into child care.

———————————————

A secure attachment gives children a positive view of self and others, dramatically affecting their self-esteem and approach to socializing with others.

Margarita has just turned 5 years old. She now appears to know the "rules" without being told and, in fact, makes sure that everyone who comes over to play knows them and follows them, as well. She is also much more likely to consistently show caring behavior to others, even to her baby sister.

Since he was about 7 months old, Markus has been very attached to his mother and has enjoyed playing close to her and checking in once in a while. Gradually, he is now able to be away from her without getting upset and seems quite self-confident about being around other children.

As the vignettes show, a significant gain in one area affects several others. For example, without a certain level of emotion regulation, children will have a lot of difficulty being accepted by other children and in making friends. A secure attachment gives children a positive view of self and others, dramatically affecting their self-esteem and approach to socializing with others. The link between moral development and empathy and prosocial behavior are clear and each arise from the discipline and modeling the child receives from caregivers and the family context in which they live. Language influences an extraordinary number of areas of development, including emotion regulation and the ability to have conversations with others that can enhance social competence. Ability to engage in pretend play, in turn, can improve language, problem-solving, planning, and popularity with peers.

The capacities described in this book are intricately linked together into a remarkably coordinated system, with each building on the other and becoming woven into a rich tapestry of abilities. Once in place, they can serve as protective factors against difficult life events, reduce vulnerability, and enhance children's resilience so that they can be happy and contributing members of society.

INDEX

Page numbers followed by *f* indicate figures; those followed by *t* indicate tables.